SIXTH EDITION

A History of
Modern Psychology

DUANE P. SCHULTZ
University of South Florida

SYDNEY ELLEN SCHULTZ

HARCOURT BRACE COLLEGE PUBLISHERS

*Fort Worth   Philadelphia   San Diego   New York   Orlando   Austin   San Antonio
Toronto   Montreal   London   Sydney   Tokyo*

Publisher	Ted Buchholz
Editor in Chief	Christopher P. Klein
Developmental Editor	Karee Galloway
Senior Project Editor	Angela Williams
Production Manager	Melinda Esco
Art Directors	Nick Welch/Melinda Welch

Illustrations courtesy of Tammi Miller.
Cover image © Garry Gay/The Image Bank.

Address for Editorial Correspondence
Harcourt Brace College Publishers, 301 Commerce Street,
Suite 3700, Fort Worth, TX 76102

Address for Orders
Harcourt Brace & Company, 6277 Sea Harbor Drive, Orlando, FL 32887
1-800-782-4479, or 1-800-433-0001 (in Florida)

ISBN: 0-15-502560-0

Library of Congress Catalogue Number: 95-75736

Printed in the United States of America

6 7 8 9 0 1 2 3 4   016   10 9 8 7 6 5 4 3

PREFACE

THE FOCUS of this book is the history of modern psychology, that period beginning in the late 19th century when psychology became a separate, independent discipline. Although we do not ignore earlier philosophical thought, we concentrate on that which relates directly to the establishment of psychology as a new and distinct field of study. We are presenting a history of modern psychology, not of psychology and all the philosophical work that preceded it.

We recount the history of psychology in terms of its great ideas and schools of thought. Since the formal beginning of the field in 1879, psychology has been defined in a variety of ways as new ideas have captured the loyalty of adherents and have come, for a time, to dominate the field. Our interest, then, is in the developing sequence of ideas that has defined psychology's subject matter, methods, and goals.

Each of the schools of thought is discussed as a movement growing out of its historical context and not as an independent or isolated entity. Contextual forces include not only the intellectual spirit of the times (the *Zeitgeist*) but also social, political, and economic factors.

Although this book is organized in terms of the schools of thought that mark psychology's evolution, we recognize that these definitions, ideas, and approaches are the work of individual scholars, researchers, and systematizers. People, not abstract forces, write the articles, conduct the research, present the papers, and teach each generation of psychologists. In so doing, these men and women have developed and promoted psychology's schools of thought. We discuss the lives of the pivotal figures who shaped the field, noting that their work was influenced not only by the times in which they flourished but also by the context of their own experiences.

We discuss each school of thought in terms of its connection to the scientific ideas and discoveries that precede and follow it. We describe how each school evolved from or revolted against the existing order, and how each in its turn inspired viewpoints that challenged, opposed, and eventually replaced it. With the hindsight of history, we can trace a pattern, a continuity of development, within modern psychology.

Preparing the sixth edition of this textbook some 30 years after writing the first one and finding so much to add, delete, and revise, is vivid testimony to the dynamic nature of the history of psychology. It is not fixed or finished but is in a continuing state of growth. There is an enormous amount of scholarly work being produced, translated, and reevaluated on significant persons, issues, methods, and theories in the history of psychology.

A significant addition to the book is a chapter dealing with gender and race issues in the history of psychology. We review the forces that limited the opportunities of women and members of ethnic minority groups to receive graduate training and obtain jobs in the developing field of psychology. The so-called politics of identity movement, that is, the push to enhance culturally diverse representation within psychology, is discussed. In addition, the contributions of many more women psychologists and Black psychologists have been noted throughout the book.

Other features of this edition include many new and expanded topics, as well as additional material on the lives of prominent psychologists that illustrates the impact of personal experiences on the subsequent development of their ideas.

The conception of the machine as a metaphor for human functioning has been expanded to include not only clocks and automata but also examples from medicine and mechanical engineering. Babbage's calculating engine is described as a forerunner of the modern computer and as the first attempt to duplicate human cognitive processes. The concept of evolution as applied to the development of machines is also noted.

In the cognitive psychology chapter we have expanded the discussion of the use of the introspective method, and we describe the return of unconscious cognition and the study of consciousness in animals.

The original source materials for structuralism, functionalism, and behaviorism have been edited to make them more accessible to today's students. The article for Gestalt psychology has been replaced with material from Köhler's book, *The Mentality of Apes,* describing his animal experiments involving the use of implements in problem-solving tasks. The article for psychoanalysis is drawn from Freud's first lecture to an American audience, at Clark University in 1909, as found in the new translation by Saul Rosenzweig. These original source materials describe in the theorists' own words their unique approach to psychology and illustrate the kind of material studied by earlier generations of college students.

Photographs, tables, and figures have been added to the new edition. Chapters contain outlines, summaries, critical thinking and discussion questions, and annotated reading lists. Important terms are highlighted in the text and defined in a marginal glossary. A comprehensive instructor's manual and test bank has been prepared by Elissa M. Lewis.

We are grateful to the many instructors and students who have contacted us over the years with valuable suggestions. The book has benefited throughout its history from the rigorous and perceptive evaluations of the eminent historian of psychology Ludy T. Benjamin, Jr., of Texas A&M University. We also wish to thank the other reviewers of this edition who offered insightful and timely comments: Gerald S. Clack, Loyola University of the South, New Orleans; Stephen R. Coleman, Cleveland State University; Catherine W. Hickman, Stephens College, Columbia, Missouri; Elissa M. Lewis, Southwest Missouri State University; and W. Scott Terry, The University of North Carolina at Charlotte.

At Harcourt Brace, developmental editor Karee Galloway was a constant source of encouragement and enthusiasm who ably helped us analyze and refine our ideas for the new edition. Senior project editor Angela Williams served as our liaison to the production team and provided stability and support throughout the process. Her professionalism and attention to detail show on every page.

D. P. S.
S. E. S.

To Russ Nazzaro,

*who said to the department's
newest assistant professor,
one day long ago,*

*"How would you like to teach
the history of psychology?"*

Brief Contents

CONTENTS

CHAPTER 16

GENDER AND RACE IN THE HISTORY OF PSYCHOLOGY 463

CHAPTER 1

THE STUDY OF THE HISTORY OF PSYCHOLOGY

THE DEVELOPMENT OF MODERN PSYCHOLOGY

WE BEGIN with a paradox, a seeming contradiction, by noting that psychology is one of the oldest of the scholarly disciplines as well as one of the newest. We have always been fascinated by our own behavior, and speculations about human nature fill many philosophical and theological volumes. As early as the 5th century B.C., Plato, Aristotle, and other Greek scholars grappled with many of the same problems that concern psychologists today: memory, learning, motivation, perception, dreaming, and abnormal behavior. Thus there is a vital continuity in subject matter from the past to the present day.

Although the intellectual precursors of psychology are as ancient as those of any discipline, the modern approach to psychology is said to have begun in 1879, not much more than one hundred years ago.

The distinction between modern psychology—the focus of this book—and its roots has less to do with the kinds of questions asked about human nature than with the methods used to seek the answers to those questions. It is the approach taken and the techniques employed that distinguish the older discipline of philosophy from modern psychology and denote the emergence of psychology as a separate and primarily scientific field of study.

Until the last quarter of the 19th century, philosophers studied human nature through speculation, intuition, and generalization based on their own limited experience. A transformation occurred when philosophers began to apply the tools and methods that had already proved successful in the biological and physical sciences to questions about human nature. Only when researchers came to rely on carefully controlled observation and experimentation to study the human mind did psychology begin to attain an identity separate from its philosophical roots. One historian described this transformation from a philosophical to a scientific enterprise as "the greatest change that has ever occurred in psychology" (Cadwallader, 1992, p. 34).

The new discipline of psychology needed to develop more precise and objective ways of dealing with its subject matter. Much of the history of psychology, after its separation from philosophy, is the story of the continual refinement of tools, techniques, and methods of study to achieve increased precision and objectivity in the questions psychologists asked and in the answers they obtained.

If we are to understand the complex issues that define and divide psychology today, then the proper starting point for the history of the field is the 19th century, the time when psychology became an independent discipline with distinctive methods of inquiry and theoretical rationales. The early philosophers such as Plato and Aristotle concerned themselves with problems that are still of general interest, but they approached these problems in ways vastly different from those of today's psychologists. Those scholars were not *psychologists* in the contemporary usage of the term. Therefore, we will discuss their ideas only as they relate directly to the establishment of modern psychology.

The idea that the methods of the physical and biological sciences could be applied to the study of mental phenomena was inherited from both the philosophical thinking and the physiological investigations of the 17th to 19th centuries. That exciting era forms the immediate background out of which modern psychology emerged. While the 19th-century philosophers were clearing the way for an experimental attack on the functioning of the mind, the physiologists were independently approaching some of the same problems from a different direction. Nineteenth-century physiologists were making great strides toward understanding the bodily mechanisms that underlie mental processes. Their methods of study differed from those of the philosophers, but the eventual union of these disparate disciplines— philosophy and physiology—produced a new field of study that quickly attained an identity and stature of its own.

Once this new field of psychology had been launched, it grew rapidly, particularly in the United States, which assumed and maintains a position of dominance in the psychological world. More than half the world's psychologists work in the U.S., and many psychologists from other nations receive at least a portion of their training at United States institutions. The major share of the world's psychological literature is published in the United States. The American Psychological Association (APA), established with 26 charter members, grew to include 1,100 psychologists by 1930. By 1995, the membership stood at more than 100,000.

This population explosion of psychologists has been paralleled by an information explosion of research reports, theoretical and review articles, computer data files, books, films, videocassettes, and other forms of publication. It is increasingly difficult for psychologists to remain knowledgeable about developments beyond their own specialty areas.

Psychology has grown not only in terms of its practitioners, researchers, scholars, and published literature, but also in its impact on our daily lives. Whatever your age, occupation, or interests, your life is likely to be directly affected in some way by the work of psychologists.

THE RELEVANCE OF THE PAST FOR THE PRESENT

Courses in the history of psychology were offered as long ago as 1911, and most psychology departments offer them today (McGovern, 1992). Some departments require a course in the history of psychology for a degree. Surveys of undergraduate and graduate psychology curricula consistently recommend that instruction in the history of psychology be required for graduation (Hilgard, Leary, & McGuire, 1991; Lloyd & Brewer, 1992; Matarazzo, 1990).

Of all the sciences, psychology is unique in this regard. Most science departments do not have similar requirements; many do not offer a course in the history of their field. Why are psychologists so interested in the historical development of their subject? One reason has to do with the point we made earlier, that many of the questions asked centuries ago are still relevant today, demonstrating a long continuity of issues and methods within psychology, a connection not apparent in other sciences. This means that psychology has a more tangible and vital link with its own past, which psychologists find satisfying and useful to explore.

The interest of psychologists in the history of their field has led to its formalization as an area of study. Just as there are psychologists who specialize in social problems, psychopharmacology, or adolescent development, so there are those who specialize in the history of psychology.

In 1965, a multidisciplinary journal, the *Journal of the History of the Behavioral Sciences*, was begun under the editorship of a psychologist. That same year the Archives of the History of American Psychology was established at the University of Akron, Ohio, to serve the needs of scholars by collecting and preserving source materials in the history of psychology. The Division of the History of Psychology (Division 26) was formed within the APA in 1966, and in 1969 the International Society for the History of the Behavioral and Social Sciences (the Cheiron Society) was founded. Graduate work in the history of psychology is offered at several universities. The growth in the number of books, articles, meetings, and archives reflects the importance psychologists attribute to the study of the history of psychology.

"That's mildly interesting," you may say, "but why does it mean that *I* have to study the history of psychology?" Consider what you have learned from your other psychology courses, namely, that there is no single form, approach, or definition of psychology on which all psychologists agree. You know that there is an enormous diversity, even divisiveness and fragmentation, in professional and scientific specialization and in subject matter.

Some psychologists focus on cognitive functions, others deal with unconscious forces, and still others work only with overt behavior or with physiological and biochemical processes. Modern psychology includes many subject areas that seem to have little in common beyond a broad interest in human nature and conduct and an approach that attempts in some way to be scientific.

The only framework that binds these diverse areas and approaches, and gives them a coherent context, is their history, the evolution of psychology as an independent discipline. Only by exploring psychology's origins and studying its development over time can we see clearly the nature of psychology today. A knowledge of history brings order to disorder and imposes meaning on what appears to be chaos, putting the past into perspective to explain the present.

Several types of psychologists practice a similar technique, agreeing that the influence of the past helps shape the present. Clinical psychologists, for example, attempt to understand the present condition of their clients by exploring their childhood, by examining the forces and events that may cause their patients to behave or to think in certain ways. By compiling case histories, clinicians reconstruct the evolution of their clients' lives, and often that process leads to explanations of present behaviors. Behavioral psychologists also accept the influence of the past in shaping the present. They believe that behavior is determined by prior conditioning and reinforcing experiences; in other words, that the current state of the person can be explained by his or her history.

So it is with the discipline of psychology. A course in the history of psychology integrates the areas and issues that constitute modern psychology. It will enable you to recognize relationships among various ideas, theories, and research efforts and to understand how different pieces of the psychology puzzle come together to form a coherent pattern. We might also describe the history of psychology as a case study, an exploration of psychology's historical events and experiences that have made it what it is today.

We should add that the history of psychology is a fascinating story on its own, offering drama, tragedy, heroism, and revolution, and even a share of sex and drugs. There have been false starts, mistakes, and misconceptions, but overall there has been a clear evolution that has shaped contemporary psychology and provides us with an explanation for its richness.

THE DATA OF HISTORY: RECONSTRUCTING PSYCHOLOGY'S PAST

The data of history—the materials historians use to reconstruct lives, events, and eras—differ markedly from the data of science. The most distinctive feature of scientific data is the way they are gathered. When psychologists want to determine, for example, the conditions under which people will help those in distress, the ways in which different reinforcement schedules influence the behavior of laboratory rats, or whether children will imitate the aggressive behavior they see on television, they construct situations or establish conditions out of which data will be generated.

They may conduct a laboratory experiment, observe behavior under controlled real-world conditions, take a survey, or calculate the statistical correlation between two variables. In using these approaches, scientists shape the situations or events they wish to study. In turn, those events can be reconstructed or replicated by other scientists at some other time and place. The data can be verified by establishing conditions similar to those of the original study and repeating the observation.

In contrast, the data of history cannot be reconstructed or replicated. Each event or situation occurred at some time in the past, perhaps centuries ago, and historians of the day may not have recorded all the details of the event as it unfolded. "History is an all-or-nothing affair; something happened once, and that is that—you cannot bring past events back into the present to study them and their determinants and effects at leisure . . . as you can examine some scientific statement in the laboratory" (Wertheimer, 1979, p. 1).

If the historical incident itself is lost to view, how can historians deal with it? What data can they use to describe it? And how can anyone possibly tell all that really happened?

Just because historians cannot repeat a situation to generate pertinent data does not mean that significant information does not exist. The data of history are available to us as fragments of past events—descriptions recorded by participants or witnesses, letters and diaries, photographs and laboratory equipment, interviews and other official accounts. And it is from these sources, these data-fragments, that historians try to re-create the events and experiences of the past.

This approach is similar to that taken by archaeologists who work with fragments of past civilizations—such as arrowheads, shards of clay pots, or human bones—and try to describe the characteristics of those civilizations. Some archaeological excavations yield more detailed data-fragments than others, allowing for more accurate reconstructions. Similarly, with excavations in history, the data-fragments may be so great as to leave little doubt about the accuracy of our reconstruction.

Lost or Suppressed Data

Sometimes historical data are incomplete. They may have been lost, deliberately suppressed, distorted by a scholar motivated by self-interest, or translated inaccurately from one language to another. The history of psychology contains many incomplete examples in the generation of historical truth.

Consider, for example, data that have been lost. It has happened that important personal papers were missing for decades before being discovered. In 1984, the papers of Hermann Ebbinghaus, prominent in the study of learning and memory, were found some 75 years after his death. In 1983, 10 large boxes containing handwritten diaries of Gustav Fechner, who developed psychophysics, were uncovered. These diaries covered the period 1828–1879, a time of great significance in the early history of psychology, yet for more than 100 years psychologists were unaware of their existence. Many books had been written about Ebbinghaus and about Fechner and their work without the authors having access to these important collections of personal papers. Uncovering these new fragments of history means that more pieces of the puzzle can be set in place.

Other data may be hidden deliberately from public view or altered to protect the image or reputation of the people involved. Sigmund Freud's first biographer, Ernest Jones, deliberately minimized Freud's use of cocaine, commenting in a letter, "I'm afraid that Freud took more cocaine than he should though I'm not mentioning that [in my biography]" (Isbister, 1985, p. 35). We will see when we discuss Freud (chapter 13) that more recently uncovered data confirm that he used cocaine for a longer period than Jones was willing to admit in print.

Another case of suppressed data was discovered during a study of the life and work of the Gestalt psychologist Wolfgang Köhler (see chapter 12). "Based on the sample of documents I had read," the researcher reported, "my impression was that they had been carefully selected to present a favorable profile of Köhler. The papers revealed nice things that Köhler said and flattering things that were said about him" (Ley, 1990, p. 197). This incident illustrates one of the difficulties faced by scholars in assessing the worth of historical materials: Are the documents or other data-fragments accurate representations of the person's life and work, or have they been chosen to foster a particular (positive or negative) image?

For a final example of suppressed data-fragments, let us return to Sigmund Freud. He died in 1939, and in the years since his death many of his papers and letters have been released to scholars and been published. A large collection of personal documents is held by the Library of Congress in Washington, D.C. At the request of the Freud estate, some of these will not be made available until well into the next century. The stated reason for this restriction is to protect the privacy of Freud's patients and their families, and perhaps Freud and his family as well.

A noted Freud scholar found considerable variation in the release dates of this material (Sulloway, 1992). For example, one letter to Freud from his eldest son is sealed until the year 2013, another until 2032. A letter from one of Freud's mentors will not be released until 2102, some 177 years after the man died, leading one to question what could be so remarkable about that letter as to require such "seemingly paranoid secrecy" (Sulloway, 1992, p. 159).

Psychologists do not know how these archival documents will affect our understanding of Freud and his work. Perhaps they will fundamentally alter our perceptions, or perhaps they will not change our knowledge at all. Until the data are available for study, however, our knowledge of one of psychology's pivotal figures remains incomplete and, possibly, inaccurate.

Data Distorted in Translation

Another problem with the data of history relates to information that has come to the historian in distorted form. The data are available, but they have been changed in some way, perhaps through faulty translation from one language to another or through distortions introduced—deliberately or carelessly—by a participant or observer in recording the relevant events.

We can refer to Freud's life and work again for examples of the misleading impact of translations. Not many psychologists are sufficiently fluent in the German language to read Freud in the original. Most people rely on a translator's choice of the most suitable or equivalent words and phrases. However, the correspondence between the translation and the original author's intended meaning is not always exact.

Three fundamental concepts in Freud's theory of the structure of the human personality are the id, the ego, and the superego, terms with which you are familiar. But these words do not represent Freud's ideas precisely. They are the Latin equivalents of Freud's German words: ego for *Ich* (I), id for *Es* (it), and superego for *Über-Ich* (above-I).

Freud wanted to describe something highly intimate and personal with his use of *Ich* (I) and to distinguish it clearly from *Es* (it), which represents something distinct from or foreign to "I." "The translation of the personal pronouns [from German] into their Latin equivalents—the 'ego' and the 'id'—rather than their English ones turned them into cold technical terms, which arouse no personal associations" (Bettelheim, 1982, p. 53). Thus, the distinction between "I" and "it" is not as pronounced in the translation as in the original.

Consider the common Freudian term *free association*. Here the word *association* implies a conscious link or connection between one idea or thought and another, as though each one acts as a stimulus to elicit the next word in a chain. This is not what Freud believed. His term in German was *Einfall*, which does not mean an association. It means, literally, an intrusion or an invasion. Freud used the word to denote something from the unconscious mind that is uncontrollably intruding on or invading a person's conscious thought.

These are important differences in meaning from what Freud intended. Our historical data—in this case, Freud's own words—have been distorted in the act of translation. An Italian proverb, "to translate is to betray," expresses this point succinctly (Baars, 1986, p. 73). Historians who rely on translations must be aware that they may be dealing with inaccurate or imprecise data-fragments. In the 1980s, the British Psycho-Analytical Society recommended that the standard translation of Freud's works be revised, because it was held to present such a distorted view of his ideas (Holder, 1988).

Self-Serving Data

The data of history may also be affected by the actions of the participants themselves in recording pivotal events. People may, consciously or unconsciously, leave us biased accounts to protect themselves or to enhance their public images. B. F. Skinner, the prominent behavioral psychologist, described in his autobiography his rigorous self-discipline while he was a graduate student at Harvard University in the late 1920s. The following paragraph has been quoted frequently in biographies of Skinner.

> *I would rise at six, study until breakfast, go to classes, laboratories, and libraries with no more than fifteen minutes unscheduled during the day, study until exactly nine o'clock at night and go to bed. I saw no movies or plays, seldom went to concerts, had scarcely any dates and read nothing but psychology and physiology.* (SKINNER, 1967, P. 398)

This description seems to be a useful data-fragment that provides insight into Skinner's character. But 12 years after this material was published, and 51 years after the event itself, Skinner denied that his graduate school days had been as spartan and difficult as he had suggested. Referring to the paragraph quoted above he wrote, "I was recalling a pose rather than the life I actually led" (Skinner, 1979, p. 5).

Although Skinner's school days may be of minor importance in the history of psychology, the two versions, both written by the participant, indicate something of the difficulty historians face. Which set of data—which version of this incident—is the more accurate? Which characterization comes closer to reality? Which has been influenced by the vagaries or the self-serving nature of memory? And how are we to know?

In some cases it is possible to find corroborating data from colleagues or observers. If Skinner's graduate school regimen were highly significant for historians of psychology, they could try to locate Skinner's classmates, or at least their diaries or letters, and compare those recollections of Skinner's behavior at Harvard with his own. This was done by biographer Daniel Bjork (Bjork, 1993). A former classmate of Skinner's told Bjork that Skinner always finished his laboratory work sooner than the other graduate students and would spend the remainder of his afternoons playing Ping-Pong.

Thus, some distortions in history can be investigated and the controversies resolved by consulting other sources. This method was applied to Sigmund Freud's descriptions of certain events in his life. Freud liked to depict himself as a martyr to his psychoanalytic cause, a visionary who was constantly scorned, rejected, and vilified by the established forces in medicine and psychiatry. Freud's first biographer, Ernest Jones, reinforced these claims in his books (Jones, 1953, 1955, 1957).

Data uncovered more recently report a different situation: Freud's work was not being ignored. By 1906, Freud's ideas were exerting an immense influence on the younger generation of intellectuals in Vienna. Freud's clinical practice was thriving, and he could even be described, in modern jargon, as a celebrity (Ellenberger, 1970). Freud himself had distorted the record, and these distortions were perpetuated by several biographers. The false impression he created has now been corrected, but for several decades—until new data-fragments were excavated—our understanding of Freud's influence during his lifetime was inaccurate.

What do these problems with the data of history suggest about our study of the history of psychology? They show primarily that our understanding of history is dynamic, not static or stagnant. The story changes and grows, refined and enhanced whenever new data are uncovered and misconceptions are corrected. A history can never be considered finished or complete but is always in progress, a story without an ending. The historian's narrative can only approximate or approach the truth, but it does so more fully with each passing year, with each new finding and examination of the fragments that are the data of history.

CONTEXTUAL FORCES IN PSYCHOLOGY

A science such as psychology does not develop in a vacuum, subject only to internal influences. It is part of the larger culture and is, therefore, subject to external influences that shape its nature and direction. An understanding of psychology's history must consider the

ZEITGEIST: The general
intellectual and cultural
climate or spirit of the times

context in which the discipline emerged and evolved; that is, the prevailing ideas in the science of the day (the **Zeitgeist** or intellectual
climate of the times), and the existing social, economic, and political
forces (Altman, 1987; Furumoto, 1989).

We describe instances throughout this book of how these contextual forces shaped psychology's past and continue to affect its present. Let us note here as examples three such influences: economic
opportunity, war, and prejudice.

Economic Opportunity as a Contextual Force

The early years of the 20th century saw a change in the nature of psychology in the United States and the type of work psychologists were
doing. Largely because of economic forces, opportunities were increasing for the application of psychological knowledge and techniques to real-world problems. The primary explanation for this
change was practical. As one psychologist said, "I became an applied
psychologist in order to earn a living" (H. Hollingworth, quoted in
O'Donnell, 1985, p. 225).

Although the number of psychology laboratories in the United
States was growing steadily toward the end of the 19th century, so
was the number of psychologists competing for jobs in those laboratories. By the turn of the century, there were three times as many psychologists with doctoral degrees as there were labs to employ them.
Fortunately, the number of teaching jobs was increasing as states
throughout the Midwest and the West established universities, but in
most of those institutions, psychology, as the youngest of the sciences,
received the smallest amount of financial support. Compared to
more established disciplines such as physics and chemistry, psychology consistently ranked lowest in annual appropriations; there was
little money for research projects, laboratory equipment, and faculty
salaries.

Psychologists quickly realized that if their academic departments, budgets, and incomes were ever to grow, they would have to
persuade university administrators, and the state legislators who
voted appropriations, that psychology could be useful in solving social, educational, and industrial problems. And so, in time, psychology departments came to be judged on the basis of their practical
worth.

At the same time, as a result of social changes in the U.S. population, there arose an exciting opportunity to apply psychology to a
practical problem. Because of the influx of immigrants to the United
States around the turn of the century, and their high birth rate, public education had become a growth industry. Between 1890 and 1918,
public school enrollments increased 700%, and new high schools
were being built across the country at the rate of one a day. More

money was being spent on education than on the military and welfare programs combined.

Many psychologists took advantage of this situation and sought
ways to apply their knowledge and research methods to education.
This was the beginning of a rapid change in emphasis in American
psychology, from the experimentation of the academic laboratory to
the application of psychology to problems of learning, teaching, and
other practical classroom issues.

War as a Contextual Force

Wars are another contextual force that helped shape modern psychology. The experiences of psychologists in aiding the war effort in
World Wars I and II accelerated the growth of applied psychology and
extended its influence into areas such as personnel selection, psychological testing, and engineering psychology. This work demonstrated
to the psychological community at large, and to the general public,
how useful psychology could be in solving problems of everyday life.

World War II also changed the face and fate of psychology in
Europe, particularly in Germany, where experimental psychology
began, and in Austria, which was the birthplace of psychoanalysis.
Many noted psychologists—among them Freud, Adler, Horney, Erikson, and the leading Gestalt psychologists—fled the Nazi menace in
the 1930s, and most of them settled in America. Their forced exile
marks the final phase of the shift of dominance in psychology from
Europe to the United States.

War also influenced the theories and systems proposed by individual psychologists. After witnessing the carnage of World War I,
Freud proposed that aggression was as important a motivating force
in human life as was sex; this represented a major change in his system of psychoanalysis. The personality theorist and antiwar activist
Erich Fromm attributed his later interest in abnormal behavior
to his exposure to the fanaticism that swept his native Germany during the war.

Prejudice as a Contextual Force

A third contextual factor is prejudice and discrimination on the basis
of race, religion, and gender, which for many years have influenced
who could become a psychologist and where he or she could work.
For decades, African Americans were largely excluded from psychology and from most fields that required advanced academic study. As
late as 1940, only four Black colleges in the United States offered undergraduate degrees in psychology, and few universities accepted
Black men and women as graduate students. Between 1920 and 1966,
the 10 most prestigious psychology departments in the United States
granted only eight PhD degrees to African Americans; more than

3,700 doctorates were awarded to Whites during those same years (Guthrie, 1976).

Jews were also victims of discrimination. The late 1800s saw the founding of Johns Hopkins University in Baltimore, Maryland, and Clark University in Worcester, Massachusetts, both important institutions in the early history of psychology. Their general policy was to exclude Jewish professors from their faculties. Well into the middle of the 20th century, Jewish men and women faced admissions quotas in graduate schools. Those who did earn doctoral degrees found it difficult to obtain academic jobs. Julian Rotter, a leading personality theorist (see chapter 11), received his PhD in 1941, and recalled that he "had been warned that Jews simply could not get academic jobs, regardless of their credentials" (Rotter, 1982, p. 346). He began his professional career working at a state mental hospital instead of a university.

Widespread prejudice against women has existed throughout psychology's history. We will discuss cases of women who were denied admission to graduate school and excluded from faculty positions. Even when women were able to obtain such appointments, they were paid lower salaries than men, and they encountered barriers to promotion and tenure. Sandra Scarr, a professor of psychology at the University of Virginia, recalls her admission interview for graduate school at Harvard University in 1960. She was told by Gordon Allport, an eminent social psychologist, that "we hate accepting women here. Seventy-five percent of you get married, have kids and never finish your degrees, and the rest of you never amount to anything anyway" (Scarr, 1987, p. 26).

Groups subject to systematic discrimination and prejudice are underrepresented in academic and professional psychology. Recognition of this situation has led some psychologists to propose a new contextual force, a challenge to psychology called *identity politics*. This is defined as "politics based on the particular life experiences of people who seek to be in control of their own identities and subjectivities and who claim that socially dominant groups have denied them this opportunity" (Sampson, 1993, p. 1219).

The identity-politics movement involves women, Blacks, gays, and minorities from developing countries who charge that psychology's conception of human nature is predominantly, if not exclusively, White, heterosexual, male, and Eurocentric. The disaffected claim that this view of human functioning and conduct not only ignores their needs and concerns, but also sustains the majority group's dominance and power. In chapter 16 we discuss the history of discrimination in psychology and psychology's response to the challenge.

Throughout this book we examine other examples of the impact of economic, political, and social forces on the development of modern psychology. Thus we see that the history of psychology has been shaped not only by the ideas, theories, and research of its leaders, but also by external influences, the contextual forces over which it had little control.

PERSONALISTIC AND NATURALISTIC CONCEPTIONS OF SCIENTIFIC HISTORY

Two approaches can be taken to explain how the science of psychology has developed: the personalistic theory and the naturalistic theory.

The Personalistic Theory of Scientific History

The **personalistic theory** of scientific history focuses on the monumental achievements and contributions of specific individuals. According to this view, progress and change are attributable directly to the will and force of unique people who alone charted and changed the course of history. A Napoleon, a Hitler, or a Darwin were, so this theory goes, the prime movers and shapers of great events. The personalistic conception implies that the events would never have occurred without the appearance of these singular figures. The theory says, in effect, that the person makes the times.

At first glance, it seems obvious that a science is the work of the intelligent, creative, and energetic men and women who have determined its direction. We often define an era by the name of the person whose discoveries, theories, or other contributions marked the period. We talk of physics "after Einstein" or sculpture "after Michelangelo." It is apparent, both in science and in the general culture, that individuals have produced dramatic (sometimes traumatic) changes that have altered the course of history.

Therefore, the personalistic theory has merit, but is it sufficient to explain entirely the development of a science or a society? No. The work of scientists, philosophers, artists, and scholars has often been ignored or suppressed during their lifetimes, only to be recognized long afterward. These occurrences imply that the cultural or spiritual climate of the times can determine whether an idea will be accepted or rejected, praised or scorned. The history of science is full of instances of the rejection of new discoveries and insights. Even the greatest thinkers and inventors have been constrained by the contextual factor called the Zeitgeist, the intellectual spirit or climate of the times. The acceptance and application of a discovery may be limited by the prevailing pattern of thought, but an idea that is too strange or unorthodox to gain acceptance in one place or time may be readily accepted a generation or a century later. Slow change is often the rule for scientific progress.

PERSONALISTIC THEORY: The idea that progress and change in scientific history are attributable to the actions of unique individuals

The Naturalistic Theory of Scientific History

NATURALISTIC THEORY: The idea that progress and change in scientific history are attributable to the Zeitgeist, which may make people receptive to some ideas but not to others

The notion that the person makes the times, then, is not entirely correct. Perhaps, as the **naturalistic theory** of history proposes, the times make the person, or at least make possible the recognition of what that person has to say. Unless the Zeitgeist and the other social forces we've described are ready for the new idea or the novel approach, its proponent may not be heard, or may be laughed at or put to death; this, too, depends on the Zeitgeist.

The naturalistic theory suggests, for example, that if Charles Darwin had died in his youth, someone else would have developed a theory of evolution in the middle of the 19th century. Another scholar would have proposed an evolutionary theory of some kind (though not necessarily precisely the same theory), because the intellectual climate was ready to accept a new way of looking at the origin of the human species. (We see in chapter 6 that someone else did propose such a theory at the same time.)

The inhibiting or delaying effect of the Zeitgeist operates not only at the cultural level but also within science itself, where its effects may be even more pronounced. As we noted, many scientific discoveries remained dormant for a long time, then were rediscovered and embraced. The concept of the conditioned response was suggested by Robert Whytt, a Scottish scientist, in 1763, but no one was interested in it then. Well over a century later, when researchers were adopting more objective methods, the Russian physiologist Ivan Pavlov elaborated on Whytt's observations and expanded them into the basis of a new system of psychology. Thus, a discovery must often await its time. "There is not much new in this world," observed one psychologist. "What passes for discovery these days tends to be an individual scientist's rediscovery of some well-established phenomenon" (Gazzaniga, 1988, p. 231).

Instances of simultaneous discovery also support the naturalistic conception of scientific history. Similar discoveries have been made by individuals working far apart geographically, often in ignorance of one another's work. In 1900, three investigators unknown to one another coincidentally rediscovered the work of the Austrian botanist Gregor Mendel, whose writings on genetics had been largely ignored for 35 years.

The dominant theoretical position in a scientific field may obstruct or prohibit consideration of new viewpoints. One theory or approach may be held so strongly by the majority of the scientists that any investigation of new issues or methods is stifled. An established theory can also determine the ways in which data are organized and analyzed, as well as the kind of research results that are permitted to be published in the scientific journals. Findings that contradict or oppose current views may be rejected by a journal's editors, who function as censors, enforcing conformity of thought by rejecting or trivi-alizing a revolutionary idea or an unusual interpretation.

An instance of this occurred in the 1970s, when psychologist John Garcia attempted to publish the results of research that challenged the prevailing S-R (stimulus-response) theory of learning. The main-stream journals refused to accept his articles, even though the work was considered to be well done and had already received professional recognition and prestigious awards. Garcia eventually published his findings in lesser known, smaller circulation journals, which delayed the dissemination of his ideas (Lubek & Apfelbaum, 1987).

The Zeitgeist within a science can have an inhibiting effect on methods of investigation, on theoretical formulations, and on the def-inition of the discipline's subject matter. We describe in the chapters that follow the early tendency in scientific psychology to focus on consciousness and the subjective aspects of human nature. Not until the 1920s could it be said that psychology finally "lost its mind," then it lost consciousness altogether! But a half century later, under the impact of a different Zeitgeist, psychology began to regain conscious-ness as an acceptable problem for investigation, in response to the changing intellectual climate of the times.

Perhaps we can more readily understand this situation if we make an analogy with the evolution of a living species. Both a science and a living species change or evolve in response to the conditions and demands of its environment. What happens to a species over time? Very little, as long as its environment remains largely constant. When the environment changes, however, the species must adapt to the new conditions or face extinction.

Similarly, a science exists in the context of an environment to which it must be responsive. The environment of that science, its Zeitgeist, is not so much physical as it is intellectual. But like the physical environment, the Zeitgeist is subject to changes.

This evolutionary process is evident throughout the history of psychology. When the Zeitgeist favored speculation, meditation, and intuition as paths to truth, psychology also favored those methods. When the intellectual spirit of the times later dictated an observa-tional and experimental approach to truth, the methods of psychology turned in that direction. When at the beginning of the 20th century one form of psychology found itself planted in two different intellec-tual soils, it became two species of psychology. This occurred when the original German form of psychology emigrated to the United States and was modified to become a uniquely American form, whereas the psychology that remained in Germany grew in a different way.

Our emphasis on the Zeitgeist does not negate the importance of the personalistic conception of the history of science, those significant contributions of its great men and women, but it does require us to consider them in a different perspective. A Charles Darwin or a Marie

Curie does not singlehandedly alter the course of history through sheer force of genius. He or she does so only because the path has, in some fashion, already been cleared; this has been true for every major figure in the history of psychology.

We believe, then, that the historical development of psychology must be considered in terms of both the personalistic and the naturalistic approaches, although the Zeitgeist appears to play the major role. When scientists and scholars propose ideas that are too far out of phase with the prevailing spirit of the times, their insights may die in obscurity. Individual creative work is more like a prism—diffusing, elaborating, and magnifying current thought—than like a beacon, although both will shed light on the path ahead.

SCHOOLS OF THOUGHT IN THE EVOLUTION OF MODERN PSYCHOLOGY

During the initial years of the evolution of psychology as a separate scientific discipline, in the last quarter of the 19th century, the direction of the new psychology was influenced profoundly by Wilhelm Wundt, a German physiologist, who had definite ideas about the form this new science—*his* new science—should take (see chapter 4). He determined the goals and subject matter, the research method, and the topics to be investigated. He was, of course, affected by the spirit of his times and the current thinking in philosophy and physiology. Nevertheless, it was Wundt, in his role as the agent of the Zeitgeist, who drew together the various philosophical and scientific lines of thought. Because he was such a compelling promoter of the inevitable, psychology was, for some time, shaped by his vision.

Before long, the situation changed. Controversy arose among the growing number of psychologists. New ideas were being advanced in other sciences and in the general culture. Some psychologists, reflecting these new currents of thought, came to disagree with Wundt's version of psychology and proposed their own. By around 1900, then, several systematic positions and schools of thought uneasily coexisted. We may think of them as, in essence, different definitions of the nature of psychology.

SCHOOL OF THOUGHT: A group of scholars who become associated ideologically with a system of ideas, sharing a theoretical orientation and working on common problems

The term **school of thought** within psychology refers to a group of psychologists who become associated ideologically, and sometimes geographically, with the leader of a movement. Typically the members of a school of thought share a theoretical or systematic orientation and work on similar problems. The emergence of various schools of thought and their subsequent decline and replacement by others is a striking characteristic of the history of psychology.

This stage in the development of a science, when it is still divided into schools of thought, has been called the preparadigmatic stage (Kuhn, 1970). (A *paradigm*, which is a model or pattern, is an accepted way of thinking within a scientific discipline that provides, for a time, the essential questions and answers for researchers in that field.) The more mature or advanced stage in the development of a science is reached when it is no longer characterized by schools of thought; that is, when the majority of the members of a discipline agree on theoretical and methodological issues. At that stage, a common paradigm or model defines the entire field, and there are no longer competing factions.

We can see paradigms at work in the history of physics. The Galilean-Newtonian concept of mechanism was accepted by physicists for some 300 years, and during that time virtually all physics research was conducted within that framework. Paradigms can change, however, once a majority of the scientists and practitioners accept a new way of viewing or working with the subject matter. In physics this occurred when the Galilean-Newtonian model was replaced by the Einsteinian model. This replacement of one paradigm by another may be thought of as a "scientific revolution" (Kuhn, 1970).

Psychology has not yet reached the paradigmatic stage. For all of psychology's history, psychologists have been seeking, embracing, and rejecting different definitions. No single system or viewpoint has succeeded in unifying the various positions. The pioneering cognitive psychologist George Miller (see chapter 15) commented that "no standard method or technique integrates the field. Nor does there seem to be any fundamental scientific principle comparable to Newton's laws of motion or Darwin's theory of evolution" (Miller, 1985, p. 42).

If there is anything on which psychologists might agree, it is that "psychology is more heterogeneous today than at any other time in the past century, and anything like a consensus as to the nature of psychology seems more distant than ever" (Evans, Sexton, & Cadwallader, 1992, p. xvi). Other psychologists offer similar views. "Approaching the end of the [20th] century, there remains no unified framework or set of principles to define the discipline of psychology and to guide research" (Chiesa, 1992, p. 1287). "Psychology . . . is not a single discipline but a collection of studies of varied cast" (Koch, 1993, p. 902). "American psychology finds itself divided into bitterly quarreling factions" (Leahey, 1992, p. 308). The field remains fragmented, with each group clinging to its own theoretical and methodological orientation, approaching the study of human nature with different techniques and promoting itself with specialized jargon, journals, and the trappings of a school of thought.

Each of the early schools of thought in psychology was a protest movement, a revolt, against the prevailing systematic position. Each school pointed out loudly what it saw as the weaknesses of the older system and offered new definitions, concepts, and research strategies to correct the perceived failures. When a new school of thought captured the attention of the scientific community, the previously held viewpoint was rejected. These intellectual conflicts between old and new positions were fought with righteous fervor on both sides.

Often, the leaders of the older school of thought never became convinced of the worth of the new system. Usually more advanced in years, these leaders remained too deeply committed to their position, intellectually and emotionally, ever to change. Younger and less committed adherents of the older school were often attracted to the new ideas and became supporters of the new position, leaving the rest to cling to their traditions, working in increasing isolation.

The German physicist Max Planck wrote that "a new scientific truth does not triumph by convincing its opponents and making them see the light, but rather because its opponents eventually die, and a new generation grows up that is familiar with it" (Planck, 1949, p. 33). "What a good thing it would be," Charles Darwin wrote to a friend, "if every scientific man was to die when sixty years old, as afterward he would be sure to oppose all new doctrines" (quoted in Boorstin, 1983, p. 468).

Different schools of thought have developed during the course of the history of psychology, each one an effective protest against what had gone before. Each new school used its older opponent as a base against which to push and gain momentum. Each position proclaimed what it was not and how it differed from the older theoretical system. As the new system developed and attracted supporters and influence, it inspired opposition, and the whole combative process began anew. What was once a pioneering, aggressive revolution became, with success, the established tradition, which then succumbed to the vigorous force of the next youthful movement. Success destroys vigor. A movement feeds on opposition. When the opposition has been defeated, the passion and ardor of the once new movement die.

The dominance of at least some of the schools of thought was only temporary, but each played a vital part in the development of psychology. And the influence of the schools can be seen in contemporary psychology, although the divisions in today's psychology bear little similarity to the earlier systems because new doctrines have again replaced the old. The function of the schools of thought in psychology has been compared to that of the scaffolding used in erecting a tall building (Heidbreder, 1933). Without the scaffolding from which to work, the structure could not be built, yet the scaffolding does not remain; it will be torn down when it is no longer needed. Likewise, the structure of today's psychology has been built within the framework and guidelines (the scaffolding) established by the schools of thought.

It is in terms of the historical development of the schools of thought that the advance of psychology can best be understood. Great men and women have made inspiring contributions, but the significance of their work is most notable when examined within the context of the ideas that preceded theirs—on which they built—and the work that followed.

Plan of the Book

We describe the philosophical and physiological precursors of experimental psychology in chapters 2 and 3. The psychology of Wilhelm Wundt (chapter 4) and the school of thought called **structuralism** (chapter 5) developed from these philosophical and physiological traditions. Structuralism was followed by **functionalism** (chapters 6, 7, and 8), **behaviorism** (chapters 9, 10, and 11), and **Gestalt psychology** (chapter 12), all of which evolved from or revolted against structuralism. On a roughly parallel course in time—though not in subject matter or methodology—**psychoanalysis** (chapters 13 and 14) evolved from ideas on the nature of the unconscious and from physicians' attempts to treat the mentally ill.

Psychoanalysis and behaviorism instigated a number of sub-schools. In the 1950s, **humanistic psychology** developed in reaction to behaviorism and psychoanalysis; it incorporated principles of Gestalt psychology. Around 1960, the **cognitive psychology** movement challenged behaviorism, and the definition of psychology was revised once again. The major aspect of that most recent change is a return to the study of consciousness and mental or cognitive processes. Having "lost its mind" in the behaviorist revolution, psychology can now be said to have regained it. These developments are described in chapter 15.

The story of psychology's evolution continues in chapter 16 with a current challenge to the field: the attempt to end discriminatory and exclusionary practices in psychology and to recognize the contributions of a more diverse group of psychologists.

DISCUSSION QUESTIONS

1. Why can psychologists claim that psychology is one of the oldest scholarly disciplines, as well as one of the newest? Explain why modern psychology is a product of both the 19th and 20th centuries.
2. What can we learn from studying the history of psychology?
3. How do the data of history differ from the data of science? Give examples of how the data of history can be distorted.
4. Discuss several contextual forces that have influenced the development of modern psychology.

STRUCTURALISM: Titchener's system of psychology, which deals with conscious experience as it is dependent on experiencing persons

FUNCTIONALISM: The system of psychology concerned with the mind as it is used in an organism's adaptation to its environment

BEHAVIORISM: Watson's science of behavior that dealt only with observable behavioral acts which could be described objectively

GESTALT PSYCHOLOGY: A system of psychology focusing largely on learning and perception, suggesting that the act of combining sensory elements produces new patterns with properties that did not exist in the individual elements

PSYCHOANALYSIS: Freud's theory of personality, as well as his system of therapy for treating mental disorders

HUMANISTIC PSYCHOLOGY: A system of psychology emphasizing the study of conscious experience and the wholeness of human nature and conduct

COGNITIVE PSYCHOLOGY: A system of psychology that focuses on the process of knowing, on how the mind actively organizes experiences

5. Describe the differences between the personalistic and the naturalistic conceptions of scientific history. Which approach is supported by instances of simultaneous discovery?
6. What is the Zeitgeist? How does the Zeitgeist affect the evolution of a science? Compare the growth of a science with the evolution of a living species.
7. What is meant by the term *school of thought*? Has the science of psychology reached the paradigmatic stage in its development? Why or why not?

SUGGESTED READINGS

Boorstin, D. (1983). *The discoverers.* New York: Random House. A dramatic account of the great discoveries in the history of human knowledge. Describes how the originators and proponents of these ideas had to fight entrenched dogma and myth to achieve acceptance of their work.

Buxton, C. E. (Ed.). (1985). *Points of view in the modern history of psychology.* Orlando, FL: Academic Press. Readings on issues in historiography (the principles and techniques of historical research). See chapter 14 on the influence of philosophical, biological, and religious viewpoints as contextual forces.

Cadwallader, T. C. (1975). Unique values of archival research. *Journal of the History of the Behavioral Sciences, 11,* 27–33. Discusses archival research (unpublished documents, diaries, correspondence, and notebooks) in tracing the development of a theory from its published form back through its earlier versions, revealing the impact of a theorist's personal circumstances on his or her ideas.

Furumoto, L. (1989). The new history of psychology. In I. S. Cohen (Ed.), *The G. Stanley Hall lecture series* (vol. 9, pp. 5–34). Washington, DC: American Psychological Association. Urges an approach based on the consideration of contextual forces in historical analysis and shows how this approach leads to a different understanding of the role of women psychologists in the development of the field.

CHAPTER 2

PHILOSOPHICAL INFLUENCES
ON PSYCHOLOGY

THE SPIRIT OF MECHANISM

IN THE royal gardens of Europe in the 17th century there appeared a whimsical form of amusement among the many marvels of an exciting age: Water running through underground pipes operated mechanical figures that performed an astonishing variety of movements, played musical instruments, and produced wordlike sounds. Hidden pressure plates, activated when people unknowingly stepped on them, sent water flowing through the pipes to the mechanisms that moved the statues.

These toys of the aristocracy reflected and reinforced the 17th-century fascination with all types of machines, then being invented and perfected for use in science, industry, and entertainment. The mechanical clock—called by one historian the "mother of machines"—had the greatest impact on scientific thought (Boorstin, 1983). Clockmakers were the first craftsmen to apply theories from physics and mechanics to the construction of machinery. In addition, engineers developed pumps, levers, pulleys, and cranes to serve the needs of agriculture and industry, and there seemed to be no limit to the machines that could be devised or the uses to which they could be put.

You may wonder what this growth of technology has to do with the history of modern psychology. We are describing a time 200 years before the founding of psychology as a science, and we are referring to physics and mechanics, disciplines far removed from the study of human nature. The relationship, however, is compelling and direct because the principles embodied by those 17th-century mechanical figures and clocks influenced the direction of the new psychology.

The Zeitgeist of the 17th to 19th centuries is the intellectual soil that nourished the new psychology. The basic contextual force of the 17th century—the underlying philosophy that would nurture the new psychology—was the spirit of **mechanism,** the image of the universe as a great machine. This doctrine held that all natural processes are mechanically determined and are capable of being explained by the laws of physics.

MECHANISM: The doctrine that natural processes are mechanically determined and capable of explanation by the laws of physics and chemistry

The idea of mechanism originated in physics, then called natural philosophy, as a result of the work of the Italian physicist Galileo Galilei (1564–1642) and the English physicist and mathematician Isaac Newton (1642–1727), who had been trained as a clockmaker. Everything that existed in the universe was assumed to be composed of particles of matter in motion. According to Galileo, matter was made up of discrete corpuscles or atoms that affected one another by direct contact. Newton revised Galileo's version of mechanism by suggesting that movement was communicated not by actual physical contact but by forces that acted to attract and repel the atoms. Newton's idea, although important in physics, did not radically change the concept of mechanism and the way it was applied to problems of a psychological nature.

If the universe consists of atoms in motion, then every physical effect (the movement of each atom) follows from a direct cause (the movement of the atom that strikes it). The effect is subject to the laws of measurement and should, therefore, be predictable. The operation of the physical universe was considered to be orderly, like a smoothly running clock or any other good machine. The universe had been designed by God with perfection—in the 17th century, scientists attributed "cause" and "perfection" to God—and it was thought that once scientists grasped the laws by which the world functioned, they could determine how it would run in the future.

The methods and findings of science were growing apace with technology during this period, and the two meshed effectively. Observation and experimentation became the distinguishing features of science, followed closely by measurement. Scholars attempted to define and describe every phenomenon by assigning it a numerical value, a process that was vital to the study of the machinelike universe. Thermometers, barometers, slide rules, micrometers, pendulum clocks, and other measuring devices were perfected during this mechanistic age, and they reinforced the notion that it was possible to measure every aspect of the natural universe.

THE CLOCKWORK UNIVERSE

The clock was the perfect metaphor for the 17th-century spirit of mechanism, and it has justly been called one of the greatest inventions of all time. Clocks were a technological sensation not unlike computers in the 20th century. No other mechanical device had such an impact on human thought at all levels of society. By the 17th century, clocks were being produced in quantity and variety. Some were small enough to fit on a tabletop. Larger ones, housed in church towers and government buildings, could be seen and heard by residents from miles around. Whereas the mechanical, water-powered figures in the royal gardens were for the entertainment only of the elite, clocks were available to everyone, regardless of class or economic circumstances. The concept of the mechanical clock "took possession of the minds and spirits of an entire civilization, in a way no other machine had ever done . . . Rarely in history has a machine so directly expressed, and in turn affected, the intellectual climate of its time" (Maurice & Mayr, 1980, pp. vii, ix).

Because of the availability, regularity, predictability, and precision of clocks, scientists and philosophers began to consider them as models for the physical universe, asking if the world itself might not be "a vast clock made and set in motion by the Creator." Many scientists—including the British physicist Robert Boyle, the German astronomer Johannes Kepler, and the French philosopher René Descartes—answered this question in the affirmative and asserted the belief that the universe was a "great piece of clock work" (quoted in Boorstin, 1983, pp. 71, 72). They and others believed that the harmony and order of the universe could be explained in terms of the clock's regularity, something built into the machine by the clockmaker, just as the regularity of the universe was thought to be built into it by God.

A German philosopher, Christian von Wolff, described the clock and the universe in simple terms: "The universe behaves no differently than a clockwork." His student, Johann Cristoph Gottsched, elaborated on this principle: "Insofar as the universe is a machine, it has to that extent a resemblance to a clock; and it is in a clock that we can on a small scale make plainer to one's understanding that which takes place in the universe on a large scale" (quoted in Maurice & Mayr, 1980, p. 290).

Determinism and Reductionism

When seen as a clocklike machine, the universe, once created by God and set in motion, will continue to function efficiently without any outside interference. Thus, the clock metaphor for the universe encompasses the idea of **determinism,** the belief that every act is determined by past events. We can predict the changes that will occur in the operation of the clock, as well as in the universe, because we understand the order and regularity with which its parts function. "He who has perfect insight into [the clock's] structure can see every

DETERMINISM: The doctrine that acts are determined by past events

future thing from its past and its present state of arrangement" (Gottsched, quoted in Maurice & Mayr, 1980, p. 290).

It was not difficult to gain insight into the structure and functioning of a clock. Anyone could easily disassemble a clock and see exactly how its springs and gears operated. This led to the idea of **reductionism.** The workings of machines such as clocks could be understood by reducing them to their basic components. Similarly, we could understand the physical universe (which was, after all, just another machine) by analyzing or reducing it to its simplest parts— its molecules and atoms. Reductionism would come to characterize every science, including the new psychology.

If the clock metaphor and the methods of science could be used to explain the workings of the physical universe, would they also be appropriate for the study of human nature? If the universe was a machine—orderly, predictable, observable, and measurable—could human beings be considered in the same way? Were people, and even animals, also some type of machine?

REDUCTIONISM: The doctrine that explains phenomena on one level, such as complex ideas, in terms of phenomena on another level, such as simple ideas

Automata

The intellectual and social aristocrats of the 17th century already had the models for such an idea in the mechanical figures in their gardens, and the proliferation of clocks had provided similar models for everyone else. As technology was refined, people had only to look around to see the mechanical contraptions called *automata* performing marvelous and amusing feats with precision and regularity.

Automata—mechanical figures built to imitate human actions— had been developed in earlier times. Ancient Greek and Arabic manuscripts contain descriptions of mechanized figures. China excelled in constructing automata. Chinese literature tells of mechanical animals and fish, and of human figures devised to pour wine, carry cups of tea, sing, dance, and play musical instruments. More than 2,000 years later, when 17th-century Western European scientists, intellectuals, and artisans proposed and developed automata, they were thought to be new. The fundamental work of those earlier civilizations had been lost to view (Mazlish, 1993).

Automata can be seen today in the central squares of European cities where mechanical figures in the town hall's clock tower march in circles, bang drums, and strike bells with hammers on the quarter hour. In France's Strasbourg Cathedral, representations of Biblical figures bow hourly to a statue of the Virgin Mary, while a rooster opens its beak, sticks out its tongue, flaps its wings, and crows. At England's Wells Cathedral, pairs of knights in armor circle each other in mock combat. As the clock strikes the hour, one knight knocks the other off his horse. The Bavarian National Museum in Munich, Germany, houses a parrot 16 inches tall. As the clock strikes the hour,

The National Museum of American History, Smithsonian Institution

FIGURE 2.1 Automaton figure of a monk

the parrot whistles, flaps its mechanical wings, rolls its eyes, and drops a small steel ball from its tail.

In Figure 2.1 you can see the inner workings of a 16-inch figure of a monk, now in the collection of the National Museum of American History in Washington, D.C. The monk is programmed to move within the space of a 2-foot square. Its feet appear to kick out from beneath its robe, but actually the statue is moving on wheels. It beats its chest with one arm and waves with the other, nods its head, and opens and shuts its mouth.

This kind of clockwork technology seemed to the philosophers and scientists of the time to be capable of fulfilling their dream of creating an artificial being. Indeed, many of the early automata clearly gave that appearance. We might consider them to be forerunners of today's Disney-like figures, and it is easy to understand why people reached the conclusion that living beings were simply another type of machine.

Look again at the inner workings of the monk (Figure 2.1). We can comprehend almost at a glance the functioning of the gears, levers, ratchets, and other devices that account for the figure's movements. Descartes and other philosophers adopted these automata as, at least to some extent, models for human beings. Not only was the universe a clockwork machine to them, but so also were its people. Descartes wrote that this idea would not "appear at all strange to those who are acquainted with the different automata, or moving machines, fabricated by human industry . . . such persons will look upon this body as a machine made by the hands of God, which is incomparably better arranged and adequate to movements more admirable than in any machine of human invention" (Descartes, 1637/1912, p. 44). People might be better and more efficient machines than the ones the clockmakers could build, but they were machines nonetheless.

Thus, clocks and automata paved the way for the idea that human functioning and behavior were governed by mechanical laws, and that the experimental and quantitative methods so successful in uncovering the secrets of the physical universe could be applied to the exploration of human nature. In 1748, the French physician Julien de La Mettrie (who died of an overdose of pheasant and truffles) reported a hallucination he had experienced during a high fever; it persuaded him that people were machines, albeit enlightened ones. The human body, he noted, is nothing but a watch that wound its own springs (Mazlish, 1993). This notion became a driving force of the 17th-century Zeitgeist in science and philosophy and drastically altered the prevailing image of human nature. The idea permeated the popular culture for a considerable time. For example, during the Civil War in the United States (1861–1865), a Northern military officer, commenting on the death of a friend, wrote that there was nothing left of him "but the broken machine that the soul once put in motion" (Lyman, quoted in Agassiz, 1922, p. 332).

This mechanical image of human nature was also spread through the literature of the 19th and early 20th centuries, in novels and children's tales that captured the public's attention. People were fascinated by the idea that lifelike figures could be re-created by machines. Hans Christian Andersen, the Danish storyteller, wrote *The Nightingale* about a mechanical bird. The English novelist Mary Wollstonecraft Shelley's perennially popular book, *Frankenstein,* is about a machine-monster who destroys its creator. The famous Oz books for children by the American writer L. Frank Baum are full of mechanical men; they became the basis for the classic movie "The Wizard of Oz."

And so there emerged during the 17th to 19th centuries the conception of humans operating as machines, along with the scientific method by which human functioning could be investigated. Bodies were likened to machines, the scientific outlook was dominant, and life was subject to mechanical laws. Mechanism was also applied, in a rudimentary way, to human mental functioning. The result was a machine that supposedly could think.

The Calculating Engine

Charles Babbage (1792–1871), an eccentric British mathematician, developed what he called a calculating engine. The machine performed mathematical calculations faster than humans and printed out the results.

Long fascinated by automata, Babbage developed his calculator not to imitate human physical actions but, rather, mental ones. In addition to tabulating the values of mathematical functions, the machine could play chess, checkers, and other games. (Babbage designed another machine to subtract, multiply, and divide, but it was never completed because of cost overruns; the British government finally refused to continue to fund it and consigned it to a museum.) Babbage's machine even had a memory capacity that held intermediate results until they were needed to complete a given calculation (Mazlish, 1993).

This calculating machine was a forerunner of the modern computer, and it marked the first successful attempt to duplicate human cognitive processes and develop a kind of artificial intelligence. Scientists and inventors speculated that there would be no limit to what machines might be designed to do or the humanlike functions they might perform.

THE BEGINNINGS OF MODERN SCIENCE

We noted that the 17th century saw far-ranging developments in science. Until that time, philosophers had looked to the past for answers, to the works of Aristotle and other ancient scholars, and to the Bible. The ruling forces of inquiry were dogma, or the doctrine proclaimed by the established church, and authority figures. In the 17th century a new force became important: **empiricism,** the pursuit of knowledge through observation and experimentation. Knowledge handed down from the past became suspect. In its place, the golden age of the 17th century became illuminated by discoveries and insights that reflected the changing nature of scientific inquiry.

EMPIRICISM: The pursuit of knowledge through the observation of nature and the attribution of all knowledge to experience

Among the many scholars whose creativity marked that period, Descartes contributed directly to the history of modern psychology. His work helped to free scientific inquiry from the rigid theological and traditional beliefs that had controlled it for centuries. Descartes symbolized the transition to the modern era of science, and he applied the idea of the clockwork mechanism to the human body. Thus, it can be suggested that he inaugurated the era of modern psychology.

René Descartes (1596–1650)

Archives of the History of American Psychology/University of Akron

RENÉ DESCARTES

Descartes was born in France on March 31, 1596. He inherited enough money from his father to support a life of study and travel. From 1604 to 1612 he was a student at a Jesuit school, where he was educated in the humanities and mathematics. He also displayed considerable talent in philosophy, physics, and physiology. Because Descartes's health was poor, the school's director excused him from morning religious services and permitted him to lie in bed until noon, a habit Descartes retained all his life. It was during these quiet mornings that he did his most creative thinking.

After completing his formal education, Descartes sampled the pleasures of life in Paris. Eventually finding this tiresome, he chose to go into seclusion to study mathematics. At the age of 21, he served as a gentleman-volunteer in the armies of Holland, Bavaria, and Hungary, being a fine swordsman and something of an adventurer. He loved to dance and to gamble, and he was a successful gambler because of his mathematical talents. He also reportedly indulged in the usual human vices, although his only lasting romantic attachment was a 3-year affair with a Dutch woman who, in 1635, gave birth to their child. Descartes adored the infant and was heartbroken when she died at the age of 5. He described the loss as the deepest sorrow of his life.

Descartes was keenly interested in applying scientific knowledge to practical concerns. He investigated techniques that might keep his hair from turning gray, and he conducted experiments on the use of wheelchairs.

While serving in the army, Descartes had a dream that changed his life. As he told it, he spent the day of November 10 alone in a stove-heated room, thinking about mathematical and scientific ideas. He fell asleep and in his dream he was—as he later interpreted it—rebuked for his idleness. The "spirit of truth" took possession of his mind and persuaded him that he should devote his life to the proposition that mathematical principles could be applied to all the sciences and thus produce certainty of knowledge.

He returned to Paris to pursue his work in mathematics but again found the life there too distracting. By selling the estates he had inherited from his father, he was able to finance a move to a country house in Holland. His need for solitude and privacy was so great that he lived in 13 towns and 24 different houses over the next 20 years, keeping his address secret from all but his closest friends, with whom he corresponded frequently. His only other apparent requirements were proximity to a Roman Catholic church and to a university.

Descartes wrote extensively on mathematics and philosophy, and his growing fame from these writings brought him to the attention of Queen Christina of Sweden, who invited him to instruct her in philosophy. Although reluctant to give up his freedom and secluded lifestyle, he nevertheless had great respect for royal demands. The queen sent a warship to fetch him, and he embarked for Sweden in the fall of 1649. Queen Christina, who was not a very good student, insisted on lessons at 5:00 A.M. in a poorly heated library during an unusually bitter winter. The frail Descartes withstood the early rising and extreme cold for nearly 4 months before contracting pneumonia. He died on February 11, 1650.

An interesting postscript to the death of a man who, as we will see, devoted considerable time to the problem of the precise interaction between the mind and the body is the disposition of his own body. Sixteen years after Descartes's death, his friends decided that the body should be brought back to France. The coffin they sent to Sweden was too short to contain the remains, so the solution reached by the Swedish authorities was to cut off the head and bury it until arrangements could be made for its return to Paris.

While the remainder of the corpse was being prepared for the journey to France, the French ambassador to Sweden decided that he wanted a souvenir, and he severed the right forefinger. The body, now minus its head and one finger, was reburied in Paris amid much pomp and ceremony. Some time later, an army officer dug up Descartes's skull as a memento, and, for 150 years, it was passed from one Swedish collector to another until it, too, was finally buried in Paris.

Descartes's personal papers and manuscripts were shipped to Paris after his death, but the boat sank just before docking, and the papers lay submerged for 3 days. It took 17 years of restoration work before they could be published (Shea, 1991).

THE CONTRIBUTIONS OF DESCARTES: MECHANISM AND THE MIND-BODY PROBLEM

Descartes's most important work for the development of modern psychology is his attempt to resolve the **mind-body problem,** an issue that had been controversial for centuries. Throughout the ages

MIND-BODY PROBLEM: The question of the distinction between mental and physical qualities

scholars had argued about how the mind, or mental qualities, could be distinguished from the body and all other physical qualities. The basic and deceptively simple question is this: Are mind and body—the mental world and the material world—distinct? For thousands of years, scholars had taken a dualistic position, that the mind (the soul or spirit) and the body were of different natures. The acceptance of that position, however, raises other questions: If the mind and body are of different natures, what is their relationship? Are they independent or does one influence the other?

The accepted theory before Descartes's time was that the interaction between mind and body was essentially in one direction. The mind could exert an enormous influence on the body, but the body had little impact on the mind. A contemporary historian suggests the following analogy: The body and mind were thought to be related in the same way that a puppet and its puppeteer are joined. The mind is like the puppeteer, pulling the strings of the body (Lowry, 1982).

Descartes accepted this dualistic position; in his view, mind and body were indeed different essences. But he deviated from tradition by redefining the relationship between the two. In his theory of mind-body interaction, Descartes insisted that the mind influences the body and that the body exerts a much greater influence on the mind than previously supposed. The relationship is not in one direction only but rather is a mutual interaction. This idea, radical in the 17th century, has important implications.

After Descartes published his doctrine, many of his contemporaries decided that they could no longer support the idea that the mind was the master of the two entities, the puppeteer pulling the strings, functioning almost independently of the body. The body, possessing qualities of a physical or material nature, came to assume a greater importance. Functions previously attributed to the mind were now considered to be functions of the body.

In the Middle Ages, for example, the mind was believed to be responsible not only for thought and reason, but also for the processes of reproduction, perception, and movement. Descartes disputed this position. He argued that the mind has a single function: thought. All other processes were functions of the body.

Descartes thus introduced an approach to the long-standing mind-body problem that focused attention on a physical/psychological duality. In so doing, he diverted attention from the abstract theological concept of soul to the scientific study of the mind and mental processes. Methods of inquiry changed from metaphysical analysis to objective observation and experimentation. Whereas one could only speculate about the nature and existence of the soul, one could observe the mind and its processes.

Mind and body, then, are two separate entities. Matter, the material substance of the body, has extension (it takes up space), and operates according to mechanical principles. The mind, however, is free; it is unextended and lacking in physical substance. But Descartes's revolutionary idea is that mind and body, although distinct, are capable of interacting within the human organism. The mind can influence the body, and the body can influence the mind.

The Nature of the Body

Let us look more closely at Descartes's conception of the body. Because the body is composed of physical matter, it must possess those characteristics common to all matter—extension in space and the capacity for movement. If the body is matter, then the laws of physics and mechanics that account for movement and action in the physical world must also apply to the body. The body is like a machine whose operation can be explained by the mechanical laws that govern the movement of objects in space. Following this line of reasoning, Descartes proceeded to explain physiological functioning in terms of physics.

Descartes was strongly influenced by the mechanistic spirit of the age, as reflected in the mechanical clocks and automata we described earlier. In Paris he had been fascinated by the mechanical marvels installed in the royal gardens and spent many hours treading on the pressure plates that caused water jets to activate the figures, making them move and dance and utter sounds.

When Descartes described the body, he referred directly to the mechanical figures he had seen. He compared the body's nerves to the pipes through which the water passed, and the body's muscles and tendons to engines and springs. The movement of the mechanical models was not caused by voluntary action on their part but by external objects; the involuntary nature of this movement was reflected in Descartes's observation that bodily movements frequently occur without a person's conscious intention.

From this line of reasoning he arrived at the idea of the *undulatio reflexa,* a movement not supervised or determined by a conscious will to move. For this work, Descartes is often called the author of the **theory of reflex action.** This theory is a precursor of modern behavioral stimulus-response (S-R) psychology, in which an external object (a stimulus) brings about an involuntary response, such as the jerk of your leg when the doctor taps your knee with a hammer. No thought or cognitive process is involved in such behavior; it is seemingly mechanical or automatic.

THEORY OF REFLEX ACTION: The idea that an external object (a stimulus) can bring about an involuntary response

Descartes's proposals are also part of a more general trend toward the notion that human behavior is predictable. The mechanical body moves and behaves in ways that can be expected or anticipated, as long as the inputs are known.

Descartes found support in the field of physiology for his mechanical interpretation of the workings of the human body. In 1628, William Harvey, an English physician, had uncovered the basic facts about the circulation of the blood, and much was also being learned about the process of digestion. Physiologists knew that the muscles of the body worked in opposing pairs, and that sensation and movement depended somehow on the nerves.

Although physiological researchers were making great strides in understanding the human body, their information was far from complete. The nerves were thought to be hollow tubes through which some sort of liquid animal spirits flowed, not unlike water flowing in the pipes that moved automata. Our concern here, however, is not with the accuracy or completeness of 17th-century physiology, but rather with its support for a mechanical interpretation of the body.

Because established dogma held that animals did not possess souls, they were believed to be automata. Thus, the difference between humans and animals, so important in Christian thought, was preserved. It was also believed that animals did not have feelings. How could they have feelings if they did not have souls? Descartes and other researchers dissected live animals, before anesthesia was available, and seemed "amused at their cries and yelps since these were nothing but the hydraulic hisses and vibrations of machines" (Jaynes, 1970, p. 224).

Animals, being machinelike, belong entirely to the category of physical phenomena. They have no immortality, no thought processes, and no free will. Animal behavior can be explained totally in mechanistic terms.

Descartes's writings refer to the clocklike nature of animals. "I know quite well that animals do many things better than we, but that does not astonish me; for precisely that serves to prove that they act . . . by such spring forces as a clock, which indicates what time it is far better than our judgment tells us" (quoted in Maurice & Mayr, 1980, p. 5).

The Mind-Body Interaction

According to Descartes, the mind is nonmaterial (it is not composed of physical matter). The mind is also capable of thought and consciousness and, consequently, provides us with information about our external world. The mind has none of the properties of matter. Its most important characteristic is the capacity to think, and this sets it apart from the material or physical world.

Because the mind thinks, perceives, and wills, it must somehow influence and be influenced by the body. When the mind decides to move from one place to another, for example, this decision is carried out by the body's muscles, tendons, and nerves. Similarly, when the body is stimulated—by light or heat, for example—it is the mind that recognizes and interprets these sensory data and determines the appropriate response.

Descartes formulated a theory about the interaction of mind and body, but he needed first to find a physical point where the mind and the body engaged in their mutual influence. He conceived of the mind as unitary, which meant that it must interact with only a single part of the body. He also believed that the point of interaction was somewhere within the brain, because research had shown that sensations travel to the brain and movement originates within the brain. It was obvious to Descartes, then, that the brain had to be the focal point for the mind's functions.

The only structure of the brain that is single and unitary (not divided and duplicated in each hemisphere) is the pineal body or *conarium,* and Descartes chose this as the logical site of interaction.

He described in mechanistic terms the manner in which the mind-body interaction occurs. He suggested that the movement of animal spirits in the nerve tubes makes an impression on the *conarium* and from this impression the mind produces a sensation. In other words, a quantity of motion (the flow of animal spirits) produces a mental quality (a sensation). The reverse can also happen; the mind can somehow make an impression on the *conarium* (in a manner Descartes never made clear), which, by inclining to one direction or another, influences the flow of animal spirits to the muscles. This results in a physical movement. Thus, a mental quality can influence motion, a property of the body.

The Doctrine of Ideas

Descartes proposed a doctrine of ideas that had a profound influence on the development of modern psychology. He suggested that the mind produces two kinds of ideas: derived and innate. **Derived ideas** are those that arise from the direct application of an external stimulus, such as the sound of a bell or the sight of a tree. Derived ideas (such as the idea of the bell or the tree) are thus products of the experiences of the senses.

DERIVED IDEAS: Ideas produced by the direct application of an external stimulus

Innate ideas are not produced by objects in the external world impinging on the senses but develop out of the mind or consciousness alone. The potential existence of innate ideas is independent of sensory experiences, although innate ideas may be realized in the presence of appropriate experiences. Some innate ideas Descartes identified are God, the self, perfection, and infinity.

INNATE IDEAS: Ideas that arise from the mind or consciousness, independent of sensory experiences or external stimuli

We see in later chapters that the concept of innate ideas led to the nativistic theory of perception (the idea that our ability to perceive is innate rather than learned) and was influential in the Gestalt school of psychology. It is also important because it inspired opposition among early empiricists and associationists, such as John Locke, and among later empiricists, such as Hermann von Helmholtz and Wilhelm Wundt.

The work of Descartes served as a catalyst for many trends that later became prominent in psychology. His noteworthy systematic contributions include the mechanistic conception of the body, the theory of reflex action, mind-body interaction, the localization of mental functions in the brain, and the doctrine of innate ideas. With Descartes we see the idea of mechanism applied to the human body. So widespread was the mechanistic philosophy in defining the Zeitgeist of that era that it was inevitable that someone would decide to apply it to the human mind. It is to that significant event—the reduction of the mind to a machine—that we now turn.

EMPIRICISM AND ASSOCIATIONISM: ACQUIRING KNOWLEDGE THROUGH EXPERIENCE

By the middle of the 19th century, 200 years after Descartes's death, the long period of prescientific psychology had come to an end. During this time, European philosophical thought had become infused with a new spirit: **positivism.** The term and the concept are the work of the French philosopher Auguste Comte (1798–1857) who, when he learned he was dying, said that his death would be an irreparable loss to the entire world.

Comte undertook a systematic survey of all human knowledge. To make this ambitious task more manageable, Comte decided to limit his work to facts that were beyond question, those facts that had been determined solely through the methods of science. His positivistic approach, then, referred to a system based exclusively on facts that are objectively observable and not debatable. Everything of a speculative, inferential, or metaphysical nature was declared to be illusory and was rejected.

The acceptance of positivism meant that scholars were now considering two types of propositions. A historian described them as follows: "One refers to the objects of sense, and it is a scientific statement. The other is nonsense!" (Robinson, 1981, p. 333). Knowledge derived from metaphysics and theology was the "nonsense." Only knowledge derived from science was believed to be valid.

Other ideas in philosophy supported this antimetaphysical positivism. The doctrine of **materialism** stated that all the facts of the universe could be described in physical terms and explained by the nature and physical properties of *matter* and energy. The materialists proposed that even human consciousness could be understood in light of the principles of physics and chemistry. Materialist consider-

POSITIVISM: The doctrine that recognizes only natural phenomena or facts that are objectively observable

MATERIALISM: The doctrine that considers the facts of the universe to be sufficiently explained in physical terms by the existence and nature of matter

ations of mental processes focused on physical properties—the anatomical and physiological structures of the brain.

A third group of philosophers, those who advocated **empiricism,** were concerned with how the mind acquires knowledge. They argued that all knowledge is derived from sensory experience.

Positivism, materialism, and empiricism became the philosophical foundations of the new science of psychology. Of these three philosophical orientations, empiricism played the major role. Empiricism could be related to the growth of the mind, to how the mind acquires knowledge. According to the empiricist view, the mind grows through the progressive accumulation of sensory experiences. This idea contrasts with the nativistic viewpoint exemplified by Descartes, which holds that some ideas are innate. We consider some of the major British empiricists: John Locke, George Berkeley, David Hume, David Hartley, James Mill, and John Stuart Mill.

EMPIRICISM: The pursuit of knowledge through the observation of nature and the attribution of all knowledge to experience

John Locke (1632–1704)

John Locke, the son of an attorney, studied at universities in London and Oxford in England, and received his bachelor's degree in 1656 and his master's degree shortly thereafter. He remained at Oxford for several years, tutoring in Greek, writing, and philosophy, then took up the practice of medicine. He developed an interest in politics and in 1667 went to London to become secretary to the Earl of Shaftesbury and, in time, the confidant and friend of this controversial statesman.

Shaftesbury's influence in the government declined, and in 1681, after participating in a plot against King Charles II, he fled to Holland. Although Locke was not involved in the plot, his relationship with the earl brought him under suspicion, and so he too left for Holland. Several years later Locke was able to return to England, where he became commissioner of appeals and wrote books on education, religion, and economics. He was concerned about religious freedom and the right of people to govern themselves. His writings brought him much fame and influence, and he was known throughout Europe as a champion of liberalism in government. Some of his work had an impact on the writers of the American Declaration of Independence.

Locke's major work of importance to psychology is *An Essay Concerning Human Understanding* (1690), which was the culmination of 20 years of study and thought. This book, which had appeared in four editions by 1700 and had been translated into French and Latin, marks the formal beginning of British empiricism.

Archives of the History of American Psychology/University of Akron

JOHN LOCKE

How the mind acquires knowledge

Locke was concerned primarily with cognitive functioning, that is, the ways in which the mind acquires its knowledge. In attacking this issue he rejected the existence of innate ideas, as proposed by Descartes, arguing that humans are not equipped at birth with any knowledge whatsoever. Locke admitted that certain concepts, such as the idea of God, may seem to us as adults to be innate, but that is only because we were taught those ideas in childhood and cannot remember any time when we were not aware of them. In this way Locke explained the apparent innateness of some ideas in terms of learning and habit.

How, then, does the mind acquire knowledge? To Locke, the answer was that the mind acquired knowledge through experience. All knowledge was empirically derived. He wrote:

> *Let us then suppose the mind to be, as we say, white paper, void of all characters, without any ideas. . . . Whence comes it by that vast store which the busy and boundless fancy of man has painted on it with an almost endless variety? Whence has it all the materials of reason and knowledge? To this I answer, in one word, from* experience. *In that all our knowledge is founded; and from that it ultimately derives itself.* (LOCKE, 1690/1959)

Aristotle had held a similar notion centuries before, that the mind at birth was a *tabula rasa,* a blank or clean slate on which experience would write.

Sensation and reflection

Locke recognized two different kinds of experiences, one deriving from sensation and the other from reflection. The ideas that derive from sensation, from direct sensory input from physical objects in the environment, are simple sense impressions. These sense impressions operate on the mind, and the mind itself also operates on these sensations, reflecting on them and forming ideas. This mental or cognitive function of reflection as a source of ideas is dependent on sensory experience, because the ideas produced by the mind's reflection are based on impressions already experienced through the senses.

In the course of human development, sensations appear first. They are a necessary forerunner of reflections because there must first be a reservoir of sense impressions for the mind to be able to reflect on. In reflecting, we recall past sensory impressions and combine them to form abstractions and other higher-level ideas. Thus, all ideas arise from sensation and reflection, but the ultimate source remains our sensory experiences.

Simple ideas and complex ideas

SIMPLE IDEAS: Elemental ideas that arise from sensation and reflection

Locke distinguished between simple ideas and complex ideas. **Simple ideas** can arise from both sensation and reflection and are received passively by the mind. Simple ideas are elemental; they cannot be analyzed or reduced to still simpler ideas. However, the mind, through the process of reflection, actively creates new ideas by combining simple ideas. These new, derived ideas are what Locke called **complex ideas.** They are compounded of simple ideas, and hence they are capable of being analyzed or resolved into their simpler component ideas.

COMPLEX IDEAS: Derived ideas that are compounded of simple ideas and thus can be analyzed or reduced to their simpler components

The theory of association

The notion of combining or compounding ideas and the reverse notion of analyzing them marks the beginning of the so-called mental-chemistry approach that characterizes the **theory of association.** In this approach, simple ideas may be linked or associated to form complex ideas. Association is an early name for the process that psychologists today call *learning*. The reduction or analysis of mental life into simple ideas or elements, and the association of these elements to form complex ideas, formed the core of the new scientific psychology. Just as clocks and other mechanical devices could be disassembled, reduced to their component parts, and reassembled to form a complex machine, so could human ideas.

THEORY OF ASSOCIATION: The notion that knowledge results from the linking or associating of simple ideas to form complex ideas

Locke treated the mind as though it behaved in accordance with the laws of the physical universe. The basic particles or atoms of the mental world are the simple ideas, which are conceptually analogous to the material atoms in the mechanistic Galilean-Newtonian system of the universe. The basic elements of the mind cannot be broken down into simpler elements, but, like their counterparts in the material world, they can combine to form more complex structures. Association theory was a significant step in the direction of considering the mind, like the body, to be a machine.

Primary and secondary qualities

Another of Locke's propositions that is important to early psychology is the notion of primary and secondary qualities as they apply to simple sensory ideas. **Primary qualities** exist in an object whether or not we perceive them. The size and shape of a building are primary qualities, whereas the color of the building is a secondary quality. Color is not inherent in the object but is dependent on the experiencing person, and not all people perceive a particular color in the same way. **Secondary qualities,** such as color, odor, sound, and taste, exist not in the object but in a person's perception of the object. The tickle of a feather is not in the feather itself but in our reaction to the touch of the feather. The pain inflicted by a knife is not in the knife itself but in our experience in response to the wound.

PRIMARY QUALITIES: Characteristics, such as size and shape, that exist in an object whether or not we perceive them

SECONDARY QUALITIES: Characteristics, such as color and odor, that exist in our perception of an object

A popular experiment described by Locke illustrates this idea. Prepare three containers of water: one cold, one lukewarm, and one hot. Place your left hand in the cold water and your right hand in the hot water, then put both hands in the pan of warm water. One hand will perceive this water as warm and the other will perceive it as cool. The lukewarm water itself is the same temperature for both hands; it cannot be warm and cool at the same time. The secondary qualities or experiences of warmth and cold exist only in our perception and not in the object (in this case, the water). For another example, if we did not bite into an apple, its taste would not exist. Primary qualities, such as the size and shape of the apple, exist in it whether or not we perceive them. Secondary qualities exist only in the act of perception.

Locke was not the first scholar to make a distinction between primary and secondary qualities. Galileo had proposed essentially the same notion: "I think that if [our] ears, tongues, and noses were removed, shapes and numbers and motions [primary qualities] would remain, but not odors nor tastes nor sounds [secondary qualities]. The latter, I believe, are nothing more than names when separated from living beings" (quoted in Boas, 1961, p. 262).

This view is in agreement with the mechanistic position, which held that matter in motion constituted the only objective reality. If matter were all that existed objectively, then perception of anything else—such as colors, odors, and tastes—must be subjective. Primary qualities, then, are all that can exist independently of the perceiver.

In making this distinction between objective and subjective qualities, Locke was recognizing the subjectivity of much of human perception, an idea that intrigued him and stimulated his desire to understand the workings of the mind and conscious experience. He proposed secondary qualities in an attempt to explain the lack of precise correspondence between the physical world and our perception of it.

Once scholars accepted the distinction, in theory, between primary and secondary qualities—that some existed in reality and others existed only in our perception—it was inevitable that someone would ask whether there was any real difference between them. Perhaps all perception exists only in terms of secondary qualities, those qualities that are subjective and dependent on the observer. The philosopher who did ask, and answer, this question was George Berkeley.

George Berkeley (1685–1753)

George Berkeley was born and educated in Ireland. A deeply religious man, he was ordained a deacon in the Anglican Church at the age of 24. Shortly thereafter, he published two philosophical works that were to exert an influence on psychology: *An Essay Towards a New Theory of Vision* (1709) and *A Treatise Concerning the Principles of*

Human Knowledge (1710). With these two books, his contribution to psychology ended.

He traveled extensively throughout Europe and held a number of jobs in Ireland, including a teaching position at Trinity College in Dublin. He became financially independent when he received a sizable gift of money from a woman he met once at a dinner party. He visited the United States, spending 3 years at Newport, Rhode Island, and donated his house and library to Yale University when he left. For the last years of his life he was Bishop of Cloyne. When he died, his body was left untended in his bed, in accordance with his instructions, until it began to decompose. Berkeley believed that putrefaction was the only sure sign of death, and he did not wish to be buried before his time.

Berkeley's fame, or at least his name, lingers in the United States today. In 1855, a clergyman from Yale, the Reverend Henry Durant, established a school in California. He named it Berkeley in honor of the good bishop, perhaps in recognition of Berkeley's poem, "On the Prospect of Planting Arts and Learning in America," which includes the often-quoted line: "Westward the course of empire takes its way."

Perception is the only reality

Berkeley agreed with Locke that all of our knowledge of the external world comes from experience, but he disagreed with Locke's distinction between primary and secondary qualities. Berkeley argued that there were no primary qualities. There were only what Locke called secondary qualities. To Berkeley, all knowledge was a function of the experiencing or perceiving person. Some years later his position was given the name **mentalism,** to denote the emphasis on purely mental phenomena.

He suggested that perception is the only reality of which we can be sure. We cannot know with certainty the nature of physical objects in the experiential world (the world that is derived from or based on our own experiences). All we can know is how we perceive or experience those objects. Because perception is within ourselves and thus is subjective, it does not mirror the external, material world. An object is nothing more than an accumulation of sensations experienced concurrently, so that they become associated in our mind by habit. Thus, to Berkeley, the experiential world becomes the summation of our sensations.

There is no material substance of which we can be sure because if we take away the perception, the quality disappears. There can be no color without the perception of color, no shape or motion without the perception of shape or motion.

MENTALISM: The notion that all knowledge is a function of mental phenomena; that is, all knowledge is dependent on the perceiving or experiencing person

Berkeley was not saying that real objects exist in the physical world only when they are perceived. His theory was that because all experience is within ourselves, relative to our own perception, we can never know precisely the physical nature of objects. We can rely only on our perception of them.

He recognized that there was some independence, stability, and consistency in the objects of the material world, and he had to find some way to account for this. He did so by invoking God; Berkeley was, after all, a bishop. God functioned as a kind of permanent perceiver of all the objects in the universe. If a tree fell in the forest (so the old riddle goes), it would, indeed, make a sound, even if no one was there to hear it, because God would always be perceiving it.

The association of sensations

Berkeley applied the theory of association to explain our knowledge of objects in the real world. This knowledge is essentially a construction or composition of simple ideas or mental elements bound by the mortar of association. Complex ideas are formed by joining simple ideas received through the senses, as he explained in *An Essay Towards a New Theory of Vision.*

> *Sitting in my study I hear a coach drive along the street; I look through the [window] and see it; I walk out and enter it. Thus, common speech would incline one to think I heard, saw, and touched the same thing . . . the coach. It is nevertheless certain the ideas [admitted] by each sense are widely different, and distinct from each other; but, having been observed constantly to go together, they are spoken of as one and the same thing.* (BERKELEY, 1709/1957a)

The complex idea of the coach is fashioned from the sound of its wheels on the cobblestone street, the sturdy feel of its frame, the fresh smell of its leather seats, and the visual image of its boxy shape. The mind constructs complex ideas by fitting together these basic mental building blocks—the simple ideas. The mechanical analogy in the use of the words *constructs* and *building blocks* is not coincidental.

Berkeley used the idea of association to explain visual depth perception. He examined the problem of how we perceive the third dimension of depth given that the human eye has a retina of only two dimensions. His answer was that we perceive depth as a result of experience, by associating visual impressions with the sensations that occur as our eyes adjust or accommodate to seeing objects at different distances, and with the movements we make in approaching or retreating from the objects we see. In other words, the continuous sensory experiences of walking toward or reaching for objects, plus the sensations from the eye muscles, become associated or linked to produce the perception of depth. When an object is brought closer to the eyes, the pupils converge; this convergence diminishes when the object is moved away. Thus, depth perception is not a simple sensory experience but an association of ideas that must be learned.

Here Berkeley was attempting to explain a purely psychological process in terms of the association of sensations. Thus he was continuing the growing associationist trend within empirical philosophy. His explanation accurately anticipated the modern view of depth perception in its consideration of the physiological cues of accommodation and convergence.

David Hume (1711–1776)

David Hume, a philosopher and historian, studied law at the University of Edinburgh, Scotland, but did not graduate. He embarked on a career in business but found this not to his liking, so he moved to France to study philosophy. He went on to England and achieved considerable fame as a writer. His most important work for psychology was *A Treatise of Human Nature* (1739). He also worked as a government official, a librarian, a judge advocate on a military expedition, and a tutor to a lunatic of noble birth.

Hume supported Locke's notion of the compounding of simple ideas into complex ideas, and he revised and clarified the theory of association. He agreed with Berkeley that the material world did not exist for the individual until it was perceived, but he took this idea a step further. Berkeley had declared that God was the permanent perceiver, as a way of guaranteeing the persistence and stability of physical objects. Hume asked what would happen if the notion of God was omitted from the picture.

In that case, Hume argued, there would be no way of knowing whether there was "anything outside of our own mind. If all knowledge of the 'outside world' is via our own ideas, and our knowledge of it is hence 'indirect,' then we cannot really be said to know, in principle, if there is an outside world or not. . . . There may be a real world; there may not; but we have no way of knowing" (Wilcox, 1992, p. 38).

Impressions and ideas

Hume drew a distinction between two kinds of mental contents: impressions and ideas. Impressions are the basic elements of mental life and are like sensations and perceptions in today's terminology. Ideas are the mental experiences we have in the absence of any stimulating object; the modern equivalent in psychology today is image.

He did not define impressions and ideas in physiological terms or in reference to external stimuli. He was careful not to assign any ultimate causes to impressions. These mental contents differed from ideas not in their source but in their relative strength. Impressions are strong and vivid whereas ideas are merely weak copies of impressions. Both of these mental contents may be simple or complex. A simple idea will resemble its simple impression. Complex ideas do not necessarily resemble any simple ideas because complex ideas evolve from a combination of simple ideas into some new pattern, compounded from these simple ideas by the process of association.

LAW OF RESEMBLANCE: The more similar two ideas, the more readily they will be associated

LAW OF CONTIGUITY: The more closely linked two ideas are in time or place, the more readily they will be associated

Two laws of association were proposed: **resemblance** or **similarity,** and **contiguity** in time or place. The more similar and contiguous are two ideas (the latter referring to how closely they are experienced in time), the more readily the ideas will be associated.

Hume's work fits within the mechanistic framework and continues the development of empiricism and associationism. He argued that just as astronomers determined the laws and forces of the physical universe by which the planets function, so it was possible to determine the laws of the mental universe. He believed that the laws governing the association of ideas were the mental counterpart of the law of gravity in physics, and that they were universal principles for the operation of the mind. With Hume we have additional support for the notion that the mind constructs complex ideas by mechanically combining simple ideas.

David Hartley (1705–1757)

David Hartley, the son of a minister, was preparing for a career in the church, but because of his quarrels with the established doctrine, he turned to medicine instead. He led a quiet and uneventful life as a doctor and pursued on his own the study of philosophy. In 1749 he published *Observations on Man, His Frame, His Duty, and His Expectations.* This was Hartley's most important work and is considered by many scholars to be the first systematic treatise on association.

Association by contiguity and repetition

DAVID HARTLEY

National Library of Medicine

Hartley's fundamental law of association is contiguity, by which he attempted to explain the processes of memory, reasoning, emotion, and voluntary and involuntary action. Ideas or sensations that occur together, simultaneously or successively, become associated, so that the occurrence of one results in the occurrence of the other. Hartley suggested that **repetition** of the sensations and ideas is also necessary for associations to be formed.

He agreed with Locke that all ideas and knowledge are derived from the experiences conveyed to us through the senses; there are no innate associations, no knowledge present at birth. As children grow and accumulate a variety of sensory experiences, mental connections or trains of association of increasing complexity are established. In this way, higher systems of thought develop by the time we reach adulthood. This higher-order mental life, such as thinking, judging, and reasoning, may be analyzed or reduced to the elements or simple sensations from which it was compounded. Hartley was the first to apply the theory of association to explain all types of mental activity.

LAW OF REPETITION: The more frequently two ideas occur together, the more readily they will be associated

The influence of mechanism

Like other philosophers before him, Hartley viewed the mental world in mechanistic terms. In one respect he exceeded the aims of other empiricists and associationists: Not only did Hartley attempt to explain psychological processes in terms of mechanical principles, but he also tried similarly to explain their underlying physiological processes. It was perhaps a natural thing for him to have attempted because of his formal training in medicine.

Isaac Newton had stated that one characteristic of impulses in the physical world is that they vibrate. Hartley applied this idea to the operation of the brain and the nervous system, and his resulting work can be said to anticipate modern ideas in neurophysiology (Smith, 1987). Vibrations in the nerves, which Hartley believed were solid structures (not hollow tubes, as Descartes had proposed), transmit impulses from one part of the body to another. These vibrations initiate smaller vibrations in the brain; Hartley believed these vibrations in the brain were the physiological counterparts of ideas. The importance of this doctrine for psychology is that it is yet another attempt to use scientific ideas about the mechanical universe as a model for understanding human nature.

James Mill (1773–1836)

James Mill was educated at the University of Edinburgh in Scotland and served for a short time as a clergyman. When he discovered that no one in his congregation could understand his sermons, he left the Church of Scotland to earn his living as a writer. His most famous literary work is the *History of British India,* which took 11 years to complete. His most important contribution to psychology is *Analysis of the Phenomena of the Human Mind* (1829).

The mind as a machine

James Mill applied the doctrine of mechanism to the human mind with a rare directness and comprehensiveness. His stated goal was to destroy the idea of subjective or psychic activities and to demonstrate that the mind was nothing more than a machine. Mill believed that empiricists who argued that the mind was merely similar to a machine in its operations had not gone far enough. The mind *was* a machine—

it functioned in the same mechanical way as a clock. It was set in operation by external physical forces and run by internal physical forces.

In his view, the mind is a passive entity that is acted on by external stimuli. We respond to these stimuli automatically; we are incapable of acting spontaneously. Obviously, Mill had no place in his theory for the concept of free will. This viewpoint persists today in the psychology that derives directly from the mechanistic tradition, most notably in the behaviorism of B. F. Skinner.

As the title of James Mill's major work suggests, he proposed that the mind be studied by the method of analysis, by reducing it to its elementary components. This is, again, the mechanistic doctrine. To understand complex phenomena, whether in the mental or the physical worlds—whether ideas or clocks—it is necessary to break them down into their smallest parts. Mill wrote that a "distinct knowledge of the elements is indispensable to an accurate conception of that which is compounded of them" (Mill, 1829, Vol. l, p. l).

He suggested that sensations and ideas are the only kinds of mental elements that exist. In the familiar empiricist-associationist tradition, all knowledge begins with sensations, from which are derived, through the process of association, the higher-level complex ideas. Association was a matter of contiguity or concurrence alone, and it could be simultaneous or successive.

Mill believed that the mind has no creative function; association is an automatic, passive process. The sensations that occur together in a certain order will be reproduced mechanically as ideas, and these ideas occur in the same order as their corresponding sensations. Association is mechanical, and the resulting ideas are merely the accumulation or sum of the individual mental elements.

John Stuart Mill (1806–1873)

James Mill subscribed to Locke's suggestion that the human mind at birth was like a blank slate or empty page on which experience would write. When his son John was born, Mill vowed that he would determine the experiences that would fill the boy's mind, and he embarked on what may be the most rigorous example of private tutoring on record. Every day, for up to 5 hours, he drilled the child in Greek, Latin, algebra, geometry, logic, history, and political economy, repeatedly questioning young John until he gave the correct answers.

At the age of 3, John Stuart Mill was reading Plato in the original Greek. At 11 he wrote his first scholarly paper, and by 12 he had mastered the standard university curriculum. At 18 he described himself as a "logical machine," and by 21 he suffered from severe depression. He wrote of his mental breakdown: "I was in a dull state of nerves . . . the whole foundation on which my life was constructed fell down. . . . I seemed to have nothing left to live for" (J. S. Mill,

1873/1961, p. 83). It took several years for him to recover a sense of self-worth.

He worked for the East India Company for many years, handling routine correspondence about England's governance of India. At the age of 24, he fell in love with Harriet Taylor, a beautiful and intelligent woman who was married. Mrs. Taylor was to have a major influence on Mill's work. When Mr. Taylor died, nearly 20 years later, she and Mill married. He later published an essay entitled "The Subjection of Women," which was written at the suggestion of his daughter and inspired by Mrs. Taylor's marital experiences with her first husband (J. S. Mill, 1873/1961).

Mill was appalled that women had no financial or property rights, and he compared the plight of women to that of other disadvantaged groups. He condemned the ideas that a wife was expected to submit to sex with her husband on demand, even against her will, and that divorce on the grounds of incompatibility was not then permitted. He proposed that marriage be more of a partnership between equals than a master/slave relationship (Rose, 1983).

The psychoanalyst Sigmund Freud later translated Mill's essay on women into German, and in letters to his fiancée sneered at Mill's notion of equality of the sexes. Freud wrote: "The position of woman cannot be other than what it is: to be an adored sweetheart in youth, and a beloved wife in maturity" (Freud, 1883/1964, p. 76).

National Portrait Gallery, London

JOHN STUART MILL

Mental chemistry

Through his writings on a variety of topics, John Stuart Mill became an influential contributor to what was soon to become the new science of psychology. He argued against the mechanistic position of his father, James Mill, who viewed the mind as passive, something acted upon by external stimuli. To John Stuart Mill, the mind played an active role in the association of ideas. Complex ideas, he suggested, are not simply the summation of simple ideas through the process of association. Complex ideas are more than the sum of the individual parts (the simple ideas) because they take on new qualities that are not found in the simple elements.

For example, if you mix blue, red, and green lights in the proper proportion, you end up with white—an entirely new quality. In this **creative synthesis** view, the combination of mental elements always produces some distinct quality.

John Stuart Mill was influenced in his thinking by research findings from the science of chemistry, which provided him with a model or context that was different from the physics and mechanics that shaped the ideas of his father and earlier empiricists and associationists. Chemists were providing demonstrations of the concept of synthesis, in which chemical compounds were found to exhibit attributes

CREATIVE SYNTHESIS: The notion that complex ideas formed from simple ideas take on new qualities; that is, the combination of mental elements creates something greater than the sum of the original elements

or qualities not found in their component parts or elements. The proper mixture of hydrogen and oxygen produces water, which has properties not found in either of the elements. Similarly, complex ideas emerge from combinations of simple ideas to take on characteristics not found in their elements. Mill called this approach to the association of ideas mental chemistry.

Another important contribution to psychology was John Stuart Mill's persuasive argument that it was possible to have a *science* of psychology. He made this assertion at a time when other philosophers, notably Auguste Comte, were denying that the mind could ever be studied scientifically. Mill also recommended the establishment of a new field of study, which he called *ethology*, devoted to the factors that influence the development of the human personality.

CONTRIBUTIONS OF EMPIRICISM TO PSYCHOLOGY

With the rise of empiricism, philosophers turned away from earlier approaches to knowledge. Although they remained concerned with many of the same problems, their method of attack on these problems became atomistic, mechanistic, and positivistic.

Reconsider the emphases of empiricism: the primary role of the processes of sensation, the analysis of conscious experience into elements, the synthesis of elements to form complex mental experiences through the process of association, and the focus on conscious processes. The major role empiricism played in shaping the new scientific psychology was about to become evident, and we will see that the concerns of the empiricists formed psychology's basic subject matter.

By the middle of the 19th century philosophy had done all it could. The theoretical rationale for a natural science of human nature had been established. What was needed to translate theory into reality was an experimental attack on the subject matter. And that was soon to occur, thanks to the physiologists, who supplied the kind of experimentation that would complete the foundation for the new psychology.

DISCUSSION QUESTIONS

1. Explain the concept of mechanism. How did mechanism come to be applied to human beings? How did the development of clocks and automata relate to the ideas of determinism and reductionism?
2. How did Descartes's views on the mind-body issue differ from earlier views? How did Descartes explain the functioning and in-

teraction of the human body and the human mind? What is the role of the *conarium?*

3. Distinguish between innate ideas and derived ideas.
4. Define positivism, materialism, and empiricism. What contributions did empiricism make to the new psychology?
5. Describe Locke's view of empiricism. Discuss his concepts of sensation and reflection, and of simple and complex ideas.
6. How did Berkeley's ideas challenge Locke's distinction between primary and secondary qualities? What did Berkeley mean by the phrase "perception is the only reality"?
7. Discuss the mental-chemistry approach to association. Compare the explanations of association offered by David Hume, David Hartley, James Mill, and John Stuart Mill. Compare the positions of James Mill and John Stuart Mill on the nature of the mind.

SUGGESTED READINGS

Landes, D. S. (1983). *Revolution in time: Clocks and the making of the modern world.* Cambridge, MA: Belknap Press of Harvard University Press. Assesses the impact of clocks on the development of science and society.

Leary, D. E. (Ed.). (1990). *Metaphors in the history of psychology.* Cambridge, England: Cambridge University Press. Explores psychology's use of metaphors to describe ideas on association, reasoning, emotion, motivation, cognition, consciousness, and behavior.

Lowry, R. (1982). *The evolution of psychological theory: A critical history of concepts and presuppositions* (2nd ed.). Hawthorne, NY: Aldine. Analyzes the major assumptions and viewpoints from which modern psychology developed, beginning with 17th-century ideas of mental and physiological mechanism.

Watson, R. I. (1971). A prescriptive analysis of Descartes's psychological views. *Journal of the History of the Behavioral Sciences, 7,* 223–248. Examines Descartes's ideas on the structure of the mind and the distinction between mind and body.

CHAPTER 3

PHYSIOLOGICAL INFLUENCES

ON PSYCHOLOGY

THE IMPORTANCE OF THE HUMAN OBSERVER

IT ALL started with a difference of five-tenths of a second in the observations made by two astronomers. The year was 1795. The royal astronomer of England, Nevil Maskelyne, noticed that his assistant's observations of the time it took for a star to pass from one point to another were slower than his own. Maskelyne rebuked the man for his mistakes and warned him to be more careful. The assistant tried, but the differences increased. In 5 months, the assistant's observations differed from Maskelyne's by eight-tenths of a second. As a result, the assistant was fired, and he passed into that crowded place known as obscurity.

For 20 years the incident was ignored, until the phenomenon was investigated by Friedrich Wilhelm Bessel, a German astronomer interested in errors of measurement. He suspected that the mistakes made by Maskelyne's assistant were not really mistakes but were attributable to individual differences, those personal differences among people over which they have no control. If so, Bessel reasoned, then differences in observation times would be found among all astronomers, a phenomenon that came to be called the *personal equation*. Bessel proceeded to test his hypothesis and found it to be correct. Disagreements were common, even among the most experienced astronomers.

Bessel's finding led to two conclusions. First, it meant that astronomers would have to take into account the nature of the human observer, because his or her personal characteristics and perceptions would influence the reported observations. Second, if the role of the human observer had to be considered in astronomy, then surely it would need to be considered in every other science that relied on the observational method.

Empirical philosophers such as Locke and Berkeley had discussed the subjective nature of human perception, arguing that there is not always—or even often—an exact correspondence between the nature of an object and our perception of it. Bessel's work provided data from a hard science—astronomy—to illustrate and support the same point.

This event, then, forced scientists to focus on the role of the human observer if they hoped to account fully for the results of their experiments. They began to investigate the psychological processes of sensing and perceiving by studying the human sense organs, those physiological mechanisms through which we receive information about our world. Once the physiologists began to study sensation in this way, the new science of psychology was but a short and inevitable step away.

DEVELOPMENTS IN EARLY PHYSIOLOGY

The physiological research that stimulated and guided the new psychology was a product of the late 19th century. As with all endeavors, it had its antecedents, the earlier work on which it built. Physiology became an experimentally oriented discipline during the 1830s, primarily under the influence of the German physiologist Johannes Müller (1801–1858), who advocated the application of the experimental method to physiology. Müller held the prestigious position of professor of anatomy and physiology at the University of Berlin. He was phenomenally productive, publishing, on the average, one scholarly paper every 7 weeks, and he maintained this pace for 38 years before committing suicide during a bout of depression.

One of his most influential publications is the *Handbook of the Physiology of Mankind,* which summarized the physiological research of the period and systematized a large body of knowledge. Volumes of the *Handbook* published between 1833 and 1840 cited much new work, indicating how widespread research in experimental physiology had become. The need for such a book was reflected in the rapid translation into English of the first volume in 1838 and the second in 1842.

Müller is also of importance to physiology and psychology for his theory of the *specific energies of nerves.* He proposed that the arousal or stimulation of a particular nerve always gives rise to a characteristic sensation, because each sensory nerve has its own specific energy. This idea stimulated a great deal of research that sought to localize functions within the nervous system and to pinpoint sensory receptor mechanisms on the periphery of the organism.

Research on Brain Functions

Several early physiologists made substantial contributions to the study of brain functions. Their work is significant for psychology because they discovered specialized areas of the brain and developed research methods that became widely used later in the field of physiological psychology.

A pioneer in the investigation of reflex behavior was Marshall Hall (1790–1857), a Scottish physician working in London. Hall observed that decapitated animals continued to move for some time when the nerve endings were stimulated. He concluded that various levels of behavior depend on different parts of the brain and nervous system. Specifically, he postulated that voluntary movement depends on the cerebrum, reflex movement on the spinal cord, involuntary movement on direct stimulation of the muscles, and respiratory movement on the medulla.

Pierre Flourens (1794–1867), a professor of natural history at the Collège de France in Paris, systematically destroyed parts of the brain and spinal cord in animals such as pigeons and observed and recorded the consequences. He concluded that the cerebrum controls the higher mental processes, parts of the midbrain control visual and auditory reflexes, the cerebellum controls coordination, and the medulla governs heartbeat, respiration, and other vital functions.

The findings of Hall and Flourens, although generally valid, are for our purposes second in importance to their use of the **extirpation method.** In this technique, the researcher attempts to determine the function of a given part of the brain by removing or destroying it and observing the resulting changes in the animal's behavior.

The mid-19th century saw two additional experimental approaches to the study of the brain: the clinical method and electrical stimulation. The **clinical method** was developed in 1861 by Paul Broca (1824–1880), a surgeon at a hospital for the insane near Paris. Broca performed an autopsy on a man who had been unable to speak intelligibly for many years. The examination revealed a lesion in the third frontal convolution of the cerebral cortex. Broca labeled this section of the brain the speech center; later it came to be called, appropriately, *Broca's area*. The clinical method is a useful supplement to extirpation because it is difficult to secure human subjects who will agree to removal of parts of their brain. As a sort of posthumous

EXTIRPATION METHOD: Technique for determining the function of a given part of an animal's brain by removing or destroying it and observing the resulting changes in the animal's behavior

CLINICAL METHOD: Posthumous examination of brain structures to detect damaged areas that are assumed to be responsible for behavioral conditions which existed before the patient died

ELECTRICAL STIMULATION METHOD: Exploration of areas of the cerebral cortex with weak electric currents to observe motor responses

extirpation, the clinical method provides the opportunity to examine the damaged area of the brain, the area assumed to be responsible for a behavioral condition that existed before the patient died.

The **electrical stimulation method** to study the brain was applied by Gustav Fritsch and Eduard Hitzig in 1870. This technique involves the exploration of the cerebral cortex with weak electric currents. Fritsch and Hitzig found that stimulating certain cortical areas in animals such as rabbits and dogs resulted in motor responses, such as movements of the legs. With the development of more sophisticated electronic equipment, electrical stimulation has become a productive technique for studying brain functions.

Research on the Nervous System

Considerable research on the structure of the nervous system and the nature of neural activity was also being conducted during the mid-19th century. Recall the two earlier theories about neural activity: the nerve tube theory held by Descartes, and Hartley's theory of vibrations.

Toward the end of the 18th century, the Italian researcher Luigi Galvani (1737–1798) had suggested that the nature of nerve impulses was electrical. His research was continued by his nephew, Giovanni Aldini, who "mixed serious research with showmanship. One of the more gruesome of Aldini's displays, designed to emphasize the effectiveness of electrical stimulation for obtaining spasmodic movements from muscles, involved using the recently severed heads of two criminals" (Boakes, 1984, p. 96).

Research proceeded so rapidly and convincingly that by the middle of the 19th century, the electrical nature of nerve impulses was accepted as fact. Scientists believed that the nervous system was essentially a conductor of electrical impulses and that the central nervous system functioned much like a switching station, shunting the impulses onto either sensory or motor nerve fibers.

Although this position was a great advance over Descartes's nerve tube theory and Hartley's theory of vibrations, it was conceptually similar to them. Both the newer and older viewpoints were reflexive. Both suggested that something from the external world (a stimulus) had an impact on a sense organ and excited a nerve impulse that traveled to the appropriate place in the brain or central nervous system. There, in response to the impulse, a new impulse was generated and transmitted via the motor nerves to trigger some response by the organism.

The anatomical structure of the nervous system was also being defined during the 19th century. Researchers learned that the nerve fibers were actually composed of separate structures called neurons, which were somehow joined or linked at points called synapses. Such findings were consistent with a mechanistic, materialistic image of human beings. It was believed that the nervous system, like the mind, was made up of atomistic structures that combined to produce the more complex product.

The spirit of mechanism was just as dominant in 19th-century physiology as it was in the philosophy of the time. Nowhere was this spirit more pronounced than in Germany. In the 1840s, a group of scientists, many of them former students of Johannes Müller, formed the Berlin Physical Society. These scientists, all in their twenties, committed themselves to one proposition—that all phenomena could be accounted for by the principles of physics. What they hoped to do was connect physiology with physics, to develop a physiology in the framework of the mechanistic view. In a dramatic gesture, four of the scientists (including Helmholtz, whom we will meet shortly) took a solemn oath, signing it, according to legend, with their own blood. The oath stated that the only forces active within an organism are the common physicochemical ones. And so the threads came together in 19th-century physiology: materialism, mechanism, empiricism, experimentation, and measurement.

These developments in early physiology indicate the kinds of research techniques and the discoveries that supported a scientific approach to the psychological investigation of the mind. While philosophers were paving the way for an experimental attack on the mind, physiologists were experimentally investigating the mechanisms underlying mental phenomena. The next step was to apply the experimental method to the mind itself.

The British empiricists had argued that sensation was the only source of knowledge. The astronomer Bessel had demonstrated the importance of sensation and perception in science. Physiologists were defining the structure and function of the senses. It was time to experiment with and to quantify this doorway to the mind—the subjective, mentalistic experience of sensation. Techniques were available to investigate the body; now they were being developed to explore the mind. Experimental psychology was ready to begin.

THE BEGINNINGS OF
EXPERIMENTAL PSYCHOLOGY

Four scientists are directly responsible for the initial applications of the experimental method to the mind, the subject matter of psychology: Hermann von Helmholtz, Ernst Weber, Gustav Theodor Fechner, and Wilhelm Wundt. All were German, trained in physiology, and aware of the impressive developments in science.

Why Germany?

Science was developing in most of the countries of Western Europe in the 19th century, particularly England, France, and Germany. No one country had a monopoly on the enthusiasm, conscientiousness, or optimism with which the tools of science were being applied. Why, then, did experimental psychology begin in Germany and not in England or France or elsewhere? The answer seems to lie in unique characteristics that made German science a more fertile breeding ground for the new psychology.

For a century, German intellectual history had paved the way for an experimental science of psychology. Experimental physiology was firmly established and was recognized to a degree not yet achieved in France and England. The so-called German temperament was well suited to the type of description and classification work needed in biology, zoology, and physiology. The deductive and mathematical approach to science was favored in France and England whereas Germany, with its emphasis on the careful and thorough collection of observable facts, had adopted an inductive approach.

Because biological and physiological sciences do not lend themselves to grand generalizations from which facts can be deduced, biology was accepted only slowly by the scientific communities of England and France. Germany, however, with its faith in taxonomic description and classification, welcomed biology to its family of sciences.

Further, the Germans defined science broadly. Science in France and England was limited to physics and chemistry, which could be approached quantitatively; but science in Germany included such areas as phonetics, linguistics, history, archeology, esthetics, logic, even literary criticism. French and English scholars were skeptical about applying science to the complex human mind. Not so the Germans, and they plunged ahead, unconstrained, using the tools of science to explore and measure the facets of mental life.

Germany also provided greater opportunities to learn and practice the new scientific techniques, and in this we see the influence of the contextual factor of prevailing economic conditions. Germany had a great many universities. Prior to 1870, the year Germany became a unified nation with a central government, it consisted of a loose confederation of autonomous kingdoms, duchies, and city–states. Each of these districts or provinces had established its own well-financed university. Each had a highly paid faculty and the most advanced scientific laboratory equipment.

In contrast, England at that time had only two universities, Oxford and Cambridge, and neither facilitated, encouraged, or supported scientific research in any discipline. Indeed, they opposed adding new fields of study to the curriculum. In 1877, Cambridge vetoed a request to teach experimental psychology because it would "insult religion by putting the human soul on a pair of scales" (Hearnshaw, 1987, p. 125). Experimental psychology would not be taught at Cambridge for another 20 years, and was not offered at Oxford until 1936. The only way to practice science in England was in the manner of the gentleman-scientist, living on an independent income, the way, as we will see, of Charles Darwin or Francis Galton. The situation was similar in France, and in the United States, there were no universities devoted to research until 1876, when Johns Hopkins University, in Baltimore, Maryland, was founded.

Thus, there were more opportunities for scientific research in Germany than elsewhere. Stated in pragmatic terms, a person could make a living as a research scientist in Germany but not in France, England, or the United States.

In the early 19th century, a wave of educational reform swept over the German universities devoted to the principles of academic freedom and to research for professors and students alike. Faculty members were encouraged to teach whatever they wished without outside interference, and to conduct research on topics of their own choosing. Students were free to take whatever courses they preferred, unrestricted by a rigid curriculum. This freedom extended to the consideration of new sciences such as psychology.

This style of university provided the ideal environment for the flourishing of scientific inquiry. Professors could not only lecture, but they could also direct students in experimental research in well-equipped laboratories. In no other country was such an approach to science fostered.

The climate of reform in German universities also encouraged their growth, and this meant that there were more jobs for those interested in academic careers in science. The chances of becoming a well-paid, respected professor were much higher in Germany, although it remained difficult to attain the top positions. The promising university scientist was required to produce research judged by experts in the field to be a major contribution, research that went beyond the typical doctoral dissertation. This meant that most of the people selected for a university career were of extremely high caliber. Once these scientists joined the faculty, the pressure on them to continue their research and to publish was fierce.

The German university system was the envy of the world, with a long tradition of outstanding academic freedom, and a reputation for scientific excellence and academic rigor. There was an old saying about German university students that a third of them succumbed to the pressures of coursework and suffered nervous breakdowns; another third responded to the pressures with avoidance, got lost in alcohol, and generally went to the devil; and the last third went on to rule Europe. (SHERRILL, 1991, P. 258)

Although the competition was intense and the demands high, the rewards were more than worth the effort. Only the best succeeded in German science of the 19th century, and the result was a series of breakthroughs in all the sciences, including the new psychology. It is no coincidence that the people directly responsible for the growth of scientific psychology were German university professors, who emerged as the rulers of science in Europe.

HERMANN VON HELMHOLTZ (1821–1894)

Helmholtz, a prolific researcher in physics and physiology, was one of the greatest scientists of the 19th century. Psychology ranked third among his areas of scientific contribution, yet his work, together with that of Fechner and Wundt, was instrumental in beginning the new psychology.

Helmholtz's Life

Born in Potsdam, Germany, where his father taught at the *Gymnasium* (in Europe, a high school/junior college preparatory for the university), Helmholtz was initially tutored at home because of his delicate health. At the age of 17 he enrolled in a Berlin medical institute where no tuition was charged to students who agreed to serve as army surgeons after graduation. Helmholtz served for 7 years, during which time he continued his studies in mathematics and physics and published several articles. He presented a paper on the indestructibility of energy, in which he mathematically formulated the law of the conservation of energy.

After leaving the army, Helmholtz accepted a position as associate professor of physiology at the University of Königsberg. Over the next 30 years he held academic appointments in physiology at universities in Bonn and Heidelberg, and in physics at Berlin.

The tremendously energetic Helmholtz wrote in several different areas. In the course of his work on physiological optics he invented the ophthalmoscope, a device for examining the retina of the eye. His three-volume work on physiological optics (*Handbook of Physiological Optics*) (1856–1866) proved to be so influential and enduring that it was translated into the English language 60 years later. He published his research on acoustical problems in 1863 in *On the Sensations of Tone,* which summarized his own findings and all the rest of the available literature. He also wrote on such diverse subjects as afterimages, color blindness, the Arabian–Persian musical scale, human eye movements, the formation of glaciers, geometrical ax-

HERMANN VON HELMHOLTZ

Archives of the History of American Psychology/University of Akron

The Helmholtz motor was powered by an electromagnetic device, and it generated energy for many laboratory instruments.

Archives of the History of American Psychology/University of Akron

ioms, and hay fever. In later years Helmholtz contributed indirectly to the invention of wireless telegraphy and radio.

In the fall of 1893, while returning from a trip to the United States that included a visit to the Chicago World's Fair, Helmholtz suffered a severe fall aboard ship. Less than a year later he had a stroke that left him semiconscious and delirious. "His thoughts ramble on confusedly," his wife wrote, "real life and dream life, time and scene, all float mistily by in his brain. . . . It is as if his soul were far, far away, in a beautiful ideal world, swayed only by science and the eternal laws" (quoted in Koenigsberger, 1965, p. 429).

The Contributions of Helmholtz: The Neural Impulse, Vision, and Audition

Of interest to psychology are Helmholtz's investigations of the speed of the neural impulse and his research on vision and audition. It had been assumed that the neural impulse was instantaneous, or at least that it traveled too fast to be measured. Helmholtz provided the first empirical measurement of the rate of conduction by stimulating a motor nerve and the attached muscle in the leg of a frog, arranged so that the precise moment of stimulation as well as the resulting movement could be recorded. Working with different nerve lengths, he recorded the delay between stimulation of the nerve near the muscle and the muscle's response, and did the same for stimulation farther from the muscle. These measurements yielded the time required for conduction of the neural impulse, the modest rate of 90 feet per second.

Helmholtz also experimented on the reaction times for sensory nerves in human subjects, studying the complete circuit from stimulation of a sense organ to the resulting motor response. The findings showed such enormous individual differences, as well as differences for the same person from one trial to the next, that Helmholtz abandoned the research.

Helmholtz's demonstration that the speed of conduction was not instantaneous suggested that thought and movement follow each other at a measurable interval and do not occur simultaneously, as had previously been thought. Helmholtz, however, was interested only in the measurement itself and not in its psychological significance. Later, the implications of his research for the new psychology were recognized by others, who went on to make reaction-time experiments a fruitful line of research. Helmholtz's work was one of the first instances of experimenting on and measuring a psychophysiological process.

His work on vision also had an influence on psychology. He investigated the external eye muscles and the mechanism by which the internal eye muscles focus the lens. He revised and extended a theory of color vision that had been published in 1802 by Thomas Young; this is now known as the Young-Helmholtz theory of color vision.

No less important is Helmholtz's research on audition, namely the perception of tones, the nature of harmony and discord, and the problem of resonance. The enduring influence of his work on vision and audition is evident from its inclusion in modern textbooks of psychology.

Helmholtz was not a psychologist, nor was psychology his main interest, but he contributed a large and important body of knowledge to the study of the human senses and helped to strengthen the experimental approach to the study of psychological problems.

ERNST WEBER (1795–1878)

Ernst Weber, the son of a theology professor, was born in Wittenberg, Germany. He earned his doctorate at the University of Leipzig in 1815 and taught anatomy and physiology there from 1817 until his retirement in 1871. His primary research interest was the physiology of the sense organs, an area in which he made outstanding and lasting contributions.

Previous research on the sense organs had been limited almost exclusively to the higher senses of vision and hearing. Weber explored new fields, notably cutaneous (skin) and muscular sensations. Particularly noteworthy is his application of the experimental methods of physiology to problems of a psychological nature.

Two-Point Thresholds

One of Weber's contributions to the new psychology involved the experimental determination of the accuracy of the two-point discrimination of the skin—the distance between two points that is necessary before subjects report feeling two distinct sensations. Without looking at the apparatus, which resembles a drawing compass, subjects are asked to report whether they feel one or two points touching the skin. When the two points of stimulation are close together, subjects report a clear sensation of being touched at only one point. As the distance between the two sources of stimulation is increased, subjects report uncertainty about whether they feel one or two sensations. Finally, a distance is reached where subjects report two distinct points of touch.

This procedure demonstrates the **two-point threshold,** the point at which the two sources of stimulation can be distinguished as such. Weber's research marks the first systematic, experimental demonstration of the concept of threshold—the point at which a psychological or physiological effect begins to be produced—an idea that has been widely used in psychology from its beginnings to the present day. (In chapter 13 we discuss the concept of threshold again, noting that the German philosopher Johann Friedrich Herbart applied it to consciousness, proposing a point at which unconscious ideas become conscious ideas.)

Archives of the History of American Psychology/University of Akron

ERNST WEBER

TWO-POINT THRESHOLD: The threshold at which two points of stimulation can be distinguished as such

Just Noticeable Differences

Weber's second major contribution led to the formulation of the first quantitative law of psychology. Weber wanted to determine the **just noticeable difference (jnd);** that is, the smallest difference between weights that could be detected. To do so, he asked his subjects to lift two weights, a standard weight and a comparison weight, and to report whether one felt heavier than the other. Small differences between the weights resulted in judgments of sameness; large differences resulted in judgments of disparity between the weights.

As the research progressed, Weber found that the just noticeable difference between two weights was a constant ratio, 1:40, of the standard weight. In other words, a weight of 41 grams was reported to be just noticeably different from a standard weight of 40 grams, and an 82-gram weight was just noticeably different from a standard weight of 80 grams.

Weber then investigated how muscle sensations contribute to the ability to distinguish between various weights. He found that subjects

JUST NOTICEABLE DIFFERENCE: The smallest difference between two physical stimuli that can be detected

could make such discriminations much more accurately when they lifted the weights themselves (receiving muscular sensations in hands and arms) than when the weights were placed in their hands by the experimenter. Hefting the weights involved both tactile (touch) and muscular sensations, whereas when the weights were placed in the hands, only tactile sensations were experienced. Because smaller differences in weights could be discriminated when the weights were lifted (a ratio of 1:40) than when the weights were placed in the hand (a ratio of 1:30), Weber concluded that the internal muscular sensations in the first case influenced the subjects' ability to discriminate.

From these experiments Weber found that discrimination seemed to depend not on the absolute difference between two weights but on their relative difference or ratio. He conducted experiments on visual discrimination and found that the ratio was smaller than for the muscle sense experiments. He suggested that there was a constant ratio for the just noticeable difference between two stimuli that is consistent for each of the senses.

Weber's research provided evidence that there is not a direct correspondence between a physical stimulus and our perception of it. Like Helmholtz, however, Weber was concerned with physiological processes and did not appreciate the significance of his work for psychology. What his research revealed was a way of investigating the relationship between body and mind, between the stimulus and the resulting sensation. This was a vital breakthrough; all that was necessary was for someone to act on its importance.

The work of Weber was experimental in the strictest sense of the term. Under well-controlled conditions, he systematically varied the stimuli and recorded the differential effects on the reported experiences of each of his subjects. His experiments stimulated a great deal of subsequent research and focused the attention of later physiologists on the usefulness of the experimental method as a means of studying psychological phenomena. Weber's research on threshold measurement was to be of paramount importance to the new psychology, and his demonstration that sensations can be measured has influenced virtually every aspect of psychology to the present day.

GUSTAV THEODOR FECHNER (1801–1887)

Fechner was a scholar who followed remarkably diverse intellectual pursuits during an active career of more than 70 years. He was a physiologist for 7 years, a physicist for 15, a psychophysicist for 14, an experimental estheticist for 11, a philosopher for 40, and an invalid for 12. Of these endeavors, it is the work on psychophysics that brought his greatest fame, although he did not wish to be so remembered by posterity.

Fechner's Life

Fechner was born in a village in southeastern Germany where his father was the minister. He began medical studies at the University of Leipzig in 1817, and while there he attended Weber's lectures on physiology. Fechner remained at Leipzig for the rest of his life.

Even before he graduated from medical school, Fechner's humanistic side showed signs of rebelling against the prevailing materialism of his scientific training. Under the pen name "Dr. Mises" he wrote satirical essays ridiculing medicine and science. This suggests a persistent conflict between the two sides of his personality—a love of science and an interest in metaphysical, or abstract, reasoning. One essay, "Proof that the Moon Is Made of Iodine," attacked the medical fad of using iodine as a remedy for all ills.

Fechner was obviously troubled by the materialistic and atomistic approach to science, and he attempted to substitute what he called his "day view"—that the universe can be regarded from the standpoint of consciousness—in opposition to the prevailing "night view" —that the universe, including consciousness, consisted of inert matter.

After completing his medical studies, Fechner began a second career in physics and mathematics at Leipzig, during which time he also translated handbooks of physics and chemistry from French into German. By 1830 he had translated more than a dozen volumes, and this activity brought him recognition as a physicist. In 1824 he began lecturing in physics at the university and conducting his own research. By the late 1830s he had developed an interest in sensation, and while investigating visual afterimages he seriously injured his eyes by looking at the sun through colored glasses.

In 1833, after many years of hard work, Fechner obtained the prestigious appointment of professor at Leipzig, whereupon he fell into a depression that endured for several years. He had difficulty sleeping and could not digest food, yet, while his body approached starvation, he felt no hunger. He was unusually sensitive to light and spent most of his time in a darkened room whose walls were painted black, listening while his mother read to him through a narrow opening in the door. He complained of chronic exhaustion and, for a time, lost all interest in living.

He tried walking—at first only at night, when it was dark, and then in daylight with his eyes bandaged—hoping to ease his boredom and depression. As a form of catharsis he composed riddles and poems. He dabbled in a variety of medical therapies, including laxatives, electric shock, steam treatments, and a type of shock therapy that involved the application of burning substances to the skin, but none of them provided a cure.

Fechner's illness may have been neurotic in nature. This idea is supported by the bizarre way in which he was cured. Recovery began

Archives of the History of American Psychology/University of Akron

GUSTAV THEODOR FECHNER

when a friend dreamed that she had made him a meal of spiced raw ham marinated in Rhine wine and lemon juice. The next day she prepared the dish and brought it to Fechner, insisting that he eat it. He tasted it, albeit reluctantly, and ate more and more of the ham every day, declaring that he felt somewhat better.

His improvement was short-lived, however, and after about 6 months, the symptoms worsened to the point where he feared for his sanity. "I had the distinct feeling," Fechner wrote, "that my mind was hopelessly lost unless I could stem the flood of disturbing thoughts. Often the least important matters bothered me in this manner and it took me often hours, even days, to rid myself of these worries" (Kuntze, 1892, quoted in Balance & Bringmann, 1987, p. 42).

Fechner forced himself to keep busy at routine, mechanical chores, as a sort of occupational therapy, but he was limited to tasks that did not make demands on his mind or his eyes. "I made strings and bandages," he wrote, "dipped candles . . . rolled yarn and helped in the kitchen sorting [and] cleaning lentils, making bread crumbs, and grinding a sugarloaf into powdered sugar. I also peeled and chopped carrots and turnips. . . . a thousand times I wished to be dead" (Kuntze, 1892, quoted in Balance & Bringmann, 1987, p. 43).

Slowly, gradually, Fechner redeveloped an interest in the world around him, and he continued the diet of spiced raw ham soaked in wine and lemon juice. Then he had a dream in which the number 77 appeared. This persuaded him that he would be cured in 77 days. And of course he was.

He felt so well that his depression turned to euphoria and delusions of grandeur, and he claimed that God had chosen him to solve all the mysteries of the world. From this experience he developed the notion of the pleasure principle, which many years later would influence the work of Sigmund Freud.

In 1844 Fechner was given a small pension from the university and officially established as an invalid. Yet not one of the next 43 years of his life passed without a serious scholarly contribution, and his health remained excellent until his death at the age of 86.

Mind and Body: A Quantitative Relationship

October 22, 1850, is an important date in the history of psychology. While lying in bed that morning, Fechner had a flash of insight about the law governing the connection between mind and body: It could be found in a quantitative relationship between a mental sensation and a material stimulus.

An increase in the intensity of a stimulus, Fechner argued, does not produce a one-to-one increase in the intensity of the sensation. Rather, a geometric series characterizes the stimulus and an arithmetic series characterizes the sensation. For example, adding the sound of 1 bell to that of an already ringing bell produces a greater increase in sensation than adding 1 bell to 10 others already ringing. The effects of stimulus intensities, therefore, are not absolute but are relative to the amount of sensation that already exists.

What this simple yet brilliant revelation means is that the amount of sensation (the mental quality) depends on the amount of stimulation (the physical or material quality). To measure the change in sensation, we must measure the change in stimulation. Thus, it is possible to relate the mental and material worlds quantitatively. Fechner crossed the barrier between body and mind by relating one to the other empirically.

Although the concept was clear, how was it to be translated into actuality? A researcher would have to measure precisely both the subjective and the objective, the mental sensation and the physical stimulus. To measure the physical intensity of the stimulus—the level of brightness or the weight of various objects, for example—was not difficult, but how was one to measure sensation, the conscious experiences that the subjects reported when they responded to the stimulus?

Fechner proposed two ways to measure sensations. First, we can determine whether a stimulus is present or absent, sensed or not sensed. Second, we can measure the stimulus intensity at which subjects report that the sensation first occurs; this is the **absolute threshold** of sensitivity, that point in stimulus intensity below which no sensation is reported and above which subjects do experience a sensation.

ABSOLUTE THRESHOLD: The point of sensitivity below which no sensations can be detected and above which sensations can be experienced

The absolute threshold, although useful, is limited because only one value of a sensation—its lowest level—is determined. To relate both intensities, we must be able to specify the full range of stimulus values and their resulting sensation values. To accomplish this, Fechner proposed the **differential threshold** of sensitivity, the least amount of change in a stimulus that will give rise to a change in sensation. For example, by how much must a weight be increased or decreased before subjects will sense the change, before they will report a just noticeable difference in sensation?

DIFFERENTIAL THRESHOLD: The point of sensitivity at which the least amount of change in a stimulus will give rise to a change in sensation

To measure how heavy a particular weight feels (how heavy the subjects sense it to be), we cannot use the physical measurement of the object's weight. We can, however, use that physical measurement as a basis for measuring the psychological intensity of the sensation. First, we measure by how much the weight must be decreased in intensity before subjects are barely able to discriminate the difference. Second, we change the weight of the object to this lower value and then measure the size of the differential threshold again. Because both weight changes are just barely noticeable, Fechner assumed that they were subjectively equal.

This process can be repeated until the object is barely felt by the subjects. If every decrease in weight is subjectively equal to every other decrease, the number of times the weight has to be decreased—the number of just noticeable differences—can be used as an objective measure of the subjective magnitude of the sensation. In this way we are measuring the stimulus values necessary to give rise to a difference between two sensations.

Fechner suggested that for each of the senses there is a certain relative increase in the stimulus that always produces an observable change in the intensity of the sensation. Thus, the sensation (the mind or mental quality), as well as the stimulus (the body or material quality), can be measured, and the relationship between the two can be stated in the form of an equation: $S = K \log R$, in which S is the magnitude of the sensation, K is a constant, and R is the magnitude of the stimulus. The relationship is logarithmic; one series increases arithmetically and the other geometrically.

Fechner wrote that this relationship had not been suggested to him by Weber's work, even though Weber was also at the University of Leipzig, where the two saw each other frequently, and Weber had written on this topic only a few years earlier. Fechner said that he did not discover Weber's work until after he had begun the experiments designed to test his hypothesis. He realized later, he reported, that the principle to which he gave mathematical form was essentially what Weber's work had shown.

Methods of Psychophysics

PSYCHOPHYSICS: The scientific study of the relations between mental and physical processes

The immediate result of Fechner's insight was the development of the research program on what he later called **psychophysics**. (The word defines itself: the relationship between the mental and material worlds.) In the course of this work—including experiments on lifted weights, visual brightness, visual distance, and tactile distance (the distance between two points touching the skin)—Fechner developed one and systematized two of the three fundamental methods of psychophysics that are still used today.

METHOD OF AVERAGE ERROR: A technique for studying sensory discrimination and reaction time that consists in having subjects adjust a variable stimulus until they perceive it to be equal to a constant standard stimulus

The **method of average error** (also called the **method of adjustment**) consists in having subjects adjust a variable stimulus until they perceive it to be equal to a constant standard stimulus. Over a number of trials, the mean or average value of the differences between the standard stimulus and the subjects' setting of the variable stimulus represents the error of observation. This technique is useful for measuring reaction time and visual and auditory discriminations. In a broader form, it is fundamental to much current psychological research. Every time we calculate a mean we are, in essence, using the method of average error.

The **method of constant stimuli** involves two constant stimuli, and the aim is to measure the stimulus difference that is required to produce a given proportion of correct judgments. For example, subjects first lift the standard weight of 100 grams and then lift a comparison weight of, say, 88, 92, 96, 104, or 108 grams. The subjects must judge whether the second weight is heavier, lighter, or equal to the first.

In the **method of limits,** two stimuli, such as weights, are presented to the subjects. One stimulus is increased or decreased until subjects report that they detect a difference. Data are obtained from a number of trials, and the just noticeable differences are averaged to determine the differential threshold.

Fechner carried on his research in psychophysics for 7 years, publishing part of it in two brief papers in 1858 and 1859. In 1860 the formal and complete exposition of his work appeared in the *Elements of Psychophysics,* a textbook of the exact science of the "functionally dependent relations . . . of the material and the mental, of the physical and psychological worlds" (Fechner, 1860/1966, p. 7). This book is one of the outstanding original contributions to the development of the science of psychology. Fechner's statement of the quantitative relationship between stimulus intensity and sensation was considered, at the time, to be of comparable importance to the discovery of the laws of gravity.

At the beginning of the 19th century, the German philosopher Immanuel Kant had insisted that psychology could never become a science because it was impossible to experiment on or to measure psychological processes. Because of Fechner's work, which did, indeed, make it possible to measure mental phenomena, Kant's assertion could no longer be regarded seriously.

It was largely because of Fechner's psychophysical research that Wilhelm Wundt conceived the plan of his experimental psychology. Fechner's methods have proved applicable to a wider range of psychological problems than he ever imagined, and with only minor modifications these methods are still applied in psychological research today. Fechner gave psychology what every discipline must possess to be a science: precise and elegant techniques of measurement.

METHOD OF CONSTANT STIMULI: A technique for measuring the stimulus difference required to produce a given proportion of correct comparative judgments of two physical stimuli

METHOD OF LIMITS: A technique for determining the differential threshold that involves comparative judgments of a standard stimulus and a variable stimulus

THE FORMAL FOUNDING OF PSYCHOLOGY

By the middle of the 19th century, the methods of natural science were being used routinely to investigate purely mental phenomena. Techniques had been developed, apparatus devised, important books written, and widespread interest aroused. British empirical philosophy and the work in astronomy emphasized the importance of the senses, and the German scientists were describing how the senses functioned. The positivistic Zeitgeist, or intellectual spirit of the times, encouraged the convergence of these two lines of thought. Still lacking, however, was someone to bring them together—in a word, to *found* the new science. This final touch was provided by Wilhelm Wundt.

Wundt is the founder of psychology as a formal academic discipline. He established the first laboratory, edited the first journal, and began experimental psychology as a science. The areas he investigated—including sensation and perception, attention, feeling, reaction, and association—became basic chapters in textbooks yet to be written. That so much of the history of psychology after Wundt consists of opposition to his view of psychology does not detract from his achievements as its founder.

Why have the honors for founding the new psychology fallen to Wundt and not to Fechner? Fechner's *Elements of Psychophysics* was published in 1860, approximately 15 years before Wundt is said to have begun psychology. Wundt himself wrote that Fechner's work represented the "first conquest" in experimental psychology (Wundt, 1888, p. 471). Wundt's disciple, E. B. Titchener, called Fechner the father of experimental psychology (Benjamin, Bryant, Campbell, Fisher, & Holtz, 1994). Historians agree on Fechner's importance; some even question whether psychology could have begun when it did were it not for Fechner's work. Why, then, does history not credit Fechner with founding the science of psychology?

The answer lies in the nature of the process of founding. Founding is a deliberate and intentional act involving abilities and characteristics that differ from those necessary for brilliant scientific achievement. Founding requires the integration of previous work and the publication and promotion of the newly organized material. "When the central ideas are all born, some promoter takes them in hand, organizes them, adding whatever else seems . . . essential, publishes and advertises them, insists upon them, and in short 'founds' a school" (Boring, 1950, p. 194). Wundt's contribution to the founding of modern psychology stems not so much from any unique scientific discovery as from his "heroic propagandizing for experimentalism" (O'Donnell, 1985, p. 16).

Founding is thus quite different from originating, although the distinction is not meant to be a disparaging one. Founders and originators are both essential to the formation of a science, as indispensable as are the architect and the builder in the construction of a house.

With this distinction in mind, we can understand why Fechner is not called the founder of psychology. Stated simply, he was not trying to found a new science. His goal was to understand the relationship between the mental and material worlds. He sought to describe a unified conception of mind and body that had a scientific basis.

Wundt, however, set out deliberately to found a new science. In the preface to the first edition of his *Principles of Physiological Psychology* (1873–1874) he wrote: "The work I here present to the public is an attempt to mark out a new domain of science." Wundt's goal was to promote psychology as an independent science. Nevertheless, it bears repeating that although Wundt is considered to have founded psychology, he did not originate it. Psychology emerged, as we have seen, from a long line of creative efforts.

During the last half of the 19th century, the Zeitgeist was ready for the application of experimental methods to problems of the mind. Wundt was a vigorous agent of what was already developing, a gifted promoter of the inevitable.

DISCUSSION QUESTIONS

1. What was the significance of Bessel's work for the new psychology? Describe how developments in early physiology supported the mechanistic image of human beings.
2. Discuss the reasons why the new experimental psychology emerged only in Germany. Describe the significance for psychology of Helmholtz's research on the speed of the neural impulse.
3. Describe Weber's research on two-point thresholds and on just noticeable differences. What was the importance of this work for psychology?
4. What was the insight Fechner had on October 22, 1850? How did Fechner measure sensations? Describe the relationship between the intensity of the stimulus and the intensity of the sensation, as represented by $S = K \log R$.
5. What psychophysical methods did Fechner use? How did psychophysics influence the development of psychology? Do you think experimental psychology would have developed when it did without Fechner's work? Why or why not?
6. Distinguish between founding and originating in science. Why is Wundt, and not Fechner, considered the founder of psychology?

SUGGESTED READINGS

Boring, E. G. (1961). Fechner: Inadvertent founder of psychophysics. *Psychometrika, 26,* 3–8. Reviews Fechner's life and assesses the importance of his work for the development of experimental psychology.

Dobson, V., & Bruce, D. (1972). The German university and the development of experimental psychology. *Journal of the History of the Behavioral Sciences, 8,* 204–207. Describes the academic freedom in German universities as a precondition for the growth of the new psychology.

Marshall, M. E. (1969). Gustav Fechner, Dr. Mises, and the comparative anatomy of angels. *Journal of the History of the Behavioral Sciences, 5,* 39–58. Examines Fechner's essays written as "Dr. Mises" and analyzes his day and night views of the universe.

Turner, R. S. (1977). Hermann von Helmholtz and the empiricist vision. *Journal of the History of the Behavioral Sciences, 13,* 48–58. Describes the impact of Helmholtz's philosophical views on his program of research.

CHAPTER 4

THE NEW PSYCHOLOGY

A CASE OF DISTORTED DATA

WILHELM WUNDT, as the founder of the new science of psychology, is one of the field's most important figures. To understand psychology's history, generations of scholars and students began their study by acquainting themselves with some version of Wundt's general approach. Yet more than a century after Wundt founded psychology, new data, and refinements of well-known data, led psychologists to conclude that the accepted view of Wundt's system was wrong. Wundt, who always feared being "misunderstood and misrepresented," had suffered just that fate (Baldwin, 1980, p. 301).

Many journal articles published in the 1970s and 1980s echoed this theme—that the prevailing description of Wundtian psychology portrayed his position inaccurately, ascribing to him beliefs that diverged from his own intentions (see, for example, Blumenthal, 1975, 1979; Leahey, 1981).

How could such a mistake be made with someone so prominent? Wundt wrote many books and articles presenting his view of psychology. His system was there for all to see—for all, that is, who were fluent in the German language and who were willing to devote the time needed to study his phenomenal number of publications.

But why go to all that trouble? Most psychologists did not think it was necessary to read Wundt's work in the original German because his most important ideas and research findings had been translated into the English language by his student E. B. Titchener, an English psychologist who spent most of his career at Cornell University in New York. Titchener pronounced himself to be Wundt's loyal follower and true interpreter. And so it came to be assumed that Titchener's approach to psychology, which he called structuralism, was essentially a mirror image of that of his mentor Wundt. If we learned about Titchener's system, then we knew Wundt's as well.

Later research on Wundt's writings casts doubt on this conclusion. Titchener did not accurately represent Wundt. Titchener apparently elected to translate only those portions of Wundt's publications that supported his own approach to psychology. Evidence suggests that he may have altered Wundt's positions to make them appear compatible with his own, to lend credibility to his views by asserting that they were consistent with those of psychology's founder.

Titchener's inaccurate and incomplete version of Wundt's system influenced several generations of psychologists, not only because of the status Titchener achieved within American psychology, but also because of the visibility attained by his student E. G. Boring, who became, for a time, the leading historian of psychology. Boring claimed that Titchener was a Wundtian in the Leipzig tradition. Although Boring also stated that Titchener's work was "distinct from the [school] of Wundt" (Boring, 1950, p. 419), many psychologists who learned their history from Boring's textbook, *A History of Experimental Psychology* (1929, 1950), came to identify Titchener's system with Wundt's.

Thus, we were offered an account of Wundt's psychology that turned out to be more myth than fact, more legend than truth. For 100 years after the formal founding of psychology, teachers and textbooks about the history of psychology (including earlier editions of this text) compounded and reinforced the error. This experience provides another example of how the changing data of history can influence our understanding of past events. As we noted in chapter 1, our understanding of history is subject to revision as new data or refinements of existing data are revealed.

WILHELM WUNDT (1832–1920)

After reviewing the life of Wilhelm Wundt, we will consider his definition of psychology and how it influenced the subsequent development of the field.

Wundt's Life

Wilhelm Wundt spent his early years in small towns near Mannheim, Germany, where his childhood was marked by loneliness and fantasies of becoming a famous writer. He earned poor grades in school and lived the life of an only child; his older brother was away at boarding school. Wundt's father was a pastor, and although both parents seem to have been sociable, Wundt's early memories of his father were unpleasant. He recalled that his father visited his school one day and hit him across the face for not paying attention to the teacher.

Beginning in the second grade, Wundt's education was undertaken by his father's assistant, a young vicar for whom the boy developed a strong emotional attachment. When the vicar was transferred to a neighboring town, Wundt became so upset that he was allowed to live with the vicar until the age of 13.

There was a strong tradition of scholarship in the Wundt family, with ancestors of intellectual renown in virtually every field. It appeared, nonetheless, that this impressive line would not be continued by the young Wundt. He spent more time daydreaming than studying, and he failed in his first year at the *Gymnasium*. He did not get along well with his classmates and was ridiculed by his teachers.

Gradually, Wundt learned to control his daydreaming, and he even became relatively popular. Although he always disliked school, he developed his intellectual interests and abilities. By the time he graduated at the age of 19, he was ready for the university.

Wundt decided to become a physician, to pursue his goal of working in science and making a living at the same time. His medical studies took him to the University of Tübingen and then to the University of Heidelberg, where he studied anatomy, physiology, physics, medicine, and chemistry. He came to realize that the practice of medicine was not to his liking, and he changed his major field to physiology.

After a semester of study at the University of Berlin with the great physiologist Johannes Müller, Wundt returned to Heidelberg to earn his doctorate in 1855. He held an appointment as lecturer in physiology at Heidelberg from 1857 to 1864, and was appointed laboratory assistant to Hermann von Helmholtz. He found the work of drilling undergraduates in their laboratory fundamentals to be dreary, so he resigned from those duties. In 1864 he was promoted to associate professor and remained at the University of Heidelberg for another 10 years.

In the course of his research in physiology, Wundt began to conceive of a field of psychology that would be an independent and experimental science. He presented his ideas in a book entitled *Contributions to the Theory of Sensory Perception,* which was published in sections between 1858 and 1862. He described his own original experiments, which he conducted in a crude laboratory built in his home, and he offered his views on the proper methods for the new psychology. In this book Wundt also used the term *experimental psychology* for the first time. Along with Fechner's *Elements of Psychophysics* (1860), Wundt's book is often considered to mark the literary birth of the new science.

National Library of Medicine

WILHELM WUNDT

The following year Wundt published *Lectures on the Minds of Men and Animals.* An indication of the importance of this book was its revision almost 30 years later, with an English translation and repeated reprintings until after Wundt's death in 1920. In it Wundt discussed many problems, such as reaction time and psychophysics, that were to occupy the attention of experimental psychologists for years.

Beginning in 1867, Wundt offered a course at Heidelberg on physiological psychology, the first formal offering of such a course anywhere in the world. Out of his lectures came a highly significant book, *Principles of Physiological Psychology,* published in two parts in 1873 and 1874. Wundt revised the book in six editions over 37 years, the last published in 1911. Undoubtedly his masterpiece, the *Principles* firmly established psychology as an independent laboratory science with its own problems and methods of experimentation.

For many years, the successive editions of the *Principles of Physiological Psychology* served experimental psychologists as a storehouse of information and a record of the progress of the new psychology. In the book's preface, Wundt stated his goal: "to mark out a new domain of science." The term *physiological psychology* in the title may be misleading. At the time, the word *physiological* was used as a synonym for the word *experimental* in German. Wundt was teaching and writing about experimental psychology, not physiological psychology as we know it today.

The Leipzig Years

Wundt began the longest and most important phase of his career in 1875 when he became professor of philosophy at the University of Leipzig, where he worked prodigiously for 45 years. He established a laboratory at Leipzig shortly after he arrived, and in 1881 began the journal *Philosophical Studies,* the official publication of the new laboratory and the new science. He had intended to call the journal *Psychological Studies,* but he changed his mind, apparently because there already was such a journal (although it dealt with occult and spiritualistic issues). In 1906, however, Wundt retitled his journal *Psychological Studies.* With a handbook, a laboratory, and a scholarly journal, psychology was well under way.

Wundt's spreading fame and his laboratory drew a large number of students to Leipzig to work with him. Among these were many subsequent contributors to psychology, including several Americans, most of whom returned to the United States to begin laboratories of their own. Through these students, the Leipzig laboratory exerted an immense influence on the development of modern psychology, serving as the model for many new laboratories.

In addition to those begun in the United States, laboratories were established in Italy, Russia, and Japan by students of those countries who had journeyed to Leipzig to study with Wundt. More of Wundt's books were translated into Russian than into any other language, and Russian adulation of Wundt led psychologists in Moscow to build a duplicate of Wundt's own lab in 1912. Another replica was built by Japanese students at Tokyo University in 1920, the year Wundt died, but it was burned in a student riot in the 1960s (Blumenthal, 1985). The students who flocked to Leipzig were united in viewpoint and purpose, at least initially, and they constituted the first formal school of thought within psychology.

Wundt's lectures at Leipzig were popular. At one time he had more than 600 students in a class. His classroom manner has been described by his student E. B. Titchener in a letter Titchener wrote in 1890, just after attending Wundt's lectures for the first time.

The [attendant] swung the door open, and Wundt came in. All in black, of course, from boots to necktie; a spare, narrow-shouldered figure, stooping a little from the hips; he gave the impression of height, though I doubt if in fact he stands more than 5 ft. 9.

He clattered–there is no other word for it–up the side-aisle and up the steps of the platform; slam bang, slam bang, as if his soles were made of wood. There was something positively undignified to me about this stamping clatter, but nobody seemed to notice it.

He came to the platform, and I could get a good view of him. Hair iron-grey, and a fair amount of it, except on the top of his head–which was carefully covered by long wisps drawn up from the side. . . .

The platform has a long desk, I suppose for demonstrations, and on that an adjustable bookrest. Wundt made a couple of mannered movements–snatched his forefinger across his forehead, arranged his chalk–and then faced his audience with both elbows set on this rest. A curious attitude, which favors the impression of height. He began his lecture in a high-pitched, weak, almost apologetic voice; but after a sentence or two, during which the room settled down to silence, his full lecturing voice came out, and was maintained to the end of the hour. It is an easy and abundant bass, somewhat toneless, at times a little barking; but it carries well, and there is a certain persuasiveness, a sort of fervor, in the delivery that holds your interest and prevents any feeling of monotony. . . . The lecture was given without reference to notes: Wundt, so far as I could tell, never looked down once at the bookrest, though he had some little shuffle of papers there between his elbows. . . .

Wundt did not keep his arms lying on the rest: the elbows were fixed, but the arms and hands were perpetually coming up, pointing and waving. . . . the movements were subdued, and seemed in some mysterious way to be illustrative. . . .

He stopped punctually at the stroke of the clock, and clattered out, stooping a little, as he had clattered in. If it wasn't for this absurd clatter I should have nothing but admiration for the whole proceeding. (Baldwin, 1980, pp. 287-289)[1]

In his personal life, Wundt was quiet and unassuming, and his days followed a carefully regulated pattern. (The diaries of his wife, Sophie, were found in the 1970s, revealing much new material about Wundt's personal life, another instance of newly discovered historical data.) In the morning Wundt worked on a book or article, read student papers, and edited his journal. In the afternoon he attended exams or visited the laboratory. A student recalled that Wundt's laboratory visits were limited to 5 or 10 minutes. Apparently, despite his great faith in laboratory research, "he was not himself a laboratory worker" (Cattell, 1928, p. 545).

Later in the day Wundt would take a walk while thinking about his afternoon lecture, which he habitually delivered at 4:00 PM. Many of his evenings were devoted to music, politics, and, at least in his younger years, concern with student and worker rights. The Wundt family enjoyed a sizable income, employed household servants, and entertained frequently.

Cultural Psychology

With the laboratory and the journal established, and an immense amount of research under direction, Wundt turned his energy to philosophy. During the years from 1880 to 1891, he wrote on ethics, logic, and systematic philosophy. He published the second edition of *Principles of Physiological Psychology* in 1880 and the third edition in 1887, and continued to contribute articles to his journal.

Another field on which Wundt later focused his considerable talent had been briefly sketched in his first book: the creation of a social psychology. When he returned to this project, he produced a 10-volume work, *Cultural Psychology,* which was published between 1900 and 1920. (The title is often translated inaccurately as "folk psychology.")

[1]Reprinted by permission of the American Psychological Association.

Wundt and his graduate students conduct an experiment on reaction time.

Archives of the History of American Psychology/University of Akron

Cultural psychology was concerned with the investigation of the various stages of human mental development as manifested in language, art, myths, social customs, law, and morals. The implications of this work for psychology are of greater significance than its actual content; it served to divide the new science of psychology into two parts: the experimental and the social.

The simpler mental functions, such as sensation and perception, can and must be studied by laboratory investigation, Wundt believed. But he argued that scientific experimentation is impossible for studying the higher mental processes, such as learning and memory, because they are conditioned by language habits and other aspects of our cultural training. To Wundt, the higher thought processes could be studied only by the non-experimental approaches as practiced in sociology, anthropology, and social psychology. The contention that social forces play a major role in the development of cognitive processes is an important one, but Wundt's conclusion that these processes cannot be studied experimentally was soon disproved.

Wundt devoted 10 years to the development of his cultural psychology, but it has had little impact on American psychology. A survey covering 90 years of articles published in the *American Journal of Psychology* showed that, of all the citations to Wundt's publications, less than 4% were to *Cultural Psychology*. In contrast, Wundt's *Principles of Physiological Psychology* accounted for more than 61% of the references to his works (Brožek, 1980).

Wundt continued to work without a break until his death in 1920. Consistent with his systematic lifestyle, he died shortly after completing his psychological reminiscences. Analyses of his productivity showed that he wrote some 54,000 pages between 1853 and 1920, an output of 2.2 pages every day (Boring, 1950; Bringmann & Balk, 1992). His childhood fantasies of becoming a famous writer had been realized.

The Study of Conscious Experience

Wundt's psychology drew on the experimental methods of the natural sciences, particularly the techniques used by the physiologists. Wundt adapted these scientific methods of investigation for the new psychology and proceeded to study its subject matter in the same way the physical scientists were studying theirs. Thus, the Zeitgeist in physiology and philosophy helped to shape both the subject matter of the new psychology and its methods of investigation.

The subject matter of Wundt's psychology was, in a word, *consciousness*. In a broad sense, the impact of 19th-century empiricism and associationism was at least partly reflected in Wundt's system. His view of consciousness was that it included many different parts and could be studied by the method of analysis or reduction. Wundt wrote: "The first step in the investigation of a fact must therefore be a description of the individual elements . . . of which it consists" (quoted in Diamond, 1980, p. 85).

With that point, however, the similarity ends between Wundt's approach and that of the majority of the empiricists and associationists. Wundt did not agree with the idea that the elements of consciousness were static—atoms of the mind—passively connected by some mechanical process of association. Instead, Wundt believed that consciousness was more active in organizing its own content. Hence, the study of the elements, content, or structure of consciousness alone would provide only a beginning to our understanding of psychological processes.

VOLUNTARISM: The idea that the mind has the capacity to organize mental contents into higher-level thought processes

Because of Wundt's focus on the self-organizing capacity of the mind, he referred to his system as **voluntarism,** which derives from the word *volition*, defined as the act or power of willing. Voluntarism refers to the power of the will to organize the contents of the mind into higher-level thought processes. Wundt emphasized not the elements themselves, as had the British empiricists and associationists (and as Titchener would later do), but rather the process of actively organizing or synthesizing those elements.

It is important to remember that although Wundt emphasized the power of the conscious mind to synthesize elements into higher-level cognitive processes, he nevertheless recognized that the elements of consciousness were basic. Without these elements, there would be nothing for the mind to organize.

According to Wundt, psychologists should be concerned with the study of immediate experience rather than mediate experience. **Mediate experience** provides us with information or knowledge about something other than the elements of the experience itself. This is the usual form in which we use experience to acquire knowledge about our world. For example, when we look at a flower and say, "The flower is red," this statement implies that our primary interest is in the flower and not in the fact that we are experiencing something called "redness."

The **immediate experience** of looking at the flower, however, is not in the object itself but, instead, is in the experience of something that is red. Thus, for Wundt, immediate experience is unbiased by any interpretation, such as describing the experience of the flower's red color in terms of the object—the flower—itself.

Similarly, when we describe our feelings of discomfort when we have a toothache, we are reporting our immediate experience. If we were simply to say, "I have a toothache," then we would be concerned with mediate experience.

In Wundt's view, our basic experiences—such as the experiences of redness or of discomfort—form the states of consciousness or the mental elements that the mind actively organizes. Wundt intended to analyze the mind into its elemental or component parts, just as the natural scientists were breaking down their subject matter, the material universe. The work of the Russian chemist Dimitri Mendeleev in developing the periodic table of chemical elements supported Wundt's aim. Historians have suggested that Wundt may have been striving to develop a "periodic table of the mind" (Marx & Cronan-Hillix, 1987, p. 76).

The Method of Introspection

Because Wundt's psychology is the science of conscious experience, the method of psychology must involve observations of conscious experience. Only the person having such an experience can observe it, so the method must involve **introspection**—the examination of one's own mental state. Wundt referred to this method as internal perception. The use of introspection did not originate with Wundt; its use can be traced to Socrates. Wundt's innovation was the application of precise experimental control over the conditions under which introspection was performed. Some critics, however, worried that continued exposure to this introspective self-observation would drive students insane (Titchener, 1921).

The use of introspection in psychology was derived from physics, in which the method had been used to study light and sound, and from physiology, in which it had been applied to the study of the

MEDIATE EXPERIENCE: Experience that provides information about something other than the elements of the experience

IMMEDIATE EXPERIENCE: Experience that is unbiased by interpretation

INTROSPECTION: Examination of one's own mind to inspect personal thoughts or feelings

sense organs. To obtain information about the sense organs, for example, an investigator applied a stimulus and asked the subject to report on the sensation produced; this is similar to Fechner's psychophysical research methods. When subjects compared two weights and reported whether one was heavier, lighter, or equal in weight to the other, they were introspecting, reporting on their conscious experiences. If you said "I am hungry," you would be introspecting, reporting on an observation you have made of your own internal condition.

Introspection, or internal perception, as practiced in Wundt's laboratory at the University of Leipzig, was conducted under stringent experimental conditions. Wundt set forth explicit rules: (1) Observers must be able to determine when the process is to be introduced; (2) They must be in a state of readiness or strained attention; (3) It must be possible to repeat the observation several times; and (4) The experimental conditions must be capable of variation in terms of the controlled manipulation of the stimuli. The last condition invokes the essence of the experimental method: varying the conditions of the stimulus situation and observing the resulting changes in the subjects' experiences.

Wundt rarely used the kind of qualitative introspection in which subjects simply described their inner experiences. The type of introspective report Wundt sought in his own laboratory dealt primarily with the subjects' conscious judgments about the size, intensity, and duration of various physical stimuli—the kinds of quantitative judgments made in psychophysical research. Only a small number of studies involved reports of a subjective or qualitative nature, such as the pleasantness of different stimuli, the intensity of images, or the quality of certain sensations. Most of Wundt's studies relied on objective measurements that involved sophisticated laboratory equipment, and many of these measurements concerned reaction times, which can be recorded quantitatively. Wundt then inferred information about conscious elements and processes from these objective measures.

Elements of Conscious Experience

Having defined psychology's subject matter and method, Wundt proceeded to outline his goals for the new field: (1) to analyze conscious processes into their basic elements, (2) to discover how these elements are synthesized or organized, and (3) to determine the laws of connection governing that organization.

Wundt suggested that sensations were one of two elementary forms of experience. Sensations are aroused whenever a sense organ is stimulated and the resulting impulses reach the brain. He classified sensations according to intensity, duration, and sense modality.

Wundt recognized no fundamental difference between sensations and images because images are also associated with excitation of the cerebral cortex.

Feelings are the other elementary form of experience. Wundt stated that sensations and feelings are simultaneous aspects of immediate experience. Feelings are the subjective complements of sensations, but they do not arise directly from a sense organ. Sensations are accompanied by certain feeling qualities, and when sensations combine to form a more complex state, a feeling quality will result.

Wundt developed a **tridimensional theory of feelings** from his own introspective observations. Working with a metronome (a device that produces audible clicks at regular intervals), Wundt reported that after he experienced a series of clicks, he felt that some rhythmic patterns were more pleasant or agreeable than others. He concluded that part of the experience of any such pattern is a subjective feeling of pleasure or displeasure. (Note that this subjective feeling occurs at the same time as the physical sensations associated with the clicks.) He then suggested that this feeling state can be located on a continuum ranging from agreeable to disagreeable.

Wundt detected a second kind of feeling while listening to the metronome's clicks, reporting a slight tension while awaiting each successive sound, followed by relief after the anticipated click occurred. From this he concluded that in addition to a pleasure/displeasure continuum, his feelings had a tension/relaxation dimension. In addition, he reported feeling mildly excited when he increased the rate of clicks, and calmer, even depressed, when he reduced the rate of clicks.

TRIDIMENSIONAL THEORY OF FEELINGS: Wundt's theory of feelings based on three dimensions: pleasure-displeasure, tension-relaxation, and excitement-depression

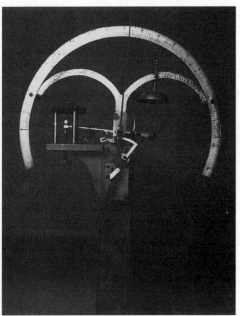

Apparatus used by Wundt to investigate the effects of attention on perception.

By repeatedly and patiently varying the speed of the metronome and introspecting and reporting on his immediate conscious experiences (his sensations and feelings), Wundt arrived at three independent dimensions of feeling: pleasure/displeasure, tension/relaxation, and excitement/depression. Every feeling could be located somewhere within this three-dimensional space.

Wundt believed that emotions are complex compounds of elementary feelings, and that all elementary feelings could be effectively described by determining their position on each of the three dimensions. In this way, he reduced emotions to mental elements. The tridimensional theory of feelings stimulated a great deal of research in the Leipzig and other laboratories, but it has not withstood the test of time.

Organizing the Elements of Conscious Experience

Despite his emphasis on the elements of conscious experience, Wundt recognized that when we look at objects in the real world, we see a unity or wholeness of perceptions. We see a tree as a unit, for example; we do not actually see each individual sensation or experience of brightness, color, or shape that observers in a laboratory report as a result of their introspections. Our visual experience comprehends the tree as a whole and not as individual elementary sensations and feelings that constitute the tree.

APPERCEPTION: The process by which mental elements are organized

How is this unified conscious experience built up from the elementary parts? Wundt proposed the doctrine of **apperception** to account for it. He called the actual process of organizing the elements into a whole creative synthesis (also called the law of psychic resultants); this process of creative synthesis creates new properties from the combination of the elements.

"Every psychic compound has characteristics which are by no means the mere sum of the characteristics of the elements" (Wundt, 1896, p. 375). Something new is created out of the synthesis of the elements of experience. We might say, as the Gestalt psychologists proclaimed in 1912, that the whole is different from the sum of its parts.

The notion of creative synthesis has its counterpart in chemistry. Combining chemical elements produces compounds or resultants that contain properties not found in the original elements. Apperception, therefore, is an active process. Our consciousness is not merely acted on by the elemental sensations and feelings we experience; rather, the mind acts on these elements in a creative way to make up the whole. You can see, then, that Wundt did not treat the process of association in the passive, mechanical fashion favored by most of the British empiricists and associationists.

Research Topics of the Leipzig Laboratory

Wundt determined the goals and problems for his experimental psychology during the early years of the Leipzig laboratory. For a long time, the issues with which the new psychology was concerned were defined primarily by the work he and his students performed there. His extensive research program showed that an experimentally based science of psychology was possible, as John Stuart Mill had claimed. Wundt believed that psychology should deal initially with problems that had already been investigated and reduced to empirical and quantitative form. For the most part, he did not occupy himself with new areas of research but rather with formally developing and extending current topics. More than 100 studies were performed in the first 20 years of the laboratory's existence.

The first series of studies at Leipzig involved psychological and physiological aspects of vision, hearing, and the minor senses. Typical issues in the area of visual sensation and perception included the psychophysics of color, color contrast, peripheral vision, negative after-images, visual contrast, color blindness, visual size, and optical illusions. Psychophysical methods were used to investigate auditory sensations. The sense of touch was studied, as was time sense (the perception or estimation of varying lengths of time).

Another topic that claimed considerable attention was reaction time, a subject that arose from the work of Bessel on the speed of reaction among astronomers. Speed of reaction had been under scientific investigation since the end of the 18th century and had been studied by Helmholtz and by F. C. Donders, a Dutch physiologist. Wundt believed that he could demonstrate experimentally three stages in a person's response to a stimulus: perception, apperception, and will.

After a stimulus is presented, subjects perceive it, then apperceive it, and finally they will themselves to react; from this will to react, muscular movement results. Wundt hoped to establish a standard table of time measurements for the human mind by determining the times for the various mental processes, such as cognition, discrimination, and will. The promise of the method was not to be realized, however, because in experienced subjects the three stages were not clearly apparent, and the times for the separate processes were not constant from person to person or from study to study.

Studies on reaction time were supplemented by research on attention and feelings. Wundt considered attention to be the most vivid perception of only a small portion of the entire content of consciousness at any one time. He was referring to what we commonly call the focus of attention. Stimuli in the focus are the most clearly perceived and are distinct from the rest of the visual field. A simple example is your focus on the words you are now reading relative to the rest of the page and the other objects on your desk, which you perceive less clearly. At the Leipzig laboratory, research was conducted on the range and fluctuation of attention as well as on attention span.

Studies of feelings were undertaken to attempt to support the tridimensional theory. Wundt used the method of paired comparisons, which requires subjects to compare stimuli in terms of the subjective feeling aroused. Other studies attempted to relate bodily changes, such as pulse and breathing rate, to corresponding feeling states.

Another area of investigation was verbal associations, continuing work begun by the English scientist Francis Galton. Subjects were asked to respond with a single word when presented with a stimulus word. Wundt proceeded to classify the types of associations discovered when single-word stimuli were presented, to determine the nature of all verbal association.

The experimental areas of the psychophysiology of the senses, reaction time, psychophysics, and association account for more than half of all the work published in the first few years of Wundt's journal. He showed some slight concern with child psychology and with animal psychology but apparently did no experiments in these areas, believing that the conditions of study could not be adequately controlled.

Comment

The act of establishing the first psychology laboratory required a person with a knowledge of contemporary physiology and philosophy who was capable of combining these disciplines effectively. To accomplish his goal of founding a new science, Wundt had to reject the nonscientific thinking of the past and cut the intellectual ties between the new scientific psychology and the old mental philosophy. By restricting the subject matter of psychology to conscious experience, and stating that psychology was a science based on experience, Wundt was able to avoid discussions about the immortal soul and its relationship to the mortal body. He said simply and emphatically that psychology did not deal with such questions. This assertion was a great step forward.

Wundt began a new domain of science, as he had announced he would, and conducted research in a laboratory he designed exclusively for that purpose. He published the results in his own journal and tried to develop a systematic theory of the nature of the human mind. Some of his students went on to found additional laboratories to continue experimenting on the problems and with the techniques Wundt set forth. Thus, Wundt provided psychology with all the trappings of a modern science.

The times, of course, were ready for the Wundtian movement, which was the natural outcome of the development of the physiological sciences, particularly in German universities. That Wundt's work was the culmination of this movement and not its origin does not diminish its stature. After all, it required a kind of genius, and a sense of dedication and courage, to bring such a movement to fulfillment. The results of Wundt's efforts represent an achievement of such overwhelming importance that Wundt is accorded a place unique among psychologists of the modern period.

It is important to note that although Wundtian psychology spread rapidly, it did not immediately or completely transform the nature of academic psychology in Germany. In Wundt's lifetime—and, indeed, as late as 1941—psychology in German universities remained primarily a subspecialty of philosophy. In part, this was because some psychologists and philosophers argued against the split of psychology and philosophy. But also it was attributable to a more practical contextual factor: Government officials in charge of funding German universities did not see sufficient practical value in psychology to warrant supplying money to establish independent academic departments and laboratories (Ash, 1987).

Nor was the new psychology, with its focus on the elements of consciousness and their synthesis, amenable to solving real-world problems. Perhaps that was one reason why Wundt's psychology did not gain popularity in the pragmatic climate of the United States. Wundt's psychology was a pure academic science, and was intended to be only that; Wundt had no interest in applying his psychology to practical concerns.

Despite its acceptance in universities throughout the world, then, Wundtian psychology at home in Germany was slow to develop as a separate science. By 1910, 10 years before Wundt's death, German psychology had three journals and several textbooks and research laboratories, but only four scholars who listed themselves in official directories as psychologists instead of philosophers. By 1925 in Germany only 25 people called themselves psychologists, and only 14 of 23 universities maintained departments of psychology (Turner, 1982). At the same time, there were a great many more psychologists and psychology departments in the United States, as well as diverse applications of psychological knowledge and techniques to practical issues. But these developments, too, as we will see, owe their origins to Wundt's psychology.

Wundt's position, like that of any innovator, was subject to criticism of many points of his system and of his experimental technique of introspection. When introspection by different people gives different results, critics asked, how do we decide who is correct? Experiments using introspection do not always yield agreement because introspective observation is self-observation, a most private experience. As such, disagreements cannot be settled by repeating the observations. Wundt believed, however, that observers with greater training and experience could improve the method.

It was difficult to criticize Wundt's system during his lifetime, primarily because he published so much. By the time a critic had prepared an attack on a specific point, Wundt had changed his argument or was working on an entirely different topic. Opponents were easily outwritten, buried under volumes of detailed and complex research findings.

The Wundtian position is not an active subject in contemporary psychology and has not been for many years. As one historian noted, "the precipitous decline of Wundtian psychology between the World Wars [1918–1939] was breathtaking. The massive body of Wundtian research and writings all but disappeared in the English-speaking world" (Blumenthal, 1985, p. 44). One explanation for this decline may have to do with Wundt's outspoken remarks about World War I. He blamed England for starting the war and defended Germany's invasion of Belgium as an act of self-defense. Both statements were self-serving and incorrect, but they served to turn many American psychologists against Wundt and his psychology (Benjamin, Durkin, Link, Vestal, & Acord, 1992; Sanua, 1993).

Wundt's system also did not fare well in the German-speaking world following World War I. In Wundt's lifetime, two other schools of thought arose in Europe to overshadow his views: Gestalt psychology in Germany and psychoanalysis in Austria. In the United States, two additional viewpoints, functionalism and behaviorism, eclipsed the Wundtian approach.

Economic and political factors—contextual forces again—contributed to the disappearance of the Wundtian system in Germany. The collapse of the economy following Germany's defeat in World War I left its universities in financial ruin. The University of Leipzig could not even afford to purchase copies of Wundt's last books for its library. Wundt's laboratory, at which he trained the first generation of psychologists, was destroyed during World War II in a British and American bombing raid on December 4, 1943. Thus, the nature, content, form, and even the home of Wundtian psychology are lost forever.

Wundt's monumental achievements are not diminished by that loss or by the fact that much of the history of psychology after Wundt consists of rebellion against some of the limitations he placed on the field. Indeed, that rebellion may enhance his greatness. Revolutions must have some target, something to push against, and as such, Wundt provided a compelling and magnificent beginning to modern experimental psychology.

A survey of 49 American historians of psychology conducted 70 years after Wundt's death revealed that he was still considered to be the most important psychologist of all time, quite an honor for a scholar whose system long ago faded from view (Korn, Davis, & Davis, 1991).

OTHER DEVELOPMENTS IN GERMAN PSYCHOLOGY

Wundt had a monopoly on the new psychology for only a short time; the science was also beginning to flourish at other laboratories in Germany. Although Wundt was obviously the most important organizer and systematizer in the early days of psychology, others were also influential in the development of this new field. These early non-Wundtian psychologists proposed different points of view, but all were engaged in the common enterprise of expanding psychology as a science. Their work, along with Wundt's, made Germany the undisputed center of the movement.

There were developments in England, however, that were to give psychology a different theme and direction. Charles Darwin proposed his theory of evolution and Francis Galton began work on the psychology of individual differences. These ideas would influence the development of psychology in the United States, even more than the work of Wundt. In addition, early American psychologists, most of whom had studied under Wundt at Leipzig, returned home and made of Wundtian psychology something uniquely American. We discuss these developments later; the important point now is that shortly after Wundt began the field of psychology, it became divided into factions. Although Wundt had founded psychology, his approach was soon only one of several. Let us consider some of Wundt's contemporaries in Germany.

HERMANN EBBINGHAUS (1850–1909)

Only a few years after Wundt claimed that it was impossible to conduct experiments on the higher mental processes, a German psychologist working alone, isolated from any academic center of psychology, began to experiment successfully on those processes. Hermann Ebbinghaus became the first psychologist to investigate learning and memory experimentally. In doing so, he not only showed that Wundt was wrong on that point, but also changed the way in which association or learning could be studied.

Before Ebbinghaus, most notably in the work of the British empiricists and associationists, the customary way to study association was to examine associations that were already formed. The investigator would, in a sense, work backward, attempting to determine how the connections had been established.

HERMANN EBBINGHAUS

Ebbinghaus began at a different point: the formation of the associations. In this way it was possible for him to control the conditions under which the associations were formed and thus to make the study of learning more objective.

Accepted as one of the great instances of original genius in experimental psychology, Ebbinghaus's work on learning and forgetting was the first venture into a truly psychological problem area, one that was not a part of physiology (as was true with so much of Wundt's research). As a result, Ebbinghaus's research considerably broadened the scope of experimental psychology.

Born near Bonn, Germany, in 1850, Ebbinghaus undertook his college studies first at the University of Bonn and then at universities in Halle and Berlin. During his academic training, his interests shifted from history and literature to philosophy, in which he received his degree in 1873, following military service in the Franco–Prussian War. He devoted 7 years to independent study in England and France, where his interests changed again, leading him this time toward science. Some 3 years before Wundt established his laboratory, Ebbinghaus bought a secondhand copy of Fechner's book, *Elements of Psychophysics,* at a London bookstore. This chance encounter was to profoundly affect his thinking, and the direction of the new psychology.

Fechner's mathematical approach to psychological phenomena was an exciting revelation to the young Ebbinghaus, and he resolved to do for psychology what Fechner had done for psychophysics, by using rigid and systematic measurement. He decided to apply the experimental method to the higher mental processes. Most likely because of the popularity of the ideas of the British associationists, Ebbinghaus chose to make his breakthrough in the area of memory.

Consider Ebbinghaus's daring course of action in light of the problem he chose and his own situation. Learning and memory had never been studied experimentally. The eminent psychologist Wilhelm Wundt had stated that they could not be. Further, Ebbinghaus had no academic appointment, no university setting in which to conduct his work, no teacher, and no laboratory. Nevertheless, he carried out alone, over a period of 5 years, a series of carefully controlled and comprehensive studies using himself as the only subject.

For the basic measure of learning Ebbinghaus adapted a technique from the associationists, who proposed the law of frequency of associations as a condition of recall. Ebbinghaus reasoned that the difficulty of learning material could be measured by counting the number of repetitions needed for one perfect reproduction of the material. This is another example of the influence of Fechner; recall that Fechner measured sensations indirectly by measuring the stimulus intensity necessary to produce a just noticeable difference in sensation. Ebbinghaus approached the problem of measuring memory similarly, by counting the number of trials or repetitions required to learn the material.

Ebbinghaus used similar, but not identical, lists of syllables as the material to be learned, and he repeated the task frequently enough to be confident of the accuracy of his results. In this way he could cancel out variable errors from trial to trial and obtain an average measure. So systematic was Ebbinghaus in his experimentation that he regulated his personal habits, keeping them as constant as possible and following a rigid routine, always learning the material at the same time each day.

Research With Nonsense Syllables

For the subject matter of his research—the material to be learned— Ebbinghaus invented what are known today as **nonsense syllables,** which revolutionized the study of learning. Titchener later commented that the use of nonsense syllables marked the first significant advance in the area since the time of Aristotle.

NONSENSE SYLLABLES: Syllables presented in a meaningless series to study memory processes

Ebbinghaus recognized an inherent difficulty in using stories or poetry as stimulus materials. Meanings or associations have already been attached to words by people familiar with the language. These existing associations can facilitate the learning of material and, because these connections are already present at the time of the experiment, they cannot be controlled by the experimenter. Ebbinghaus wanted to use material that would be uniformly unassociated, completely homogeneous, and equally unfamiliar—material with which there could be few past associations. His nonsense syllables, typically formed of two consonants with a vowel in between (as in *lef, bok,* or *yat*), satisfied these criteria. He wrote all possible combinations of consonants and vowels on cards, yielding a supply of 2,300 syllables from which to draw at random those to be learned.

New data of history—supplied by a German psychologist who read all the footnotes in Ebbinghaus's publications and the workbook for a set of his experiments, and who compared the English translations with Ebbinghaus's work in German—give a new interpretation to our understanding of nonsense syllables (Gundlach, 1986). They were not necessarily nonsense at all, nor were they limited to three letters.

This meticulous investigation of the data of history—in this case, Ebbinghaus's own writings—revealed that some of the syllables he constructed were four, five, or six letters long. More important, what Ebbinghaus called a "meaningless series of syllables" as the subject matter of his research was incorrectly translated into the English language as a "series of nonsense syllables." To Ebbinghaus, it was not the individual syllables that were designed to be meaningless (although many of them were), but rather that the entire list of "words" would be meaningless; that is, constructed to be free of connections or associations.

This new look at Ebbinghaus's writings also revealed that he was fluent in English and French as well as German, and had studied Latin and Greek. "He would have had a very hard time, indeed, to construct any syllable at all that would be nonsense to him. The vain struggle for the definitively nonsensical, association-free syllable is the endeavor of some of his followers" (Gundlach, 1986, pp. 469–470).

Ebbinghaus designed a number of experiments using his meaningless series of syllables to determine the influence of various conditions on human learning and retention. One of these studies investigated the difference between his speed in memorizing lists of syllables versus his speed in memorizing more meaningful material. To determine the difference, he memorized stanzas of Byron's poem "Don Juan." Each stanza has 80 syllables, and Ebbinghaus found that it required about nine readings to memorize one stanza. He then memorized a list of 80 nonsense syllables and discovered that the task required almost 80 repetitions. He concluded that meaningless or unassociated material is approximately nine times harder to learn than meaningful material.

He also studied the effect of the length of the material to be learned on the number of repetitions necessary for a perfect reproduction. He found that longer material requires more repetitions and, consequently, more time to learn. The average time to memorize one syllable increased when he increased the number of syllables to be learned. These results are predictable in a general way: The more we have to learn, the longer it will take us. The significance of Ebbinghaus's work, however, is in his careful control of the experimental conditions, his quantitative analysis of the data, and his conclusion that learning time per syllable and total learning time increase with longer lists of syllables.

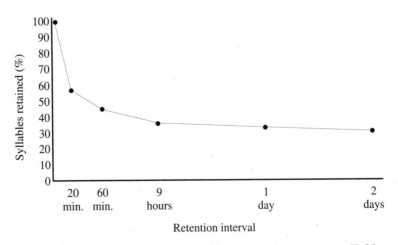

FIGURE 4.1 *Ebbinghaus's curve of forgetting for nonsense syllables*

Ebbinghaus studied other variables he thought would influence learning and memory, such as the effects of overlearning (repeating the lists more times than necessary for one perfect reproduction), of associations within lists, of reviewing the material, and of the time between learning and recall. His research on the effect of time yielded the famous Ebbinghaus forgetting curve, which demonstrates that material is forgotten rapidly in the first few hours after learning and more slowly thereafter (see Figure 4.1).

In 1880 Ebbinghaus received an academic appointment at the University of Berlin, where he continued his research, replicating and verifying his earlier studies. He published his research results in a book entitled *On Memory* in 1885, which is perhaps the most brilliant single investigation in the history of experimental psychology. In addition to beginning a new field of study, which is still important today, it provides an example of technical skill, perseverance, and ingenuity. We cannot find in the history of psychology any other investigator working alone who subjected himself to such a painstaking regimen of experimentation. The research was so exacting, thorough, and systematic that it continues to be cited in psychology textbooks, more than 100 years later.

Ebbinghaus's Other Contributions to Psychology

Ebbinghaus was content to let others develop the field of learning and memory, and to extend and refine the methodology. He published relatively little after 1885, and a year later he was promoted to assistant professor at Berlin. He established a laboratory, and in 1890 he founded a journal, with the physicist Arthur König, the *Journal of Psychology and Physiology of the Sense Organs*. A new journal was needed in Germany, because Wundt's journal, the primary organ of the Leipzig laboratory, could not publish all the psychological research being conducted at the time. The need for another journal, just nine years after Wundt had begun his, is significant testimony to the phenomenal growth of the new psychology, in both size and diversity.

In the first issue of their journal, Ebbinghaus and König made a bold claim for the two disciplines named in their title: psychology and physiology. These fields, they wrote, have "consequently grown together . . . to form one whole; they promote and presuppose one another, and so constitute two coequal members of one great double science" (Turner, 1982, p. 151). Such a declaration, only 11 years after Wundt opened his experimental laboratory, also shows how far Wundt's idea of psychology as a science had come.

Ebbinghaus was not promoted again at the University of Berlin, apparently because of his lack of publications, and in 1894 he accepted a position at the University of Breslau, where he remained until 1905. He developed a sentence-completion test, probably the first successful test of the higher mental processes; a modified form of that test is included today in tests of general intelligence or cognitive ability.

In 1902 Ebbinghaus published a highly successful general textbook, *The Principles of Psychology*, dedicated to Fechner's memory, and in 1908 a more popular text, *A Summary of Psychology*. Both books appeared in several editions and were revised by others after Ebbinghaus's death. Ebbinghaus accepted an appointment at the University of Halle in 1905 and died suddenly of pneumonia in 1909.

Ebbinghaus did not make any theoretical contributions to psychology; he created no formal system and had no disciples of importance to psychology. He did not found a school, nor did he seem to want to do so. Yet he is of great importance not only to the study of learning and memory, which he began, but also to experimental psychology as a whole.

One measure of the overall historical worth of a scientist is how well his or her position and conclusions stand the test of time. By that standard, it can be suggested that Ebbinghaus is more influential than Wundt. Ebbinghaus's research brought objectivity, quantification, and experimentation to the study of learning, a topic that is central to modern psychology. It is because of Ebbinghaus that work on the concept of association changed from speculation about its attributes to formal scientific investigation. Many of his conclusions about the nature of learning and memory remain valid, a century after he published them.

GEORG ELIAS MÜLLER (1850–1934)

GEORG ELIAS MÜLLER

Archives of the History of American Psychology/University of Akron

Georg Müller, who never went to bed before midnight, was born near Leipzig and developed an interest in philosophy from reading German translations of English poetry. He fought in the Franco–Prussian War and studied physiology at the University of Leipzig and the University of Göttingen, where he spent his 40-year academic career. From 1881 to 1921, his well-equipped laboratory rivaled Wundt's at Leipzig and attracted many students from Europe and the United States.

One of his American students, Eleanor Gamble, was a graduate of Wellesley College who later earned her PhD from E. B. Titchener at Cornell. She published a now-classic monograph on the method of reconstruction for measuring memory (Gamble, 1909).

Müller was one of the first to work in the area begun by Ebbinghaus, the experimental study of learning and memory, and his research verified and extended many of Ebbinghaus's findings. Ebbinghaus's approach had been strictly objective; he had not recorded introspections about his mental processes while engaged in his learning tasks.

Müller believed that Ebbinghaus's approach tended to make the learning process seem too mechanical and automatic. He believed that the mind was more actively involved in learning. He used Ebbinghaus's objective methods, but he added introspective report. His results confirmed that learning did not proceed mechanically. Subjects were actively involved in consciously grouping and organizing the material, and they even found meanings in the lists of nonsense syllables.

On the basis of his research, Müller concluded that association by contiguity alone cannot adequately account for learning, because the subjects seem to actively seek relationships among the stimuli to be learned. He suggested that a set of mental phenomena, such as readiness, hesitation, and doubt (the so-called conscious attitudes), actively influence learning. Similar findings followed, as we will see, from the work of Oswald Külpe at the University of Würzburg.

Müller was the first to propose and to demonstrate in the laboratory the **interference theory of forgetting.** In his view, forgetting was less a function of memory decay over time than of newly learned material interfering with the recall of material that had been learned earlier.

One final contribution to the study of learning deserves mention. Along with Friedrich Schumann, his laboratory assistant, Müller developed the memory drum, a revolving drum that makes possible the uniform presentation of material to be learned. This apparatus was significant because it increased the precision and objectivity of research on learning and memory problems.

INTERFERENCE THEORY OF FORGETTING: The idea that the act of forgetting results from the learning of new material, which interferes with the recall of previously learned material

FRANZ BRENTANO (1838–1917)

At about the age of 16, Franz Brentano began training for the priesthood, studying at universities in Berlin, Munich, and Tübingen in Germany, and receiving his degree in philosophy from Tübingen in 1864. He was ordained the same year, and 2 years later began teaching philosophy at the University of Würzburg and writing and lecturing on the writings of Aristotle. In 1870 the Vatican Council in Rome accepted the doctrine of papal infallibility, an idea Brentano disputed. He resigned his professorship, to which he had been appointed as a priest, and left the church.

Brentano's most famous book, *Psychology from an Empirical Standpoint*, was published in 1874, the year in which the second part of Wundt's *Principles of Physiological Psychology* appeared. Brentano's book stood in direct opposition to the Wundtian view, attesting to the dissent already apparent in the new psychology. Also in 1874, Brentano was appointed professor of philosophy at the University of Vienna, Austria. He remained there for 20 years, and during that time his influence grew considerably. He was a popular lecturer, and among his students were several who later achieved prominence in psychology: Carl Stumpf, Christian von Ehrenfels, and Sigmund Freud. In

FRANZ BRENTANO

National Library of Medicine

ACT PSYCHOLOGY: Brentano's system of psychology that focuses on mental activities such as seeing, rather than on mental contents, such as that which is seen

1894 Brentano retired and spent his remaining years in Italy and Switzerland engaged in study and writing.

Brentano was one of the more important early psychologists because of his diverse influences. We will see that he is an intellectual precursor of Gestalt psychology and humanistic psychology. He shared with Wundt the goal of making psychology a science. Whereas Wundt's psychology was experimental, however, Brentano's was empirical. The primary method of psychology for Brentano was observation, not experimentation, although he did not reject the experimental method. An empirical approach generally is broader in scope, in that it obtains data from observation and individual experience as well as from experimentation.

Brentano opposed Wundt's fundamental idea that psychology should study the content of conscious experience. He argued that the proper subject matter for psychology is mental activity—the mental act of seeing, for example, rather than the mental content of that which is seen. Thus, Brentano's **act psychology** countered the Wundtian view that mental processes involve contents or elements.

Brentano argued that a distinction should be drawn between experience as a structure and experience as an activity. In looking at a red flower, for example, the sensory content of redness is different from the act of sensing redness. Brentano said that the act of experiencing was the true subject matter of psychology. He stated that a color is not a mental quality but strictly a physical quality. The act of seeing the color, however, is a mental activity. Of course, an act always involves an object; some sensory content is always present because the act of seeing is meaningless unless there is something to be seen.

This new definition of psychology's subject matter meant that a different method of study was necessary, because acts, unlike sensory contents, are not accessible through the introspective method—the method Wundt and his students were using at the Leipzig laboratory. The study of mental acts required observation on a larger scale than that practiced by Wundt. Brentano's act psychology was more empirical than experimental in its methodology. It was not a return to speculative philosophy, however; although not experimental, Brentano did rely on systematic observation.

Specifically, Brentano argued that mental acts could be studied in two ways: through memory (recalling the mental processes involved in a particular mental state), and through imagination (imagining a mental state and observing the accompanying mental processes).

His position attracted followers, but Wundtian psychology maintained prominence in the new psychology. Because Wundt published more than Brentano, his position became the better known. Also, it was easier to study sensations or conscious contents with the methods of psychophysics than it was to study the more elusive acts.

CARL STUMPF (1848–1936)

Born into a medical family in Bavaria, Carl Stumpf came in contact with science at an early age but developed a greater interest in music. At the age of 7 he began studying the violin and eventually mastered five other instruments. By age 10 he was composing music. As a student at the University of Würzburg, he became interested in Brentano's work and turned his attention to philosophy and science. At Brentano's suggestion, Stumpf went to the University of Göttingen, where he received his doctoral degree in 1868. Stumpf held a number of academic appointments over the following years while he began his work in psychology.

In 1894 Stumpf was awarded an appointment at the University of Berlin, the most prized professorship in German psychology. His years at Berlin were extremely productive, and his original laboratory of three small rooms grew into a large and important institute. Although the research programs at Stumpf's laboratory never equaled Wundt's in scope, Stumpf may be considered Wundt's major rival. Stumpf trained two of the psychologists who later founded Gestalt psychology, a school of thought that opposed Wundt's views.

Stumpf's early writings in psychology were concerned with the perception of space, but his most influential work, in keeping with his lifelong interest in music, is *Psychology of Tone,* which appeared in two volumes in 1883 and 1890. This work, and his later studies of music, earned him a place second only to Helmholtz in the field of acoustics, and were considered a pioneering effort in the psychological study of music.

The influence of Brentano may explain why Stumpf accepted a less rigorous approach to psychology than what Wundt considered appropriate. Stumpf argued that the primary data of psychology are phenomena. **Phenomenology,** the kind of introspection Stumpf favored, refers to the examination of unbiased experience; that is, experience just as it occurs. He disagreed with Wundt about breaking experience down into elements. To analyze experience in this way, Stumpf believed, made the experience artificial and abstract, and thus it was no longer natural.[2]

In a series of publications, Stumpf and Wundt waged a bitter fight about the introspection of tones. Stumpf initiated the debate on a theoretical level, but Wundt made it personal. Essentially, the issue involved the question of whose introspectionists' reports were the more credible. When dealing with tones, should we accept the results of highly trained laboratory observers, as Wundt required, or of

Archives of the History of American Psychology/University of Akron

CARL STUMPF

PHENOMENOLOGY: Stumpf's method of introspection, which examines experience as it occurs and does not try to reduce it to elements

---

[2]A student of Stumpf's, Edmund Husserl, later proposed a philosophy of phenomenology; this movement is a precursor of Gestalt psychology (see chapter 12).

expert musicians, as Stumpf did? Stumpf refused to accept the results on this problem obtained at Wundt's Leipzig laboratory.

While continuing to write about music and acoustics, Stumpf established a center for the collection of recordings of primitive music from all over the world. He also founded the Berlin Association for Child Psychology. He published a theory of emotion in which he attempted to reduce feelings to sensations; this idea is considered relevant to cognitive theories of emotion in contemporary psychology (Reizenzein & Schönpflug, 1992). Stumpf was one of a number of German psychologists who worked independently of Wundt to expand the boundaries of psychology.

OSWALD KÜLPE (1862–1915) AND THE WÜRZBURG SCHOOL

Archives of the History of American Psychology/University of Akron

OSWALD KÜLPE

Initially a follower of Wundt, Oswald Külpe led a group of students in a protest movement against the limitations of Wundt's ideas. Although Külpe's movement was not a revolution, it was a declaration of freedom. Throughout his career in psychology, Külpe worked on problems that Wundt's psychology had ignored.

At the age of 19 Külpe began his studies at the University of Leipzig. He planned to study history, but under the influence of Wundt he switched to philosophy and experimental psychology, which, in 1881, was still in its infancy. Külpe remained interested in the field of history, however, and after a year with Wundt he resumed its study at Berlin. Two more academic forays alternating between psychology and history followed before he returned to Wundt in 1886, and Külpe remained at Leipzig for 8 years.

After receiving his degree at Leipzig, Külpe stayed on as assistant professor and assistant to Wundt, carrying on research in the laboratory. He wrote a textbook, *Outline of Psychology*, which was published in 1893 and dedicated to Wundt. In it Külpe defined psychology as the science of the facts of experience as dependent on the experiencing individual.

In 1894 Külpe became a professor at the University of Würzburg, and 2 years later he established a laboratory that soon threatened to rival Wundt's in importance. Among the students attracted to Würzburg were several Americans; one, James Rowland Angell, became a pivotal figure in the development of the school of thought called functionalism.

Külpe's Differences With Wundt

In the *Outline of Psychology*, Külpe did not discuss the higher mental process of thought; at that time, his position was still compatible with Wundt's. Only a few years later, however, Külpe became convinced that the thought processes could be studied experimentally. Memory, another of the higher mental processes, had been studied experimentally by Ebbinghaus. If memory could be studied in the laboratory, why not thought? Asking this question put Külpe in direct opposition to his former teacher, because Wundt claimed that the higher mental processes could not be studied experimentally.

Another difference between psychology at Würzburg and at Wundt's Leipzig laboratory relates to introspection. Külpe developed a method he called **systematic experimental introspection.** This method involved the performance of a complex task (such as establishing logical connections between concepts), after which the subjects were required to make a retrospective report about their cognitive processes during the experimental task. In other words, subjects performed some mental process, such as thinking or judging, and then examined how they had thought or judged. Wundt prohibited the use of such retrospective, or after-the-fact, reporting in his laboratory. He believed in studying conscious experience as it occurred, not the memory of it after it had occurred. Wundt referred to Külpe's form of introspection as "mock" introspection.

Külpe's introspective method was systematic, in that the whole experience was described precisely by dividing it into time periods. Similar tasks were repeated many times so that the reports could be corrected, corroborated, and amplified. These reports were often supplemented by additional questions, directing the subjects' attention to particular points.

There were several other differences between the introspective approaches of Külpe and Wundt. Wundt was not in favor of having his subjects describe their conscious experiences in detail. Most of his research focused on objective, quantitative measurements, such as reaction times or the judgments of weights in psychophysical research.

In contrast, Külpe's systematic experimental introspection emphasized subjective, qualitative, and detailed reports from subjects about the nature of their thought processes. In Külpe's laboratory, subjects were expected to do more than make simple judgments about the intensity of a stimulus. They were supposed to describe the complex mental processes they performed during their exposure to some experimental task. Külpe's approach was aimed directly at investigating what was going on in a subject's mind during a conscious experience. Külpe's stated goal was to expand Wundt's conception of psychology's subject matter to include the higher mental processes, and to refine the method of introspection.

What were the results of Külpe's attempt to expand and refine psychology's subject matter and method? Wundt's system emphasized that conscious experience could be reduced to its component parts, its sensations or images. All experience, Wundt said, is composed of sensations or images. The results of Külpe's direct introspection of the thought processes supported the opposite viewpoint, that

SYSTEMATIC EXPERIMENTAL INTROSPECTION: Külpe's method of introspection, which uses retrospective reports of subjects' cognitive processes after the completion of an experimental task

IMAGELESS THOUGHT: Külpe's
idea that meanings in thought
can occur without having any
sensory or imaginal components

thought can occur *without* any sensory or imaginal content. This finding came to be identified as **imageless thought,** to represent the idea of meanings in thought that do not seem to involve any specific images. Thus, Külpe's research identified a nonsensory form or aspect of consciousness.

Research Topics of the Würzburg Laboratory

The research topics of the Würzburg school were varied. An important contribution was a study by Karl Marbe on the comparative judgment of weights. Marbe found that, although sensations and images were present during the task, they seemed to play no part in the process of judgment. Subjects could not report on how the judgments of lighter or heavier weights came into their minds. This contradicted the current notion that in making such judgments, subjects retained a mental image of the first weight and compared it with a sensory impression of the second.

A study by Henry Watt demonstrated that in a word-association task (asking subjects to respond to a stimulus word), subjects had little relevant information to report about their conscious process of judgment. This finding reinforced Külpe's contention that conscious experience could not be reduced solely to sensations and images. Watt's subjects were able to respond correctly without being consciously aware of any intention to do so at the time they made their response. Watt concluded that the conscious work was done before the task was performed, at the time when the instructions were given and understood.

The subjects apparently established an unconscious set or determining tendency to respond in the desired way. Once the rules for the task had been understood and the determining tendency adopted, the actual task was performed with little, if any, conscious effort. This research suggested that predispositions outside of consciousness were somehow able to control conscious activities. This demonstration that experience depends not only on conscious elements but also on unconscious determining tendencies suggests that the unconscious plays a role in behavior, an idea adopted by Sigmund Freud for his psychoanalytic school of thought.

COMMENT

We can see that divisions and controversies enveloped psychology almost as soon as it was founded. For all their differences, however, the early psychologists were united in their goal: to develop an independent science of psychology.

Wundt, Ebbinghaus, Brentano, Stumpf, and others irrevocably changed the study of human nature. Because of their efforts, psychology was no longer "a study of the soul [but] a study, by observation and experiment, of certain reactions of the human organism not included in the subject matter of any other science. The German psychologists, in spite of their many differences, were to this extent engaged in a common enterprise; and their ability, their industry, and the common direction of their labors all made the developments in the German universities the center of the new movement in psychology" (Heidbreder, 1933, p. 105).

Germany did not remain the center of the new movement for long, however. A version of Wundt's psychology was soon brought to the United States by his student E. B. Titchener.

DISCUSSION QUESTIONS

1. Describe how Wundt's system, as translated by Titchener, is an example of distorted data of history. What was Wundt's cultural psychology? How did it lead to a division within the new psychology?
2. How was Wundt's psychology influenced by the work of the German physiologists and the British empiricists? Describe Wundt's concept of voluntarism. What is the role of the elements of consciousness?
3. Distinguish between mediate and immediate experience. Describe Wundt's use of introspection. What is the purpose of apperception in Wundt's system?
4. What topics did Wundt and his students investigate in the Leipzig laboratory? Trace the growth of Wundtian psychology in Germany. On what grounds was Wundt's system criticized?
5. Describe Ebbinghaus's research on learning and memory. How did Fechner's work influence Ebbinghaus? How did G. E. Müller expand on Ebbinghaus's work?
6. How does Brentano's act psychology differ from Wundtian psychology? How did Stumpf differ with Wundt on the reduction of experience to elements and on the use of introspection?
7. What did Külpe mean by systematic experimental introspection? How did Külpe's approach differ from Wundt's? How did the idea of imageless thought challenge Wundt's conception of conscious experience?

SUGGESTED READINGS

Baldwin, B. T. (1921). In memory of Wilhelm Wundt by his American students. *Psychological Review, 28,* 153–158. Reminiscences of Wundt's American students.

Langfeld, H. S. (1937). Stumpf's "Introduction to Psychology." *American Journal of Psychology, 50,* 33–56. Describes the beginning psychology course taught by Stumpf at the University of Berlin in 1906–1907.

Lindenfeld, D. (1978). Oswald Külpe and the Würzburg School. *Journal of the History of the Behavioral Sciences, 14,* 132–141. Assesses Külpe's importance and relates his conception of psychology to his philosophical views.

Postman, L. (1968). Hermann Ebbinghaus. *American Psychologist, 23,* 149–157. Describes Ebbinghaus's contributions to the experimental study of memory.

CHAPTER 5

STRUCTURALISM

INTRODUCTION

E. B. TITCHENER dramatically altered Wundt's system of psychology when he brought it from Germany to the United States, while professing to be a loyal follower. He offered his own approach, which he called **structuralism,** and claimed that it represented the form of psychology set forth by Wundt. Yet the two systems were radically different, and the label, structuralism, can properly be applied only to Titchener's psychology. Structuralism attained a prominence in the United States that lasted for some 2 decades around the turn of the century, until it was challenged and overthrown by newer movements. Although Titchener was undoubtedly an influential figure in the history of American psychology, his contemporaries were already developing different definitions of psychology.

Wundt recognized elements or contents of consciousness, but his overriding concern was their organization or synthesis into higher-level cognitive processes through apperception. In Wundt's view, the mind had the power to organize mental elements voluntarily, a position that contrasted with the passive, mechanistic notion of association favored by most of the British empiricists and associationists.

Titchener accepted the focus on mental elements or contents and their mechanical linking through the process of association. He discarded Wundt's doctrine of apperception, however, and concentrated on the elements themselves. In Titchener's view, the fundamental task of psychology was to discover the nature of these elementary conscious experiences—that is, to analyze consciousness into its component parts and thus determine its structure.

EDWARD BRADFORD TITCHENER (1867–1927)

Titchener spent his most productive years at Cornell University in New York. For Titchener, who invariably wore his academic gown to class, every lecture was a dramatic production. The stage was carefully prepared by assistants under his watchful eye. The junior faculty, who attended all his lectures, entered through one door to take front-row seats. Professor Titchener came through another door that led directly to the lecture platform. Titchener assumed that his Oxford University cap and gown gave him the right to be dogmatic. Although he studied with Wundt for only 2 years, he resembled his mentor in many ways, copying his autocratic style, his formal lecture manners, and his beard.

Titchener's Life

Born in Chichester, England, into an old family that had little money, Titchener relied on his considerable intellectual abilities to win scholarships to advance his education. He attended Malvern College and then Oxford University, where he studied philosophy and the classics and became a research assistant in physiology.

While at Oxford, Titchener became interested in Wundt's new psychology, an interest that was not shared or encouraged by anyone at the university. It was natural, then, that he should journey to Leipzig, the mecca for scientific pilgrims, to study under Wundt, earning his doctoral degree in 1892.

Titchener planned to become the English pioneer of the new experimental psychology. When he returned to Oxford, however, Titchener found that his colleagues were skeptical of a scientific approach to one of their favorite philosophical subjects. Therefore, after only a few months at Oxford, Titchener left England for the United States to teach psychology and direct the laboratory at Cornell University. He was then 25 years old, and he remained at Cornell for the rest of his life.

Titchener spent the years from 1893 to 1900 establishing his laboratory, conducting research, and writing more than 60 articles. As his brand of psychology attracted more and more students to Cornell, he relinquished the task of participating personally in the research studies, leaving his students to conduct the experiments. Thus, it was through the direction of his students' research that Titchener's systematic position reached fruition. He supervised more than 50 doctoral candidates in psychology in 35 years, and most of their dissertations

Archives of the History of American Psychology/University of Akron

EDWARD BRADFORD TITCHENER

STRUCTURALISM: Titchener's system of psychology, which deals with conscious experience as it is dependent on experiencing persons

bear the imprint of his ideas. He exercised his authority in selecting their research problems, assigning topics that were related to issues about which he was curious. In this way he built his system of structuralism, what he called the "only scientific psychology worthy of the name" (Roback, 1952, p. 184).

Titchener translated Wundt's books from German into English. When he had completed work on Wundt's third edition of the *Principles of Physiological Psychology,* he found that Wundt had already finished the fourth edition. Titchener translated the fourth edition, only to learn that the tireless Wundt had published a fifth edition.

Titchener's own books include *An Outline of Psychology* (1896), *Primer of Psychology* (1898), and the four-volume *Experimental Psychology: A Manual of Laboratory Practice* (1901–1905), the last considered "among the most important books in the history of psychology" (Benjamin, 1988a, p. 210). These *Manuals,* as the individual volumes of that work came to be called, stimulated the growth of laboratory work in psychology in the United States and influenced a generation of experimental psychologists. All of Titchener's textbooks were popular and were translated into Russian, Italian, German, Spanish, and French.

Titchener had several hobbies that diverted time and energy from his work in psychology. He conducted a small musical ensemble at his home every Sunday evening and for many years was "professor in charge of music" at Cornell, before a music department was established. His interest in coin collecting led him, with typical thoroughness, to learn Chinese and Arabic so that he could read the characters on the coins. He corresponded with numerous colleagues; most of these letters were typewritten with additional notes written by hand.

As he grew older, Titchener withdrew from social and university life. He was considered a living legend at Cornell, although many faculty members had never met him or even seen him. He did a great deal of his work in his study at home and spent relatively little time at the university. After 1909, he lectured only on Monday evenings during the spring semester of each academic year. His wife screened all callers and protected him from intrusions; it was understood that no student would telephone him except in an emergency.

Although he was autocratic in the manner of the German professor, he was also kind and helpful to students and colleagues, as long as they accorded him the deference and respect he felt were his due. Stories are told of how junior faculty members and graduate students washed his car and helped install window screens at his house in the summer, not on command but out of respect and admiration.

One former student, Karl Dallenbach, quotes Titchener as saying that "a man could not hope to become a psychologist until after he had learned to smoke" (Dallenbach, 1967, p. 91). Accordingly, many of his students took to smoking cigars, at least in Titchener's presence. Another doctoral student, Cora Friedline, "was discussing her research in Titchener's office when his ever-present cigar caught his beard on fire. He was talking at the time and his imposing manner made her reluctant to interrupt. Finally she said, 'I beg your pardon, Dr. Titchener, but your whiskers are on fire.' By the time he extinguished the flames, the fire had burned through his shirt and his underwear."[1]

Titchener's concern for his students did not end when they left Cornell, nor did his impact on their lives. Dallenbach, on receiving his PhD, intended to go to medical school, but Titchener obtained a teaching position for him at the University of Oregon. Dallenbach thought that Titchener would approve of medical school, but he was wrong. "I had to go to Oregon, as [Titchener] did not intend to have his training and work with me wasted" (Dallenbach, 1967, p. 91).

Titchener's relations with psychologists outside his own group were sometimes strained. Elected to the American Psychological Association by the charter members in 1892, he resigned shortly thereafter because the association declined to expel a member he had accused of plagiarism. The story is told that a friend paid Titchener's dues for years so that his name would be listed as a member.

In 1904, a group of psychologists, calling themselves the Titchener Experimentalists, began meeting regularly to compare research notes. Titchener selected the topics and the guests and generally dominated the meetings. One of his rules was that no women were allowed. His student E. G. Boring said that Titchener wanted "oral reports that could be interrupted, dissented from, and criticized in a smoke-filled room with no women present—for . . . women were considered too pure to smoke" (Boring, 1967, p. 315).

Titchener Experimentalists at a meeting in 1916; at least 5 members can be seen with cigars.

Archives of the History of American Psychology/University of Akron

[1]From L. T. Benjamin, Jr., based on material in the Cora Friedline papers, Archives of the History of American Psychology, University of Akron, Ohio.

Several women students from Bryn Mawr College in Pennsylvania tried to attend the meetings but were told to leave. Once they succeeded in hiding under a table throughout a session. Boring's fiancée and another woman waited in the next room "with the door ajar to hear what unexpurgated male psychology was like. They came through unscathed" (Boring, 1967, p. 322).

Although Titchener continued to exclude women from the Experimentalists' meetings, he was otherwise advanced in his thinking about women's rights. He accepted women in his graduate studies program at Cornell, at a time when Harvard and Columbia universities refused to admit them. More than one-third of the 56 doctorates he awarded were to women (Furumoto, 1988). More women "completed their PhD degrees with him than with any other male psychologist of his generation" (Evans, 1991, p. 90). He also favored hiring women as faculty members, an idea many of his colleagues considered radical. In one instance, he insisted on hiring a woman faculty member despite the objection of the dean.

The first woman graduate student to earn a doctoral degree in psychology was Margaret Floy Washburn; she was also Titchener's first doctoral student. "He did not quite know what to do with me," she recalled (Washburn, 1932, p. 340). Her first choice was Columbia University, but they would not admit women to graduate programs. Titchener accepted her, and after she received her degree at Cornell, Washburn began a highly successful career in psychology. She wrote an important book on comparative psychology (*The Animal Mind,* 1908) and was the first woman psychologist elected to the National Academy of Sciences. She served as president of the American Psychological Association and established at Vassar College "one of the most significant psychological centers in the country" (Scarborough, 1990, p. 344).

We mention Washburn's success briefly here to highlight Titchener's continuing support of women in psychology throughout his lifetime. He worked to open doors to women that were kept firmly closed by most other male psychologists of his day.

Around 1910 Titchener began writing what he envisioned as a complete exposition of his system. Unfortunately, he died of a brain tumor at the age of 60, before he could finish the work. A few chapters were published in a journal and reprinted in a book after his death. It is said that somewhere on the Cornell campus, Titchener's pickled brain is on display.

Archives of the History of American Psychology/University of Akron

MARGARET FLOY WASHBURN

Titchener's System: The Content of Conscious Experience

According to Titchener, the subject matter of psychology is conscious experience as that experience is dependent on experiencing persons. This kind of experience is different from that studied by scientists in other disciplines. For example, light and sound are studied by both physicists and psychologists. Physicists examine the phenomena from the standpoint of the physical processes involved; psychologists consider them in terms of how they are observed and experienced by humans.

Other sciences, Titchener said, are independent of experiencing persons, and he offered, from physics, the example of temperature. The temperature in a room may be, say, 85°Fahrenheit whether or not anyone experiences it. When observers are present in that room and report that they feel uncomfortably warm, that feeling is thus experienced by and dependent on those experiencing individuals—those people in the room. To Titchener, this type of experience was the only proper subject matter for psychology.

Titchener warned that in studying conscious experience, we must not commit what he called the **stimulus error;** that is, confusing the mental process with the object we are observing. For example, observers who see an apple and describe it as an apple, instead of reporting the color, brightness, and shape they are experiencing, are committing the stimulus error. The object of observation is not to be described in everyday language but rather in terms of the conscious content of the experience.

When observers focus on the stimulus object instead of on the conscious process, they fail to distinguish what they have learned in the past about the object (that it is called an apple, in our example) from their own immediate experience. All observers *really* know about the apple are that it is red, shiny, and round. When they describe anything other than these color, brightness, and spatial characteristics, they are interpreting the object, not observing it, and thus they are dealing with mediate—not immediate—experience.

Titchener defined *consciousness* as the sum of our experiences as they exist at a given time, and *mind* as the sum of our experiences accumulated over a lifetime. Consciousness and mind are similar, except that consciousness involves mental processes occurring at the moment whereas mind involves the sum total of these processes.

The structural psychology Titchener proposed was a pure science; he had no applied or utilitarian concerns. Psychology was not in the business of curing "sick minds," he said, or of reforming individuals or society. Its only legitimate purpose was to discover the facts, or structure, of the mind. He believed that scientists had to remain free of concerns about the practical worth of their work. For this reason he opposed the development of child psychology, animal psychology, and other areas that did not fit with his introspective experimental psychology of the content of consciousness.

STIMULUS ERROR: Confusing the mental process under study with the stimulus or object being observed

Introspection

Titchener's form of introspection, or self-observation, relied on observers who were trained to describe their conscious state and not the observed or experienced stimulus. Titchener realized that everyone learns to describe experience in terms of the stimulus—such as calling a red shiny round object an apple—and that in everyday life this is beneficial and necessary. In the laboratory, however, this practice had to be unlearned.

Titchener adopted Külpe's label, systematic experimental introspection, to describe his method. Like Külpe, he used detailed, qualitative, subjective reports of his subjects' mental activities during the act of introspecting. He opposed Wundt's approach, with its focus on objective, quantitative measurements, because he believed it was incapable of uncovering the elementary sensations and images of consciousness. These were the core of his psychology—not the synthesis of the elements through apperception but the analysis of complex conscious experience into its component parts. Titchener emphasized the parts, whereas Wundt emphasized the whole. In line with most of the British empiricists and associationists, Titchener's goal was to discover the atoms of the mind.

Titchener was also influenced by philosophy's mechanistic spirit, as is evident in the structuralist image of the observers who supplied his data. In his published research reports, subjects were sometimes called *reagents,* a term used by scientists, especially chemists, to denote substances that, because of their capacity for certain reactions, are used to detect, examine, or measure other substances. A reagent is generally a passive agent, one that is applied to something to elicit certain responses (Schultz, 1969).

Applying this concept to the human observers in Titchener's laboratory, we see that he considered his subjects to be like mechanical recording instruments, objectively noting the characteristics of the stimulus they were observing. Thus, the subjects were nothing more than impartial and detached machines. Titchener wrote that trained observation should become so mechanized and habitual that it would no longer be a conscious process.

If human observers in the laboratory can be considered to be machines, then it is easy to think that all human beings are machines. This viewpoint shows the continuing impact of the Galilean-Newtonian mechanical view of the universe, an idea that did not disappear with the eventual death of structuralism. As the history of psychology unfolds, we will see that this image of human-as-machine characterized experimental psychology through the first half of the 20th century.

Titchener believed that introspective observation in psychology should also be experimental. He diligently followed the rules of scientific experimentation, noting that

an experiment is an observation that can be repeated, isolated, and varied. The more frequently you can repeat an observation, the more likely are you to see clearly what is there and to describe accurately what you have seen. The more strictly you can isolate an observation, the easier does your task of observation become, and the less danger is there of your being led astray by irrelevant circumstances, or of placing emphasis on the wrong point. The more widely you can vary an observation, the more clearly will the uniformity of experience stand out, and the better is your chance of discovering laws. All experimental appliances, all laboratories and instruments, are provided and devised with this one end in view: that the student shall be able to repeat, isolate and vary his observations. (TITCHENER, 1909, P. 20)

The reagents or subjects in Titchener's laboratory introspected on a variety of stimuli and provided lengthy, detailed observations of the elements of their experiences. Introspection was a serious endeavor, and the graduate student subjects were highly dedicated to the work.

Titchener's student Cora Friedline recalled the time when the Cornell laboratory was studying organic sensitivity. The observers were asked to swallow a stomach tube in the morning and to keep it in place until evening, while going about their normal routines. Many of them vomited at first, but they gradually got used to it. Throughout the day they reported to the laboratory. There hot water was poured down the tube, and the students introspected on the sensations they were experiencing. The process was later repeated with iced water.

Introspection sometimes carried over into the graduate students' private lives. For a time, the students were required to carry notebooks when they used the toilet and to record their sensations and feelings during urination and defecation.

Another bit of introspective research provides an example of data lost to history. Married students were asked to make notes of their elementary sensations and feelings during sexual intercourse and to attach measuring devices to their bodies to record physiological responses.

This research went generally unpublicized at the time and was revealed by Cora Friedline in 1960. It did become known around the Cornell University campus, however, giving the psychology laboratory a reputation as an immoral place. The housemother in the women's dormitory would not allow her students to visit the laboratory after dark. When word spread that condoms had been attached to the stomach tubes the graduate students were swallowing, the talk in the dormitory was that the lab "wasn't a safe place for anyone to go."[2]

The more routine research conducted in Titchener's laboratory is described in the original source material reprinted from his textbook (see pages 109–116).

Elements of Consciousness

To Titchener, the three essential problems for psychology were: (1) to reduce conscious processes to their simplest components, (2) to de-

---

[2]Friedline spoke about these experiences at Randolph-Macon College in Lynchburg, Virginia, in April 1960. We are grateful to F. B. Rowe for providing a copy of her remarks.

Titchener's study at home, where he typically met with students.

Archives of the History of American Psychology/University of Akron

termine the laws by which these elements of consciousness were associated, and (3) to connect the elements with their physiological conditions. Thus, the aims of Titchener's structural psychology coincide with those of the natural sciences. After scientists decide which part of the natural world they wish to study, they proceed to discover its elements, to demonstrate how those elements are compounded into complex phenomena, and to formulate laws governing those phenomena. The bulk of Titchener's research efforts were devoted to the first problem—discovering the elements of consciousness.

Titchener proposed three elementary states of consciousness: sensations, images, and affective states. Sensations are the basic elements of perception and occur in the sounds, sights, smells, and other experiences evoked by physical objects in our environment. Images are the elements of ideas, and they are found in the process that reflects experiences not actually present at the moment, such as a memory of a past experience. Affective states, or affections, are the elements of emotion and are found in experiences such as love, hate, and sadness.

In *An Outline of Psychology* (1896), Titchener presented a list of the elements of sensation he discovered through his research. The list includes more than 44,000 sensation qualities; of these, 32,820 were identified as visual sensations, and 11,600 as auditory. Each element was believed to be conscious and distinct from all others, and each could be combined with others to form perceptions and ideas.

Although basic and irreducible, these elements could be categorized, just as chemical elements are grouped into classes. Despite their simplicity, mental elements have characteristics that allow us to distinguish among them. To the Wundtian attributes of quality and intensity, Titchener added duration and clearness. He considered these four attributes to be basic characteristics of all sensations; they are present, to some degree, in all experience.

Quality is the characteristic—such as "cold" or "red"—that clearly distinguishes each element from every other. *Intensity* refers to the strength, weakness, loudness, or brightness of a sensation. *Duration* is the course of a sensation over time. *Clearness* refers to the role of attention in conscious experience; that which is the focus of our attention is clearer than that toward which our attention is not directed.

Sensations and images possess all four of these attributes, but affective states have only quality, intensity, and duration. They lack clearness; Titchener believed it was impossible to focus attention directly on an element of feeling or emotion. When we try to do so, the affective quality—the sadness or the pleasantness, for example—disappears. Some sensory processes, particularly those involving vision and touch, also possess the attribute of *extensity*, in that they take up space.

All conscious processes can be reduced to one of these attributes. The findings from Külpe's laboratory at Würzburg did not cause Titchener to modify his position. He recognized that some poorly defined qualities may occur during thought, but he suggested that these were still sensations or images. Külpe's subjects had succumbed, Titchener said, to the stimulus error because they paid more attention to the stimulus object than to their conscious processes.

Titchener's graduate students at Cornell carried out a great deal of research on affective states, and their findings led him to reject Wundt's tridimensional theory of feelings. Titchener suggested that affections had only one dimension, that of pleasure/displeasure. He denied Wundt's other dimensions of tension/relaxation and excitement/depression.

Toward the end of his life, Titchener began to alter his system in fundamental ways. He dropped the concept of mental elements from his lectures as early as 1918, suggesting that psychology should study not basic elements but the larger dimensions or processes of mental life; these he listed as quality, intensity, duration, clearness, and extensity. Seven years later he wrote to a graduate student that "You must give up thinking in terms of sensations and affections. That was all right ten years ago; but now . . . it is wholly out of date. . . . You must learn to think in terms of dimensions rather than in terms of systematic constructs like sensation" (Evans, 1972, p. 174).

Titchener even questioned the term *structural psychology* by the early 1920s, and he took to calling his approach an existential psychology. He was also reconsidering his introspective method in favor of a phenomenological approach, examining experience just as it occurs, without trying to break it down into elements.

These are dramatic shifts in viewpoint, and had Titchener lived long enough to implement them, they would have radically altered the face (perhaps the fate) of structural psychology. They also suggest a flexibility and openness that scientists like to think they possess, but which not all demonstrate. The evidence for these changes was pieced together from meticulous examination of Titchener's letters and lectures (Evans, 1972; Henle, 1974). Although the ideas were not formally incorporated into Titchener's system, they indicate the direction toward which he was moving, but death prevented him from reaching his goal.

Original Source Material on Structuralism: From *A Textbook of Psychology* by E. B. Titchener

The following material, drawn from Titchener's popular A Textbook of Psychology *(1909),[3] describes the orthodox structuralist conception of the subject matter and methodology of the new science of psychology.*

You may be wondering why we are asking you to read something Titchener wrote nearly 90 years ago. After all, you have just read about Titchener's system, and your instructor has discussed it in class. This should have given you a broad overview of Titchener's approach to psychology. Please remember, however, that both textbook authors and teachers provide their own versions, visions, and perceptions of the material under study. They must reduce, abstract, and synthesize the original data to distill them to manageable proportions. In that process something of the unique form and style, if not content, of the original may be lost.

To understand a system of thought, one should, ideally, read the original data of history on which writers base their books and professors base their lectures. In practice, this is not possible in the space of a semester. That is why we are providing a sample of the original data, the theorists' own words, for each of the major schools of thought. These excerpts will show you how the theorists described their unique approaches to psychology and will acquaint you with the style of writing and explanation studied by previous generations of psychology students.

Before each of the five original articles included in this book, we outline the important points, to give you a framework for understanding what each theorist is saying.

In Titchener's description of his structural psychology, reprinted below, he discusses:

I.   *the difference between experience that is independent of the experiencing person and experience that is dependent on the experiencing person, with examples of each;*

[3]Reprinted with permission of Macmillan Publishing Co., Inc., from *A textbook of psychology* by E. B. Titchener (pp. 6–9, 15–25, 36–41). Copyright 1909 by Macmillan Publishing Co., Inc. Revised 1937 by Sophia K. Titchener.

2. *his form of observation or* introspection *and its relationship to the kind of* observation or inspection *used in other sciences;*

3. *the goal of structuralism and the similarity between psychology and the natural sciences in terms of attempting to answer the basic questions of "what," "how," and "why."*

All human knowledge is derived from human experience; there is no other source of knowledge. But human experience, as we have seen, may be considered from different points of view. Suppose that we take two points of view, as far as possible apart, and discover for ourselves what experience looks like in the two cases. First, we will regard experience as altogether independent of any particular person; we will assume that it goes on whether or not anyone is there to have it. Secondly, we will regard experience as altogether dependent upon the particular person; we will assume that it goes on only when someone is there to have it. We shall hardly find standpoints more diverse. What are the differences in experience, as viewed from them?

Take, to begin with, the three things that you first learn about in physics: space, time, and mass. Physical space, which is the space of geometry and astronomy and geology, is constant, always and everywhere the same. Its unit is the centimeter, and the centimeter has precisely the same value wherever and whenever it is applied. Physical time is similarly constant, and its constant unit is the second. Physical mass is constant; its unit, the gram, is always and everywhere the same. Here we have experience of space, time, and mass considered as independent of the person who experiences them.

Change, then, to the point of view which brings the experiencing person into account. The two vertical lines in [Figure 5.1] are physically equal; they measure alike in units of one centimeter. To you, who see them, they are not equal. The hour that you spend in the waiting room of a village station and the hour that you spend in watching an amusing play are physically equal; they measure alike in units of one second. To you, the one hour goes slowly, the other quickly; they are not equal. Take two circular cardboard boxes of different diameter (say, two centimeters and eight centimeters) and pour sand into them until they both weigh, say, fifty grams. The two masses are physically equal; placed on the pans of a balance [a scale], they will hold the beam level. To you, as you lift them in your two hands, or raise them in turn by the same hand, the box of smaller diameter is considerably the heavier. Here we have experience of space, time, and mass considered as dependent upon the experiencing person. It is the same experience that we were discussing just now. But our first point of view gives us facts and laws of physics; our second gives us facts and laws of psychology.

Now take three other topics that are discussed in the physical textbooks: heat, sound, and light. Heat proper, the physicists tell us, is the energy of molecular motion; that is to say, heat is a form of energy due to a move-

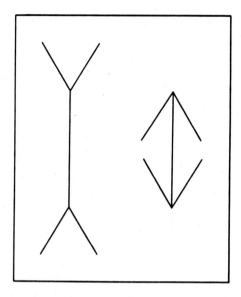

FIGURE 5.1

ment of the particles of a body among themselves. Radiant heat belongs, with light, to what is called radiant energy—energy that is propagated by wave movements of the luminiferous ether with which space is filled. Sound is a form of energy due to the vibratory movements of bodies, and is propagated by wave movements of some elastic medium, solid, liquid, or gaseous. In brief, heat is a dance of molecules; light is a wave motion of the ether; sound is a wave motion of the air.

The world of physics, in which these types of experience are considered as independent of the experiencing person, is neither warm nor cold, neither dark nor light, neither silent nor noisy. It is only when the experiences are considered as dependent upon some person that we have warmth and cold, blacks and whites and colors and grays, tones and hisses and thuds. And these things are the subject matter of psychology. . . .

The method of psychology   Scientific method may be summed up in the single word *observation;* the only way to work in science is to observe those phenomena which form the subject matter of science. And observation implies two things: attention to the phenomena, and record of the phenomena; that is, clear and vivid experience, and an account of the experience in words or formulas. . . .

The method of psychology then, is observation. To distinguish it from the observation of physical science, which is inspection, a looking-at, psychological observation has been termed introspection, a looking-within. But this difference of name must not blind us to the essential likeness of the methods. Let us take some typical instances.

We may begin with two very simple cases.

1. Suppose that you are shown two paper discs: the one of a uniform violet, the other composed half of red and half of blue. If this second disc is rapidly rotated, the red and blue will mix, as we say, and you will see a certain blue-red, that is, a kind of violet. Your problem is, so to adjust the proportions of red and blue in the second disc that the resulting violet exactly matches the violet of the first disc. You may repeat this set of observations as often as you like; you may isolate the observations by working in a room that is free from other, possibly disturbing colors; you may vary the observations by working to equality of the violets first from a two-color disc that is distinctly too blue, and secondly from a disc that is distinctly too red.

2. Suppose, again, that the chord c-e-g is struck, and that you are asked to say how many tones it contains. You may repeat this observation; you may isolate it, by working in a quiet room; you may vary it, by having the chord struck at different parts of the scale, in different octaves.

It is clear that, in these instances, there is practically no difference between introspection and inspection. You are using the same method that you would use for counting the swings of a pendulum, or taking readings from a galvanometer scale, in the physical laboratory. There is a difference in subject matter: the colors and the tones are dependent, not independent experiences; but the method is essentially the same.

Now let us take some cases in which the material of introspection is more complex.

1. Suppose that a word is called out to you, and that you are asked to observe the effect which this stimulus produces upon consciousness: how the word affects you, what ideas it calls up, and so forth. The observation may be repeated; it may be isolated—you may be seated in a dark and silent room, free from disturbances; and it may be varied—different words may be called out, the word may be flashed upon a screen instead of spoken, and so forth. Here, however, there seems to be a difference between introspection and inspection.

The observer who is watching the course of a chemical reaction, or the movements of some microscopical creature, can jot down from moment to moment the different phases of the observed phenomenon. But if you try to report the changes in consciousness, while these changes are in progress, you interfere with consciousness; your translation of the mental experience into words introduces new factors into that experience itself.

2. Suppose, again, that you are observing a feeling or an emotion: a feeling of disappointment or annoyance, an emotion of anger or chagrin. Experimental control is still possible; situations may be arranged, in the psychological laboratory, such that these feelings may be repeated, isolated, and varied. But your observation of them interferes, even more seriously than before, with the course of consciousness. Cool consideration of an emotion

is fatal to its very existence; your anger disappears, your disappointment evaporates, as you examine it.

To overcome this difficulty of the introspective method, students of psychology are usually recommended to delay their observation until the process to be described has run its course, and then to call it back and describe it from memory. Introspection thus becomes retrospection; introspective examination becomes *post mortem* examination. The rule is, no doubt, a good one for the beginner; and there are cases in which even the experienced psychologist will be wise to follow it. But it is by no means universal. For we must remember that the observations in question may be repeated. There is, then, no reason why the observer to whom the word is called out, or in whom the emotion is set up, should not report at once upon the first stage of his experience: upon the immediate effect of the word, upon the beginnings of the emotive process.

It is true that this report interrupts the observation. But, after the first stage has been accurately described, further observations may be taken, and the second, third, and following stages similarly described; so that presently a complete report upon the whole experience is obtained. There is, in theory, some danger that the stages become artificially separated; consciousness is a flow, a process, and if we divide it up we run the risk of missing certain intermediate links. In practice, however, this danger has proved to be very small; and we may always have recourse to retrospection, and compare our partial results with our memory of the unbroken experience.

Moreover, the practiced observer gets into an introspective habit, has the introspective attitude ingrained in his system; so that it is possible for him, not only to take mental notes while the observation is in progress, without interfering with consciousness, but even to jot down written notes, as the histologist does while his eye is still held to the ocular [eyepiece] of the microscope.

In principle, then, introspection is very like inspection. The objects of observation are different; they are objects of dependent, not of independent experience; they are likely to be transient, elusive, slippery. Sometimes they refuse to be observed while they are in passage; they must be preserved in memory, as a delicate tissue is preserved in hardening fluid, before they can be examined. And the standpoint of the observer is different; it is the standpoint of human life and of human interest, not of detachment and aloofness. But, in general, the method of psychology is much the same as the method of physics.

It must not be forgotten that, while the method of the physical and the psychological sciences is substantially the same, the subject matter of these sciences is as different as it can well be. Ultimately, as we have seen, the subject matter of all the sciences is the world of human experience; but we have also seen that the aspect of experience treated by physics is radically different from the aspect treated by psychology. The likeness of method may tempt us to slip from the one aspect to the other, as when a textbook of physics contains a chapter on vision and the sense of color, or a text-book of physiology contains paragraphs on delusions of judgment; but this confusion of subject matter must inevitably lead to confusion of thought. Since all the sciences are concerned with the one world of human experience, it is natural that scientific method, to whatever aspect of experience it is applied, should be in principle the same.

On the other hand, when we have decided to examine some particular aspect of experience, it is necessary that we hold fast to that aspect, and do not shift our point of view as the inquiry proceeds. Hence it is a great advantage that we have the two terms, introspection and inspection, to denote observation taken from the different standpoints of psychology and of physics. The use of the word *introspection* is a constant reminder that we are working in psychology, that we are observing the dependent aspect of the world of experience.

Observation, as we said above, implies two things: attention to the phenomena, and record of the phenomena. The attention must be held at the highest possible degree of concentration; the record must be photographically accurate. Observation is, therefore, both difficult and fatiguing; and introspection is, on the whole, more difficult and more fatiguing than inspection. To secure reliable results, we must be strictly impartial and unprejudiced, facing the facts as they come, ready to accept them as they are, not trying to fit them to any preconceived theory; and we must work only when our general disposition is favorable, when we are fresh and in good health, at ease in our surroundings, free from outside worry and anxiety.

If these rules are not followed, no amount of experimenting will help us. The observer in the psychological laboratory is placed under the best possible external conditions; the room in which he works is fitted up and arranged in such a way that the observation may be repeated, that the process to be observed may stand out clearly upon the background of consciousness, and that the factors in the process may be separately varied. But all this care is of no avail, unless the observer himself comes to the work in an even frame of mind, gives it his full attention, and is able adequately to translate his experience into words....

The problem of psychology   Science seeks always to answer three questions in regard to its subject matter, the questions of what, how, and why. What precisely, stripped of all complications and reduced to its lowest terms, is this subject matter? How, then, does it come to appear as it does; how are its elements combined and arranged? And, finally, why does it appear now in just this particular combination or arrangement? All three questions must be answered, if we are to have a science. . . .

To answer the question ''what'' is the task of analysis. Physical science, for example, tries by analysis to reduce the world of independent experience to its lowest terms, and so arrives at the various chemical elements. To answer the question ''how'' is the task of synthesis. Physical science traces the behavior of the elements in their various combinations, and presently succeeds in formulating the laws of nature. When these two questions have been answered, we have a description of physical phenomena.

But science inquires, further, why a given set of phenomena occurs in just this given way, and not otherwise; and it answers the question "why" by laying bare the cause of which the observed phenomena are the effect. There was dew on the ground last night because the surface of the earth was colder than the layer of air above it; dew forms on glass and not on metal because the radiating power of the one is great and of the other is small. When the cause of a physical phenomenon has thus been assigned, the phenomenon is said to be explained.

So far, now, as description is concerned, the problem of psychology closely resembles the problem of physics. The psychologist seeks, first of all, to analyze mental experience into its simplest components. He takes a particular consciousness and works over it again and again, phase by phase and process by process, until his analysis can go no further. He is left with certain mental processes which resist analysis, which are absolutely simple in nature, which cannot be reduced, even in part, to other processes. This work is continued, with other consciousnesses, until he is able to pronounce with some confidence upon the nature and number of the elementary mental processes.

Then he proceeds to the task of synthesis. He puts the elements together, under experimental conditions: first, perhaps, two elements of the same kind, then more of that kind, then elementary processes of diverse kinds; and he presently discerns that regularity and uniformity of occurrence which we have seen to be characteristic of all human experience. He thus learns to formulate the laws of connection of the elementary mental processes.[4] . . .

If, however, we attempted to work out a merely descriptive psychology, we should find that there was no hope in it of a true science of mind. A descriptive psychology would stand to scientific psychology very much as the old-fashioned natural histories stand to modern textbooks of biology, or as the view of the world which a boy gets from his cabinet of physics experiments stands to the trained physicist's view. It would tell us a good deal about mind; it would include a large body of observed facts, which we might classify and, in large measure, bring under general laws. But there would be no unity or coherence in it; it would lack that single guiding principle which biology has, for instance, in the law of evolution, or physics in the law of the conservation of energy. In order to make psychology scientific we must not only describe, we must also explain mind. We must answer the question "why."

---

[4]By using the phrase "connection of the elementary mental processes," Titchener reveals the influence of the empiricists and associationists and their mechanical view of association. In Wundt's view, the elements were synthesized or organized by the active power of the mind, not connected passively and mechanically.

But here is a difficulty. It is clear that we cannot regard one mental process as the cause of another mental process, if only for the reason that, with change of our surroundings, entirely new consciousnesses may be set up. When I visit Athens or Rome for the first time, I have experiences which are due, not to past consciousnesses, but to present stimuli.

Nor can we, on the other hand, regard nervous processes as the cause of mental processes. The principle of psychophysical parallelism lays it down that the two sets of events, processes in the nervous system and mental processes, run their course side by side, in exact correspondence but without interference: they are, in ultimate fact, two different aspects of the same experience. The one cannot be the cause of the other.

Nevertheless, it is by reference to the body, to the nervous system and the organs attached to it, that we explain mental phenomena. The nervous system does not cause, but it does explain mind. It explains mind as the map of a country explains the fragmentary glimpses of hills and rivers and towns that we catch on our journey through it. In a word, reference to the nervous system introduces into psychology just that unity and coherence which a strictly descriptive psychology cannot achieve. . . .

Physical science, then, explains by assigning a cause; mental science explains by reference to those nervous processes which correspond with the mental processes that are under observation. We may bring these two modes of explanation together, if we define explanation itself as the statement of the proximate circumstances or conditions under which the described phenomenon occurs. Dew is formed under the condition of a difference of temperature between the air and the ground; ideas are formed under the condition of certain processes in the nervous system. Fundamentally, the object and the manner of explanation, in the two cases, are one and the same.

In [conclusion], just as the method of psychology is, on all essential points, the method of the natural sciences, so is the problem of psychology essentially of the same sort as the problem of physics. The psychologist answers the question "what" by analyzing mental experience into its elements. He answers the question "how" by formulating the laws of connection of these elements. And he answers the question "why" by explaining mental processes in terms of their parallel processes in the nervous system.

His program need not be carried out in this order: he may get the hint of a law before his analysis is completed, and the discovery of a sense organ may suggest the occurrence of certain elementary processes before he has found these processes by introspection. The three questions are intimately related, and an answer to any one helps toward the answers to the other two. The measure of our progress in scientific psychology is our ability to return satisfactory answers to all three.

CRITICISMS OF STRUCTURALISM

People often gain prominence in history because they oppose an older view, but the situation was reversed with Titchener, who stood firm when everyone else opposed him. The intellectual climate of thought in American and European psychology was changing by the second decade of the 20th century, but the formal published statement of Titchener's system was not. As a result, many psychologists came to regard his structural psychology as a futile attempt to cling to antiquated principles and methods.

Titchener believed he was establishing the foundation for psychology, but his efforts proved to be only one phase in its history. The era of structuralism collapsed when he died. That it was sustained for so long is an effective tribute to his commanding personality.

Criticisms of Introspection

The most severe criticisms of structuralism have been directed at the method of introspection. These charges are much more relevant to introspection as practiced at Titchener's and Külpe's laboratories, which dealt with subjective reports of the elements of consciousness, than to Wundt's internal perception method, which dealt with more objective and quantitative responses to external stimuli.

Introspection, broadly defined, had been in use for a long time, and attacks on the method were not new. The German philosopher Immanuel Kant had written, a century before Titchener's work, that any attempt at introspection necessarily alters the conscious experience being studied, because it introduces an observing element into the content of the conscious experience.

The positivist philosopher Auguste Comte also attacked the introspective method, arguing that if the mind were capable of observing its own activities, it would have to divide itself into two parts—one doing the observing and the other being observed. This, Comte claimed, was impossible (Wilson, 1991). Several decades before Titchener proposed his structural psychology, Comte wrote: "The mind may observe all phenomena but its own. . . . The observing and observed organ are here the same, and its action cannot be pure and natural. In order to observe, your intellect must pause from activity; yet it is this very activity that you want to observe. If you cannot effect it, you cannot observe; if you do effect it, there is nothing to observe. The results of such method are in proportion to its absurdity" (Comte, 1830/1896, Vol. I, p. 9).

Additional criticism of introspection came in 1867 from the English physician Henry Maudsley, who wrote extensively about psychopathology:

> There is little agreement among introspectionists. Where agreement does occur, it can be attributed to the fact that introspectionists must be meticulously trained, and thereby have a bias built into their observations. . . . Due to the extent of the pathology of mind, self-report is hardly to be trusted. Introspective

knowledge cannot have the generality we expect of science. It must be restricted to the class of sophisticated, trained adult subjects. Much of behavior (habit and performance) occurs without conscious correlates. (QUOTED IN TURNER, 1967, P. 11)

There were, then, substantial doubts about introspection long before Titchener modified and refined the method to make it conform to the requirements of science. But as his approach to introspection became more precise, the attacks continued.

One point relates to the definition of introspection. Titchener apparently had difficulty defining the method precisely, and he attempted to do so by relating it to specific experimental conditions. "The course that an observer follows," Titchener wrote, "will vary in detail with the nature of the consciousness observed, with the purpose of the experiment, [and] with the instruction given by the experimenter. Introspection is thus a generic term, and covers an indefinitely large group of specific methodical procedures" (Titchener, 1912b, p. 485).

A second point of the attack on Titchener's methodology relates to the question of what, precisely, the structuralist introspectors were trained to do. Titchener's graduate student observers learning to introspect were instructed to ignore certain classes of words (so-called meaning words) that had become a fixed part of their vocabulary. The phrase, "I see a table," for example, has no scientific meaning to a structuralist; the word *table* is a meaning word, based on previously established and generally agreed-upon knowledge about the specific combination of sensations we have learned to identify and label as a table.

Thus, the observation, "I see a table," told the structural psychologist nothing about the observers' conscious experience. The structuralist was interested not in the collection of sensations summarized in a meaning word but in the specific elementary forms of the experience. Observers who said "table" were committing the stimulus error.

If these ordinary words were stricken from the vocabulary, how were observers to describe their experiences? An introspective language would have to be developed. Because Titchener (and Wundt, as well) emphasized that the external conditions of the experiment must be carefully controlled, so that the conscious experience could be precisely determined, two observers should have the identical experiences and their results should corroborate one another. And because of these highly similar experiences under controlled conditions, it was theoretically possible to develop a working vocabulary free of meaning words for the observers. After all, it is because of our shared experiences in everyday life that we are able to agree on common meanings for familiar words.

The idea of developing an introspective language was never realized. There was frequent disagreement among the observers, even under the most rigidly controlled experimental conditions. Introspectors at different laboratories reported different results. Even subjects at the same laboratory often failed to agree. Titchener nevertheless maintained that agreement would be reached eventually, and had there been sufficient agreement on introspective findings, the school of structuralism might have lasted longer than it did.

Critics also charged that introspection was really a form of *retro*spection, because some time elapsed between the experience and the reporting of it. Our rate of forgetting, Ebbinghaus demonstrated, is most rapid immediately after an experience, so it seemed likely that some of the experience was lost before introspection could be performed and reported on. The structuralists answered this charge, first, by specifying that observers work with the briefest time intervals, and, second, by proposing the existence of a primary mental image that was alleged to maintain the experience for the observers until it could be reported.

We noted that the act of examining an experience in an introspective manner may, in itself, change it. Consider the difficulty in introspecting the conscious state of anger. In the process of rationally paying attention to and trying to dissect the experience into its elementary components, the anger may subside or disappear. Titchener believed, however, that experienced and well-trained introspectors, with continued practice, performed their observational task automatically, without consciously altering the experience.

Other Criticisms of Titchener's System

The method of introspection was not the only target of criticism. The structuralist movement was accused of artificiality and sterility for its attempt to analyze conscious processes into elements. Critics charged that the whole of an experience cannot be recaptured by any later association of the elemental parts. Experience, they argued, does not come to us in individual sensations, images, or affective states but rather in unified wholes. Something of the conscious experience must inevitably be lost in any artificial effort to analyze it. We will see that the Gestalt school of psychology made effective use of this point in launching their revolt against structuralism.

The structuralist definition of psychology came under attack. By Titchener's later years, the scope of psychology was growing in several specialty areas that the structuralists chose to exclude, because these areas did not fit with their definition and method. For example, Titchener regarded animal psychology and child psychology as not psychology at all. His conception of the field was too limited to embrace all the new work being performed. Psychology was moving beyond Titchener, and moving very quickly.

CONTRIBUTIONS OF STRUCTURALISM

Despite these criticisms, there is no denying that Titchener and the structuralists made important contributions to psychology. Their subject matter—conscious experience—was clearly defined. Their research methods were in the best tradition of science, involving observation, experimentation, and measurement. Because consciousness was best perceived by the person having the conscious experience, the best method for that subject matter was self-observation.

Although the subject matter and aims of the structuralists are no longer vital, introspection—defined as the giving of a verbal report based on experience—is still used in many areas of psychology. Contemporary researchers in psychophysics ask subjects to report whether a second tone sounds louder or softer than the first. Self-reports are requested from people exposed to unusual experimental environments, such as conditions of weightlessness for space flights. Clinical reports from patients, and responses on personality tests and attitude scales, are also introspective in nature.

Introspective reports involving the higher-level cognitive processes, such as reasoning, are obtained from subjects in many areas. Industrial/organizational psychologists study introspective reports from employees about their interaction with computer terminals, for consideration in the development and refinement of such computer equipment and furniture. These and other, similar verbal reports based on personal experience are legitimate forms of data collecting. We will see that cognitive psychology, with its renewed interest in conscious processes, has conferred greater legitimacy on introspection. The method remains alive and well in psychology today.

Another contribution of structuralism is its service as a target of criticism. Structuralism provided a strong, established orthodoxy against which newly developing movements in psychology could array their forces. These newer schools of thought owed their existence in no small measure to their progressive reformulation of the structuralist position. We noted that advances in science require something to oppose. With the help of structuralism, as an idea to oppose, psychology moved far beyond Titchener's initial boundaries.

DISCUSSION QUESTIONS

1. Discuss the differences between the approaches of Titchener and Wundt to psychology. Describe Titchener's views on women in psychology.

2. According to Titchener, what is the proper subject matter for psychology? What is the stimulus error? What distinction did Titchener draw between consciousness and mind?

3. Describe Titchener's method of introspection and note how it differed from Wundt's method. What did Titchener's use of the term *reagent* indicate about his views of the human subject?

4. Define the three elementary states of consciousness and the four attributes of mental elements, according to Titchener. In what ways did Titchener alter his system late in his career?

5. What questions must a science strive to answer about its subject matter? In Titchener's view, how does psychology answer these questions?

6. Discuss the criticisms of introspection. What additional criticisms have been made of Titchener's structuralism? What contributions has structuralism made to psychology?

Suggested Readings

Angell, F. (1928). Titchener at Leipzig. *Journal of General Psychology, 1,* 195–198. A fellow student describes the time at Leipzig and recalls Titchener's research and personal characteristics.

Boring, E. G. (1953). A history of introspection. *Psychological Bulletin, 50,* 169–189. Discusses introspection as practiced in Titchener's psychology and the use of introspective methods in later schools of thought.

Evans, R. B. (1972). E. B. Titchener and his lost system. *Journal of the History of the Behavioral Sciences, 8,* 168–180. Describes the development of Titchener's structural psychology and speculates on the changes in his thinking toward the end of his life.

Hindeland, M. J. (1971). Edward Bradford Titchener: A pioneer in perception. *Journal of the History of the Behavioral Sciences, 7,* 23–28. Describes Titchener's experimental approach to sensation and perception.

CHAPTER 6

FUNCTIONALISM:
ANTECEDENT INFLUENCES

THE FUNCTIONALIST PROTEST

FUNCTIONALISM, AS the name suggests, is concerned with the mind as it functions or is used by an organism in adapting to its environment. The functional psychology movement focused on a practical question: What do mental processes accomplish? Functionalists studied the mind not from the standpoint of its composition (its structure or its mental elements) but rather as a conglomerate or an accumulation of functions and processes that lead to practical consequences in the real world.

The studies of the mind undertaken by Wundt and by Titchener revealed nothing of the outcomes or accomplishments of our mental activity; this was not their goal. Such utilitarian concerns were inconsistent with their pure scientific approach to psychology. Functionalism, as the first uniquely American system of psychology, was a deliberate protest against Wundt's experimental psychology and Titchener's structuralism, both of which were seen as too restrictive. They could not answer the questions the functionalists were asking: What does the mind do? How does it do it?

Although functionalism was a protest against the current schools of thought, its promoters did not intend formally to found a school. The primary reason for this was personal, not ideological: None of the major proponents of the functionalist position had the ambition to establish a movement or system of thought in the way Wundt and Titchener did.

In time, functionalism did attain many of the characteristics of a school of thought, but that was not the aim of its leaders. They appeared content to modify the existing orthodoxy without striving to replace it.

As a result, functionalism was never as rigid or as formally differentiated a systematic position as was Titchener's structuralism. There was not a single functional psychology, as there was a single structural psychology. Several functional psychologies existed, and although they differed somewhat, they all shared an interest in the functions of consciousness. And as an outgrowth of this emphasis on the functioning of an organism in its environment, functionalists became interested in potential applications of psychology to solving everyday problems. Thus, applied psychology developed rapidly in the United States, where today it is the most important legacy of the functionalist movement.

FORERUNNERS OF FUNCTIONALISM

FUNCTIONALISM: The system of psychology concerned with the mind as it is used in an organism's adaptation to its environment

We consider in this chapter the roots of the functional psychology movement, including the works of Charles Darwin, Francis Galton, and early students of animal behavior. It is important to note the time when these forerunners of functionalism were developing their ideas—the period prior to and during the years in which the new psychology was first developing.

Darwin's pioneering book about evolution, *On the Origin of Species* (1859) was published 1 year before Fechner's *Elements of Psychophysics* (1860) and 20 years before Wundt established his laboratory at the University of Leipzig. Galton began work on the problem of individual differences in 1869, before Wundt wrote his *Principles of Physiological Psychology* (1873–1874). Animal psychology experiments were conducted in the 1880s, before Titchener had journeyed to Germany to come under Wundt's influence.

Thus, major work on the functions of consciousness, on individual differences, and on animal behavior was being performed at the same time Wundt and Titchener were deliberately excluding these areas from their definitions of psychology. It would remain for the new American psychologists to bring mental functions, individual differences, and the laboratory rat to positions of prominence in psychology.

THE EVOLUTION REVOLUTION: CHARLES DARWIN (1809–1882)

Charles Darwin's *On the Origin of Species by Means of Natural Selection,* published in 1859, is one of the world's most important books.

The theory of evolution presented in this work was to have a tremendous impact on contemporary American psychology, which owes its form and substance as much to Darwin as to any other idea or individual. (As we will see, evolutionary theory also affected the work of Sigmund Freud.)

The suggestion that living things change with time, which is the fundamental notion of evolution, did not originate with Darwin. Intellectual anticipations of this idea can be traced to the 5th century B.C., although it was not until the late 18th century that the theory was investigated systematically. Erasmus Darwin (the 340-pound English physiologist and grandfather of Charles Darwin and Francis Galton, who composed erotic poetry and fathered 14 children by two wives and a governess) wrote that all warm-blooded animals had evolved from a single living filament and were given animation by God.

In 1809 the French naturalist Jean-Baptiste Lamarck formulated a behavioral theory of evolution that emphasized the modification of an animal's bodily form through its efforts to adapt to its environment. These modifications, Lamarck suggested, were inherited by succeeding generations. According to this theory, the giraffe, for example, developed its long neck over generations of having to reach for higher and higher branches to find food.

In the mid-1800s, the British geologist Charles Lyell introduced the notion of evolution into geological theory, arguing that the earth had passed through various stages of development in evolving to its present structure.

Why, after so many centuries of acceptance of the biblical account of creation, were scholars driven to seek an alternative explanation? One reason is that scientists were learning more about the other species that inhabited the earth. Explorers were discovering new forms of animal life that were previously unknown. It was inevitable, therefore, that someone would ask how the biblical Noah could possibly have put a pair of each of these animals into the Ark. There were simply too many species to allow for continued belief in that story.

Explorers and scientists had also uncovered fossils and bones of creatures that did not match those of existing species—bones that apparently belonged to animals that had once roamed the earth and then disappeared. Thus, living forms could no longer be seen as constant, unchanged since the beginning of time, but rather as being subject to modification and change. Old species became extinct and new species appeared, some of them alterations of current forms. Some scientists speculated that everything in nature results from change and is still in the process of evolving.

The impact of continuing change was being observed not only in intellectual and scientific circles but also in everyday life. The social Zeitgeist was being transformed by the impact of the Industrial

The American Museum of Natural History

CHARLES DARWIN

Revolution. Society's values, relationships, and cultural norms, constant for generations, were being disrupted as masses of people migrated from rural areas and small towns to the rapidly developing urban manufacturing centers.

Over all was the growing domination of science. People were less content to base their ideas about human nature and society on what the Bible and ancient authorities claimed was true. Instead, they were ready to shift their allegiance, to put their faith in science.

Change was the order of the day. It affected the peasant farmer, whose life now pulsed to the rhythm of the machine instead of to the seasons, as much as it affected the scientist, whose time was spent puzzling over a newly unearthed set of bones. The intellectual and social climate of the times rendered the idea of evolution scientifically respectable. For a long time, however, scholars and thinkers speculated and suggested and hypothesized, but could offer little supporting evidence. Then Darwin's *On the Origin of Species* provided so much well-organized data that evolutionary theory could not be ignored. The times, the Zeitgeist, demanded such a theory, and Charles Darwin became its agent.

Darwin's Life

As a boy, Charles Darwin gave little indication of becoming the keen, hard-working scientist the world would later know. He was boisterous and mischievous, playing pranks, lying, and stealing to get attention. One of his early memories was of trying to break the windows in a room in which he had been locked as punishment for misbehaving (Desmond & Moore, 1991). He showed so little promise that his father, a wealthy physician, worried that young Charles would disgrace the family name. Although Charles never liked school and did poorly at his studies, he showed an early interest in natural history and in collecting coins, shells, and minerals. Sent by his father to the University of Edinburgh to study medicine, he soon pronounced it dull. His father decided that Charles should become a clergyman instead.

Darwin spent 3 years at Cambridge University and described the experience as wasted, at least from an academic standpoint. Socially, he had a wonderful time, the happiest period of his life. He collected beetles, hunted, and spent much time drinking, singing, and playing cards as part of a group of students he referred to as dissipated and low-minded.

One of Darwin's instructors, the noted botanist John Stevens Henslow, secured Darwin's appointment as a naturalist aboard the ship *H.M.S. Beagle,* which the British government was preparing for a scientific voyage around the world. This famous excursion, which lasted from 1831 to 1836, began in South American waters, proceeded to Tahiti and New Zealand, and returned to England by way of Ascension Island and the Azores. The journey afforded Darwin a unique opportunity to observe a variety of plant and animal life, and he was able to collect an immense amount of data. The trip also changed Darwin's character. No longer the pleasure-loving dilettante, he returned to England a serious, dedicated scientist with a single passion in life: to develop his theory of evolution.

In 1839 Darwin married, and 3 years later he and his wife moved to Down, a village 16 miles from London, where he could concentrate on his work without the distractions of city life. Never in robust health, he was plagued by physical ailments, complaining of vomiting, flatulence, boils, skin rashes, dizziness, trembling, and depression. These symptoms were apparently neurotic in origin, triggered by any disruption to his daily routine. Whenever the outside world intruded, preventing him from working, he would suffer another attack. Illness became a useful device, protecting him from mundane affairs and allowing him the solitude and concentration he needed to create his theory. One writer termed Darwin's condition a "creative malady" (Pickering, 1974).

> *He cut himself off, ducked parties and declined engagements; he even installed a mirror outside his study window to spy on visitors as they came up his drive. Day after day, week after week, his stomach plagued him, and for years after reaching his rural retreat he refused to sleep anywhere else, unless it was a safe house, a close relative's home. This was a worried man.* (DESMOND & MOORE, 1991, PP. xviii–xix)

Darwin had good reason to be worried. The idea of evolution was being condemned by conservative authorities in the church and even in some academic circles. The clergy viewed it as morally degenerative and subversive, and preached that if people were seen as no different from animals, they would behave accordingly. The resulting savagery would surely cause the collapse of civilization. Darwin sometimes referred to himself as the "devil's chaplain," telling a friend that working on an evolutionary theory was like confessing to a murder (Desmond & Moore, 1991). Darwin knew that when he finally published his ideas, he would be damned as a heretic.

He waited 22 years before presenting his work to the world, wanting to be certain that when his findings were published, his theory would be supported by irrefutable scientific evidence. And so Darwin proceeded slowly, with painstaking caution.

In 1842, Darwin wrote a brief 35-page sketch of his theory. Two years later he expanded this into a 200-page essay, but still he was not satisfied. He continued to keep his ideas private, sharing them only with the geologist Lyell and with Joseph Hooker, a botanist. For 15 more years Darwin fretted and pored over his data, rechecking, elaborating, revising, wanting all aspects of the theory to be unassailable.

No one knows how much longer Darwin might have delayed if he had not received, in June of 1858, a shocking letter from one Alfred Russel Wallace, a naturalist some 14 years younger than Darwin. Wallace, while in the East Indies to recover from an illness, had outlined a theory of evolution remarkably similar to Darwin's, although it did not rest on the wealth of data Darwin had accumulated. What was worse, Wallace said his work had taken 3 days. He asked for Darwin's opinion of his theory and for help in getting it published. Imagine Darwin's feelings after he had spent more than 2 decades of laborious and painstaking work!

Darwin was highly ambitious, a trait not uncommon among scientists. Even before his journey on the *Beagle* he had written in his diary that he was "ambitious to take a fair place among scientific men." Later he added, "I wish I could set less value on the bauble fame. . . . I rather hate the idea of writing for priority, yet I certainly should be vexed if anyone were to publish my doctrines before me" (Merton, 1957, pp. 647–648).

Darwin knew, as he told his friend Lyell, that if he helped Wallace get his paper published, then all his years of hard work and the credit for originating evolutionary theory would be forfeited (Benjamin, 1993). While he was still agonizing over the options open to him, his infant son died of scarlet fever, leaving Darwin in despair. He brooded about the implications of Wallace's letter, but with an enviable sense of fair play, he decided that "It seems hard on me that I should lose my priority of many years' standing, but I cannot feel at all sure that this alters the justice of the case. . . . It would be dishonorable in me now to publish" (Merton, 1957, p. 648).

Lyell and Hooker suggested that both Wallace's paper and portions of Darwin's forthcoming book be read at a meeting of the Linnean Society (a scientific society named after the Swedish naturalist Linnaeus) on July 1, 1858. And the rest is history. Every one of the 1,250 copies of the first printing of Darwin's *On the Origin of Species* was sold on the day of publication. The book generated immediate excitement and controversy, and Darwin, although subjected to considerable criticism, won his "bauble fame."

On the Origin of Species *and Other Works*

The Darwinian theory of evolution is so well known that only an overview of the fundamental points is necessary here. Starting with the obvious fact of variation among individual members of a species, Darwin reasoned that this spontaneous variability was inheritable. In nature, a process of natural selection results in the survival of those organisms best suited for their environment and the elimination of those not fit. A continuing struggle for survival takes place, Darwin suggested, and those forms that survive are the ones that have made successful adaptations or adjustments to the environmental circumstances to which they are exposed. Species that cannot adapt do not survive.

Darwin formulated the idea of a struggle for survival after reading *Essay on the Principle of Population,* written by the economist Thomas Malthus in 1789. (Alfred Russel Wallace had been inspired by the same book.) Malthus had noted that the world's food supply increases arithmetically, whereas the human population tends to increase geometrically. The inevitable result, which Malthus described as having a "melancholy hue," is that many human beings will live under near-starvation conditions. Only the most forceful and cunning will survive.

Darwin extended this principle to all living organisms and developed the concept of natural selection. Those forms of organisms that survive the struggle and reach maturity tend to transmit to their offspring the skills or advantages that enabled them to thrive. Further, because variation is another general law of heredity, offspring will show variation among themselves; some will possess the advantageous qualities developed to a higher degree than their parents. The qualities tend to survive, and in the course of many generations great changes in form may occur. These changes can be so extensive as to account for the differences among species that are found today.

Natural selection was not the only mechanism of evolution Darwin recognized. He also believed in Lamarck's doctrine that changes in form brought about by experience during an animal's lifetime can be passed to subsequent generations.

Although some church leaders were surprisingly receptive to the idea of evolutionary theory, others saw it as a threat because they believed it to be inconsistent with a literal interpretation of the biblical account of creation. One distinguished minister called it "an attempt to dethrone God," adding that "If the Darwinian theory is true, Genesis is a lie . . . and the revelation of God to man, as we Christians know it, is a delusion" (White, 1896/1965, p. 93). The controversy was intense and long-lasting.

Within a year of the publication of *On the Origin of Species* a debate took place at Oxford University, at a meeting of the British Association for the Advancement of Science. The speakers were the biologist Thomas Henry Huxley, who defended Darwin and evolution, and Bishop Samuel Wilberforce (nicknamed Soapy Sam, because of his long-winded speeches), who defended the Bible. "Referring to the ideas of Darwin, [Wilberforce] congratulated himself . . . that he was not descended from a monkey. The reply came from Huxley: 'If I had to choose, I would prefer to be a descendant of a humble monkey rather than of a man who employs his knowledge and eloquence in misrepresenting those who are wearing out their lives in the search for truth'" (White, 1896/1965, p. 92).

Another speaker at the debate was Robert Fitzroy, captain of the *Beagle* during Darwin's voyage. A religious fundamentalist, Fitzroy blamed himself for his part in aiding Darwin's research. Fitzroy hefted a large Bible over his head as he spoke, urging the audience to believe the word of God, but the crowd shouted him down. Five years later, the brooding captain committed suicide (Desmond & Moore, 1991).

Recently discovered data of history have led to a reevaluation of this famous confrontation (Richards, 1987). Apparently, the account of the Oxford debate stems from Huxley's anti-church attitude and his attempt (perhaps unwitting) to bolster his scientific image. The event was less a debate than a series of speeches, and it was Darwin's friend, Joseph Hooker, not Huxley, who offered the more effective rebuttal to Bishop Wilberforce. Darwin remained on good terms with Wilberforce; he found the bishop's remarks "uncommonly clever, [though] not worth anything scientifically" (Gould, 1986, p. 31).

The battle is not yet finished. In 1925, at the famous Scopes "monkey trial" in Dayton, Tennessee, a high school teacher, John T. Scopes, was prosecuted for teaching the theory of evolution. Almost a half century later, in 1972, a Tennessee minister charged that Darwin's theory "breeds corruption, lust, immorality, greed, and such acts of criminal depravity as drug addiction, war, and atrocious acts of genocide" (*New York Times,* October 1, 1972). The United States Supreme Court in 1968 struck down the final law that banned the teaching of evolution in the public schools, but a 1985 survey showed that half of a national sample of American adults rejected evolutionary theory (*Washington Post,* June 3, 1986).

In 1987 the U.S. Supreme Court ruled against a bill in the state of Louisiana requiring that if evolution were taught in the public schools, then creationism, a biblical view of the origin of species, had to be given equal time. In 1990, the Texas state board of education approved science textbooks that cover the theory of evolution, but one-third of its members objected.

Darwin remained aloof from the disputes of his time and wrote other books of importance for psychology. His second major report on evolution, *The Descent of Man* (1871), gathered the evidence for human evolution from lower forms of life, emphasizing the similarity between animal and human mental processes. The book quickly became popular. A prominent magazine writer noted that "In the drawing room it is competing with the latest novel, and in the study it is troubling alike the man of science, the moralist, and the theologian. On every side it is raising a storm of mingled wrath, wonder, and admiration" (Richards, 1987, p. 219). Wonder, admiration, and acceptance soon won out over wrath.

Darwin made an intensive study of emotional expressions in humans and animals, suggesting that the changes in gestures and postures typical of the major emotional states could be interpreted in evolutionary terms. In his book, *The Expression of the Emotions in Man and Animals* (1872), he stated that emotional expressions were remnants of movements that once had served some practical function.

Beginning in 1840, Darwin kept a diary about his infant son, recording the child's development. He published it as "A Biographical Sketch of an Infant" in the journal *Mind* in 1877. It is considered to be one of the early sources for modern child psychology.

The Evolution of Machines

Let us return to a discussion of mechanical models. We noted that machines had been created to duplicate human movement (automata) and human thought (Babbage's calculating engine). Was it possible that machines could evolve to higher forms the way humans and animals were said to do? At the time Darwin's theory was published, the mechanical metaphor for human life had become widespread in intellectual and social circles, and the question seemed inevitable.

The person who asked the question, and who extended the theory of evolution to machines, was Samuel Butler, an eccentric English writer, painter, and musician who emigrated to New Zealand to raise sheep the year Darwin's *On the Origin of Species* was published (Mazlish, 1993). Butler and Darwin later carried on an extensive correspondence.

In several essays, including one entitled "Darwin among the Machines," Butler wrote that the evolution of machines had already occurred. We only had to compare, he said, primordial, rudimentary machines such as levers, wedges, screws, and pulleys with the modern, complex machinery of the factories of the Industrial Revolution or the great steam-driven ocean liners.

Mechanical evolution was said to occur through the same processes that guide human evolution: natural selection and the struggle for existence. Inventors are constantly creating new machines, Butler argued, to gain some competitive advantage. The new machines eliminate or render extinct the older, inferior machines that can no longer adapt or compete in the struggle for life. As a result, the obsolete machines disappeared completely, just as the dinosaurs did.

The rapid development of technology made it clear to Butler that machines had made greater evolutionary strides than had animals, and he speculated about the result of that situation. He predicted that machines would become self-regulating and self-acting, capable of simulating human intelligence. That, he warned, raised the possibility that machines would become superior to humans, to the point where they would become dominant in our lives. Would humankind become totally dependent on machines, unable to survive without them?

One historian of science wrote that Butler had posed the "Frankenstein-like fear of the monster as machine, now evolving, and threatening our own survival, or at least our dominion over species" (Mazlish, 1993, p. 151). It required only a small additional step to predict that machines would evolve to the point of becoming conscious. "There is no security," Butler wrote, "against the ultimate development of mechanical consciousness. . . . who can say that the vapour-engine has not a kind of consciousness? Where does consciousness begin, and where end? Who can draw the line?" (quoted in Mazlish, 1993, p. 153). These questions are being asked today about computers, a highly evolved form of machine, and we consider the issue further in chapter 15.

Butler advanced his ideas in several essays, but because they were published in obscure journals, they had little impact on mainstream scientific thought. In 1872, the notion of the evolution of machines received wider circulation when Butler incorporated it into a novel, *Erewhon* (approximately "nowhere," spelled backward). The story describes a Utopian society in which machines were destroyed because they had become too threatening to humans.

The popularity of Butler's theme attests to the 19th-century fascination with machines and the mechanized image of human nature. This, of course, was the theme at the core of the newly emerging science of psychology.

Darwin's Influence on Psychology

Darwin's work in the last part of the 19th century was a major force in shaping modern psychology. The theory of evolution raised the intriguing possibility that a continuity existed in mental functioning between humans and the lower animals. If the human mind had evolved from more primitive minds, then did it follow that there might be similarities in mental functioning between animals and humans? The gap between animals and humans described 2 centuries earlier by Descartes thus became a reopened question. Scholars saw that the study of animal behavior was vital to an understanding of human behavior, and they turned to investigating animal mental functioning, introducing a new topic into the psychology laboratory. The subsequent field of animal psychology was to have far-reaching implications.

Evolutionary theory also brought about a change in the subject matter and goal of psychology. The focus of the structuralist school of thought was the analysis of the contents of consciousness. Darwin's work inspired some psychologists, particularly those in the United States, to consider the *functions* that consciousness might serve. This seemed to many researchers to be more important than finding any so-called elements of consciousness. And so as psychology came to be more concerned with how the organism functioned in adapting to its environment, the detailed investigation of mental elements began to lose its appeal.

Darwin's theory also influenced psychology by broadening the methods the new science could legitimately use. The methods employed in Wundt's laboratory at Leipzig were derived primarily from physiology, notably the psychophysical methods of Fechner. Darwin's methods, which produced results applicable to both humans and animals, bore no resemblance to those physiologically based techniques. Darwin's data came from a variety of sources including geology, archaeology, demography, observations of wild and domesticated animals, and research on breeding. Information from all these fields provided support for his theory.

Here was tangible and impressive evidence that scientists could study human nature by techniques other than experimental introspection. Following Darwin's example, the psychologists who were influenced by evolutionary theory and its emphasis on the functions of consciousness became more eclectic with regard to their research methods. As a result, the kinds of data psychologists collected were expanded.

Another effect of evolution on psychology was seen in the growing focus on individual differences. The fact of variation among members of the same species was obvious to Darwin as a result of his observation, during the *Beagle* voyage, of so many species and forms. Evolution could not occur if each generation were identical to its forebears. Variation, therefore, was an important tenet of evolutionary theory.

While the structural psychologists continued their search for general laws to encompass all minds, the psychologists influenced by Darwin's ideas began to search for the ways in which individual minds differed, and for techniques to measure those differences. The psychology of the structuralists had little room for the consideration of animal minds or individual differences. It remained for scientists of a functionalist persuasion to pursue those problems. As a result, the form and nature of the new psychology began to change.

INDIVIDUAL DIFFERENCES: FRANCIS GALTON (1822–1911)

Galton effectively brought the spirit of evolution to bear on psychology with his work on the problems of mental inheritance and individual differences in human capacity. Before Galton's efforts, the phenomenon of individual differences had not been considered an appropriate subject for study in psychology. Only a few isolated attempts had been made, notably by Weber, Fechner, and Helmholtz, who had reported individual differences in their experimental results but had not investigated them systematically. Wundt and Titchener did not consider individual differences to be a part of psychology.

Galton's Life

FRANCIS GALTON

Archives of the History of American Psychology/University of Akron

Francis Galton possessed an extraordinary intelligence (an estimated IQ of 200) and a wealth of novel ideas. A few of the topics he investigated are fingerprints (which the police force adopted for identification purposes), fashions, the geographical distribution of beauty, weightlifting, and the effectiveness of prayer. He also invented an early version of the teletype printer, a device for picking locks, and a periscope to enable him to see over the heads of the crowd while watching a parade.

Galton was born in 1822 near Birmingham, England, the youngest of nine children. His father was a prosperous banker whose wealthy and socially prominent family included important people in major spheres of influence: the government, the church, and the military. At the age of 16, at his father's insistence, Galton began the study of medicine at Birmingham General Hospital. He worked as an apprentice to the physicians; he dispensed pills, studied medical books, set broken bones, amputated fingers, pulled teeth, vaccinated children, and amused himself by reading the classics. Overall, however, it was not a pleasant experience, and only the continued pressure from his father kept him there.

One incident during this medical apprenticeship illustrates Galton's mental curiosity. Wanting to learn the effects of the various medications in the pharmacy, Galton began taking small doses of each and noting his reaction, beginning in systematic fashion with those under the letter "A." This scientific venture ended at the letter "C" when he took a dose of croton oil, a powerful laxative.

After serving a year at the hospital Galton continued his medical education at King's College, London. A year later he changed his plans and enrolled at Trinity College of Cambridge University, where, with a bust of Isaac Newton opposite his fireplace, he pursued his interest in mathematics. Although his work was interrupted by a severe mental breakdown, he did manage to earn his degree. He returned to the study of medicine, which by now he disliked intensely, until his father's death released him from that profession.

Travel and exploration claimed Galton's attention. He journeyed throughout Africa and published accounts of his travels, earning a medal from the Royal Geographic Society. In the 1850s he stopped traveling, because of marriage and poor health, he said, but maintained his interest in exploration and wrote a guidebook called *The Art of Travel*. He organized expeditions for other explorers and gave lectures on camp life to soldiers training for overseas duty.

Restlessness led him next to meteorology and the design of instruments to plot weather data. He summarized his findings in a book considered to be the first attempt to chart large-scale weather patterns.

When his cousin Charles Darwin published *On the Origin of Species,* Galton immediately turned his attention to the new theory. The biological aspect of evolution captivated him first, and he undertook an investigation of the effects of blood transfusions between rabbits, to determine whether acquired characteristics could be inherited. Although the genetic side of evolutionary theory did not hold his interest for long, the social implications guided Galton's subsequent work and determined his influence on modern psychology.

Mental Inheritance

Galton's first important book for psychology was *Hereditary Genius,* published in 1869. (When Darwin read it, he wrote to Galton that never in all his life had he read anything more interesting or original.) In it Galton sought to demonstrate that individual greatness or genius occurred within families far too often to be explained solely by environmental influences. His thesis, briefly, was that eminent men have eminent sons. (Daughters at that time had few opportunities to achieve eminence, except through marriage to someone of importance.)

Most of the biographical studies Galton reported in this book were investigations into the ancestries of influential scientists and physicians. His data showed that each famous person inherited not only genius but a specific form of genius. A great scientist, for example, was born into a family that had attained eminence in science.

Galton's ultimate aim was to encourage the birth of the more eminent or fit individuals and to discourage the birth of the unfit. To help achieve this goal, he founded the science of eugenics, dealing with factors that may improve the inherited qualities of the human race. He argued that humans, not unlike farm animals, could be improved by artificial selection. If people of considerable talent were selected and mated generation after generation, a highly gifted race of people would result. He proposed that intelligence tests be developed to choose exceptional men and women for selective breeding, and he recommended that those who scored high be offered financial incentives for marrying and producing children. (Galton himself had no children; neither did his brothers. Apparently the problem was genetic.)

In attempting to verify his eugenic theory, Galton pursued problems of measurement and statistics. In *Hereditary Genius* he applied statistical concepts to the problems of heredity, sorting the prominent men in his sample into categories according to the frequency with which their level of ability occurred in the population. His data showed that eminent men have a higher probability of fathering eminent sons than do average men. His sample consisted of 977 famous men, each so outstanding as to be one in 4,000. On a chance basis, this group would be expected to have only one important relative; instead it had 332.

The probability of eminence in certain families was not high enough for Galton to consider seriously any possible influence of a superior environment, better educational opportunities, or social advantages granted to the sons of the outstanding families he studied. Eminence—or the lack of it—was a function of heredity, he argued, not of opportunity.

Galton wrote *English Men of Science* (1874), *Natural Inheritance* (1889), and more than 30 papers on problems of inheritance. He started the journal *Biometrika* in 1901, established the Eugenics Laboratory at University College, London, in 1904, and founded an organization for promoting the idea of racial improvement.

Statistical Methods

Throughout his career Galton was never fully satisfied with a problem until he had found some way to quantify the data and analyze them statistically, developing his own methods when necessary. A Belgian statistician, Adolph Quetelet, had been the first to apply statistical methods and the normal curve of distribution to biological and social data. The normal curve had been used in work on the distribution of measurements and errors in scientific observation, but had not been applied to human variability until Quetelet showed that measures of height taken from 10,000 subjects approximated the normal curve. He used the phrase *l'homme moyen* (the average man) to express the finding that most physical measurements cluster around the average or center of the distribution, and fewer are found toward either extreme.

Galton was impressed by Quetelet's data and assumed that similar results would be true for mental characteristics. He found, for example, that the grades given on university examinations followed the normal curve. Because of the simplicity of the normal curve and its consistency over a variety of traits, Galton suggested that any large set of measurements or values of human characteristics could be meaningfully described by two numbers: the average value of the distribution (the mean), and the dispersion or range of variation around this average value (the standard deviation).

Galton's work in statistics yielded one of science's most important measures: the correlation. The first report of what he called "correlations" appeared in 1888. Modern techniques for determining the validity and reliability of tests, as well as factor-analytic methods, are direct outgrowths of Galton's discovery of correlation, which resulted from his observation that inherited characteristics tend to regress toward the mean. For example, he noted that tall men are, on the average, not as tall as their fathers, whereas the sons of very short men are, on the average, taller than their fathers. He devised the graphic means to represent the basic properties of the correlation coefficient and developed a formula for its calculation, although the formula is no longer in use.

With Galton's encouragement, his student Karl Pearson developed the currently used mathematical formula for calculating the correlation coefficient—the Pearson product-moment coefficient of correlation. The symbol for the correlation coefficient, *r*, is taken from the first letter of the word *regression,* in recognition of Galton's discovery of the tendency of inherited human traits to regress toward the average or mean. Correlation is a fundamental tool in the social and behavioral sciences, and in engineering and the natural sciences. Many other statistical techniques have been developed from Galton's pioneering work.

Mental Tests

Galton originated **mental tests,** although the term came from James McKeen Cattell, an American disciple of Galton and a former student of Wundt. Galton's fundamental assumption was that intelligence could be measured in terms of a person's sensory capacities—the higher the intelligence, the higher the level of sensory functioning. He derived this assumption from John Locke's empiricist view that all knowledge comes through the senses. If that is true, Galton concluded, then it follows that the "most capable individuals have the most acute senses. The fact that the lowest grade of idiots often have sensory deficits seemed to confirm this line of thinking" (Loevinger, 1987, p. 98).

To carry out his work, Galton needed to invent the apparatus with which sensory measurements could be made quickly and accurately for large numbers of people. For example, to determine the highest frequency of sound that could be heard, he invented a whistle, which he tested on animals as well as people. (He liked to walk through the London zoo with the whistle affixed to a hollow walking stick; he would

MENTAL TESTS: Tests of motor skills and sensory capacities

The Galton whistle was an instrument used to detect the highest pitch to which humans and animals react.

squeeze a rubber bulb to activate the whistle and observe the reactions of the animals.) Galton's whistle became a standard piece of psychology laboratory equipment until it was replaced in the 1930s by a more sophisticated electronic device.

Other instruments included a photometer to measure the precision with which a subject could match two spots of color, a calibrated pendulum to measure reaction time to sounds and lights, and a series of weights to be arranged in order of heaviness to measure kinesthetic or muscle sensitivity. He provided a bar with a variable distance scale to test estimation of visual extension, and sets of bottles containing different substances to test olfactory discrimination. Most of Galton's tests served as prototypes for the standard equipment that was used for decades in psychology laboratories.

Armed with his new tests, Galton proceeded to collect a mass of data. He established his Anthropometric Laboratory in 1884 at the International Health Exhibition, and later moved it to London's South Kensington Museum. The laboratory remained active for 6 years, during which time Galton collected data from more than 9,000 people. Instruments for the anthropometric and psychometric measurements were arranged on a long table at one end of a narrow room. For a small admission fee, a person would pass down the length of the table to be assessed by an attendant who recorded the data on a card.

In addition to the measurements noted above, information was obtained on height, weight, breathing power, strength of pull and squeeze, quickness of blow, hearing, vision, and color sense. The aim of this large-scale testing program was no less than the definition of the range of human capacities of the entire British population to determine its collective mental resources.

A century later a group of psychologists in the United States analyzed Galton's data (Johnson et al., 1985). They found substantial test/retest correlations, indicating that the data were statistically reliable. In addition, Galton's data provided useful information on developmental trends during childhood, adolescence, and maturity within the population tested. Measures such as weight, arm span, breathing power, and strength of squeeze were shown to be similar to those reported in more recent psychology literature, except that the rate of development in Galton's time appears to have been slightly slower. Thus, the psychologists concluded that Galton's data continue to be instructive.

The Association of Ideas

Galton worked on two problems in the area of association: the diversity of the associations of ideas, and the time required to produce associations (reaction time).

One of his methods for studying the diversity of associations was to walk 450 yards along Pall Mall, the London street that runs between Trafalgar Square and St. James Palace, focusing his attention on an object until it suggested one or two associated ideas to him. The first time he tried this he was amazed at the number of associations that developed from the nearly 300 objects he had seen. He found that many of these associations were recollections of past experiences, including incidents long forgotten. Repeating the walk a few days later he found considerable repetition of the associations that had occurred during the first walk. This quashed his interest in the problem, and he turned instead to reaction-time experiments, which produced more useful results.

For these reaction-time experiments Galton prepared a list of 75 words, writing each one on a separate slip of paper. After a week he viewed them one at a time and used a chronometer to record the time necessary to produce two associations for each word. Many of the associations were single words, but some were images or mental pictures that required several words to describe. His next task was to determine the origin of these associations. He discovered that about 40% of them could be traced to events in his childhood and adolescence, an early demonstration of the influence of childhood experiences on the adult personality.

Of greater importance than Galton's results was the method he developed to study associations, the word-association test, which was the first experimental attempt to examine associations. Wundt adapted the technique, as we noted, limiting his subjects' responses to a single word, and used it for research in his Leipzig laboratory. The analyst Carl Jung elaborated on it for his own word-association studies.

Mental Imagery

Galton's investigation of mental imagery marks the first extensive use of the psychological questionnaire. Subjects were asked to recall a scene, such as their breakfast table that morning, and to try to elicit images of it. They were told to indicate whether the images were dim or clear, bright or dark, colored or not colored, and so on. To Galton's amazement, his first group of subjects, scientific acquaintances, reported no clear images at all! Some were not even sure what Galton was talking about.

Turning to a broader cross-section of the population, Galton obtained reports of clear and distinct images, full of color and detail. He found that the imagery of women and children was particularly concrete and detailed. He determined that imagery, like so many other characteristics, was distributed normally in the population.

As with much of Galton's research, the work on imagery was rooted in his attempt to demonstrate hereditary similarities. He found that similar images were more likely to occur between siblings than between people who were unrelated.

Additional Research

The richness of Galton's talent is evident in the variety of his research studies. He once tried to put himself into the state of mind of the insane by imagining that everyone or everything he saw while he was taking a walk was spying on him. "By the end of the morning stroll, every horse seemed to be watching him either directly or, just as suspicious, disguising their espionage by elaborately paying no attention" (Watson, 1978, pp. 328–329).

Galton lived at a time when the controversy between evolutionary theory and fundamentalist theology was at its height. With typical objectivity he studied the problem and concluded that although large numbers of people held strong religious beliefs, this was not sufficient evidence that those beliefs were valid. He investigated the power of prayer to produce results and decided that it was of no use to physicians in curing patients or to meteorologists in invoking changes in the weather, or even to ministers in affecting their everyday lives. He believed that there was little difference between people who professed a religious belief and those who did not, in terms of how they dealt with other people or with their own problems. Galton hoped to give the world a new set of beliefs structured in terms of science. He thought that the evolutionary development of a better human race through eugenics should be one's goal, rather than a place in heaven.

Galton always seemed to be counting something. He occupied himself at lectures and the theater by counting the yawns and coughs of the audience, discussing the results as a measure of boredom. While having his portrait painted he counted the artist's brushstrokes, some 20,000. At one time he decided to count by odors instead of numbers. Training himself to forget what numbers meant, he assigned numerical values to smells such as peppermint and learned to add and subtract by thinking of them. Out of this intellectual exercise came a paper entitled "Arithmetic by Smell," published in the first issue of the American journal *Psychological Review.*

Comment

Galton spent only 15 years investigating issues of a psychological nature, but his efforts influenced the direction of the new psychology. He was not truly a psychologist any more than he was a eugenicist or an anthropologist. He was an extremely gifted person whose talent and temperament could not be bound by the confines of a single discipline. Consider the topics in which psychologists later became interested: adaptation, heredity versus environment, comparison of species, child development, the questionnaire method, statistical techniques, individual differences, mental tests. In the scope of his interests and his methods, Galton had a greater impact on American psychology than the science's founder, Wilhelm Wundt.

ANIMAL PSYCHOLOGY AND THE DEVELOPMENT OF FUNCTIONALISM

Darwin's evolutionary theory proved to be a stimulus for the development of animal psychology. Before Darwin published his theory, there was no reason for scientists to be concerned about the animal mind because animals were considered to be automata that had no minds or souls. Descartes had stated emphatically that animals had no similarity with humans.

On the Origin of Species altered this comfortable view. Darwin's evidence led to the suggestion that there was no sharp distinction between human minds and animal minds. Scientists could propose a continuity between all mental and physical aspects of humans and animals, because humans were believed to be derived from animals by the continuous evolutionary process of change and development. Darwin wrote: "There is no fundamental difference between man and the higher mammals in their mental faculties" (1871, p. 66).

He believed that the lower animals experience pleasure and pain, feel happiness and sadness, have vivid dreams, and even some degree of imagination. Even worms, Darwin wrote, show pleasure from eating and demonstrate sexual passion and social feeling, all evidence, to Darwin, of some form of animal mind.

If mental abilities could be demonstrated to exist in animals, and if a continuity between animal minds and human minds could be shown, then such evidence would disprove the human/animal dichotomy espoused by Descartes. A quest was begun for evidence of intelligence in animals.

Darwin defended his theory in a book, *The Expression of the Emotions in Man and Animals* (1872), in which he argued that human emotional behavior results from the inheritance of behavior that was once useful to animals but was no longer relevant for humans. One of many examples he described to support this idea was the way people curl their lips when they sneer. He held this gesture to be a remnant of the way animals bare their canine teeth in rage.

In the years following the publication of *On the Origin of Species*, the topic of animal intelligence grew in popularity, not only among scientists but also with the general public. In the 1860s and 1870s many people wrote to both scientific and popular magazines to report instances of animal behavior that were taken to suggest hitherto unsuspected mental capacities. Thousands of stories circulated about remarkable feats of intelligence of pet cats and dogs, horses and pigs, snails and birds.

Even the great experimentalist Wilhelm Wundt was not immune to this trend. In 1863, before he became the world's first psychologist, he wrote about the intellectual abilities of a wide range of living beings, from beetles to beavers. He argued that animals that showed even minimal sensory capacities must also possess powers of judgment and conscious inference. The so-called inferior animals differed from humans not so much in their abilities as in the fact that they had not received as much education and training. Thirty years later Wundt became much less generous in attributing intelligence to animals, but for a time his voice was added to the many suggesting that animals might be as mentally well endowed as humans.

Studies of Animal Intelligence

The person who formalized and systematized the study of animal intelligence was the British physiologist George John Romanes (1848–1894), who, as a child, was considered by his parents to be "a shocking dunce" (Richards, 1987, p. 334). As a young man, Romanes had been impressed by Darwin's writings. Later, after he and Darwin had become friends, Darwin gave Romanes his notebooks on animal behavior. Darwin thus chose Romanes to carry on that portion of his work, to apply the theory of evolution to the mind as Darwin had applied it to the body.

Romanes became a worthy successor. Because he was quite wealthy, he did not have to be concerned about finding a job to earn a living. The only job he held was that of part-time lecturer at the

University of Edinburgh, which required his presence 2 weeks a year! He spent winters in London and Oxford and summers on the seacoast, where he built a private laboratory that was as well equipped as that of any university.

In 1883 Romanes published *Animal Intelligence,* generally considered to be the first book on comparative psychology. He collected data on the behavior of protozoa, ants, spiders, reptiles, fish, birds, elephants, monkeys, and domestic animals. His purpose was to demonstrate the high level of animal intelligence as well as its similarity to human intellectual functioning, thus illustrating a continuity in mental development. As Romanes put it, he wanted to show that "there is no difference in kind between the acts of reason performed by the crab and any act of reason performed by a man" (quoted in Richards, 1987, p. 347).

Romanes's methodology is referred to as the **anecdotal method;** that is, the use of observational, often casual, reports or narratives about animal behavior. Many of the reports he accepted came from uncritical and untrained observers and were, therefore, vulnerable to the criticisms that they were incorrect observations, careless descriptions, and biased interpretations.

How did Romanes derive his findings on animal intelligence from these anecdotal observations? He worked through a curious and eventually discarded technique known as **introspection by analogy.** In this approach, investigators assume that the same mental processes that occur in their own minds also occur in the minds of the animals being observed. The existence of mind and of specific mental functions is inferred by observing animal behavior and then drawing an analogy—a correspondence or a relationship—between human mental processes and those assumed to be taking place in the animals.

Romanes described the process of introspection by analogy in these terms: "Starting from what I know subjectively of the operations of my own individual mind, and of the activities which in my own organism these operations seem to prompt, I proceed by analogy to infer from the observable activities displayed by other organisms the fact that certain mental operations underlie or accompany these activities" (quoted in Mackenzie, 1977, pp. 56–57).

Through the use of this technique, Romanes suggested that animals are capable of the same kinds of rationalization, ideation, complex reasoning, and problem-solving ability as humans. Some of his followers credited animals with a level of intelligence far superior to that of the average person.

In a study of cats, which Romanes considered to be more intelligent than all other animals except monkeys and elephants, he wrote about the behavior of the cat that belonged to his driver. Through a series of intricate movements, the cat was able to open a door leading to the stables. Introspecting by analogy, Romanes reached the following conclusion: "Cats in such cases have a very definite idea as to the

ANECDOTAL METHOD: The use of observational reports about animal behavior

INTROSPECTION BY ANALOGY: A technique for studying animal behavior by assuming that the same mental processes that occur in the observer's mind also occur in the minds of the animals

mechanical properties of a door; they know that to make it open, even when unlatched, it requires to be pushed. . . . First the animal must have observed that the door is opened by the hand grasping the handle and moving the latch. Next she must reason, by 'the logic of feelings,' if a hand can do it, why not a paw? . . . The pushing with the hind feet after depressing the latch must be due to adaptive reasoning" (Romanes, 1883, pp. 421–422).

Romanes's work fell far short of modern scientific rigor, and the line between fact and subjective interpretation in his data is unclear. Although the deficiencies in his data and method are recognized, he is respected for his pioneering efforts in stimulating the development of comparative psychology and for preparing the way for the experimental approach that followed. We have seen that in many areas of science, reliance on observational data precedes the development of refined experimental methodology, and it was Romanes who launched the observational stage of comparative psychology.

The weaknesses inherent in the anecdotal method and in introspection by analogy were recognized by Conwy Lloyd Morgan (1852–1936), whom Romanes designated as his successor. Morgan, a professor of psychology and education at the University of Bristol, England, and one of the first persons ever to ride a bicycle within the city limits, was also a geologist and a zoologist. He proposed a **law of parsimony** (also called Lloyd Morgan's Canon), in an effort to counter the tendency to attribute too much intelligence to animals.

Morgan's dog, Tony, learns by trial-and-error to operate the latch of a gate.

The law of parsimony states that an animal's behavior must not be interpreted as the outcome of a higher mental process when it can be explained in terms of a lower mental process. Morgan advanced this idea in 1894 and may have derived it from a law of parsimony published by Wundt 2 years earlier. Wundt had noted that "complex explanatory principles can be used only when the simpler have proved insufficient" (Richards, 1980, p. 57).

It was not Morgan's intent to exclude anthropomorphism but rather to reduce its use and to give the methodology of comparative psychology a more scientific basis. He agreed with Romanes that anthropomorphism was necessary and could not be avoided, but he was trying to keep anecdotal inferences to a minimum (Costall, 1993).

Morgan followed essentially the same approach as Romanes, observing an animal's behavior and trying to explain it through an introspective examination of his own mental processes. Applying his law of parsimony, however, Morgan refrained from ascribing higher-level mental processes to animals when their behavior could be explained in terms of lower-level processes. He believed that most animal behavior resulted from learning or association based on sensory experience, learning being a process of a lower level than rational thought or ideation. With Morgan's canon, the use of introspection by analogy became more restricted and was eventually superseded by more objective methods.

Morgan was the first to conduct large-scale experimental studies in animal psychology. Although his early experiments were not performed under rigid scientific conditions, they did involve careful observations of animal behavior, mostly in natural environments but with some artificially induced modifications. These studies did not permit the same degree of control as laboratory experiments, but they were an important advance over Romanes's anecdotal method.

This initial work in comparative psychology was British in origin, but leadership in the field quickly passed to the United States. Romanes died young, in his forties, from a brain tumor, and Morgan decided to leave research for a career in university administration.

Comparative psychology was an outgrowth of the excitement and controversy engendered by Darwin's suggestion of the continuity of the species. Basic to Darwinian theory are the notion of function and the assertion that as a species evolves, its physical structure is determined by its requirements for survival. This premise led biologists to regard each anatomical structure as a functioning or utilitarian element in a total living, adapting system. When psychologists began to examine mental processes in the same way, they created a new movement: functional psychology.

Chapters 7 and 8 describe the development of functionalism in the United States. We continue the story of the development of animal psychology in chapter 9.

LAW OF PARSIMONY (LLOYD MORGAN'S CANON): The idea that an animal's behavior must not be attributed to a higher mental process when it can be explained in terms of a lower mental process

DISCUSSION QUESTIONS

1. With what aspects of consciousness were the functionalists concerned? Describe the nature of their protest against Wundt's psychology and Titchener's structuralism.
2. How was Darwin's concept of natural selection influenced by Malthus's doctrine of population and food supply?
3. Discuss the notion of the evolution of machines. Why was this said to be a threat to humans?
4. How did Darwin's ideas and Galton's research change the subject matter and methods of psychology?
5. How was Galton's work on mental tests influenced by Locke's empiricistic view? What statistical tools did Galton use to measure human characteristics?
6. How did Darwin's evolutionary theory stimulate the development of animal psychology? What was Wundt's initial reaction to this development?
7. How was animal intelligence studied by Romanes and by Morgan?

SUGGESTED READINGS

Angell, J. R. (1909). The influence of Darwin on psychology. *Psychological Review, 16,* 152–169. Discusses Darwin's ideas on evolution and assesses their impact on functional psychology.

Boring, E. G. (1950). The influence of evolutionary theory upon American psychological thought. In S. Persons (Ed.), *Evolutionary theory in America* (pp. 268–298). New Haven, Conn.: Yale University Press. Describes the influence of Darwin's work on Baldwin, Dewey, Hall, James, and Watson—all contributors to the development of psychology in the United States.

Costall, A. (1993). How Lloyd Morgan's Canon backfired. *Journal of the History of the Behavioral Sciences, 29,* 113–122. Compares the views of Morgan and Romanes on animal psychology.

Diamond, S. (1977). Francis Galton and American psychology. *Annals of the New York Academy of Sciences, 291,* 47–55. Describes the influence of Galton's work on such American pioneers as Cattell and Jastrow.

Domjan, M. (1987). Animal learning comes of age. *American Psychologist, 42,* 556–564. Reviews animal learning in terms of its historical context (Darwin, Romanes, Morgan, and Thorndike) and relates it to contemporary learning theory.

CHAPTER 7

FUNCTIONALISM:

DEVELOPMENT

AND FOUNDING

ONLY IN AMERICA

BY ABOUT 1900, psychology in the United States had assumed a character all its own, distinct from Wundt's psychology and from Titchener's structuralism, neither of which was concerned with the purpose or usefulness, the function, of consciousness. The functionalist movement that was evolving from the works of Darwin and Galton focused on how conscious processes operated, rather than on their structure or content. For the formal development of functional psychology as a school of thought, we move from England to the United States at the end of the 19th and the beginning of the 20th century.

Why did functional psychology thrive in the United States and not in England, where the functional spirit originated? The answer lies in the American temperament—its unique social, economic, and political characteristics. The American Zeitgeist was ready to accept evolution and the functionalist attitude that derived from it.

HERBERT SPENCER (1820–1903) AND SYNTHETIC PHILOSOPHY

In 1882 a 62-year-old self-taught English philosopher, who often wore earmuffs to keep the outside world from intruding on his

HERBERT SPENCER

thoughts, arrived in the United States where he was hailed as a national hero. He was met in New York by Andrew Carnegie, the multimillionaire patriarch of the American steel industry, who praised the philosopher as a messiah. In the eyes of many leaders of American business, science, politics, and religion, the man was indeed a savior. He was wined and dined; honors and appreciation were lavished upon him.

His name was Herbert Spencer, the scholar Darwin called "our philosopher," and his impact on the American scene was monumental. Spencer's mind was prolific, and he produced a large number of books, many of which he dictated to a secretary between sets of tennis or while lounging in a rowboat. His works were serialized in popular magazines, his books sold hundreds of thousands of copies, and his system of philosophy was taught in universities by scholars in almost every discipline. "Spencer struck American universities like lightning in the early 1860s and dominated them for thirty years" (Peel, 1971, p. 2). His ideas, read by people at all levels of society, influenced a generation of Americans. Had television been available, Spencer would have appeared on talk shows and received even greater publicity and acclaim.

He might have written more had he not developed, at the age of 35, a neurotic condition that was aggravated by the unwanted presence of other people, or by any disturbance of his routine. The earmuffs helped assure that he would not be annoyed by the sounds of people talking. In this way he was able to work, though only for short periods. Whenever the outside world intruded, he developed insomnia, heart palpitations, and digestive disorders. Like Darwin, his problem began just as he started to develop the system to which he would devote his life.

Social Darwinism

The philosophy that brought Spencer so much recognition and acclaim was Darwinism—the notion of evolution and survival of the fittest—though Spencer extended it far beyond Darwin's own work.

In the United States, interest in Darwin's theory of evolution was intense, and Darwin's ideas had been accepted eagerly. Evolutionary theory was discussed and embraced not only in universities and scholarly societies but also in popular magazines and even some religious publications.

Spencer argued that the development of all aspects of the universe, including human character and social institutions, is evolutionary. It operates in accordance with the principle of survival of the fittest, a phrase he coined. It was this emphasis on what came to be called social Darwinism, the application of the theory of evolution to human nature and society, that met with such enthusiasm in America.

In Spencer's utopian view, if the principle of survival of the fittest was allowed to operate freely, obviously only the best would survive. Human perfection, therefore, was inevitable as long as nothing was done to interfere with the natural order of things. He promoted individualism and a laissez-faire economic system and criticized government attempts to regulate the lives of its citizens, even opposing subsidies for education and housing.

People and organizations were to be left to develop themselves and their society in their own ways, just as other living species were left to develop and adapt in their natural environment. Any assistance from the state would interfere with the natural evolutionary process. Those individuals or businesses or institutions that could not adapt to the environment were unfit for survival and should be allowed to perish or become extinct, for the betterment of society as a whole. If governments continued to support poorly functioning enterprises (people, groups, or organizations), then these enterprises would endure, ultimately weakening society and violating the law that only the strongest and most fit shall survive. Spencer emphasized that by ensuring that only the best survive, societies will eventually achieve perfection.

This message was compatible with America's individualistic spirit, and the phrases "survival of the fittest" and "the struggle for existence" quickly became part of the national consciousness. They reflected the American society of the late 19th century; the United States was a living example of Spencer's ideas.

This pioneer nation was being settled by hardworking people who believed in free enterprise, self-sufficiency, and independence from government regulation. And they knew all about the survival of the fittest from their daily lives. Land was still freely available to those with the courage, cunning, and ability to take it and to make a living from it. The principles of natural selection were vividly demonstrated in everyday experiences, particularly on the Western frontier, where survival and success depended on the ability to adapt to the demands of a hostile environment; those who could not adapt did not survive.

The American historian Frederick Jackson Turner described the survivors in these terms: "That coarseness and strength combined with acuteness and inquisitiveness; that practical, inventive turn of mind, quick to find expedients; that masterful grasp of material things . . . powerful to effect great ends; that restless, nervous energy; that dominant individualism" (Turner, 1947, p. 235).

The people of the United States were oriented toward the practical, the useful, and the functional, and American psychology in its pioneering stages mirrored these qualities. For this reason, the United States was more accepting than other nations of evolutionary theory. American psychology became a functional psychology, because evolution and the functional spirit were in keeping with its basic temperament. And because Spencer's views were compatible with the

American ethos, his philosophical system influenced every field of learning.

Spencer formulated a system he called **synthetic philosophy.** (He used the word *synthetic* in the sense of synthesizing or combining, not to mean something artificial or unnatural.) He based this all-encompassing system on the application of evolutionary principles to all human knowledge and experience. His ideas were published in a series of 10 books between 1860 and 1897. The volumes were hailed by many of the leading scholars of the time as works of genius. Conwy Lloyd Morgan wrote to Spencer that "to none of my intellectual masters do I owe a larger debt of gratitude than to you." Alfred Russel Wallace named his first son after Spencer. Darwin said after reading one of Spencer's books that Spencer was "a dozen times my superior" (quoted in Richards, 1987, p. 245).

Two of the volumes on synthetic philosophy constitute *The Principles of Psychology,* published first in 1855, and later used by William James as a textbook for the psychology course he taught at Harvard University. In this book Spencer discussed the notion that the mind exists in its present form because of past and continuing efforts to adapt to various environments. He emphasized the adaptive nature of nervous and mental processes and wrote that an increasing complexity of experiences, and hence of behavior, is part of the normal evolutionary process. The organism needs to adapt to its environment if it is to survive.

WILLIAM JAMES (1842–1910): ANTICIPATOR OF FUNCTIONAL PSYCHOLOGY

There is much that is paradoxical about William James and his role in American psychology. His work was the major American precursor of functional psychology, and he was a pioneer of the new scientific psychology in the United States. A recent survey of historians of psychology revealed that James ranked second only to Wundt among psychology's most important figures and was the leading American psychologist on the list (Korn, Davis, & Davis, 1991).

However, James was viewed by some of his colleagues as a negative force in the development of a scientific psychology. He maintained a widely publicized interest in mental telepathy, clairvoyance, spiritualism, attempts to communicate with the dead at séances, and other mystical events. Many American psychologists, including Titchener and Cattell, criticized James for his enthusiastic espousal of the very mentalistic and psychical phenomena that they, as experimental psychologists, were trying to banish from the field.

James founded no formal system of psychology and trained no disciples. There would be no Jamesian school of thought. Although

Archives of the History of American Psychology/University of Akron

WILLIAM JAMES

the form of psychology with which he was associated was attempting to be scientific and experimental, James was not an experimentalist in attitude or deed. Psychology, which he once called that "nasty little science," was not his lifelong passion, as it was for Wundt and Titchener. James worked in psychology for a while and moved on.

This fascinating and complex man who contributed so much to psychology turned his back on it later in life. (Prior to delivering a talk at Princeton University, he asked that he *not* be introduced as a psychologist.) He said that psychology was an "elaboration of the obvious." Although he allowed it to stumble on without his commanding presence, his place in the history of psychology is significant and assured.

James did not found functional psychology, but he wrote and thought clearly and effectively in the functionalist atmosphere that pervaded American psychology at the time. In doing so, he influenced the functionalist movement through the inspiration he provided to subsequent generations of psychologists.

James's Life

William James was born in the Astor House, a New York City hotel, into a prominent and wealthy family. His father devoted himself with enthusiasm to the education of his children, alternating between Europe (because he believed American schools were too restrictive) and the United States (because he also believed his children should be educated among their fellow citizens). Thus, James's early schooling took place in England, France, Germany, Italy, Switzerland, and the United States. These stimulating experiences exposed James to the intellectual and cultural advantages of England and Europe, and he frequently journeyed abroad throughout his life.

Although his father thought that none of the children need be concerned with learning a vocation or earning a living, he did try to encourage William's early interest in science. The boy had a chemistry set—a "Bunsen burner and vials of mysterious liquids which he mixed, heated, and transfused, staining his fingers and clothes, to his father's annoyance, and sometimes even causing alarming explosions" (Allen, 1967, p. 47).

James decided at the age of 18 to become an artist. Six months at the studio of the painter William Hunt, in Newport, Rhode Island, persuaded him that he lacked talent, so he enrolled in the Lawrence Scientific School at Harvard. It was then that his health and self-confidence began to decline, transforming him into the intensely troubled neurotic he would remain for most of his life. He abandoned his interest in chemistry, apparently because of the demands of laboratory work, and entered medical school. He had little enthusiasm for medicine, however, noting that "there is much humbug therein. . . . With the exception of surgery, in which something positive is sometimes accomplished, a doctor does more by the moral effect of his presence on the patient and family, than by anything else. He also extracts money from them" (quoted in Allen, 1967, p. 98).

James left his medical studies to assist the zoologist Louis Agassiz on an expedition to Brazil to collect specimens of marine animals in the Amazon River basin. The trip gave James the opportunity to sample a career in biology, but he could not tolerate the required precise collecting and categorizing or the physical demands of field work. "I am cut out for a speculative rather than an active life," he wrote (quoted in Lewis, 1991, p. 174). His reaction to chemistry and biology was prophetic of his later distaste for experimentation in psychology.

Although medicine proved no more attractive after the 1865 expedition than it had been before, James reluctantly resumed his studies because nothing else appealed to him. He was frequently ill, complaining of depression, digestive disorders, insomnia, visual disturbances, and a weak back. "It was obvious to everyone that he was suffering from America; Europe was the only cure" (Miller & Buckhout, 1973, p. 84).

James recuperated at a German spa, dabbled in literature, and wrote long letters to friends, but his depression persisted. He attended some physiology lectures at the University of Berlin and speculated afterward that perhaps it was time for "psychology to begin to be a science" (quoted in Allen, 1967, p. 140). He also said that—if he survived his illness and lived through the winter—he might be interested in learning more about psychology from the great Helmholtz and "a man named Wundt." James did live through the winter, but he did not meet Wundt at that time. The fact that he had heard of Wundt, however, shows his awareness of scientific and intellectual trends some 10 years before Wundt started his laboratory.

James earned his medical degree from Harvard in 1869, but his feelings of insecurity and depression worsened. He thought of suicide and was plagued by nameless and horrible dreads. He was unable to go out at night alone, so intense was his fear. In those dark months he began to build a philosophy of life, compelled not so much by intellectual curiosity as by despair.

He read much work in philosophy, including essays on freedom of the will by the philosopher Charles Renouvier, and he became persuaded of its existence. He decided that his first act of free will would be to believe in free will. Next, he resolved to believe that he could cure himself of his depression by believing in the power of the will. He apparently succeeded to some extent, because in 1872 he felt well enough to accept a teaching position at Harvard in physiology, commenting that "it is a noble thing for one's spirits to have some responsible work to do" (James, 1902, p. 167). After a year on the job he took time off to visit Italy, but then he returned to teaching.

In the 1875–1876 academic year James taught his first course in psychology, which he called "The Relations Between Physiology and Psychology." Thus, Harvard became the first university in the United States to offer instruction in the new experimental psychology. James had never done formal course work in psychology; the first psychology lecture he attended was his own. He secured $300 from the college to purchase laboratory and demonstration equipment for his classes.

In 1878 two important events occurred: He married Alice Howe Gibbens and he signed a publishing contract with Henry Holt, which resulted in one of psychology's classic books. It took James 12 years to write the book; he began the work on his honeymoon.

One reason James took so long to complete the book was that he was a compulsive traveler. If he was not in Europe, then he could be found in the mountains of New York or New Hampshire.

> *His letters give the impression that he periodically needed to be alone, that any intimate relationship was fatiguing for him over time, and that he saw travel as a crucial means of coping with restlessness. It was well known to James's friends that he arranged a journey in the aftermath of each child's birth, and then wrote to [his wife] about his guilt for having done so. He was often absent, if only as far away as Newport, on holidays such as Christmas, New Year's Day, and birthdays. . . . James's flights from his family were escapes from human entanglements to nature, solitude, and mystical relief.* (MYERS, 1986, PP. 36–37)

The births of his children were particularly unsettling to James's sensitive temperament. He found it impossible to work and resented his wife's attention to the newborns. After the second child was born, he left for Europe for a year, moving restlessly among several cities.

From Venice he wrote to his wife that he had fallen in love with an Italian woman. "You will get used to these enthusiasms of mine and like them," he told her (Lewis, 1991, p. 344). He believed that his attraction to other women was somehow a tribute to his wife; her thoughts on the matter were not recorded. Several months later he changed his mind, announcing that he was homesick. He asked if he might rent a room near their house and visit her a few hours each day.

James continued to teach at Harvard, when he was in town, and was promoted to professor of philosophy in 1885. Four years later, the title was changed to professor of psychology. He had by then met many European psychologists, including Wundt, who, he wrote, "made a pleasant and personal impression on me, with his agreeable voice and ready, tooth-showing smile." A few years later, however, he noted that Wundt "isn't a genius, he is a professor—a being whose duty is to know everything, and have his own opinion about everything" (quoted in Allen, 1967, pp. 251, 304).

James's book, *The Principles of Psychology,* was finally published in two volumes in 1890 and was a tremendous success. It is still considered a major contribution to the field. Almost 80 years after its publication one psychologist wrote: "James's *Principles* is without question the most literate, the most provocative, and at the same time the most intelligible book on psychology that has ever appeared in English or in any other language" (MacLeod, 1969, p. iii). It became the most influential textbook ever written in psychology and was required reading for several generations of students (Weiten & Wight, 1992). Indeed, it is still read by many who are not required to do so.

Not everyone reacted favorably to the book. Wundt and Titchener, whose views James attacked, did not like it. "It is literature," Wundt wrote, "it is beautiful, but it is not psychology" (Bjork, 1983, p. 12). James's own reaction to the book on its completion was not favorable either. In a letter to his publisher he described the manuscript as a "loathsome, distended, tumefied, bloated, dropsical mass, testifying to nothing but two facts: first, that there is no such thing as a science of psychology, and second, that [William James] is an incapable" (quoted in Allen, 1967, pp. 314–315).

With the publication of *The Principles,* James decided that he had nothing more to say about psychology and was no longer interested in supervising the psychology laboratory. He arranged for Hugo Münsterberg, then at the University of Freiburg, Germany, to become director of the Harvard laboratory and to teach the psychology courses, freeing James for work in philosophy. Münsterberg never fulfilled the role James intended for him—to provide leadership in experimental research for Harvard. Instead, Münsterberg worked in a variety of applied fields and paid scant attention to the laboratory. As we will see, he is important for helping to popularize psychology and to make it a more applied discipline.

Although James began and equipped Harvard's psychology laboratory, he was not an experimentalist. He was never convinced of the value of laboratory work and did not like it personally. He remarked that American universities had too many laboratories, and in *The Principles* he stated that the results of laboratory work were not in proportion to the amount of painstaking effort involved. It is not surprising, therefore, that he contributed little important experimental work to psychology.

James spent the last 20 years of his life refining his philosophical system, and by the 1890s was recognized as America's leading philosopher. He also published *Talks to Teachers,* to show how psychology could be applied to the classroom learning situation. The book marked the beginning of educational psychology and became the first textbook in the field (Berliner, 1993). *The Varieties of Religious Experience* appeared in 1902, followed by three additional works in philosophy.

At the age of 53, James became smitten with Pauline Goldmark, "a perfect little serious rosebud," who was a 21-year-old senior student at Bryn Mawr College (quoted in Rosenzweig, 1992, p. 182). "I fairly dote upon her," he wrote to a friend, "and were I younger and 'unattached' should probably be deep in love" (quoted in Rosenzweig, 1992, p. 188).

Three years later, while on a camping trip in the Adirondack Mountains with Ms. Goldmark and several companions, James overexerted himself and aggravated a heart lesion that would prove fatal. Excited by Ms. Goldmark's presence and fatigued by a lengthy hike and lack of sleep, James unwisely insisted on carrying an extra load of camping equipment the next day, in a "brave display of prowess" (Rosenzweig, 1992, p. 183). The strain caused irreparable damage to his heart. He died in 1910, 2 days after returning from a final trip to Europe.

The Principles of Psychology

Why is James considered by many to be the greatest American psychologist? Three reasons have been suggested for his overwhelming stature and influence. First, James wrote with a clarity rare in science. His writing style has magnetism, spontaneity, and charm. Second, he opposed the Wundtian position that the goal of psychology was the analysis of consciousness into elements. Third, James offered an alternative way of looking at the mind, an approach congruent with the new American functional approach to psychology. In brief, the times were ready for what James had to say.

In *The Principles of Psychology* James presents what subsequently became the central tenet of American functionalism: the goal of psychology is not the discovery of the elements of experience but rather the study of living people as they adapt to their environment. The function of consciousness, James wrote, is to guide us to those ends required for survival. Consciousness is vital to the needs of complex beings in a complex environment; without it, human evolution could not have occurred.

The book treats psychology as a biological science. This approach was not new, but James's writings steered psychology in a different direction from Wundt's formulations. James was concerned with mental processes as useful, functional activities of living organisms as they attempt to maintain themselves and adapt to their world.

James also emphasized nonrational aspects of human nature. People are creatures of action and passion as well as of thought and reason. Even when discussing purely intellectual processes, James stressed the nonrational. He noted that intellect operates under the physiological influences of the body, that beliefs are determined by emotional factors, and that reason and concept formation are affected by human wants and needs. Thus, James did not consider human beings to be wholly rational creatures.

We describe several of the major areas James wrote about in *The Principles.*

The Subject Matter of Psychology: A New Look at Consciousness

James stated at the beginning of *The Principles* that "Psychology is the Science of Mental Life, both of its phenomena and their conditions" (James, 1890, Vol. 1, p. 1). In terms of subject matter, the key words are *phenomena* and *conditions.* "Phenomena" is used to indicate that the subject matter is to be found in immediate experience; "conditions" refers to the importance of the body, particularly the brain, in mental life.

According to James, the physical substructures of consciousness form a basic part of psychology. He recognized the importance of considering consciousness in its natural setting, which is the physical human being. This awareness of biology, of the action of the brain on consciousness, is a unique feature of James's approach to psychology.

James rebelled against the artificiality and narrowness of the Wundtian position. Conscious experiences are simply what they are, James wrote, not groups or collections of elements. The discovery of discrete elements through introspective analysis does not show that these elements exist independently of an observer. Psychologists may read into an experience whatever their systematic position or viewpoint tells them should be there.

A trained food taster learns to discriminate individual elements in a flavor that may not be perceived by the untrained person. The untrained person experiences while eating a fusion of flavor elements, a total blend not capable of analysis. Similarly, James argued, the fact that some people can analyze their conscious experiences in a psychology laboratory does not mean that the discrete elements they report are present in the consciousness of anyone else exposed to the same experience. James considered such an assumption to be the *psychologists' fallacy.*

Striking at the heart of Wundt's approach to psychology, James declared that simple sensations do not exist in conscious experience but exist only as the result of a convoluted process of inference or abstraction. In a blunt and eloquent statement, James wrote: "No one ever had a simple sensation by itself. Consciousness, from our natal day, is of a teeming multiplicity of objects and relations, and what we call simple sensations are results of discriminative attention, pushed often to a very high degree" (James, 1890, Vol. 1, p. 224).

In place of the artificial analysis and reduction of conscious experience to its alleged elements, James called for a new program for psychology. Mental life is a unity, he proclaimed, a total experience that changes. Consciousness is a continuous flow—he coined the phrase **stream of consciousness** to express this property—and any attempt to divide it into temporally distinct elements or phases can only distort it.

Because consciousness is always changing, we can never experience a thought or sensation more than once. We may think of an object or a stimulus on more than one occasion, but our thoughts will not be identical. They will differ because of the effect of intervening experiences. Consciousness, then, is cumulative and not recurrent.

The mind is also continuous. There are no sharp disruptions in the flow of consciousness. There may be gaps in time, such as during sleep, but on our awakening we have no difficulty making connection with the ongoing stream of consciousness. In addition, the mind is selective. Because we can attend to only a small part of our experiential world, the mind chooses from among the many stimuli to which it is exposed, filtering out some, combining or separating others, selecting or rejecting still others. The criterion of selection, according to James, is relevance. The mind selects relevant stimuli so that consciousness can operate in a logical manner, and a series of ideas can lead to a rational conclusion.

Above all, James emphasized the purpose of consciousness. He believed that consciousness must have some biological utility or it would not have survived over time. The purpose or function of consciousness is to enable us to adapt to our environment by allowing us to choose. James distinguished between conscious choice and habit; he believed habits to be involuntary and nonconscious. When we encounter a new problem and need to choose a new way of coping, consciousness comes into play. This emphasis on purposiveness reflects the impact of evolutionary theory.

STREAM OF CONSCIOUSNESS: James's idea that consciousness is a continuous, flowing process and that any attempt to reduce it to elements will distort it

The Methods of Psychology

Because psychology deals with a personal and immediate consciousness, introspection must be a basic tool. James wrote: "Introspective observation is what we have to rely on first and foremost and always. . . . the looking into our own minds and reporting what we there discover. Everyone agrees that we there discover states of consciousness" (James, 1890, Vol. 1, p. 185).

James was aware of the difficulties of introspection, and he accepted it as a less-than-perfect form of observation. He believed, however, that introspective results could be verified by appropriate checks and by comparing the findings obtained from several observers.

Although he did not make widespread use of the experimental method, James acknowledged its use as a means to psychological knowledge, primarily for psychophysics, for the analysis of space perception, and for research on memory.

To supplement introspective and experimental methods, James suggested the use of the comparative method in psychology. By inquiring into the psychological functioning of different populations—such as animals, infants, preliterate peoples, and mentally disturbed individuals—James believed that psychology could discover meaningful variations in mental life.

The methods James cited in his book point up a major difference between structural and functional psychologies: The American functionalism movement would not be restricted to a single technique, such as Wundtian introspection. It would apply other methods as well, and this eclecticism broadened the scope of psychology.

PRAGMATISM: The doctrine that the meaning of ideas is to be sought in their practical consequences

James emphasized the value for psychology of **pragmatism,** the basic tenet of which is that the validity of an idea or conception is to be tested by its practical consequences. The popular expression of the pragmatic viewpoint is "anything is true if it works." Pragmatism had been advanced in the 1870s by Charles Sanders Peirce, a mathematician and philosopher and a lifelong friend of James. Peirce's work remained largely unrecognized until James wrote a book entitled *Pragmatism* (1907), which formalized the doctrine as a philosophical movement. (It was Peirce, in an article published in 1869, who first described the new psychology of Fechner and Wundt for scholars in the United States [Cadwallader, 1992].)

The Theory of Emotions

James's theory of emotions, published in an article in 1884 and later in *The Principles,* contradicted current thinking about the nature of emotional states. Psychologists had assumed that the subjective mental experience of an emotional state precedes the bodily expression or action. The traditional example—we see a wild animal, we feel fear, and we run away—illustrates the idea that the emotion (fear) comes before the body's reaction (running away).

James reversed the order and stated that the arousal of the physical response precedes the appearance of the emotion, especially for what he termed the "coarser" emotions such as fear, rage, grief, and love. For example, we see the wild animal, we run, and *then* we experience the emotion of fear. "Our feeling of the [bodily] changes as they occur IS the emotion" (James, 1890, Vol. 2, p. 449). To support this contention James noted the introspective observation that if the bodily changes—such as increased heart rate, rapid breathing, and muscle tension—did not occur, then there would be no emotion! James's view of emotion stimulated considerable controversy and a great deal of research.

In an instance of simultaneous discovery, the Danish physiologist Carl Lange published a similar theory in 1885. The similarity between the two led to the designation **James-Lange theory of emotions.**

JAMES-LANGE THEORY OF EMOTIONS: The notion, simultaneously proposed by William James and Carl Lange, that arousal of a physical response precedes the appearance of an emotion

Habit

The chapter in *The Principles* dealing with habit is in keeping with James's interest in physiological influences. He described all living creatures as "bundles of habits" (James, 1890, Vol. 1, p. 104), and he considered habit to involve the nervous system. Repetitive or habitual actions serve to increase the plasticity of neural matter. As a result, habits become easier to perform on subsequent repetitions and require less conscious attention.

James also believed that habits have enormous social implications, as noted in this frequently quoted passage.

> *Habit . . . alone is what keeps us all within the bounds of ordinance. . . . It dooms us all to fight out the battle of life upon the lines of our nurture or our early choice, and to make the best of a pursuit that disagrees, because there is no other for which we are fitted, and it is too late to begin again. . . .*

> *Already at the age of twenty-five you see the professional mannerism settling down on the young commercial traveler, on the young doctor, on the young minister, on the young counselor-at-law. You see the little lines of cleavage running through the character, the tricks of thought, the prejudices . . . from which the man can by-and-by no more escape than his coatsleeve can suddenly fall into a new set of folds. On the whole, it is best he should not escape. It is well for the world that in most of us, by the age of thirty, the character has set like plaster, and will never soften again.* (JAMES, 1890, VOL. 1, P. 121)

Comment

James is one of the most important psychologists the United States has ever produced. *The Principles* was a major influence, and its publication has been acclaimed as a great event in the history of psychology, inspiring a series of reflective essays a century later (Donnelly, 1992; Johnson & Henley, 1990). The book affected the views of thousands of students and inspired psychologists to shift the new science of psychology away from the structuralist view and toward the formal founding of the functionalist school of thought.

It is also worth noting that James was instrumental in facilitating the graduate education of Mary Whiton Calkins and helping her overcome the barriers of prejudice and discrimination. Calkins later developed the paired-associate technique used in the study of memory and made significant and lasting contributions to psychology (Madigan & O'Hara, 1992).

Calkins became the first woman president of the American Psychological Association. In 1906 she was ranked 12th among the 50 most important psychologists in the United States, high praise from colleagues for a woman who was refused her PhD (Furumoto, 1990). She had never been allowed to enroll formally at Harvard, but James welcomed her into his seminars and urged the university to grant her the degree. The administration resisted, and James wrote to Calkins that it was "enough to make dynamiters of you and all women. I hope and trust that your application will break the barrier. I will do what I can" (quoted in Benjamin, 1993, p. 72). Despite James's efforts, Harvard would not award the doctoral degree to a woman, even though her examination (administered informally by James and other faculty members) was described as "brilliant."

Seven years later, in 1902, when Calkins was a professor at Wellesley and undertaking her memory research, Harvard offered to grant her a degree from Radcliffe College, established by Harvard to provide undergraduate education for women. Calkins declined to accept, arguing that she had completed the graduate degree requirements at Harvard, and that Harvard was discriminating against her because she was a woman. Harvard continued to refuse her requests for the degree she had earned; she was awarded an honorary degree by Columbia University (Denmark & Fernandez, 1992).

THE FOUNDING OF FUNCTIONALISM

The scholars associated with the founding of functionalism had no ambition to start a new school of thought. They protested against the restrictions and limitations of Wundt's version of psychology and of Titchener's structuralism, but they did not want to replace these with another formal "ism." A graduate student at the University of Chicago, which became a major center of functional psychology, recalled that the psychology department there was functional in orientation but "without self-consciousness and certainly without promoting functional psychology as a school" (McKinney, 1978, p. 145). Paradoxically, the formalization of this protest movement was imposed on it by the founder of structuralism: E. B. Titchener.

Titchener may have indirectly "founded" functional psychology when he adopted the word *structural* as opposed to *functional* in an article, "The Postulates of a Structural Psychology," published in the *Philosophical Review* in 1898. In this article Titchener pointed out the differences between structural and functional psychology and argued that structuralism was the only proper study for psychology.

By establishing functionalism as an opponent, Titchener unwittingly brought it into focus. "What Titchener was attacking was in fact nameless until he named it; hence he thrust the movement into high relief and did more than anyone else to get the term *functionalism* into psychological currency" (Harrison, 1963, p. 395).

THE CHICAGO SCHOOL

Not all the credit for founding functionalism can go to Titchener, of course, but those whom history has labeled the founders of functional psychology were reluctant founders, at best.

Two psychologists who contributed directly to the founding of functionalism were John Dewey and James Rowland Angell. In 1894 they arrived at the newly established University of Chicago; some time later, each man appeared on the cover of *Time* magazine.

JOHN DEWEY (1859–1952)

John Dewey had an undistinguished early life and showed little intellectual promise until his junior year at the University of Vermont. After graduation he taught high school for a few years and studied philosophy on his own, publishing several scholarly articles. He enrolled in graduate school at Johns Hopkins University in Baltimore, received his PhD in 1884, and taught at the universities of Michigan and Minnesota. In 1886 he published the first American textbook in the new psychology (entitled, appropriately, *Psychology*), which was popular until it was eclipsed by James's *The Principles of Psychology* in 1890.

Dewey spent 10 years at the University of Chicago, where he became a vital force in psychology. He established a laboratory school, then considered a radical innovation in education, which served as the cornerstone for the progressive education movement. He went to Columbia University in New York in 1904 to work on the application of psychology to educational and philosophical problems, another example of the practical orientation of many functional psychologists.

Dewey was brilliant but he was not a good teacher. One of his students recalled that he wore a green beret. "He would come [to class], sit down at a desk, and he'd lay the green cap down in front of him,

JOHN DEWEY

and then he would lecture to the green cap—in a monotone. . . . If there was anything that would put students to sleep, it was that. But if you could pay attention to what that guy had to say, it was well worth it" (May, 1978, p. 655).

The Reflex Arc

Dewey's 1896 article, "The Reflex Arc Concept in Psychology," published in the *Psychological Review*, was the point of departure for functional psychology. In this work—his most important and, unfortunately, his last contribution to psychology proper—Dewey attacked the psychological molecularism, elementism, and reductionism of the reflex arc with its distinction between stimulus and response. In doing so, he was arguing that neither behavior nor conscious experience could be reduced to parts or elements, as Wundt and Titchener claimed to do. Thus, Dewey was attacking the core of their approaches to psychology.

The proponents of the reflex arc argued that a behavior unit ends with the response to a stimulus, such as when a child withdraws his or her hand from a flame. Dewey suggested that the reflex forms more of a circle than an arc because the child's perception of the flame changes, thus serving a different function. Initially the flame attracted the child, but after feeling its effects, the child will now be repelled by the flame. The response has altered the child's perception of the stimulus (the flame) and so perception and movement (stimulus and response) must be considered as a unit and not as a composition of individual sensations and responses. Thus, Dewey argued that the behavior involved in a reflexive response cannot be meaningfully reduced to basic sensorimotor elements any more than consciousness can be meaningfully analyzed into elementary components.

This type of artificial analysis and reduction causes behavior to lose all meaning, leaving only abstractions in the minds of the psychologists performing the exercise. Dewey wrote that behavior should be treated not as an artificial scientific construct but in terms of its significance to the organism in adapting to the environment. Thus, the proper subject matter for psychology was the study of the total organism as it functions in its environment.

Dewey was strongly influenced by the theory of evolution. In the struggle for survival, both consciousness and behavior function for the organism, with consciousness bringing about the appropriate behavior that enables the organism to survive. A functional psychology, therefore, was the study of the organism in use.

It is interesting to note that Dewey never called his psychology *functionalism.* He did not believe that structure and function could be meaningfully separated, despite his attack on structuralism's basic premise. It remained for Angell and others to proclaim that functionalism and structuralism were opposing forms of psychology (Tolman, 1993).

Dewey's significance for psychology lies in his influence on psychologists and other scholars and his development of the philosophical framework for the new school of thought. When he left the University of Chicago in 1904, the leadership of the functionalist movement passed to Angell.

JAMES ROWLAND ANGELL (1869–1949)

James Rowland Angell molded the functionalist movement into a working school of thought. He made the psychology department at the University of Chicago the most influential of the day, the major training ground for functional psychologists.

Angell was born into an academic family in Vermont. His grandfather had been president of Brown University in Providence, Rhode Island, and his father was president of the University of Vermont and, later, the University of Michigan. Angell did his undergraduate work at Michigan, where he studied under Dewey and read James's *The Principles of Psychology,* which, Angell reported, influenced his thinking more than any other book he ever read. He worked with James for a year at Harvard and received his master's degree in 1892.

He continued his graduate studies at the University of Halle, Germany, disappointed to learn that Wundt would not accept any more students at Leipzig that year. Angell did not receive his doctoral degree. His dissertation was accepted conditionally—he needed to rewrite it in better German—but to do so he would have to remain at Halle without any source of income. He chose, instead, to accept an appointment at the University of Minnesota, where the salary, although low, was better than nothing, particularly for a young man eager to end a 4-year engagement and get married. Although he never earned a PhD, Angell was instrumental in granting doctorates to many others, and in the course of his career he received 23 honorary degrees.

After a year at Minnesota, Angell went to the University of Chicago, where he remained for 25 years. Following in the family tradition, he became president of Yale University, where he helped to develop the Institute of Human Relations. In 1906 he was elected the 15th president of the American Psychological Association. After retiring from academic life, he served on the board of the National Broadcasting Company (NBC).

JAMES ROWLAND ANGELL

The Province of Functional Psychology

In 1904 Angell published a textbook, *Psychology,* that embodied the functionalist approach. The book was so successful that it appeared in four editions by 1908, indicating the appeal of the functionalist position. In it he maintained that the function of consciousness is to improve the organism's adaptive abilities. The goal of psychology was to study how the mind assists this adjustment of the organism to its environment.

A more important contribution to functional psychology is Angell's 1906 presidential address to the American Psychological Association, published in the *Psychological Review* (1907). In this paper, entitled "The Province of Functional Psychology," he articu-lated the functionalist viewpoint. We have seen that new movements gain vitality and momentum only with reference to, or in opposition to, an established position. Angell drew the battle lines from the beginning, but he concluded his introductory remarks modestly: "I formally renounce any intention to strike out new plans; I am engaged in what is meant as a dispassionate summary of actual conditions."

Functional psychology, Angell said, was not at all new but had been a significant part of psychology from the earliest times. It was structural psychology that had set itself apart from the older and more truly pervasive functional form of psychology.

He brought together three major themes of the functionalist movement:

1. Functional psychology is the psychology of mental operations in contrast to the psychology of mental elements (structuralism). Titchenerian elementism was still strong, and Angell promoted functionalism in direct opposition to it. The task of functionalism is to discover how a mental process operates, what it accomplishes, and under what conditions it occurs.

2. Functional psychology is the psychology of the fundamental utilities of consciousness. Consciousness, viewed in this utilitarian spirit, mediates between the needs of the organism and the demands of its environment. Structures and functions of the organism exist because, by allowing the organism to adapt to its environment, they have enabled it to survive. Angell believed that because consciousness has survived, it, too, must perform an essential service for the organism. Functionalism had to discover precisely what this service was, not only for consciousness, but also for more specific mental processes, such as judging and willing.

3. Functional psychology is the psychology of psychophysical (mind/body) relations, concerned with the total relationship of the organism to its environment. Functionalism encompasses all mind/body functions and holds that there is no real distinction between mind and body. It considers them not as different entities but as belonging to the same order and assumes an easy transfer from one to the other.

Comment

Angell's address to the American Psychological Association was given at a time when the spirit of functionalism was already firmly established. He shaped that spirit into an active, prominent enterprise with a laboratory, a body of research data, an enthusiastic staff of teachers, and a dedicated core of graduate students. In guiding functionalism to the status of a formal school, he gave it the focus and stature necessary to make it effective. He continued to insist, however, that functionalism did not really constitute a school of thought and should not become identified exclusively with the University of Chicago. The formal school of functionalism flourished, however, despite Angell's disclaimers, and was often referred to as the "Chicago school." It became permanently associated with the kind of psychology taught and practiced there.

HARVEY A. CARR (1873–1954)

Harvey Carr majored in mathematics at DePauw University in Indiana and at the University of Colorado, and switched to psychology because of the friendliness of his professor. Because there was no psychology laboratory at Colorado, Carr transferred to the University of Chicago, where his first course in experimental psychology was taught by the young assistant professor Angell. In Carr's 2nd year at Chicago, in which he served as a laboratory assistant, he worked with John B. Watson, then an instructor and later the founder of the behaviorist school of psychology. Watson introduced Carr to animal psychology.

After Carr received his PhD in 1905, he taught at a Texas high school and then at a state teachers college in Michigan. In 1908 he returned to Chicago to replace Watson, who had moved to Johns Hopkins University. Carr eventually succeeded Angell as head of Chicago's psychology department and went on to extend Angell's theoretical position on functionalism. During Carr's tenure as chair (1919–1938), the psychology department awarded 150 doctoral degrees.

HARVEY A. CARR

FUNCTIONALISM: THE FINAL FORM

The work of Carr represents functionalism when it no longer needed to crusade against structuralism; it had become a recognized position in its own right. Under Carr, functionalism at Chicago reached its peak as a formally defined system. He held the view that functional psychology was *the* American psychology. Other versions of psychology that were then developing—such as behaviorism, Gestalt psychology, and psychoanalysis—were regarded as needlessly exaggerated forms operating on limited aspects of psychology. Carr thought that these schools had little to add to the all-encompassing functionalist psychology.

Because Carr's book, *Psychology* (1925), is an expression of the finished form of functionalism, it is instructive to consider two of its major points. First, Carr defined the subject matter of psychology as mental activity—processes such as memory, perception, feeling, imagination, judgment, and will. Second, the function of mental activity is to acquire, fixate, retain, organize, and evaluate experiences and to use these experiences to determinate one's actions. Carr called the specific form of action in which mental activities appear adaptive or adjustive behavior.

We see in Carr's ideas functional psychology's familiar emphasis on mental processes rather than on the elements and content of consciousness. And we see also a description of mental activity in terms of what it accomplishes in enabling the organism to adapt to its environment. It is significant that by 1925 these issues were accepted as fact, no longer as matters for dispute. By then, functionalism was the mainstream psychology. "Since most psychologists considered themselves functionalists to one degree or another, the label began to lose its significance. One was simply a psychologist; the functional attitude went without saying since it was part of being a psychologist" (Wagner & Owens, 1992, p. 10).

Carr accepted data from both introspective and experimental methods, and believed, as did Wundt, that the study of cultural creations, such as literature and art, could provide information on the mental activities that produced them. Although functionalism did not adhere to a single methodology, as did structuralism, in practice there was an emphasis on objectivity. A great deal of the research undertaken at the University of Chicago used methods other than introspection, and where it was used, it was limited as much as possible by objective controls. It is also important to note that both animals and humans served as subjects in the research.

The Chicago school of functionalism promoted the shift away from the exclusive study of the subjective mind or consciousness toward the study of objective, overt behavior. Functionalism helped to move American psychology to the point where eventually it focused *only* on behavior, dropping the study of the mind altogether. In this way the functionalists provided a bridge between structuralism and the next revolutionary movement: Watson's behaviorism.

Original Source Material on Functionalism:
From *Psychology*
by Harvey A. Carr

The following discussion is reprinted from Chapter I of Carr's Psychology, *published in 1925.[1] It discusses the finished form of functionalism and covers these topics:*

[1] From Harvey A. Carr, *Psychology* (New York: Longmans, Green, 1925), pp. 1–14.

1. *the subject matter of functional psychology, with illustrations of the kinds of adaptive acts in which the mind engages;*

2. *the psychophysical nature of mental activity, showing the relationship between mental activities and their physiological basis;*

3. *the research methods of functional psychology, indicating the variety of data collection methods;*

4. *the relationship between functional psychology and the other sciences, noting that psychology gathers data from and can be applied to other disciplines, as well as to problems of everyday life.*

The subject matter of psychology   Psychology is primarily concerned with the study of *mental activity*. This term is the generic name for such activities as perception, memory, imagination, reasoning, feeling, judgment, and will. The essential features of these various activities can hardly be characterized by a single term, for the mind does various things from time to time. Stated in comprehensive terms, we may say that mental activity is concerned with the acquisition, fixation, retention, organization, and evaluation of experiences, and their subsequent utilization in the guidance of conduct.

The type of conduct that reflects mental activity may be termed *adaptive or adjustive behavior. . . .* An adaptive act is a response on the part of an organism in reference to its physical or social environment of such a character as to satisfy its motivating conditions. Illustrations of these mental operations may be drawn from the professional education of a physician. At times his mind is mainly engaged in the task of acquisition from lectures, books, and clinics, or from his experiences as a practitioner. At other moments his mind is primarily engaged in the attempt to memorize certain important data. Again, the reflective activities may predominate, and his mind is concerned with the task of analyzing, comparing, classifying, and relating the data in hand to other aspects of his medical knowledge. Finally comes the aspect of adaptive conduct—the use of this knowledge and skill in diagnosis, treatment, or surgical operation. . . .

The importance of these various aspects of mental activity is apparent on a moment's reflection. Retention is essential to all learning, mental development, and social progress. The acquisition of an act of skill involves a series of successive trials or practice periods during which the act is gradually perfected and established. Each step of progress is a result of the preceding trials. The effects of each practice period are retained and it is these accumulated effects that render the succeeding attempts more facile. Without retention there could be no mind. If any individual should suddenly lose all his past experiences, he would become almost as helpless as an infant.

Our experiences must be properly organized and systematized in order to be utilized effectively. In popular speech, we often say that an insane person has lost his mind. As a matter of fact these people do have minds. They accumulate, organize, and evaluate their experiences in some sort of fashion, and they react to the world on the basis of these experiences. These people have disordered minds. Their experiences are improperly organized and evaluated.

Theoretically, any group of experiences can be organized in various ways. An individual's manner of thinking and the character of his conduct are functions to a large extent of his previous organization. Certain types of organization are conducive to irrational modes of thought and to antisocial forms of behavior. Experiences must not only be organized, but they must be properly organized in order to be utilized effectively in reacting to the world in an intelligent and rational fashion.

The mind is also continuously evaluating the various aspects of experience. The mind not only labels things as good, bad, and indifferent, but it also arranges the good things of life in a crude scale of relative worth. Aesthetic appreciation in the realms of literature, music, and the graphic arts illustrates this function. Ethical values may also be cited. We label social conduct as right and wrong and develop concepts of such virtues as charity, chastity, honesty, sobriety, and punctuality. An individual's system of values constitutes perhaps the most important aspect of his personality.

Some students overemphasize the relative value of study and become bookworms and grinds. Some boys attach too great an importance to the value of financial independence, and leave school to seek a job. Some people underestimate the importance of neatness of dress, correct habits of speech, courtesy, kindliness, and many other traits that make for an effective personality in social relations. Some individuals take their politics, their religion, or their science too seriously, and overestimate the relative importance of those aspects of life. . . . The mind does evaluate its experiences, and an individual's conduct is to a large extent a function of his ideals and system of values.

All experiences of an individual during life are thus organized into a complex but unitary system of reaction tendencies that determine to a large extent the nature of his subsequent activity. The reactive disposition of an individual, in other words, what he does and what he can and cannot do, is a function of his native equipment, of the nature of his previous experiences, and of the way in which these have been organized and evaluated. The term *self* is generally employed to characterize an individual from the standpoint of his reactive disposition.

We also speak of an individual's personality when we wish to refer to all those traits and characteristics of his self that make or mar his efficiency in dealing with other individuals, while the term mind is used when we wish to characterize an individual from the standpoint of his intellectual characteristics and potentialities. . . .

Psychology is thus concerned with the study of personality, mind, and the self, but these are conceptual objects that can be studied only indirectly through their manifestations—only insofar as they express themselves in the reactions of the individual. The various concrete activities involved in an act of adjustment are the observable data and the subject matter of psychology.

The psychophysical nature of mental activity   These various mental operations that are involved in the performance of an adjustive response are usually termed *psychophysical processes.* By their physical character, we mean that they are acts of which the individual has some knowledge. For example, an individual not only perceives and reacts to an object, but he is at least aware of the fact and he may have some knowledge of the nature and significance of those acts. Individuals are not accustomed to reason, make decisions and react on the basis of those decisions and be wholly oblivious of the fact. The performance of any mental act on the part of an individual implies some sort of experiential contact with that act. For this reason we shall refer to these mental acts from time to time as *experiences or experiential activities.*

These acts are not only experienced, but they are also the reactions of a physical organism. They are acts that directly involve such structures as the sense organs, muscles, and nerves. The participation of sense organs and muscles in such activities as perception and voluntary acts is obvious. The nervous system is also concerned in every mental act. While this fact is not one of the obvious sort, yet the truth of the doctrine has been thoroughly established.

The integrity of these structures is essential to normal mental activity. An excision or lesion in any part of the brain is usually correlated with some sort of a mental disturbance. All conditions that affect the metabolism of these structures also influence the character of the mental operations. We shall make no attempt to explain the nature of this psychophysical relationship. We merely note the fact that these mental acts are psychophysical events and insist that they must be studied as such. . . .

Methods of approach   Mental acts can be studied from several avenues of approach. Mental acts can be directly observed, they can be studied indirectly through their creations and products, and finally they can be studied in terms of their relation to the structure of the organism.

Mental acts may be subjectively or objectively observed. Objective observation refers to the apprehension of the mental operations of another individual insofar as these are reflected in his behavior. Subjective observation refers to the apprehension of one's own mental operations. Subjective observation is often termed *introspection,* and in times past it was regarded as a unique mode of apprehension different in kind from that involved in perceiving an external event. As a matter of fact, the two processes are essentially alike in nature and they can be differentiated only in terms of the objects cognized [perceived or recognized]. Each mode of observation possesses certain advantages and limitations.

1.   Introspection gives us a more intimate and comprehensive knowledge of mental events. Some mental events cannot be objectively apprehended. For example, we might know from an individual's behavior that he is engaged in thought without being able to tell what he is thinking about.

The individual himself not only knows that he is thinking but is keenly aware of the topic under consideration. Neither will objective observation give us any clue as to whether these thoughts are mediated in terms of words or visual imagery. Introspection often reveals the motives and considerations derived from past experience that influence us in any particular act. It would be very difficult to obtain knowledge of this character by the exclusive use of the objective method.

2. Subjective observations are rather difficult. Many mental operations consist of a series of complex and rapidly shifting events that are difficult to analyze and apprehend in a comprehensive manner. Inasmuch as our minds are usually engaged in dealing with objective situations, many people encounter a considerable amount of difficulty in the attempt to break this habit and become introspective.

3. The validity of a subjective observation cannot always be tested. Given a report by a subject that he thinks by means of visual imagery, any verification or disproof of this statement is practically impossible inasmuch as this particular mental event can be observed only by that individual. Neither can we decide that the statement is untrue because other people assert that they think in verbal terms, for it is possible that individuals may differ in their manner of thinking. On the other hand, any objective act can be observed by several people and their reports compared.

4. Naturally the use of the subjective method must be confined to subjects of training and ability. Psychology must thus rely upon the objective method in the study of animals, children, primitive peoples, and many cases of insanity.

5. Instruments may be used to record and measure any of the objective manifestations of mind. These records can then be analyzed at leisure. Acts can be detected in this manner that would otherwise escape our notice. For example, photography has been utilized as a means of studying the finer eye movements that are involved in an act of perception. This method has been extensively employed in the study of perceptual activities involved in reading and in certain visual illusions.

Subsidiary to observation is the method of experimentation. In an experiment, the mental operations are observed under certain prescribed and defined conditions. An experiment is often called a controlled observation. An experiment may be relatively simple or quite complex according to the degree of control that is exercised. As an illustration of a simple type of experiment, we may cite the case of memorizing a list of words for the purpose of analyzing this process and discovering some of the conditions that influence our ability to recall this material on some subsequent occasion. In general, the performance of any mental act for the purpose of studying that act may be termed an experiment.

A psychological experiment does not necessarily involve the employment of an elaborate technique and complicated forms of apparatus. The character of the apparatus is a function of the problem. Instruments are employed as a means of controlling the experimental conditions, or as a means of measuring and recording any feature of the experimental situation.

The primary value of an experiment depends upon the fact that the observations are made under certain prescribed and specified conditions. An experiment is thus a means of discovering facts and relations that would escape detection during the ordinary course of experience. Furthermore, the results of any experiment can be tested by other investigators.

The experimental method has its limitations in the field of psychology. Not all aspects of the human mind are subject to control. An individual's mental reactions are to a very large extent a function of his previous experiences. A complete experimental control of a human mind implies a freedom in manipulating its development throughout life in ways that are both impossible and socially undesirable.

The nature of mind may also be studied indirectly through its creations and products—industrial inventions, literature, art, religious customs and beliefs, ethical systems, political institutions, and so forth. This method might well be termed the social avenue of approach. Naturally this method will not be used when the mental operations themselves can be studied. Consequently the method is mainly utilized in the study of primitive races or of past civilizations. The method in practice is essentially historical or anthropological. Obviously our knowledge of the human mind would be exceedingly limited if we were forced to rely exclusively upon such data. Facts of this character, however, are significant for an understanding of the developmental aspects of mind.

Mental acts can also be studied from the standpoint of anatomy and physiology. The structure of any organ and its functional possibilities are intimately related. The neurologist attempts to conceive of the structural arrangements of the nervous system in terms of their relation to the various activities in which they are involved. A study of the mutual relations between mental acts and the architectural features of the nervous system will obviously clarify the conceptions of both psychology and neurology.

We know that the character of mental acts is influenced by the metabolic conditions of the nervous system. Neural defects are frequently correlated with disturbances of perception, memory, recall, and voluntary activity. A considerable portion of our accurate and detailed knowledge of the relation of mental operations to the nervous structures has been gained in this way. Certain parts of the nervous structures are excised in animals and the effect of this loss of nerve tissue upon the subsequent ability of the organism is noted. Many features of mind must be explained in terms of the physiological peculiarities of the nervous system. The fact of retention, certain temperamental peculiarities of mind, and some aspects of the process of forgetting must be explained in this manner.

It is thus apparent that any fact is a psychological datum whenever it can be utilized in comprehending the nature and significance of the mental operations. The same fact may be significant to several sciences such as neurology, psychology, and physiology, and such a fact will constitute a part of the data of each of these branches of knowledge.

Psychology like the other sciences utilizes any fact that is significant for its purposes irrespective of how or where or by whom it was obtained. No single avenue of approach can give a complete knowledge of a mental act. The various sources of knowledge supplement each other and psychology is concerned with the task of systematizing and harmonizing the various data in order to form an adequate conception of all that is involved in the operations of mind. . . .

Relation to other sciences   Psychology gathers materials from a great many fields of human endeavor. Psychology appropriates any facts that are significant for an understanding of mind. A professional psychologist naturally encounters a very limited range of mental phenomena and hence must gather his materials from a great variety of sources. Psychology takes facts from sociology, education, neurology, physiology, biology, and anthropology, and hopes in time to be able to borrow from biochemistry. Most of our factual knowledge concerning the great variety of mental disorders has been contributed by physicians and psychiatrists. Peculiar facts of mind and personality are frequently contributed by the legal profession. The various practices of business and industry contribute many suggestive data. In fact, psychological materials can be gathered from any line of human endeavor.

Psychology in turn is interested in making whatever contributions it can to all allied fields of thought and endeavor such as philosophy, sociology, education, medicine, law, business, and industry. Naturally, any knowledge of human nature will be extremely serviceable to any field of endeavor that is in any way concerned with human thought and action.

FUNCTIONALISM AT COLUMBIA UNIVERSITY

We noted that there was not a single approach to, or form of, functional psychology, as there was a single structural psychology. Although the primary development and founding of functionalism occurred at the University of Chicago, another approach was being shaped by Robert Woodworth at Columbia University. We will see that Columbia was also the academic base for two other psychologists with a functional orientation: James McKeen Cattell, whose work on mental tests embodied the American functionalist spirit, and E. L. Thorndike, whose research on problems of animal learning reinforced the functionalist trend toward greater objectivity.

ROBERT SESSIONS WOODWORTH (1869–1962)

Robert Woodworth did not belong formally to the functionalist school in the tradition of Angell and Carr. He expressed dislike for the constraints imposed by membership in any school of thought. Nevertheless, much of what Woodworth wrote about psychology was in the functionalist spirit of the Chicago school, and he went on to add an important new ingredient.

Woodworth was active in psychology for more than 70 years as a researcher, beloved teacher, writer, and editor. After receiving his bachelor's degree from Amherst College in Massachusetts, he taught high school science and then mathematics at a small college. During that period he reported two experiences that changed his life. First, he heard the noted psychologist G. Stanley Hall give a talk, and second, he read William James's *The Principles of Psychology*. He knew then that he had to become a psychologist.

He enrolled at Harvard University, where he earned his master's degree, and received his PhD in 1899 from Cattell at Columbia. Woodworth taught physiology in New York City hospitals for 3 years and spent another year working with the physiologist Charles Scott Sherrington in England. In 1903 he returned to Columbia, where he remained until his first retirement in 1945. He was so popular, however, that he continued to lecture to large classes until 1958, when he retired from Columbia for a second time, at the age of 89.

A former student, Gardner Murphy, remembered Woodworth as the best teacher he had ever had in a psychology course. Murphy described Woodworth "entering the classroom in an unpressed, baggy old suit, and wearing army shoes." He would walk to the blackboard and "utter some inimitable word of insight or whimsy, which would go into our notebooks to be remembered in the decades that followed" (Murphy, 1963, p. 132).

Woodworth described his view of psychology in a number of journal articles and in two books, *Dynamic Psychology* (1918) and *Dynamics of Behavior* (1958). He wrote an introductory text, *Psychology,* published in 1921, which appeared in five editions by 1947 and is said to have outsold every other psychology text for 25 years. His *Experimental Psychology* (1938, 1954) also became a classic. In 1956 Woodworth received the first Gold Medal Award of the American Psychological Foundation for having made "unequaled contributions to shaping the destiny of scientific psychology" as an "integrator and organizer of psychological knowledge."

Archives of the History of American Psychology/University of Akron

ROBERT SESSIONS WOODWORTH

Dynamic Psychology

Woodworth maintained that his approach was not really new but was the one followed by "good" psychologists even in the days before psychology became a science. Psychological knowledge must begin, he said, with an investigation of the nature of the stimulus and the response—that is, with objective, external events. But when psychology considers *only* the stimulus and the response in attempting to explain behavior, it misses what may be the most important part—the living organism itself. The stimulus is not the complete cause of a particular response. The organism, with its varying levels of energy and its current and past experiences, also acts to determine the response.

Psychology must consider the organism itself as interpolated between the stimulus and the response. It follows, Woodworth said, that the subject matter for psychology must be both consciousness and behavior (a position later adopted by the humanistic psychologists and the social-learning theorists). The external stimulus as well as the overt response may be uncovered by the objective observation of behavior, but what occurs inside the organism can be known only through introspection. Woodworth accepted introspection as a useful tool for psychology, along with observational and experimental methods.

DYNAMIC PSYCHOLOGY:
Woodworth's system of psychology concerned with the causal factors and motivations in feelings and behavior

Woodworth introduced into functionalism a **dynamic psychology** that elaborated on the teachings of Dewey and James. (The word *dynamic* had been used as early as 1884 by Dewey and 1908 by James.) A dynamic psychology is concerned with motivation. As Woodworth put it, he intended to develop a "motivology."

Although there are similarities between Woodworth's position and that of the Chicago functionalists, Woodworth emphasized the physiological events underlying behavior. His dynamic psychology focused on cause-and-effect relationships, and he believed that psychology's goal should be to determine why people behave as they do. Thus his primary interest was in the forces that drive or motivate the human organism.

Woodworth did not feel the need to adhere to a single system, nor did he desire to develop his own school of thought. His viewpoint was built not from protest but from extension, elaboration, and synthesis as he sought to select the best features from the other systematic approaches.

CRITICISMS OF FUNCTIONALISM

Attacks on the functionalist movement came quickly and vehemently from the structuralists. For the first time, at least in the United States, the new psychology was divided into warring factions. Titchener's laboratory at Cornell and the functionalist psychology department at Chicago became the respective headquarters of the structuralist and functionalist enemy camps. Accusations, charges, and countercharges were flung back and forth between the universities with all the righteousness typical of those convinced they possess the only truth.

One criticism directed against functionalism was that the term itself had not been clearly defined. In 1913, C. A. Ruckmick, a student of Titchener's, examined 15 general psychology textbooks to determine how function was defined by the various writers. The two most common usages were "an activity or process," and "a service to other processes or to the whole organism."

In the first usage, function is essentially the same as activity; for example, remembering and perceiving are functions. In the second usage, function is defined in reference to the usefulness of some activity to the organism, such as the function of digesting food or breathing. Ruckmick charged that the functionalists sometimes used the word *function* to describe an activity and sometimes to refer to its use.

It was some 17 years before anyone in the functionalist school answered this charge of inconsistent and ambiguous usage. Writing in 1930, Harvey Carr argued that the two definitions were not inconsistent because both referred to the same processes. Functional psychologists were interested in a particular activity both for its own sake (the first definition) *and* for its relationship to other conditions or activities (the second definition). A similar practice was followed in biology, he noted. However, it has been suggested that "Functionalism used the concept first and defined it later; and this sequence of events is characteristic of the movement" (Heidbreder, 1933, p. 228).

Another criticism, particularly from Titchener, related to the definition of psychology. Titchener's structuralists claimed that functionalism was not psychology at all because it did not adhere to the subject matter and methodology of structuralism! In Titchener's view, any approach other than the introspective analysis of the mind into elements was not really psychology. Of course, it was his definition of psychology that the functionalists were questioning in the first place.

Other critics found fault with the functional psychologists' interest in practical or applied concerns, a manifestation of the long-standing controversy between pure and applied science. The structuralists did not look favorably on applied psychology. The functionalists, however, were unconcerned with maintaining psychology as a pure science and never apologized for their practical interests.

Carr suggested that rigorous scientific procedures could be adhered to in both pure and applied psychology and that valid research could be performed in a factory, office, or classroom, as well as in a university laboratory. It is the method and not the subject matter, Carr noted, that determines how scientific a field of inquiry is. This controversy between pure and applied science is no longer so extreme in American psychology, largely because applied psychology is so pervasive. We may consider this practical application of psychology to real-life problems to be functionalism's most important contribution.

CONTRIBUTIONS OF FUNCTIONALISM

Functionalism's vigorous opposition to structuralism was of immense value to the development of psychology in the United States. The long-range consequences of the shift in emphasis from structure to function were also significant. One result was that research on animal behavior, which was not part of the structuralist approach, became an important part of psychology.

The functionalists' broadly defined psychology also incorporated studies of infants, children, and people with mental disabilities. In addition, functionalism allowed psychologists to supplement the introspective method with other ways of obtaining data, such as physiological research, mental tests, questionnaires, and objective descriptions of behavior. All these methods, rejected by the structuralists, became, to the functionalists, respectable sources of information for psychology.

DISCUSSION QUESTIONS

1. Describe Spencer's notion of social Darwinism. How did social Darwinism influence American psychology?
2. How did James's view of consciousness differ from Wundt's view? According to James, what was the purpose of consciousness? What methods did James consider appropriate for the study of consciousness?
3. Describe the contributions of Titchener and Dewey in founding functional psychology.
4. According to Angell, what were three major themes of the functionalist movement? What research methods did Carr consider appropriate for functional psychology?
5. Describe Woodworth's dynamic psychology and his views on the use of introspection.
6. Compare functionalism's contributions to psychology with the contributions of structuralism.

SUGGESTED READINGS

Crissman, P. (1942). The psychology of John Dewey. *Psychological Review, 49,* 441–462. Reviews and evaluates concepts in Dewey's approach to psychology.

Donnelly, M. E. (Ed.). (1992). *Reinterpreting the legacy of William James.* Washington, DC: American Psychological Association. Essays on James's ideas as anticipations of issues in modern psychology.

Lewis, R. W. B. (1991). *The Jameses: A family narrative.* New York: Farrar, Straus and Giroux. An account of the remarkable James family, including William (psychologist), Henry (novelist), Alice (political radical), Wilky (war hero), and Bob (alcoholic).

McKinney, F. (1978). Functionalism at Chicago: Memories of a graduate student, 1929–1931. *Journal of the History of the Behavioral Sciences, 14,* 142–148. Describes the faculty, students, course work, and intellectual Zeitgeist of the psychology department at the University of Chicago.

Owens, D. A., & Wagner, M. (Eds.). (1992). *Progress in modern psychology: The legacy of American functionalism.* Westport, Conn. Praeger/Greenwood. Examines the idea of functional psychology as a distinct school of thought and evaluates its impact on contemporary psychology.

Thorne, F. C. (1976). Reflections on the Golden Age of Columbia's psychology. *Journal of the History of the Behavioral Sciences, 12,* 159–165. Describes the faculty and research orientation of the psychology department at Columbia University from 1920 to 1940.

CHAPTER 8

FUNCTIONALISM'S LEGACY:

APPLIED PSYCHOLOGY

THE GROWTH OF PSYCHOLOGY
IN THE UNITED STATES

EVOLUTIONARY DOCTRINE and the functional psychology that derived from it rapidly took hold in the United States toward the
end of the 19th century, and we have seen that American psychology was guided much more by the ideas of Darwin and Galton
than by the work of Wundt. This was a curious, even paradoxical, historical phenomenon. Wundt trained many of the first generation of
American psychologists in his form of psychology. Yet they brought
few of his ideas home with them. When these students of Wundt's,
these new psychologists, returned to the United States, they set about
establishing a psychology that bore little resemblance to what Wundt
had taught them. Thus, the new science, not unlike a living species,
was changing to adapt to its new environment.

Wundt's psychology and Titchener's structuralism could not long
survive in their original form in the American intellectual climate,
the American Zeitgeist, and so they evolved into functionalism. They
were not practical kinds of psychology; they did not deal with the
mind in use and could not be applied to the everyday demands and
problems of life. American culture was oriented toward the practical;
people valued what worked. "We need a psychology that is usable,"
wrote G. Stanley Hall, America's pioneer applied psychologist.
"Wundtian thoughts can never be acclimated here, as they are an-
tipathetic to the American spirit and temper" (Hall, 1912, p. 414).

The newly trained American psychologists returned from Germany and in typically direct and aggressive American fashion transformed the German species of psychology. They began to study not what the mind *is* but what it *does*. While some American psychologists—notably James, Angell, and Carr—were developing the functionalist approach in academic laboratories, others were applying it in settings outside the universities. The move toward a practical psychology was occurring at the same time that functionalism was being founded as a separate school of thought.

The applied psychologists took their psychology into the real world, into the schools, factories, advertising agencies, courthouses, child guidance clinics, and mental health centers, and made of it something functional in both subject matter and use. In doing so, they changed the nature of American psychology as radically as did the academic founders of functionalism. The professional literature of the day reflects their impact. By around 1900, 25% of the research articles published in American psychology journals dealt with applied psychology, and less than 3% involved introspection (O'Donnell, 1985). The approaches of Wundt and Titchener, themselves so recently the new psychology, were rapidly being overtaken by a newer psychology.

Even Titchener, the great structural psychologist, recognized this sweeping change in American psychology. In 1910 he wrote: "If, then, one were asked to sum up, in a sentence, the trend of psychology during the past ten years, one's reply would be: Psychology has leaned, very definitely, toward application" (quoted in Evans, 1992, p. 74).

Psychology grew and prospered rapidly in the United States. The vibrant and dynamic development of American psychology during the years 1880 to 1900 is a striking event in the history of science. In 1880 there were no laboratories in the United States; by 1900 there were 42, and they were better equipped than laboratories in Germany. In 1880 there were no American psychology journals; by 1895 there were three. In 1880, Americans had to go to Germany to study psychology; by 1900 they could enter graduate programs at home. By 1903, more PhDs were awarded by American universities in psychology than in any other science except chemistry, zoology, and physics.

In 1910, more than 50% of all published articles in psychology were written in the German language; only 30% were in English. By 1933, 52% of the articles published were in English and only 14% in German (Wertheimer & King, 1994). The British publication *Who's Who in Science* for 1913 stated that the United States was predominant in psychology, having more of the world's leading psychologists—numbering 84—than Germany, England, and France combined (Jonçich, 1968).

In little more than 20 years after psychology began in Europe, American psychologists had assumed undisputed leadership in the field. James McKeen Cattell reported in his presidential address to the American Psychological Association in 1895 that the "academic growth of psychology in America during the past five years is almost without precedent. . . . Psychology is a required subject in the undergraduate curriculum . . . and among university courses psychology now rivals the other leading sciences in the number of students attracted and in the amount of original work accomplished" (Cattell, 1896, p. 134). In 1898 a Harvard psychology professor lamented that, "My elementary psychology course . . . has 360 students—what will this country do with all these psychologists?" (Brown, 1992, p. 65).

Psychology made its debut before an eager American public at the World's Fair of 1893, held in Chicago, Illinois. In a program similar to Francis Galton's Anthropometric Laboratory in England, psychologists organized exhibits of research apparatus and a testing laboratory in which, for a fee, visitors could have their sensory capacities measured. A more extensive exhibition was mounted at the 1904 Louisiana Purchase Exposition in St. Louis, Missouri. This star-studded event featured lectures by the leading psychologists of the day— E. B. Titchener, C. Lloyd Morgan, Pierre Janet, G. Stanley Hall, and John B. Watson. Such a popular display of psychology would not have found favor with Wundt, and nothing like it ever took place in Germany. The popularizing of psychology reflected the American temperament that so substantially remade Wundt's form of psychology into functional psychology and extended it far beyond the experimental laboratory.

Thus, America embraced psychology with enthusiasm, and the field quickly became established in college classrooms and in people's daily lives. Its scope today is far broader than its founders ever thought possible, or even desirable.

ECONOMIC INFLUENCES ON APPLIED PSYCHOLOGY

Although the American Zeitgeist, the intellectual spirit and temper of the times, helped to foster the emergence of applied psychology, other more practical contextual forces were also responsible for its development. In chapter 1 we discussed the role of economic factors in shifting the focus of American psychology from pure research to application. While the number of psychology laboratories was increasing toward the end of the 19th century, the number of Americans with doctoral degrees in psychology was growing three times as fast. Many of these new PhDs, particularly those without an independent source of income, had to look beyond the university for economic survival.

The psychologist Harry Hollingworth (1880–1956), for example, could not afford to live on his annual salary of $1,000 for teaching at Barnard College in New York City. He supplemented it by teaching courses at other universities, proctoring examinations for $.50 an hour, and conducting workshops on psychology for advertising executives to try to support his goal of a life devoted to research and scholarly activities. He soon found, however, that he had no choice but to become an applied psychologist to make a living (Benjamin, Rogers, & Rosenbaum, 1991).

Hollingworth was not alone. Other pioneers in applied psychology acted out of economic necessity. This does not mean that they did not find practical work to be stimulating and challenging. Most did, and they also came to recognize that human behavior and mental life could be studied in real-world settings as effectively as in the academic laboratory. It should also be noted that some psychologists chose to work in applied areas out of genuine desire. Yet the fact remains that many of the first generation of applied psychologists in the United States were compelled to abandon their dreams of pure academic experimental research as the only way to escape a life of poverty.

The situation was more critical for psychologists who taught at less well endowed state universities in the Midwest and West at the turn of the century. By 1910, one third of all American psychologists held such positions, and as their numbers grew, so did the pressure on them to deal with practical problems and thus prove that this new field of psychology had some financial worth.

In 1912, C. A. Ruckmick surveyed his fellow psychologists and concluded that psychology was held in low esteem in American colleges and universities, despite its popularity with students. It was poorly funded and equipped, and there seemed to be little hope for improvement (Leary, 1987). Perhaps the only way to increase departmental budgets and faculty salaries was to demonstrate to college administrators and state legislators that the science of psychology could help cure society's ills.

G. Stanley Hall advised a colleague in the Midwest to make psychology's influence felt "outside the university, lest some irresponsible, sensational man or party criticize it in the legislature." Cattell urged his colleagues to "make practical applications and develop a profession of applied psychology" (quoted in O'Donnell, 1985, pp. 215, 221).

The solution, then, was obvious: make psychology more valuable by applying it. But to what? Fortunately, the answer soon became clear. Public school enrollments were increasing dramatically; between 1870 and 1915 they rose from 7 to 20 million. The amount of money spent on public education during that period grew from $63 million to $605 million (Siegel & White, 1982). Education was suddenly big business, and it got the psychologists' attention.

Hall proclaimed in 1894 that the "one chief and immediate field of application for [psychology] was its application to education" (quoted in Leary, 1987, p. 323). Even William James, who could not be considered an applied psychologist, wrote a book, *Talks to Teachers,* on the uses of psychology in the classroom (James, 1899). By 1910 more than one third of all American psychologists expressed interest in applying psychology to problems in education. Three fourths of those calling themselves applied psychologists were already working in that area. Psychology had found its place in the real world.

We discuss in this chapter the careers and contributions of five applied psychologists who extended the new science into education, business and industry, psychological testing, the criminal justice system, and mental health clinics. All of these men were trained at Leipzig by Wilhelm Wundt to become academic psychologists, but all moved away from Wundt's teachings when they began their careers in American universities. They provide striking examples of how American psychology came to be influenced more by Darwin and Galton than by Wundt, and how the Wundtian approach was refashioned when transplanted to American soil. We also describe the beginnings of three major areas of applied psychology: psychological testing, industrial/organizational psychology, and clinical psychology.

GRANVILLE STANLEY HALL (1844–1924)

Hall compiled an outstanding record of firsts in American psychology. He received the first American doctoral degree in psychology, and he claimed to be the first American student in the first year of the first psychology laboratory.[1] Hall began what is often considered to be the first psychology laboratory in the United States as well as the first American journal of psychology. He was the first president of Clark University, the organizer and first president of the American Psychological Association, and one of the first applied psychologists.

Hall's Life

G. Stanley Hall was born on a farm in Massachusetts and from an early age exhibited a high level of ambition. At 14, he pledged to "do and be something in the world" (quoted in Ross, 1972, p. 12). At 17, he was deeply ashamed when, at the onset of the American Civil War, his father purchased a draft exemption for him. Hall said he felt the need to do penance, to atone for not doing his duty by serving in the army (Vande Kemp, 1992).

[1] New data of history reveal that he was actually the second; see Benjamin, Durkin, Link, Vestal, & Acord, 1992.

Archives of the History of American Psychology/University of Akron

GRANVILLE STANLEY HALL

In 1863 he entered Williams College. By the time he graduated, Hall had won a number of honors and had developed an enthusiasm for philosophy, especially evolutionary theory, which was to influence his career in psychology. After graduation, "still being very uncertain as to what I would be and do in the world" (quoted in Bringmann, Bringmann, & Early, 1992, p. 282), he enrolled in the Union Theological Seminary in New York City, although without a strong commitment to the ministry. His interest in evolution was no advantage in this situation, and he was not noted for his religious orthodoxy. The story is told that when Hall gave his trial sermon to the faculty and students, the seminary president knelt and prayed for Hall's soul.

On the advice of the famous preacher Henry Ward Beecher, Hall went to the University of Bonn, Germany, to study philosophy and theology. He traveled to Berlin, where he added studies in physiology and physics. He supplemented this phase of his education by visits to theaters and beer gardens, daring experiences for a young man of pious upbringing. He wrote of his amazement at seeing a theology professor drinking beer on a Sunday. Hall also recorded his romantic interludes, noting that two passionate affairs revealed capacities in himself "hitherto unusually dormant and repressed and [that] thus made life seem richer and more meaningful" (quoted in Lewis, 1991, p. 317). Hall's European sojourn was a time of liberation.

He returned home in 1871, 27 years old, with no degree and heavily in debt. He completed his seminary studies (although he was not ordained) and preached in a country church in Cowdersport, Pennsylvania, for all of 10 weeks. After working as a private tutor for more than a year, Hall secured a teaching job at Antioch College in Ohio. He taught English literature, French and German languages and literature, and philosophy, served as librarian, led the choir, and preached in the chapel.

In 1874 he read Wundt's *Physiological Psychology,* and it aroused his interest in the new science, causing him some uncertainty about his career. He took a leave of absence from Antioch, settled in Cambridge, Massachusetts, and became a tutor in English at Harvard. In addition to teaching sophomore English, Hall began his own graduate studies and conducted research at the medical school. In 1878 he presented his dissertation on the muscular perception of space and was awarded the first degree in psychology in the United States.

Immediately after receiving his doctoral degree, Hall left for Europe again, first to study physiology at Berlin and then to become Wundt's student at Leipzig, where he lived next door to Fechner. The anticipation of working with Wundt was apparently greater than the reality. Although Hall attended Wundt's lectures and dutifully served as a subject in the laboratory, he conducted his own research along more physiological lines, and his subsequent career clearly shows that

Wundt ultimately had little influence on him. When Hall returned to the United States in 1880 he had no prospect of a job, yet within a span of 10 years he had become a figure of national importance.

Hall recognized, when he returned from Germany, that the best chance to satisfy his ambition was in the application of psychology to education. In 1882 he gave a talk to a meeting of the National Education Association (NEA), urging that the psychological study of the child be made a major component of the teaching profession. He repeated this message at every opportunity. The president of Harvard invited him to deliver a series of Saturday morning talks on education. These speeches brought Hall much favorable publicity and an invitation to lecture part-time at Johns Hopkins University, established 5 years earlier as the first graduate school in the United States.

Hall's lectures were a great success, and he was offered a professorship at Hopkins in 1884. During his time there he began what is usually considered to be the first American psychology laboratory (formally established in 1883), which he called his "laboratory of psychophysiology" (Pauly, 1986, p. 30). He taught a number of students who later became prominent psychologists, among them John Dewey and James McKeen Cattell.

In 1887 Hall founded the *American Journal of Psychology,* the first psychology journal in the United States and still an important publication. It provided a platform for theoretical and experimental ideas and a sense of solidarity and independence for American psychology. In a burst of enthusiasm Hall had printed an excessive number of copies of the first issue; it took 5 years for the journal and Hall to pay back those initial costs.

In 1888 Hall became the first president of Clark University in Worcester, Massachusetts. Before taking the job, he embarked on an

Ferdinand Hamburger, Jr. Archives, The Johns Hopkins University

Hall's psychology laboratory at Johns Hopkins University is considered to be the first in the United States.

extended tour abroad to study European universities and to hire faculty for his new school. The trip also served as a "paid vacation for labors not yet commenced. . . . it included a number of stops wholly irrelevant to the task ahead, such as Russian military academies, ancient Greek historical sites, and [the] standard run of brothels, circuses, and curiosities" (Koelsch, 1987, p. 21).

Hall aspired to make Clark a graduate university along the lines of Johns Hopkins and the German universities, with the emphasis on research rather than on teaching. Unfortunately, the founder—the wealthy merchant Jonas Gilman Clark—had different ideas and did not provide as much money as Hall had been led to expect. After Clark died in 1900, the endowment was designated for the founding of an undergraduate college, which had been opposed by Hall but long advocated by Clark.

Hall made Clark University more receptive to women and minority students than were most other schools in the United States at that time. Although he shared the nationwide opposition to coeducation for undergraduates, he did admit women as graduate students and junior faculty. He also took the unusual step of encouraging Japanese students to enroll at Clark, and the unprecedented step of encouraging African Americans to become graduate students. The first Black American to earn a PhD in psychology, Francis Sumner, studied with Hall. Sumner went on to a distinguished career as chair of the psychology department at Howard University in Washington, D.C., where he "established a solid program that was critical in bringing psychology to Blacks and Blacks to psychology" (Dewsbury & Pickren, 1992, p. 137). Hall refused to restrict the hiring of Jewish faculty members at a time when most universities would not hire them (Guthrie, 1976; Sokal, 1990).

At Clark University, Hall was professor of psychology as well as university president, and he taught in the graduate school for several years. He established, at his own expense, the journal *Pedagogical Seminary* (now the *Journal of Genetic Psychology*), to serve as an outlet for research in child study and educational psychology. In 1915 he founded the *Journal of Applied Psychology*, bringing the number of American psychology journals to 16.

The American Psychological Association (APA) was founded in 1892, largely through Hall's efforts. At his invitation, approximately a dozen psychologists met in the study of his home to plan the organization, and they elected him the first president. By 1900 the group included 127 members.

Hall maintained his interest in religion with the founding of the Clark School of Religious Psychology and of the *Journal of Religious Psychology* (1904), which ceased publication after a decade. In 1917 he published a book entitled *Jesus, the Christ, in the Light of Psychology*. His depiction of Jesus as a kind of "adolescent superman" was not well received by organized religion (Ross, 1972, p. 418).

Psychology at Clark prospered under Hall. During his 36 years there, 81 doctorates were awarded in psychology. His students remember the exhausting but exhilarating Monday evening seminars at Hall's home, when doctoral candidates were quizzed by the faculty and other graduate students. After the meetings, which lasted up to 4 hours, a household servant would bring in a gigantic tub of ice cream.

Hall's comments on his students' papers were often devastating. "Hall would sum things up," Lewis Terman recalled, "with an erudition and fertility of imagination that always amazed us and made us feel that his offhand insight into the problem went immeasurably beyond that of the student who had devoted months of slavish drudgery to it." And when the evening sessions ended, Terman said he "always went home dazed and intoxicated, took a hot bath to quiet my nerves, then lay awake for hours rehearsing the drama and formulating the clever things I should have said and did not" (quoted in Sokal, 1990, p. 119).

The graduate students were awed by Hall. One recalled:

Hall was a man of powerful build, standing taller than six feet. He was frequently seen operating his hand lawn mower along the three-foot bank that sloped from his front yard down to the sidewalk. . . . Striding easily along the top edge of the slope, his left hand in his pocket, he manipulated the mower up and down with his right, in successively brisk push and pull from one end of the bank to the other, a good one hundred feet away. Sometimes as he moved he carried on a conversation with a student pacing the sidewalk beside him. (AVERILL, 1990, P. 125)

Adept at nurturing intelligent students, as long as they were properly deferential, Hall could be generous and supportive. At one time it could be claimed that the majority of American psychologists had been associated with Hall either at Clark or at Johns Hopkins, although he was not the primary source of inspiration for all of them. Perhaps his personal influence is reflected best in the fact that one third of his doctoral students eventually went into college administration, as he had done.

Hall was one of the first Americans to become interested in psychoanalysis and was largely responsible for the early attention it received in the United States. In 1909, to celebrate the 20th anniversary of the founding of Clark University, he invited Sigmund Freud and Carl Jung to participate in a series of conferences, an invitation that was courageous because of the suspicion with which psychoanalysis was viewed. Hall also invited his former teacher, Wilhelm Wundt, who declined because of age and because he was scheduled to be the featured speaker at the 500th anniversary of his own university.

Hall continued to write after his retirement from Clark in 1920. He died 4 years later, a few months after his election to a second term as president of the APA. After his death a survey was taken of APA members to evaluate Hall's contributions to psychology. Of the 120 people who responded, 99 ranked Hall among the world's top 10 psychologists. Many of them praised his teaching ability, his efforts in promoting psychology, and his defiance of orthodoxy, but they, and others who knew him, were critical of his personal qualities. He was described as difficult to get along with, untrustworthy, unscrupulous, devious, and aggressively self-promoting. William James once called him the "queerest mixture of bigness and pettiness I ever knew" (quoted in Myers, 1986, p. 18). Even his critics, however, would have agreed with the judgment of the APA survey: "[Hall] has been the cause of more writing and research than any other three men in the field" (Koelsch, 1987, p. 52).

Evolution as a Framework for Human Development

Although Hall was interested in many areas, his intellectual wanderings had a single theme: evolutionary theory. His work on a variety of topics in psychology was governed by the conviction that the normal growth of the mind involved a series of evolutionary stages. Thus, using the theory of evolution as a framework for broad theoretical and applied speculations, Hall contributed more to educational psychology than to experimental psychology. Only in the early phase of his career did he focus on experimental psychology. He agreed that the experimental method was important for psychology, but he became impatient with its limitations. Laboratory work in the new psychology proved too narrow for Hall's more general goals and efforts.

Hall is often called a genetic psychologist because of his concern with human and animal development and with the related problems of adaptation. At Clark, Hall's genetic interests led him to the psychological study of childhood, which he made the core of his psychology. In a speech at the 1893 Chicago World's Fair he said, "Hitherto we have gone to Europe for our psychology. Let us now take a child and place him in our midst and let America make her own psychology" (Siegel & White, 1982, p. 253). Hall intended to apply his psychology to the functioning of the child in the real world. As a former student aptly remarked, "The child became, as it were, his laboratory" (Averill, 1990, p. 127).

In his child studies Hall made extensive use of questionnaires, a procedure he had learned in Germany. By 1915 Hall and his students had developed and used 194 questionnaires covering many topics (White, 1990). So extensive was his use of questionnaires that for a time the method came to be associated in the United States with Hall's name, even though the technique had been developed earlier by Galton.

These early studies of children generated great public enthusiasm and led to the formalization of the **child study movement.** The movement disappeared in a few years because of poorly executed research, however. The subject samples were inadequate, the questionnaires unsound, the data collectors untrained, and the data poorly analyzed—an effort considered "very poor psychology, inaccurate, inconsistent and misguided" (Thorndike quoted in Berliner, 1993, p. 54). Despite such deserved criticism, the child study movement established the importance of both the empirical study of the child and the concept of psychological development.

CHILD STUDY MOVEMENT: A program based on Hall's research to study psychological development in children

Hall's most influential work is the lengthy (some 1,300 pages), two-volume *Adolescence: Its Psychology, and Its Relations to Physiology, Anthropology, Sociology, Sex, Crime, Religion, and Education,* published in 1904. This encyclopedia contains the most complete statement of Hall's **recapitulation theory of psychological development.** He believed that children in their personal development repeat the life history of the human race. The book went through several printings, one done 20 years after its initial publication.

RECAPITULATION THEORY OF PSYCHOLOGICAL DEVELOPMENT: Hall's idea that children, in their personal development, repeat the life history of the human race

Adolescence also became controversial because of what some considered an excessive focus on sex. Hall was accused of having prurient interests. In a book review, the psychologist E. L. Thorndike wrote that "the acts and feelings, normal and morbid, resulting from sex are discussed in a way without precedent in English science." Thorndike was even more critical in a letter to a colleague, saying that Hall's book was "chock full of errors, masturbation and Jesus. He is a mad man" (quoted in Ross, 1972, p. 385). At the time, Hall was giving a series of lectures at Clark on sex. This was considered to be scandalous, even though he did not allow women to attend. He eventually stopped the talks because "too many outsiders got in and even listened surreptitiously at the door" (Koelsch, 1970, p. 119).

Many psychologists were uneasy about Hall's enthusiasm for sex. "Is there no turning Hall away from this d——d sexual rut?" wrote Angell to Titchener. "I really think it is a bad thing morally and intellectually to harp so much on the sexual string" (quoted in Boakes, 1984, p. 163). They need not have worried; the productive and energetic Hall soon moved on to other interests.

As Hall grew older he naturally became curious about the final stage of human development. At the age of 78 he published *Senescence* (1922), which was the first large-scale survey of psychological issues of old age. In the last few years of his life he wrote two autobiographies, *Recreations of a Psychologist* (1920) and *The Life and Confessions of a Psychologist* (1923).

Comment

Hall was once introduced to an audience as the "Darwin of the mind." The characterization evidently pleased him, and it vividly expressed his aspirations and the attitude that permeated his work. He was introduced to another audience as the "greatest authority in the world on the study of the child," and reportedly said that the praise was correct (Koelsch, 1987, p. 58). Throughout his career he remained versatile and agile. His enthusiasm was bold, diverse, and nontechnical, and it is perhaps this characteristic that made him so stimulating and influential.

In his second autobiography he wrote, "All my active conscious life has been made up of a series of fads or crazes, some strong, some weak; some lasting long . . . and others ephemeral" (Hall, 1923, pp. 367–368). It was a perceptive observation. Hall was aggressive, quixotic, and often at odds with colleagues, but never dull.

JAMES MCKEEN CATTELL

Archives of the History of American Psychology/University of Akron

JAMES MCKEEN CATTELL (1860–1944)

The functionalist spirit of American psychology was also well represented in the life and work of James McKeen Cattell, who directed the movement toward a practical, test-oriented approach to the study of mental processes. Cattell's psychology was concerned with human abilities rather than conscious content, and in this respect he comes close to being a functionalist.

Cattell's Life

James McKeen Cattell was born in Easton, Pennsylvania. He earned his bachelor's degree in 1880 at Lafayette College, where his father was president. Following the custom of going to Europe for graduate study, Cattell went first to the University of Göttingen and then to Leipzig and Wilhelm Wundt.

A paper in philosophy won him a fellowship to Johns Hopkins University in 1882. At the time, his major interest was philosophy, and during his first semester at Hopkins no psychology courses were offered. It appears that Cattell became interested in psychology as a result of his own experiments with drugs. He tried a variety of substances ranging from hashish, morphine, and opium to caffeine, tobacco, and chocolate. He found the results to be of both personal and professional interest. Some drugs, notably hashish, cheered him considerably and reduced the depression he had been experiencing. He also took note of the effects of the drugs on his mental functioning.

"I felt myself making brilliant discoveries in science and philosophy," he confided to his journal, "my only fear being that I could not remember them until morning." Later he wrote, "Reading has become uninteresting. I keep reading without paying much attention. It takes a long time to write a word. I'm rather confused" (quoted in Sokal, 1981a, pp. 51, 52). Cattell was not so confused, however, that he failed to recognize the psychological importance of the drugs, and he observed his own behavior and mental state with increasing fascination. "I seemed to be two persons," he wrote, "one of whom could observe and even experiment on the other" (quoted in Sokal, 1987, p. 25).

During Cattell's second semester at Johns Hopkins, G. Stanley Hall began to teach classes in psychology, and Cattell enrolled in Hall's laboratory course. Cattell began to conduct experiments on reaction time—the time required for different mental activities—and the results of this work reinforced his desire to become a psychologist.

Cattell's return to Wundt in Germany in 1883 is the subject of some popular stories in the history of psychology, which provide additional examples of how historical data can be distorted. Cattell allegedly appeared at the University of Leipzig and boldly announced to Wundt, "Herr Professor, you need an assistant, and I shall be your assistant" (Cattell, 1928, p. 545). Cattell made it clear to Wundt that he would choose his own research project, on the psychology of individual differences, a topic that was not central to Wundtian psychology. Wundt is said to have characterized Cattell and his project as *ganz Amerikanisch* ("typically American"), which was a prophetic remark. The interest in individual differences, a natural outcome of an evolutionary point of view, has since been a feature of American and not German psychology.

Cattell supposedly gave Wundt his first typewriter, on which most of Wundt's books were written. For this gift Cattell was teased by his colleagues for having "done a serious disservice . . . for it had enabled Wundt to write twice as many books as would otherwise have been possible" (Cattell, 1928, p. 545).

Careful archival research on Cattell's letters and journals indicates that these stories are questionable (see Sokal, 1981a). Cattell's account of these events, written many years later, is not supported by his own correspondence and journal entries written at the time the events occurred. Wundt apparently thought highly of Cattell and appointed him as his laboratory assistant in 1886. Also, there is no evidence that Cattell wanted to study individual differences at that time. Cattell introduced Wundt to the use of the typewriter, but he did not give him one.

After Cattell obtained his doctorate in 1886, he returned to the United States to lecture on psychology at Bryn Mawr College and the University of Pennsylvania. He became a lecturer at Cambridge University in England, where he met Francis Galton. The two had similar interests and views on individual differences, and Galton, then at the peak of his fame, "provided [Cattell] with a scientific goal—the

measurement of the psychological differences between people"
(Sokal, 1987, p. 27). Cattell admired Galton's versatility and his emphasis on measurement and statistics. As a result, Cattell became one
of the first American psychologists to stress quantification, ranking,
and ratings, even though personally he was "mathematically illiterate" (Sokal, 1987, p. 37). Cattell developed the order of merit method
(also called the ranking method), which is widely used in psychology,
and was the first psychologist to teach the statistical analysis of experimental results.

Wundt did not favor the use of statistical techniques, so it was the
direct influence of Galton on Cattell that was responsible for the fact
that the new American psychology came to resemble Galton's work
more than Wundt's. This also explains why American psychologists
began to focus on studies of large groups of subjects, for which statistical comparisons could be made, rather than on individual subjects
(the approach favored by Wundt).

Cattell was also interested in Galton's work in eugenics, and he
argued for the sterilization of delinquents and "defectives," and for
the offering of incentives to healthy, intelligent people if they would
intermarry. He offered his seven children $1,000 each if they would
marry the sons or daughters of college professors (Sokal, 1971).

In 1888 Cattell became professor of psychology at the University
of Pennsylvania, an appointment arranged for him by his father.
Learning that an endowed chair in philosophy was to be established
at the university, the elder Cattell lobbied the school's provost, an old
friend, to secure the post for his son. The elder Cattell urged his son
to publish more articles to enhance his professional reputation, and
he even traveled to Leipzig to obtain Wundt's personal letter of rec-
ommendation. He told the provost that because the family was
wealthy, salary was not a consideration, and thus Cattell was hired
for an extremely low salary (O'Donnell, 1985). Cattell would later
claim, inaccurately, that his was the first psychology professorship in
the world, but his appointment was actually in philosophy. He stayed
at Pennsylvania only 3 years, then left to become professor of psychology and head of the department at Columbia University, where
he remained for 26 years.

Because of his dissatisfaction with Hall's *American Journal of
Psychology,* Cattell began the *Psychological Review* in 1894 with J.
Mark Baldwin. Cattell acquired from Alexander Graham Bell the
weekly journal *Science,* which was about to cease publication for lack
of funds. Five years later it became the official journal of the
American Association for the Advancement of Science (AAAS). In
1906 Cattell began a series of reference books, including *American
Men of Science* and *Leaders in Education.* He bought *Popular Science
Monthly* in 1900; after selling the name in 1915, he continued to publish it as *Scientific Monthly.* Another weekly, *School and Society,* was
established in 1915. The phenomenal organizing and editing work

required a great deal of his time and, not surprisingly, his research productivity in psychology declined.

During his career at Columbia more doctorates in psychology were awarded there than at any other graduate school in the United States. Cattell emphasized the importance of independent work and gave his students considerable freedom to conduct research on their own. He believed that a professor should maintain some distance from the university and the students, so he lived 40 miles from the campus. He established a laboratory and an editorial office at home and visited the university only a few days each week.

This aloofness was only one of several factors that strained relations between Cattell and the university administration. He urged increased faculty participation in university affairs, arguing that many decisions should be made by faculty and not by administrators. To this end, he helped to found the American Association of University Professors (AAUP). He was not considered tactful in his dealings with the Columbia University administration, and has been described as difficult, "ungentlemanly, irretrievably nasty, and lacking in decency" (Gruber, 1972, p. 300).

On three occasions between 1910 and 1917 the trustees considered retiring Cattell. The deciding blow fell during World War I, when Cattell wrote two letters to United States congressmen protesting the practice of sending draftees into combat. This was an unpopular position to take, but Cattell remained adamant. He was dismissed from Columbia in 1917 on the grounds that he had been disloyal to his country. He sued the university for libel, and although he was awarded $40,000, he was not reinstated. He isolated himself from his colleagues and wrote satirical pamphlets about the university administration. He made many enemies and remained embittered by the experience.

Cattell never returned to academic life. He devoted himself to his publications and to the AAAS and other learned societies. His promotional efforts for psychology elevated the new science to a higher standing in the scientific community.

In 1921 Cattell realized one of his ambitions, the promotion of applied psychology as a business. He organized the Psychological Corporation, with stock purchased by members of the APA, to provide psychological services to industry, the psychological community, and the public. The venture was a failure; in its first 2 years, the company made a profit of only $51. The situation did not improve as long as Cattell remained president. After he resigned, the organization's outlook improved. In 1969, the Psychological Corporation had $5 million in sales and was sold to the publisher Harcourt Brace Jovanovich, which 10 years after that reported $30 million in sales from the venture Cattell began (Landy, 1993).

Cattell remained active as an editor and spokesman for psychology until his death in 1944.

Mental Testing

MENTAL TESTS: Tests of motor skills and sensory capacities; intelligence tests use more complex tests of mental ability

In an article published in 1890 Cattell coined the term **mental tests,** and while at the University of Pennsylvania he administered a series of such tests to his students. "Psychology," Cattell wrote, "cannot attain the certainty and exactness of the physical sciences unless it rests on a foundation of experiment and measurement. A step in this direction could be made by applying a series of mental tests and measurements to a large number of individuals" (Cattell, 1890, p. 373). This is precisely what he was attempting to do. He continued the testing program at Columbia and collected data from several classes of entering students.

The kinds of tests Cattell used in trying to measure the range and variability of human capacities differed from the intelligence or cognitive ability tests psychologists developed later; intelligence tests use more complex tasks of mental ability. Cattell's tests, like Galton's, dealt primarily with elementary sensorimotor measurements: dynamometer pressure, rate of movement (how quickly the hand can move 50 cm), the two-point threshold for skin sensation, amount of pressure on the forehead necessary to cause pain, just noticeable differences in judging weights, reaction time for sound, time for naming colors, bisection of a 50-cm line, judgment of a 10-second time period, and number of letters remembered after a single presentation.

An instrument to measure vital capacity, the maximum volume of air that is exhaled after deep inhalation. Vital capacity was believed to be related to intelligence.

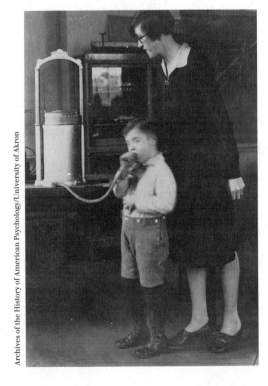

Archives of the History of American Psychology/University of Akron

By 1901 he had amassed enough data to correlate the test scores with measures of the students' academic performance. The correlations proved disappointingly low, as did intercorrelations among individual tests. Because similar results had been obtained in Titchener's laboratory, Cattell concluded that tests of this type were not valid predictors of college achievement, or, by assumption, of intellectual ability.

Comment

Cattell exerted his strongest impact on American psychology through his work as an organizer, executive, and administrator of psychological science and practice, and as an articulate link between psychology and the greater scientific community. He became an ambassador of psychology, delivering lectures, editing journals, and promoting the practical applications of the field.

Building on Galton's work, Cattell investigated the nature and origin of scientific ability, using his order of merit ranking technique. Stimuli ranked by a number of judges were arranged in a final rank order by calculating the average rating given to each stimulus item. The method was applied to eminent American scientists by having competent people in each scientific field rank in order a number of their outstanding colleagues. The source book *American Men of Science* emerged from this work. Despite the book's title, it also included American women of science. The 1910 edition lists 19 women psychologists, about 10% of the total number of psychologists cited (O'Donnell, 1985).

Cattell also contributed to the development of psychology through his students. During his years at Columbia he trained, as we noted, more graduate students in psychology than anyone else in the United States, and several—Robert Woodworth and E. L. Thorndike among them—became prominent in the field. Through his work on mental testing, the measurement of individual differences, and the promotion of applied psychology, Cattell energetically reinforced the functionalist movement in American psychology. When Cattell died, the historian E. G. Boring wrote to Cattell's children: "In my opinion your father did more than William James even to give American psychology its peculiar slant, to make it different from the German psychology from which it stemmed" (quoted in Bjork, 1983, p. 105).

THE PSYCHOLOGICAL TESTING MOVEMENT

Alfred Binet (1857–1911)

Although Cattell coined the term *mental tests,* it remained for Alfred Binet, an independently wealthy and self-taught French psychologist,

Alfred Binet (shown here with his daughters) developed the first truly psychological test of mental ability, which has evolved into the widely used Stanford-Binet Intelligence Scale.

The Bettmann Archive

to develop the first truly psychological test of mental ability. Binet used more complex measures than those selected by Cattell. Binet's approach provided an effective measure of human cognitive abilities and marked the beginning of modern intelligence testing.

Binet disagreed with the approach taken by Galton and Cattell, which used tests of sensorimotor processes in the attempt to measure intelligence. He believed that assessment of such cognitive functions as memory, attention, imagination, and comprehension would provide a better measure of intelligence. In 1904, the opportunity to prove his point arose in response to a practical need. The French ministry of public instruction appointed a commission to study the learning abilities of children who were having difficulties in school. Binet and a psychiatrist, Théodore Simon, were appointed to the commission, and together they investigated the kinds of intellectual tasks that most children could master at different ages.

From their delineation of these tasks they constructed the first intelligence test. It consisted of 30 problems arranged in ascending order of difficulty, and it focused on three cognitive functions: judgment, comprehension, and reasoning.

MENTAL AGE: The age at which children of average ability can perform certain tasks

Three years later the test was revised and expanded, and the concept of **mental age** was introduced. Binet and Simon defined mental age as the age at which children of average ability could perform certain tasks. For example, if a child with a chronological age of 4 passed all the tests that the sample of average 5-year-olds had passed, that 4-year-old child was assigned a mental age of 5.

A third revision of the test was prepared in 1911, but after Binet's death the development of intelligence tests shifted to the United States. Binet's work in testing became more widely accepted in the United States than in France. Large-scale intelligence testing programs did not become popular in France until some 35 years after Binet's death (Schneider, 1992).

Binet's test was translated from the French language and introduced to psychologists in the United States by Henry Goddard, a student of Hall's, who worked with mentally retarded children at a private school in Vineland, New Jersey. Goddard coined the word *moron,* derived from the Greek word for *slow.* He called his translation of the test the *Binet-Simon Measuring Scale for Intelligence.*

In 1916 Lewis M. Terman, who had also studied with Hall, developed a version of the test that has since become standard. He named it the *Stanford-Binet,* after the university with which he was affiliated, and adopted the concept of the **intelligence quotient (IQ).** (The IQ measure, defined as the ratio between mental age and chronological age, had originally been developed by the German psychologist William Stern.) The *Stanford-Binet* has undergone several revisions and continues to be widely used.

INTELLIGENCE QUOTIENT (IQ): A number denoting a person's intelligence, determined by multiplying mental age by 100 and dividing by chronological age

The Impact of World War I

On the day the United States entered World War I in 1917, a meeting of Titchener's Society of Experimental Psychologists was being held at Harvard University. The president of the APA, Robert Yerkes, was in attendance. Yerkes urged the psychologists present to consider how psychology could aid in the war effort. Titchener declined, explaining that he was a British subject. It is more likely that Titchener disdained war work because he disliked the idea of applying psychology to practical problems, fearing that psychology would be trading "a science for a technology" (O'Donnell, 1979, p. 289).

The army was faced with the problem of assessing the intelligence of great numbers of recruits, to classify them and assign them to suitable tasks. The *Stanford-Binet* was an individual test of intelligence, and a highly trained person was needed to administer it properly. Such a test could not be used for a large-scale testing program where many people must be evaluated in a short time. For that purpose, the army needed a group test that was simple to administer.

Yerkes, given an army commission as a major, assembled a staff of 40 psychologists to develop a group intelligence test. They examined a number of tests, none of which was in general use, and selected as a model one prepared by Arthur S. Otis, who had studied with Terman. Otis's contribution was the development of the multiple-choice type of question. The Yerkes group prepared the *Army Alpha* and *Army Beta,* based on Otis's test. (The *Beta* is a version of the *Alpha* for non-English-speaking and illiterate people. Instead of oral or written directions, instructions for the *Beta* are given by demonstration or pantomime.)

Work on the testing program proceeded slowly, and the formal order to actually begin testing recruits was not given until 3 months before the war ended. More than 1 million men were tested, but by then, the military no longer needed the results. Although the program had little direct effect on the war effort, it had a major impact on psychology. The publicity did a great deal to enhance psychology's stature, and the army tests became prototypes for many that were devised later.

Development and application of group testing for personality characteristics was also spurred by the war effort. Prior to that time only limited attempts had been made to assess the human personality. In the closing years of the 19th century the German psychiatrist Emil Kraepelin had used what he called a free-association test, in which a patient responded to a stimulus word with the first word that came to mind; the technique had been originated by Galton. In 1910 Carl Jung had developed a similar device, the word-association test, which he used to measure personality complexes in his patients. Both of these were individual personality tests. When the army expressed interest in separating out recruits who were highly neurotic, Robert Woodworth constructed the *Personal Data Sheet,* a self-report inventory on which respondents checked off the neurotic symptoms that applied to them. Like the *Army Alpha* and *Army Beta,* the *Personal Data Sheet* served as a prototype for the development of additional group tests.

Psychological testing won its own victory in the war, the victory that came with public acceptance. Before long, millions of employees, school children, and college applicants found themselves facing batteries of tests, the results of which could determine the course of their lives. In the early 1920s, as many as 4 million intelligence tests were being sold every year, mostly for use in public schools. Terman's *Stanford-Binet* sold over a half million copies in 1923, and the American public education system was reorganized around the concept of the intelligence quotient. IQ scores became the most important criterion for student placement (Brown, 1992).

An epidemic of testing swept the United States, but in the haste to answer the call of business and education, it was inevitable that some poorly designed and inadequately researched tests would appear, leading to disappointing results. The most notorious instance was a so-called intelligence test published in 1921 by the inventor Thomas Edison. He did little more than assemble a random series of questions, which he thought were exceedingly simple. Consider a few examples: "What telescope is the largest in the world?" "What is the weight of air in a room twenty by thirty by ten feet?" "What city in the United States leads in making laundry machines?"

The questions may have been simple for the genius Edison but not for the 36 college graduates to whom he administered his test. They could answer correctly few of the items, leading Edison to comment that, "Men who have gone through college I find to be amazingly ignorant. They don't seem to know anything" (Dennis, 1984,

p. 25). Edison's phony test received extraordinary publicity—the *New York Times* alone published 23 articles about it in one month—and it contributed significantly to the public's loss of faith in testing and to a decline in scientific prestige. The poorly researched work of Edison and others led many organizations to abandon the use of psychological tests during the mid-1920s.

Metaphors From Medicine and Engineering

In an attempt to lend authority and scientific credibility to their fledgling enterprise, intelligence testers adopted terminology from the long-established disciplines of medicine and engineering. Their purpose was to persuade people that psychology was just as legitimate, scientific, and essential as the older sciences (Keiger, 1993).

Psychologists described the people they tested not as subjects but as patients. The tests were said to be analogous to thermometers, which, at that time, were available only to physicians; no one without proper training was permitted to use a thermometer, a claim also made for psychological tests. Tests were promoted as X-ray machines that enabled psychologists to see inside the mind, to dissect the mental mechanisms of their patients. "The more [psychologists] sounded like doctors, the more willing the public was to accord them similar status" (Keiger, 1993, p. 49).

Metaphors from engineering were also used. Schools were referred to as education factories, and tests as ways to measure the products of those factories; that is, the intelligence levels of the children. Society was likened to a bridge, and intelligence tests were the scientific tool required to preserve the strength of that bridge by detecting its weakest elements—the feebleminded—which could be removed from society and placed in institutions.

Goddard wrote that mental tests "enable us to know a very fundamental fact about the human material, its mental strength. The mechanical engineer could never build bridges or houses if he did not know the strength of his materials, how much of a load each will support. Of how infinitely greater importance it is then when we seek to build up a social structure that we should know the strengths of our materials" (quoted in Brown, 1992, pp. 116–117).

By applying these metaphors, these analogies with other sciences, psychologists hoped to enhance their importance and credibility and to apply psychological testing to every level and facet of society.

Racial Issues

The growth of the testing movement became part of a great social controversy that still lingers today. In 1912, Goddard, who had translated the Binet test and coined the term *moron*, visited Ellis Island in

Archives of the History of American Psychology/University of Akron

HENRY GODDARD

A mental examination for an immigrant at Ellis Island; typically, 3 different examiners administered tests with the aid of an interpreter.

Archives of the History of American Psychology/University of Akron

New York, the point of entry for millions of European immigrants. He believed that the Binet test would be a useful screening device for keeping mentally defective people out of the United States (Gould, 1981).

On Goddard's first visit to Ellis Island, he selected a young man whom he thought looked mentally defective, and confirmed his diagnosis by administering the test with the aid of an interpreter. The interpreter pointed out that he could not have answered most of the questions when he was a new arrival in the United States and that the test was unfair to people who were unfamiliar with American culture, but Goddard disagreed.

Later testing of large immigrant populations revealed that the majority—some 87% of Russians, 83% of Jews, 80% of Hungarians, and 79% of Italians—were feebleminded, with a mental age below 12 (Gould, 1981). This so-called evidence from the application of intelligence tests was later used to support federal legislation to restrict the immigration of racial and ethnic groups alleged to be inferior in intelligence.

The idea of racial differences in intelligence received additional support in 1921 when the results obtained from testing the army recruits during World War I were made public. The data showed that the mental age of the draftees, and by extension of the White population as a whole, was only 13. Further, the data showed that Blacks had a lower measured IQ than Whites, as did immigrants from Mediterranean and Latin American countries. Only Northern European immigrants had IQs equal to White Americans.

These findings raised questions among scientists, politicians, and journalists. How could the American form of government survive if the populace was so stupid? Should groups with low IQs be allowed to vote? Should the government refuse entry to immigrants from low-IQ countries? How could the notion that people were created equal be meaningful?

The concept of racial differences in intelligence had been advanced in the United States as early as the 1880s, and there had been many calls for restrictions on immigrants from Mediterranean and Latin American countries. The allegedly inferior intelligence level of Blacks in the United States had also been widely accepted, even before the development of psychological tests to measure intelligence.

One of the most vocal and articulate critics of that view was Horace Mann Bond (1904–1972), an African American scholar and president of Lincoln University in Pennsylvania. Bond, who earned a doctoral degree in education from the University of Chicago, published a number of books and articles in which he argued that any differences in the IQ scores of Blacks and Whites were attributable to environmental rather than inherited factors. His research showed that Blacks from northern states scored higher on intelligence tests than did Whites from southern states, a finding that severely damaged the charge that Blacks were genetically inferior in intelligence (Urban, 1989).

Many psychologists responded to the claim of racial differences in intelligence by suggesting that the tests were biased. In time the controversy faded, only to be revived most recently in the book, *The Bell Curve* (Herrnstein & Murray, 1994), which argues, based on intelligence test scores, that Blacks are inferior in intelligence to Whites.

Psychologists are working to develop tests that are free of cultural and educational bias and that more accurately assess the full range of human abilities.

LIGHTNER WITMER (1867–1956)

While Hall was changing forever the nature of American psychology by applying it to the child and the schoolroom, and Cattell was applying psychology to the measurement of mental abilities, a student of Cattell's and Wundt's was applying it to the assessment and treatment of abnormal behavior. Only 17 years after Wundt founded the new science of psychology, another of his former students was using psychology in a practical manner that was inconsistent with Wundt's intentions.

In 1896 Lightner Witmer, who replaced Cattell at the University of Pennsylvania, and who insisted that the temperature in his lecture room be kept at 68°F, opened the world's first psychology clinic.

LIGHTNER WITMER

Described as "hopelessly contentious and antisocial" and a "conceited dwarf," Witmer began the field he called *clinical psychology* (Landy, 1992, pp. 793–794).

What Witmer practiced in his psychology clinic was not clinical psychology as we know it today. His work was devoted to assessing and treating learning and behavioral problems in school children, an applied specialty area now called *school psychology*. Modern clinical psychology deals with a wider range of psychological disorders, from mild to severe, in people of all ages. Although Witmer was instrumental in the development of clinical psychology, and used that label freely, the field has broadened far beyond what he envisioned.

Witmer went on to offer the first college course on clinical psychology and started the first journal, *Psychological Clinic,* which he edited for 29 years. He was one of those pioneers of the functionalist approach to psychology who believed that the new science should be used to help people solve problems rather than to study the contents of their minds.

Witmer's Life

Born in 1867 in Philadelphia, Pennsylvania, Lightner Witmer was the son of a prosperous pharmacist who believed in the importance of education. Witmer graduated from the University of Pennsylvania in 1888, then taught history and English at a private school in Philadelphia before returning to the university to enroll in law courses.

He apparently had no thought of a career in psychology but, for reasons that remain obscure, he studied experimental psychology with Cattell and was given a graduate assistantship in the psychology department. Witmer began research studies on individual differences in reaction time and expected to earn his PhD at Pennsylvania.

Cattell had other plans. He thought so highly of Witmer that he chose him to be his successor when he left for Columbia University. It was a remarkable opportunity for the young man, but Cattell placed one condition on the appointment: Witmer would have to go to Leipzig to earn his doctorate from Wundt. The prestige of a German PhD was still paramount, and so Witmer agreed to go.

He studied with Wundt and with Külpe, and one of his classmates was E. B. Titchener. Witmer was not impressed with Wundt's approach to research, and he later said he got nothing out of his Leipzig experience but his degree. Wundt refused to allow Witmer to continue the reaction-time work he had begun with Cattell and forced him to pursue introspective research on the elements of consciousness.

Witmer criticized what he called Wundt's "slovenly research methods," describing how Wundt made Titchener repeat an observation "because the results obtained by Titchener were not such as he, Wundt, had anticipated" (O'Donnell, 1985, p. 35). Nevertheless,

Witmer received his degree and returned to his new position at the University of Pennsylvania in the summer of 1892, the same time Titchener got his degree and went to Cornell, and the same year another student of Wundt's, Hugo Münsterberg, was brought to Harvard by William James. Also in that year Hall started the American Psychological Association, with Witmer as one of its charter members. The functional, applied spirit had begun to take hold of American psychology.

For 2 years Witmer worked as an experimental psychologist, conducting research and presenting papers on individual differences and on the psychology of pain. All the while, however, he was searching for an opportunity to apply psychology to abnormal behavior. The chance came in March 1896, as a result of an incident that had its origins in the economic circumstances we mentioned earlier—the growing amount of money available for public education.

Many state boards of education were establishing college departments of pedagogy (instruction in the principles and methods of teaching), and psychologists were being asked to offer courses to education majors as well as public school teachers working for advanced degrees. Psychologists were also being urged to shift the focus of their laboratory research, to find ways to train students to become educational psychologists. Psychology departments profited handsomely from this sudden influx of students because then, as now, departmental budgets were contingent on enrollments.

The University of Pennsylvania established courses for public school teachers in 1894, and Witmer taught some of them. Two years later, one of the teachers, Margaret Maguire, consulted Witmer about problems she was having with a 14-year-old student who was having difficulty learning to spell, although he did well in some other subjects. Could psychologists help solve this problem? "It appeared to me," Witmer wrote, "that if psychology was worth anything to me or to others, it should be able to assist in a retarded case of this kind" (quoted in McReynolds, 1987, p. 853). Witmer organized a makeshift clinic and thus began his lifelong work.

Within a few months Witmer was preparing courses on methods for treating mentally defective, blind, and disturbed children, and he published an article entitled "Practical Work in Psychology," in the journal *Pediatrics*. He presented a paper on the topic at the annual meeting of the APA, and it was there that he used the term *clinical psychology* for the first time.

In 1907 he founded the journal *Psychological Clinic,* which became the first, and for many years the only, journal in the field. In its first issue Witmer proposed a new application of psychology—indeed a new profession—to be called clinical psychology. The following year he established a boarding school for retarded and disturbed children, and in 1909 his university clinic expanded and was established as a separate administrative unit.

Witmer remained at the University of Pennsylvania throughout his working life, teaching, promoting, and practicing his clinical psychology. He retired from the university in 1937 and died in 1956 at the age of 89, the last of the small group of psychologists who had met in G. Stanley Hall's study in 1892 to found the American Psychological Association.

Psychology Clinics

As the world's first clinical psychologist, Witmer had no examples or precedents on which to base his actions, and he developed his own methods of diagnosis and treatment as he went along. With his first case, the boy who had trouble spelling, Witmer examined the child's level of intelligence, reasoning, and reading ability and concluded that the last was deficient. After exhaustive analyses over many hours Witmer concluded that the boy was suffering from what Witmer called visual verbal amnesia. Although the child could recall geometric figures, he had trouble remembering words. Witmer developed an intensive remedial program that produced some improvement, but the boy never became proficient at reading or spelling.

Teachers sent to Witmer's new clinic many other children with a broad range of deficiencies and problems, including hyperactivity, learning disabilities, and poor speech and motor development. As Witmer's experience with these problems increased, he developed standard programs of assessment and treatment, and he added physicians, social workers, and psychologists to his staff.

Witmer recognized that physical problems could interfere with psychological functioning, and so he had a physician examine the children to determine if malnutrition or visual and hearing defects were contributing to any child's difficulties. The patients were tested and interviewed extensively by psychologists, while social workers prepared case histories on their family backgrounds.

At first, Witmer believed that genetic factors were largely responsible for many of the behavioral disturbances and cognitive deficits he saw, but he later realized, as his clinical experience grew, that environmental factors were more important. He emphasized the need to provide a variety of sensory experiences early in a child's life, anticipating the Head Start enrichment programs of more recent times. He also believed in direct intervention in the lives of his patients and their families, arguing that if home and school conditions were changed for the better, so too might a child's behavior.

Comment

Witmer's example was followed by many other psychologists. By 1914 nearly 20 psychological clinics were in operation in the United

States, the majority of them patterned on Witmer's clinic. In addition, the students he trained spread his approach, teaching the next generation of students about clinical work. Witmer was also influential in the area of special education, training many of the early workers in the field. One of his students, Morris Viteles, extended Witmer's work by establishing a clinic devoted to vocational guidance, the first such facility in the United States. Others applied Witmer's clinical approach to adults.

THE CLINICAL PSYCHOLOGY MOVEMENT

In addition to Witmer's efforts at the University of Pennsylvania to apply psychology to the assessment and treatment of abnormal behavior, two books provided an early impetus to the field. *A Mind That Found Itself* (1908), written by a former mental patient, Clifford Beers, became immensely popular and focused public attention on the need to deal humanely with mentally ill people. Hugo Münsterberg's *Psychotherapy* (1909), also widely read, described techniques for treating a variety of mental disorders. It promoted clinical psychology by showing specific ways in which disturbed persons could be helped.

The first child guidance clinic was established in 1909 by William Healey, a Chicago psychiatrist. Many more such clinics soon followed. Their purpose was to treat childhood disorders early, so that these problems would not develop into more serious disturbances in adulthood. These clinics used the team approach, introduced by Witmer, in which all aspects of a patient's problem were evaluated and treated by psychologists, psychiatrists, and social workers.

The ideas of Sigmund Freud were crucial to the development of clinical psychology and would move the field far beyond its origins in Witmer's clinic. Freud's work on psychoanalysis fascinated—and outraged—segments of the psychology establishment and the American public. His ideas provided clinical psychologists with their first psychological techniques of therapy.

Despite these events, clinical psychology advanced slowly, and as late as 1940 it was still a minor part of psychology. There were few treatment facilities for disturbed adults and, consequently, few job opportunities for clinical psychologists. There were no educational programs to train clinical psychologists, and their duties were limited, in general, to administering tests.

The situation changed in 1941, when the United States entered World War II. It was that event, more than any other, that made clinical psychology the large and dynamic applied specialty area it has since become. The army established training programs for several hundred clinical psychologists who were needed to treat emotional disturbances among military personnel.

After the war the need for clinical psychologists was even greater. The Veterans Administration (VA) found itself responsible for more than 40,000 veterans with psychiatric problems. Over 3 million others needed vocational and personal counseling to help them return comfortably to civilian life. Some 315,000 veterans needed counseling to help them adjust to physical disabilities resulting from war wounds. The demand for mental health professionals was staggering and far exceeded the supply.

To help meet this need, the VA funded graduate programs at universities and paid the tuition of graduate students in return for work at VA hospitals and clinics. These programs changed the kind of patient typically treated by clinical psychologists. Prior to the war, most of their work had been with children with delinquency and adjustment problems, but the postwar needs of the veterans meant that most of those treated were adults with more severe emotional problems. The VA (now the Department of Veterans Affairs) remains the largest single employer of psychologists in the United States, and its impact on the field of clinical psychology has been enormous (Moore, 1992; VandenBos, Cummings, & Deleon, 1992).

Clinical psychologists are also employed in mental health centers, schools, businesses, and private practice. Clinical psychology today is the largest of the applied areas, with more than one third of all graduate students enrolled in clinical programs. Seven of the eight largest APA divisions are devoted to mental health issues in both academic and applied settings. Nearly 70% of APA members work in areas that are health service oriented (Shapiro & Wiggins, 1994). In 1993, *Money* magazine listed psychology fourth among the top 50 occupations with the brightest career prospects for the 21st century (Wiggins, 1994).

WALTER DILL SCOTT (1869–1955)

Another student of Wundt, Walter Dill Scott, left the world of pure introspective psychology he had learned at Leipzig to apply the new science to advertising and business. Scott dedicated much of his adult life to making the marketplace and the workplace more efficient, and to determining how business leaders could motivate both employees and consumers.

Scott's work reflects functional psychology's concern with practical issues. "Upon returning from Wundt's Leipzig to turn-of-the-century Chicago, Scott's publications shifted from Germanic theorizing to American usefulness. Instead of explaining motives and impulses in general, Scott described how to influence people, including consumers, lecture audiences, and workers" (Von Mayrhauser, 1989, p. 61).

Scott compiled an impressive list of firsts. He was the first person to apply psychology to advertising and to personnel selection and management, the first to hold the title of professor of applied psychology, founder of the first psychological consulting company, and the first psychologist to receive the Distinguished Service Medal from the U.S. Army.

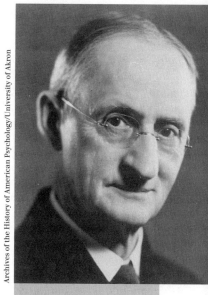

WALTER DILL SCOTT

Scott's Life

Walter Dill Scott was born on a farm near the town of Normal, Illinois. He was captivated by the idea of working efficiently at the age of 12 while plowing a field. Because his father was often ill, the boy essentially ran the small family farm. One day he paused at the end of a furrow he had plowed to give his two horses a rest. Staring at the campus buildings of Illinois State Normal University in the distance, he suddenly realized that if he was ever going to achieve anything, he would have to stop wasting time. Here he was losing 10 minutes out of every hour of plowing to rest the horses! That added up to about an hour and a half every day, time he could use for studying. From that day on, Scott always carried a book with him and read every spare moment.

To earn his college tuition, he picked and canned blackberries, salvaged scrap metal to sell, and took on odd jobs. He saved some of the money and spent the rest on books. At the age of 19 he enrolled at Illinois State Normal University and began his long journey away from the farm. Two years later he won a scholarship to Northwestern University in Evanston, Illinois, where he took tutoring jobs to make extra money, played varsity football, and met Anna Marcy Miller, the woman he would marry.

He also chose his career: He decided to become a missionary to China. That meant 3 additional years of education, and by the time Scott graduated from a Chicago theological seminary, prepared to depart for China, he found there were no vacancies; China was full. It was then that he thought of a career in psychology. He had taken a course in the field and liked it, and he had read a magazine article about Wundt's laboratory at Leipzig. Through his scholarships, tutoring, and frugal living, Scott had saved several thousand dollars, enough not only to go to Germany but also to get married.

On July 21, 1898, Scott and his bride departed. While he studied with Wundt at Leipzig, Anna Scott worked on her PhD in literature at the University of Halle, 20 miles away. They saw each other on weekends. They received their doctoral degrees 2 years later and returned home, where Scott joined the faculty at Northwestern University as an instructor of psychology and pedagogy, showing that he was already influenced by the trend toward applying psychology to problems in education.

His switch to a different field of application came in 1902 when an advertising executive sought out Scott, who had been recommended by a former professor, and asked him to apply psychological principles to advertising to make it more effective. Scott was intrigued by the idea. In keeping with the spirit of American functionalism, he had moved away from Wundtian psychology, seeking ways to make psychology more applicable to real-world concerns. Now he had his chance.

He wrote *The Theory and Practice of Advertising* (1903), the first book on the topic, and followed it with other magazine articles and books as his expertise, reputation, and contacts in the business community widened. He then turned his attention to problems of personnel selection and management. In 1905 he was promoted to professor at Northwestern, and in 1909 became professor of advertising in the university's school of commerce. In 1916 he was appointed professor of applied psychology and director of the bureau of salesmanship research at Carnegie Technical University in Pittsburgh.

When the United States entered World War I Scott offered his skills to the army to help select military personnel. At first, he and his proposals were not well received; not everyone was convinced of psychology's practical value. The army general with whom Scott dealt was outraged, and voiced his suspicions of professors. "He said it was his function to see that college professors did not get in the way of progress, that we were at war with Germany and that we had no time to fool with experiments" (quoted in Von Mayrhauser, 1989, p. 65). Scott calmed the irate man, took him to lunch, and persuaded him of the value of his selection techniques. By the end of the war Scott had proved his point, and the army awarded him the Distinguished Service Medal, the highest honor bestowed on civilians.

In 1919 Scott formed his own company (called, imaginatively, The Scott Company), which provided consulting services to more than 40 major corporations that sought help with personnel selection and methods for increasing worker efficiency. A year later, he became president of Northwestern University and retired in 1939. (Scott Hall at Northwestern University is named for both Walter Dill Scott and Anna Miller Scott.)

Advertising

The imprint of Scott's training in Wundtian experimental psychology and his attempt to extend it into the realm of the practical are evident in Scott's writings on advertising. He wrote, for example, that the sense organs were the *windows of the soul. The more sensations we receive from an object, the better we know it. The function of the nervous system is to make us aware of the sights, sounds, feelings, tastes, et cetera, of the objects in our environment. The nervous system which does not respond to sound or to any other sensible quality is defective.*

Advertisements are sometimes spoken of as the nervous system of the business world. The advertisement of musical instruments which contains nothing to awaken images of sounds is a defective advertisement. . . . As our nervous system is arranged to give us all the possible sensations from every object, so the advertisement which is comparable to the nervous system must awaken in the reader as many different kinds of images as the object itself can excite. (QUOTED IN JACOBSON, 1951, P. 75)

Scott argued that consumers are not rational beings and can be easily influenced. He focused on emotion and sympathy as important factors in heightening this suggestibility. He also believed, as was common then, that women were more easily influenced than men by advertisements that played on their emotions and sentimentality. Applying what he called the law of suggestibility to advertising, he recommended that companies use direct commands—such as "Use Pears Soap"—to sell their products. He also promoted the use of return coupons because they required consumers to take some direct action, tearing the coupon out of the magazine or newspaper, filling it in, and mailing it to receive a free sample. Both techniques—direct commands and coupon returns—were quickly adopted by advertisers and were in widespread use by 1910 (Kuna, 1976).

Personnel Selection

For selecting the best employees—especially salespeople, executives, and military personnel—Scott devised rating scales and group tests to measure the characteristics shown by people who were already successful in those occupations (see Table 8.1). Like Witmer in clinical psychology, Scott had no prior work on which to base his approach, so he had to develop his own. He questioned army officers and business managers, asking them to rank their subordinates on appearance, demeanor, sincerity, productivity, character, and value to the organization. Job applicants could then be ranked on those qualities found to be necessary for successful performance of the job in question, a procedure not so different from that in use today.

Scott developed psychological tests to measure intelligence and other abilities, but instead of assessing each applicant individually, he constructed tests that could be administered to groups. Business

I. PHYSICAL QUALITIES. Physique, bearing, neatness, voice, energy, endurance. Consider how he impresses his command in these respects.	Highest	15
	High	12
	Middle	9
	Low	6
	Lowest	3
II. INTELLIGENCE. Accuracy, ease in learning; ability to grasp quickly the point of view of commanding officer, to issue clear and intelligent orders, to estimate a new situation, and to arrive at a sensible decision in a crisis.	Highest	15
	High	12
	Middle	9
	Low	6
	Lowest	3
III. LEADERSHIP. Initiative, force, self reliance, decisiveness, tact, ability to inspire men and to command their obedience, loyalty and co-operation.	Highest	15
	High	12
	Middle	9
	Low	6
	Lowest	3
IV. PERSONAL QUALITIES. Industry, dependability, loyalty; readiness to shoulder responsibility for his own acts; freedom from conceit and selfishness; readiness and ability to co-operate.	Highest	15
	High	12
	Middle	9
	Low	6
	Lowest	3
V. GENERAL VALUE TO THE SERVICE. Professional knowledge, skill and experience; success as administrator and instructor; ability to get results.	Highest	40
	High	32
	Middle	24
	Low	16
	Lowest	8

CCP 1102B 9–18

TABLE 8.1   *This rating scale was designed by Scott to aid in the assessment of subordinate officers. Each rater recorded the name of an officer he believed to be representative of each attribute at each level of competence.*

and the military demanded that large numbers of candidates be assessed and evaluated rapidly, and it was more efficient and less expensive to test them in groups.

Scott's tests differed from those being developed by Cattell and others. Scott was not attempting only to measure a person's general intelligence, but rather to determine how that person used his or her intelligence. In other words, he wanted to understand how intelligence functioned in the everyday world. He defined intelligence not in terms of specific cognitive abilities but in practical terms such as judgment, quickness, and accuracy—the characteristics needed to perform well on a job. Thus, he was interested in how job applicants' test scores compared with the scores of successful employees, not in what those test scores might signify about mental elements or content.

Comment

Scott, like Witmer, has received only passing attention in the history of psychology. There are several reasons for this neglect. Like most applied psychologists, Scott formulated no theories, founded no school of thought, and trained no loyal core of students to continue his work. He conducted little pure research and published rarely in the mainstream journals of the day. His work for private corporations and for the military was strictly practical, designed to solve their problems and satisfy their needs. Many academic psychologists, particularly those in tenured positions with major universities and well-funded laboratories, discounted the work of applied psychologists, believing that it did not contribute to the advancement of psychology as a science.

Scott and other applied psychologists disputed this position. They saw no conflict between useful applications and the advancement of the science. They believed that "psychology's empirical progress depended greatly upon the results of extra-academic experience" (Von Mayrhauser, 1989, p. 63). Applied psychologists argued that bringing psychology to the public's attention demonstrated its worth, which, in turn, increased the recognition of psychological research in the universities. Thus, the early applied psychologists were reflecting the legacy and impact of the functionalist spirit in American psychology, to make that psychology useful.

THE INDUSTRIAL/ORGANIZATIONAL PSYCHOLOGY MOVEMENT

The Impact of the World Wars

World War I brought about a monumental increase in the scope, popularity, and growth of industrial/organizational psychology. We noted that Scott volunteered his services to the United States Army and developed a rating scale for selecting army captains, based on scales he had developed for rating business leaders. By the end of the war he had evaluated the job qualifications of 3 million soldiers, and his work provided another highly publicized example of the practical worth of psychology. After the war

A two-hand coordination test used to select air crew trainees during World War II.

Archives of the History of American Psychology/University of Akron

business, industry, and government clamored for the services of industrial psychologists to reorganize their personnel procedures and to introduce psychological tests as employee selection devices.

We also mentioned that World War II brought many psychologists directly into the war effort. As in World War I, their major contribution was the testing, screening, and classifying of recruits, and by the 1940s far more sophisticated tests had been devised. Operation of the increasingly complex weapons of war, such as high-speed aircraft, required more complex skills. The need to identify people who possessed the ability to learn those skills led psychologists to refine their selection and training procedures.

The necessities of war spawned a specialty within industrial psychology variously called engineering psychology, human engineering, human factors engineering, and ergonomics. Working closely with weapons systems engineers, engineering psychologists supplied information about human capabilities and limitations. Their work directly influenced the design of military equipment to make it more compatible with the skills and abilities of the people who had to use it. Engineering psychologists today work not only on military hardware but also on consumer products such as computer keyboards, office furniture, home appliances, and automobile dashboard displays.

The Hawthorne Studies and Organizational Factors

The primary focus of industrial psychology during the 1920s was the selection and placement of job applicants—matching the right person with the right job. The scope of the field was broadened in 1927 by an innovative research program conducted by the Western Electric Company at its Hawthorne plant in Illinois (Roethlisberger & Dickson, 1939). These studies extended the field beyond selection and placement to complex problems of human relations, motivation, and morale.

The research began as a straightforward investigation of the effects of the physical work environment—lighting and temperature, for example—on employee efficiency. The results astonished the psychologists and the plant managers: It was found that social and psychological conditions of the work environment were much more important than the physical conditions under which the job was performed.

The Hawthorne studies led psychologists to explore factors such as the nature of leadership, informal groups of workers on the job, employee attitudes, communication between employees and managers, and other forces capable of influencing motivation, productivity, and satisfaction.

Since the 1950s business leaders have accepted the influence of motivation, leadership, and other psychological factors on job performance. These aspects of the work environment have assumed greater importance, as has the entire social-psychological climate in which work takes place. Psychologists today study different types of organizations, their styles of communication, and the formal and informal social structures they produce. Recognizing this emphasis on organizational variables, the Division of Industrial Psychology of the American Psychological Association was renamed the Society for Industrial and Organizational Psychology.

Courtesy, Western Electric

Studies conducted during the 1920s and 1930s at the Hawthorne, Illinois, plant of the Western Electric Company led applied psychologists into the complex areas of human relations, leadership styles, and employee motivation and morale.

Industrial/organizational (I/O) psychology continues to grow at a rapid rate. It is also worth noting that I/O psychology as a profession has been open to women. The first person to receive a PhD in the field was Lillian Moore Gilbreth (Brown University, 1915), who, with her husband, promoted time-and-motion analysis as a technique to improve efficiency in job performance. I/O psychology boasts a higher rate of increase in women awarded doctoral degrees than any other specialty in psychology (Koppes, Landy, & Perkins, 1993).

HUGO MÜNSTERBERG (1863–1916)

Hugo Münsterberg, the stereotypical German professor, was for a time a phenomenal success in American psychology and the psychologist best known to the public. He wrote hundreds of popular magazine articles and almost two dozen books. He was a frequent visitor to the White House in Washington, D. C., as the guest of two American presidents, Theodore Roosevelt and William Howard Taft. Münsterberg was sought as a consultant by business and government leaders and counted among his acquaintances the rich and famous and powerful, including Germany's Kaiser Wilhelm, steel magnate Andrew Carnegie, philosopher Bertrand Russell, as well as movie stars and intellectuals.

He was, for a time, an honored professor at Harvard University who was elected to the presidency of both the American Psychological Association and the American Philosophical Association. He was a founder of applied psychology in the United States as well as Europe. In addition, he was one of only two psychologists ever accused of being a spy (Spillmann & Spillmann, 1993).

Münsterberg has been described as a "prolific propagandizer for applied psychology" (O'Donnell, 1985, p. 225), who was interested in many areas. According to his biographer, Münsterberg was also a successful publicist, "blessed with an uncanny flair for the sensational. [His] life can be read as a series of promotions—of himself, his science, and his [German] fatherland" (Hale, 1980, p. 3).

Toward the end of his life, Münsterberg became a figure of scorn and ridicule, the subject of newspaper cartoons and caricatures, and an embarrassment to the university he had served for so many years. When he died in 1916 there were few eulogies for the man who had once been called a giant of American psychology.

HUGO MÜNSTERBERG

Archives of the History of American Psychology/University of Akron

Münsterberg's Life

In 1882, at the age of 19, Münsterberg left his birthplace in Danzig, Germany, and traveled to Leipzig, intending to study medicine. But when he took a course with Wilhelm Wundt, his career plans changed.

The new psychology excited him, promising opportunities that medical research and practice did not. He received his PhD from Wundt in 1885 and earned an MD at the University of Heidelberg 2 years later, to be better equipped for a career in academic research. He accepted a teaching job at the University of Freiburg and set up a laboratory in his home, at his own expense, because there were no facilities at the university.

Münsterberg published several articles on his experimental work in psychophysics, which Wundt criticized because the research dealt with the mind's cognitive contents, to the exclusion of feeling states. Münsterberg's work attracted followers, however, and soon students from throughout Europe were flocking to his laboratory. He seemed well on his way to securing a professorship at a major university and a reputation as a respected scholar.

William James lured Münsterberg from this path in 1892 by offering him the chance to become the highly paid director of Harvard's psychology laboratory. James used flattery in his appeal, writing to Münsterberg that Harvard was the greatest university in the United States and needed a genius to run its laboratory. Münsterberg would have preferred to stay in Germany, but his ambition led him to accept James's offer.

Münsterberg did not make the transition from Germany to the United States—and from pure experimental psychology to applied psychology—quickly or easily. At first he disapproved of the spread of applied psychology and scolded university administrators for paying scholars so little that they were forced to take on more practical pursuits. He criticized American psychologists who wrote popular books for lay audiences, gave paid lectures to business leaders, and offered, for a fee, their services as experts. Before long, however, Münsterberg would be doing all these things.

After 10 years in the United States, and perhaps realizing that no German university was going to offer him a professorship, he wrote his first book in English. Called *American Traits* (1902), it was a psychological, social, and cultural analysis of American society. A rapid and gifted writer, Münsterberg was able to dictate to a secretary a 400-page book in less than a month. James remarked that Münsterberg's brain never seemed to get tired.

The enthusiastic response to Münsterberg's book encouraged him to write more for the public than for his colleagues, and soon he was publishing in popular magazines rather than in psychology journals. He abandoned his psychophysical research on the contents of the mind to deal instead with everyday problems psychologists could solve. His articles covered courtroom trials and the criminal justice system, the advertising of consumer products, vocational counseling, mental health and psychotherapy, education, problems of business and industry, and the psychology of motion pictures. Branching out into other media, he prepared correspondence courses on learning and business, and made films about mental tests, which were shown in movie theaters.

Münsterberg never shied from controversy. During a sensational murder trial he administered almost 100 mental tests to the confessed killer of 18 people who had accused a labor union leader of paying for the murders. On the basis of the test results, Münsterberg announced—before the jury reached its verdict in the labor leader's trial—that the murderer's confession implicating the labor leader was true. When the jury acquitted the labor leader, the decision damaged Münsterberg's credibility; a newspaper took to calling him "Professor Monsterwork."

In 1908 Münsterberg became involved in the fight over prohibition, the movement to ban the sale of alcoholic beverages. He argued against prohibition, citing his expertise as a psychologist, and expressed the position that alcoholic beverages in moderation were beneficial. German-American beer brewers, including Adolphus Busch and Gustave Pabst, were delighted to have Münsterberg's support, and they made sizable financial contributions to Münsterberg's efforts to bolster Germany's image in the United States.

In an unfortunate and suspicious bit of timing, Busch donated $50,000 for Münsterberg's proposed Germanic Museum only a few weeks after Münsterberg published an article denouncing the idea of prohibition. The coincidence received a great deal of attention in the news media.

Münsterberg's beliefs about women were also hard to ignore. Although he was supportive of several women graduate students at Harvard, including Mary Whiton Calkins, he believed that graduate work was too demanding for most women. His view was that women should not be trained for careers, because that would take them away from the home. He argued that women should not teach in the public schools, because they could not teach as well as men and were poor role models for boys. And he said that women should not be allowed to serve on juries because they were incapable of rational deliberation, a remark that generated international newspaper headlines.

The president of Harvard University, and most of Münsterberg's colleagues, were not pleased with this sensationalism, nor did they approve of his interest in applying psychology to practical problems. Strained relations reached the breaking point over Münsterberg's vocal defense of his German homeland during World War I; war had broken out in Europe in 1914, although the United States did not enter the conflict directly until 1917. American public opinion was decidedly anti-German. Germany was the aggressor in a war that had already claimed millions of lives, and Münsterberg insisted openly on defending Germany, an increasingly unpopular position.

Newspapers reported that Münsterberg, who had never become a United States citizen, was really a secret agent, a spy, and a high-ranking German military officer. The Boston newspapers called for his resignation from Harvard. His neighbors suspected that the pigeons his daughter was seen feeding in the backyard of his house were being used to carry messages to other spies. A Harvard alumnus offered the university $10 million if they would fire Münsterberg.

Münsterberg received death threats in the mail and was snubbed by his colleagues. The ostracism and virulent public attacks eventually broke his spirit. But on a cold, blustery December 16, 1916, the newspapers published speculations about peace talks in Europe. "By spring we shall have peace," he announced to his wife (Münsterberg, 1922, p. 302). He set off on foot through deep snows to teach his morning class. By the time he reached the lecture hall he felt exhausted. Münsterberg entered the classroom and lectured "for about a half hour when he appeared to hesitate and a moment later stretched his right hand toward the desk as though to steady himself" (*New York City Evening Mail*, December 16, 1916).[2] He fell to the floor without saying another word and died instantly of a massive stroke.

Forensic Psychology

The first applied area in which Münsterberg worked, forensic psychology, deals with psychology and the law. He wrote magazine articles on such topics as crime prevention, the use of hypnosis to question suspects, the use of mental tests to detect guilty people, and the lack of trustworthiness of eyewitness testimony. He was particularly interested in the latter—the fallibility of human perception of an event such as a crime and the subsequent recollection of the event. He conducted research on simulated crimes in which witnesses were asked, immediately after seeing the crime, to describe what had occurred. The subjects could not agree on the details of what they had witnessed, even though the scene was still fresh in their memories. How accurate can such testimony be in a courtroom, Münsterberg asked, when the event under discussion would have taken place many months earlier?

In 1908 he published *On the Witness Stand*, which described the problems with eyewitness testimony. The book also considered other psychological factors that can affect the outcome of a trial, such as false confessions, the power of suggestion in the questioning of witnesses, and the use of physiological measurements (heart rate, blood pressure, and skin resistance) to detect heightened emotional states in a suspect or defendant. The book was reprinted as recently as 1976, almost 70 years after its publication.

[2] We are grateful to Dr. Ludy T. Benjamin, Jr., for supplying this information based on his research on the Münsterberg papers in the Boston Public Library.

The late 1970s brought a resurgence of interest in the issues Münsterberg raised (Loftus, 1979; Loftus & Monahan, 1980), and the American Psychology-Law Society was established as a division of the American Psychological Association to promote basic and applied research on forensic psychology.

Clinical Psychology

Münsterberg published a book entitled *Psychotherapy* in 1909, beginning work in a different applied area. He treated patients in his laboratory rather than in a clinic, and he never charged a fee. He relied on the authority of his position as a therapist and did not hesitate to make direct suggestions to his patients about how they could be cured.

Mental illness, he believed, was a problem of behavioral maladjustment, not something that was attributable to deep underlying unconscious conflicts as Sigmund Freud claimed. "There is no subconscious," Münsterberg announced (quoted in Landy, 1992, p. 792). When Freud visited Clark University in 1909, at the invitation of Hall, Münsterberg left the country. He returned only after Freud went back to Europe, thus avoiding a confrontation.

Münsterberg's therapeutic approach was to force the patient's disturbing ideas out of awareness, to suppress those behaviors that were undesirable or troubling, and to urge the patient to forget the emotional difficulty. He treated a variety of problems, including alcoholism, drug abuse, hallucinations, obsessive thoughts, phobias, and sexual disorders. For a time he used hypnosis as a method of treatment but stopped after a woman patient threatened him with a gun. The story made the newspapers, and Harvard's president demanded that Münsterberg refrain from hypnotizing women.

His book on psychotherapy did much to bring the field of clinical psychology to public attention, but it was not well received by Witmer, who had opened his clinic at the University of Pennsylvania several years before. Witmer had never achieved, nor had he desired, the kind of popular acclaim Münsterberg thrived on. In an article published in his journal, *Psychological Clinic*, Witmer complained that Münsterberg had "cheapened" the profession by hawking claims of cures in the marketplace. He called Münsterberg little better than a faith healer because of the "jaunty way in which the professor of psychology at [Harvard] goes about the country, claiming to have treated in his psychological laboratory hundreds and hundreds of cases of this or that form of nervous disorder" (quoted in Hale, 1980, p. 110).

Industrial Psychology

Münsterberg also promoted industrial psychology. He embarked on this work in 1909 with an article entitled "Psychology and the

Market." It covered several areas to which he believed psychology could contribute: vocational guidance, advertising, personnel management, mental testing, employee motivation, and the effects on job performance of fatigue and monotony.

He was hired as a consultant by several companies, and for them he performed a great deal of research. He published his findings in *Psychology and Industrial Efficiency* (1913), written for the general public. The book was so successful that it made the best-seller list. He argued that the best way to increase job efficiency and employee productivity and satisfaction was to select workers for positions that matched their mental and emotional abilities. How could employers do this? By developing psychological selection techniques, such as mental tests and job simulations in which the applicants' knowledge, skills, and abilities could be assessed.

Münsterberg conducted research on such diverse occupations as ship's captain, streetcar driver, telephone operator, and salesperson, showing how his selection techniques could bring about improvements in job performance. With regard to problems of efficiency, he described the results of studies that showed, for example, that talking while working decreased efficiency. His solution was not to prohibit conversation among the workers (that, he recognized, would engender hostility), but to design the workplace so that it would be difficult for workers to talk to one another. That goal could be achieved by increasing the distance between machines in the factory or separating the office work stations with partitions.

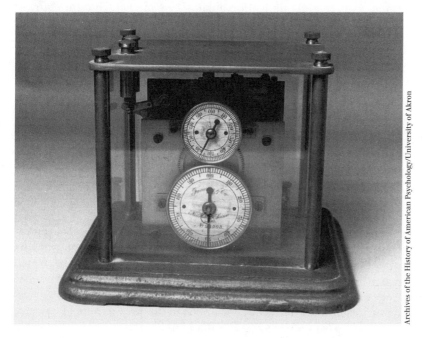

Chronoscope designed by Münsterberg to measure time intervals in units of hundredths of a second.

Comment

Münsterberg formulated no theories, started no new school of thought, and—once he began work in applied psychology—conducted no academic research. He insisted that his research serve a definite purpose, that it be functional and oriented toward helping people in some way. Although he had been trained by Wundt in the introspective method, he criticized psychologists who clung to that technique and were unwilling to use the methods and findings of psychology for the betterment of all humanity.

If there is one theme that characterizes Münsterberg's colorful and controversial career, it is that psychology must be functional and useful. In that sense he was, for all his Germanic temperament, the quintessential American psychologist, reflecting and demonstrating the spirit of his times.

APPLIED PSYCHOLOGY IN THE UNITED STATES

The contributions of psychologists during World War I put psychology, Cattell said, "on the map and on the front page" (quoted in O'Donnell, 1985, p. 239). Hall wrote that the war had "given applied psychology a tremendous impulse. This will, on the whole, do good for psychology. . . . [we] must not try to be too pure" (Hall, 1919, p. 48). Some psychology journals, such as the *Journal of Experimental Psychology,* ceased publication during the war years, but the *Journal of Applied Psychology* thrived. By the time the war ended in 1918, applied psychology had become far more respectable within the profession as a whole. "Applied psychology," said Thorndike, "is scientific work. Making psychology for business or industry or the army is harder than making psychology for other psychologists, and intrinsically requires higher talents" (quoted in Camfield, 1992, p. 113).

Academic psychology also benefited from this applied success during the war. For the first time, there were enough jobs and financial support for university psychologists. New departments of psychology were established, new buildings and laboratories constructed, and more money appropriated for faculty salaries. Membership in the APA increased threefold, from 336 in 1917 to over 1,100 in 1930 (Camfield, 1992).

In the 1920s, psychology became something of a "national mania" (Dennis, 1984, p. 23). People assumed that psychologists could fix everything from marital disharmony to job dissatisfaction, or sell everything from cars to mouthwash. An increasing clamor for solutions to real-world problems drew more psychologists away from academic research and into applied areas. In the 1921 edition of Cattell's *American Men of Science,* more than 75% of the psychologists listed said they were engaged in applied work; in 1910 the figure had been 50% (O'Donnell, 1985). The meetings of the New York branch of the APA in the early 1920s show a substantial increase from prewar days in the number of papers dealing with research on applied issues (Benjamin, 1991).

By the 1930s, however, the decade of the worldwide economic depression, applied psychology came under attack for its failure to live up to its promise. Business leaders complained that industrial psychologists were not curing all their corporate ills. Bad experiences with poorly designed selection tests, for example, had led them to hire unproductive workers.

Perhaps the expectations of psychologists and their clients had been too high, but whatever the reason, a disenchantment with applied psychology set in. One vocal critic was Grace Adams, who had been one of Titchener's students. In "The Decline of Psychology in America," an article published in a popular magazine, Adams argued that psychology had "forsaken its scientific roots so that individual psychologists might achieve popularity and prosperity" (quoted in Benjamin, 1986, p. 944). The *New York Times* and other influential newspapers criticized psychologists for overstating their abilities and for failing to ameliorate the malaise created by the depression. The public attention paid to psychology declined, and psychology's image was not restored until 1941, when the United States entered World War II. Thus we have another example of war as a contextual influence on the development of psychology.

World War II (1941–1945) provided a different set of problems for psychology to solve, and it revived and expanded the influence of the field. Fully 25% of American psychologists were directly involved in the war effort, and many others made indirect contributions through their research and writing. Ironically, the war also revived a flagging psychology in Germany, where the field had declined after the Nazis expelled all Jewish psychologists from their jobs. The needs of the German military created a fresh demand for psychologists to assist in the selection of officers, pilots, submariners, and other specialists (Geuter, 1987).

In the half century since the end of the war American psychology has experienced a dramatic surge of growth. Within the field as a whole, the most significant advancement has occurred in the applied areas. Applied psychology has outstripped the academic, research-oriented side of psychology that for many years was dominant. No longer is it true that the majority of psychologists can be found in universities, conducting experimental research. Before World War II almost 70% of the doctorates awarded in psychology were in experimental psychology; by 1984 that figure had dropped to 8% (Goodstein, 1988). Before the war, 75% of all psychologists with doctoral degrees worked in academic settings. By 1989, that number had fallen to 30% (Kohout & Wicherski, 1990). One result has been a shift in power within the American Psychological Association, where applied psychologists (particularly clinical psychologists) assume a commanding position. In 1988, a group of academic and research-oriented members revolted and founded their own organization, the American Psychological Society (APS).

COMMENT

The nature of American psychology has changed immensely in the years since Hall, Cattell, Witmer, Scott, and Münsterberg studied under Wundt in Germany and brought that psychology to the United States. As a result of their efforts, psychology is no longer restricted to the lecture halls, libraries, and laboratories but extends into many areas of everyday life. In addition to testing, educational and school psychology, clinical and counseling psychology, industrial/organizational psychology, and forensic psychology, psychologists are working in community and social action research, consumer psychology, population and environmental psychology, health and rehabilitation psychology, family services, exercise and sports psychology, military psychology, and media psychology. They are also concerned with addictive behaviors, religion, the arts, peace, and ethnic minority issues.

None of these areas of application would have been possible had psychology remained concerned with mental elements or the contents of conscious experience. The people, ideas, and events we have described in these chapters on the functionalist school of thought compelled American psychology to move far beyond the confines of Wundt's Leipzig laboratory.

Consider the following factors:

1.   Darwin's notion of adaptation and function,

2.   Galton's measurement of individual differences,

3.   the American intellectual focus on the practical and the useful,

4.   the shift within academic research laboratories from content to function brought about by James, Angell, Carr, and Woodworth,

5.   economic and social factors and the forces of war.

All of these factors intertwined to bring forth a psychology designed to change our lives—an active, assertive, engaging, influential science. This overall movement in American psychology toward the practical was reinforced by behaviorism, the next school of thought in psychology's evolution.

DISCUSSION QUESTIONS

1.   Describe the economic forces that influenced the development of applied psychology. Do you think applied psychology would have developed in the absence of those forces?

2.   What "firsts" in American psychology are attributed to G. Stanley Hall? How was Hall's work influenced by Darwin's evolutionary theory? Why was Hall called a genetic psychologist?

3.   Compare the approaches of Cattell and Binet to the development of mental tests. What was the impact of World War I on the testing movement?

4.   How did metaphors from medicine and engineering lend scientific authority to intelligence testing? How were tests used in the United States to support the notion of racial differences in intelligence and the alleged inferiority of immigrants?

5.   Describe the impact of Witmer, Münsterberg, and World War II on the growth of clinical psychology.

6.   Discuss the roles of Scott and Münsterberg in the origin of industrial/organizational psychology. How was the field affected by the Hawthorne studies and by the world wars?

SUGGESTED READINGS

Katzell, R. A., & Austin, J. T. (1992). From then to now: The development of industrial-organizational psychology in the United States. *Journal of Applied Psychology, 77,* 803–835. Reviews the growth of I/O psychology since the turn of the century and assesses its influence on contemporary psychology and on America's industrial society.

Landy, F. J. (1992). Hugo Münsterberg: Victim or visionary? *Journal of Applied Psychology, 77,* 787–802. Examines Münsterberg's contributions to applied psychology and possible reasons for his obscurity.

McReynolds, P. (1987). Lightner Witmer: Little-known founder of clinical psychology. *American Psychologist, 42,* 849–858. Sketches Witmer's life and career and the beginning of his clinic at the University of Pennsylvania, and assesses his importance for psychology.

Sokal, M. M. (Ed.). (1987). *Psychological testing and American society: 1890–1930.* New Brunswick, NJ: Rutgers University Press. Discusses the ideas, programs, and practices in the mental testing movement.

Von Mayrhauser, R. T. (1989). Making intelligence functional: Walter Dill Scott and applied psychological testing in World War I. *Journal of the History of the Behavioral Sciences, 25,* 60–72. Describes the efforts of Scott, Thorndike, and others in constructing group intelligence tests.

White, S. H. (1990). Child study at Clark University: 1894–1904. *Journal of the History of the Behavioral Sciences, 26,* 131–150. Describes the questionnaire studies of child development initiated by G. Stanley Hall.

CHAPTER 9

BEHAVIORISM: ANTECEDENT

INFLUENCES

A SCIENCE OF BEHAVIOR

B Y THE second decade of the 20th century, fewer than 40 years after Wilhelm Wundt formally launched psychology, the science had undergone drastic revision. No longer did psychologists agree on the value of introspection, on the existence of mental elements, or on the need for psychology to remain a pure science. The functional psychologists were rewriting the rules, using psychology in ways that could not be accepted at Leipzig or Cornell.

The movement to functionalism was less revolutionary than it was evolutionary. The functionalists did not deliberately set out to destroy the establishment of Wundt and Titchener. Instead, they modified it, adding a bit here, changing something there, so that over the years a new form of psychology emerged. It was more a chipping away from the inside than an attack from outside. The leaders of the functionalist movement were not ambitious to solidify or formalize their position. They saw their role, not so much as a breaking with the past as a building upon it. The change from structuralism to functionalism was, therefore, not so noticeable at the time it was taking place.

This was the situation in psychology in the second decade of the 20th century in the United States. Functionalism was maturing and structuralism still held a strong but no longer exclusive position.

In 1913 a protest erupted against both of these positions. It was deliberately intended to be an abrupt and open break, a total war designed to shatter both of the older points of view. Its author wanted no modification of the past, no compromise with it.

This new movement was called **behaviorism,** and its leader was the 35-year-old psychologist John B. Watson. Just 10 years earlier Watson had received his PhD from Angell at the University of Chicago. At that time—1903—Chicago was the center of functional psychology, one of the two movements Watson set out to smash.

BEHAVIORISM: Watson's science of behavior that dealt only with observable behavioral acts which could be described objectively

The basic tenets of Watson's behaviorism were simple, direct, and bold. He called for a scientific psychology that dealt only with observable behavioral acts that could be described objectively in terms such as *stimulus* and *response.* Further, Watson's psychology would reject all mentalistic concepts and terms. Such words as *image, mind,* and *consciousness*—which had been carried over from the days of mental philosophy—were meaningless for a science of behavior.

Watson was particularly vehement in rejecting the concept of consciousness. He said that consciousness has "never been seen, touched, smelled, tasted, or moved. It is a plain assumption just as unprovable as the old concept of soul" (Watson & McDougall, 1929, p. 14). The technique of introspection, which assumed the existence of conscious processes, was, therefore, irrelevant, of no use at all to a science of behavior.

These basic ideas of the behaviorist movement were not original with Watson but had been developing in psychology and in biology for years. Watson, like all founders, organized and promoted ideas and issues already acceptable to the intellectual Zeitgeist. We examine here the major forces Watson so effectively brought together to form his new system of psychology: (1) the philosophical tradition of objectivism and mechanism; (2) animal psychology; and (3) functional psychology.

Watson's insistence on the need for greater objectivity in psychology was not unusual by 1913. The notion has a long history, traced back to Descartes, whose attempts at mechanistic explanations of the operation of the body were among the first steps toward greater objectivity. More important in the history of objectivism is the French philosopher Auguste Comte (1798–1857), founder of the movement called **positivism,** which emphasized positive knowledge (facts), the truth of which was not debatable. According to Comte, the only valid knowledge is that which is social in nature and is objectively observable. These criteria rule out introspection, which depends on a private individual consciousness and cannot be objectively observed.

POSITIVISM: The doctrine that recognizes only natural phenomena or facts that are objectively observable

In the early years of the 20th century, positivism was part of the Zeitgeist in science. Watson rarely discussed positivism, nor did most American psychologists of the day, but they "acted like positivists, even if they did not assume the label" (Logue, 1985b, p. 149). Thus, by the time Watson set to work on behaviorism, the objectivist, mechanist, and materialist influences were strong. Their impact was so pervasive that they led inevitably to a new kind of psychology, one without consciousness or mind or soul, one that focused on only what could be seen and heard and touched. A science of behavior that viewed human beings as machines was the inescapable result.

THE INFLUENCE OF ANIMAL PSYCHOLOGY ON BEHAVIORISM

Watson offered a clear statement of the relationship between animal psychology and behaviorism: "Behaviorism is a direct outgrowth of studies in animal behavior during the first decade of the twentieth century" (Watson, 1929, p. 327). We can say, then, that the most important antecedent of Watson's program was animal psychology, which grew out of evolutionary theory. It led to attempts to demonstrate the existence of mind in lower organisms and the continuity between animal and human minds.

We noted in chapter 6 the work of two pioneers in animal psychology—George John Romanes and Conwy Lloyd Morgan. With Morgan's law of parsimony and his reliance on experimental instead of anecdotal techniques, the field of animal psychology became more objective. Consciousness remained its focus, however. Thus, whereas the methodology was becoming more objective, the subject matter was not.

In 1889, Alfred Binet published *The Psychic Life of Micro-Organisms*, in which he proposed that single-celled protozoa possess the ability to perceive and discriminate between objects and to display behavior that has some purpose. In 1908, Francis Darwin (son of Charles Darwin) discussed the role of consciousness in plants. In the early years of animal psychology in the United States, we find, not surprisingly, a continuing interest in the conscious processes of animals. The influence of Romanes and Morgan persisted for quite some time.

A Note on Jacques Loeb

A significant step toward greater objectivity in animal psychology was taken by Jacques Loeb (1859–1924), a German physiologist and zoologist who liked to water his lawn whenever it rained. He worked at several institutions in the United States, including the University of Chicago. Reacting against the anthropomorphic tradition of Romanes and the method of introspection by analogy, Loeb developed a theory of animal behavior based on the concept of **tropism,** an involuntary forced movement (Pauly, 1990). Loeb believed that an animal's response to a stimulus is a direct and automatic reaction. That behavioral response is said to be *forced* by the stimulus, and

TROPISM: An involuntary forced movement

thus it does not require any explanation in terms of the animal's consciousness.

Although Loeb's work represented the most objective and mechanistic approach to animal psychology then proposed, he had not completely cast off the past. He did not reject consciousness totally, particularly in animals, such as human beings, that were high on the evolutionary scale.

ASSOCIATIVE MEMORY: An association between stimulus and response used to indicate evidence of consciousness in animals

Loeb argued that consciousness among animals was revealed by **associative memory;** that is, the animals had learned to react to certain stimuli in a desired way. For example, when an animal responds to the calling of its name, or when it reacts to a specific sound by going repeatedly to the place where it receives food, this is evidence of some mental connection, an associative memory. Thus, even in Loeb's otherwise mechanistic approach, he still invoked the idea of consciousness (Loeb, 1918).

Watson took courses with Loeb at the University of Chicago and hoped to do research under his direction, showing that he was then in sympathy with (or at least curious about) Loeb's mechanistic views. Angell and another faculty member, the neurologist H. H. Donaldson, talked Watson out of this plan. They argued that Loeb was "unsafe," a word open to interpretation but perhaps indicating their disapproval of Loeb's objectivism.

Rats, Ants, and the Animal Mind

By the beginning of the 20th century, experimental animal psychologists were hard at work. Robert Yerkes began animal studies in 1900,

A hungry rat placed in the maze is allowed to wander freely until it finds food.

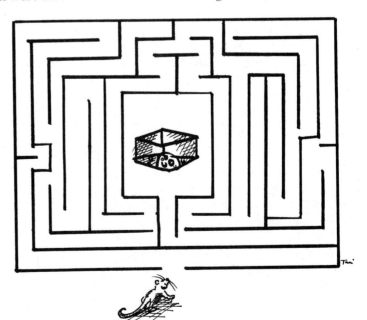

using a variety of animals, and his research strengthened the position and influence of comparative psychology.

Also in 1900 the rat maze was introduced by W. S. Small at Clark University, and the white rat and maze became a standard method for the study of learning. Yet consciousness continued to intrude in animal psychology, even with the white rat running the maze. In interpreting the rat's behavior, Small used mentalistic terms, writing about the rat's "ideas" and "images."

Although Small's conclusions were more objective than those produced by Romanes's brand of anthropomorphizing, they reflected a concern with mental processes, even with mental elements. Watson, in the early years of his career, fell under the same influence. His doctoral dissertation, completed in 1903, was entitled "Animal Education: The *Psychical* Development of the White Rat" (italics added). As late as 1907 he was discussing the conscious experience of sensation in his rats.

In 1906, Charles Henry Turner, a noted African-American researcher in comparative psychology, published an article entitled "A Preliminary Note on Ant Behavior." Watson reviewed the paper in the prestigious journal *Psychological Bulletin* and had high praise for it. In his review Watson used the word *behavior*, taken from Turner's title. This may have been the first time Watson used the word in print, although he had written it earlier in a grant application (Cadwallader, 1984, 1987).

By 1910, some eight laboratories of comparative psychology had been established; the earliest were at Clark, Harvard, and the University of Chicago. Many universities offered courses in the field. Margaret Floy Washburn, who had been Titchener's first doctoral student, taught animal psychology at Cornell. She wrote the first textbook on comparative psychology, *The Animal Mind* (1908).

Note the title of Washburn's book: *The Animal Mind.* The attribution of consciousness to animals persisted, as did the method of introspecting the animal mind by analogy with the human mind. Washburn noted that "we are obliged to acknowledge that all psychic interpretation of animal behavior must be on the analogy of human experience. . . . We must be anthropomorphic in the notions we form of what takes place in the mind of an animal" (Washburn, 1908, p. 88).

Although Washburn's book was the most thorough treatment of the research in animal psychology of its day, it also marked the end of an era. "After it, no other text would use the approach of inferring mental states from behavior. The questions that had interested [Herbert] Spencer, Lloyd Morgan, and Yerkes went out of fashion and mostly disappeared from the literature. Almost all subsequent textbooks in the field were behaviorist in orientation, and primarily concerned with the issues and problems of learning" (Demarest, 1987, p. 144).

Manuscripts and Archives, Yale University Library

Robert Yerkes

Whether one dealt with mind or with behavior, it was not easy to be an animal psychologist. The field was not considered by state legislators and university administrators to have any practical value. The president of Harvard "saw no future in Yerkes's brand of comparative psychology. It was smelly and expensive and seemed to have no relation to practical public service" (Reed, 1987a, p. 94).

The students Yerkes trained in his laboratory entered applied fields, unable to find jobs in comparative psychology. Those with university positions knew they were the most expendable members of their psychology departments. In times of financial hardship, animal psychologists were generally the first to be fired.

Watson himself had difficulties early in his career. "I am very hampered in my research at present," he wrote to Yerkes in 1904. "We have absolutely no place to keep animals and no funds to run the 'menagerie' if we had the place" (quoted in O'Donnell, 1985, p. 190).

In 1908 only six animal studies were published, some 4% of all the psychological research for the year. In 1909, when Watson suggested to Yerkes that all animal psychologists arrange to have dinner together during the APA meeting, he knew they could be seated at one table—all nine of them. In the 1910 edition of Cattell's *American Men of Science,* only six out of 218 psychologists listed said they were active in animal research. Career prospects were obviously poor, yet the field expanded because of the dedication of the few who stayed with it.

The *Journal of Animal Behavior,* later the *Journal of Comparative Psychology,* was begun in 1911. In 1909 the work of the Russian physiologist Ivan Pavlov became known in the United States through an article written by Yerkes and a Russian student, Sergius Morgulis. Pavlov's work supported an objective psychology and Watson's behaviorism in particular.

Animal psychology became established and grew increasingly objective in its methods and subject matter. The kinds of conscious experiences being assumed and described by animal researchers narrowed and eventually disappeared from the literature.

Before we consider additional influences on the development of Watson's behaviorism, let us tell the tale of the most famous horse in the history of psychology.

Clever Hans, the Clever Horse

In the early 1900s virtually every literate person in the Western world had read about Hans the Wonder Horse, surely the most intelligent four-legged creature who ever lived. The horse, who resided in Berlin, Germany, was a celebrity throughout Europe and the United States. Songs, books, and magazine articles had been written about him, and advertisers were using the horse's name to sell their products. Hans was a sensation.

The horse could add and subtract, use fractions and decimals, read, spell, tell time, distinguish among colors, identify objects, and perform phenomenal feats of memory. Hans replied to the questions put to him by tapping his hoof a specified number of times or by nodding his head in the direction of the correct object.

"How many of the gentlemen present are wearing straw hats?" the horse was asked.

Clever Hans tapped the answer with his right foot, being careful to omit the straw hats worn by the ladies.

"What is the lady holding in her hand?"

The horse tapped out "Schirm," meaning parasol, indicating each of the letters by means of a special chart. He was invariably successful at distinguishing between canes and parasols and also between straw and felt hats.

More important, Hans could think for himself. When asked a completely novel question, such as how many corners in a circle, he shook his head from side to side to say there were none. (Fernald, 1984, p. 19)

No wonder people were dazzled. No wonder Hans's owner, Wilhelm von Osten, a retired mathematics teacher, was pleased with what he had accomplished. He had spent several years teaching Hans the fundamentals of human intelligence. The motivation for his painstaking efforts was purely scientific. His goal was to prove that Darwin was correct in suggesting that humans and animals have similar mental processes. Von Osten believed that the only reason horses and other animals appear to be less intelligent than they are is that they have not been given sufficient education. He was convinced that with the right kind of training, the horse could show that it was an intelligent being.

Von Osten did not profit financially from Hans's performances. He never charged admission fees for the demonstrations he put on in the courtyard of his apartment building, and he never benefited from the resulting publicity.

A government committee was established to examine Clever Hans's powers and to determine if any deception or trickery was involved. The group included a circus manager, a veterinarian, horse trainers, an aristocrat, the director of the Berlin Zoo, and the psychologist Carl Stumpf from the University of Berlin.

In September 1904, after a lengthy investigation, the committee concluded that Hans was not receiving any intentional signs or cues

Clever Hans, the clever horse.

from his owner. No fraud, no deceit. But Stumpf was not completely satisfied. He was curious about how the horse was able to respond correctly to so many different kinds of questions. He assigned the problem to one of his graduate students, Oskar Pfungst, who approached the task in the careful manner of an experimental psychologist.

One of Pfungst's first experiments occurred after a demonstration that Hans could answer questions even when his owner, von Osten, was not present. Pfungst formed two groups of questioners, one composed of people who knew the answers to the questions put to the horse, and the second composed of people who did not know the answers. This led to a crucial finding: The horse could give the correct answers only when the questioners themselves knew the answers. Obviously Hans was somehow receiving information from the person questioning him, even when that person was a stranger.

Following a series of well-controlled experiments, Pfungst concluded that Hans had been unintentionally conditioned to begin tapping his hoof whenever he perceived the slightest downward movement of von Osten's head. When the correct number of taps had been reached, von Osten's head would automatically move slightly upward and the horse would stop. Pfungst demonstrated that everyone—even people who had never been around a horse before— made the same barely perceptible head gestures when speaking to a horse.

Thus, it was shown that Hans did not have a storehouse of knowledge. He had simply been trained to start tapping his hoof, or to incline his head toward an object, whenever his questioner made a certain movement. Further, the horse had been conditioned to stop tapping in response to the opposite movement. During the training period von Osten had reinforced Hans by giving him pieces of carrot or sugar lumps every time he made a correct response. As the training progressed, von Osten no longer had to reinforce Hans's behavior for every correct reply, but rewarded him instead on a partial or intermittent basis. The behavioral psychologist B. F. Skinner would later demonstrate the effectiveness of partial reinforcement in the conditioning process.

The case of Clever Hans illustrated the value (indeed, the necessity) of an experimental approach to the study of animal behavior. It made psychologists more skeptical of claims of great intelligence in animals. It was clear, however, that animals were capable of learning and could be conditioned to alter their behavior. Therefore, the experimental study of animal learning came to be seen as much more profitable than speculation about what might be going on in an animal's mind in terms of some alleged consciousness or intelligence. Pfungst's report about his experiments with Clever Hans was reviewed by John B. Watson, and its conclusions influenced Watson's growing inclination to promote a psychology that would deal only with behavior, not with consciousness (Watson, 1908).

Edward Lee Thorndike (1874–1949)

Thorndike, who was never able to learn how to drive a car, is one of the most important researchers in the development of animal psychology. He fashioned an objective, mechanistic theory of learning that focuses on overt behavior. He believed that psychology must study behavior, not mental elements or conscious experience, and he reinforced the trend toward greater objectivity begun by the functionalists. He interpreted learning not in subjective terms but rather in terms of concrete connections between stimuli and responses, although he did permit some reference to consciousness and mental processes.

The works of Thorndike and Ivan Pavlov provide an example of independent simultaneous discovery. Thorndike developed his law of effect in 1898, and Pavlov proposed a similar law of reinforcement in 1902, but it was many years before psychologists recognized the resemblance between the two.

Thorndike's Life

Edward Lee Thorndike was one of the first American psychologists to receive all of his education in the United States. It is significant that this was possible—that he did not have to go to Germany for graduate study—just 2 decades after psychology was founded. His interest in psychology was awakened, as it was for so many others, when he read William James's *The Principles of Psychology* while an undergraduate at Wesleyan University in Middletown, Connecticut. He

National Library of Medicine

Edward Lee Thorndike

later studied under James at Harvard, where he began his investigation of learning.

He had planned to conduct research using children as subjects, but he was forbidden to do so by the university administration, which was sensitive about a recent scandal when an anthropologist had "loosenèd" children's clothing to take their body measurements. When Thorndike learned that he could not study children, he chose chicks instead, apparently inspired by lectures given by Morgan, who described his own research with chicks.

Thorndike trained his chicks to run through mazes that he improvised by standing books on end. The story is told of Thorndike's difficulties in finding room for his chicks. Because his landlady refused to allow him to keep chicks in his bedroom, he turned to James for advice. James was unsuccessful in finding space in the laboratory or the university museum, so he took Thorndike and the chicks into the basement of his home, to the delight of the James children.

Thorndike did not complete his education at Harvard. Believing that a certain young lady did not return his interest, he applied to Cattell at Columbia, so that he could get away from the Boston area. When Cattell offered him a fellowship, Thorndike went to New York, taking his two best-trained chicks with him. He continued his animal research at Columbia, working with cats and dogs in puzzle boxes of his own design. In 1898 he was awarded his doctorate. His dissertation, "Animal Intelligence: An Experimental Study of the Associative Processes in Animals," was published, along with subsequent research on associative learning in chicks, fish, and monkeys.

Fiercely ambitious and competitive, Thorndike wrote to his fiancée, "I've decided to get to the top of the psychology heap in five years, teach ten more, and then quit" (quoted in Boakes, 1984, p. 72). He did not remain an animal psychologist for long, admitting that he had no real interest in it. He had stuck with it only to complete his degree and establish a reputation. Animal psychology was not the field for someone with such an intense drive to succeed.

Thorndike became an instructor in psychology at Teachers College of Columbia University in 1899. There he worked with human subjects, applying his animal research techniques to children and young people. The remainder of his long career was spent on problems in human learning and the applied areas of educational psychology and mental testing. He wrote several textbooks and got to the top of the psychology heap, as he put it; in 1912 he was elected president of the American Psychological Association. He became wealthy from royalties from his tests and textbooks and by 1924 enjoyed an income of nearly $70,000 a year, a tremendous sum at that time (Boakes, 1984).

Thorndike's 50 years at Columbia are among the most productive ever recorded. His bibliography lists 507 items, many of which are lengthy books. He retired in 1939 but continued to work until his death 10 years later.

Connectionism

Thorndike created an experimental approach to association that he called **connectionism.** He wrote that if he were to analyze the human mind he would "find connections of varying strength between (a) situations, elements of situations, and compounds of situations, and (b) responses, readinesses to respond, facilitations, inhibitions, and directions of responses. If all these could be completely inventoried, telling what the man would think and do and what would satisfy and annoy him, in every conceivable situation, it seems to me that nothing would be left out. . . . Learning is connecting. The mind is man's connection-system" (Thorndike, 1931, p. 122).

This position was a direct extension of the older philosophical notion of association (see chapter 2), with one significant difference: Instead of talking about associations or connections between ideas, Thorndike was dealing with connections between situations and responses. Although he incorporated a more objective frame of reference into his psychological theory, he did invoke mental or subjective processes. He spoke about "satisfaction," "annoyance," and "discomfort" when discussing the behavior of his experimental animals, terms that are clearly more mentalistic than behavioristic. Thorndike thus showed the influence of Romanes and Morgan. "Detailed analysis of an animal's mental operations on the basis of objective inference was followed by descriptions of the animal's private experience on the basis of subjective inference" (Mackenzie, 1977, p. 70).

It must be noted that Thorndike, like Loeb, was not granting high levels of consciousness and intelligence to animals as freely and extravagantly as Romanes had. We can see a steady reduction in the role of consciousness in animal psychology from its beginnings to the time of Thorndike, along with a greater focus on the use of the experimental method to study more objective behavior.

In spite of the mentalistic tinge to Thorndike's work, we must not lose sight of the mechanistic nature of his approach. He argued that to study behavior, it must be broken down or reduced to its simplest elements: the stimulus-response units. He thus shared with the structuralists an analytic and atomistic point of view. The stimulus-response units are the elements of behavior (not of consciousness), the building blocks from which more complex behaviors are compounded.

CONNECTIONISM: Thorndike's approach to learning based on connections between situations and responses

The Puzzle Box

Thorndike's theories were derived from research using a piece of equipment he designed, the puzzle box (see Figure 9.1). An animal placed in the box had to learn to operate a latch in order to escape. Thorndike placed a cat that had been deprived of food in the slatted box. Food was put outside the box as a reward for escaping. The door of the box was fastened by several latches. The cat had to pull a lever

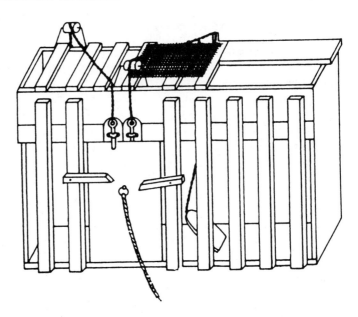

FIGURE 9.1   Thorndike's puzzle box.

or a chain, and sometimes engage in several acts in succession, to open the door.

At first the cat displayed random behaviors, poking, sniffing, and clawing to get at the food. Eventually the cat hit on the correct behavior and unlatched the door. During the first trial the correct behavior occurred by accident. On subsequent trials the random behaviors were displayed less frequently, until learning was complete. Then the cat would exhibit the correct behavior as soon as it was placed in the box.

Thorndike used quantitative measures of learning. One technique was to record the number of wrong behaviors, acts that did not lead to escape. Over a series of trials these behaviors occurred less often. Another technique was to record the time that elapsed from the moment the cat was placed in the box until it succeeded in escaping. As learning took place, this time period became shorter.

Thorndike wrote of the stamping in or stamping out of a response tendency by its favorable or unfavorable results. Unsuccessful response tendencies (those that did nothing to get the cat out of the box) disappear; they are stamped out over a number of trials. Response tendencies that lead to success are stamped in after a number of trials. This kind of learning has been called **trial-and-error learning;** Thorndike preferred to call it "trial and accidental success" (Jonçich, 1968, p. 266).

TRIAL-AND-ERROR LEARNING:

Learning based on the repetition of response tendencies that lead to success

Laws of Learning

The stamping in or stamping out of a response tendency was formalized as the **law of effect:** "Any act which in a given situation produces satisfaction becomes associated with that situation, so that when the situation recurs the act is more likely than before to recur also. Conversely, any act which in a given situation produces discomfort becomes disassociated from that situation, so that when the situation recurs the act is less likely than before to recur" (Thorndike, 1905, p. 203).

A companion law—the **law of exercise** or the **law of use and disuse**—states that any response made in a particular situation becomes associated with that situation. The more the response is used in the situation, the more strongly it becomes associated with it. Conversely, prolonged disuse of the response tends to weaken the association. In other words, repeating a response in a given situation tends to strengthen that response. Thorndike's later research persuaded him that the reward consequences of a response (a situation that produces satisfaction) are more effective than mere repetition of the response.

In the early 1930s Thorndike reexamined the law of effect in an extensive research program using human subjects. The results revealed that rewarding a response did indeed strengthen it, but punishing a response did not produce a comparable negative effect. He revised the law of effect to place greater emphasis on reward than on punishment.

LAW OF EFFECT: Acts that produce satisfaction in a given situation become associated with that situation, so that when the situation recurs the act is likely to recur

LAW OF EXERCISE: The more an act or response is used in a given situation, the more strongly the act becomes associated with that situation

Comment

Thorndike's investigations of human and animal learning are among the greatest in the history of psychology. His work heralded the rise of learning theory to prominence in American psychology, and the objective spirit in which he conducted his research was an important contribution to behaviorism. Watson wrote that Thorndike's research laid the foundation for behaviorism.

Ivan Pavlov also paid tribute to Thorndike:

> *Some years after the beginning of the work with our new method I learned that somewhat similar experiments had been performed in America, and indeed not by physiologists but by psychologists. Thereupon I studied in more detail the American publications, and now I must acknowledge that the honor of having made the first steps along this path belongs to E. L. Thorndike. By two or three years his experiments preceded ours and his book must be considered a classic, both for its bold outlook on an immense task and for the accuracy of its results.*
> (PAVLOV, 1928, QUOTED IN JONÇICH, 1968, PP. 415–416)

IVAN PETROVITCH PAVLOV (1849–1936)

Pavlov's work on learning helped to shift associationism from its traditional emphasis on subjective ideas to objective and quantifiable

Archives of the History of American Psychology/University of Akron

IVAN PETROVITCH
PAVLOV

physiological events, such as glandular secretions and muscular movements. As a result, Pavlov's work provided Watson with a new method for studying behavior and a means of attempting to control and modify it.

Pavlov's Life

Ivan Pavlov was born in the town of Ryazan in central Russia, the eldest of 11 children of a village priest. His position in such a large family brought him responsibility and hard work at an early age, characteristics he retained all his life. He was unable to attend school for several years because of an accident involving a severe blow to his head at the age of 7. His father tutored him at home, and in 1860 he entered the theological seminary, intending to prepare for the priesthood. Later, after reading about Darwin's theories, Pavlov changed his mind. He walked several hundred miles to the city of St. Petersburg to attend the university there. He chose to specialize in animal physiology.

With this university training, Pavlov became part of the intelligentsia, the emerging class in Russian society, distinct from the other classes—the aristocracy and the peasantry. Pavlov was "too well-educated and too intelligent for the peasantry from which he came, but too common and too poor for the aristocracy into which he could never rise. These social conditions often produced an especially dedicated intellectual, one whose entire life was centered on the intellectual pursuits that justified his existence. And so it was with Pavlov, whose almost fanatic devotion to pure science and to experimental research was supported by the energy and simplicity of a Russian peasant" (Miller, 1962, p. 177).

Pavlov obtained his degree in 1875 and began medical training, not to practice as a physician but in the hope of a career in physiological research. He studied in Germany for 2 years, then returned to St. Petersburg for several years as a laboratory research assistant.

Pavlov's dedication to research was almost total. He was not distracted by practical issues such as salary, clothing, or living conditions. His wife, Sara, whom he married in 1881, devoted herself to protecting him from mundane matters. They made a pact early in their marriage, agreeing that she would take care of everyday concerns and allow nothing to distract him from his work. He promised, in return, never to drink or play cards and to socialize only on Saturday and Sunday evenings. He adhered to a rigorous schedule, working 7 days a week from September to May; summers were spent in the country.

Characteristic of his indifference to ordinary life is the story that Sara often had to remind him to collect his pay. She said that he couldn't be trusted to buy clothes for himself. When he was in his seventies, riding the streetcar to his laboratory, he jumped off before it stopped and broke his leg. "He was impetuous. He wouldn't wait for it to stop. A woman standing near saw it and said, 'My, here is a man of genius, but he doesn't know how to get off a streetcar without breaking his leg'" (Gantt, 1979, p. 28).

The family lived in poverty until 1890 when, at the age of 41, Pavlov finally became professor of pharmacology at the Military Medical Academy in St. Petersburg. In 1883, while Pavlov was preparing his doctoral dissertation, their first child was born. Frail and sickly, the infant would not survive, the doctor said, unless mother and child could rest in the country. Pavlov was able to borrow enough money for the journey, but it was too late and the child died. For a time Pavlov slept on a cot in his laboratory while his wife and second child lived with relatives, because they could not afford an apartment.

A group of Pavlov's students, knowing of his financial difficulties, gave him money on the pretext of covering the expenses of lectures they had asked him to present. Pavlov spent the money on dogs for his laboratory and kept nothing for himself. So strong was his dedication to his work that he did not seem bothered by the hardship. He said it never caused him concern.

In 1923, Pavlov visited the United States to attend a conference in New York City and was robbed of $2,000 at Grand Central Station. He had sat down on a bench to rest and had placed his briefcase on the seat beside him. He became so absorbed watching the crowds that he failed to watch the bag, and when he got up to leave it was gone. "Ah well," he said, "one must not put temptation in the way of the needy" (quoted in Gerow, 1986, p. 42).

Pavlov was known to have a temper; he was given to explosive emotional tirades at work, often directed at his research assistants. During the Bolshevik Revolution of 1917 he berated an assistant for being 10 minutes late. Gunfire in the streets was no excuse and should not be permitted to interfere with laboratory work. Usually these outbursts were quickly forgotten. His students knew what was expected of them, because Pavlov never hesitated to tell them. He was honest and direct, if not always considerate, in his dealings with other people.

He was aware of his own volatile nature. When one laboratory worker could no longer tolerate the insults, he asked to be relieved of his duties. "Pavlov replied that his abusive behavior was just a habit. . . . it was not of itself a sufficient reason to quit the laboratory" (Windholz, 1990, p. 68). A research failure could cause Pavlov to become depressed, but a success was met with such joy that he would congratulate not only his assistants but the dogs as well.

Pavlov was one of the few Russian scientists to allow women students and Jewish students to work in his laboratory, and he became angry at any hint of anti-Semitism. He had a good sense of humor and knew how to enjoy a joke. During the ceremony at which he received an honorary degree from Cambridge University, students lowered a toy dog into his lap by a rope from the balcony. Pavlov kept the dog by his desk in his apartment.

His relations with the Soviet government were difficult; he was openly critical of the 1917 revolution and the Soviet system. He wrote strong letters of protest to Joseph Stalin, the tyrannical Russian leader who killed and exiled millions, and he boycotted Russian scientific meetings to demonstrate his disapproval of the regime. Not until 1933 did Pavlov acknowledge that the Soviets had achieved some success. Despite his attitude toward the authorities, Pavlov received generous research support from the Soviet bureaucracy and was permitted to conduct his research free of government interference.

Pavlov remained a scientist to the last. He had the habit of self-observation whenever he was ill, and the day of his death was no exception. Weak from pneumonia, he called in a physician and described his symptoms: "My brain is not working well, obsessive feelings and involuntary movements appear; mortification may be setting in." He discussed his condition with the doctor for a while and then fell asleep. When he awoke, Pavlov raised himself up in bed and began to search for his clothes, with the same impatient energy he had shown all his life. "It is time to get up," he cried. "Help me, I must dress!" And with that, he fell back on the pillows and died (Gantt, 1941, p. 35).

Conditioned Reflexes

During his distinguished and productive career Pavlov worked on three research problems. The first concerned the function of the nerves of the heart, and the second was on the primary digestive glands. His brilliant research on digestion won him worldwide recognition and, in 1904, the Nobel Prize. His third research area, for which he occupies a prominent place in the history of psychology, was the study of **conditioned reflexes.**

CONDITIONED REFLEXES:
Reflexes that are conditional or dependent on the formation of an association or connection between stimulus and response

The notion of conditioned reflexes originated, as so many scientific breakthroughs, in an accidental discovery. In his work on the digestive glands in dogs, Pavlov used the method of surgical exposure to permit the collection of digestive secretions outside the body where they could be observed, measured, and recorded (Pavlov, 1927).

One aspect of this work dealt with the function of saliva, which was involuntarily secreted whenever food was placed in the dog's mouth. Pavlov noticed that sometimes saliva would flow before the food was given. The dogs salivated when they saw the food or the man who regularly fed them, and even when they heard his footsteps. The unlearned response of salivation had somehow become connected with or conditioned to stimuli that had, on previous occasions, been associated with food.

These psychic reflexes, as Pavlov first called them, were aroused in the dogs by stimuli other than the original one (the food). Pavlov reasoned that this occurred because these other stimuli (such as the sight and sounds of the attendant) had so often been associated with feeding.

Pavlov, in accordance with the prevailing Zeitgeist in animal psychology (like Thorndike, Loeb, and others before him), initially focused on the mentalistic experiences of his laboratory animals; we can see this focus in his original term for conditioned reflexes— *psychic reflexes*. He wrote about the animals' desires, judgment, and will, interpreting the animals' mental events in subjective and human terms.

In time, Pavlov dropped all mentalistic references in favor of a more objective, descriptive approach. "At first in our psychical experiments . . . we conscientiously endeavored to explain our results by imagining the subjective state of the animal. But nothing came of this except sterile controversy and individual views that could not be reconciled. And so we could do nothing but conduct the research on a purely objective basis" (quoted in Cuny, 1965, p. 65).

Studies on Conditioned Reflexes

Pavlov's first experiments were simple. He showed a dog a piece of bread in his hand before giving it to the dog to eat. In time, the dog began to salivate as soon as it saw the bread. The dog's response of salivating when the bread was placed in its mouth is a natural reflexive response of the digestive system; no learning is necessary for it to occur. Pavlov called this an innate or unconditioned reflex.

Salivating at the sight of food, however, is not reflexive but must be learned. This response Pavlov now called a conditional reflex (instead of the mentalistic "psychic" reflex) because it was conditional or dependent on the formation of an association or connection between the sight of the food and the subsequent eating of it.

In translating Pavlov's work from the Russian into the English language, an American student, W. H. Gantt, used the word *conditioned* instead of *conditional*. Gantt later said he regretted the change. Nevertheless, conditioned reflex remains the accepted term (Fishman & Franks, 1992).

Pavlov discovered that many stimuli could produce the conditional salivary response in his laboratory animals as long as it was capable of attracting the animal's attention without arousing fear or anger. He tested buzzers, lights, whistles, tones, bubbling water, and ticking metronomes, and achieved similar results.

His thoroughness and precision are evident in the elaborate and sophisticated technique he devised to collect the saliva. A rubber tube was connected to a surgical opening made in the dog's cheek through which saliva flowed. When each drop of saliva fell onto a platform that rested on a sensitive spring, it activated a marker on a revolving drum (see Figure 9.2). This arrangement, which made it possible to

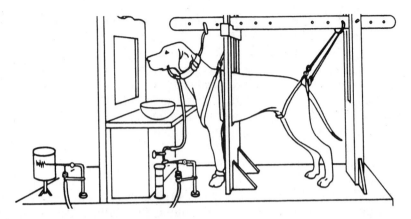

FIGURE 9.2   *Pavlov's apparatus for studying the conditional salivary response in dogs.*

record the precise number of drops and the moment at which each fell, is but one example of Pavlov's painstaking efforts to follow the scientific method—to standardize experimental conditions, apply rigorous controls, and eliminate sources of error.

He was so concerned about preventing outside influences from affecting the research that he designed special cubicles. The experimental animal was placed in a harness in one cubicle and the experimenter occupied another. The researcher could operate the various conditioning stimuli, collect saliva, and present food without being seen by the animal.

These precautions did not completely satisfy Pavlov. He believed that extraneous environmental stimuli could still operate to contaminate his results. Using funds supplied by a Russian businessman, Pavlov designed a three-story research building—known as the "Tower of Silence"—in which the windows were covered with extra-thick glass. The rooms had double steel doors that formed an airtight seal when closed, and the steel girders that supported the floors were embedded in sand. A moat filled with straw encircled the building. Vibration, noise, temperature extremes, odors, and drafts were eliminated. Pavlov wanted nothing to influence the experimental animals except the conditioning stimuli to which they were exposed.

Let us follow a typical conditioning experiment in Pavlov's laboratory. The conditioned stimulus (a light, let us say) is presented (in this case, the light is switched on). Immediately, the unconditioned stimulus (the food) is presented. After a number of pairings of the light and the food, the animal will salivate at the sight of the light alone. The animal has become conditioned to respond to the conditioned stimulus. An association or bond has been formed between the light and the food. This conditioning or learning will not occur unless the light is followed by the food a sufficient number of times. Thus, **reinforcement** (being fed) is necessary for learning to take place.

REINFORCEMENT: Something that increases the likelihood of a response

In addition to studying the formation of these conditioned responses, Pavlov and his associates investigated related phenomena such as reinforcement, the extinction of responses, spontaneous recovery, generalization, discrimination, and higher-order conditioning—all well-known problems in the field today. Some 200 collaborators came to work with Pavlov, and his experimental program extended over a longer time period and involved more people than any research effort since Wundt's.

A Note on E. B. Twitmyer

An interesting historical sidelight involves the independent discovery of the same phenomenon at the same time. In 1904 a young American named Edwin Burket Twitmyer (1873–1943), a former student of Lightner Witmer at the University of Pennsylvania, presented a paper at the APA meeting based on his doctoral dissertation, completed 2 years earlier. His work concerned the familiar knee jerk reflex. In the course of his study Twitmyer noticed that subjects began to respond to stimuli other than the original stimulus, which was the tap of the hammer just below the knee. He described the subjects' reactions as a new and unusual kind of reflex and suggested that it be studied further.

No one was interested in Twitmyer's report at the meeting. There were no questions from the audience after he finished his presentation. His research was ignored. Discouraged, he did not pursue the issue.

Several reasons have been advanced to explain Twitmyer's continued residence in obscurity. Perhaps the American Zeitgeist was not yet ready to accept such a notion as a conditioned reflex. Perhaps Twitmyer was too young and inexperienced or lacked the skills and economic resources to persevere and publicize his finding. Or perhaps it was simply a matter of bad timing.

Twitmyer delivered his talk on reflexes just before lunch as part of a series of papers in a long session chaired by William James. The meeting was running late, and James (perhaps hungry, maybe bored as well) adjourned the meeting without allowing much time for any discussion of Twitmyer's paper.

Although the story of Twitmyer is revived periodically as another example of simultaneous discovery (see Coon, 1982; Misceo & Samelson, 1983; Windholz, 1986), it is also a tragic tale of a scientist who might have become famous for making one of the most important discoveries in all of psychology. "Surely Twitmyer must have wrestled with that realization most of his life—an awareness of what his legacy to psychology might have been" (Benjamin, 1987, p. 1119).

Comment

Pavlov demonstrated that higher mental processes could be studied in physiological terms with animal subjects and without any mention of consciousness. Further, conditioning methods have had broad practical applications in areas such as behavior therapy. Thus, Pavlov's work influenced psychology's shift toward greater objectivity in subject matter and method and reinforced the trend toward the functional and practical.

Pavlov also continued the long tradition of mechanism and atomism, which shaped the new psychology from its beginnings. In his view, dogs and humans, like all animals, were machines. He maintained the belief that "the living organism showed itself to be merely a machine—a very complicated one, of course, but just as submissive and obedient as any other machine" (Mazlish, 1993, p. 124).

Pavlov's conditioning techniques provided the science of psychology with a basic element of behavior, a workable concrete unit to which complex human behavior could be reduced and experimented on under laboratory conditions. John B. Watson seized on this unit of behavior and made it the core of his program. Pavlov was pleased with Watson's work, noting that the growth of behaviorism in the United States represented a confirmation of his ideas and methods.

It is ironic that Pavlov's greatest influence has been in psychology, a field toward which he was not altogether favorable. He was familiar with the structural and functional psychologies, and he agreed with James that psychology had not yet reached the status of a science. Consequently, Pavlov excluded psychology from his own work. He levied fines on laboratory assistants who used psychological rather than physiological terminology, and in his lectures he made reference to the "untenable pretensions of psychology" (Woodworth, 1948, p. 60).

Toward the end of his life Pavlov changed his attitude and even referred to himself as an experimental psychologist. However, his initially negative view of the field did not prevent psychologists from making effective use of his work.

VLADIMIR M. BEKHTEREV (1857–1927)

Vladimir Bekhterev is another important figure in the development of animal psychology, helping to lead the field away from subjective ideas toward objectively observed overt behavior. Although less well known than Pavlov, this Russian physiologist, neurologist, and psychiatrist was a pioneer in several research areas. He was a political radical who was openly critical of the Czar and the Russian government. He accepted women and Jews as students and colleagues at a time when they were largely excluded from Russian universities.

Bekhterev received his degree from the Military Medical Academy in St. Petersburg in 1881. He studied at the University of Leipzig with Wilhelm Wundt, took courses in Berlin and Paris, and returned to Russia to accept a professorship in mental diseases at the University of Kazan. In 1893, he was appointed chair of mental and nervous diseases at the Military Medical Academy, where he organized a mental hospital. In 1907, he founded the Psychoneurological Institute, which now bears his name, and began a program of neurological research.

Bekhterev and Pavlov became enemies after Pavlov published a negative review of one of Bekhterev's books. "The enmity between Bekhterev and Pavlov was so pronounced that they would insult each other in the street. If they ran into each other at the same congress they would soon be embroiled in dispute. Forming cliques and slinging snide shots at each other, they were engaged in a constant struggle to expose one another's faults and weaknesses. No sooner had some pupil of Bekhterev made a public statement than it was parried by Pavlov's retort—which followed virtually as a conditioned reflex" (Ljunggren, 1990, p. 60).

In 1927, 10 years after the Bolshevik Revolution that toppled the Czar, Bekhterev was summoned to Moscow and asked to treat the Soviet dictator, Joseph Stalin, said to be experiencing periods of depression. Bekhterev told Stalin he was suffering from severe paranoia. Suspiciously, Bekhterev died that afternoon. No autopsy was permitted to determine the cause of death, and the body was cremated. It was thought that Stalin had Bekhterev poisoned as revenge for Bekhterev's diagnosis. Stalin later suppressed Bekhterev's work and ordered his son shot (Ljunggren, 1990).

Associated Reflexes

Whereas Pavlov's conditioning research had been conducted almost exclusively on glandular secretions, Bekhterev was interested in the motor conditioning response. He extended Pavlov's conditioning principles to the muscles. Bekhterev's basic discoveries were the **associated reflexes,** revealed through his study of motor responses. He found that reflexive movements—such as withdrawing one's finger from the source of an electric shock—could be elicited not only by the unconditioned stimulus (the electric shock), but also by stimuli that had become associated with the original stimulus. For example,

ASSOCIATED REFLEXES: Reflexes that can be elicited not only by unconditioned stimuli but also by stimuli that have become associated with the unconditioned stimuli

sounding a buzzer at the time of the shock soon brought forth the withdrawal of the finger.

The associationists explained such connections in terms of mental processes, but Bekhterev considered the reactions to be reflexive. Further, he believed that higher-level behaviors of greater complexity could be explained in the same way; that is, as an accumulation or compounding of lower-level motor reflexes. Thought processes were of similar character in that they depended on inner actions of the speech musculature, an idea later adopted by Watson. Bekhterev argued for a completely objective approach to psychological phenomena and against the use of mentalistic terms and concepts.

He presented his views in the book *Objective Psychology*, published in 1907. It was translated into German and French in 1913, when it was read by Watson. A third edition was published in English in 1932 as *General Principles of Human Reflexology*.

COMMENT

From the beginnings of animal psychology in the work of Romanes and Morgan we can see a steady movement toward increased objectivity in both subject matter and methodology. The initial work in the field invoked the concepts of consciousness and mental processes and relied on subjective research methods. By the early 20th century, however, animal psychology was completely objective in subject matter and methods. Glandular secretions, conditional responses, acts, behaviors—such terms left no doubt that animal psychology had finally discarded its subjective past.

Animal psychology was shortly to serve as a model for behaviorism, whose leader—Watson—much preferred animal to human subjects for his psychological research. Watson adopted the findings and techniques of the animal psychologists as the foundation for a science of behavior applicable to animals and humans alike.

THE INFLUENCE OF FUNCTIONAL PSYCHOLOGY ON BEHAVIORISM

Another direct antecedent of behaviorism was functionalism. Although not totally objective, functional psychology in Watson's day did represent greater objectivity than its predecessors. Cattell and other functionalists, who were emphasizing behavior and objectivity, had expressed dissatisfaction with introspection. Applied psychologists had little use for consciousness and introspection, and their various specialty areas essentially constituted an objective functional psychology. Thus, even before Watson came on the scene, the functional psychologists had moved away from the pure psychology of conscious experience of Wundt and Titchener. In their writings and lectures, some functional psychologists were quite specific in calling for an objective psychology, a psychology that would focus on behavior instead of consciousness.

Cattell, speaking at the 1904 World's Fair in St. Louis, Missouri, said: "I am not convinced that psychology should be limited to the study of consciousness. . . . The rather widespread notion that there is no psychology apart from introspection is refuted by the brute argument of accomplished fact. It seems to me that most of the research work that has been done by me or in my laboratory is nearly as independent of introspection as work in physics or in zoology. . . . I see no reason why the application of systematized knowledge to the control of human nature may not in the course of the present century accomplish results commensurate with the nineteenth-century applications of physical science to the material world" (Cattell, 1904, pp. 179-180, 186).

Watson was present for Cattell's speech. The similarity between his later public position and Cattell's statement is so striking that one historian has suggested that Cattell be called the "grandfather" of Watson's behaviorism (Burnham, 1968, p. 149).

In the decade before Watson formally founded behaviorism, the intellectual climate in the United States favored and reinforced the idea of an objective psychology, and the overall movement of American psychology was in a behavioristic direction. Robert Woodworth at Columbia University noted that American psychologists were "slowly coming down with behaviorism . . . as more and more of them, from 1904 on, expressed a preference for defining psychology as the science of behavior rather than as an attempt to describe consciousness" (Woodworth, 1943, p. 28).

In 1911, Walter Pillsbury, who had studied with Titchener, defined psychology in his textbook as the "science of *behavior*" (italics added). He argued that it was possible to treat human beings as objectively as any other aspect of the physical universe. Also in that year, William Montague presented a paper before the New York branch of the APA entitled, "Has Psychology Lost Its Mind?" He spoke of the "movement to dispense with the concept of mind or consciousness and to substitute the concept of behavior as the sufficient object of psychological study" (Benjamin, 1993b, p. 77). Max Meyer published a book entitled *The Fundamental Laws of Human Behavior*. William McDougall wrote *Psychology: The Study of Behavior*. And Knight Dunlap, a psychologist at Johns Hopkins University, where Watson was teaching, proposed that introspection be banned from psychology.

Angell, perhaps the most progressive of the functional psychologists, predicted that American psychology was ready for greater objectivity. In 1910 he commented that it seemed possible that the term *consciousness* would disappear from psychology, much as had the term *soul*. Three years later, shortly before Watson's behaviorist manifesto was published, Angell suggested that it would be profitable if consciousness were forgotten and if animal and human behavior were described objectively instead.

Thus, the notion that psychology should be the science of behavior was already gaining converts. Watson's greatness was not in being the first to propose the idea but in seeing, perhaps more clearly than anyone else, what the times were calling for. He responded vigorously and articulately as the agent of a revolution whose inevitability and success were assured, because it was already under way.

Discussion Questions

1. What were the basic tenets of Watson's behaviorism? Describe the three major forces Watson brought together to form his new psychology.
2. Describe the development of animal psychology since the work of Romanes and Morgan. How did the Clever Hans incident affect animal psychology?
3. Relate Thorndike's connectionism to the older philosophical notion of association. Describe Thorndike's puzzle-box research and define the laws of learning that resulted from this research.
4. Describe Pavlov's research on conditioning. Discuss his initial focus on mentalistic experiences and his attempt to control outside influences.
5. How did Pavlov's work influence Watson's behaviorism? Compare Pavlov's concept of the conditioned reflex with Bekhterev's associated reflex.
6. Describe the Zeitgeist in American psychology in the second decade of the 20th century; specifically, the positions of structuralism and functionalism. How did functionalist ideas influence Watsonian behaviorism?

Suggested Readings

Bitterman, M. E. (1969). Thorndike and the problem of animal intelligence. *American Psychologist, 24,* 444–453. Discusses Thorndike's career at Columbia University and his puzzle-box experiments on animal learning.

Fernald, D. (1984). *The Hans legacy: A story of science*. Hillsdale, NJ: Erlbaum. Recounts the Clever Hans story and its implications for scientific inquiry.

Windholz, G. (1990). Pavlov and the Pavlovians in the laboratory. *Journal of the History of the Behavioral Sciences, 26,* 64–74. Describes the daily routine in Pavlov's laboratory (1897–1936) and his influence on associates and students.

Yerkes, R. M., & Morgulis, S. (1909). The method of Pavlov in animal psychology. *Psychological Bulletin, 6,* 257–273. The article that brought Pavlov's work to the attention of American psychologists.

CHAPTER 10

BEHAVIORISM:
THE BEGINNINGS

JOHN B. WATSON (1878–1958)

WE HAVE discussed several antecedents of the behaviorist movement that influenced Watson in his attempt to construct a new school of thought for psychology. He recognized that founding is not the same as originating, and he described his efforts as a crystallization of current trends in psychology. Like Wundt, psychology's first promoter-founder, Watson announced as his goal the founding of a new school. This deliberate intention clearly distinguishes him from others whom history now labels as precursors of behaviorism.

Watson's Life

John B. Watson was born on a farm near Greenville, South Carolina, where his early education was conducted in a one-room schoolhouse. His mother was intensely religious, his father just the opposite. The elder Watson drank heavily, was given to violence, and had several extramarital affairs.

Because Watson's father rarely held any job for long, the family lived on the edge of poverty, subsisting on the output of their farm. Their neighbors looked on them with pity and contempt. When Watson was 13, his father ran off with another woman, never to return, and

JOHN B. WATSON

Bachrach Studios

Watson resented him all his life. Many years later, when Watson was rich and famous, his father came to New York to see him, but Watson refused to meet him.

In Watson's youth and teenage years, he was described as a delinquent. He characterized himself as lazy and insubordinate, and he never earned better than passing grades in school. Teachers remember him as indolent, argumentative, and sometimes uncontrollable. He got into fistfights and was twice arrested, once for shooting a gun within the city limits. Nevertheless, he enrolled at Baptist-affiliated Furman University in Greenville at the age of 16, determined to become a minister, something he had promised his mother, many years earlier. He studied philosophy, mathematics, Latin, and Greek, and expected to graduate in 1899 and enter Princeton Theological Seminary the following fall.

A curious thing happened during Watson's senior year at Furman. A professor warned the students that anyone who handed in the final examination with the pages in reverse order would receive a failing grade for the course. Watson took the professor up on the challenge, turned in his exam backward, and failed; at least that is how Watson reported the story. A recent examination of the pertinent data of history—in this case, Watson's grades—shows that he did not fail that particular course. His biographer suggests that the story Watson chose to tell reveals something of his personality; that is, "his ambivalence toward success. Watson's constant striving for achievement and approval was often sabotaged by acts of sheer obstinacy and impulsiveness more characteristic of a flight from respectability" (Buckley, 1989, p. 11).

Another of Watson's professors at Furman remembered him as a nonconformist, "a brilliant but somewhat lazy and insolent student—a bit heavy but handsome—who thought too highly of himself and was more interested in his own ideas than in people" (Brewer, 1991, p. 174).

Watson remained at Furman for another year and received a master's degree in 1900, but during that year his mother died, releasing him from his vow to become a clergyman. Instead of attending Princeton Theological Seminary, Watson went to the University of Chicago. He was at this time "an ambitious, extremely status-conscious young man, anxious to make his mark upon the world but wholly unsettled as to his choice of profession and desperately insecure about his lack of means and social sophistication. He arrived on campus with fifty dollars to his name" (Buckley, 1989, p. 39).

He had chosen Chicago to pursue graduate work in philosophy with John Dewey but after a while found Dewey incomprehensible. "I never knew what he was talking about then," Watson recalled, "and, unfortunately for me, I still don't know" (Watson, 1936, p. 274). His enthusiasm for philosophy diminished.

He became attracted to psychology through the work of Angell, the functional psychologist, and he also studied biology and physiology with Jacques Loeb, who introduced him to the concept of mechanism. Watson worked at several jobs—a waiter in a boarding house, a rat caretaker, and an assistant janitor (his duties included dusting Angell's desk). Toward the end of his graduate studies he experienced a period of acute anxiety attacks and for a time was unable to sleep without a light on in his room.

In 1903 Watson received his PhD, the youngest person to earn a doctorate from the University of Chicago. Although he graduated with honors (*magna cum laude* and Phi Beta Kappa), he felt a deep sense of inferiority when Angell and Dewey told him that his doctoral examination was not as good as that of Helen Thompson Woolley, who had graduated 2 years earlier.[1]

That same year Watson married one of his students, 19-year-old Mary Ickes, who was from a socially and politically prominent family. This young woman had written a long love poem to Watson on one of her examination papers. It is not known what grade she got, but she did get Watson.

Watson stayed on as an instructor at the University of Chicago until 1908. He published his dissertation on the neurological and psychological maturation of the white rat, demonstrating early his preference for animal subjects. "I never wanted to use human subjects," he wrote. "I hated to serve as a subject. I didn't like the stuffy, artificial instructions given to subjects. I always was uncomfortable and acted unnaturally. With animals I was at home. I felt that, in studying them, I was keeping close to biology with my feet on the ground. More and more the thought presented itself: Can't I find out by watching their behavior everything that the other students are finding out by using [human observers]?" (Watson, 1936, p. 276).

Watson's colleagues recalled that he was not a good introspector. Whatever talent or temperament was needed for introspection, Watson did not have it. This lack may have helped to direct him toward an objective behavioral psychology. After all, if he was no good at practicing introspection, the primary technique in his field, then his career prospects were dim. He would have to develop another approach. Also, if psychology was a science that studied only behavior—which, of course, could be done by experimenting on animals as well as humans—then the professional interests of animal psychologists could be brought into the mainstream of the field.

In 1908, Watson was offered a professorship at Johns Hopkins University in Baltimore. Although he was reluctant to leave Chicago,

---

[1] Woolley, described by Dewey as one of the most brilliant students he had ever seen, had graduated *summa cum laude* and later became a pioneer in the area of the psychology of women (see chapter 16) (James, 1994).

the promotion, the opportunity to direct the laboratory, and the substantial salary increase offered by Johns Hopkins left him little choice. Watson spent 12 years there, his most productive years for psychology.

The person who offered Watson the job at Johns Hopkins was James Mark Baldwin (1861–1934), who, with Cattell, had started the journal *Psychological Review*. A year after Watson arrived, Baldwin was forced to resign because of a scandal: He had been caught in a police raid on a house of prostitution. Baldwin's explanation for his presence in the brothel was not accepted by the university's president. "I foolishly yielded," Baldwin said, "to a suggestion, made after a dinner, to visit [the brothel] and see what was done there. I did not know before going that immoral women were harbored there" (Evans & Scott, 1978, p. 713).

Baldwin became an outcast from American psychology and spent the remainder of his life in Europe. Eleven years later history repeated itself when the same university president asked for Watson's resignation because of a scandal.

At the time of Baldwin's resignation, however, Watson was promoted. He became chair of the psychology department and replaced Baldwin as editor of the influential *Psychological Review*. Thus, at the age of 31 Watson became an important figure in American psychology. He was in the right place at the right time.

Watson was extremely popular with the students at Johns Hopkins. They dedicated their yearbook to him and voted him the handsomest professor, surely a unique accolade in the history of psychology. He remained ambitious and intense, often driven to the edge of exhaustion. He struggled with the "fear of losing control, and he usually reacted by working even harder" (Buckley, 1989, p. 67).

He began to think seriously about a more objective approach to psychology around 1903, and he first expressed these ideas publicly in 1908, in a lecture at Yale University and in a paper presented at the annual meeting in Baltimore of the Southern Society for Philosophy and Psychology. In that paper Watson argued that psychic or mental concepts are "valueless to the science" of psychology (Pate, 1993, p. 5). In 1912, at the invitation of Cattell, Watson spoke on the subject in a series of lectures at Columbia University. The following year he published his now famous article in the *Psychological Review* (Watson, 1913), and behaviorism was officially launched.

Behavior: An Introduction to Comparative Psychology appeared in 1914. In this book Watson argued for the acceptance of animal psychology, and he described the advantages of using animals as subjects in psychological research. Many younger psychologists and graduate students found his proposals for a behavioral psychology appealing, believing that Watson was cleansing the muddled atmosphere of psychology by casting out long-standing mysteries carried over from philosophy.

Mary Cover Jones (1896–1987), then a graduate student and later president of the APA's Division of Developmental Psychology, remembered the excitement that greeted the publication of each of Watson's books. "It shook the foundations of traditional European-bred psychology, and we welcomed it. . . . It pointed the way from armchair psychology to action and reform and was therefore hailed as a panacea" (Jones, 1974, p. 582). Older psychologists were not universally captivated by Watson's program. Indeed, most rejected his approach.

Only 2 years after the publication of the *Psychological Review* article, Watson was elected president of the American Psychological Association, at the age of 37. His election may not have represented an official endorsement of his position, however, as much as a recognition of his visibility within the field and his personal connection with many prominent psychologists.

Watson wanted his new behaviorism to be of practical value. His ideas were not only for the laboratory but for the real world as well, and he worked hard to promote psychology's applied specialties. In 1916 he became a personnel consultant for a large insurance company, and he offered a course at Johns Hopkins on the psychology of advertising for business students.

Watson's professional activities were interrupted by World War I, when he served as a major in the Army Aviation Service. After the war, in 1918, he began research on children, one of the earliest attempts at experimental work on human infants.

His next book, *Psychology from the Standpoint of a Behaviorist*, was published in 1919. It presented a more complete statement of his behavioral psychology and argued that the methods and principles he recommended for animal psychology were appropriate for the study of humans.

Meanwhile, Watson's marriage had deteriorated; his infidelity left his wife embittered. In a letter to Angell Watson wrote that his wife no longer cared for him. "She instinctively loathes my touch. . . . Haven't we made a mess of our lives?" (quoted in Buckley, 1994, p. 27). Watson was about to make an even greater mess.

He fell in love with his graduate assistant, Rosalie Rayner, who was half his age and from a wealthy Baltimore family who had donated a considerable sum of money to the university. Watson wrote her torrid (and somewhat scientifically minded) love letters, 15 of which were found by his wife. Excerpts of the letters were printed in the *Baltimore Sun* during the sensational divorce proceedings that followed.

"Every cell I have is yours, individually and collectively," Watson had written. "My total reactions are positive and toward you. So likewise each and every heart reaction. I can't be more yours than I am, even if a surgical operation made us one" (quoted in Pauly, 1979, p. 40).

Thus ended Watson's promising university career. He was forced to resign from Johns Hopkins. "Watson was stunned. Until the end, he had refused to believe that he would actually be fired. . . . He had been convinced that his professional stature would have rendered him impervious to any censure of his private life" (Buckley, 1994, p. 31). Although he married Rosalie Rayner, he was never permitted to return to a full-time academic position. No university would have him because of the notoriety attached to his name, and he soon realized that he would have to make a new life. "I can find a commercial job," he wrote to a friend. "But I frankly love my work. I feel that my work is important for psychology and that the tiny flame which I have tried to keep burning for the future of psychology will be snuffed out if I go" (quoted in Pauly, 1986, p. 39).

Many academic colleagues, including his mentor Angell at the University of Chicago, publicly criticized Watson. He became embittered toward them and "never forgave the academic community, which he thought had betrayed him" (Brewer, 1991, pp. 179–180). Ironically, considering their radically different temperaments and theoretical positions, it was E. B. Titchener at Cornell who provided emotional support to Watson during this personal crisis.

Unemployed and ordered to pay two thirds of his former salary in alimony and child support, Watson began a second professional career as an applied psychologist in the field of advertising. He joined the J. Walter Thompson advertising agency in 1921 for an annual salary of $25,000, four times his academic salary. He conducted house-to-house surveys, sold coffee, and clerked in Macy's department store to learn about the business world. Acting with his characteristic ingenuity and drive, within 3 years he was a vice president. In 1936 he joined another agency, where he remained until his retirement in 1945.

Watson believed that people acted like machines and that their behavior as consumers could be predicted and controlled, just like the behavior of other machines. To control a consumer "it is only necessary to confront him with either fundamental or conditional emotional stimuli. . . . tell him something that will tie up with fear, something that will stir up a mild rage, that will call out an affectionate or love response, or strike at a deep psychological or habit need" (quoted in Buckley, 1982, p. 212).

He proposed that consumer behavior be studied under laboratory conditions and emphasized that advertising messages should focus on style rather than substance, striving to convey the impression of a new design or image. The purpose was to make consumers dissatisfied with the products they were using and instill the desire for new goods.

For many years Watson was given credit for pioneering the use of celebrity endorsements of products and services and for devising techniques to manipulate human motives, emotions, and needs. Recent research has shown that, although he vigorously promoted these techniques, they were already in use before he joined the advertising field (Coon, 1994; Kreshel, 1990). Nevertheless, Watson's contributions to advertising were highly successful and led to a position of prominence and wealth.

After 1920, Watson's contact with academic psychology was only indirect. He spent a great deal of time presenting his ideas for a behavioral psychology to the public through various media. He gave talks and radio addresses and wrote articles for popular magazines such as *Harper's, Cosmopolitan, McCall's, Collier's,* and *The Nation,* which increased his visibility and popularity.

In these articles Watson attempted to convey the message of behaviorism to a wide audience. He wrote in a clear and readable, if somewhat simplistic, style. In his autobiography he commented that because he could no longer publish in the professional psychology journals, he saw no reason why he should not "sell his wares" to the public (Watson, 1936). Although this work popularized his ideas, it further alienated him from the academic community. "Those who were not particularly tolerant of the application of psychological principles more generally, or of the behaviorist doctrine itself, were even less tolerant of Watson's 'campaigns' to spread the doctrine" (Kreshel, 1990, p. 56).

Watson's only formal contact with academic psychology came through a series of lectures he delivered at the New School for Social Research in New York City. These talks formed the basis of his book, *Behaviorism* (1925, 1930), which described his program for the improvement of society.

In 1928 he published a book on child care, *Psychological Care of the Infant and Child,* in which he outlined a regulatory rather than a permissive system of child rearing, in keeping with his strong environmentalist position. The book was full of stern advice on the behaviorist way of bringing up children.

For example, parents should never "hug and kiss them, never let them sit on your lap. If you must, kiss them once on the forehead when they say goodnight. Shake hands with them in the morning. Give them a pat on the head if they have made an extraordinarily good job of a difficult task. . . . you will find how easy it is to be perfectly objective with your child and at the same time kindly. You will be utterly ashamed at the mawkish, sentimental way you have been handling it" (Watson, 1928, pp. 81–82).

The book transformed American child-rearing practices and had a greater impact than anything else Watson wrote. A generation of children, including his own, was raised in accordance with these prescriptions. Watson's son James, a California businessman, re-called in 1987 that his father was unable to show affection to the children and never kissed or held them.

He described his father as "unresponsive, emotionally uncommunicative, unable to express and cope with any feelings or emotions of his own, and determined unwittingly to deprive, I think, my brother and me of any kind of emotional foundation. He deeply believed that any expression of tenderness or affection would have a harmful effect on us. He was very rigid in carrying out his fundamental philosophies as a behaviorist" (quoted in Hannush, 1987, pp. 37–138).

Rosalie Rayner Watson wrote an article for *Parent's Magazine* entitled "I Am the Mother of a Behaviorist's Sons," in which she admitted to some disagreement with her husband's child-rearing practices. She found it difficult, she said, to restrain completely her affection for her children and occasionally wanted to break all the behaviorist rules, although her son James could not recall that ever happening.

Watson was intelligent and articulate, and his handsome appearance and legendary charm made him a celebrity. He was much in the public eye throughout most of his life, and he courted and relished the attention. His clothes were always stylish. He raced speedboats. He mingled with the cream of New York society and "prided himself on being able to take on all challengers in extensive drinking bouts" (Buckley, 1989, p. 177).

He also considered himself to be a great lover and romantic adventurer, and attracted a host of beautiful young women (Brewer, 1991, p. 180; Burnham, 1994, p. 69). He built a mansion in Connecticut and staffed it with servants, yet delighted in donning old clothes and doing the yard work himself.

Watson's life changed in 1935 when Rosalie died. His son James recalled that this was the only time he saw his father cry, and for a brief moment Watson put his arms around his sons' shoulders. Myrtle McGraw, a psychologist in New York, met Watson not long afterward. He told her how unprepared he was to deal with his wife's death; because he was 20 years older than Rosalie, he had always assumed that he would die first. He talked to McGraw at some length and "wondered how he could ever recover from this grief" (McGraw, 1990, p. 936).

Watson never did recover. He became a recluse, shutting himself off from social contact and plunging into work. He sold the estate and moved to a wooden farmhouse that resembled his boyhood home.

In 1957, when Watson was 79, the American Psychological Association voted to award him a citation, praising his work as "one of the vital determinants of the form and substance of modern psychology . . . the point of departure for continuing lines of fruitful research." A companion drove Watson to the New York hotel where the presentation ceremony was to be held, "but at the last minute Watson refused to go inside and insisted that his eldest son attend in his stead. . . . Watson was afraid that in that moment his emotions would overwhelm him, that the apostle of behavior control would break down and weep" (Buckley, 1989, p. 182).

Watson died the following year, but first he burned all of his letters, manuscripts, and notes, feeding them into the fireplace one by one, refusing to leave them to history.

Original Source Material on Behaviorism: From *Psychology as the Behaviorist Views It* by John B. Watson

There is no better starting point for a discussion of Watson's behaviorism than the article that began the movement: "Psychology as the Behaviorist Views It" from the Psychological Review *of 1913.[2] In his clear and readable style Watson discussed the following ideas:*

1. *the definition and goal of his new psychology,*

2. *his criticisms of structuralism and functionalism,*

3. *the role of "hereditary and habit equipments" in enabling organisms to adapt to their environment,*

4. *the view that the areas of applied psychology are truly scientific because they seek general laws that can be used to control behavior,*

5. *the importance of maintaining uniform experimental procedures in both human and animal research.*

Psychology as the behaviorist views it is a purely objective experimental branch of natural science. Its theoretical goal is the prediction and control of behavior. Introspection forms no essential part of its methods, nor is the scientific value of its data dependent upon the readiness with which they lend themselves to interpretation in terms of consciousness. The behaviorist, in his efforts to get a unitary scheme of animal response, recognizes no dividing line between man and brute. The behavior of man, with all of its refinement and complexity, forms only a part of the behaviorist's total scheme of investigation.

It has been maintained by its followers generally that psychology is a study of the science of the phenomena of consciousness. It has taken as its problem, on the one hand, the analysis of complex mental states (or processes) into simple elementary constituents, and on the other the construction of complex states when the elementary constituents are given. The world of

[2] From J. B. Watson. "Psychology as the behaviorist views it." *Psychological Review, 20,* 158–177. Copyright 1913 by the American Psychological Association. Reprinted by permission.

the physical objects (stimuli, including here anything which may excite activity in a receptor), which forms the total phenomena of the natural scientist, is looked upon merely as a means to an end. That end is the production of mental states that may be "inspected" or "observed." The psychological object of observation in the case of an emotion, for example, is the mental state itself. The problem in emotion is the determination of the number and kind of elementary constituents present, their loci [locations], intensity, order of appearance, and so forth.

It is agreed that introspection is the method *par excellence* by means of which mental states may be manipulated for purposes of psychology. On this assumption, behavior data (including under this term everything which goes under the name of comparative psychology) have no value *per se*. They possess significance only insofar as they may throw light upon conscious states. Such data must have at least an analogical or indirect reference to belong to the realm of psychology. . . .

I do not wish unduly to criticize psychology. It has failed signally, I believe, during the fifty-odd years of its existence as an experimental discipline to make its place in the world as an undisputed natural science. Psychology, as it is generally thought of, has something esoteric in its methods. If you fail to reproduce my findings, it is not due to some fault in your apparatus or in the control of your stimulus, but it is due to the fact that your introspection is untrained. The attack is made upon the observer and not upon the experimental setting.

In physics and in chemistry the attack is made upon the experimental conditions. The apparatus was not sensitive enough, impure chemicals were used, and so forth. In these sciences a better technique will give reproducible results. Psychology is otherwise. If you can't observe three to nine states of clearness in attention, your introspection is poor. If, on the other hand, a feeling seems reasonably clear to you, your introspection is again faulty. You are seeing too much. Feelings are never clear.

The time seems to have come when psychology must discard all reference to consciousness; when it need no longer delude itself into thinking that it is making mental states the object of observation. We have become so enmeshed in speculative questions concerning the elements of the mind, the nature of conscious content . . . that I, as an experimental student, feel that something is wrong with our premises and the types of problems which develop from them.

There is no longer any guarantee that we all mean the same thing when we use the terms now current in psychology. Take the case of sensation. A sensation is defined in terms of its attributes. One psychologist will state with readiness that the attributes of a visual sensation are quality, extension, duration, and intensity. Another will add clearness. Still another that of order. I doubt if any one psychologist can draw up a set of statements describing what he means by sensation which will be agreed to by three other psychologists of different training.

Turn for a moment to the question of the number of isolable sensations. Is there an extremely large number of color sensations—or only four:

red, green, yellow, and blue? Again, yellow, while psychologically simple, can be obtained by superimposing red and green spectral rays upon the same diffusing surface! If, on the other hand, we say that every just noticeable difference in the spectrum is a simple sensation, and that every just noticeable increase in the white value of a given color gives simple sensations, we are forced to admit that the number is so large and the conditions for obtaining them so complex that the concept of sensation is unusable, either for the purpose of analysis or that of synthesis.

Titchener, who has fought the most valiant fight in this country for a psychology based upon introspection, feels that these differences of opinion as to the number of sensations and their attributes; as to whether there are relations (in the sense of elements) and on the many other [questions] which seem to be fundamental in every attempt at analysis, are perfectly natural in the present undeveloped state of psychology. While it is admitted that every growing science is full of unanswered questions, surely only those who are wedded to the system as we now have it, who have fought and suffered for it, can confidently believe that there will ever be any greater uniformity than there is now in the answers we have to such questions.

I firmly believe that two hundred years from now, unless the introspective method is discarded, psychology will still be divided on the question as to whether auditory sensations have the quality of extension, whether intensity is an attribute which can be applied to color, whether there is a difference in texture between image and sensation, and upon many hundreds of other [questions] of like character. . . .

My psychological quarrel is not with the systematic and structural psychologist alone. The last fifteen years have seen the growth of what is called functional psychology. This type of psychology decries the use of elements in the static sense of the structuralists. It throws emphasis upon the biological significance of conscious processes instead of upon the analysis of conscious states into introspectively isolable elements.

I have done my best to understand the difference between functional psychology and structural psychology. Instead of clarity, confusion grows upon me. The terms *sensation, perception, affection, emotion, volition* are used as much by the functionalist as by the structuralist. . . . Surely if these concepts are elusive when looked at from a content standpoint, they are still more deceptive when viewed from the angle of function, and especially so when function is obtained by the introspection method. . . .

I was greatly surprised some time ago when I opened Pillsbury's book and saw psychology defined as the "science of behavior." A still more recent text states that psychology is the "science of mental behavior." When I saw these promising statements I thought, now surely we will have texts based upon different lines. After a few pages the science of behavior is dropped and one finds the conventional treatment of sensation, perception, imagery, and so forth, along with certain shifts in emphasis and additional facts which serve to give the author's personal imprint.

I believe we can write a psychology, define it as Pillsbury, and never go back upon our definition: never use the terms *consciousness, mental states, mind, content, introspectively verifiable, imagery,* and the like. . . . It can be done in terms of *stimulus* and *response,* in terms of *habit formation, habit integrations* and the like. Furthermore, I believe that it is really worthwhile to make this attempt now.

The psychology which I should attempt to build up would take as a starting point, first, the observable fact that organisms, man and animal alike, do adjust themselves to their environment by means of hereditary and habit equipments. These adjustments may be very adequate or they may be so inadequate that the organism barely maintains its existence. Secondly, that certain stimuli lead the organism to make the responses. In a system of psychology completely worked out, given the response the stimuli can be predicted; given the stimuli the response can be predicted. Such a set of statements is crass and raw in the extreme, as all such generalizations must be. Yet they are hardly more raw and less realizable than the ones which appear in the psychology texts of the day. . . .

What gives me hope that the behaviorist's position is a defensible one is the fact that those branches of psychology which have already partially withdrawn from the parent, experimental psychology, and which are consequently less dependent upon introspection are today in a most flourishing condition. Experimental pedagogy, the psychology of drugs, the psychology of advertising, legal psychology, the psychology of tests, and psychopathology are all vigorous growths. These are sometimes wrongly called "practical" or "applied" psychology. Surely there was never a worse misnomer. In the future there may grow up vocational bureaus which really apply psychology. At present these fields are truly scientific and are in search of broad generalizations which will lead to the control of human behavior.

For example, we find out by experimentation whether a series of stanzas may be acquired more readily if the whole is learned at once, or whether it is more advantageous to learn each stanza separately and then pass to the succeeding. We do not attempt to apply our findings. The application of this principle is purely voluntary on the part of the teacher.

In the psychology of drugs we may show the effect upon behavior of certain doses of caffeine. We may reach the conclusion that caffeine has a good effect upon the speed and accuracy of work. But these are general principles. We leave it to the individual as to whether the results of our tests shall be applied or not.

Again, in legal testimony, we test the effects of recency upon the reliability of a witness's report. We test the accuracy of the report with respect to moving objects, stationary objects, color, and so forth. It depends upon the judicial machinery of the country to decide whether these facts are ever to be applied.

For a "pure" psychologist to say that he is not interested in the questions raised in these divisions of the science because they relate indirectly to the application of psychology shows, in the first place, that he fails to understand the scientific aim in such problems, and secondly, that he is not interested in a psychology which concerns itself with human life. The only fault

I have to find with these disciplines is that much of their material is stated in terms of introspection, whereas a statement in terms of objective results would be far more valuable. There is no reason why appeal should ever be made to consciousness in any of them. Or why introspective data should ever be sought during the experimentation, or published in the results.

In experimental pedagogy especially one can see the desirability of keeping all the results on a purely objective plane. If this is done, work there on the human being will be comparable directly with the work upon animals. For example, at Hopkins, Mr. Ulrich has obtained certain results upon the distribution of effort in learning—using rats as subjects. He is prepared to give comparative results upon the effect of having an animal work at the problem once per day, three times per day, and five times per day. Whether it is advisable to have the animal learn only one problem at a time or to learn three abreast. We need to have similar experiments made upon man, but we care as little about his "conscious processes" during the conduct of the experiment as we care about such processes in the rats.

I am more interested at the present moment in trying to show the necessity for maintaining uniformity in experimental procedure and in the method of stating results in both human and animal work, than in developing any ideas I may have upon the changes which are certain to come in the scope of human psychology.

Let us consider for a moment the subject of the range of stimuli to which animals respond. I shall speak first of the work upon vision in animals. We put our animal in a situation where he will respond (or learn to respond) to one of two monochromatic lights. We feed him at the one (positive) and punish him at the other (negative). In a short time the animal learns to go to the light at which he is fed.

At this point questions arise which I may phrase in two ways: I may choose the psychological way and say, "Does the animal see these two lights as I do, in other words, as two distinct colors, or does he see them as two grays differing in brightness, as does the totally colorblind?" Phrased by the behaviorist, it would read as follows: "Is my animal responding upon the basis of the difference in intensity between the two stimuli, or upon the difference in wavelengths?"

He nowhere thinks of the animal's response in terms of his own experiences of colors and grays. He wishes to establish the fact whether wavelength is a factor in that animal's adjustment. If so, what wavelengths are effective and what differences in wavelength must be maintained in the different regions to afford bases for differential responses? If wavelength is not a factor in adjustment he wishes to know what difference in intensity will serve as a basis for response, and whether that same difference will suffice throughout the spectrum. Furthermore, he wishes to test whether the animal can respond to wavelengths which do not affect the human eye. He is as much interested in comparing the rat's spectrum with that of the chick as in comparing it with man's. The point of view when the various sets of comparisons are made does not change in the slightest.

However we phrase the question to ourselves, we take our animal after the association has been formed and then introduce certain control experiments which enable us to return answers to the questions just raised. But there is just as keen a desire on our part to test man under the same conditions, and to state the results in both cases in common terms.

The man and the animal should be placed as nearly as possible under the same experimental conditions. Instead of feeding or punishing the human subject, we should ask him to respond by setting a second apparatus until standard and control offered no basis for a differential response. Do I lay myself open to the charge here that I am using introspection? My reply is not at all; that while I might very well feed my human subject for a right choice and punish him for a wrong one and thus produce the response if the subject could give it, there is no need of going to extremes even on the platform I suggest.

But be it understood that I am merely using this second method as an abridged behavior method. We can go just as far and reach just as dependable results by the longer method as by the abridged. In many cases the direct and typically human method cannot be safely used.

Suppose, for example, that I doubt the accuracy of the setting of the control instrument, in the above experiment, as I am very likely to do if I suspect a defect in vision. It is hopeless for me to get his introspective report. He will say: "There is no difference in sensation, both are reds, identical in quality." But suppose I confront him with the standard and the control and so arrange conditions that he is punished if he responds to the control but not with the standard. I interchange the positions of the standard and the control at will and force him to attempt to differentiate the one from the other. If he can learn to make the adjustment even after a large number of trials, it is evident that the two stimuli do afford the basis for a differential response. Such a method may sound nonsensical, but I firmly believe we will have to resort increasingly to just such a method where we have reason to distrust the language method. . . .

The situation in regard to the study of memory is hardly different. Nearly all of the memory methods in actual use in the laboratory today yield the type of results I am arguing for. A certain series of nonsense syllables or other material is presented to the human subject. What should receive the emphasis are the rapidity of the habit formation, the errors, peculiarities in the form of the curve, the persistence of the habit so formed, the relation of such habits to those formed when more complex material is used, and so forth. Now such results are taken down with the subject's introspection. The experiments are made for the purpose of discussing the mental machinery involved in learning, in recall, recollection and forgetting, and not for the purpose of seeking the human being's way of shaping his responses to meet the problems in the terribly complex environment into which he is thrown, nor for that of showing the similarities and differences between man's methods and those of other animals.

The situation is somewhat different when we come to a study of the more complex forms of behavior, such as imagination, judgment, reasoning, and conception. At present the only statements we have of them are in content terms. Our minds have been so warped by the fifty-odd years which have been devoted to the study of states of consciousness that we can envisage these problems only in one way.

We should meet the situation squarely and say that we are not able to carry forward investigations along all of these lines by the behavior methods which are in use at the present time. In extenuation I should like to call attention to the . . . point that the introspective method itself has reached a *cul-de-sac* with respect to them. The topics have become so threadbare from such handling that they may well be put away for a time. As our methods become better developed it will be possible to undertake investigations of more and more complex forms of behavior. Problems which are now laid aside will again become imperative, but they can be viewed as they arise from a new angle and in more concrete settings. . . .

The plans which I most favor for psychology lead practically to the ignoring of consciousness in the sense that that term is used by psychologists today. I have virtually denied that this realm of psychics is open to experimental investigation. I don't wish to go further into the problem at present because it leads inevitably over into metaphysics. If you will grant the behaviorist the right to use consciousness in the same way that other natural scientists employ it—that is, without making consciousness a special object of observation—you have granted all that my thesis requires.

In concluding, I suppose I must confess to a deep bias on these questions. I have devoted nearly twelve years to experimentation on animals. It is natural that such a one should drift into a theoretical position which is in harmony with his experimental work. Possibly I have put up a straw man and have been fighting that. There may be no absolute lack of harmony between the position outlined here and that of functional psychology. I am inclined to think, however, that the two positions cannot be easily harmonized. Certainly the position I advocate is weak enough at present and can be attacked from many standpoints. Yet when all this is admitted I still feel that the considerations which I have urged should have a wide influence upon the type of psychology which is to be developed in the future. What we need to do is to start work upon psychology, making *behavior*, not *consciousness*, the objective point of our attack.

THE REACTION TO WATSON'S PROGRAM

Watson's attack on the old psychology and his call for a new approach was a stirring appeal. Consider again the major points. Psychology was to be the science of *behavior*—not the introspective study of consciousness—and a purely objective experimental branch of natural science. Both human and animal behavior would be investigated.

The new psychology would discard all mentalistic concepts and use only behavior concepts such as stimulus and response. The goal of psychology would be the prediction and control of behavior.

Despite its appeal, Watson's program was not embraced immediately or universally. At first, behaviorism received relatively little attention in the professional journals. It was not until the publication of Watson's 1919 book, *Psychology from the Standpoint of a Behaviorist*, that the movement began to have an impact (Todd, 1994).

One psychologist who disagreed with Watson was Mary Whiton Calkins. Questioning his rejection of introspection, she spoke for many psychologists who believed that certain psychological processes could be studied *only* by introspection. The argument persisted for several years and was sometimes heated; Margaret Floy Washburn went so far as to call Watson an enemy of psychology.

Support for Watson's movement grew, however, particularly among younger psychologists, and by the 1920s, universities were offering courses in behaviorism and the word *behaviorist* was appearing in the professional journals. William McDougall, an opponent of behaviorism, became sufficiently worried about behaviorism's popularity to issue a public warning. E. B. Titchener complained that behaviorism had engulfed the country like a tidal wave. By 1930 Watson proudly proclaimed that behaviorism had become so important that no university could avoid teaching it.

Behaviorism succeeded, of course, but it did so slowly. The changes Watson called for in 1913 were a long time coming. When they finally arrived, his was not the only form of behavioral psychology being promoted.

THE METHODS OF BEHAVIORISM

We have seen that when scientific psychology began, it was eager to ally itself with the older, well-established, more respectable natural science of physics. The new psychology consistently tried to adapt the methods of the natural sciences to its own needs. This tendency is seen most strongly in the behaviorist school of thought.

Watson argued that psychology must restrict itself to the data of the natural sciences, to what could be observed—in other words, to behavior. Therefore, only the most truly objective methods of investigation were admissible in the behaviorist's laboratory. Watson's methods included the following: observation, with and without the use of instruments; testing methods; the verbal report method; and the conditioned reflex method.

The method of observation is a necessary basis for the other methods. Objective testing methods were already in use, but Watson proposed that test results be treated as samples of behavior, not as measures of mental qualities. To Watson, a test did not measure intelligence or personality; it measured, instead, the responses the subject made to the stimulus situation of taking the test, and nothing more.

The verbal report method is more controversial. Because Watson was so strongly opposed to introspection, his use of verbal reporting in the laboratory had been challenged. Some psychologists considered it a compromise whereby he let introspection sneak in the back door after throwing it out the front. Why did Watson admit verbal reports? Despite his aversion to introspection, he could not ignore the work in psychophysics, which made use of introspection. He suggested, therefore, that speech reactions, because they are objectively observable, are as meaningful to the behaviorist as any other type of motor response. Watson said: "Saying is doing—that is, behaving. Speaking overtly or to ourselves (thinking) is just as objective a type of behavior as baseball" (Watson, 1930, p. 6).

The verbal report method in behaviorism was a concession widely debated by Watson's critics, who contended that Watson was proposing merely a semantic change. He admitted that verbal report could be imprecise and was not a satisfactory substitute for more objective observational methods, and he limited its use to situations in which it could be verified; for example, observing and reporting on differences between tones (Watson, 1914). Unverifiable verbal reports, such as imageless thoughts or reports about feeling states, were ruled out.

The most important research method of the behaviorists, the conditioned reflex method, was adopted in 1915, 2 years after Watson's formal founding of behaviorism. Conditioning methods were already in limited use, but Watson was largely responsible for their widespread application in American psychological research. Watson told psychologist Ernest Hilgard that his interest in conditioned reflexes grew out of his study of Bekhterev's work, although he later gave credit to Pavlov as well (Hilgard, 1994).

Watson described conditioning in terms of stimulus substitution. A response is conditioned when it becomes attached or connected to a stimulus other than the one that originally aroused it. (The salivating of Pavlov's dogs to the sound of a tone instead of to the sight of food is a conditioned response.) Watson chose this approach because it provided an objective method of analyzing behavior—reducing behavior to its elementary units, the stimulus-response (S-R) bonds. Because all behavior could be reduced to these elements, the conditioned reflex method permitted the laboratory investigation of complex human behaviors.

Watson was thus continuing in the atomistic and mechanistic tradition established by the British empiricists and adopted by the structural psychologists. He would study human behavior in the same way physical scientists study the universe, by breaking it down into its component parts, the atoms or elements.

The exclusive focus on the use of objective methods and the elimination of introspection meant a change in the nature and role of the human subject in the psychology laboratory. For Wundt and Titchener, subjects were both observer and observed; that is, they observed their own conscious experience. As such, their role was much more important than that of the experimenter.

In behaviorism, subjects assumed a less important role. They no longer observed but were, instead, observed by the experimenter. With this change in focus and status, experimental subjects came to be called *subjects* rather than *observers* (Danziger, 1988; Scheibe, 1988). The true observers were now the experimenters—the research psychologists—who set up the conditions of the experiment and observed how the subjects responded to them. Thus, human subjects were demoted in status. They no longer observed, they merely behaved. And almost anyone can behave—infants and children, mentally ill persons, pigeons and white rats. This point of view reinforced psychology's image of humans as machines: "you put a stimulus in one of the slots and out comes a packet of reactions" (Burt, 1962, p. 232).

THE SUBJECT MATTER OF BEHAVIORISM

The primary subject matter or data for Watson's behavioral psychology was items or elements of behavior: muscular movements or glandular secretions. Psychology, as the science of behavior, must deal only with acts that can be described objectively, without resorting to mentalistic concepts and terminology.

Despite the stated goal of reducing behavior to stimulus-response (S-R) units, Watson argued that, ultimately, behaviorists must understand the overall behavior of the total organism. Although a response can be something as simple as a knee jerk or some other reflex, it can also be more complex; in the latter instance, Watson applied the term *act*. He considered response acts to include such things as eating, writing a book, playing baseball, or building a house. Thus, an act involves the organism's response through movement in space such as talking, reaching, or running.

Watson seems to have conceived of a response act in terms of accomplishing some result—acting on one's environment—rather than as an assemblage of muscular elements. Nevertheless, to Watson, behavioral acts, no matter how complex, were capable of being reduced to lower-level motor or glandular responses.

Responses can be either explicit or implicit. Explicit responses are overt and directly observable. Implicit responses, such as visceral movements, glandular secretions, and nerve impulses, occur inside the organism. Although such internal movements are not overt, they are considered items of behavior. With the notion of implicit responses, Watson was modifying his requirement that the subject matter of psychology must be actually observable. He accepted, instead, that it must be potentially observable. The movements or responses that occur within the organism are observable through the use of instruments.

Like responses, the stimuli with which behaviorism deals may be simple or complex. Light waves striking the retina of the eye may be considered relatively simple stimuli, but stimuli can also be physical objects or a more complex situation (a constellation of specific stimuli). Just as the constellation of responses involved in an action can be reduced to component responses, so the stimulus situation can be resolved into specific component stimuli.

Thus, behaviorism deals with the behavior of the whole organism in relation to its environment. Specific laws of behavior can be worked out by analyzing the stimulus-response complexes into their elementary stimulus and response units.

In methodology and subject matter, Watson's behavioral psychology was an attempt to construct a science that was free of mentalistic notions and subjective methods, a science as objective and sound as physics. Let us consider how Watson treated three traditional topics in psychology: instinct, emotion, and thought. Like all systematic theorists, Watson developed his psychology in accordance with an underlying belief. In his case, all areas of behavior were to be considered in objective stimulus-response terms.

Instincts

Initially Watson accepted the role of instincts in behavior. In his book *Behavior: An Introduction to Comparative Psychology* (1914), he described 11 instincts, including one dealing with random behaviors. He had studied the instinctive behavior of the tern, an aquatic bird, in the Dry Tortugas Islands off the coast of Florida. Accompanying him was Karl Lashley, a student at Johns Hopkins University. Lashley said that the expedition was cut short when he and Watson ran out of cigarettes and whiskey.

By 1925 Watson changed his position and eliminated the concept of instinct. Those aspects of human behavior that seem instinctive, he argued, are really socially conditioned responses. By adopting the view that learning is the key to understanding the development of human behavior, Watson became an extreme environmentalist. He then went further: Not only did he deny instincts in his system, he refused to admit that there were inherited capacities, temperaments, or talents of any kind!

Things that seemed inherited could be traced to early childhood training. Children were not born with the ability to be great athletes

Watson tests the grasping reflex of an infant (a still photo made from a 1919 film).

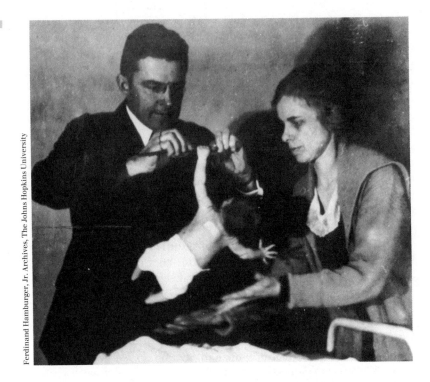

Ferdinand Hamburger, Jr. Archives, The Johns Hopkins University

or musicians, for example, but were slanted in that direction by their parents or caregivers, who encouraged and reinforced the appropriate behaviors. This emphasis on the overwhelming nurturing effect of the parental and social environment—with the conclusion that children can be trained to be whatever one wants them to be—was one reason for Watson's overwhelming popularity.

Watson was not alone in suggesting that environmental influences were more important than any traits we might have been born with; a trend was already evident in psychology to minimize the role of instincts in determining behavior. Watson's position reflected a shift in viewpoint already in progress. In addition, his stand may have been influenced by the applied orientation of early 20th-century American psychology. Psychology could not be used to change or control behavior unless behavior was capable of being changed. If behavior was governed by instinctive forces, then it could not be modified, but if behavior depended on learning or training, then, indeed, it could be changed.

Emotions

To Watson, emotions were bodily responses to specific stimuli. A stimulus, such as the presence of an attacker, produces internal bodily changes, such as rapid heart rate, and the appropriate learned overt responses. This theory implies no conscious perception of the emotion or sensations from the internal organs.

Each emotion involves a particular pattern of physiological changes. Although Watson recognized that emotional responses involve overt movements, he believed that the internal responses are predominant. Emotion, then, is a form of implicit behavior in which the internal responses are evident, to some extent, in physical manifestations such as blushing, perspiring, or increased pulse rate.

Watson's theory of emotions is less complex than that of William James. In James's theory, the bodily changes followed immediately the perception of the stimulus, and the feeling of those bodily changes was the emotion. Watson criticized James's position. Discarding the conscious process of the perception of the situation and the feeling state, Watson claimed that emotions can be described and understood completely in terms of the objective stimulus situation, the overt bodily response, and the internal physiological changes.

In a now classic study, Watson investigated the stimuli that produce emotional responses in infants. He said that infants show three fundamental emotions: fear, rage, and love. Fear is produced by loud noises and sudden loss of support; rage is produced by the restriction of bodily movement; and love is evoked by caressing the skin or by rocking and patting.

He also found typical response patterns to these stimuli. He believed that fear, rage, and love were unlearned emotional responses. Other human emotional responses are compounded of these basic emotions through the process of conditioning. They may become attached to stimuli that were not originally capable of eliciting them.

Albert, Peter, and the Rabbits

Watson demonstrated his theory of conditioned emotional responses in his experimental study of 11-month-old Albert, who was conditioned to fear a white rat, something he had not feared before the conditioning trials (Watson & Rayner, 1920). The fear was established by making a loud noise (striking a steel bar with a hammer) behind Albert's head whenever he was shown the rat. Within a short time, the mere sight of the rat produced signs of fear in the child.

This conditioned fear could be generalized to similar stimuli such as a rabbit, a white fur coat, and a set of Santa Claus whiskers. Watson suggested that adult fears, aversions, and anxieties are likewise conditioned in early childhood.

The Albert study has never been successfully replicated. Watson described the research as preliminary—a pilot study—and psychologists have since noted serious flaws in his methodology. Nevertheless, the results of the Albert study have been accepted as scientific evidence and are cited in virtually every basic psychology textbook, usually incorrectly (see Harris, 1979; Samelson, 1980). A survey of 130 introductory psychology textbooks published between 1920 and 1989 revealed that the Albert study was the most frequently cited experiment (Todd, 1994).

Although Albert may have been conditioned to fear white rats, rabbits, and Santa Claus, he was no longer available as a subject when Watson wanted to try to eliminate those fears. Not long after this experiment Watson left academics, and he did not pursue the problem. Some time later, when he was working in advertising in New York, he gave a talk about his research. In the audience was Mary Cover Jones, a classmate of Rosalie Rayner's at Vassar. Watson's remarks sparked her interest, and she wondered whether the conditioning technique could be used to remove children's fears. She asked Rosalie to introduce her to Watson and then undertook a study that has become another classic in the history of psychology.

Her subject was named Peter, and he already showed a fear of rabbits, although his fear had not been conditioned in the laboratory (Jones, 1924). While Peter was eating, a rabbit was brought into the room but kept at a distance great enough so as not to trigger a fearful response. Over several trials, the rabbit was brought progressively closer, always while the child was eating. Eventually Peter got used to the rabbit and could touch it without showing fear. Other, generalized fear responses to similar objects were eliminated by this procedure.

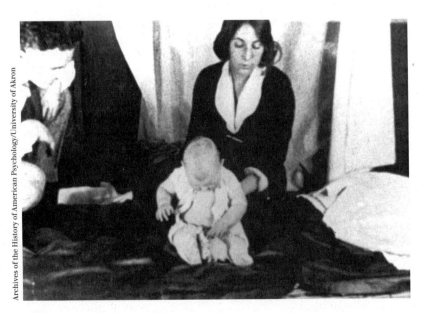

John B. Watson, with Rosalie Rayner holding Little Albert. The child seems to be reaching for the white rat between his feet. Albert was conditioned to fear the rat and similar stimuli.

Archives of the History of American Psychology/University of Akron

Jones's study has been described as a precursor of behavior therapy (the application of learning principles to change maladaptive behavior), almost 50 years before the technique became popular. Jones, long associated with the Institute of Child Welfare at the University of California, Berkeley, received the G. Stanley Hall award in 1968 for her outstanding contributions to developmental psychology.

MARY COVER JONES

Thought Processes

The traditional view of thought processes was that they occurred in the brain "so faintly that no neural impulse passes out over the motor nerve to the muscle, hence no response takes place in the muscles and glands" (Watson, 1930, p. 239). According to this theory, because thought processes occur in the absence of muscular movements, they are not accessible to observation and experimentation. Thought was regarded as intangible, something that was exclusively mental and that had no physical reference points.

Watson's behaviorist system attempted to reduce thinking to implicit motor behavior. He argued that thought, like all other aspects of human functioning, was sensorimotor behavior of some sort. He reasoned that the behavior of thinking must involve implicit speech reactions or movements. Thus, he reduced thinking to subvocal talking that relies on the same muscular habits we learn for overt speech. As children grow up, these muscular habits become inaudible and invisible because parents and teachers warn children to stop talking aloud to themselves. In this way, thinking becomes a way of silently talking to ourselves.

Watson suggested that the focal points for much of this implicit behavior are the muscles of the tongue and the larynx (the so-called voice box). He also considered thought to be expressed by gestures, such as frowns and shrugs, which are overt reactions to stimuli.

An obvious source of corroboration for Watson's theory of thinking is that most of us are aware that we talk to ourselves while we are thinking. For example, a study of college students' introspective reports found that 73% of the thoughts sampled involved talking to themselves while they were thinking (Farthing, 1992).

This kind of evidence is unacceptable to behaviorists, however, because it is introspective, and Watson could hardly call on introspection to support his behavioral theory. Behaviorism required objective evidence of implicit speech movements, so experimental attempts were made to record tongue and larynx movements during thought.

These measurements revealed slight movements some of the time that the subjects were thinking. Measurements taken from hands and fingers of hearing-impaired people also revealed movements some of the time during thought. Despite his inability to secure more positive results, Watson remained convinced of the

The Bancroft Library, University of California

existence of implicit speech movements, assuming that their demonstration required only the development of more sophisticated laboratory equipment.

BEHAVIORISM'S POPULAR APPEAL

Why did Watson's bold pronouncements win him such a large public following? Surely most people didn't care that some psychologists pretended to be conscious while others proclaimed that psychology had lost its mind, or that some said thinking took place in the head and others voted for the neck. These issues aroused considerable comment among psychologists, but they hardly concerned anyone else.

What stirred the public was Watson's call for a society based on scientifically shaped and controlled behavior, free of myths, customs, and conventional ways. His ideas offered hope to people who had become disenchanted with older ideas. In fervor and in faith, then, behaviorism took on some of the aspects of a religion. Among the hundreds of articles and books written about behaviorism was *The Religion Called Behaviorism* (Berman, 1927). It was read by a young man of 23 by the name of B. F. Skinner, who wrote a review of the book and sent it to a popular literary magazine. "They did not publish [my review]," Skinner wrote later, "but in writing it I was more or less defining myself for the first time as a behaviorist" (Skinner, 1976, p. 299). Skinner was to refine and extend Watson's work.

Some of the excitement generated by Watson's ideas is evident in the newspaper reviews of his book *Behaviorism* (Watson, 1925). The *New York Times* reviewer said, dramatically, "It marks an epoch in the intellectual history of man" (August 2, 1925). The *New York Herald Tribune* called it "the most important book ever written. One stands for an instant blinded with a great hope" (June 21, 1925).

The hope stemmed in part from Watson's emphasis on the nurturing effect of one's childhood environment in determining behavior and in his minimizing of the influence of inherited tendencies. The following paragraph from *Behaviorism* is frequently quoted to support his point:

> *Give me a dozen healthy infants, well-formed, and my own specified world to bring them up in, and I'll guarantee to take any one at random and train him to become any type of specialist I might select—doctor, lawyer, artist, merchant-chief, and, yes, even beggarman and thief, regardless of his talents, penchants, tendencies, abilities, vocations, and race of his ancestors.* (WATSON, 1930, P. 104)

Watson's conditioned reflex experiments, such as the Albert study, persuaded him that emotional disturbances in adulthood cannot be traced to sexual factors alone, as Sigmund Freud was proposing. Watson argued that adult problems are linked to conditioned responses established in infancy, childhood, and adolescence. And if adult disturbances are a function of faulty childhood conditioning, then a proper program of childhood conditioning should prevent the emergence of adult disorders.

Watson believed that this type of practical control over childhood behavior (and hence over the later adult behavior) was not only possible but was absolutely necessary. He developed a plan for the improvement of society—a program of experimental ethics—based on the principles of his behaviorism.

No one gave him a dozen healthy infants so that he might test his claim, and he later admitted that in making it he was going beyond the facts. He noted, however, that people who disagreed with him—the ones who believed the impact of heredity was greater than that of the environment—had been stating their case for thousands of years and still had no real evidence for their view.

The following passage from *Behaviorism* shows the vitality with which Watson described his program for life under a behavioristic system, and it may help explain why so many people flocked to behaviorism as to a new faith.

Behaviorism ought to be a science that prepares men and women for understanding the principles of their own behavior. It ought to make men and women eager to rearrange their own lives, and especially eager to prepare themselves to bring up their own children in a healthy way. I wish I could picture for you what a rich and wonderful individual we should make of every healthy child if only we could let it shape itself properly and then provide for it a universe in which it could exercise that organization—a universe unshackled by legendary folklore of happenings thousands of years ago; unhampered by disgraceful political history; free of foolish customs and conventions which have no significance in themselves, yet which hem the individual in like taut steel bands.

I am not asking here for revolution; I am not asking people to go out to some Godforsaken place, form a colony, go naked and live a communal life, nor am I asking for a change to a diet of roots and herbs. I am not asking for "free love." I am trying to dangle a stimulus in front of you, a verbal stimulus which, if acted upon, will gradually change this universe. For the universe will change if you bring up your children, not in the freedom of the libertine, but in behavioristic freedom—a freedom which we cannot even picture in words, so little do we know of it. Will not these children in turn, with their better ways of living and thinking, replace us as society and in turn bring up their children in a still more

> *scientific way, until the world finally becomes a place fit for human habitation?* (WATSON, 1930, PP. 303–304)

Watson's plan to replace the older speculative ethics based on religion with a program of experimental ethics based on behaviorism remained only a hope; it was never carried out. He outlined his program and left it as a framework for future research. Years later, B. F. Skinner conceived a more detailed program for a scientifically shaped utopia in the spirit of the one Watson espoused.

AN OUTBREAK OF PSYCHOLOGY

Psychology had already become popular by the 1920s. Under Watson's influence, given his charm, charisma, persuasiveness, and message of hope, Americans were almost overwhelmed by what one writer called an "outbreak" of psychology. Much of the American public was convinced that the way to health, happiness, and prosperity was through psychology, and soon psychological advice columns sprouted in the pages of the daily newspapers.

Psychologist Joseph Jastrow's column, "Keeping Mentally Fit," was syndicated in more than 150 papers. Albert Wiggam, who was not a psychologist, wrote a column called "Exploring Your Mind." Many people agreed with his views:

> *Men and women never needed psychology so much as they need it today. Young men and women need it in order to measure their own mental traits and capacities with a view to choosing their careers early and wisely. . . . businessmen need it to help them select employees; parents and educators need it as an aid in rearing and educating children; all need it in order to secure the highest effectiveness and happiness. You cannot achieve these things in the fullest measure without the new knowledge of your own mind and personality that the psychologists have given us.* (WIGGAM, 1928, QUOTED IN BENJAMIN, 1986, P. 943)

The Canadian humorist Stephen Butler Leacock noted that in the past, psychology was safely confined to college campuses, where it had no connection with reality and did no visible harm to anyone who studied it. By 1924, however, psychology could be seen everywhere. "For almost every juncture of life," wrote Leacock, "we now call in the services of an expert psychologist as naturally as we send for an emergency plumber. In all our great cities there are already, or soon will be, signs that read 'Psychologist—Open Day and Night'" (quoted in Benjamin, 1986, p. 944).

Thus was psychology welcomed throughout the United States, and Watson may have done more than any other individual to help it spread.

EDWIN B. HOLT (1873–1946) AND KARL LASHLEY (1890–1958)

Although behaviorism had captured the attention of American psychologists, not all of them adopted Watson's formulations. Some developed their own behavioral psychologies, taking the school of thought in different directions. Two of these early behaviorists are Edwin Holt and Karl Lashley.

Edwin B. Holt received his PhD from William James at Harvard University in 1901 and spent his academic career there and at Princeton. He disagreed with Watson's rejection of consciousness and mental phenomena, and he thought it was possible to relate conscious experience to physical referents. Like Watson, Holt believed in the determining influence of the environment over instinctive forces.

In addition, he suggested that learning can occur in response to inner motivation (internal needs and drives such as hunger and thirst) as well as outer motivation (external stimuli). Thus, Holt was one of the first theorists to propose the existence of such internal drives, anticipating later work on the problem of motivation.

Holt did not attempt to reduce behavior to stimulus-response units but preferred to deal with larger behaviors that had some purpose for the organism, behaviors that accomplished some goal. The term and concept of purpose was, of course, disallowed in Watson's system. Holt's emphasis on purpose served as a stimulus for the work of the neobehaviorist E. C. Tolman.

Karl Lashley was a student of Watson's at Johns Hopkins, where he earned his PhD. His career as a physiological psychologist took him to the universities of Minnesota and Chicago, to Harvard, and finally to the Yerkes Laboratory of Primate Biology. He was an ardent supporter of Watson's behaviorism, even though his research on brain mechanisms in rats challenged a basic point in Watson's system.

He summarized his findings in *Brain Mechanisms and Intelligence* (1929) and postulated two now famous principles: the **law of mass action,** which states that the efficiency of learning is a function of the intact mass of the cortex—that is, the more cortical tissue available, the better the learning; and the **principle of equipotentiality,** which states that one part of the cortex is essentially equal to another in terms of its contribution to learning.

LAW OF MASS ACTION: The efficiency of learning is a function of the total mass of cortical tissue

PRINCIPLE OF EQUIPOTENTIALITY: One part of the cerebral cortex is essentially equal to another in its contribution to learning

Lashley had expected to find specific sensory and motor centers in the cerebral cortex as well as corresponding connections between sensory and motor apparatus. Those findings would have supported the primacy and simplicity of the reflex arc as an elemental unit of behavior. His results, however, challenged Watson's idea of a simple point-to-point connection in reflexes, according to which the brain serves merely to switch incoming sensory nerve impulses into outgoing motor impulses.

Lashley's findings suggested that the brain plays a more active role in learning than Watson could accept, and he contested Watson's assumption that behavior is compounded bit by bit through conditioned reflexes.

Although Lashley's research discredited a fundamental part of Watson's system, it did not weaken the behaviorist contention that only objective research methods should be used. Indeed, Lashley's work confirmed the value of objective methods in psychological research.

The work of the early behaviorists was undertaken only shortly after Watson introduced his system. Although differing somewhat from Watson's approach, their research contributed to the overall growth of behaviorism and reinforced the notion of an objective natural science of behavior.

CRITICISMS OF WATSON'S BEHAVIORISM

Any systematic program that proposes sweeping revisions and blatantly attacks the existing order—indeed, suggests that the earlier version of the truth be discarded—is bound to be criticized. We know that American psychology was already moving toward greater objectivity when Watson founded behaviorism, but not all psychologists were ready to accept the extreme form of objectivity Watson proposed. Many, including some who supported objectivity, believed that Watson's system omitted important components of psychology, such as sensory and perceptual processes.

One of Watson's more forceful opponents was William McDougall (1871–1938), an English psychologist who came to the United States in 1920 and was affiliated first with Harvard and later with Duke University. McDougall is noted for his instinct theory of behavior and for the impetus his book on social psychology gave to that field (McDougall, 1908).

It is interesting that McDougall, who contributed so much to social psychology, was not very social himself. "I have never fitted neatly into any social group," he wrote, "never been able to find myself wholly at one with any party or any system; and, though not insensible to the attractions of group life, group feeling and thinking, have always stood outside, critical and ill-content" (McDougall, 1930, p. 192).

He was a supporter of unpopular causes including free will, Nordic superiority, and psychic research, and was regularly denounced by the American press for his views. McDougall was also vilified in the psychological community because of his criticism of behaviorism in the 1920s, when most psychologists had, to some degree, accepted its influence.

By 1928, McDougall was so "ostracized by America's psychological mainstream that he believed himself to be an object of contempt" (Jones, 1987, p. 931). Ten years later, when McDougall was dying of cancer, Knight Dunlap, Watson's successor at Johns Hopkins, said that "the sooner he died, the better it would be for psychology" (quoted in Smith, 1989, p. 446).

McDougall's instinct theory states that human behavior results from innate tendencies to thought and action. His ideas were initially well received but rapidly lost ground to behaviorism. Watson rejected the notion of instincts, and on this issue, and many others, the two men clashed.

American Psychological Association

WILLIAM McDOUGALL

They met to debate their differences on February 5, 1924, at the Psychology Club in Washington, D.C. The fact that Washington had a psychology club that was not affiliated with a university attests to the widespread popularity of the field. One thousand people attended the debate. Only a few were psychologists; there were only 464 members of the APA nationwide at that time. Thus, the size of the crowd also reflects the popularity of Watson's behaviorism. The judges of the debate, however, voted McDougall the winner. Watson and McDougall published their arguments jointly in *The Battle of Behaviorism* (1929).

McDougall began the debate on an optimistic note: "I have an initial advantage over Dr. Watson," he said, "an advantage which I feel to be so great as to be unfair; namely, all persons of common sense will of necessity be on my side from the outset" (Watson & McDougall, 1929, p. 40). He said he agreed with Watson that the data of behavior are a proper focus for psychological research, but he argued that the data of consciousness are also indispensable. His position was later upheld by the humanistic psychologists and the social-learning theorists.

If psychologists do not use introspection, McDougall asked, how can they determine the meaning of a subject's response or the accuracy of speech behavior (what Watson called verbal report)? Without self-report, how can we know anything about daydreams and fantasies? How can we understand or appreciate aesthetic experiences? He challenged Watson to explain how a behaviorist would account for the experience of enjoying a violin concert. McDougall said,

> I come into this hall and see a man on this platform scraping the guts of a cat with hairs from the tail of a horse, and, sitting silently in attitudes of rapt attention, are a thousand persons, who presently break into wild applause. How will the behaviorist explain these strange incidents? How explain the fact that the vibrations emitted by the catgut stimulate all the thousands into absolute silence and quiescence, and the further fact that the cessation of the stimulus seems to be a stimulus to the most frantic activity?

Common sense and psychology agree in accepting the explanation that the audience heard the music with keen pleasure, and vented their gratitude and admiration for the artist in shouts and handclappings. But the behaviorist knows nothing of pleasure and pain, of admiration and gratitude. He has relegated all such "metaphysical entities" to the dust heap, and must seek some other explanation. Let us leave him seeking it. The search will keep him harmlessly occupied for some centuries to come.
(Watson & McDougall, 1929, pp. 62–63)

Then McDougall questioned Watson's assumption that human behavior is fully determined, that everything we do is the direct result of past experience and can be predicted once the past events are known. Such a psychology, McDougall said, leaves no room for free will or freedom of choice.

If the determinist position were true—that humans have no free will and therefore cannot be held responsible for their actions—then there would be no human initiative, no creative effort, no desire to improve ourselves or our society. No one would attempt to prevent war, alleviate injustice, or achieve any personal or social ideal.

Additional criticism was directed against Watson's use of the verbal report method in his research. He was charged with being inconsistent, accepting it when it could be verified and rejecting it when it could not. Of course, that was Watson's point, and the goal of the entire behaviorist movement—to use only data that could be verified.

The Watson-McDougall debate came 11 years after Watson formally founded the behaviorist school of thought. McDougall predicted that in a few more years Watson's position would disappear without a trace. In a postscript to the published version of the debate, McDougall wrote that his forecast had been too optimistic: "It was founded upon a too generous estimate of the intelligence of the American public. . . . Dr. Watson continues, as a prophet of much honor in his own country, to issue his pronouncements" (Watson & McDougall, 1929, pp. 86, 87).

CONTRIBUTIONS OF WATSON'S BEHAVIORISM

Watson's productive career in psychology lasted less than 20 years, but he profoundly affected the course of psychology's development for many years to come. He was an effective agent of the Zeitgeist, and the times were changing not only in psychology but in general scientific attitudes as well.

The 19th century had witnessed magnificent advances in every branch of science; the 20th century promised even more marvels. It was thought that scientists, if given enough time, would find solutions to every problem, answers to every question.

Watson made psychology more objective in methods and terminology. Although his positions on specific topics stimulated a great deal of research, his original formulations are no longer useful. Watsonian behaviorism as a separate school of thought has been replaced by the newer forms of psychological objectivism that built on it. The historian E. G. Boring said in 1929 that behaviorism was already past its prime. Because revolutionary movements depend on protest for their strength, it is an effective tribute to Watson's behaviorism that only 16 years after its introduction, it no longer needed to protest.

Watsonian behaviorism effectively overcame the earlier positions in psychology. A graduate student at the University of Wisconsin in 1926 reported that by then, few students had heard of Wundt and Titchener (Gengerelli, 1976). Objective methods and language became part of the mainstream of American psychology, and so Watson's system died, as have other successful movements, by being absorbed into the main body of thought to provide a strong conceptual base for modern psychology.

Although Watson's program did not realize its ambitious goals, Watson himself is widely recognized for his founding role. The centennial of his birth was celebrated in April of 1979, the same year as the centennial of the birth of psychology as a science. A symposium at Furman University (where the psychology laboratory is named for

Historical marker beside U.S. Route 276 at the village of Travelers Rest, South Carolina (about 8 miles from Greenville).

Archives of the History of American Psychology/University of Akron

Watson) drew psychologists from all over the United States. The speakers included B. F. Skinner, whose talk was entitled "What J. B. Watson Meant to Me."

Apparently, Watson is remembered less favorably by his hometown residents, many of whom recalled him as "an upstart and an atheist who had turned his back on his Southern heritage and Baptist upbringing" (*Greenville News,* April 5, 1979). In 1984, a commemorative marker was placed on the highway near his birthplace.

To some degree, the acceptance of Watsonian behaviorism was a function of Watson's own personality. Charismatic and attractive, he projected his ideas with enthusiasm, optimism, and self-confidence. He was a strong and appealing figure who scorned tradition and rejected the current version of psychology. These personal qualities, interacting with the spirit of the times that he so ably manipulated, define John B. Watson as one of psychology's pioneers.

DISCUSSION QUESTIONS

1. How were Watson's ideas about behaviorism received by most younger psychologists? What did Watson believe about the value of applied psychology? How did he implement those beliefs?
2. What criticisms of structuralism and functionalism did Watson make in his pivotal 1913 article?
3. Describe the controversy over Watson's use of verbal reports. How did behaviorism change the role and task of the human subject?
4. Discuss how Watson's subject matter and methodology continued the atomistic, mechanistic tradition of the empiricists. How did Watson distinguish between responses and acts? Between explicit and implicit responses?
5. Discuss Watson's views on instinct and thought. How do the studies of Albert, Peter, and the rabbits support Watson's views on emotion?
6. Discuss the reasons for behaviorism's popular appeal. Note some of McDougall's criticisms of Watsonian behaviorism.
7. How did Holt's conception of behaviorism differ from Watson's? Describe Lashley's law of mass action and his principle of equipotentiality. In what way did Lashley's research results discredit a portion of Watson's system?

SUGGESTED READINGS

Buckley, K. W. (1989). *Mechanical man: John Broadus Watson and the beginnings of behaviorism.* New York: Guilford. Presents Watson's life and work and assesses his academic and business careers, his role as a popularizer of psychology, and his status in the development of modern psychology.

Duke, C., Fried, S., Pliley, W., & Walker, D. (1989). Rosalie Rayner Watson: The mother of a behaviorist's sons. *Psychological Reports, 65,* 163–169. A sketch of Watson's second wife, who co-authored the study on conditioned emotional reactions and assisted in the preparation of Watson's popular book on child care.

Harris, B. (1979). Whatever happened to little Albert? *American Psychologist, 34,* 151–160. Questions the design, interpretation, and popular understanding of Watson's classic study of conditioned fear.

Samelson, F. (1981). Struggle for scientific authority: The reception of Watson's behaviorism, 1913–1920. *Journal of the History of the Behavioral Sciences, 17,* 399–425. Traces the impact of Watson's ideas after the publication of his behaviorist manifesto.

CHAPTER 11

BEHAVIORISM:

AFTER THE FOUNDING

NEOBEHAVIORISM

WATSON'S INTENDED revolution did not transform psychology overnight, as he had hoped. It took time. Yet by 1924, little more than a decade after Watson launched behaviorism, even his greatest opponent, E. B. Titchener, conceded that behaviorism had engulfed the nation. By 1930 Watson was able to proclaim, with considerable justification, that his victory was complete. Although other varieties of behaviorism had been proposed—such as those of Holt and Lashley—they reinforced Watson's movement toward defining psychology as a totally objective natural science. Thus, by 1930, behavioral psychology had routed all earlier approaches to the field.

The first stage in the evolution of behaviorism, Watsonian behaviorism, lasted from 1913 to about 1930. The second stage, neobehaviorism, can be dated from 1930 to about 1960, and includes the work of Edward Tolman, Edwin Guthrie, Clark Hull, and B. F. Skinner. These neobehaviorists agreed on several points about the systems they designed to explain their data: (1) the core of psychology is the study of learning; (2) most behavior, no matter how complex, can be accounted for by the laws of conditioning; and (3) psychology must adopt the principle of operationism. The third stage in behaviorism's evolution, neo-neobehaviorism or sociobehaviorism, dates from about 1960 and is characterized by a return of cognitive processes (Segal & Lachman, 1972).

OPERATIONISM

Operationism is an attitude or general principle, the purpose of which is to render the language and terminology of science more objective and precise, and to rid science of those problems that are not actually observable or physically demonstrable (the so-called pseudo-problems). Briefly, operationism holds that the validity of a given scientific finding or theoretical construct depends on the validity of the operations used in arriving at that finding.

The operationist viewpoint was championed by Harvard University physicist Percy W. Bridgman in his book, *The Logic of Modern Physics* (1927), which captured the attention of many psychologists. Bridgman proposed that physical concepts be defined in precise and rigid terms and that all concepts lacking physical referents be discarded. He wrote:

> *We may illustrate by considering the concept of length. What do we mean by the length of an object? We evidently know what we mean by length if we can tell what the length of any and every object is, and for the physicist nothing more is required. To find the length of an object, we have to perform certain physical operations. The concept of length is therefore fixed when the operations by which length is measured are fixed; that is, the concept of length involves as much as and nothing more than a set of operations;* the concept is synonymous with the corresponding set of operations. (BRIDGMAN, 1927, P. 5)

Thus, a physical concept is the same as the set of operations or procedures by which it is determined. Many psychologists found this principle to be of use in the science of psychology and were eager to apply it.

Bridgman's concern with discarding pseudo-problems—those questions that defy answer by any known objective test—was particularly appealing to the behaviorists. Notions or propositions that cannot be put to experimental test, such as the existence and nature of the soul, are meaningless for science. What is the soul? Can it be observed in the laboratory? Can it be measured and manipulated under controlled conditions to determine its effects on behavior? If not, it has no use or meaning or relevance for science.

It follows that the concept of an individual or private conscious experience is a pseudo-problem for psychology. Neither the existence of consciousness nor its characteristics can be determined or even investigated by objective methods. Therefore, according to the operationist viewpoint, consciousness has no place in a scientific psychology.

It can be argued that operationism is little more than a formal statement of principles already used by psychologists to define words and concepts in terms of their physical referents. There is little in operationism that cannot be traced to the works of the British empiricists. We have noted the long-term trend in American psychology toward increasing objectivity in methodology and subject matter, so it can be said that the idea of operationism, as an attitude and a framework within which to conduct research and formulate theories, had already been accepted by many American psychologists before the publication of Bridgman's 1927 book.

Since the days of Wundt, however, physics had been the paragon of scientific respectability for the newer psychology—its role model—and when physicists proclaimed their acceptance of operationism as a formal doctrine, psychologists had to follow. Indeed, psychologists used operationism more extensively than did physicists.

Operationism did not win universal acceptance in psychology. Controversy arose about the utility or futility of limiting psychology's subject matter to only that which had empirical reference. Also, "the reduction of concepts to their operations turned out to be dull business. No one wants to trouble with it when there is no special need" (Boring, 1950, p. 658). Bridgman himself had doubts about the use psychologists made of his concept. Some 27 years after proposing the operationist viewpoint he wrote, "I feel that I have created a Frankenstein which has certainly gotten away from me. I abhor the word *operationism*. . . . The thing I have envisaged is too simple to be so dignified by so pretentious a name" (Bridgman, 1954, p. 224).

This appears to be another case of the disciples becoming more fanatical than their leader. Nevertheless, the important point about operationism is that the generation of neobehaviorists that came of age in the late 1920s and 1930s promoted operationism in their approach to psychology.

EDWARD CHACE TOLMAN (1886–1959)

One of the early converts to behaviorism, Edward Tolman studied engineering at the Massachusetts Institute of Technology. He switched to psychology and worked under Edwin Holt at Harvard, where he received his PhD in 1915. In the summer of 1912, Tolman studied with the Gestalt psychologist Kurt Koffka in Germany, and in Tolman's final year of graduate school, while being trained in the Titchener tradition of structural psychology, he became acquainted with Watsonian behaviorism. As a graduate student Tolman had already questioned the scientific usefulness of introspection. In his *Autobiography* (1952), he

Archives of the History of American Psychology/University of Akron

EDWARD CHACE TOLMAN

PURPOSIVE BEHAVIORISM:
Tolman's system combining the objective study of behavior with the consideration of purposiveness or goal-orientation in behavior

wrote that Watson's behaviorism came to him as a "tremendous stimulus and relief."

After completing his degree, Tolman became an instructor at Northwestern University in Evanston, Illinois, and in 1918 went to the University of California at Berkeley. It was at Berkeley, where he taught comparative psychology and conducted research on learning in rats, that he became dissatisfied with Watson's behaviorism and began to develop his own.

His career at Berkeley was interrupted by World War II, when he served in the Office of Strategic Services (the OSS, which was the forerunner of the CIA). From 1950 to 1953, he helped lead the commendable faculty opposition to the California state loyalty oath.

Purposive Behaviorism

The definitive statement of Tolman's position is presented in *Purposive Behavior in Animals and Men* (1932). His system of **purposive behaviorism** may appear at first glance to be a curious blend of two contradictory terms: *purpose* and *behavior*. Attributing purpose to an organism seems to imply consciousness, a mentalistic concept that had no place in a behavioral psychology. Tolman made it clear, however, that he was very much the behaviorist in subject matter and methodology. He was not urging psychology to accept consciousness. Like Watson, he rejected introspection and had no interest in any presumed internal experiences of the organism that were not accessible to objective observation.

Purposiveness in behavior, Tolman wrote, can be defined in objective behavioral terms without resorting to introspection or to reports about how the organism might "feel" about an experience. It seemed obvious to him that all behavior is directed toward some goal. The cat, for example, tries to get out of the puzzle box, the rat tries to master the maze, the child tries to learn to play the piano.

Behavior, Tolman said, "reeks of purpose." All behavior is oriented toward achieving some goal, toward learning the means to an end. The rat persistently runs the maze, making fewer errors each time, to reach the goal faster. In other words, the rat is learning, and the fact of learning—whether in rat or human—is objective behavioral evidence of purpose. Note that Tolman is dealing with the organism's response. His measures are in terms of the changes in response behavior as a function of learning. These measures yield objective data.

Watsonian behaviorists were quick to criticize any attribution of purpose to behavior because, they said, purposiveness relied on the assumption of consciousness. Tolman replied that it made no difference to him whether the organism was conscious or not. The conscious experience, if there was any, associated with purposive behavior did not influence the organism's behavioral responses. Tolman concerned himself only with the overt response.

Intervening Variables

As a behaviorist, Tolman believed that the initiating causes of behavior, and the final resulting behavior, must be capable of objective observation and operational definition. He suggested that the causes of behavior include five independent variables: environmental stimuli, physiological drives, heredity, previous training, and age. Behavior is a function of these variables, which he expressed in a mathematical equation.

Between these observable independent variables and the resulting response behavior (the observable dependent variable), Tolman inferred a set of unobserved factors, which he called the **intervening variables.** These intervening variables are the actual determinants of behavior. They are the internal processes that connect the stimulus situation with the observed response. The behaviorists' statement *S-R* (for stimulus-response) must now read *S-O-R*. The intervening variable is what is going on within *O* (the organism) that brings about a given behavioral response to a given stimulus.

Because this intervening variable cannot be objectively observed, it is of no use to psychology unless it can be clearly related to both the experimental (independent) variables and the behavior (dependent) variable.

The classic example of an intervening variable is hunger, which cannot actually be seen in a person or a laboratory animal. However, hunger can be precisely and objectively related to an experimental variable, such as the length of time since the organism was last given food. It can also be related to an objective response or behavior variable, such as the amount of food eaten or the speed with which it was consumed. Thus, the unobservable, inferred factor of hunger can be given precise empirical referents and is, therefore, amenable to quantification and experimental manipulation.

By specifying the independent and dependent variables, which are observable events, Tolman was able to provide operational definitions of unobservable, internal states. He initially called his approach *operational behaviorism,* before selecting the term *intervening variable.*

Intervening variables appeared to be useful in developing a theory of behavior, as long as they were empirically related to experimental and behavior variables. To do this comprehensively, however, turned out to be such an enormous task that Tolman later abandoned hope "of ever making a complete definition of any intervening variables" (Mackenzie, 1977, p. 146).

INTERVENING VARIABLES:
Unobserved and inferred factors within the organism that are the actual determinants of behavior

Learning Theory

Learning played a major role in Tolman's purposive behaviorism. He rejected Thorndike's law of effect, saying that reward or reinforcement has little influence on learning. In its place Tolman proposed a cognitive theory of learning, suggesting that the repeated performance of a task strengthens the learned relationship between cues in the environment and the organism's expectations. In this way the organism gets to know its environment. Tolman called these learned relationships *sign Gestalts,* and they are built up by the continued performance of a task.

Let us keep Tolman's ideas in mind as we watch a hungry rat in a maze. The rat moves about in the maze, sometimes exploring correct alleys and sometimes blind alleys. Eventually it discovers food. In subsequent trials in the maze, the goal (finding the food) gives purpose and direction to the rat's behavior. At each choice point, expectations are established. The rat comes to expect that certain cues associated with the choice point will or will not lead to the food.

When the rat's expectation is confirmed and it gets food, the sign Gestalt (the cue expectancy associated with a particular choice point) is strengthened. Over all the choice points in the maze, the animal thus establishes a pattern of sign Gestalts, which Tolman called a *cognitive map.* This pattern is what the animal learns—a cognitive map of the maze, not a set of motor habits. In a sense, then, the rat establishes a comprehensive knowledge of the maze or of any familiar environment. Something like a field map is developed in its brain, enabling it to go from one spot in the environment to another, without being restricted to a fixed series of bodily movements.

A classic experiment that supports Tolman's theory of learning investigated whether the rat in the maze learns a cognitive map or a set of motor responses. A cross-shaped maze was used. One group of rats always found food at the same place, even though, using different starting points, the rats sometimes had to turn to the right and other times to the left to reach the food. The motor responses differed, but the food remained in the same place.

The second group of rats always made the same response regardless of the starting point, but the food was found in different places. For example, starting from one end of the cross-shaped maze, the rats would find food only by turning to the right at the choice point; when starting from the other end of the cross, they also found food only by turning to the right.

The results showed that the first group, the place learners, performed significantly better than the second group, the response learners. Tolman concluded that the same phenomenon occurs with people who are familiar with their neighborhood or town. They can go from one point to another by a number of different routes because of the cognitive map they have developed of the area.

Another experiment involved **latent learning,** which is learning that cannot be observed at the time it is taking place. A hungry rat was placed in a maze and allowed to wander freely. At first, there was no food for it to find. Would the rat learn anything in the absence of reinforcement? After a number of no-reinforcement trials, the rat did find food. The improvement thereafter in the time the rat needed to run the maze was extremely rapid, indicating that some learning had occurred during the no-reinforcement period. The rat's performance quickly came to equal that of control group rats that had been reinforced with food on every trial.

LATENT LEARNING: Learning that cannot be observed at the time it is occurring

Comment

Tolman had a great influence on psychology, particularly in the area of learning, and his work is recognized as a forerunner of the cognitive movement in modern psychology. He also initiated many research topics in learning and introduced the concept of the intervening variable. Because intervening variables are a way of operationally defining unobservable internal states such as hunger, they have made these conditions scientifically respectable. Intervening variables became a necessary format for dealing with hypothetical constructs and were used by neobehaviorists such as Guthrie, Hull, and Skinner.

Another significant contribution was Tolman's support for the rat as an appropriate subject for psychological study. At the start of his career, however, Tolman was not enthusiastic about rats. "I don't like them," he told a friend. "They make me feel creepy" (Tolman, 1919, quoted in Innis, 1992, p. 191).

By 1945, he had changed his attitude. He wrote: "Let it be noted that rats live in cages; they do not go on binges the night before one has planned an experiment; they do not kill each other off in wars; they do not invent engines of destruction, and, if they did, they would not be so inept about controlling such engines; they do not go in for either class conflicts or race conflicts; they avoid politics, economics, and papers on psychology. They are marvelous, pure, and delightful" (Tolman, 1945, p. 166).

EDWIN RAY GUTHRIE (1886–1959)

Edwin Guthrie received his PhD in 1912 from the University of Pennsylvania and spent his academic career of some 40 years at the University of Washington. While in graduate school he became a supporter of the behavioral approach to psychology, although he cannot be described as a Watsonian behaviorist.

Archives of the History of American Psychology/University of Akron

EDWIN RAY GUTHRIE

ONE-TRIAL LEARNING:
Guthrie's notion that a single pairing of a stimulus and a response is sufficient to establish a connection

One-Trial Learning

Guthrie's most important contribution to psychology was his formulation of a simple learning theory, set forth in his book, *The Psychology of Learning* (1935). It is based on a single principle: contiguity. In accounting for the strengthening of learned responses, Guthrie rejected Thorndike's laws of effect and frequency as well as Pavlovian reinforcement, and relied instead on what he called simultaneous conditioning, which he considered to be psychology's most general law.

To Guthrie, all learning depends on the contiguity of stimulus and response. When a stimulus accompanies a response just once, the S-R association is formed. It is, in essence, a **one-trial learning** situation. Repetition and reinforcement are not required to establish a connection between stimulus and response. One pairing of the stimulus and the resulting movement or response establishes the association, and thus the behavior is learned. Guthrie's only formal law of learning states: "A combination of stimuli which has accompanied a movement will on its recurrence tend to be followed by that movement" (Guthrie, 1935, p. 26).

Guthrie's law refers to movements, which he was careful to distinguish from acts, much as Watson had done. He defined a movement as a pattern of motor and glandular responses. An act is a movement or series of movements that brings about some result. An act is of a larger scale than a movement. Hitting a nail with a hammer, for example, is an act composed of a number of separate movements, and it brings about a certain result. Guthrie noted that when psychologists study learning, the performance of the complete act is usually taken as the measure of learning; to Guthrie, it is the movements that are actually conditioned or learned.

He considered this focus on movements to be a distinguishing feature of his system. He said that Thorndike was concerned with the total act, such as acquiring a skill (the cat trying to escape from a puzzle box, for example), but that skill is actually a function of a number of individual muscular movements. And it is these individual movements, Guthrie argued, that are developed or acquired in single trials (one-trial learning). Learning the total act calls for repeated practice.

The movements (the individual parts of the learned act) are the raw data in Guthrie's system. Because they are smaller than acts, these movements are more difficult to observe in a typical learning situation and are often overlooked.

Just as an organism's response is made up of separate components, so too is the stimulation to which the organism is exposed. Because stimulus and response are each composed of many parts, it is necessary to have a large number of pairings of the total stimulus and response situations to achieve any consistency in behavior. Therefore, practice is necessary to bring about improvement in learning any combination of movements (the act), but each component movement or response is learned after a single pairing with the stimulus.

Comment

Much of the appeal of Guthrie's system rests on its simplicity and its consistency over the years. It is easy to understand, especially when compared with more complex and mathematically based learning theories such as Hull's. But the inherent simplicity of Guthrie's theory draws praise from some psychologists and criticism from others.

It has been suggested that Guthrie avoided dealing with problems in learning that defied explanation within his framework. These critics insist that additional principles and assumptions are necessary to account for the major issues in the field.

Nevertheless, Guthrie maintained his position and stature as a leading learning theorist. His contributions received formal recognition in 1958, when the American Psychological Foundation presented him with its Gold Medal Award.

CLARK LEONARD HULL (1884–1952)

First and foremost a behaviorist, Clark Hull, and later his followers, dominated American psychology from the 1940s until the 1960s. Perhaps no other psychologist was so consistently and keenly devoted to the problems of the scientific method. Hull had a prodigious command of mathematics and formal logic, and he applied them to psychological theory in a way no one had done before.

Hull's Life

For most of his life, Hull was plagued by poor health and poor eyesight. At the age of 24 he contracted polio, which left him disabled in one leg and forced to wear an iron brace of his own design. His family was poor (he had been born in a log cabin), and he had to interrupt his education several times to take teaching jobs. Hull's greatest asset was an intense aspiration to greatness, and he persevered in the face of many obstacles.

In 1918, at the relatively advanced age of 34, Hull received his PhD from the University of Wisconsin, where he had studied mining engineering before switching to psychology. He remained on the faculty at Wisconsin for 10 years. His early research interests foretell his lifelong emphasis on objective methods and functional laws.

He investigated concept formation, the effects of tobacco on behavioral efficiency, and tests and measurements, and published an

Archives of the History of American Psychology/University of Akron

CLARK LEONARD HULL

important textbook in the applied area of aptitude testing (Hull, 1928). He worked to develop practical methods of statistical analysis and invented a machine for calculating correlations, which has been exhibited at the Smithsonian in Washington, D.C. He devoted 10 years to the study of hypnosis and suggestibility, publishing 32 papers and a book that summarized the research (Hull, 1933).

In 1929 Hull became a research professor at Yale University, where he pursued his final research interest: a theory of behavior based on Pavlov's laws of conditioning. He first read Pavlov in 1927 and became interested in problems of conditioned reflexes and learning. He referred to Pavlov's book, *Conditioned Reflexes,* as "that great book," and he selected animal subjects for his research. He had not used rats before because he hated the odors associated with a rat lab, but at Yale he visited the meticulously clean rat colony established by Ernest R. Hilgard. Hull looked at the rats, "sniffed them and said that he guessed he could use rats after all" (Hilgard, 1987, p. 201).

In the 1930s Hull wrote articles about conditioning, arguing that complex higher-order behaviors could be explained in terms of basic conditioning principles. In 1940 he published, with five colleagues, *Mathematico-Deductive Theory of Rote Learning: A Study in Scientific Methodology.* Although the book was recognized as a notable achievement in the development of scientific psychology, it was difficult to understand and was read by few people.

Hull's next major publication, *Principles of Behavior* (1943), outlined in detail and with characteristic precision a theoretical framework comprehensive enough to include all behavior. Hull soon became the most frequently cited psychologist in the field; in the 1940s, up to 40% of all experimental articles and 70% of all articles on learning and motivation published in the two leading American psychology journals cited Hull's work (Spence, 1952). Hull revised his system over the years, incorporating the results of research that put earlier versions to experimental test. The final form of his system appears in *A Behavior System* (1952).

The Spirit of Mechanism

Hull was committed to an objective behaviorist psychology. There was no place in his program for consciousness, purpose, or any other mentalistic notion. He used mechanistic terms to describe his behaviorism and his image of human nature, and he regarded human behavior as automatic and capable of being reduced to the language of physics. He warned against anthropomorphizing; that is, giving subjective interpretation to the behavior under observation, as the early animal psychologists had done. Hull sought a safeguard against such subjectivism and found it in the notion that the organism is "a completely self-maintaining robot, constructed of materials as unlike ourselves as may be" (Hull, 1943, p. 27).

Thus, to Hull, behaviorists needed to view their subject matter as robotlike, and he believed that machines could be constructed that would think and display other human cognitive functions, an enterprise under way today with computers. "It has struck me many times," Hull wrote in 1926, "that the human organism is one of the most extraordinary machines—and yet a machine. And it has struck me more than once that so far as the thinking processes go, a machine could be built which would do every essential thing that the body does" (quoted in Amsel & Rashotte, 1984, pp. 2–3). The spirit of mechanism represented by the mechanical figures of the 17th-century European clocks and automata was faithfully incorporated into Hull's work.

Objective Methodology and Quantification

Hull's mechanistic, reductionistic, and objective behaviorism provides a clear view of what his methods of study had to be. Obviously, they would be as objective as possible. In addition, Hull's approach to psychology would, of necessity, be quantitative, and his laws of behavior expressed in the precise language of mathematics. In *Principles of Behavior* (1943), Hull explained how such a mathematically defined psychology would proceed:

> *Progress will consist in the laborious writing, one by one, of hundreds of equations; in the experimental determination, one by one, of hundreds of the empirical constants contained in the equations; in the devising of practically usable units in which to measure the quantities expressed by the equations; in the objective definition of hundreds of symbols appearing in the equations; in the rigorous deduction, one by one, of thousands of theorems and corollaries from the primary definitions and equations; in the meticulous performance of thousands of critical quantitative experiments.* (HULL, 1943, PP. 400–401)

This statement provides a good indication of the rigor, and the patience, required of any follower of Hull's system.

Hull described four methods he considered to be useful to science. Three were already in use: simple observation, systematic controlled observation, and the experimental testing of hypotheses. Hull proposed a fourth method, the **hypothetico-deductive method,** which uses deduction from a set of formulations that are determined a priori. The method involves establishing postulates from which experimentally testable conclusions can be deduced. These conclusions are then submitted to experimental test. If they are not supported by experimental evidence, they must be revised. If they are supported and verified, they may be incorporated into the body of science.

HYPOTHETICO-DEDUCTIVE METHOD: Hull's method for establishing postulates from which experimentally testable conclusions can be deduced

Hull believed that if psychology were to become an objective science like the other natural sciences, which was a central part of the behaviorist program, the only appropriate method would be the hypothetico-deductive one.

Drives

To Hull, the basis of motivation was a state of bodily need arising from a deviation from optimal biological conditions. However, rather than introducing the concept of biological need directly into his system, he postulated the intervening variable of *drive,* a term that had already come into use in psychology. Drive was defined as a stimulus arising from a state of tissue need that arouses or activates behavior. In Hull's view, reduction or satisfaction of a drive is the sole basis for reinforcement. The strength of the drive can be empirically determined by the length of deprivation, or by the intensity, strength, and energy expenditure of the resulting behavior. Hull considered length of deprivation to be an imperfect measurement, and he placed greater emphasis on the strength of the organism's response.

Drive was also assumed to be nonspecific. In other words, any kind of deprivation—food, water, or sex, for example—contributed in the same way (though in differing degrees) to the drive. This nonspecificity means that drive does not direct behavior but only energizes it. The direction of behavior is determined by environmental stimuli.

Hull postulated two kinds of drive: primary and secondary. Primary drives are associated with biological need states and are directly involved with the organism's survival. These drives, which arise from a state of physical need, include food, water, air, temperature regulation, defecation, urination, sleep, activity, sexual intercourse, and relief from pain. These are basic innate processes that are vital to the organism's survival.

He recognized that humans and animals are also motivated by forces other than primary drives. Accordingly, Hull proposed the secondary or learned drives, which refer to situations or environmental stimuli associated with the reduction of primary drives, and which, as a result, may become drives themselves. This means that previously neutral stimuli may acquire the characteristics of a drive because they are capable of eliciting responses that are similar to the responses aroused by the primary drive or original state of need.

A simple example involves touching a hot stove and getting burned. The painful burn, caused by damage to bodily tissues, produces a primary drive, the desire for relief from the pain. Other environmental stimuli associated with this primary drive, such as the sight of the stove, may, in the future, lead to the withdrawal of the hand when this visual stimulus is perceived. In this way, the sight of the stove may become the stimulus for the learned drive of fear. These secondary or learned drives that motivate behavior develop on the basis of the primary drives. Because of his focus on learned drives, then, Hull awarded the study of learning a key role in his behavioristic system.

Learning

Hull's learning theory focuses mainly on the principle of reinforcement, which is essentially Thorndike's law of effect. Hull's **law of primary reinforcement** states that when a stimulus-response relationship is followed by a reduction in need, the probability increases that on subsequent occasions the same stimulus will evoke the same response.

Note that reward or reinforcement is defined not in terms of Thorndike's notion of satisfaction but rather in terms of the reduction of a primary need. Thus, primary reinforcement—the reduction of a primary drive—is the basis of Hull's theory of learning.

Just as his system contains secondary or learned drives, it also deals with secondary reinforcement. If the intensity of the stimulus is reduced as the result of a secondary or learned drive, the drive will act as a secondary reinforcement.

> *It follows that any stimulus consistently associated with a reinforcement situation will through that association acquire the power of evoking the conditioned inhibition, i.e., reduction in stimulus intensity, and so of itself producing the resulting reinforcement. Since this indirect power of reinforcement is acquired through learning, it is called* secondary *reinforcement.* (HULL, 1951, PP. 27–28)

Hull believed that the stimulus-response connection is strengthened by the number of reinforcements that have occurred. He called the strength of the S-R connection **habit strength,** which is a function of reinforcement and refers to the persistence of the conditioning.

Learning cannot take place in the absence of reinforcement, which is necessary to bring about a reduction of the drive. Because of this emphasis on reinforcement, Hull's system has been called a need-reduction theory, as opposed to Guthrie's contiguity theory and Tolman's cognitive theory.

Hull's system is presented in verbal and mathematical form in 18 postulates and 12 corollaries (Hull, 1952). Although the system is based on conditioning principles, Hull believed it could be expanded to include complex processes such as problem solving, social behavior, and forms of learning other than conditioning. He lived to see only a portion of this ambition realized.

LAW OF PRIMARY REINFORCEMENT: When a stimulus-response relationship is followed by a reduction in a bodily need, the probability increases that on subsequent occasions the same stimulus will evoke the same response

HABIT STRENGTH: The strength of the stimulus-response connection, which is a function of the number of reinforcements

Comment

Hull's program achieved such visibility that it inevitably generated a great deal of criticism. As a leading exponent of neobehaviorism, Hull was subject to the same attacks aimed at Watson and others who worked in the behaviorist tradition. Psychologists who opposed the idea of a behavioral approach to psychology included Hull in the enemy camp.

His system can be faulted for its lack of generalizability. In his attempt to define his variables so exactly, in quantitative terms, he necessarily operated on a narrow plane. He often formulated postulates from results obtained in a single experimental situation. Opponents argued that it is questionable whether one can generalize to all behavior on the basis of such specific experimental demonstrations as "the most favorable interval for human eyelid conditioning (Postulate 2)" or "the weight in grams of food needed to condition a rat (Postulate 7)" (Hilgard, 1956, p. 181). Although precise quantification is necessary and commendable, Hull's extreme approach tended to reduce the range of applicability of his research findings.

Hull's influence on psychology cannot be minimized, however. The amount of research inspired by his work, perhaps more than by any other theory, assures his stature in the history of psychology. It is also a tribute to Hull's greatness to note a few of the psychologists who were his disciples and followers: John Dollard, Carl Hovland, Neal Miller, Robert Sears, Hobart Mowrer, and Kenneth Spence. Few psychologists have had such a pronounced effect on the professional motivation of so many other psychologists.

Hull defended, extended, and expounded the objective behaviorist approach to psychology as had never been done before. Although there are still unanswered questions about his theory, there is respect and admiration for the rigorous methods he used to develop it. "It is not often in any field that a true theoretical genius comes along; of the very few to whom psychology can lay claim, Hull must surely rank among the foremost" (Lowry, 1982, p. 211).

B. F. Skinner (1904–1990)

B. F. Skinner was for decades the most influential person in psychology. One historian of psychology called him "without question the most famous American psychologist in the world" (Gilgen, 1982, p. 97). A survey of historians of psychology and chairs of psychology departments ranked him as the most important contemporary psychologist (Korn, Davis, & Davis, 1991). When Skinner died in 1990, the editor of the journal *American Psychologist* praised him as "one of the giants of our discipline," who has "made a permanent mark on psychology" (Fowler, 1990, p. 1203). And an obituary in the *Journal of the History of the Behavioral Sciences* described him as the "leading figure in behavior science of this century" (Keller, 1991, p. 3).

For many years, beginning in the 1950s, Skinner was America's leading behaviorist, and he attracted a large, loyal, and enthusiastic band of followers. He developed a program for behavioral control of society, invented an automatic crib for the care of infants, and was largely responsible for the advancement of behavior modification techniques and teaching machines. He wrote a novel, *Walden Two*, which remains popular 50 years after its publication. In 1971 his book *Beyond Freedom and Dignity* was a national best-seller, and Skinner became "the hottest item on national and big-city talk shows" (Bjork, 1993, p. 192). He became a celebrity—a status few academics achieve—as well known to the general public as to other psychologists.

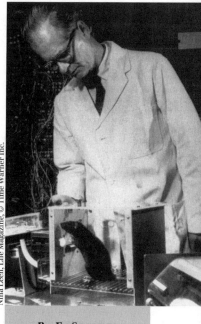

B. F. SKINNER

Skinner's Life

Skinner was born in Susquehanna, Pennsylvania, where he lived until he went away to college. According to his own recollections, his childhood environment was affectionate and stable. He attended the same small high school from which his parents had graduated; there were only seven other students in Skinner's graduating class. He liked school and was the first student to arrive each morning. As a child and adolescent he was interested in building things: wagons, rafts, merry-go-rounds, slingshots, model airplanes, and a steam cannon with which he shot potato and carrot plugs over the roofs of his neighbors' houses. He spent years trying to develop a perpetual motion machine. He read a great deal about the behavior of animals and kept an assortment of turtles, snakes, lizards, toads, and chipmunks. At a county fair he saw a flock of performing pigeons; years later he trained pigeons to perform tricks.

Skinner's system of psychology reflects his early life experiences. In his view, one's life is a product of past reinforcements. He claimed that his own life was just as predetermined, lawful, and orderly as his system dictates all human lives will be. He believed that all aspects of his own experience could be traced solely to environmental sources.

Skinner enrolled in Hamilton College in New York, but was not happy there. He wrote:

> *I never fitted into student life. I joined a fraternity without knowing what it was all about. I was not good at sports and suffered acutely as my shins were cracked in ice hockey or better players bounced basketballs off my cranium. . . . In a paper I wrote at the end of my freshman year, I complained that the college was pushing me around with unnecessary requirements (one of them daily*

Nina Leen, Life Magazine, © Time Warner Inc.

*chapel) and that almost no intellectual interest was shown by
most of the students. By my senior year I was in open revolt.*
(Skinner, 1967, p. 392)

As part of his revolt Skinner played practical jokes that disrupted
the college community, and he spoke openly and critically about the
faculty and administration. His disobedience continued on graduation day when, at commencement ceremonies, the college president
warned Skinner and his friends that if they did not settle down they
would not be allowed to graduate.

Skinner did graduate, with a degree in English, a Phi Beta Kappa
key, and a desire to become a writer. At a summer writing workshop,
the poet Robert Frost had commented favorably on Skinner's poems
and stories. For 2 years after graduation Skinner worked at writing,
then decided that he had "nothing important to say." His lack of success as a writer depressed him so greatly that he thought about consulting a psychiatrist. He considered himself to be a failure; his sense
of self-worth had been shattered.

He was also disappointed in love; at least a half dozen young
women had rejected him, leaving him in what he described as intense
physical pain. He was so upset that he once branded a woman's initial on his arm, where it remained for years. A biographer noted that
Skinner's "love interests were always tempered to some degree with
ambivalence and disappointment. And, indeed, Skinner would have a
reputation as a womanizer" (Bjork, 1993, p. 116).

After reading about the conditioning experiments of Watson and
Pavlov, Skinner turned from a literary interest in human behavior to
a scientific one. In 1928, he enrolled as a graduate student in psychology at Harvard University, though he had never before taken a
psychology course. He went to graduate school, he said, "not because
I was a fully committed convert to psychology, but because I was
escaping from an intolerable alternative" (Skinner, 1979, p. 37).
Committed or not, he received his PhD 3 years later. After completing
postdoctoral fellowships, he taught at the University of Minnesota
(1936–1945) and Indiana University (1945–1947), before returning to
Harvard.

His dissertation topic provides a hint of the position to which he
consistently adhered throughout his career. He proposed that a reflex
is the correlation between a stimulus and a response, and nothing
more. His 1938 book, *The Behavior of Organisms,* describes the basic
points of his system. The book sold only 500 copies in its first 8 years
and received largely negative reviews. Fifty years later it was judged
to be "one of the handful of books that changed the face of modern
psychology" (Thompson, 1988, p. 397).

What changed the book, and the system it described, from an
initial failure to a subsequent overwhelming success was primarily

its usefulness for the applied areas of psychology. "In the 1960s, Skinner's star began to rise, partly because of the reception of his ideas in the field of education and partly because of the use of Skinner's principles in the growing clinical field of behavior modification" (Benjamin, 1993, p. 177). Such widespread practical application of Skinner's ideas was entirely appropriate, because he was keenly interested in the solution of real-world problems. A later work, *Science and Human Behavior* (1953), became the basic textbook for Skinner's behavioral psychology.

Skinner remained productive until his death at the age of 86, working with as much enthusiasm as when he began some 60 years before. He built, in the basement of his home, his own personal "Skinner box"—a controlled environment that provided positive reinforcement. He slept there in a yellow plastic tank, just large enough to contain a mattress, a few shelves for books, and a small television set. He went to bed each night at 10:00, slept for 3 hours, worked for an hour, slept for 3 more hours, and arose at 5:00 in the morning to work for 3 more hours. Then he walked to his office at the university for more work and administered self-reinforcement every afternoon by listening to music. He also received considerable positive reinforcement from his writing. "Writing is the thing I most enjoy and I would be very unhappy to give it up" (Skinner, 1985, quoted in Fallon, 1992, p. 1439).

At the age of 78 he wrote a paper entitled "Intellectual Self-Management in Old Age," citing his own experiences as a case study (Skinner, 1983a). He described how it is necessary for the brain to work fewer hours each day, with rest periods between spurts of effort, in order to cope with failing memory and the diminished intellectual abilities of age.

In 1989, Skinner was diagnosed with leukemia and given 2 months to live. In a radio interview he described his feelings:

> *I'm not religious, so I don't worry about what will happen after I'm dead. And when I was told that I had this and would be dead in a few months, I didn't have any emotion of any kind at all. Not a bit of panic, or fear, or anxiety. Nothing at all. The only thing that touched me was, and really, my eyes watered when I thought of this, I will have to tell my wife and my daughters. You see, when you die, you hurt people, if they love you. And you can't help it. . . . I've had a very good life. It would be very foolish of me to complain, in any way, about it. So I'm enjoying these last few months as well as I ever enjoyed life.* (QUOTED IN CATANIA, 1992, P. 1527)

Eight days before he died, frail and weak, he presented a paper at the 1990 American Psychological Association convention in Boston, in which he vigorously attacked the growth of cognitive psychology, which was challenging his form of behaviorism. The evening before his death, he was working on his final article, "Can Psychology Be a Science of Mind?" (Skinner, 1990), another indictment of the cognitive movement that threatened to supplant his definition of psychology.

Skinner's Behaviorism

In several respects Skinner's position represents a renewal of Watson's behaviorism. One psychologist wrote that "Watson's spirit is indestructible. Cleaned and purified, it breathes through the writings of B. F. Skinner" (MacLeod, 1959, p. 34).

Although Hull is also considered to be a rigorous behaviorist, there is a marked difference between Hull's and Skinner's views. Whereas Hull emphasized the importance of theory, Skinner advocated an empirical system with no theoretical framework within which to conduct research.

Skinner summarized his approach in this way: "I never attacked a problem by constructing a hypothesis. I never deduced theorems or submitted them to experimental check. So far as I can see I had no preconceived model of behavior—certainly not a physiological or mentalistic one, and I believe not a conceptual one" (Skinner, 1956, p. 227).

Skinner's form of behaviorism is devoted to the study of responses. He was concerned with describing behavior rather than explaining it. His research dealt only with observable behavior, and he believed that the task of scientific inquiry is to establish functional relationships between the experimenter-controlled stimulus conditions and the organism's subsequent response.

In *Science and Human Behavior* (1953), Skinner wrote about the mechanical figures in the royal gardens of 17th-century Europe and the mechanical image of human beings they portrayed. Under the heading "Man a Machine" he described how his ideas are compatible with that early mechanical image. The human organism, Skinner wrote, is a machine, and like any other machine, a human being behaves in lawful and predictable ways in response to the external forces (the stimuli) that impinge on it.

Skinner was not concerned with theorizing or speculating about what might be going on inside the organism. His program includes no presumptions about internal entities, whether they are called intervening variables or physiological processes. Whatever might occur between the stimulus and the response does not represent objective data for a Skinnerian behaviorist. Skinner's purely descriptive behaviorism has been called, with good reason, the "empty organism" approach. Human organisms are operated by forces in the environment—the external world—and not by forces within themselves.

It is important to note that Skinner was not completely opposed to all theorizing. Rather, he warned against premature theorizing in the absence of adequate supporting data. In a 1968 interview, Skinner said that he hoped for "an overall theory of human behavior which will bring together a lot of facts and express them in a general way. That kind of theory I would be very much interested in prompting" (quoted in Evans, 1968, p. 88).

In contrast to many contemporary psychologists, Skinner did not believe it was necessary to use large numbers of subjects or to make statistical comparisons between the mean or average responses of groups. His focus was the thorough investigation of a single subject.

> *A prediction of what the* average *individual will do is often of little or no value in dealing with a particular individual. . . . A science is helpful in dealing with the individual only insofar as its laws refer to individuals. A science of behavior which concerns only the behavior of groups is not likely to be of help in our understanding of the particular case.* (Skinner, 1953, p. 19)

Skinner insisted that valid and replicable results could be obtained from a single subject without the use of statistical analysis, as long as sufficient data were collected under well-controlled experimental conditions. He argued that the use of large groups of subjects forced the experimenter to concentrate on average behavior. As a result, individual response behavior and individual differences in behavior would be lost.

In 1958 Skinnerian behaviorists established their own publication, the *Journal of the Experimental Analysis of Behavior,* largely because of the unwritten requirements of the mainstream psychology journals concerning the use of statistical analysis and the size of the subject sample. That journal now has the second largest circulation of all psychology journals that deal with applications of psychology (Lattal, 1992). Another journal, the *Journal of Applied Behavior Analysis,* was started to serve as an outlet for research on behavior modification, another applied outgrowth of Skinner's behavioral psychology.

Operant Conditioning

Generations of psychology students have studied Skinner's **operant conditioning** experiments and how they differ from the respondent behavior investigated by Pavlov. In the Pavlovian conditioning situation, a known stimulus is paired with a response under conditions of reinforcement. The behavioral response is elicited by a specific

Operant Conditioning: A learning situation that involves behavior, which is emitted by an organism rather than elicited by a detectable stimulus

observable stimulus; Skinner called this behavioral response a *respondent behavior.*

Operant behavior occurs without any observable external stimulus. The organism's response appears to be spontaneous in that it is not related to any known observable stimulus. This does not mean that there is no stimulus eliciting the response, but rather that no stimulus is detected when the response occurs. As far as the experimenters are concerned, there is no stimulus because they have not applied a stimulus and cannot see one.

Another difference between respondent and operant behavior is that operant behavior *operates* on the organism's environment whereas respondent behavior does not. The harnessed dog in Pavlov's laboratory can do nothing but respond (salivate, for example) when the experimenter presents the stimulus. The dog cannot act on its own to secure the stimulus (the food).

The operant behavior of the rat in the Skinner box, however, is instrumental in securing the stimulus (the food). When the rat presses the bar, it receives food, and it does not get any food until it does press the bar and thus operate on the environment. (Skinner disliked the term *Skinner box,* first used by Hull in 1933. He referred to the equipment as an operant conditioning apparatus. *Skinner box* has become so popular a label, however, that it is listed in most dictionaries and is accepted usage in psychology.)

Skinner believed that operant behavior is much more representative of everyday learning. Because behavior is mostly of the operant type, the most effective approach to a science of behavior is to study the conditioning and extinguishing of these operant behaviors.

His classic experimental demonstration involved bar pressing in a Skinner box constructed to eliminate extraneous stimuli. In this experiment a rat that had been deprived of food was placed in the apparatus and allowed to explore. In the course of this exploration the rat sooner or later accidentally depressed a lever or bar that activated a mechanism that released a food pellet into a tray. After receiving a few food pellets, the reinforcers, conditioning was usually rapid. Note that the rat's behavior (pressing the bar or lever) operated on the environment and was instrumental in securing food. The dependent variable in this experiment is simple and direct: the rate of response.

Law of Acquisition: The strength of an operant behavior is increased when it is followed by the presentation of a reinforcing stimulus

From this basic experiment Skinner derived his **law of acquisition,** which states that the strength of an operant behavior is increased when it is followed by the presentation of a reinforcing stimulus. Although practice is important in establishing a high rate of bar pressing, the key variable is reinforcement. Practice by itself will not increase the rate; all it does is provide the opportunity for additional reinforcement to occur.

Skinner's law of acquisition differs from the positions of Thorndike and Hull on learning. Skinner did not deal with the pleasure-pain or satisfaction-dissatisfaction consequences of reinforcement, as did Thorndike. Nor did Skinner make any attempt to interpret reinforcement in terms of reducing drives, as did Hull. The systems of Thorndike and Hull are explanatory; Skinner's is strictly descriptive.

Skinner and his followers conducted a great deal of research on problems of learning, such as the role of punishment in acquiring responses, the effect of various schedules of reinforcement, the extinction of operant responses, secondary reinforcement, and generalization.

They also worked with other animals and with human subjects, using the same basic approach as the Skinner box. With pigeons the operant behavior involves pecking at a key or a spot; the reinforcer is food. The operant behavior for human subjects involves problem solving, reinforced by verbal approval or by the knowledge of having given the correct answer.

Skinner reported an attempt to use back-rubbing as a reinforcer for his 3-year-old daughter, but the experiment backfired. He was talking to her at bedtime while rubbing her back and decided to test this as a reinforcer. "I waited," he wrote, "until she lifted her foot slightly and then rubbed briefly. Almost immediately she lifted her foot again, and again I rubbed. Then she laughed. 'What are you laughing at?' I said. 'Every time I raise my foot you rub my back!'" (Skinner, 1987a, p. 179).

Schedules of Reinforcement

The initial research on bar pressing in the Skinner box demonstrated the necessary role of reinforcement in operant behavior. In that situation the rat's behavior was reinforced for every bar press; that is, it received food every time it made the correct response. Skinner noted, however, that reinforcement in the real world is not always consistent or continuous, yet learning occurs and behaviors persist even when they are reinforced only occasionally or intermittently.

> *We do not always find good ice or snow when we go skating or skiing. . . . We do not always get a good meal in a particular restaurant because cooks are not always predictable. We do not always get an answer when we telephone a friend because the friend is not always at home. . . . The reinforcements characteristic of industry and education are almost always intermittent because it is not feasible to control behavior by reinforcing every response.*
> (SKINNER, 1953, P. 99)

Even if you study consistently, you may not get an A on every test. On the job, you do not receive praise or a pay increase every day. How is behavior affected by such variable reinforcement? Is one **reinforcement schedule** or pattern better than another in terms of its influence on behavior? Skinner and his colleagues devoted years of research to these questions (Ferster & Skinner, 1957; Skinner, 1969).

The impetus for the research came not from intellectual curiosity but from expediency, and it illustrates that science sometimes operates quite differently from the idealized picture presented in some textbooks. One Saturday afternoon Skinner found that his supply of food pellets was running low. At that time (the 1930s), food pellets could not be purchased from a laboratory supply company; the experimenter had to compound them by hand, a laborious and time-consuming process.

Rather than spend his weekend making food pellets, Skinner asked himself what would happen if he reinforced his rats only once a minute regardless of the number of responses they were making. That way, he would need far fewer food pellets over the weekend. Skinner went on to design a lengthy series of experiments to test different rates and times of reinforcement.

In one set of studies, Skinner compared the response rates of animals reinforced for every response with those reinforced only after a certain time interval. The latter condition is called the *fixed interval* schedule of reinforcement. A reinforcer could be given, for example, once per minute or once every 4 minutes. The important point is that the animal will be reinforced only after the passage of a stated period of time. (A job in which the salary is paid once a week or once a month provides reinforcement on a fixed interval schedule; employees are paid not for the number of items they produce—the number of responses they make—but for the number of days or weeks that pass.) Skinner's research showed that the shorter the interval between reinforcers, the more rapidly the animal responded. Conversely, as the interval between reinforcers lengthened, the rate of responding declined.

Frequency of reinforcement also affects the extinction of a response. Behaviors are extinguished more quickly when they have been reinforced continuously, and the reinforcers are then stopped, than when they have been reinforced intermittently. Some pigeons responded as many as 10,000 times without reinforcement when they had originally been conditioned on an intermittent reinforcement basis.

Skinner also investigated a *fixed ratio* schedule of reinforcement. In this case, reinforcement is presented not after a certain time interval but rather after a predetermined number of responses. The animal's behavior determines how often it will be reinforced. It is required to respond, for example, 10 times or 20 times after receiving one reinforcer before it gets another one. Animals on a fixed ratio schedule respond much faster than those on a fixed interval schedule. More rapid responding on fixed interval reinforcement will not bring about additional reinforcement; the animal on a fixed interval schedule may press the bar 5 times or 50 times, and it will still be reinforced only when the predetermined time interval has elapsed.

The higher rate of responding on the fixed ratio schedule has been found to hold for rats, pigeons, and humans. For example, a fixed ratio schedule of payment is used in the workplace where an employee's pay depends on the number of units produced, or a sales commission depends on the number of items sold. This reinforcement schedule is effective as long as the ratio is not set too high (that is, an impossible amount of work required for each unit of pay), and the specific reinforcement is worth the effort.

Verbal Behavior

The sounds the human organism makes in speech, Skinner said, are a kind of behavior—verbal behavior. They are responses that can be reinforced by other speech sounds or by gestures in the same way a rat's bar-pressing behavior can be reinforced by food.

Verbal behavior requires two people in interaction—one speaking and one listening. The speaker makes a response; that is, he or she utters a sound. The listener, by his or her behavior in reinforcing, not reinforcing, or punishing the speaker for what has been said, can control the speaker's subsequent behavior.

For instance, if every time the speaker uses a certain word, the listener smiles, the listener increases the likelihood that the speaker will use that word again. If the listener responds by frowning, making hostile gestures, or uttering a nasty comment, the listener increases likelihood that the speaker will avoid that word in the future.

We can see examples of this process in the behavior of parents when their children are learning to speak. Unacceptable words, incorrect usage, or poor pronunciation elicit different reactions from polite phrases, correct usage, and clear pronunciation. In this way the child is taught proper speech, at least as the parents or caregivers understand it.

Because speech is behavior, it is subject to contingencies of reinforcement, prediction, and control, just like any other type of behavior. Skinner summarized his research in the book entitled *Verbal Behavior* (Skinner, 1957).

Aircribs and Teaching Machines

The Skinner box in the psychology research laboratory brought Skinner prominence among psychologists, but it was the aircrib—a device to mechanize infant care—that brought him public notoriety.

He described the development of the aircrib in an article in *Ladies' Home Journal* in 1945. When he and his wife decided to have a second child, she told him that baby care through the first 2 years required too much attention and menial labor, so Skinner invented an automated device to relieve parents of those routine tasks. The aircrib was made available commercially but was never a big success.

The aircrib has been described as "a large, air-conditioned, temperature controlled, germ free, soundproof compartment in which a baby can sleep and play without blankets or clothing other than a diaper. It allows complete freedom of movement, and relative safety from the usual colds and heat rashes" (Rice, 1968, p. 98). Skinner's daughter apparently bore no ill effects from the aircrib experience.

Another piece of equipment Skinner promoted was the teaching machine, invented in the 1920s by psychologist Sidney Pressey. Unfortunately for Pressey, the device was far ahead of its time, and no one expressed any interest in it.

Contextual forces may have been responsible for the lack of interest then, and for the enthusiastic acceptance of the teaching machine some 30 years later (Benjamin, 1988b). In the 1920s, when Pressey introduced the machine, he promised that it could be used to teach students at a faster pace with fewer classroom teachers. At the time, however, there was a surplus of teachers and no public pressure to improve the learning process. In the 1950s, when Skinner introduced a similar device, there was a shortage of teachers, an unusually large number of students, and public pressure to improve the quality of education so that Americans could compete with the Russians in space exploration. Skinner reported that he had not known about Pressey's invention when he developed his own teaching machine, but he gave due credit to his predecessor.

Skinner promoted the teaching machine after visiting his daughter's fourth-grade class, deciding that something had to be done to improve the teaching process. He summarized his work in this field in *The Technology of Teaching* (1968). Teaching machines were widely used throughout the late 1950s and early 1960s, until they were superseded by computer-assisted instructional methods.

Walden Two—*A Behaviorist Society*

Skinner mapped out a program of behavioral control, a technology of behavior, in which he attempted to apply his laboratory findings to society at large. Whereas John B. Watson spoke in general terms about a foundation for saner living through the principles of conditioning, Skinner outlined the operation of such a society in detail.

In 1948 he published a novel, *Walden Two,* that describes a 1,000-member rural community in which every aspect of life is controlled by positive reinforcement. The book was the outgrowth of a depression, a midlife crisis, that Skinner suffered at the age of 41. He apparently resolved it by returning to his earlier identity as a writer. Gripped by personal and professional conflicts, he expressed his despair in the book, speaking through the story's main character, T. E. Frazier. "Much of the life in *Walden Two* was my own at the time," Skinner admitted. "I let Frazier say things I myself was not yet ready to say to anyone" (Skinner, 1979, pp. 297–298).

The book received both praise and condemnation by the press and sold only a few thousand copies a year until the early 1960s, when sales increased sharply. By 1990, the year of Skinner's death, *Walden Two* had sold almost 2.5 million copies (Bjork, 1993).

The society depicted in Skinner's novel, and Skinner's basic assumption that humans are, by nature, like machines, reflect the culmination of the long line of thought from Galileo and Newton through the British empiricists to Watson. "If we are to use the methods of science in the field of human affairs, we must assume that behavior is lawful and determined. . . . that what a man does is the result of specifiable conditions and that once these conditions have been discovered, we can anticipate and to some extent determine his actions" (Skinner, 1953, p. 6).

The mechanistic, analytic, and deterministic approach of natural science, reinforced by Skinner's conditioning experiments, persuaded behavioral psychologists that human behavior could be controlled, guided, modified, and shaped by the proper use of positive reinforcement.

Behavior Modification

Skinner's program for a society based on positive reinforcement exists only in fictional terms, but the control or modification of the behavior of people and small groups is widespread. **Behavior modification** through positive reinforcement is a popular technique in mental hospitals, factories, prisons, and schools where it is used to change abnormal or undesirable behaviors to more acceptable and desirable ones. The behavior modification technique works with people in the same way the operant conditioning approach works to change the behavior of rats and pigeons, by reinforcing the desired behavior and not reinforcing undesired behavior.

BEHAVIOR MODIFICATION: The use of positive reinforcement to control or modify the behavior of individuals and groups

Consider the child who throws temper tantrums to get food or attention. When parents give in to the child's demands, they reinforce the undesirable behavior. In behavior modification, such behavior as kicking and screaming would never be reinforced. Only more desirable and pleasant behaviors would be reinforced. After a time the child's behavior will be modified, because the temperamental displays no longer work to bring rewards, whereas more pleasant behaviors will.

Operant conditioning and reinforcement have been applied in the workplace, where behavior modification has been used to reduce absenteeism and the abuse of sick-leave time and to improve job performance and safe work practices. Behavior modification techniques have also been used to teach job skills.

Behavior modification programs have been shown to be successful in changing the behavior of patients in mental institutions. By rewarding patients with tokens, which can be exchanged for possessions or privileges, when they behave in the desired ways, and by not reinforcing negative or disruptive behavior, positive behavioral changes can be induced. Unlike traditional clinical techniques, there is no concern with what might be going on in a patient's mind, any more than there is concern about what might be going on inside the rat in the Skinner box. The focus is exclusively on overt behavior and positive reinforcement.

Punishment is not used; people are not punished for failing to behave in desirable ways. Instead, they are reinforced or rewarded when their behavior changes in positive ways. Skinner believed that positive reinforcement is much more effective than punishment in altering behavior, a position supported by considerable human and animal research. (Skinner wrote that as a child he was never physically punished by his father and only once by his mother; she washed out his mouth with soap and water for saying a naughty word [Skinner, 1976]. He did not report whether the punishment was effective in changing his behavior.)

Criticisms of Skinner's Behaviorism

A frequently voiced objection to Skinner's form of behaviorism is directed at his extreme positivism and his opposition to theory. Opponents argue that it is impossible to eliminate all theorizing. Because the details of an experiment must be planned in advance of its execution, this in itself is evidence of theorizing, however simple. It has also been noted that Skinner's acceptance of the basic principles of conditioning as the framework for his research constitutes some degree of theorizing.

Skinner made confident assertions about economic, social, political, and religious issues that he apparently derived from his system. In 1986, for example, he wrote an article with the all-embracing title, "What Is Wrong with Life in the Western World?" In it he stated that "human behavior in the West has grown weak, but it can be strengthened through the application of principles derived from an experimental analysis of behavior" (Skinner, 1986, p. 568). Critics charge that this willingness to extrapolate from the data, particularly with regard to proposals about complex human problems, is inconsistent with an antitheoretical stand and shows that Skinner went beyond the observable data in presenting his blueprint for the redesign of society.

The narrow range of behavior studied in Skinnerian laboratories (such as bar pressing and key pecking) has also been attacked. Critics argue that such studies ignore many aspects of behavior. Skinner's position that all behavior is learned has been challenged by a former student, who conditioned more than 6,000 animals of 38 species to perform in television commercials, tourist attractions, and state fairs (Breland & Breland, 1961). Pigs, chickens, hamsters, porpoises, whales, cows, and other animals all demonstrated a tendency toward instinctive drift; that is, they substituted instinctive behaviors for behaviors that had been reinforced, even when these instinctive behaviors interfered with obtaining food. Thus, reinforcement was not all-powerful, as Skinner had claimed.

Skinner's position on verbal behavior, particularly his explanation of how infants learn to speak, has been challenged on the grounds that some behavior must be inherited. Critics argue that an infant does not learn a language on a word-by-word basis because of reinforcement received for the correct usage or pronunciation of each word. Instead, the infant masters the grammatical rules necessary to produce sentences. The potential to construct those rules, so this argument runs, is inherited, not learned (Chomsky, 1959, 1972).

Contributions of Skinner's Behaviorism

Despite these criticisms, Skinner remained the uncontested leader and champion of behavioral psychology. For at least 3 decades, American psychology was shaped more by his work than by the work of any other psychologist.

The American Psychological Association granted Skinner the Distinguished Scientific Contribution Award in 1958, noting that "few American psychologists have had so profound an impact on the development of psychology and on promising younger psychologists." In 1968, Skinner received the National Medal of Science, the highest accolade bestowed by the United States government for contributions to science. In 1971, the American Psychological Foundation presented Skinner with its Gold Medal Award, and he appeared on the cover of *Time* magazine. And in 1990, Skinner was awarded the APA's Presidential Citation for Lifetime Contribution to Psychology.

It is important to note that Skinner's goal was the betterment of human lives and of society. Despite the mechanistic nature of his system, Skinner was a humanitarian, a quality that was apparent in his efforts to modify behavior in the real-world settings of homes, schools, businesses, and hospitals. He hoped that his technology of behavior would relieve human suffering, and he felt increasingly frustrated that his system, though popular and influential, had not been applied more widely.

As Skinner aged, he became more pessimistic about the ability of science and, in the end, even behavioral science to make changes in time. He expressed a gathering despair about the future of the world. (Bjork, 1993, p. 226)

There is no question that Skinner's radical behaviorism achieved and maintained a strong position within psychology. The *Journal of the Experimental Analysis of Behavior* and the *Journal of Applied Behavior Analysis* continue to flourish, as does the Division for the Experimental Analysis of Behavior of the APA. The application of Skinnerian principles in the form of behavior modification remains popular, and the results of this work provide additional support for his approach. By any standard of professional and public acclaim, Skinner's behaviorism clearly overshadowed all other behavioral psychologies.

SOCIAL LEARNING THEORIES: THE COGNITIVE CHALLENGE

We have seen that behaviorism, like other systematic positions, has a long history. John B. Watson gave voice to the changing Zeitgeist, the spirit of the times in American psychology, when he rebelled against its mentalistic background and formally established an objective science of behavior. This vigorous movement marked the beginning of the positivist era in American psychology.

Enthusiastic formulations of different kinds of behaviorism followed. Fifty years after the publication of Watson's article, which launched behaviorism, B. F. Skinner marked the anniversary with a paper entitled "Behaviorism at Fifty" (Skinner, 1963), in which he noted that the tremendous progress in experimental psychology in the United States was due primarily to the influence of behaviorism.

For all its popularity and influence, however, behaviorism came under attack from many psychologists, including some who identified themselves as behaviorists. They questioned behaviorism's disavowal of mental or cognitive processes and formed a new movement, the social learning or sociobehaviorist approach, which reflects the broader cognitive revolution in psychology. This movement marks the third stage—the neo-neobehaviorist stage—in the development of the behaviorist school of thought.

Since about 1960 there has been a trend within psychology away from the "restrictive shackles of behaviorism toward a more flexible emphasis on cognitive processes" (Bruner, 1982, p. 42). Today, consciousness has returned to psychology in full measure. As you might expect, Skinner decried this trend, noting that "mentalism returned in a flood . . . It became fashionable to insert the word 'cognitive' wherever possible" (Skinner, 1983b, p. 194).

We discuss the origins and impact of the larger-scale cognitive movement in contemporary psychology in chapter 15. Here we describe two examples of how the readmission or reconsideration of consciousness changed the nature of behaviorism: the works of the neo-neobehaviorists Albert Bandura and Julian Rotter.

ALBERT BANDURA (1925–   )

Albert Bandura was born in Canada, in a town so small that his high school had only 20 students and 2 teachers. Following his graduation, he worked with construction crews in the Yukon Territory, filling potholes in the Alaska Highway. Bandura became fascinated by the people he met in this northern exposure. "Finding himself in the midst of a curious collection of characters, most of whom had fled creditors, alimony, and probation officers, [Bandura] quickly developed a keen appreciation for the psychopathology of everyday life, which seemed to blossom in the austere tundra" ("Distinguished Scientific," 1981, p. 28).

Bandura received his PhD from the University of Iowa in 1952 and joined the faculty of Stanford University. Beginning in the early 1960s he proposed a version of behaviorism that he initially defined as a sociobehavioristic approach but later called a social cognitive theory (Bandura, 1986).

Social Cognitive Theory

Bandura's social cognitive theory is a less extreme form of behaviorism than Skinner's, and it reflects and reinforces the impact of psychology's renewed interest in cognitive factors. Bandura's approach remains behavioristic, however. His research focuses on the observation of the behavior of human subjects in interaction. He does not use introspection, and he emphasizes the role of reinforcement in acquiring and modifying behaviors.

In addition to being behavioral, Bandura's system is cognitive. He stresses the influence on external reinforcement schedules of such thought processes as beliefs, expectations, and instructions. In Bandura's view, behavioral responses are not automatically triggered by external stimuli in the manner of a robot or a machine. Instead, reactions to stimuli are self-activated. When an external reinforcer alters behavior, it does so because the person is consciously aware of what is being reinforced and anticipates the same reinforcement for behaving in the same way again.

Although Bandura agrees with Skinner that human behavior can be changed as a result of reinforcement, he also believes—and has demonstrated empirically—that individuals can learn virtually all kinds of behavior without directly experiencing any reinforcement.

VICARIOUS REINFORCEMENT:
Bandura's notion that learning
can occur by observing the
behavior of other people and
the consequences of their
behavior, rather than always
experiencing reinforcement
personally

We do not always have to be reinforced ourselves; we can learn through **vicarious reinforcement,** by observing the behaviors of other people and the consequences of those behaviors.

This ability to learn by example and by vicarious reinforcement assumes that we have the capacity to anticipate and appreciate consequences that we have only observed in others and have not yet experienced ourselves. We can regulate and guide our own behavior by visualizing or imagining as yet unexperienced consequences of that behavior and by making a conscious decision to behave or not behave in the same way. There is not, Bandura suggests, a direct link between a stimulus and a response, or between behavior and reinforcement, as in Skinner's system. Instead, a mediating mechanism is interposed between stimulus and response, and that mechanism is the person's cognitive processes.

Thus, cognitive processes assume a powerful role in social cognitive theory and distinguish Bandura's views from those of Skinner. To Bandura, it is not the actual schedule of reinforcement that is effective in changing behavior but rather what the person thinks that schedule is. Rather than learning by experiencing reinforcement directly, we learn through modeling, by observing other people and patterning our behavior on theirs. In Skinner's view, whoever controls the reinforcers controls behavior. In Bandura's view, whoever controls the models in a society controls behavior.

Bandura has conducted extensive research on the characteristics of the models that influence our behavior. He has found that we are much more likely to model our behavior after a person of our same sex and age, peers who have solved problems similar to our own. We also tend to be impressed by models high in status and prestige. The type of behavior involved affects the extent of our imitation. Simple behaviors are more likely to be imitated than highly complex behaviors. Hostile and aggressive behaviors tend to be strongly imitated, especially by children (Bandura, 1986). Thus, what we see—in real life or in the media—can determine our behavior.

Bandura's approach is a *social* learning theory, because it studies behavior as it is formed and modified in social situations. Bandura criticized Skinner's research using only individual subjects, and mostly rats and pigeons, instead of human subjects interacting with one another. Few people actually live in social isolation. Bandura suggests that psychology cannot expect research findings that ignore social interaction to be relevant to the modern world.

Self-Efficacy

SELF-EFFICACY: One's sense of
self-esteem and competence in
dealing with life's problems

Bandura has conducted considerable research on **self-efficacy,** which he describes as our sense of self-esteem or self-worth, our feeling of adequacy and efficiency in dealing with life's problems (Bandura,

1982). His work has shown that people who are high in self-efficacy believe that they are capable of coping with the diverse events in their lives. They expect to be able to overcome obstacles. They will seek challenges, persevere at their tasks, and maintain a high level of confidence in their ability to succeed.

On the other hand, people who are low in self-efficacy feel helpless and hopeless in coping with life events and believe they have little or no ability to influence the conditions or situations that affect them. When they encounter problems they are likely to give up trying to solve those problems if their initial attempts fail. They believe that nothing they can do will make a difference.

Research has shown that self-efficacy beliefs affect many aspects of human functioning. People higher in self-efficacy tend to consider a wider range of career possibilities and have greater career success, earn better grades in school, set higher personal goals, and enjoy better physical and mental health than people lower in self-efficacy. In general, men have been found to be higher in self-efficacy than women. For men and for women, self-efficacy seems to peak in middle age and to decline after the age of 60.

Behavior Modification

Bandura's goal in developing his social cognitive approach to behaviorism has been a practical and applied one: to change or modify behavior that society considers to be abnormal or undesirable. He reasoned that if all behavior, including the abnormal, is learned by observing others and modeling our behavior on theirs, then behavior can be relearned or changed in the same way.

Like Skinner, Bandura focuses on the external aspects of abnormality—the behavior—and not on any presumed internal conscious or unconscious conflicts. Treating the symptom means treating the disorder, because symptom and disorder are considered to be the same.

Modeling is used to change behavior by having subjects observe a model in a situation they find to be frightening or anxiety provoking. For example, children who are afraid of dogs watch a child of their age approach and play with a dog. Observing from a safe distance, the fearful children see the model make progressively closer and bolder movements toward the dog. The model may pet the dog through the bars of a playpen, then enter the pen to play happily with the dog. As a result of this observational learning situation, the children's fear of dogs will be markedly reduced.

In a variation of this technique, subjects watch models play with the feared object, such as a snake. Then the subjects themselves make progressively closer movements toward the object and are eventually able to handle it.

Bandura's form of behavior therapy is widely used in clinical, business, and classroom situations and has been supported by hundreds of experimental studies. It has proved to be effective in eliminating phobias about snakes, closed spaces, open spaces, and heights. It is also useful in treating obsessive-compulsive disorders, sexual dysfunctions, and some forms of anxiety. In addition, observation of models can be used to enhance self-efficacy.

Comment

Traditional behaviorists have been critical of Bandura's social cognitive approach to behaviorism, arguing that cognitive processes such as belief and anticipation have no causal effect on behavior. Bandura's response is as follows: "It is amusing to see radical behaviorists, who contend that thoughts have no causal influence, devoting considerable time to speeches, articles, and books in an effort to convert people's beliefs to their way of thinking" (quoted in Evans, 1989, p. 83).

Social cognitive theory has gained a high degree of acceptance in psychology as an effective way to study behavior in the laboratory and to modify it in the clinic. Bandura's contributions to contemporary psychology have been recognized by his peers. He was president of the American Psychological Association in 1974 and received the APA's Distinguished Scientific Contribution Award in 1980. His theory and the modeling therapy that derives from it fit the functional, practical cast of much of 20th-century American psychology. His approach is objective, amenable to precise laboratory methods, responsive to the current intellectual climate that recognizes the impact of internal cognitive variables, and applicable to real-world issues. To many psychologists, Bandura's work represents an exciting and productive innovation in behaviorism's long history.

JULIAN ROTTER (1916–   )

Julian Rotter grew up in Brooklyn, New York, and discovered books on psychoanalysis by Sigmund Freud and Alfred Adler while in high school. He decided then that he wanted to be a psychologist. There were few jobs for psychologists at that time, during the Great Depression, so he chose to major instead in chemistry at Brooklyn College. While there he met Adler (see chapter 14) and switched to psychology after all, even though he knew it was impractical. He wanted to pursue an academic career, but the widespread prejudice against Jewish people kept him from that goal. "At Brooklyn College and again in graduate school I had been warned that Jews simply could not get academic jobs, regardless of their credentials. The warnings seemed justified" (Rotter, 1982, p. 346).

After Rotter received his PhD from Indiana University in 1941, he found a job at a state mental hospital in Connecticut. He served as a psychologist with the U.S. Army during World War II, taught at The Ohio State University until 1963, then went to the University of Connecticut. In 1988 Rotter received the APA's Distinguished Scientific Contribution Award.

Cognitive Processes

Rotter was the first to use the term *social learning theory* (Rotter, 1947). He developed a cognitive approach to behaviorism, which, like Bandura's, invokes the existence of internal subjective experiences. Thus, his behaviorism (again, like Bandura's) is less radical than Skinner's. Rotter criticized Skinner for studying individual subjects in isolation, arguing that we learn our behavior primarily through social experiences. Rotter's approach relies on rigorous, well-controlled laboratory research of the kind that is typical of the behaviorist movement, and he studies only human subjects in social interaction.

Rotter's system deals with cognitive processes more extensively than Bandura's. Rotter believes that we always perceive ourselves as conscious beings who are capable of influencing the experiences that affect our lives. Both external stimuli and the reinforcement they provide can affect human behavior, but the nature and extent of their influence are mediated by cognitive factors (Rotter, 1982).

Four cognitive principles determine behavioral outcomes:

1. We have a subjective expectation of the outcome or result of our behavior in terms of the amount and kind of reinforcement that is likely to follow it.

2. We form an estimate of the likelihood that behaving in a particular way will lead to a certain reinforcement, and we adjust our behavior accordingly.

3. We place different values on different reinforcers, and we assess their relative worth in different situations.

4. Because we function in different psychological environments that are unique to us as individuals, the same reinforcement can have different values for different people.

Thus, to Rotter, our subjective expectations and experiences, which are internal cognitive states, determine the effects that different external experiences will have on us.

Locus of Control

Rotter's social learning theory also deals with our beliefs about the source of our reinforcement. His research has shown that some people think reinforcement depends on their own behavior; these people are

INTERNAL LOCUS OF CONTROL:
The belief that reinforcement depends on one's own behavior

EXTERNAL LOCUS OF CONTROL:
The belief that reinforcement depends on outside forces

said to have an **internal locus of control.** Others believe reinforcement depends on outside forces; they are said to have an **external locus of control** (Rotter, 1966).

These two sources of control exert differing influences on behavior. To external-locus-of-control people, their own abilities and actions make little difference in the reinforcers they receive, and so they make little or no attempt to improve or change their situation. Internal-locus-of-control people think they are in charge of their lives and behave accordingly.

Rotter's research has shown that internal-locus-of-control people tend to be physically and mentally healthier than external-locus-of-control people. Internals generally have lower blood pressure, fewer heart attacks, and less anxiety and depression. Internals tend to receive better grades in school and to believe that they have greater personal choice in their lives. They are more socially skillful and popular, and rank higher in self-esteem than externals. College students are more likely to be internally rather than externally oriented.

In addition, Rotter's work suggests that one's locus of control is learned in childhood from the way the parents or caregivers treat the child. Parents of internal-locus-of-control people tend to be supportive, generous with praise for achievement (supplying positive reinforcement), consistent in their discipline, and nonauthoritarian in their attitudes.

Comment

Rotter's social learning theory has attracted a large and loyal band of followers who are primarily experimentally oriented and who agree on the importance of cognitive variables in influencing behavior. His research is considered to be as rigorous and well controlled as his subject matter allows, and he has defined his concepts with the precision that makes them amenable to experimental testing. Large numbers of research studies, particularly on internal/external locus of control, support his cognitive approach to behaviorism. Indeed, Rotter claims that his concept of locus of control has become "one of the most studied variables in psychology and the other social sciences" (Rotter, 1990, p. 489).

THE FATE OF BEHAVIORISM

Although the cognitive challenge to behaviorism from within succeeded in modifying the behaviorist movement that we have followed from John B. Watson through B. F. Skinner, it is important to remember that Bandura, Rotter, and the other neo-neobehaviorists who support the cognitive approach still consider themselves behaviorists. They are what have been called *methodological behaviorists;*

that is, they invoke internal cognitive processes as part of psychology's subject matter. *Radical behaviorists,* on the other hand, believe that psychology must study only overt behavior and environmental stimuli; they do not deal with any presumed internal states. Watson and Skinner were radical behaviorists; Hull and Tolman were methodological behaviorists. Bandura's and Rotter's work as methodological behaviorists has changed the nature of behaviorism in American psychology today.

A loyal core of Skinnerians remain active within the radical behaviorist tradition Skinner fostered, but their popularity and influence peaked in the 1980s, and the decline of this movement was hastened by Skinner's death in 1990. In 1987 Skinner conceded that his form of behaviorism was losing ground and that the importance of the cognitive approach was growing (Goleman, 1987). Other scholars agree, noting that Skinnerian behaviorism has "fallen from favor among the majority of active workers in the field. . . . Fewer scholars at major universities now call themselves behaviorists in the traditional sense. In fact, 'behaviorism' is often referred to in the past tense" (Baars, 1986, pp. viii, 1).

The behaviorism that remains intact and vital in today's psychology—which is especially visible within applied psychology where behavior modification techniques are popular—is a different behaviorism from what flourished in the decades between Watson's 1913 manifesto and Skinner's death. As with all evolutionary movements in science and in nature, the species continues to evolve. In that sense, behaviorism survives in the spirit, if not the reality, of its founder's intent.

DISCUSSION QUESTIONS

1. What is operationism? How did it influence the neobehaviorists of the 1920s and 1930s? How are intervening variables defined operationally?
2. Compare Tolman's approach to learning with Guthrie's approach to learning. Describe the classic experiment that supports Tolman's theory.
3. Describe Hull's behaviorism and contrast it with the views of Watson and Tolman.
4. Define primary and secondary drives, and primary and secondary reinforcement, according to Hull. What is the hypothetico-deductive method? What are some of the criticisms of Hull's system?
5. Describe Skinner's views on theorizing, on mechanism, on intervening variables, and on the use of statistics. Distinguish between operant conditioning and respondent conditioning.

6. How is operant conditioning used to modify behavior? What is the difference between a fixed-interval and a fixed-ratio schedule of reinforcement? What criticisms have been offered of Skinner's system?

7. How do Bandura's and Rotter's views of the role of cognitive factors differ from Skinner's views? Distinguish between self-efficacy and locus of control in terms of their effect on behavior. How is modeling used to change behavior?

SUGGESTED READINGS

Bandura, A. (1976). Albert Bandura. In R. I. Evans (Ed.), *The making of psychology: Discussions with creative contributors.* New York: Knopf. Interviews with Bandura about his life and work.

Bergmann, G., & Spence, K. W. (1941). Operationism and theory in psychology. *Psychological Review, 48,* 1–14. Describes problems with the use of operationism and assesses Hull's theory in the context of these problems.

Catania, A. C. (1992). B. F. Skinner, organism. *American Psychologist, 47,* 1521–1530. Describes parallels in the lives and ideas of Skinner and Darwin.

Skinner, B. F. (1953). *Science and human behavior.* New York: Free Press. Presents Skinner's approach to the scientific analysis of human behavior and its implications for government, religion, and education.

Tolman, E. C. (1922). A new formula for behaviorism. *Psychological Review, 29,* 44–53. Suggests that a less physiologically based approach to behaviorism will allow psychologists to deal more comprehensively with such issues as motivation and emotion.

CHAPTER 12

GESTALT PSYCHOLOGY

THE WHOLE IS DIFFERENT FROM THE SUM OF ITS PARTS

WE HAVE traced the development of psychology from the initial ideas of Wilhelm Wundt and their elaboration by E. B. Titchener, through the growth of the functionalist school of thought, to the spread of the behaviorism of Watson and Skinner and the cognitive challenge within that movement. While these ideas were forming in the United States, the Gestalt revolution was taking hold in Germany. It was yet another protest against Wundtian psychology, further testimony to the importance of Wundt's ideas as an inspiration for new viewpoints and as a basis for launching new systems of psychology.

In its attack on the Wundtian establishment, **Gestalt psychology** focused primarily on one aspect of Wundt's work—elementism. The Gestalt psychologists seized on Wundt's recognition of the fundamental status of sensory elements and made that their target of opposition. "We had been shocked," wrote Wolfgang Köhler, a founder of Gestalt psychology, "by the thesis that all psychological facts . . . consist of unrelated inert atoms and that almost the only factors which combine these atoms and thus introduce action are associations" (Köhler, 1959, p. 728).

To understand the nature of the Gestalt protest, we go back to around 1912, a contentious year for psychology. Behaviorism was beginning its attack on Wundt and Titchener and on functionalism.

GESTALT PSYCHOLOGY: A system of psychology focusing largely on learning and perception, suggesting that the act of combining sensory elements produces new patterns with properties that did not exist in the individual elements

Animal research from Thorndike's and Pavlov's laboratories was having a significant impact. Thorndike presented his first full statement of his position in the years 1911 to 1913, and the importance for psychology of Pavlov's conditioned reflex had been discussed in an American journal in 1909. Another approach to psychology, Sigmund Freud's psychoanalysis, was more than a decade old.

The Gestalt psychologists' movement against Wundt's elementistic position occurred at the same time as the rise of the behaviorist movement in the United States. Although they were independent of one another, both schools of thought started by opposing the same ideas; later they would oppose each other.

There were clear differences between Gestalt psychologists and behaviorists. Gestalt psychologists accepted the value of consciousness but criticized the attempt to analyze it into atoms or elements. Behavioral psychologists refused even to acknowledge the existence of consciousness for psychology.

Gestalt psychologists referred to Wundt's approach (as they understood it) as "brick and mortar" psychology, implying that the elements (the bricks) were held together by the mortar of the process of association. They argued that when we look out a window we see trees and sky, not alleged sensory elements such as brightnesses and hues that may constitute our perception of trees and sky.

Further, they accused the Wundtians of claiming that the perception of objects consists merely of the summation of elements into bundles of some sort. The Gestalt psychologists maintained that when sensory elements are combined, they form some new pattern or configuration. Put together a group of musical notes, they said, and something new—a melody or a tune—emerges from their combination, something that did not exist in any of the individual elements (the notes). Stated succinctly: The whole is different from the sum of its parts. It should be noted, however, that Wundt recognized this point in his doctrine of apperception.

To illustrate the difference between the Gestalt and the Wundtian approaches to perception, imagine you are a subject in a psychology laboratory in Germany around 1915. The psychologist in charge asks you to describe what you see on the table. You say:

"A book."

"Yes, of course, it is a book," he agrees, *"but what do you really see?"*

"What do you mean, 'What do I really see?' you ask, puzzled. "I told you that I see a book. It is a small book with a red cover."

The psychologist is persistent. "What is your perception really?" he insists. "Describe it to me as precisely as you can."

"You mean it isn't a book? What is this, some kind of trick?"

There is a hint of impatience. "Yes, it is a book. There is no trickery involved. I just want you to describe to me exactly what you can see, no more and no less."

You are growing very suspicious now. "Well," you say, "from this angle the cover of the book looks like a dark red parallelogram."

"Yes," he says, pleased. "Yes, you see a patch of dark red in the shape of a parallelogram. What else?"

"There is a grayish white edge below it and another thin line of the same dark red below that. Under it I see the table–" He winces. "Around it I see a somewhat mottled brown with wavering streaks of lighter brown running roughly parallel to one another."

"Fine, fine." He thanks you for your cooperation.

As you stand there looking at the book on the table you are a little embarrassed that this persistent fellow was able to drive you to such an analysis. He made you so cautious that you were not sure any longer what you really saw and what you only thought you saw. . . . In your caution you began talking about what you saw in terms of sensations, where just a moment earlier you were quite certain that you perceived a book on a table.

Your reverie is interrupted suddenly by the appearance of a psychologist who looks vaguely like Wilhelm Wundt. "Thank you, for helping to confirm once more my theory of perception. You have proved," he says, "that the book you see is nothing but a compound of elementary sensations. When you were trying to be precise and say accurately what it was you really saw, you had to speak in terms of color patches, not objects. It is the color sensations that are primary, and every visual object is reducible to them. Your perception of the book is constructed from sensations just as a molecule is constructed from atoms."

This little speech is apparently a signal for battle to begin. "Nonsense!" shouts a voice from the opposite end of the hall. "Nonsense! Any fool knows that the book is the primary, immediate, direct, compelling, perceptual fact!" The psychologist who charges down upon you now bears a faint resemblance to William James, but he seems to have a German accent, and his face is so flushed with anger that you cannot be sure. "This reduction of a perception into sensations that you keep talking about is nothing but an intellectual game. An object is not just a bundle of sensations. Any man who goes about seeing patches of dark redness where he ought to see books is sick!"

As the fight begins to gather momentum you close the door softly and slip away. You have what you came for, an illustration that there are two different attitudes, two different ways to talk about the information that our senses provide. (MILLER, 1962, PP. 103–105) [1]

Gestalt psychologists believe there is more to perception than meets the eye, that our perception somehow goes beyond the sensory elements, the basic physical data provided to the sense organs.

ANTECEDENT INFLUENCES ON GESTALT PSYCHOLOGY

As with all movements, the ideas of the Gestalt protest have their historical antecedents. The basis of the Gestalt position—its focus on the wholeness of perception—can be found in the work of the German philosopher Immanuel Kant (1724–1804), who wrote all his books in his bathrobe and slippers. Kant argued that when we perceive what we call objects, we encounter mental states that might seem to be composed of bits and pieces; these are the sensory elements the empiricists and associationists dealt with. These elements are meaningfully organized in a priori fashion, however, and not through some mechanical process of association. Instead, the mind, in the process of perceiving, forms or creates a unitary experience.

According to Kant, perception is not a passive impression and combination of sensory elements, as the empiricists and associationists suggested, but an active organizing of elements into a coherent experience. Thus, the mind gives shape and form to the raw data of perception.

The psychologist Franz Brentano (1838–1917), at the University of Vienna, opposed Wundt's focus on the elements or content of conscious experience and proposed instead that psychology study the process or act of experiencing. He considered Wundtian introspection to be artificial and favored a less rigid and more direct observation of experience as it occurred. Thus, Brentano's approach was much like the later Gestalt method.

Ernst Mach (1838–1916), a professor of physics at the University of Prague, exerted a more direct influence on the Gestalt revolution with his book, *The Analysis of Sensations* (1885). In it he discussed spatial patterns such as geometric figures and temporal patterns

[1] From pp. 103–105 in *Psychology* by George A. Miller. Copyright 1962 by George A. Miller. Reprinted by permission of Harper & Row, Publishers, Inc.

such as melodies, and considered them to be sensations. These space-form and time-form sensations were independent of their elements. For example, the space-form of a circle might be white or black, large or small, and lose nothing of its elemental quality of circularity.

Mach argued that our perception of an object does not change, even if we change our spatial orientation to it. A table remains a table in our perception whether we look at it from the side or from the top or from an angle. Similarly, a tune remains the same in our perception even when its time-form is changed, that is, when it is played faster or slower.

Mach's ideas were expanded by Christian von Ehrenfels (1859–1932), who suggested that there are qualities of experience that cannot be explained in terms of combinations of elementary sensations. He called these qualities *Gestalt qualitäten* (form qualities), perceptions based on something beyond the individual sensations. A melody, for example, is a form quality because it sounds the same even when transposed to different keys. The melody is independent of the particular sensations of which it is composed. To Ehrenfels, and the Austrian school of *Gestalt qualität* headquartered at Graz, form itself was an element—a new element created by the action of the mind as it operates on the sensory elements. Thus, the mind creates form out of elementary sensations.

Max Wertheimer, a founder of Gestalt psychology, studied with Ehrenfels at Prague, and he noted that the "most important impulse" for the Gestalt movement came from Ehrenfels's work.

William James's work, opposing the notion of elementism in psychology, is also a precursor of Gestalt psychology. James regarded elements of consciousness as artificial abstractions. He emphasized that we see objects as wholes, not as bundles of sensations.

Another early influence is the phenomenological movement in German philosophy and psychology. **Phenomenology** refers to an unbiased description of immediate experience just as it occurs. It is uncorrected observation in which the experience is not analyzed into elements or otherwise artificially abstracted. It involves the almost naïve experience of common sense rather than experience as reported by a trained introspector with a particular systematic orientation.

PHENOMENOLOGY: A doctrine based on an unbiased description of immediate experience as it occurs, not analyzed or reduced to elements

A group of phenomenological psychologists worked at G. E. Müller's laboratory at the University of Göttingen in Germany from 1909 to 1915, the period when the Gestalt movement was beginning to develop. Their work anticipated the formal Gestalt school of thought, which later adopted their approach.

THE CHANGING ZEITGEIST IN PHYSICS

Not to be neglected among the antecedent influences on Gestalt psychology is the Zeitgeist, especially the intellectual climate in physics.

Fields of Force: A region or space traversed by lines of force, such as of a magnet or electric current

In the closing decades of the 19th century, that discipline was becoming less atomistic as physicists recognized and accepted the idea of **fields of force** (regions or spaces crossed by lines of force, such as from an electric current or a magnet).

The classic instance of this new direction in physics is magnetism, a property or quality difficult to define or understand in traditional Galilean-Newtonian terms. For example, when iron filings are shaken onto a sheet of paper that is resting on a magnet, the filings become arranged in a characteristic pattern. The iron filings do not touch the magnet, yet they are obviously affected by the field of force around the magnet. Light and electricity were considered to operate similarly. These fields of force were thought to possess the properties of spatial extension and pattern or configuration. They were believed to be new structural entities, not summations of the effects of individual elements or particles.

Thus, the notion of atomism or elementism, which had been so influential in the establishment of the new science of psychology, was being reconsidered in physics. Physicists were coming to think in terms of fields and organic wholes, a concept that was supportive of what the Gestalt psychologists were proposing for perception. The ideas offered by the Gestalt psychologists were reflecting the new ideas in the physics of the day. Once again psychologists were striving to emulate the older, well-established natural sciences.

The impact on psychology of this changing emphasis in physics came about in a personal way. Wolfgang Köhler had a strong background in physics and had studied with Max Planck, one of the architects of modern physics. Köhler wrote that it was because of Planck's influence that he perceived a connection between field physics and the Gestalt emphasis on wholes. He recognized in physics an increasing reluctance to deal with elemental atoms and molecules, and noted that this was being replaced by a focus on larger concepts, the systems or fields. "Gestalt psychology has since become a kind of application of field physics to essential parts of psychology" (Köhler, 1969, p. 77).

The founder of behaviorism, John B. Watson, in contrast, apparently had no training in the new physics, and so he continued to develop a reductionistic approach to psychology that focused on elements—the elements of behavior—a view that was compatible with the principles of the older atomistic physics.

The Phi Phenomenon: A Challenge to Wundtian Psychology

The formal movement known as Gestalt psychology grew out of a research study conducted in 1910 by Max Wertheimer. While riding on a train during his vacation, Wertheimer got an idea for an experiment about how we see motion when no actual motion had occurred. Abandoning his vacation plans, he got off the train at Frankfurt, bought a toy stroboscope, and verified his insight in a preliminary way in his hotel room. (The stroboscope, a forerunner of the motion picture camera, is an instrument that rapidly projects a series of different pictures on the eye, producing apparent motion.) Wertheimer later carried out more extensive research on this problem at the University of Frankfurt. Two other psychologists, Kurt Koffka and Wolfgang Köhler, who had been students at the University of Berlin, were also at Frankfurt, and shortly they all embarked on a joint crusade.

Wertheimer's research problem, for which Koffka and Köhler served as subjects, involved the perception of apparent movement; that is, the perception of motion when no actual physical movement has taken place. Wertheimer referred to it as the "impression of movement." Using the tachistoscope, he projected light through two slits, one vertical and the other 20° or 30° from the vertical.

If light was shown first though one slit and then through the other, with a relatively long interval between (more than 200 milliseconds), the subjects saw what appeared to be two successive lights, first a light at one slit and then a light at the other. When the interval between the lights was shorter, the subjects saw what appeared to be two lights on continuously. With an optimal time interval between the lights, about 60 milliseconds, the subjects saw a single line of light that appeared to move from one slit to the other and back again.

These findings may seem straightforward. Scientists had been aware of the phenomenon for years, and it may even be considered common sense. However, according to the then prevailing position in psychology—the Wundtian viewpoint—all conscious experience could be analyzed into sensory elements. Yet how could this perception of apparent movement be explained in terms of a summation of individual elements, which were simply two stationary slits of light? Could one stationary stimulus be added to another to produce a sensation of movement? It could not, and this was precisely the point of Wertheimer's brilliantly simple demonstration: It defied explanation by the Wundtian system.

Wertheimer believed that the phenomenon he verified in his laboratory was, in its own way, as elementary as a sensation, yet it obviously differed from a sensation or even a series of sensations. He gave it the name **phi phenomenon.** And how did Wertheimer explain the phi phenomenon when the accepted psychology of the day could not? His answer was as simple and ingenious as his research: Apparent movement did not need explaining. It existed as it was perceived, and it could not be reduced to anything simpler.

PHI PHENOMENON: The illusion that two stationary flashing lights are moving from one place to another

According to Wundt, introspection of the stimulus would produce two successive lines and nothing more, but no matter how rigorously one introspected the two exposures of light, the experience of a single line in motion persisted. Any further attempt at analysis was a failure. The whole (the apparent movement of the line from one slit to another) was different from the sum of its parts (two stationary lines). Thus, the traditional associationist-atomist psychology had been challenged, and it was a challenge it could not meet.

Wertheimer published the results of his research in 1912 in "Experimental Studies of the Perception of Movement," an article considered to mark the beginning of the Gestalt psychology school of thought.

MAX WERTHEIMER (1880–1943)

Born in Prague, Max Wertheimer attended local schools until the age of 18 and studied law at the University of Prague. He changed his major to philosophy, attending lectures by Ehrenfels, and later went to the University of Berlin to study philosophy and psychology. He earned his doctoral degree in 1904 at the University of Würzburg under Oswald Külpe. For several years, Wertheimer spent time at universities in Prague, Vienna, and Berlin before settling at the University of Frankfurt. There he conducted research and lectured, receiving a professorship in 1929. During World War I, he conducted military research on listening devices for submarines and harbor fortifications.

In 1921, Wertheimer, Koffka, and Köhler, assisted by Kurt Goldstein and Hans Gruhle, founded the journal *Psychological Research*, which became the official publication of the Gestalt school of thought. Printing was suspended in 1938 by the Nazi regime, but publication resumed in 1949.

Wertheimer was among the first group of refugee scholars to flee Nazi Germany, and he arrived in New York City in 1933. He became associated with the New School for Social Research, where he remained until his death in 1943. Although his years in the United States were productive, he became increasingly exhausted by his efforts to adapt to a new language and culture.

Wertheimer made a strong impression on a young American psychologist, Abraham Maslow, who was apparently so in awe that he began to study Wertheimer's personal characteristics and abilities. It was from these observations of Wertheimer and others that later Maslow developed his concept of self-actualization and promoted the humanistic school of thought in psychology.

KURT KOFFKA (1886–1941)

Kurt Koffka, born in Berlin, was probably the most inventive of the founders of Gestalt psychology. He received his education at the

MAX WERTHEIMER

Archives of the History of American Psychology/University of Akron

University of Berlin and developed an interest in science and philosophy. He studied psychology with Carl Stumpf and received his PhD in 1909. In 1910 Koffka began his long and fruitful association with Wertheimer and Köhler at the University of Frankfurt. The following year he accepted a position at the University of Giessen, 40 miles from Frankfurt, and remained there until 1924. During World War I he worked with brain-damaged and aphasic patients at the psychiatric clinic.

After the war, as psychologists in the United States became aware that a new school of thought was taking shape in Germany, Koffka wrote an article for the American journal *Psychological Bulletin*. This article, "Perception: An Introduction to Gestalt-Theorie" (Koffka, 1922), presented the basic concepts of Gestalt psychology and the results and implications of considerable research. Although the article was important as the first explanation of the Gestalt movement to American psychologists, it may have done the movement a disservice. The article's title, "Perception," created a misunderstanding that lingered for many years; namely, the idea that Gestalt psychology deals exclusively with perception and therefore has no relevance for other areas of psychology.

In reality, Gestalt psychology was more broadly concerned with problems of thinking and learning and, ultimately, with all aspects of conscious experience.

Archives of the History of American Psychology/University of Akron

KURT KOFFKA

> *The main reason why the early Gestalt psychologists concentrated their systematic publications on perception was because of the Zeitgeist: Wundt's psychology, against which the Gestaltists rebelled, had obtained most of its support from studies of sensation and perception, so the Gestalt psychologists chose perception as the arena in order to attack Wundt in his own stronghold.*
> (MICHAEL WERTHEIMER, 1979, P. 134)

In 1921 Koffka published *The Growth of the Mind,* a book on developmental child psychology that became a success both in Germany and in the United States. He came to America as visiting professor at Cornell University and the University of Wisconsin, and in 1927 was appointed professor at Smith College in Northampton, Massachusetts, where he remained until his death in 1941. In 1935 he published *Principles of Gestalt Psychology,* which was a difficult book to read and so did not become the definitive treatment of Gestalt psychology he had intended it to be.

WOLFGANG KÖHLER (1887–1967)

Wolfgang Köhler was the spokesman for the Gestalt movement. His books, written with care and precision, became the standard works

WOLFGANG KÖHLER

on several aspects of Gestalt psychology. Köhler's training in physics with Max Planck persuaded him that psychology must ally itself with physics and that *Gestalten* (forms or patterns) occur in psychology as well as in physics.

Born in Estonia, Köhler was 5 years old when his family moved to northern Germany. His university education was at Tübingen, Bonn, and Berlin, and he received his doctorate from Carl Stumpf at the University of Berlin in 1909. He went to the University of Frankfurt, arriving just before Wertheimer and his toy stroboscope.

In 1913, at the invitation of the Prussian Academy of Science, Köhler embarked on a voyage to Tenerife in the Canary Islands, off the northwest coast of Africa, to study chimpanzees. Six months after his arrival, World War I began, and he reported he was unable to leave, although other German citizens did manage to return home during the war years. One psychologist has suggested, based on his interpretation of new data of history, that Köhler may have been a spy for Germany and that his research facility was actually a cover for espionage activities (Ley, 1990). It is charged that on the top floor of his home Köhler concealed a powerful radio transmitter that he used to broadcast information about allied ship movements. The evidence to support this claim is circumstantial, however, and has been challenged by historians and Gestalt psychologists.

Whether a spy or simply a scientist marooned by war, Köhler spent the next 7 years studying the behavior of chimpanzees. He produced the now classic volume *The Mentality of Apes* (1917), which appeared in a second edition in 1924 and was translated into English and French.

In 1920, Köhler returned to Germany and 2 years later succeeded Stumpf as professor of psychology at the University of Berlin, where he remained until 1935. The apparent reason for his appointment to this coveted position was the publication of his book *Static and Stationary Physical Gestalts* (1920), which won considerable acclaim for its high level of scholarship.

The mid-1920s were difficult years in Köhler's personal life. He divorced his wife, married a young Swedish student, and after that had no contact with the four children of his first marriage. He developed a tremor in his hands, which became more noticeable when he became annoyed. As a way to gauge his temper, his laboratory assistants would observe him every morning, to see how badly his hands were shaking.

In the 1925–1926 academic year, Köhler lectured at Harvard University and at Clark University, where, in addition to his academic duties, he taught the graduate students to dance the tango. In 1929 he published *Gestalt Psychology,* a comprehensive account of the Gestalt movement.

He left Nazi Germany in 1935, because of conflicts with the regime. After he spoke against the government in his lectures, a gang of Nazi thugs invaded his classroom. He wrote a courageous anti-Nazi letter to a Berlin newspaper, because he was incensed by the dismissal of Jewish professors from German universities. On the evening his letter was published, he and a few friends waited at his home, expecting the Gestapo to arrest him. The dreaded knock on the door never came.

After Köhler emigrated to the United States, he taught at Swarthmore College in Pennsylvania, published several books, and edited the Gestalt journal *Psychological Research*. In 1956 he received the Distinguished Scientific Contribution Award from the American Psychological Association and shortly thereafter was elected its president.

THE NATURE OF THE GESTALT REVOLT

Gestalt ideas were in direct opposition to much of the academic tradition of German psychology. Behaviorism was a less immediate revolt against Wundt and structuralism because functionalism had already brought about changes in American psychology. No such tempering paved the way for the Gestalt revolt in Germany. The pronouncements of the Gestalt psychologists were considered nothing less than heresy.

Like most revolutionaries, the leaders of the Gestalt school of thought demanded a complete revision of the old order, almost like "intellectual missionaries, spreading a new gospel" (Sokal, 1984, p. 1257). Köhler wrote that "We were excited by what we found, and even more by the prospect of finding further revealing facts. . . . it was not only the stimulating newness of our enterprise which inspired us. There was also a great wave of relief—as though we were escaping from a prison. The prison was psychology as taught at the universities when we still were students" (Köhler, 1959, p. 728).

After the studies on the perception of apparent movement, the Gestalt psychologists seized on other perceptual phenomena. The experience of **perceptual constancies** afforded additional support for their position. When we stand directly in front of a window, for example, a rectangular image is projected onto the retina of the eye, but when we stand off to one side and look at the window, the retinal image becomes a trapezoid, although we will continue to perceive the window as a rectangle. Our perception of the window remains constant, even though the sensory data (the images projected on the retina) have changed.

Similarly, with brightness and size constancy, the actual sensory elements may change but our perception does not. In these cases, as with apparent movement, the perceptual experience has a quality of wholeness or completeness that is not found in any of the parts.

PERCEPTUAL CONSTANCIES:
A quality of wholeness or completeness in perceptual experiences that does not vary even when the actual sensory elements change

There exists, then, a difference between the character of the actual perception and the character of the sensory stimulation. The perception cannot be explained simply as a collection of sensory elements or as the mere sum of the parts.

The perception is a whole, a *Gestalt,* and any attempt to analyze or reduce it to elements will destroy it.

> *To begin with elements is to begin at the wrong end; for elements are products of reflection and abstraction, remotely derived from the immediate experience they are invoked to explain.* Gestalt *psychology attempts to get back to naïve perception, to immediate experience . . . and it insists that it finds there not assemblages of elements, but unified wholes; not masses of sensations, but trees, clouds, and sky. And this assertion it invites any one to verify simply by opening his eyes and looking at the world about him in his ordinary everyday way.* (Heidbreder, 1933, p. 331)

The word *Gestalt* has caused difficulty because it does not clearly indicate, as does *functionalism* or *behaviorism*, what the movement stands for. Also, it has no precise counterpart in English. Several equivalents in common use are *form, shape,* and *configuration.* The word *Gestalt* itself has become part of the English language.

In his book, *Gestalt Psychology* (1929), Köhler noted that the word was used in two ways in the German language.

1. One usage denotes shape or form as a property of objects; in this sense, *Gestalt* refers to general properties that can be expressed in such terms as *angular* or *symmetrical,* and describes characteristics such as triangularity in geometric figures or tempos in a melody.

2. The second usage denotes a whole or concrete entity that has as one of its attributes a specific shape or form; in this sense the word may refer, for example, to triangles rather than the notion of triangularity.

Thus, the word *Gestalt* can be used for reference to objects as well as to their characteristic forms. Also, the term is not restricted to the visual field or even the total sensory field. "The processes of learning, of recall, of striving, of emotional attitude, of thinking, acting, and so forth, may have to be included" (Köhler, 1947, pp. 178–179). It is in this general, functional sense of the word that the Gestalt psychologists attempted to deal with the entire province of psychology.

Let us consider some of the topics studied by the Gestalt psychologists.

GESTALT PRINCIPLES OF PERCEPTUAL ORGANIZATION

Wertheimer's principles of perceptual organization were presented in a paper in 1923. He took the position that we perceive objects in the same manner in which we perceive apparent motion; that is, as unified wholes, not as clusters of individual sensations. The principles of perceptual organization, which are described in most introductory psychology textbooks, are essentially laws or rules by which we organize or arrange our perceptual world.

A basic premise of these principles is that perceptual organization occurs instantly, whenever we see or hear different shapes or patterns. Parts of the perceptual field become connected, uniting to form structures that are distinct from their background. Perceptual organization is spontaneous and inevitable whenever we look around. We do not have to learn to form patterns, as the associationists claimed, although some higher-level perception, such as labeling objects by name, does depend on learning.

According to Gestalt theory, the primary brain process in visual perception is not a collection of separate activities. The visual area of

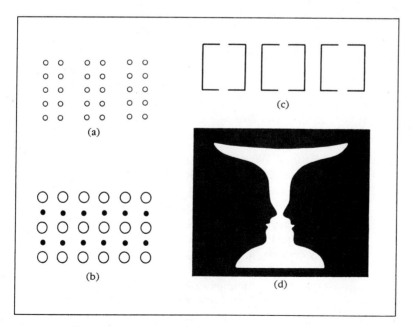

FIGURE 12.1   Examples of perceptual organization.

the brain does not respond to individual elements of visual input, connecting these elements by some mechanical process of association. Rather, the brain is a dynamic system in which all elements active at a given time interact. Elements that are similar or close together tend to combine, and elements that are dissimilar or far apart do not tend to combine.

Several of the principles of perceptual organization are listed here and illustrated in Figure 12.1.

1. *Proximity.* Parts that are close together in time or space appear to belong together and tend to be perceived together. In Figure 12.1(a) you see the circles in three double columns rather than as one large collection.

2. *Continuity.* There is a tendency in our perception to follow a direction, to connect the elements in a way that makes them seem continuous or flowing in a particular direction. In Figure 12.1(a) you tend to follow the columns of small circles from top to bottom.

3. *Similarity.* Similar parts tend to be seen together as forming a group. In Figure 12.1(b) the circles and the dots each appear to belong together, and you tend to perceive rows of circles and rows of dots instead of columns.

4. *Closure.* There is a tendency in our perception to complete incomplete figures, to fill in gaps. In Figure 12.1(c) you perceive three squares even though the figures are incomplete.

5. *Simplicity.* We tend to see a figure as being as good as possible under the stimulus conditions; the Gestalt psychologists called this *prägnanz* or "good form." A good Gestalt is symmetrical, simple, and stable, and cannot be made simpler or more orderly. The squares in Figure 12.1(c) are good Gestalts because they are clearly perceived as complete and organized.

6. *Figure/ground.* We tend to organize perceptions into the object being looked at (the figure) and the background against which it appears (the ground). The figure seems to be more substantial and to stand out from its background. In Figure 12.1(d) the figure and the ground are reversible; you may see two faces or you may see a vase, depending on how your perception is organized.

These organizing principles do not depend on higher mental processes or on past experiences; they are present in the stimuli themselves. Wertheimer called them peripheral factors, but he also recognized that central factors within the organism will influence perception; for example, the higher mental processes of familiarity and attitude can affect perception. In general, however, the Gestalt psychologists tended to focus more on the peripheral factors of organization than on the effects of learning or experience.

GESTALT STUDIES OF LEARNING: INSIGHT AND THE MENTALITY OF APES

We mentioned Köhler's stay on the island of Tenerife from 1913 to 1920, when he investigated the intelligence of chimpanzees as demonstrated in their ability to solve problems (Köhler, 1917). These studies were conducted in and around the animals' cages and involved simple props, such as the bars of the cages (used to block access), bananas, sticks for drawing bananas into the cages, and boxes on which the animals could climb. Consistent with the Gestalt view of perception, Köhler interpreted the results of his animal research in terms of the whole situation and the relationships among the various stimuli. For example, he considered problem solving to be a matter of restructuring the perceptual field.

In one study, a banana was placed outside the cage and a string attached to the banana led into the cage. The ape pulled the banana into the cage with little hesitation. Köhler concluded that in this situation the problem as a whole was easy for the animal to grasp. However, if several strings led from the cage in the general direction of the banana, the ape would not recognize at first which string to pull to get the banana. This indicated to Köhler that the problem could not be envisioned clearly all at once.

Yerkes Primate Research Center

A chimpanzee uses sticks of different lengths to reach a piece of fruit.

In another study, a piece of fruit was placed outside the cage just beyond the chimp's reach. If a stick was placed near the bars of the cage in front of the fruit, the stick and the fruit would be perceived as part of the same situation, and the animal would use the stick to pull the fruit into the cage. But if the stick was placed at the back of the cage, then the two objects (the stick and the fruit) would be less readily seen as parts of the same situation. In this case, a restructuring of the perceptual field would be necessary to solve the problem.

Another experiment involved positioning a banana outside the cage, beyond reach, and placing two hollow bamboo sticks inside the cage. Each stick by itself was too short to retrieve the banana. To reach the banana, the animal had to push the two sticks together (inserting the end of one into the end of the other) to make a stick of sufficient length. Thus, to solve this problem and reach the banana, the animal had to visualize a new relationship between the sticks.

The following original source material describes some other studies conducted by Köhler on learning in chimpanzees.

Original Source Material on Gestalt Psychology:
From *The Mentality of Apes*
by Wolfgang Köhler

In this excerpt from Köhler's classic book, The Mentality of Apes *(1927),[2] he discusses the efforts of his chimps to learn to use implements to retrieve food that was otherwise unobtainable. These experiments show how the animals learned to use boxes to reach the objective (the stimulus object), which was typically a banana suspended from the roof.*

Note the nontechnical language Köhler used to describe his work. He focused on the personalities of his subjects and the individual differences he found among them. He used no formal experimental design, no pre- and post-experiment measurements, no formal experimental treatments, control groups, or statistical analysis. Köhler simply described his observations of how the animals reacted to the situations he created.

When a chimpanzee cannot reach an objective hung high up with one box, there is a possibility that he will pile two or more boxes on top of one another and reach it in that way. Whether he actually does this seems a simple question that can soon be decided. But if experiments are made, it is quickly seen that the problem for the chimpanzee falls into two very distinct parts: one of which he can settle with ease, while the other presents

[2] From Wolfgang Köhler, *The Mentality of Apes* (London: Routledge & Kegan Paul, 1927), pp. 135–172.

considerable difficulties. We think the first is the whole problem; where the animal's difficulties begin, we do not, at first, see any problem at all. If in the description this curious fact is to be emphasized as much as it impressed itself on the observer, the report of the experiment should be divided into two parts in accordance with this fact. I shall begin with the answer to the question that seems to be the only one.

In one of the experiments described previously, Sultan [Köhler's most intelligent chimp] came very near putting one box on the top of another, when he found one insufficient; but instead of placing the second box, which he had already lifted, upon the first, he made uncertain movements with it in the air around and above the other; then other methods replaced these confused movements.

The test is repeated; the objective is placed very high up, the two boxes are not very far away from each other and about four meters away from the objective; all other means of reaching it have been taken away. Sultan drags the bigger of the two boxes toward the objective, puts it just underneath, gets up on it, and looking upward, makes ready to jump, but does not jump; gets down, seizes the other box, and, pulling it behind him, gallops about the room, making his usual noise, kicking against the walls and showing his uneasiness in every other possible way.

He certainly did not seize the second box to put it on the first; it merely helps him to give vent to his temper. But all of a sudden his behavior changes completely; he stops making a noise, pulls his box from quite a distance right up to the other one, and stands it upright on it. He mounts the somewhat shaky construction, several times gets ready to jump but again does not jump; the objective is still too high for this bad jumper. But he has achieved the essential part of his task. . . .

Some days previously [the chimps] Chica and Grande learned from Sultan and myself how to use one box; they do not yet know how to work with two. The situation is the same as in Sultan's experiment. Each of the animals forthwith seizes a box; first Chica, then Grande, will stand under the objective with her box, but there is no sign of an attempt to put one on top of the other.

On the other hand, they hardly get up on their own boxes; though their feet are lifted, they put them down again as soon as they glance upward. It is certainly not a matter of accident, but the result of that upward glance at the objective, when both Chica and Grande proceed to stand the box upright. . . .

A measurement of the distance with the eye leads to this change of plan; it is a sudden and obvious attempt to meet the needs of the situation. Finally, Grande seizes her box and tears about the room with it, in a rage, as Sultan did before. Just as he did, she calms down unexpectedly, pulls her box close to the other one, after a glance at the objective, lifts it with an effort, puts it clumsily on the lower one, and quickly tries to get up on it; but when the upper box slips to one side during this operation, she makes no move, and lets it fall altogether, quite discouraged.

In principle, Grande solved the problem too, so the box is lifted by the observer, placed firmly on the lower one, and held there, while Grande climbs up and reaches the objective. But she does all this with the greatest mistrust.

[The chimps] Grande, Chica, and Rana are present. Grande carries first one, then the other box underneath the objective, but handles them in such a way as to create the impression that she is perplexed; she does not put one box on the other. This looks very like the condition of "lack of direction" which sometimes influenced Sultan and Chica when dealing with the two bamboo sticks.

Suddenly Chica springs up beside Grande, puts one box on the other without further delay, and gets up on top. It is hard to say whether this was an aftereffect of the previous attempt and Grande's example, or an independent solution, helped perhaps by Grande's "messing around."

A new objective is hung up; Rana now puts one of the boxes flat underneath the objective and the second one immediately on top of it (also flat); but the arrangement is too low, and the animals prevent each other from improving it, as they now all want to build on their own, and at the same time. Knowing Rana, I am inclined to assume that this is a case of imitation of what she has just seen, or, at any rate, what she saw was of great help to her; but this question is not important here. . . .

After the animals had become accustomed to putting one box on another as soon as the situation called for it, the question arose as to whether they would make further progress in the same direction.

The tests (higher objective, three boxes at some distance) first resulted in Sultan carrying out more difficult constructions, with two boxes on top of each other, perpendicularly so that they looked like columns, and, of course, enabled him to reach very high; he took the third box, to begin with, to the place of construction, but left it standing beside him without using it, as he could then reach the objective by means of his column without it.

The objective hangs still higher up; Sultan has fasted all the forenoon and, therefore, goes at his task with great zeal. He lays the heavy box flat underneath the objective, puts the second one upright upon it, and, standing on the top, tries to seize the objective. As he does not reach it, he looks down and round about, and his glance is caught by the third box, which may have seemed useless to him at first, because of its smallness. He climbs down very carefully, seizes the box, climbs up with it, and completes the construction.

Grande in particular progressed with time. Of the smaller animals she was the strongest and by far the most patient. She would not allow herself to be diverted by any number of mishaps, the collapse of the structure, or any other difficulties (partly created involuntarily by herself), and soon was able to put three boxes on top of each other, like Sultan. She even managed once a beautiful construction of four boxes when she found a fairly big cage nearby, whose flat surface allowed of the addition of the three remaining parts with safety. . . .

Chica also builds towers composed of three boxes without too many mishaps, but has not become so expert as Grande, because, impatient and quick by nature, she prefers dangerous jumps (with or without a stick) from the floor or from some low structure to the slow process of building. And in these she is often successful, while Grande in her own way has still a good deal of hard work to get done.

Rana scarcely gets beyond two boxes. Whenever she has got so far, she stops, and either goes on endlessly trying out miniature vaulting poles, or else (a frequent occurrence) she places the upper box open side up, and then carries out an irresistible impulse to sit down beside it; once she is there, she feels too comfortable to get up again and to continue building. Konsul never built, Tercera and Tschego got no further than some feeble attempts, Nueva and Koko died before they could be experimented with.

Without doubt, constructions such as those achieved by Grande are considerable feats, especially when one considers that the constructions of insects (ants, bees, spiders) and other vertebrates (birds, beavers), though they may, when finished, be more perfect, yet are built by a very different and much more primitive process, from an evolutionary point of view.

The following accounts will show that the difference between the clever but clumsy constructions of a gifted chimpanzee, and the firm and objectively elegantly spun web of a spider, for instance, is one of *genus,* which, of course, should be obvious from what has been already said. But, unfortunately, I have been asked by otherwise intelligent spectators of these constructions, whether this is not instinct. Therefore I feel obliged to emphasize the following particularly: the spider and similar artists achieve true wonders, but the main special conditions for this particular work alone are within them, long before the incentive to use them occurs.

The chimpanzee is not simply provided for life with any special disposition which will help him to attain objects placed high up, by heaping up any building material, and yet he can accomplish this much by his own efforts, when circumstances require it, and when the material is available.

Adult human beings are inclined to overlook the chimpanzee's real difficulty in such construction, because they assume that adding a second piece of building material to the first is only a repetition of the placing of the first one on the ground (underneath the objective); that when the first box is standing on the ground, its surface is the same thing as a piece of level ground, and that, therefore, in the building-up process the only new factor is the actual lifting up. So the only questions seem to be, whether the animals proceed at all tidily in their work, whether they handle the boxes very clumsily, and so forth. . . .

That another special difficulty exists, however, should become obvious from the further details of Sultan's first attempt at building: When Sultan for the first time fetches a second box and lifts it, he waves it about enigmatically above the first, and does not put it on the other. The second time he places it upright on the bottom one, seemingly without any hesitation, but the construction is still too low, as the objective has accidentally been hung too high up.

The experiment is continued at once, the objective hung about two meters to one side at a lower spot in the roof, and Sultan's construction is left in its old place, but Sultan's failure seems to have a disturbing aftereffect; for a long time he pays no attention at all to the boxes, quite contrary to other cases, where a new solution was found and usually repeated readily. It may well be that for the chimpanzee (as for man) the practical success of a method is more important as an estimate of its value, than is really justifiable. . . .

Further on in the experiment a curious incident occurs: the animal reverts to older methods, wants to lead the keeper by his hand to the objective, is shaken off, attempts the same thing with me, and is again turned away. The keeper is then told that if Sultan tries to fetch him again, he is apparently to give in, but, as soon as the animal climbs on his shoulders, he is to kneel down very low.

Soon this actually happens: Sultan climbs onto the man's shoulders, after he has dragged him underneath the objective, and the keeper quickly bends down. The animal gets off, complaining, takes hold of the keeper by his seat with both hands, and tries with all his might to push him up. A surprising way to try to improve the human implement!

When Sultan now takes no further notice of the box, since he once discovered the solution by himself, it seems justifiable to remove the cause of his failure. I put the boxes on top of each other for Sultan, underneath the objective, exactly as he had himself done the first time, and let him pull down the objective.

As to Sultan's effort to push the keeper into an erect position, I should like at the very beginning to rebut the reproach of misunderstanding, of "reading into the animal"; the procedure has merely been described, and there is no possibility at all of its being misunderstood. But lest suspicions should arise, this case being an isolated one (an unjustifiable suspicion in any case, considering that Sultan tries to utilize both the keeper and me, not once, but over and over again, as a footstool), I shall briefly add a description of similar cases:

Sultan cannot solve a problem, in which the objective is outside the bars beyond reach; I am near him inside. After vain attempts of all sorts, the animal comes up to me, seizes me by the arm, pulls me toward the bars, at the same time pulling my arm with all his might down to himself, and then pushes it through the bars toward the objective. As I do not seize it, he goes to the keeper, and tries the same thing with him.

Later he repeats this proceeding, with the only difference that he first has to call me with plaintive pleading to the bars, as this time I am standing outside. In this case, as in the first, I offered so much resistance that the animal could barely overcome it, and he did not release me until my hand was actually on the objective; but I did not do him the favor (in the interests of future experiments) of bringing it in.

I must mention further, that one hot day the animals had had to wait longer than usual for their water course, so that finally they simply grabbed hold of the keeper's hand, foot, or knee, and pushed him with all their strength toward the door, behind which the water jug usually stood. This became their custom for some time; if the man tried to continue feeding them on bananas, Chica would calmly snatch them out of his hand, put them aside, and pull him toward the door (Chica is always thirsty).

It would be erroneous to consider the chimpanzee unenlightened and stupid in these matters. I must add that the animals understand the human body particularly easily in its local costume of shirt and trousers without any coat. If anything puzzles them, they will investigate it on occasion, and any large change in the manner of dressing or appearance (for example, a beard) will make Grande and Chica undertake an immediate and very interested examination.

After the encouraging assistance to Sultan, the boxes are again put aside. A new objective is hung in the same place on the roof. Sultan immediately builds up both boxes, but at the place where the objective had been hung at the very beginning of the experiment and where his own first construction had stood. In about a hundred cases of using boxes for building, this is the only one in which a stupidity of this kind was committed. Sultan is quite confused while doing this, and is probably quite exhausted, as the experiment has lasted over an hour in this hot place.[3] As Sultan keeps on pushing the boxes to and fro quite aimlessly, they are once more put on top of each other underneath the objective; Sultan reaches it, and is allowed to go. Only on one occasion did I see him similarly confused and disturbed.

The next day it is clear that a particular difficulty must lie in the problem itself. Sultan carries one box underneath the objective, but does not bring the second one; finally it is built up for him and he attains the goal. The new one immediately replacing it (the construction was again destroyed) does not induce him to work at all; he keeps on trying to use the observer as a footstool; so once more the construction is made for him. Underneath the third objective Sultan places a box, pulls the other one up beside it, but stops at the critical moment, his behavior betraying complete perplexity; he keeps on looking up at the objective, and meanwhile fumbling about with the second box. Then, quite suddenly, he seizes it firmly, and with a decided movement places it on the first. His long uncertainty is in the sharpest contrast to this sudden solution.

Two days later the experiment is repeated; the objective is again hung at a new spot. Sultan places a box a little aslant underneath the objective, brings the second one up, and has begun to lift it, when, all the while looking at the objective, he lets it drop again. After several other actions (climbing along the roof, pulling the observer up) he again starts to build; he carefully stands the first box upright underneath the objective, and now takes great pains to get the second one on top of it; in the turning and twisting, it gets stuck on the lower one, with its open side caught on one of

---

[3] I only noticed later that I used to strain the animals a little too much during the first months; only with time did I develop the slowness of procedure adequate to the apes and to the climate.

the corners. Sultan gets up on it, and straightaway tumbles with the whole thing to the floor.

Quite exhausted, he remains lying in one corner of the room, and from here gazes at both box and objective. Only after a considerable time does he resume work; he stands one box upright and tries to reach his goal thus; jumps down, seizes the second, and finally, with tenacious zeal, succeeds in making it stand upright also, on the first one; but it is pushed so far to one side that, at every attempt to climb up, it begins to topple. Only after a long attempt, during which the animal obviously acts quite blindly, letting everything depend on the success or failure of planless movements, the upper box attains a more secure position, and the objective is attained.

After this attempt Sultan always used the second box at once and, above all, was never uncertain as to where he had to put it.

Comment

INSIGHT: Immediate apprehension or cognition

Köhler interpreted these and similar studies as providing evidence of **insight,** the apparently spontaneous apprehension or understanding of relationships. Sultan finally achieved an insight into the problem by grasping, after many trials, the relationship between the boxes and the banana suspended overhead. Köhler's word in German to describe this phenomenon was *Einsicht,* which translates into English as *insight* or *understanding.* In another example of independent, simultaneous discovery, the American animal psychologist Robert Yerkes found evidence in orangutans to support the concept of insight, which he called *ideational learning.*

In 1974, the keeper of Köhler's chimps, Manuel Gonzalez y Garcia, then 87 years old, told an interviewer many stories about the animals, particularly Sultan, who used to help him feed the other apes. Gonzalez would give Sultan bunches of bananas to hold. "On the oral command, 'two each,' Sultan would walk about the compound and dole out two bananas to each of the other apes" (Ley, 1990, pp. 12–13).

One day Sultan watched as the keeper painted a door. When the keeper left, Sultan picked up the paintbrush and began to imitate the behavior he had observed. On another occasion, Köhler's young son Claus sat in front of a cage, trying unsuccessfully to pull a banana out between the bars. Sultan, inside the cage and apparently not hungry, turned the banana 90° so it would fit between the bars, whereupon Köhler told his son that Sultan was smarter than he was.

Problem solving and insight, as demonstrated in Köhler's studies with chimps, differed from the trial-and-error learning described by Thorndike. Köhler was a forceful critic of Thorndike's work, arguing that its experimental conditions were artificial and allowed only random behavior to be displayed. Köhler said the cats in Thorndike's puzzle box could not survey the entire release mechanism (all the elements pertaining to the whole situation), and thus could engage only in trial-and-error behavior.

Similarly, an animal in a maze could not see the overall pattern or design but only each alley it encountered, and so it could do nothing but blindly try each path. In the Gestalt view, the organism must be able to see the relationships among the various parts of the problem before insight can occur.

The studies of insight lend support to the Gestalt psychologists' molar or global conception of behavior, as opposed to the molecular or atomistic view promoted by the behaviorists. The research also reinforces the Gestalt idea that learning involves a reorganization or restructuring of the psychological environment.

PRODUCTIVE THINKING IN HUMANS

Max Wertheimer's book on productive thinking (Wertheimer, 1945) was published after his death. In it, he applied the Gestalt principles of learning to creative thinking in humans, proposing that thinking is done in terms of wholes. Not only does the learner regard the situation as a whole, but the teacher must also present the situation as a whole.

This approach differs from Thorndike's trial-and-error learning, in which a solution to the problem is, in a sense, hidden, and the learner may make several mistakes before happening on the correct answer.

The cases presented in Wertheimer's book range from children solving geometric problems to the complex thought processes of the physicist Albert Einstein that led to his famous theory of relativity. At different ages and at various levels of problem difficulty, Wertheimer found evidence to support the idea that the whole problem must dominate the parts. He believed that the details of a problem should be considered only in relation to the total situation, and that problem solving should proceed from the whole problem downward to the parts, not the reverse.

Wertheimer suggested that if a teacher arranges or organizes the elements of classroom exercises into meaningful wholes, then students would more easily display insight and grasp the problems and solutions. He demonstrated that once the principle of a problem's solution had been understood, that principle could be transferred readily to other situations.

He attacked traditional educational practices, such as mechanical drill and rote learning, which derive from the associationist approach to learning. Repetition is rarely productive, Wertheimer argued, and he cited as evidence a student's inability to solve a variation of a problem when the solution had been learned by rote rather than by insight. He did agree, however, that material such as names and dates should be learned by rote through association strengthened by repetition. Thus, he conceded that repetition was useful to a point, but he maintained that its habitual use led to mechanical performance rather than to truly creative or productive thinking.

ISOMORPHISM

Having established that we perceive organized wholes rather than bundles of sensations, the Gestalt psychologists turned to the problem of the brain mechanisms involved in perception. They attempted to develop a theory about the underlying neurological correlates of perceived Gestalts. Gestalt psychologists view the cerebral cortex as a dynamic system, in which the elements active at a given time interact. This idea contrasts with the machine-like conception that compares neural activity to a telephone switchboard mechanically linking sensory inputs according to the principles of association. In the associationist view, the brain functions passively and is incapable of actively organizing or modifying the sensory elements it receives; this view also implies a direct correspondence between the perception and its neurological counterpart.

In his research on the apparent movement phenomenon, Wertheimer suggested that brain activity is a configural whole process. Because apparent and actual motion are experienced identically, the cortical processes for apparent and actual motion must be similar. On the assumption that these two kinds of motion are identical, then, corresponding brain processes must be operative.

ISOMORPHISM: The doctrine that there is a correspondence between psychological or conscious experience and the underlying brain experience

In other words, to account for the phi phenomenon, there must be a correspondence between the psychological or conscious experience and the underlying brain experience. This idea is called **isomorphism,** a principle already accepted in biology and chemistry. The Gestalt psychologists likened a perception to a map, in that it is identical (*iso*) in form or shape (*morph*) to what it represents, without being a literal copy of the terrain. It does, however, serve as a reliable guide to the perceived real world.

Wertheimer's position was extended by Köhler in his book *Static and Stationary Physical Gestalts* (1920). Köhler considered that cortical processes behave in a manner similar to fields of force, and he suggested that, like the behavior of an electromagnetic field of force around a magnet, fields of neuronal activity may be established by electromechanical processes in the brain in response to sensory impulses.

THE SPREAD OF GESTALT PSYCHOLOGY

By the mid-1920s, the Gestalt movement was a coherent, dominant, and forceful school of thought in Germany, centered at the Psychological Institute of the University of Berlin, where it attracted large numbers of students from many countries. Housed in a wing of the former Imperial Palace, it had one of the largest and best equipped laboratories in the world. The Gestalt journal *Psychological Research* was widely read and respected, and Gestalt researchers were investigating a variety of psychological issues.

After the Nazis came to power in Germany in 1933, their rampant anti-intellectualism and anti-Semitism and their repressive actions forced many scholars, including the leaders of Gestalt psychology, to leave the country. The movement was reduced to a minor position in the German academic system of the day, and the center of Gestalt psychology shifted to the United States.

The spread of the Gestalt movement within the United States occurred through personal contacts as well as published works. And even before Gestalt psychology was formally founded, soon-to-be prominent American psychologists were studying with future leaders of the Gestalt school and absorbing their ideas. Herbert Langfeld of Princeton University met Koffka in Berlin in the first decade of the century and sent his student E. C. Tolman to Germany, where Tolman served as a subject in Koffka's Gestalt research. Robert Ogden of Cornell University also knew Koffka. The personality researcher Gordon Allport of Harvard University spent a year in Germany and declared he was much impressed with the quality of the experimental research from the Gestalt school.

In the 1920s, a few books by Koffka and Köhler were translated from German into English and reviewed in American psychology journals. A series of articles by the American psychologist Harry Helson, published in the *American Journal of Psychology*, also helped spread Gestalt theory in the United States (Helson, 1925, 1926).

Koffka and Köhler visited the United States to lecture at universities and conferences. Koffka gave 30 talks about Gestalt psychology in 3 years, and Köhler was one of the keynote speakers at the Ninth International Congress of Psychology held at Yale University in 1929. (The other keynote speaker was Ivan Pavlov, who was spat on by one of Robert Yerkes's chimps.)

Although Gestalt psychology attracted attention in the United States, for several reasons its acceptance as a school of thought was slow. First, behaviorism was then at the peak of its popularity in American psychology. Second, there was the language barrier. The major Gestalt publications were in German, and the need for translation delayed the full and accurate dissemination of the principles of the Gestalt viewpoint. Third, many psychologists incorrectly believed that Gestalt psychology dealt only with perception. And fourth, Wertheimer, Koffka, and Köhler settled at small American colleges that did not have graduate programs, so it was difficult for them to attract disciples to carry on the movement.

The most important reason, however, for the relatively slow progress of Gestalt psychology as a school of thought in the United

States was that American psychology had already advanced far beyond the ideas of Wundt and Titchener. Behaviorism was the second phase of American opposition. Hence, American psychology was already further removed from Wundt's elementistic position than was European psychology at that time. American psychologists tended to think the Gestalt psychologists were fighting an enemy who had already been beaten, that they had come to the United States protesting something that was no longer of any concern.

This situation was hazardous for the survival of the Gestalt school. We have seen many times that revolutionary movements need something to oppose, something to push against, if they are to be successful in promoting their ideas.

THE BATTLE WITH BEHAVIORISM

When the Gestalt psychologists became aware of the trends within American psychology, they readily found a new target. If they didn't need to protest against Wundtian psychology, they could attack the reductionistic and atomistic qualities of the behaviorist school of thought.

The Gestalt psychologists argued that behaviorism, like the earlier Wundtian psychology, also dealt with artificial abstractions. It made little difference whether analysis was in terms of introspective reduction to mental elements or of objective reduction to conditioned stimulus-response units. The result was the same: a molecular instead of a molar approach.

Gestalt psychologists also criticized the behaviorists' denial of the validity of introspection and elimination of consciousness. Koffka argued that it was senseless to develop a psychology that lacked consciousness, as the behaviorists had done, because that meant psychology could offer little more than a collection of animal research studies.

The battles between the Gestalt psychologists and the behavioral psychologists grew emotional and personal. On a social occasion in 1941, when Clark Hull, E. C. Tolman, Wolfgang Köhler, and several other psychologists went out for a few beers after a scientific meeting in Philadelphia, Köhler said he had heard that Hull used the insulting phrase "those goddamned Gestalters" in his classroom lectures. Hull was embarrassed, and he told Köhler that scientific matters should not be turned into some kind of warfare.

Köhler replied that he was "willing to discuss most things in a logical and scientific manner, but when people try to make man out to be a kind of slot machine, then he would fight." And he emphasized his point by bringing "his fist down on the table with a resounding smack" (Amsel & Rashotte, 1984, p. 23).

FIELD THEORY: KURT LEWIN (1890–1947)

The trend in late 19th-century science was to think in terms of field relationships and to move away from an atomistic and elementistic framework. Gestalt psychology reflected this trend. Field theory arose within psychology as a counterpart to the concept of fields of force in physics. In psychology today the term **field theory** usually refers to the ideas of Kurt Lewin. Lewin's work is Gestalt in its orientation, but he extended his ideas beyond the framework of the orthodox Gestalt position to include human needs, personality, and social influences on behavior.

FIELD THEORY: Lewin's system of psychology using the concept of fields of force to explain behavior in terms of one's field of social influences

Lewin's Life

Kurt Lewin was born in Mogilno, Germany, and undertook his education at universities in Freiburg, Munich, and Berlin. He received his PhD in psychology from Carl Stumpf at Berlin in 1914, where he also studied mathematics and physics. During World War I Lewin served in the German army, was wounded in action, and received Germany's Iron Cross decoration. Afterward he returned to the University of Berlin and became such a productive member of the Gestalt group that he was considered to be a colleague of the three senior Gestaltists. He conducted research on association and motivation and began to develop his field theory, which he presented to psychologists in the United States at the 1929 International Congress of Psychology at Yale.

Lewin was already well known in the United States when, in 1932, he became a visiting professor at Stanford University. The following year he decided to leave Germany permanently because of the Nazi menace. "I now believe there is no other choice for me but to emigrate," he wrote to Köhler, "even though it will tear my life apart" (quoted in Benjamin, 1993, pp. 158, 160). Lewin's mother and sister later died in Nazi concentration camps.

He spent 2 years at Cornell and in 1935 he went to the University of Iowa to conduct research on the social psychology of the child. As a result of this work he was invited to develop and head the new Research Center for Group Dynamics at the Massachusetts Institute of Technology. Although he died within a few years of accepting the position, his program was so effective that the research center, now at the University of Michigan, remains active today.

Archives of the History of American Psychology/University of Akron

KURT LEWIN

Throughout his 30 years of professional activity Lewin devoted himself to the broadly defined area of human motivation. His research was based on the study of human behavior within its total physical and social context (Lewin, 1936, 1939).

The Life Space

Field theory in physics led Lewin to consider that a person's psychological activities occur within a kind of psychological field, which he called the *life space*. The life space encompasses all past, present, and future events that may affect us. From a psychological standpoint, each of these events can determine behavior in a given situation. Thus the life space consists of the person's needs interacting with the psychological environment.

A life space shows varying degrees of development as a function of the amount and kind of experience the person has accumulated. Because an infant lacks experiences, it has few differentiated regions in the life space. A highly educated, sophisticated adult has a complex and well-differentiated life space, showing a variety of past experiences.

Lewin sought a mathematical model to represent his theoretical conception of psychological processes. Because he was interested in the individual person, the single case, instead of in groups or averages, statistics were not useful for his purpose. He chose a form of geometry, called topology, to diagram the life space, to show at any given moment a person's possible goals and the paths leading to them.

Within his topological maps Lewin used arrows or vectors to represent the direction of a person's movement toward a goal. To com-

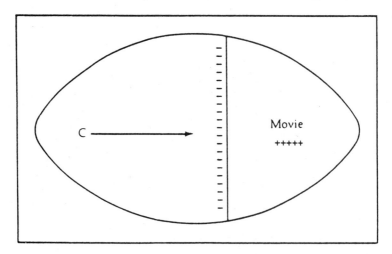

FIGURE 12.2 *A simplified example of a life space.*

plete the illustration he chose the notion of valences or weights to refer to the positive or negative value of objects within the life space. Objects that are attractive to the individual or that satisfy his or her needs have a positive valence; objects that are threatening have a negative valence.

Thus, Lewin's so-called "blackboard psychology" includes complex schematic diagrams to represent psychological phenomena. To Lewin, all forms of behavior can be represented by a diagram. A simple bit of behavior is mapped in Figure 12.2, which illustrates a situation in which a child wants to go to the movies but is forbidden to do so by its parents. The ellipse represents the life space; C represents the child. The arrow is the vector indicating that C is motivated toward the goal of going to the movie, which has a positive valence for the child. The vertical line is the barrier to the goal, established by the parents, and it has a negative valence.

Motivation

Lewin proposed a state of balance or equilibrium between the person and his or her environment. When this equilibrium is disturbed, tension arises, which leads to some movement in an attempt to restore the balance. This is the basis of Lewin's conception of motivation. Thus he believed that behavior involves a cycle of tension or need followed by action and relief. Whenever a need is felt and a state of tension exists, the person attempts to relieve the tension by acting to restore the balance.

The first experimental attempt to test this proposition was performed under Lewin's supervision by Bluma Zeigarnik in 1927. Subjects were given a series of tasks and allowed to complete some of them, but they were interrupted before they could complete others. Lewin predicted that (1) a tension-system develops when subjects are given a task to perform; (2) when the task is completed, the tension is dissipated; and (3) when the task is not completed, the persistence of the tension results in a greater likelihood the task will be recalled.

Zeigarnik's results confirmed the predictions. The subjects remembered the uncompleted tasks more readily than they recalled the completed tasks. Much subsequent research has been performed on what is now known as the **Zeigarnik effect.**

ZEIGARNIK EFFECT: The tendency to recall uncompleted tasks more easily than completed tasks

Social Psychology

By the 1930s Lewin became interested in social psychology. His pioneering efforts in this field alone are sufficient to justify his importance in the history of psychology.

The outstanding feature of Lewin's social psychology is group dynamics, the application of concepts dealing with individual and group behavior. Just as the individual and his or her environment form a psychological field, so the group and its environment form a social field. Social behaviors occur within, and result from, concurrent social entities such as subgroups, group members, barriers, and channels of communication. Thus, group behavior at any given time is a function of the total field situation.

Lewin conducted research on behavior in various social situations. A classic experiment involved authoritarian, democratic, and laissez-faire leadership styles and their effects on the productivity and behavior of groups of boys (Lewin, Lippitt, & White, 1939). Studies such as this one opened up new areas of social research and contributed to the growth of social psychology.

In addition, Lewin emphasized the importance of social action research, the study of relevant social problems with a view to introducing change. Reflecting his concern about racial problems, he conducted community studies on several topics—integrated housing and prejudice, equal employment opportunities, and the development and prevention of prejudice in childhood. His social action research transformed these issues into controlled research studies, applying the rigor of the experimental method without the artificiality of the academic laboratory.

Lewin was also instrumental in fostering sensitivity training, which has been applied to situations in education and business to reduce intergroup conflict and develop individual potential. His sensitivity training groups (T-groups) were forerunners of the encounter groups popular in the 1960s and 1970s.

Comment

Lewin's experimental programs and research findings are, in general, more acceptable to psychologists than his theoretical views. His influence on social and child psychology is considerable. Many of his concepts and experimental techniques are widely used in the areas of personality and motivation. "Nearly alone among the leading émigré psychologists, Kurt Lewin succeeded in creating both a successful career for himself and a 'school' of followers in America" (Ash, 1992, p. 204).

CRITICISMS OF GESTALT PSYCHOLOGY

Critics of Gestalt psychology have charged that the organization of perception, as in the phi phenomenon, was not approached as a problem that needed investigating, but rather as a phenomenon whose existence was simply accepted; to them, this was like denying there was a problem at all! Experimental psychologists have asserted that the

Gestalt position is vague, and that the basic concepts and terms are not defined with sufficient rigor to be scientifically meaningful. Gestalt psychologists countered these charges by insisting that in a young science attempts at explanation and definition may be incomplete, but that being incomplete was not the same as being vague.

Others alleged that Gestalt psychology was too occupied with theory at the expense of research and empirical supporting data. Although the Gestalt school has been theoretically oriented, since the time of its founders it has also emphasized experimentation and has been responsible for a considerable amount of research.

Related to this point is the suggestion that the experimental work of the Gestalt psychologists is inferior to that of behavioral psychologists because it lacks adequate controls and because its unquantified data are not amenable to statistical analysis. Gestalt psychologists take the position that because qualitative results take precedence in their system, much of their research has deliberately been less quantitative than other psychologists consider necessary. Gestalt research, in general, is exploratory, investigating problems within a different framework.

Köhler's notion of insight has also been challenged. Attempts to replicate Köhler's two-stick experiment with chimps have provided little support for the role of insight in learning. These later studies suggest that the apes' solution of the problem does not occur suddenly and may depend on prior learning or experience (Windholz & Lamal, 1985).

A final criticism relates to what some psychologists consider to be poorly defined physiological assumptions. Gestalt psychologists admit that their theorizing in this area is tentative, but they believe their speculations are a useful adjunct to their system.

CONTRIBUTIONS OF GESTALT PSYCHOLOGY

The Gestalt movement has left an indelible imprint on psychology and has influenced the areas of perception, learning, thinking, personality, social psychology, and motivation. Recent work deriving from the Gestalt school suggests that the movement still has contributions to make.

Unlike its chief competitor at the time—behaviorism—Gestalt psychology retained much of its separate identity, in that its major tenets were not fully absorbed into the mainstream of psychological thought. It continued to foster interest in conscious experience as a legitimate problem for psychology during the years when behaviorism was the dominant school of thought.

The focus on conscious experience was not of the Wundt/Titchener variety but centered instead on a modern version of phenomenology. Contemporary adherents of the Gestalt position are convinced that conscious experience does occur and must be studied. They recognize, however, that it cannot be investigated with the same precision and objectivity as overt behavior.

A phenomenological approach to psychology is more widespread in Europe than in the United States, but its influence on American psychology can be seen in the humanistic psychology movement. Many aspects of contemporary cognitive psychology owe their origins to the work of Wertheimer, Koffka, and Köhler, and the movement they founded nearly 90 years ago.

DISCUSSION QUESTIONS

1. On what grounds did the Gestalt psychologists attack Wundt's approach to psychology? Discuss the historical antecedents to the Gestalt school of thought. What was the impact of the changing Zeitgeist in physics?
2. What is the phi phenomenon? How is it produced? Why couldn't the phi phenomenon be explained by Wundtian psychology?
3. Why did some people mistakenly assume that Gestalt psychology dealt only with perception? Discuss Wertheimer's principles of perceptual organization.
4. How do studies of perceptual constancies support the Gestalt viewpoint? Why has the word *Gestalt* caused problems for the movement?
5. Describe Köhler's research on insight. How does insight learning differ from the trial-and-error learning described by Thorndike? How did Wertheimer apply Gestalt principles of learning to creative thinking in humans?
6. What factors impeded acceptance of Gestalt psychology in the United States? Discuss the criticisms that have been made of the Gestalt approach.
7. Describe Lewin's field theory. How was it influenced by physics? How does field theory deal with motivation and with social psychology?

SUGGESTED READINGS

Helson, H. (1925, 1926). The psychology of Gestalt. *American Journal of Psychology, 36,* 342–370, 494–526; *37,* 25–62, 189–223. A series of articles that did much to spread the Gestalt viewpoint in the United States.

Henle, M. (1978). One man against the Nazis—Wolfgang Köhler. *American Psychologist, 33,* 939–944. Describes Köhler's last years in Berlin and his struggle to preserve the integrity of the Psychological Institute in the face of Nazi repression.

Henle, M. (1987). Koffka's *Principles* after fifty years. *Journal of the History of the Behavioral Sciences, 23,* 14–21. Evaluates the impact of Koffka's *Principles of Gestalt Psychology.*

Köhler, W. (1959). Gestalt psychology today. *American Psychologist, 14,* 727–734. Describes the differences between Gestalt psychology and behavioral psychology.

Sokal, M. M. (1984). The Gestalt psychologists in behaviorist America. *American Historical Review, 89,* 1240–1263. Describes the spread of the Gestalt movement in the United States.

CHAPTER 13

PSYCHOANALYSIS:
THE BEGINNINGS

THE PLACE OF PSYCHOANALYSIS IN THE HISTORY OF PSYCHOLOGY

THE TERM **psychoanalysis** and the name Sigmund Freud are recognized throughout the modern world. Other prominent figures in the history of psychology, such as Fechner, Wundt, and Titchener, are little known outside psychology, but Freud has maintained his popularity among the general public. More than 40 years after Freud's death, *Newsweek* magazine noted that his ideas had become so pervasive that "it would be difficult to imagine twentieth-century thought without him" (November 30, 1981). He is one of a small group of individuals who have been pivotal in the history of civilization by changing the way we think about ourselves.

Freud suggested that in all of history, there have been three great shocks to the collective human ego (Freud, 1917). The first was delivered by Copernicus (1473–1543), the Polish astronomer who showed us that the earth was not the center of the universe but merely one of many planets revolving around the sun. The second revelation came from Charles Darwin in the 19th century when he demonstrated that human beings are not a unique and separate species with a privileged place in creation but merely a higher form of animal species that has evolved from lower forms of life.

Sigmund Freud administered the third shock by proclaiming we are not the rational rulers of our lives but instead are controlled

PSYCHOANALYSIS: Freud's
theory of personality, as well
as his system of therapy for
treating mental disorders

by unconscious forces of which we are not aware. Thus, "Copernicus had displaced humanity from the center of the world, Darwin had compelled it to recognize its kinship with the animals, [and] Freud had shown that reason is not master in its own house" (Gay, 1988, p. 580).

Chronologically, psychoanalysis overlaps psychology's other schools of thought. Consider the situation in 1895, the year Freud published his first book marking the formal beginning of his new movement. In that year Wundt was 63 years old. Titchener, just 28, had been at Cornell University only 2 years and was beginning to develop his system of structural psychology. The spirit of functionalism was beginning to flourish in the United States. Neither behaviorism nor Gestalt psychology had been founded; Watson was then 17 and Wertheimer 15.

Yet, by the time of Freud's death in 1939, the entire psychological world had changed. Wundtian psychology, Titchener's structuralism, and functional psychology were history. Gestalt psychology was being transplanted from Germany to the United States, and behaviorism had become the dominant form of American psychology.

Despite their fundamental disagreements, the schools of thought we have discussed shared an academic heritage and owed much of their inspiration and form to Wundt. Their concepts and methods had been refined in laboratories, libraries, and lecture halls, and they were concerned with topics such as sensation, perception, and learning. They attempted to maintain a pure science. Psychoanalysis, in contrast, was neither a product of the universities nor a pure science, but, instead, arose within the psychiatric tradition with its efforts to treat persons society labeled "mentally ill." Thus, psychoanalysis was not, and still is not, a school of psychological thought directly comparable with the others.

From the beginning, psychoanalysis was distinct from mainstream psychological thought in goals, subject matter, and methods. Its subject matter is abnormal behavior, which had been relatively neglected by other schools of thought, and its primary method is clinical observation, not controlled laboratory experimentation. Also, psychoanalysis deals with the unconscious, a topic virtually ignored by the other systems of thought.

Wundt and Titchener did not accept the unconscious into their systems for one reason: It is impossible to introspect the unconscious. And because the unconscious cannot be introspected, it cannot be reduced to its elementary components. The functionalists, too, with their exclusive focus on consciousness, had no use for the unconscious. In Angell's lengthy textbook published in 1904, he devoted no more than two pages at the end to the unconscious. Woodworth's 1921 textbook had little more to say about it, covering the topic as an afterthought. Watson, of course, had no more room in his behavioristic system for the unconscious than he did for consciousness. He referred to the unconscious as merely that which the individual has not yet verbalized, but he accorded it no role in his system.

Despite these differences, psychoanalysis shares some background characteristics with functionalism and behaviorism. All were influenced by the spirit of mechanism, by the work in psychophysics of Fechner, and by the evolutionary ideas of Darwin.

ANTECEDENT INFLUENCES ON PSYCHOANALYSIS

Two major sources of influence on the psychoanalytic movement were (1) philosophical speculations about unconscious psychological phenomena and (2) early work in psychopathology.

Theories of the Unconscious Mind

In the early 18th century, the German philosopher and mathematician Gottfried Wilhelm Leibnitz (1646–1716) developed an idea he called **monadology.** Monads, which Leibnitz considered to be the individual elements of all reality, were not physical atoms. They were not composed wholly of matter, in the usual sense of the word. Each monad was an unextended psychic entity, which, although mental in nature, had some of the properties of physical matter. When enough monads were grouped together, they created an extension.

Monads can be likened to perceptions. Leibnitz believed that mental events (the activity of monads) had different degrees of consciousness, ranging from completely unconscious to clearly conscious. Lesser degrees of consciousness were called *petites perceptions;* the conscious realization of these was called *apperception.*

For example, the sound of waves breaking on the beach is an apperception. This apperception is composed of all the individual falling drops of water (the *petites perceptions*). We do not consciously perceive each drop of water in itself, but when enough of them collect, they summate to produce an apperception.

A century later the German philosopher and educator Johann Friedrich Herbart (1776–1841) developed Leibnitz's notion of the unconscious into the concept of **threshold** or **limen of consciousness.** Reflecting the impact of the mechanistic Zeitgeist, Herbart argued that "the ways ideas influence one another can be described in terms of the mechanics of forces" (quoted in Hoffman, Cochran, & Nead, 1990, p. 185).

In Herbart's view, ideas below the proposed threshold are unconscious. When an idea rises to a conscious level of awareness it is apperceived (to use Leibnitz's term). But Herbart went further. For an

National Library of Medicine

GOTTFRIED WILHELM LEIBNITZ

MONADOLOGY: Leibnitz's theory of psychic entities called monads

LIMEN OF CONSCIOUSNESS: The threshold below which ideas are unconscious idea to rise into consciousness, it must be compatible with the ideas already in consciousness. Incongruous ideas cannot exist in consciousness at the same time, and ideas that are irrelevant are forced out of consciousness to become inhibited ideas.

Inhibited ideas exist below the threshold of consciousness; they are similar to Leibnitz's *petites perceptions.* According to Herbart, there is a conflict among ideas as they struggle for conscious realization, and he proposed mathematical formulas to account for the mechanics of ideas as they enter into or are pushed out of consciousness.

Gustav Fechner also contributed to the development of theories about the unconscious. Although he, too, used the notion of threshold, it was his suggestion that the mind is analogous to an iceberg that had a greater impact on Freud. Fechner speculated that like the greater portion of an iceberg, much of the mind is hidden below the surface, where it is influenced by unobservable forces.

It is interesting that Fechner's work, to which experimental psychology owes so great a debt, was also a precursor of psychoanalysis. Freud quoted from Fechner's book, *Elements of Psychophysics,* in several of his own, and he derived major concepts (such as the pleasure principle, psychic energy, and the importance of aggression) from Fechner's work. Fechner was, a Freud biographer claimed, "the only psychologist from whom Freud ever borrowed any idea" (Jones, 1957, p. 268).

Ideas about the unconscious were very much a part of the intellectual climate of the 1880s in Europe, the time when Freud was beginning his clinical practice. Not only was the issue of interest to professionals, but it was also a fashionable topic of conversation among the public. A book entitled *Philosophy of the Unconscious* (Hartmann, 1869/1884) was so popular that it appeared in nine editions between 1869 and 1882. In the 1870s, at least a half dozen other books published in Germany contained the word *unconscious* in their titles.

Freud, therefore, was not the first person to discover or discuss seriously the unconscious human mind. He conceded that philosophers before him had dealt with it extensively. What he had discovered, he claimed, was a way to study it.

Ideas About Psychopathology

We have seen that a new movement always requires something to revolt against, something to push away from in order to gain momentum. Because psychoanalysis did not develop within academic psychology, the existing movement it opposed was not Wundtian psychology or any other school of psychological thought. To find out what Freud did oppose, we must consider the prevailing thought in the area in which he worked—the understanding and treatment of mental disorders.

The history of the treatment of mentally ill persons is both fascinating and depressing. Recognition of mental illness dates back to

2100 B.C. (Brems, Thevenin, & Routh, 1991). The Babylonians believed that the cause of mental illness was possession by demons, a condition they treated humanely with a combination of magic and prayer.

Ancient Hebrew cultures regarded mental illness as a punishment for sin, and they, too, relied on magic and prayer to cure it. Greek philosophers—notably Socrates, Plato, and Aristotle—argued that mental illness arose from disordered thought processes. They prescribed the healing and persuasive power of words.

When Christianity became established in the 4th century, mental illness came once again to be blamed on evil spirits and the devil. The treatment mandated by the established church involved blame, torture, and barbaric execution for persons so possessed. Beginning in the 15th century and continuing for some 300 years, the infamous Inquisition carried out by the church pursued heresy and witchcraft, describing in detail the symptoms of mental disorders, for which severe punishment was deemed to be the only cure.

By the 18th century, mental illness was considered to be irrational behavior. No longer put to death, mentally ill persons were imprisoned instead in institutions similar to jails. No treatment was offered. The patients were kept in chains and sometimes put on public display like animals in a zoo.

More humane approaches to treatment

By the 19th century more humane and rational attitudes began to emerge. One of the leaders of this approach was Philippe Pinel (1745–1826), a French physician who argued that mental illness was a natural phenomenon and should be treated by the methods of natural science. He released patients from their chains and treated them more humanely. He was the first to maintain precise case history files and careful records of cure rates. Under Pinel's direction, the number of patients pronounced cured and released from asylums grew dramatically. Because of his example, the chains were struck from more and more mentally ill patients in both Europe and the United States, and mental illness increasingly became the subject of scientific study. "Scientific enlightenment resulted . . . in the treatment of human beings as machines that, when broken, needed to be fixed. This repair was to take place in insane asylums equipped with gadgets and apparatuses reflective of the industrial inventions of the industrial revolution" (Brems, Thevenin, & Routh, 1991, p. 12).

The first psychiatrist to practice in the United States was Benjamin Rush (1745–1813). He believed that some irrational behaviors were caused by too much or too little blood, and his remedy was to drain blood out of or pump blood into his patients. He developed a

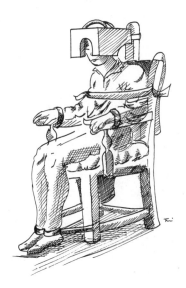

Rush's tranquilizing chair was a method of patient restraint.

rotating chair that spun the unfortunate person at high speed, a procedure that often led to fainting. In an early form of shock treatment Rush dunked patients in a tub of cold water. He is also credited with the first tranquilizing technique. Patients were strapped in a so-called tranquilizing chair, and pressure was applied to their heads by large wooden blocks gripped in a vise.

Although these techniques sound cruel today, remember that Rush was trying to help mentally ill persons instead of dumping them in custodial institutions where their needs would be ignored. He recognized that his patients were sick, not possessed by evil spirits, and he established the first hospital in the United States solely for the treatment of emotional disturbances.

During the 19th century there were two major schools of thought in psychiatry, the somatic and the psychic. The somatic school held that abnormal behavior had physical causes such as brain lesions, understimulated nerves, or nerves that were too tight. The psychic school subscribed to mental or psychological explanations for abnormal behavior. In general, the somatic viewpoint was dominant and was supported by the ideas of the eminent German philosopher Immanuel Kant, who ridiculed the view that emotional problems could somehow lead to mental illness.

Psychoanalysis developed as a revolt against this somatic orientation. As the treatment of mentally ill persons progressed, some scientists became convinced that emotional factors were of far greater importance than brain lesions or other potential physical causes.

The use of hypnosis

Hypnosis played a role in fostering interest in the psychic causes of abnormal behavior. In the late 18th century, hypnosis was brought to the attention of the medical profession by Franz Anton Mesmer (1734–1815), an Austrian physician, but for a century the medical establishment rejected it, equating mesmerism with quackery and fraud. The public, however, embraced the phenomenon, making of it a sort of party game.

In England, James Braid (1795–1860) called the hypnotic state *neurypnology,* from which the term *hypnosis* was eventually derived. Braid's careful work and his disdain for exaggerated claims earned for hypnosis some degree of scientific respectability.

Hypnosis achieved professional acceptance with the work of the French physician Jean Martin Charcot (1825–1893), head of a neurological clinic at Salpêtrière, a Paris hospital for insane women. Charcot treated hysterical patients by means of hypnosis with some success. More important, he described the symptoms of hysteria and his application of hypnosis in medical terminology, making them more acceptable to other physicians and to the French Academy of Science.

Charcot's work was primarily neurological, emphasizing physical disturbances and symptoms such as paralysis. Doctors continued to ascribe hysteria to somatic or physical causes until 1889, when Charcot's student, Pierre Janet (1859–1947), became director of the psychological laboratory at Salpêtrière.

Janet rejected the opinion that hysteria was a physical problem and conceived of it instead as a mental disorder. He posited mental phenomena—especially memory impairments, fixed ideas, and unconscious forces—as causal factors, and he chose hypnosis as the method of treatment. Thus, during the early years of Sigmund Freud's medical career, the professional literature about hypnosis and the psychological causes of mental illness was growing. Janet's work anticipated many of Freud's ideas. Personally, however, Janet later expressed contempt for Freud (Abel, 1989).

The work of Charcot and Janet in treating mental disturbances helped to change beliefs in psychiatry from the somatic or physical to the psychic or mental point of view. Physicians began to think in terms of curing emotional disturbances by treating the mind instead of the body. By the time Freud started to publish his ideas, the term *psychotherapy* was already in widespread use.

The Work of Charles Darwin

In 1979, Frank J. Sulloway, a distinguished historian of science, published *Freud: Biologist of the Mind,* in which he argued that Freud's thinking had been influenced by the work of Charles Darwin. Sulloway based his conclusions on new data of history; more precisely, he examined data that had existed for years but that no one else had viewed in the same way.

Sulloway examined the books in Freud's personal library and found copies of Darwin's works. Freud had read them all, had written notes in their margins, and was known to have praised them. Sulloway suggested that Darwin "probably did more than any other individual to pave the way for Sigmund Freud and the psychoanalytic revolution" (Sulloway, 1979, p. 238).

Darwin discussed several ideas that Freud later made central issues in his psychoanalysis, including unconscious mental processes and conflicts, the significance of dreams, the hidden symbolism of certain behavioral symptoms, and the importance of sexual arousal. Overall, Darwin focused, as Freud did later, on nonrational aspects of thought and behavior.

Darwin's theories also had an impact on Freud's ideas about childhood development. Darwin gave his notes and unpublished materials to Romanes, who later wrote two books, based on Darwin's material, about mental evolution in humans and animals. Sulloway found copies of Romanes's books in Freud's library, also with Freud's handwritten comments in the margins. Romanes elaborated on Darwin's notion of a continuity in emotional behavior from childhood to adulthood, and on the suggestion that the sex drive appears in infants as young as 7 weeks. Both of these themes became central to Freudian psychoanalysis.

Darwin insisted that humans were driven by biological forces, particularly love and hunger, which he believed were the foundation of all behavior. Less than a decade later, the German psychiatrist Richard von Krafft-Ebing expressed the same view, that sexual gratification and self–preservation were the only instincts in human physiology. Thus, respected scientists were already following Darwin's lead and recognizing sex as a basic human motivation.

Other Influences

During Freud's university training, he was exposed to the idea of mechanism, as represented by a group of physiologists, including Helmholtz, who were students of Johannes Müller. They had united to take the position that there are no forces active within the organism other than the common physical and chemical ones. Freud was influenced by this mechanistic orientation espoused by Ernst Brücke, his major professor, and later formulated a deterministic theory of human behavior, which he called *psychic determinism.*

Another aspect of the Zeitgeist that influenced and reinforced Freud's work was the attitude toward sex in late 19th-century Vienna, where Freud lived and worked. It has been popularly, but wrongly, assumed that because society in Freud's day was so repressive, his frank discussion of sexual matters was shocking and daring.

Although sexual inhibitions may have been typical of the upper-middle-class neurotic women who were Freud's patients—as well as of Freud himself—this was not the attitude of the culture as a whole. Turn-of-the-century Vienna was a permissive and open society. Even Victorian England and Puritan America were not really characterized by the excessive prudery and inhibitions usually associated with those cultures (Gay, 1983). The 1880s and 1890s saw a breakdown of the Victorian sublimation of sexuality and a concurrent "explosion of erotic imagery" (Tuzin, 1994, p. 123). Passion, prostitution, and pornography flourished.

Interest in sexual matters was visible in everyday Viennese life as well as in the scientific literature. In the years before Freud advanced his sex-based theory, many studies had been published on sexual pathologies, infantile sexuality, and the suppression of sexual impulses and its effects on mental and physical health. In 1845 the German physician Adolf Patze argued that the sex drive was present in children as young as 3, a point reiterated in 1867 by Henry Maudsley, a well-known British psychiatrist. In 1886 Krafft-Ebing published his sensational book, *Psychopathia Sexualis.* And in 1897 a Viennese physician, Albert Moll, wrote a book about childhood sexuality and the child's love for the parent of the opposite sex (Steele, 1985a).

A colleague of Freud's in Vienna, the neurologist Moritz Benedikt, had achieved dramatic cures with hysterical women by getting them to talk about problems with their sex lives. The French psychologist Alfred Binet published work on sexual perversions. Even the word *libido,* which was to assume such importance in Freud's psychoanalysis, was already in use and had the same meaning Freud later emphasized. Thus, much of the sexual component of Freud's work had been anticipated in one form or another. Because the professional and the public Zeitgeists were already receptive, Freud's ideas received a great deal of attention.

The concept of **catharsis** was also popular before Freud published any of his work. In 1880, a year before Freud received his medical degree, an uncle of his future wife wrote a book about Aristotle's concept of catharsis. There ensued a "craze for the topic of catharsis. [It] was one of the most discussed subjects among scholars and one of the topics of conversation in sophisticated Viennese salons" (Ellenberger, 1972, p. 272). By 1890 there were more than 140 publications in German about catharsis (Sulloway, 1979).

Finally, many of Freud's ideas about dreams had been anticipated in the literature in philosophy and physiology as far back as the

CATHARSIS: The process of reducing or eliminating a complex by recalling it to conscious awareness and allowing it to be expressed

17th century. Although Freud claimed he was the only scientist of his time to show an interest in dreams, the facts of history tell a different story. Three of Freud's contemporaries were already conducting studies of dreams. Charcot had proposed that the psychological trauma associated with hysteria was revealed in the patient's dreams. Janet believed that the causes of hysteria were contained in dreams, and he used dreams as a therapeutic tool. And Krafft-Ebing argued that unconscious sexual wishes could be found in dreams (Sand, 1992).

We can see that there were many diverse influences on Freud's thinking. No small part of his genius, and the genius of all founders, was his ability to draw together the threads of these various ideas to weave a coherent system.

SIGMUND FREUD (1856–1939) AND THE DEVELOPMENT OF PSYCHOANALYSIS

Sigmund Freud was born on May 6, 1856, in Freiberg, Moravia (now Pribor, Czech Republic). In 1990, the town renamed its Stalin Square as Freud Square. Freud's father was a wool merchant who, when his business failed in Moravia, moved the family to Leipzig and later, when Freud was 4 years old, to Vienna. Freud remained in Vienna for nearly 80 years.

Freud's father was 20 years older than his mother and was strict and authoritarian. As a young boy, Freud felt both fear and love toward his father. Freud's mother was protective and loving, and toward her he felt a passionate attachment. This fear of the father and sexual attraction to the mother is what Freud later called the *Oedipus complex,* and it derived from his boyhood experiences and recollections. We will see that much of his theory is autobiographical in nature.

One of eight children, Freud demonstrated great intellectual ability, which the family tried to encourage. His was the only room in the house to have an oil lamp, providing better light for study than the candles the other children used. The rest of the children, toward whom Freud displayed considerable resentment, were not allowed to study music, lest their practicing disturb the young scholar.

Freud entered high school a year earlier than normal and was considered a brilliant student, graduating with distinction at the age of 17. His study of Darwin's theory of evolution awakened in him an interest in the scientific approach to knowledge, and he decided to study medicine. Freud felt no great desire to be a practicing physician, but he hoped a medical degree would lead to a career in scientific research.

He began his studies at the University of Vienna in 1873. Because he wanted to take courses in subjects, such as philosophy, that were

SIGMUND FREUD

Archives of the History of American Psychology/University of Akron

not directly connected with medical training, he spent 8 years getting his degree. At first he concentrated on biology; he dissected more than 400 male eels to determine the structure of the testicles. His findings were inconclusive, but it is interesting that his first attempt at research concerned sex. He moved on to physiology and work on the spinal cord of fish, spending 6 years over a microscope in the physiological institute.

During his medical training Freud began experimenting with the drug cocaine. He used it himself, made it available to his fiancée, his sisters, and his friends, and was responsible for introducing it into medical practice. He was enthusiastic about the substance and claimed it eased his depression and helped his chronic indigestion. He was convinced that in cocaine he had discovered a miracle drug that would cure everything from sciatica to seasickness and win him the fame and recognition he craved.

This was not to be. One of Freud's medical colleagues, after hearing Freud's casual conversation about the drug, conducted his own experiments and found that cocaine could be used to anesthetize the human eye, thus facilitating the use of surgery for the treatment of eye disorders.

Freud published a paper on the beneficial uses of cocaine in 1884, and this work was considered partly responsible for an epidemic of cocaine use in Europe and the United States, lasting well into the 1920s. Freud was criticized severely for advocating the use of cocaine for purposes other than eye surgery and for unleashing this plague upon the world. For the rest of his life he tried to erase any memory of his endorsement of cocaine, even omitting reference to his work in his own bibliography.

For many years it was believed that Freud stopped using cocaine after his medical school days, but more recently uncovered data of history—Freud's own letters—reveal that he used the drug for at least 10 years more, well into middle age (Masson, 1985).

Freud wanted to continue his scientific research within an academic setting, but Ernst Brücke, the medical school professor who was director of the physiological institute where Freud was working, discouraged him because of his financial circumstances. Freud was too poor to support himself during the many years he would have to wait to secure one of the few university professorships. Reluctantly Freud agreed that Brücke was right, so he decided to take his medical examinations and enter private practice.

He received his MD in 1881 and opened a practice as a clinical neurologist. He did not find medical practice to be any more attractive than he had anticipated, but economic realities won out. He had become engaged to Martha Bernays, who also had no money, and they had postponed their marriage several times for financial reasons.

During their years of courtship, Freud showed intense jealousy toward anyone who claimed Martha's attention or affection, even members of her own family. "From now on you are but a guest in your family," he wrote to her. "I will not leave you to anyone. . . . If you can't be fond enough of me to renounce for my sake your family, then you must lose me, wreck your life, and not get much yourself out of your family. . . . I do have a tyrannical streak in my nature" (quoted in Appignanesi & Forrester, 1992, pp. 30, 31).

Finally, after a frustrating 4-year engagement, they were married, but first Freud had to borrow money and pawn their watches. Their situation eventually improved, but Freud never forgot those early years of poverty.

Freud's long working hours prevented him from spending a great deal of time with his wife and children (of whom there were eventually six). He took vacations alone or with his sister-in-law, Minna, because Martha could not keep up with his pace of hiking and sightseeing.

The Case of Anna O.

Freud developed a friendship with the physician Josef Breuer (1842–1925), who had gained fame for his study of respiration and his discovery of the functioning of the semicircular canals in the ears. The successful and sophisticated Breuer offered the young Freud advice and even loaned him money. To Freud, Breuer was a father-figure; Breuer apparently viewed Freud as a precocious younger brother. "Freud's intellect is soaring at its highest," Breuer wrote to a friend. "I gaze after him as a hen at a hawk" (quoted in Hirschmüller, 1989, p. 315). They frequently discussed Breuer's patients, including Anna O., whose case became pivotal in the development of psychoanalysis.

An intelligent and attractive 21-year-old woman, Anna O. suffered from a wide range of severe hysterical symptoms, including paralysis, memory loss, mental deterioration, nausea, and disturbances of vision and speech. The symptoms first appeared while she was nursing her dying father. Breuer began treating her by using hypnosis. He found that under hypnosis she would remember specific experiences that seemed to have given rise to certain symptoms. Talking about the experiences while in a hypnotic state seemed to relieve those symptoms.

Breuer saw Anna O. every day for more than a year. During their meetings Anna would recount the disturbing incidents of the day, after which she often reported relief from her symptoms. She referred to her conversations with Breuer as "chimney sweeping" or "the talking cure." As the treatment continued, Breuer realized—and described to Freud—that the incidents Anna recalled under hypnosis involved some thought or event that she found repulsive. Reliving the disturbing experience under hypnosis reduced or eliminated the symptoms.

Breuer's wife grew jealous of the close emotional relationship that was developing between Breuer and Anna O., who exhibited what was later called a **positive transference** to Breuer. In other words, she transferred her feelings for her father to her doctor. This transference was aided by the physical resemblance between her father and Breuer. Breuer, too, may have experienced an emotional attachment to his patient; "her youthful attractions, her charming helplessness, and her very name . . . reawakened in Breuer his dormant Oedipal longings for his own mother" (Gay, 1988, p. 68).

Breuer finally perceived the situation as a threat and told Anna that he could no longer treat her. A few hours later Anna was stricken by the pains of hysterical childbirth. Breuer terminated this event through hypnosis and, according to legend, took his wife on a second honeymoon in Venice, at which time she became pregnant.

This tale turns out to be a myth perpetuated by several generations of psychoanalysts and historians and provides another example of distorted data of history. In this case the myth persisted for almost 100 years. Breuer and his wife may indeed have gone to Venice, but the birthdates of their children reveal that none could have been conceived at that time (Ellenberger, 1972).

Also, on further study it appears that Anna O. (whose real name was Bertha Pappenheim) was not cured by Breuer's cathartic treatments. After Breuer stopped treating her, she was institutionalized for some time and would spend hours sitting beneath a portrait of her father, talking about visiting his grave. Breuer told Freud she was deranged, and he expressed the hope that she might die and end her suffering. It is not known how she overcame her mental illness, but Anna O. later became a social worker and a feminist, endorsing education for women. She wrote short stories of "intelligence, passion, and wit" and published a play about women's rights (Shepherd, 1993, p. 210).

Breuer's report of the Anna O. case is important in the development of psychoanalysis, because it introduced Freud to the method of catharsis, the talking cure, that later figured so prominently in his work.

POSITIVE TRANSFERENCE: The process by which a patient responds to the therapist as if the therapist was a significant person, such as a parent, in the patient's life

Sex and Free Association

In 1885, Freud received a small postgraduate grant that enabled him to spend several months studying in Paris with Charcot. He observed Charcot's use of hypnosis in the treatment of hysteria and came to regard the man as another father-figure, even imagining how advantageous it would be to his career if he were married to Charcot's daughter. He wrote to Martha about how attractive he thought the young woman was (Gelfand, 1992).

Charcot also alerted Freud to the role of sex in hysterical behavior. At a party one evening, Freud overheard Charcot say that a particular patient's difficulties had a sexual basis. "In this sort of case it's always a question of the genitals—always, always, always" (quoted in Freud, 1914, p. 14).

After his return from Paris, Freud was again reminded of the possible sexual basis of emotional disturbance. A colleague asked Freud if he would take the case of a woman patient who suffered anxiety attacks that were relieved only when she knew where her doctor was at every moment. The physician told Freud that the anxiety was caused by the woman's impotent husband; after 18 years, their marriage had not been consummated. "The sole prescription for such a malady," the doctor told Freud, "is familiar enough to us, but we cannot order it. It runs: R_x *Penis normalis dosim repetatur*!" (Freud, 1914).

Freud had adopted Breuer's methods of hypnosis and catharsis to treat his patients, but he gradually became dissatisfied with hypnosis. Although it was apparently successful in relieving or eliminating symptoms, it did not seem able to effect a long-term cure. Many patients returned with a new set of complaints. Also, Freud found that some neurotic patients could not be easily or deeply hypnotized. He soon abandoned hypnosis, but he retained catharsis as a treatment method and developed from it the technique of **free association.** (We noted in chapter 1 that Freud meant, in German, free intrusion or invasion, not free association.)

FREE ASSOCIATION: A technique in which the patient says whatever comes to mind

In free association, the patient lies on a couch and is encouraged to talk openly and spontaneously, giving complete expression to every idea, no matter how embarrassing, unimportant, or foolish it may seem. The goal of Freud's system of psychoanalysis was to bring into conscious awareness repressed memories or thoughts, which were assumed to be the source of the patient's abnormal behavior.

Freud believed there was nothing random about the material revealed during free association, and that it was not censored by the patient's conscious choice. The experiences recounted during a free-association session were predetermined. The nature of the patient's conflict forced this material to come out. It intruded on the patient's consciousness so that the patient had to express it to the therapist.

Through the free-association technique Freud found that his patients' memories reached far back into childhood, and that many of the repressed experiences they recalled concerned sexual matters. Already sensitive to sexual factors as possible causes of his patients' illnesses, and aware of the current writings on sexual pathology, Freud paid increasing attention to the sexual material revealed in his patients' narratives.

The Break With Breuer

In 1895 Freud and Breuer published *Studies on Hysteria,* which is considered to mark the formal beginning of psychoanalysis, although

Freud did not use the word *psychoanalysis* until a year later (Rosenzweig, 1992). The book contained papers by both authors and several case histories, including that of Anna O. Although the book received some negative reviews, it was largely praised in scientific and literary journals throughout Europe and considered to be a valuable contribution to the field. It was a firm, if modest, beginning of the recognition Freud desired.

Breuer had been hesitant to publish the book. They had argued about Freud's contention that sex was the sole cause of neurotic behavior. Breuer agreed that sexual factors were important, but he was not persuaded that they were the only explanation. He told Freud there wasn't enough evidence on which to base his conclusion. The decision to proceed with publication anyway led to a rift in their relationship.

Freud was convinced he was correct and that there was no need to accumulate additional data to support his position. He may have been unwilling to wait for more research support because any delay might allow someone else to publish the idea and claim priority. Freud's ambition for success may have taken precedence over any scientific caution about rushing into print with insufficient evidence.

Freud's dogmatic attitude about his work disturbed Breuer, and within a few years the break between them was complete. Freud became embittered toward Breuer, who had done so much for him, remarking that the mere sight of Breuer made him want to leave the country! However, Freud did give Breuer credit for his pioneering work on the treatment of hysteria. By the time Breuer died in 1925, Freud had mellowed. He wrote a sensitive obituary for Breuer, acknowledging his mentor's accomplishments. And he sent a letter of condolence to Breuer's son, noting the "magnificent part played by your late father in the creation of our new science" (quoted in Hirschmüller, 1989, p. 321).

The Childhood Seduction Controversy

By the mid-1890s Freud's conviction that sex played the determining role in neurosis was firm. He observed that most of his patients reported traumatic sexual experiences in childhood, often involving members of their families. He also came to believe that neurosis could not develop in a person who led a normal sex life.

In a paper presented to the Viennese Society of Psychiatry and Neurology in 1896, Freud reported that, in free association, his patients had revealed childhood experiences that appeared to be seduction, with the seducer usually being an older relative, often the father. These seduction traumas, Freud believed, were the cause of adult neurotic behavior.

He further reported that his patients were hesitant about describing details of the seduction experience. Somehow, the events seemed unreal. Patients spoke haltingly, in a manner suggesting that they could not fully recall the experiences, almost as though they had never really happened.

Freud's paper was received with skepticism. The group's president, Krafft-Ebing, said it sounded like a "scientific fairy tale" (quoted in Jones, 1953, p. 263). Freud responded that his critics were asses and could all go to hell.

About a year later, Freud reversed his position and claimed that, in most cases, the childhood seduction experiences his patients described were not real; they had never actually occurred. This marks another turning point in the development of psychoanalysis. At first, the awareness that patients were reporting fantasies came as a shock to Freud, because his theory of neurosis was based on his belief that his patients *had* experienced some sexual trauma in childhood, which accounted for their irrational behavior as adults.

On reflection, however, Freud decided the patients' fantasies were quite real to them. And, because the fantasies focused on sex, sex remained the root of their problem. Thus, Freud was able to preserve the basic idea of sex as the cause of neurosis.

Nearly a century later, in 1984, controversy erupted when a psychoanalyst who had briefly been the director of the Freud Archives, Jeffrey Masson, charged that Freud lied about the reality of his patients' childhood sexual experiences. Masson claimed that the sexual abuses reported by Freud's patients had indeed occurred, and that Freud decided to call them fantasies only to make his system more acceptable to his colleagues and to the public (Masson, 1984).

Most reputable scholars denounced Masson's claims, arguing that his evidence was unconvincing (Gay, 1988; Krüll, 1986; Malcolm, 1984). The dispute received nationwide media coverage. In an interview in the *Washington Post* (February 19, 1984), Freud scholars Paul Roazen and Peter Gay described Masson's theory as a hoax and a slander, "a severe distortion of the history of psychoanalysis." It should be noted that Freud had never abandoned his belief that childhood sexual abuse had sometimes taken place; what he changed was his view that these experiences, as reported by his patients, had *always* actually occurred, and he stated that such widespread abuse was hardly credible.

Yet, more recent evidence indicates that childhood sexual abuse is far more common than had generally been supposed, leading some psychoanalysts to suggest that Freud's original conception of the seduction theory as an explanation for neuroses may have been correct. We do not know whether Freud deliberately suppressed the truth, as Masson claimed, or whether he genuinely believed that his patients were reporting fantasies. However, it is possible that "more of Freud's patients were telling the truth about their childhood experiences than he was ultimately prepared to believe" (Crewsdon, 1988, p. 41).

The same conclusion had been reached in the 1930s by Freud's disciple Sandor Ferenczi. On the basis of the reports of his own patients, Ferenczi decided the Oedipus complex resulted from real acts of sexual abuse and not from fantasies. When he described his findings at a psychoanalytic congress in 1932, Freud tried to prevent him from speaking. When that failed, Freud led the opposition to Ferenczi's position.

It has also been suggested that Freud may have modified the seduction theory because he realized that if it were true, then all fathers, including his own, would be judged guilty of perverse acts against their children (Krüll, 1986).

Beginning in the late 1980s and continuing into the 1990s, the issue of the reality of repressed memories of childhood sexual abuse resurfaced in sensational reports about people recalling incidents presumed to have occurred years earlier. In 1990, a man was convicted of murder on the basis of an unearthed repressed memory his daughter had of an incident 20 years before: She suddenly recalled seeing him kill her childhood friend.

A number of women have brought criminal charges against fathers, uncles, and family friends for sexual abuse alleged to have taken place during childhood, long-repressed events that they had only recently recalled.

Self-Analysis and the Interpretation of Dreams

Whatever the ultimate judgment of the seduction theory, it is clear that Freud, who emphasized the role of sex in emotional life, held a negative attitude toward sex and experienced sexual difficulties of his own. He wrote of the dangers of sexuality, even for people who were not neurotic, and argued that we should strive to rise above that "common animal need." He considered the sex act to be degrading, arguing that it contaminated both the mind and the body. In 1897, when he was 41 years old, Freud reported that personally he had given up sex: "Sexual excitation is of no more use to a person like me" (Freud, 1954, p. 227). Freud occasionally experienced periods of impotence and had sometimes abstained from sex because he disliked condoms and coitus interruptus, the standard methods of birth control of the day (Gay, 1988).

In the same year he decided to give up sex, he began the monumental task of self-analysis. He had suffered from a number of neurotic symptoms and diagnosed his condition as anxiety neurosis, which he attributed to the accumulation of sexual tension. He reported migraine headaches, urinary problems, and spastic colon, and he became anxious about dying, travel, open spaces, and heart disease. This was a time of intense inner turmoil for Freud, yet it was also one of his most creative periods. Indeed, much of his theory of neurosis derived from his own neurotic difficulties and his attempt to analyze them. "The most important patient for me was my own person," he wrote (quoted in Gardner, 1993, p. 71). He undertook the self-analysis as a way of better understanding himself and his patients, and the method he chose was **dream analysis.**

DREAM ANALYSIS: A technique involving interpreting dreams to uncover unconscious conflicts

In the course of his work Freud had discovered that a patient's dreams could be a rich source of significant emotional material. Dreams often contained clues to the underlying causes of a disturbance. Because of his positivist belief that everything had a cause, he thought that events in a dream could not be completely without meaning but must result from something in the patient's unconscious.

Realizing he could not analyze himself by the technique of free association—it being difficult to be patient and therapist at the same time—Freud decided to analyze his dreams instead. On awakening each morning, he wrote down his dream stories from the night before and then free-associated to them.

This self-analysis continued for about 2 years, culminating in the publication of *The Interpretation of Dreams* (1900), a book now considered Freud's major work. In it he outlined for the first time the nature of the Oedipus complex, drawing largely on his own childhood experiences. The book was not universally praised, but it drew much favorable comment. Professional journals reviewed it, as did magazines and newspapers in Vienna, Berlin, and other major European cities. In Zurich, Switzerland, a young man by the name of Carl Jung read the book and quickly became a convert to the new psychoanalysis.

The Interpretation of Dreams was eventually so successful that it appeared in eight editions during Freud's lifetime. He adopted dream analysis as a standard technique for psychoanalysis, and thereafter devoted the last half-hour of each day to self-analysis.

Recognition—But Dissension in the Ranks

In the years after 1900 Freud developed and expanded his ideas. In 1901 he published *The Psychopathology of Everyday Life,* which contains a description of the now famous **Freudian slip.** Freud suggested that in our everyday behavior, unconscious ideas that are struggling for expression can modify our thoughts and actions. What might seem to be casual slips of the tongue or acts of forgetting are actually reflections of real, although unacknowledged, motives.

FREUDIAN SLIP: An act of forgetting or a lapse in speech that reflects unconscious motives or anxieties

Freud's next book, *Three Essays on the Theory of Sexuality,* appeared in 1905. Three years earlier some students had urged him to conduct a weekly discussion group, to teach them about psychoanalysis. (The topic of their first meeting was the psychology of cigar making [Kerr, 1993].) These disciples, described as a "collection of marginal neurotics" (Gardner, 1993, p. 51), included Carl Jung and

Alfred Adler, who later achieved distinction through their opposition to Freud.

As we saw with the breakdown of Freud's relationship with Breuer, Freud tolerated no disagreement about the role of sexuality in his theory. Anyone who did not accept it, or who sought to alter it, was excommunicated. Freud wrote: "Psychoanalysis is my creation; for ten years I was the only person who concerned himself with it. . . . No one can know better than I do what psychoanalysis is" (Freud, 1914, p. 7).

During the years 1900 to 1910, Freud's professional standing improved. His private practice was thriving, and his colleagues were taking his pronouncements seriously. In 1909, he received international recognition when he and Jung were invited by G. Stanley Hall to speak at the 20th anniversary celebration of Clark University in Massachusetts. Freud delivered a series of lectures and was awarded an honorary doctorate in psychology.

He found the experience deeply moving, another turning point in his career. "Perhaps the person most profoundly affected by Freud's lectures was Freud himself. Here, to an audience far, far superior to any he had ever commanded in Europe, he proposed himself as a scientist and a therapist who had made important empirical discoveries, and they responded with adulation" (Kerr, 1993, pp. 243–244).

He met many prominent American psychologists at Clark, including William James, E. B. Titchener, and James McKeen Cattell. Freud's lectures were printed in the *American Journal of Psychology* and translated into several languages (Freud, 1909/1910). A few

Clark University

At Clark University, 1909. Seated, from left: Sigmund Freud, G. Stanley Hall, Carl Jung. Standing, from left: Ernest Jones, A. A. Brill, Sandor Ferenczi.

months after the ceremonies, the annual meeting of the American Psychological Association devoted a 3-hour session to Freud's work, evidence of the impact of his appearance in the United States.

Freud's conception of the unconscious mind received an enthusiastic reception from the American public. People were already interested in the idea, thanks to the writings of the Canadian psychologist H. Addington Bruce. Between 1903 and 1917, Bruce wrote 63 magazine articles and 7 books about the unconscious, helping to stimulate public interest in Freud's work (Dennis, 1991).

Although Freud was welcomed and honored on his visit to the United States, he left with many unfavorable impressions, feelings he retained for years. He complained about the quality of American cooking, the scarcity of public toilets, the difficulty of the language, and the informality of manners. He was offended when a tourguide at Niagara Falls referred to him as "the old fellow." He never returned to the United States and told his biographer that "America is a mistake; a gigantic mistake, it is true, but nonetheless a mistake" (Jones, 1955, p. 60). In fairness, we note that Freud also claimed to dislike Vienna, the city in which he lived for so many years.

It was not long before the official psychoanalytic family was torn by discord and dissension about certain of Freud's ideas, a situation that resulted, finally, in defections. Freud's break with Adler came in 1911, and with Jung—whom Freud considered his spiritual son and heir to the system of psychoanalysis—in 1914. Freud was furious. At a family dinner party he complained about the disloyalty of those who had once been so faithful to his cause. "The trouble with you, Sigi," Freud's aunt remarked, "is that you just don't understand people" (Hilgard, 1987, p. 641).

Freud's Final Years

In 1923, at the peak of his fame, Freud was diagnosed as having cancer of the mouth. Over the next 16 years he suffered continuous pain and had 33 operations; portions of his palate and upper jaw were removed. He took X-ray and radium treatments and also had a vasectomy, which some physicians believed would reverse the growth of the cancer. The artificial device made necessary by his mouth surgery affected his speech, and it became difficult to understand what he was saying. Although he continued to see patients and disciples, he shunned other personal contact. He was used to smoking 20 cigars a day, and he did not stop after his illness was diagnosed. (The writer Anthony Burgess described in the *New York Times* [October 7, 1984] his visit to Freud's home in Vienna, which is now a museum. There you can buy a vivid reminder of Freud's last grim years, "a phonograph record in which [Freud] speaks from the dead in precise English tortured by the clicks of his prosthesis.")

After Adolf Hitler came to power in Germany in 1933, the official Nazi position on psychoanalysis was made clear: Freud's books were publicly burned in May 1933, at a rally in Berlin. As the volumes were flung onto the bonfire, a Nazi leader shouted, "Against the soul-destroying overestimation of the sex life—and on behalf of the nobility of the human soul—I offer to the flames the writings of one Sigmund Freud!" (Schur, 1972, p. 446). Freud commented: "What progress we are making. In the Middle Ages they would have burnt me; nowadays they are content with burning my books" (quoted in Jones, 1957, p. 182).

By 1934, the more farsighted Jewish psychologists and psychoanalysts had emigrated. The Nazi campaign to eradicate psychoanalysis in Germany was effective; knowledge of Freud, once so widespread, was almost obliterated. A student at the Institute for Psychological Research and Psychotherapy, established by the Nazis in Berlin, recalled that "Freud's name was never mentioned, and his books were kept in a locked bookcase" (*New York Times,* July 3, 1984). Even today, more than 60 years later, many important books on psychoanalysis are unavailable in Germany.

Freud insisted on remaining in Vienna. In March 1938, German troops were welcomed into Austria, and on March 15, his home was invaded by a gang of Nazis. A week later his daughter Anna was arrested and detained. This finally persuaded Freud that, for his own safety, he should leave. Partly through the intervention of the American government, the Nazis agreed to let Freud go to England. (Four of Freud's sisters who stayed in Vienna died in Nazi concentration camps.) To secure an exit visa, Freud had to sign a document attesting to his respectful and considerate treatment by the Gestapo (the secret police), and noting that he had no reason to complain. He signed the form and supposedly added the sarcastic comment: "I can heartily recommend the Gestapo to anyone" (quoted in Jones, 1957, p. 226). So noted Ernest Jones, Freud's friend and biographer, who related the incident presumably as Freud told it to him. Newly uncovered data of history—the original document Freud signed—reveal no such comment (Decker, 1991).

Although Freud was received well in England, he was unable to enjoy his last year because of failing health. In his diary and in letters to friends, he wrote about his bad days and the pain from the spreading cancer. "I had to cancel my work for twelve days, and I lay with pain and hot-water bottles on the couch which is meant for others" (Freud, 1992, p. 229). He remained mentally alert and worked almost to the end.

Some years before, when he selected Max Schur to be his personal physician, Freud made Schur promise he would not let him suffer unnecessarily. On September 21, 1939, he reminded Schur of his vow. "You promised me then not to forsake me when my time comes. Now it's nothing but torture and makes no sense anymore" (Schur,

1972, p. 529). The doctor gave Freud an overdose of morphine over a 24-hour period, bringing Freud's many years of suffering to an end.

Original Source Material on Psychoanalysis: From Freud's First Lecture at Clark University, September 9, 1909

Freud's initial lecture at Clark University is presented here in the 1992 translation by the American psychologist, Saul Rosenzweig.[1] His goal was to correct inaccuracies in previous translations (1910, 1924) and to render the style more faithful to Freud's own prose. In this excerpt from Rosenzweig's translation, Freud discusses the case of Anna O. He considers the following points:

1.   *Breuer's role in the development of psychoanalysis,*

2.   *Anna's symptoms,*

3.   *hypnosis as a method of treatment,*

4.   *the effect of catharsis, having the patient talk about her symptoms,*

5.   *the importance of recalling the circumstances under which the symptoms first appeared,*

6.   *the importance of expressing the emotions that accompanied the onset of the symptoms,*

7.   *the splitting of Anna's personality into conscious and unconscious states.*

Ladies and Gentlemen: It is a novel and confusing experience for me to appear as lecturer before an eager audience in the New World. I assume that I owe this honor only to the connection of my name with the topic of psychoanalysis and, consequently, it is of psychoanalysis that I intend to speak. I shall attempt to give you in very brief compass a historical survey of the origin and further development of this new method of investigation and treatment.

If merit is due to the originator of psychoanalysis, the merit is not mine. I did not participate in its earliest beginnings. I was a student, occupied with the preparation for my final examinations, when another Viennese physician, Dr. Josef Breuer, applied this method for the first time in the case of a hysterical girl (1880–1882). We shall start by examining the history of this case and its treatment. You can find it described in detail in *Studies on Hysteria* later published by Dr. Breuer and myself.

---

[1] From Saul Rosenzweig. *Freud, Jung, and Hall the king-maker: The historic expedition to America (1909)* (Seattle: Hogrefe & Huber, 1992), pp. 397–406. Reprinted with permission of Dr. Rosenzweig.

First, however, an incidental remark. I have discovered with satisfaction that the majority of my audience are not of the medical profession. Now have no concern that a medical education is necessary to follow my discourse. We shall at the outset accompany the physicians for a short time, but soon we shall separate from them and go with Dr. Breuer along a unique path.

Dr. Breuer's patient was a highly intelligent girl of twenty-one. She had developed, in the course of her more than two years of illness, a series of physical and mental disturbances which well deserve to be taken seriously. She had a severe paralysis of both right extremities, with anaesthesia, and at times she had the same disturbance in the limbs of her left side; she had disordered eye movements, and many visual restrictions; difficulty in keeping her head in an upright position, an intense *Tussis nervosa* [uncontrollable cough]; nausea when attempting to take nourishment, and, at one time, during a period of several weeks, an inability to drink despite tormenting thirst. There was a reduction in her capacity for language which progressed to the point of her being unable either to speak or to understand her mother tongue; and, finally, she was subject to states of "absence," or confusion, delirium—alterations of her whole personality—which we shall later have to consider separately.

When one hears of such a syndrome one does not need to be a physician to incline to the opinion that one is here concerned with a serious illness, probably of the brain, for which there is little hope of recovery and which will probably lead to the early death of the patient. However, physicians inform us that in a certain type of case with such severe symptoms a different and quite favorable prognosis is justified. When such a syndrome appears in a young female whose vital internal organs (heart, kidneys) are shown by objective investigations to be normal but who has experienced intense *emotional* agitations, and if the individual symptoms are exceptional in certain of their minute characteristics, then physicians do not regard such a case too gravely.

They maintain that an organic lesion of the brain is not present but, rather, an enigmatic condition, known since the time of Greek medicine as *hysteria,* which can simulate a large number of syndromes of serious illness. They then judge that the life of the patient is not threatened and that even a complete restoration to health is probable. The differentiation of such a case of hysteria from one of severe organic illness is not always easy to make. But we do not need to know how a differential diagnosis of this kind is made; it is sufficient for us to be assured that Breuer's patient was just such a case in which no competent physician would fail to make a diagnosis of hysteria. We can also at this point add from the case report that her illness arose while she was nursing her dearly loved father, during his serious and fatal illness, and that she had to withdraw from this duty as a consequence of falling ill herself.

Thus far it has been an advantage to go along with the doctors, but we shall soon take leave of them. You should not, indeed, expect that the prospects of a patient to receive medical aid are, in fact, increased by a diagnosis of hysteria instead of serious brain disease. Medical skill is powerless in most cases involving serious brain disease, but the physician is likewise helpless in combating hysterical illness. He is obliged to rely upon benign Nature as to when and how the hopeful prognosis is to be realized. . . .

It had been noticed that the patient in her states of absence—alterations of consciousness with confusion—used to mutter a few words to herself which appeared to derive from some connection with the thoughts preoccupying her. The doctor, after recovering these words, put her into a kind of hypnosis and reiterated these words in order to encourage her associations to them. The patient complied and reproduced for the physician the mental images which controlled her mind during her states of absence and had betrayed themselves in the mentioned fragmentary utterances. These were deeply tragic, often poetically beautiful fantasies—we might call them daydreams—which usually took as their starting point the situation of a girl at the sickbed of her father. Once she had narrated a number of such fantasies, she seemed to be set free and restored to her normal mental condition. The state of ensuing well-being, which continued for several hours, yielded on the next day to a new state of absence which would be removed in the same manner through the narration of other fantasies.

One could not escape the impression that the mental alterations which expressed themselves in the states of absence were a consequence of stimuli derived from these highly emotional fantasy formations. The patient herself, who at this stage of her illness, rather remarkably spoke and understood only English, named this novel method of treatment "talking cure" or, as a joke, designated it as "chimney sweeping."

It was soon realized that by such purging of the mind more could be accomplished than a temporary removal of the constantly recurring mental turbulence. Symptoms of the illness could be brought to disappear when during hypnosis the patient recalled on what occasion and in which connections the symptoms had first appeared if at the same time she gave vent to her feelings.

During the summer there had been a time of intense heat and the patient was suffering very severely from thirst; for, without being able to assign any reason, it had suddenly become impossible for her to drink. She reached for a desired glass of water but as soon as it touched her lips she pushed it away from her like a hydrophobiac. As she did so, she was for a few seconds clearly in a state of absence. She took only fruit, melons, and the like, in order to assuage her tormenting thirst. After this condition had lasted for about six weeks, she was once ruminating, under hypnosis, about her English lady companion, whom she did not like. She related with every sign of disgust how she had come into that lady's room and had seen her little dog, a nauseating creature, drinking out of a glass. She had said nothing for she wanted to be polite. After she had given energetic expression to her stifled anger, she asked for water, drank a large quantity of it uninhibitedly, and woke from hypnosis with the glass at her lips. Thereupon the disturbance disappeared forever.

Permit me to dwell on this experience for a moment. No one had ever previously cured a hysterical symptom by such means or had, by doing so, entered so deeply into the understanding of its causation. It would have to be a discovery of great consequence if one were able to confirm the expectation that still other symptoms, perhaps the majority of them, arose in the patient in such a manner and could be removed in this way. Breuer spared no pains to convince himself of this assertion and he methodically investigated the pathogenesis of the other and more serious symptoms.

Such was actually the case; almost all the symptoms had arisen in this way, as residues, as precipitates—if you will—of affect-laden events which we later labeled "psychic traumas," the peculiarity of which was explained through their relationship to the causative injurious situations. They were, to use the technical term, *determined* by the scenes, the memory traces of which they embodied, and need not any longer be described as capricious or enigmatic aspects of neurosis.

Only one qualification must be noted: it was not always a single event which left the symptom behind. Most symptoms, instead, arose through the effective convergence of numerous, often very many similar, repeated traumas. This entire chain of pathogenic memories would then have to be reproduced in chronological order, but, in fact, reversed, the last ones first, and the first ones last. It was quite impossible to push through to the earliest, and often most cogent trauma, by skipping those which came later.

You will certainly now want to hear about other examples of the origin of her hysterical symptoms in addition to the one concerning the drinking inhibition which resulted from her disgust at seeing the dog drink from a glass. However, if I am to adhere to my program, I must limit myself to very few instances. Breuer relates that her visual disturbances could be traced to occasions such as when the patient, sitting at her father's sickbed with tears in her eyes, was suddenly asked by him what the time was, whereupon trying to look but seeing only indistinctly, she brought the watch up so close to her face that the dial appeared much enlarged (compare the later macropsia and convergent squint). Again, she exerted herself to suppress her tears so that the sick man would not see them.

In like manner, all the pathogenic impressions stemmed from the period when she shared in the care of her sick father. Once, at night, she was very anxiously attending the sick man, who had a high fever, and she was in suspense because a surgeon was expected from Vienna to perform an operation. Her mother had gone out for a while and Anna was sitting by the sickbed with her right arm over the back of the chair. She fell into a state of daydreaming in which she saw a black snake approaching the sick man as if to bite him. (It is very probable that in the meadow behind the house there actually were some snakes which had previously frightened the girl and thus furnished the material for the hallucination.)

She wanted to drive away the animal but seemed paralyzed. Her right arm, hanging over the back of the chair, had "fallen asleep." It had become anaesthetic and paretic [numb and tingling], and when she looked at it, the fingers were transformed into little snakes with death-heads (fingernails). She probably made an attempt to drive off the snake with her paralyzed right hand and in this way the anaesthesia and the paralysis became associated with the snake hallucination. When this image vanished, she tried in her anxiety to pray, but all speech failed her. She could not talk in any language until at last an English children's verse occurred to her and thereafter she continued to think and to pray in that language.

With the recall of this scene under hypnosis, the paralysis of the right arm which had existed since the start of the illness, was eliminated, and the treatment came to an end.

When, a number of years later, I began to employ Breuer's method of investigation and treatment with my own patients, I discovered that my experience agreed completely with his. . . .

Ladies and Gentlemen, if you will permit me a generalization, which is inescapable in so abbreviated a presentation, we can summarize our findings up to this point in the formula: *Our hysterical patients suffer from reminiscences.* Their symptoms are residues and memory symbols for certain (traumatic) events. A comparison with other memory symbols in other areas will perhaps lead us to a deeper understanding of this symbolism. The memorials and monuments with which we decorate our large cities are just such symbols. If you take a walk through London, you find in front of one of the largest railway stations of the city an elaborately decorated gothic pillar—*Charing Cross.* One of the old Plantagenet kings in the thirteenth century, who had the body of his beloved Queen Eleanor carried to Westminster, erected gothic crosses at each of the stations where the coffin was set down, and *Charing Cross* is the last of the monuments preserving the memory of the sad procession.

At another place in the city, not far from London Bridge, one sees a more modern, lofty pillar which is merely called "The Monument." It commemorates the great fire which broke out in that neighborhood in the year 1666 and destroyed a great part of the city.

These monuments are therefore memory symbols similar to the symptoms of hysteria, and up to this point the comparison seems justified. But what would you say to a Londoner who today stood in sorrow before the monument to the funeral of Queen Eleanor instead of going about his business, with the haste demanded by modern industrial conditions while rejoicing in the youthful queen of his own heart? Or to another who, standing before the "Monument," bemoaned the burning down of his beloved native city which has long since been restored in more splendor than before? Hysterical patients, indeed all neurotics, behave like these two impractical Londoners, not only in that they remember the painful experiences of the distant past but because they are still strongly affected by them. They cannot free themselves from the past; by dwelling on it they neglect the reality of the present. This fixation of the mental life on pathogenic traumas is one of the most important and practically significant characteristics of neurosis.

I am willing to yield to an objection which you are probably framing as you think over the case history of Breuer's patient. All traumas stemmed from the time when she was nursing her sick father, and her symptoms can be regarded as memory traces of his illness and death. They therefore express a state of mourning, and fixation on memories of the dead person such a short time after his decease signify nothing pathological. Instead, such conduct is a normal expression of feeling.

I concede this point; the fixation on such traumas in the case of Breuer's patient is not at all surprising. But in other cases . . . the mark of an abnormal adherence to the past is very clear, and Breuer's patient would probably also have developed it had she not benefited from the *cathartic* treatment so soon after experiencing the traumas and developing the symptoms.

We have thus far discussed only the relationship of the hysterical symptoms to the life history of the patient. By considering two further aspects which Breuer observed, we can gain a clue as to how to conceptualize the process of falling ill and of recovering. With regard to the first, it is especially to be noted that in almost all pathogenic situations Breuer's patient had suppressed any strong excitement instead of permitting its discharge by appropriate emotion, by word and deed. In the minor episode of the lady-companion's dog, the patient suppressed, out of deference, every manifestation of her very intense disgust. While she was sitting by the bed of her father she was continually careful not to let the sick man observe any sign of her anxiety or of her sorrowful mood. When she later reproduced the same scene for the physician, the emotion which she had previously inhibited burst forth with special intensity as though it had been long pent up. In fact, the symptom which had been left over from that scene achieved its highest intensity when the doctor got close to the cause of it, and it vanished after the cause had been fully aired.

On the other hand, experience shows that the recollection of a scene in the presence of the physician remained without effect if, for any reason whatever, it occurred without emotional expression. The fate of these affects [emotions], which can hence be conceived as displaceable quantities, were thus the decisive basis for the development of the illness as well as for the recovery.

One is impelled to the assumption that the illness came into existence because the emotions developed in the pathological situations were denied a normal outlet; the essence of the illness consisted in an abnormal use of this underlying "strangulated" affect. In part they remained as a persisting burden on the psychic life and constituted a source of constant excitement for it; in part they underwent a transformation into unusual physical *innovations* and *inhibitions* which manifested themselves as the somatic symptoms of the case. We have coined the term "hysterical conversion" for this latter process.

A certain portion of our own psychical excitement is, apart from this special process, led into the path of somatic innovation and yields what we know as "the expression of emotions." Now, hysterical conversion exaggerates that portion of the discharge of an affectively cathected mental process [the discharge of the psychic energy attached to some object or person]; it bespeaks a much more intense expression of the emotions directed into new paths. If the bed of a stream flows in two channels, there will be an overflow of one of them as soon as the stream meets with an obstruction of the other.

You will note that we have arrived in our thinking at a purely psychological theory of hysteria in which we assign the affective processes the chief place. But now a second observation of Breuer obliges us to assign a role of great significance to the condition of consciousness in characterizing the pathological proceedings. Breuer's patient displayed numerous peculiar mental states—conditions of absence, confusion, and character alterations along with her normal condition. In the normal state she knew nothing of the pathogenic scenes and of their relation to her symptoms; she had forgotten these events or, at any rate, had split away the pathogenic connection. When she was hypnotized, it became possible, but only after considerable exertion, to recall these scenes to her memory, and by this process of recall the symptoms were removed.

One would have encountered great difficulty in finding a way to interpret this situation had not previous experiences and experiments in hypnotism pointed the way. Through the investigation of hypnotic phenomena the conception had become familiar, though it seemed at first preposterous, that in one and the same individual mind several mental groupings are possible and that these can remain quite independent of one another, "know nothing" of one another, and can, by splitting, alternate in consciousness.

Cases of this kind, known as "double conscience" [dual personality], occasionally come under observation as spontaneous occurrences. When in such splitting of the personality consciousness remains persistently attached to one of these two states, it is called the *conscious* mental condition, and the split-off portion is termed *unconscious*.

In the well-known phenomenon of posthypnotic suggestion, in which a command given in hypnosis is involuntarily carried out in the later normal state, one has an excellent prototype of the influence which can be exerted upon consciousness by what is unconscious. Moreover, on this model one can interpret the phenomena of hysteria. Breuer arrived at the postulate that hysterical symptoms originate in such special mental states, which he called *hypnoidal*. Affective stimulation which occurs in such hypnoidal states readily becomes pathogenic because such states do not provide the conditions for a normal discharge of aroused emotion.

There ensues, after the emotional arousal, an unusual product, namely, the symptom, which intrudes itself like a foreign body into the normal state of consciousness and the latter lacks any knowledge of the hypnoidal, pathogenic situation. When a symptom arises one thus finds an amnesia, a memory gap, and the closing of the gap is accomplished by the removal of the originating conditions of the symptom.

I am afraid that this part of my exposition may not have seemed very clear. However, you must bear in mind that we are dealing here with new and difficult views which can perhaps not be made much clearer. This circumstance proves that we have not yet advanced very far in our knowledge. Breuer's concept of the *hypnoidal* states has, moreover, proved to be a handicap, and to be superfluous, and it has been dropped from contemporary psychoanalysis. Presently you will learn at least something of the influences and processes discovered behind the dubious construct of hypnoidal states advanced by Breuer. You may also quite rightly have received the impression that Breuer's formulation was able to give only a very incomplete and unsatisfying explanation of the observed phenomena. But complete theories do not fall from heaven, and you would be even more justified to be skeptical if anyone at the beginning of his observations offered you a well-rounded theory without any gaps. Such a theory could certainly be only a child of speculation, not the product of an unprejudiced and objective investigation.

PSYCHOANALYSIS AS A METHOD OF TREATMENT

Freud found that the method of free association did not always operate so freely. Sooner or later his patients reached a point in their recollections where they were unable or unwilling to continue. He believed that these **resistances** indicated that the patients had called into consciousness memories that were too shameful or repulsive to be faced. Freud thought resistance was a form of protection against emotional pain. The presence of the pain indicated that the analysis was coming close to the source of the problem and that the analyst should continue to probe along those lines.

RESISTANCES: In free association, a blockage or refusal to disclose painful memories

Freud's discovery of resistances led him to formulate a fundamental principle, **repression,** which he described as the process of ejecting or excluding unacceptable ideas, memories, and desires from conscious awareness, leaving them to operate in the unconscious. Freud regarded repression as the only possible explanation for the occurrence of resistances. Unpleasant ideas or impulses are pushed out of consciousness and forcefully kept out. The therapist must help patients bring repressed material back into the conscious mind so they can confront it and learn to cope with it.

REPRESSION: The process of barring unacceptable ideas, memories, or desires from conscious awareness, leaving them to operate in the unconscious mind

Freud recognized that the effective treatment of neurotic patients depended on the development of an intimate personal relationship between patient and therapist. We noted earlier how the transference Anna O. developed toward Breuer so disturbed him that he ended her therapy. To Freud, transference was a necessary part of the therapeutic process. One goal of his therapy was to wean patients from this childish dependence on the therapist and help them assume a more adult role.

Another important treatment method in Freudian psychoanaly-sis is dream analysis. Freud believed that dreams represent a dis-guised satisfaction of repressed desires and that the essence of a dream is wish fulfillment. Dreams have both a manifest and a latent content. The manifest content is the actual story told in recalling the events that occurred in the dream. The significance of the dream, however, lies in the latent content, which is the dream's hidden or symbolic meaning.

Freud believed that when patients describe their dreams, their forbidden desires (the latent dream content) are expressed only in symbolic form. Although many dream symbols are relevant only to the person reporting the dream, other symbols are common to all of us (see Table 13.1). Despite the apparent universality of these sym-bols, interpreting a particular dream requires knowledge of the patient's specific conflicts.

Not all dreams are caused by emotional conflicts. Some arise from simpler stimuli such as the temperature of the bedroom, con-tact with a partner, or overeating before bedtime. Therefore, not all dreams will contain hidden or symbolic material.

Table 13.1   *Dream symbols or events and their latent psychoanalytic meaning.*

Symbol	Interpretation
Smooth-fronted house	Male body
House with ledges, balconies	Female body
King and queen	Parents
Small animals	Children
Children	Genital organs
Playing with children	Masturbation
Baldness, tooth extraction	Castration
Elongated objects (e.g., tree trunks, umbrellas, neckties, snakes, candles)	Male genitals
Enclosed spaces (e.g., boxes, ovens, closets, caves, pockets)	Female genitals
Climbing stairs or ladders; driving cars; riding horses; crossing bridges	Sexual intercourse
Bathing	Birth
Beginning a journey	Dying
Being naked in a crowd	Desiring to be noticed
Flying	Desiring to be admired
Falling	Desiring to return to a state (such as childhood) where one is satisfied and protected

No Passion for Helping

Despite the growing use of psychoanalysis as a method of treatment, Freud had little personal interest in the potential therapeutic value of his system. He was not primarily concerned with curing people. His desire, instead, was to explain the dynamics of human behavior. He identified himself more as a scientist than a therapist, and he viewed the techniques of free association and dream analysis as research tools for the collection of data for his case studies. The fact that these techniques also had therapeutic applications was, to Freud, secondary to their scientific use.

Perhaps because of his relative lack of interest in treating patients, then, he has been described as impersonal, indifferent, and brisk in dealing with them. He placed his chair at the head of the psychoanalytic couch because he did not want the patients staring at him. Sometimes he fell asleep during analytic sessions. "I lack that passion for helping," he admitted (quoted in Jones, 1955, p. 446). His passion was the research on which he built a theory to explain the functioning of the human personality.

FREUD'S METHOD OF RESEARCH

Freud's system differed greatly in content and methodology from the traditional experimental psychology of the time. Despite his scientific training, Freud did not use experimental research methods. He did not collect data from controlled experiments or use statistics to analyze his results.

He had little faith in the experimental approach, yet he believed his work was scientific and that the case histories of his patients, and his own self-analysis, provided ample support for his conclusions. Freud wrote:

> *When I set myself the task of bringing to light what human beings keep hidden within them, not by the compelling power of hypnosis, but by observing what they say and what they show, I thought the task was a harder one than it really is. He that has eyes to see and ears to hear may convince himself that no mortal can keep a secret. If the lips are silent, he chatters with his fingertips; betrayal oozes out of him at every pore. And thus the task of making conscious the most hidden recesses of the mind is one which it is quite possible to accomplish.* (FREUD, 1901/1905b, PP. 77–78)

Freud formulated, revised, and extended his ideas in terms of the evidence as he alone interpreted it. His own critical abilities were his most important guide in the construction of his theory. He insisted that only psychoanalysts who used his methods were qualified to judge the scientific worth of his work, and he ignored criticism from others, particularly from those who were not sympathetic to psychoanalysis. Only rarely did he respond to his critics. Psychoanalysis was his system, and his alone.

Psychoanalysis as a System of Personality

Freud's system of thought did not encompass all the topics that are usually included in psychology textbooks. He explored areas that psychologists of the day tended to ignore—unconscious motivating forces, the conflicts among those forces, and the effects of those conflicts on behavior.

Instincts

INSTINCTS: Mental representations of internal stimuli, such as hunger, that drive a person to take certain actions

Instincts are the propelling or motivating forces of the personality, the biological forces that release mental energy. Although the word *instinct* has become accepted usage in the English language, it does not convey Freud's intended meaning. He did not use the German equivalent, *Instinkt,* when referring to the human personality, but only when describing innate drives in animals. Freud's term when referring to humans was *Trieb,* best translated as *driving force* or *impulse* (Bettelheim, 1982).

Freudian instincts are not inherited predispositions—the usual meaning of *instinct*—but rather refer to sources of stimulation within the body. The goal of the instincts is to remove or reduce the stimulation through some behavior such as eating, drinking, or sexual activity.

Freud did not attempt to offer a detailed list of every human instinct, but he grouped them in two categories: the life instincts and the death instinct. The life instincts include hunger, thirst, and sex, and are concerned with self-preservation and the survival of the species. These are the creative forces that sustain life. The form of energy through which they are manifested is called **libido.** The death instinct is a destructive force that can be directed inward as in masochism or suicide, or outward as in hatred and aggression. As he grew older, Freud became convinced that the aggressive instinct could be as powerful as the sex instinct in motivating human behavior.

LIBIDO: The form of psychic energy that drives a person toward pleasurable behaviors and thoughts

With the concept of the death instinct, we have another example of the autobiographical nature of Freud's system. He developed the notion of a death instinct only when death became a personal concern: His cancer worsened, he witnessed the horrors of war, and his daughter Sophie died at the age of 26, leaving two young children.

Freud was devastated by that loss, and less than 3 weeks later was writing about a death instinct.

Freud also became aware of an aggressive tendency within himself. Colleagues have described him as a good hater, and some of his writings, as well as the bitterness and finality of his breaks with dissenters within the psychoanalytic movement, suggest a high personal level of aggression.

The concept of aggression as a motivating force has been better received by psychoanalysts than his suggestion of a death instinct. One wrote that the idea of the death instinct should be "relegated to the dustbin of history" (Becker, 1973, p. 99). Another suggested that if Freud was a genius, then the proposal of the death instinct was an instance of a genius having a bad day (Eissler, 1971).

Conscious and Unconscious Aspects of Personality

In his early work Freud expressed the belief that mental life consists of two parts, the conscious and the unconscious. The conscious part, like the visible portion of an iceberg, is small and insignificant, presenting but a superficial aspect of the total personality. The vast and powerful unconscious—like the larger portion of the iceberg that exists beneath the surface of the water—contains the instincts that are the driving power behind all human behavior.

Freud later revised this simple conscious/unconscious distinction, proposing instead the id, ego, and superego. The **id,** which corresponds roughly to Freud's earlier notion of the unconscious, is the most primitive and least accessible part of the personality. The powerful forces of the id include the sexual and aggressive instincts. "We call it . . . a cauldron full of seething excitations," Freud wrote. The id "knows no judgments of value, no good and evil, no morality" (Freud, 1933, p. 74). Id forces seek immediate satisfaction without regard for the circumstances of reality, operating in accordance with the pleasure principle, which is concerned with reducing tension by seeking pleasure and avoiding pain. We noted that Freud's word in German for the id was *es,* meaning *it,* a term suggested by the psychoanalyst Georg Groddeck, who sent Freud the manuscript of a book he was writing entitled *The Book of It* (Isbister, 1985).

Our basic psychic energy or libido is contained in the id and is expressed through tension reduction. Increases in libidinal energy result in increased tension; we then attempt to reduce this tension to a more tolerable level. To satisfy our needs and maintain a comfortable or livable level of tension, we must interact with the real world. Hungry people, for example, must act to find food if they are to discharge the tension induced by hunger. Therefore, some appropriate link between the demands of the id and the circumstances of reality must be established.

The **ego** serves as the mediating agent between the id and the external world to facilitate their interaction. The ego represents reason

Id: The source of psychic energy and the aspect of personality allied with the instincts

Ego: The rational aspect of personality responsible for directing and controlling the instincts

or rationality, in contrast to the unthinking and insistent passions of the id. Freud called the ego *ich*, which translates into English as *I*. He did not like the word *ego* and rarely used it (Holt, 1989).

The id craves blindly, unaware of reality. The ego is aware of reality, manipulates it, and regulates the id accordingly. The ego follows the reality principle, holding off the pleasure-seeking demands of the id until an appropriate object can be found to satisfy the need and reduce the tension.

The ego does not exist independently of the id; indeed, it derives its power from the id. The ego exists to help the id, and it is constantly striving to bring about satisfaction of the id instincts. Freud compared the interaction of ego and id to a rider on a horse. The horse supplies the energy to move the rider along the trail, but the horse's power must be constantly guided or reined in, or else the horse may throw the rider to the ground. Similarly, the id must be guided and checked or it will overthrow the rational ego.

Superego: The moral aspect of personality; the internalization of parental and societal values and standards

The third part of Freud's structure of personality, the **superego,** develops early in life when the child assimilates the rules of conduct taught by parents or caregivers through a system of rewards and punishments. Behaviors that are wrong and bring punishment become part of the child's conscience, which is one part of the superego. Behaviors that are acceptable to the parents or social group and that bring rewards become part of the ego-ideal, the other part of the superego. Thus, childhood behavior is initially controlled by parental behavior, but once the superego has formed a pattern of conduct, behavior is determined by self-control. At that point, the person administers his or her own rewards and punishments. Freud's term for the superego was a word he coined, *über-ich*, meaning, literally, *above I.*

The superego represents morality, Freud said, and is the "advocate of a striving toward perfection—it is, in short, as much as we have been able to grasp psychologically of what is described as the higher side of human life" (Freud, 1933, p. 67). Obviously, then, the superego is in conflict with the id. Unlike the ego, which attempts to postpone id satisfaction to a more appropriate time and place, the superego attempts to inhibit it completely.

Thus, Freud envisioned a continuous struggle within the personality as the ego is pressured by insistent and opposing forces. It must try to delay the urgings of the id, perceive and manipulate reality to relieve tension, and cope with the superego's striving for perfection. Whenever the ego is too greatly stressed, the result is the condition known as anxiety.

Anxiety

Anxiety functions as a warning that the ego is being threatened. Freud described three types of anxiety: objective, neurotic, and moral. Objective anxiety arises from fear of actual dangers in the real world. The other two types derive from it.

Neurotic anxiety comes from recognizing the potential dangers inherent in gratifying the id instincts. It is not fear of the instincts themselves but fear of the punishment that is likely to follow indiscriminate, id-dominated behavior. In other words, neurotic anxiety is a fear of being punished for expressing impulsive desires.

Moral anxiety arises out of a fear of one's conscience. When a person performs or even thinks of performing some action that is contrary to the conscience's moral values, he or she may experience guilt or shame. Moral anxiety, then, depends on how well developed one's conscience is. Less virtuous people will experience less moral anxiety.

Anxiety induces a state of tension, motivating the individual to act to reduce it. Freud proposed that the ego develops protective defenses against anxiety—the **defense mechanisms**—which are unconscious denials or distortions of reality (see Table 13.2). For example, in the mechanism of *identification,* a person adopts the mannerisms of someone who appears admirable and less vulnerable to the conditions that give rise to the anxiety. *Sublimation* involves substituting socially acceptable goals for ones that cannot be satisfied directly, such as diverting energy from sexual behaviors into artistically creative endeavors. In the defense mechanism of *projection,* the source of the anxiety is attributed to someone else. In *reaction formation,* a person conceals a disturbing impulse by converting it into its opposite; for example, replacing hate with love. The defense mechanism of *regression* involves behavior that indicates a reversion to an earlier developmental stage, one at which there was greater security and less anxiety.

DEFENSE MECHANISMS: Modes of behavior adopted to protect against anxiety generated by conflicts in everyday life

Psychosexual Stages of Personality Development

Freud was convinced that his patients' neurotic disturbances had originated in their childhood experiences, and he became one of the first theorists to emphasize the importance of child development. He believed that the personality pattern of the adult was formed almost completely by the age of 5.

In the psychoanalytic theory of development, children pass through a series of **psychosexual stages.** During these stages children are considered to be autoerotic; that is, they derive sensual pleasure by stimulating the erogenous zones of the body or by being stimulated by parents or caregivers in their normal caretaking activities. Each developmental stage tends to be centered around a specific erogenous zone.

The *oral stage* lasts from birth into the second year of life. During this stage, stimulation of the mouth, such as sucking, biting, and

PSYCHOSEXUAL STAGES: Developmental stages of childhood, centering around erogenous zones, through which all children pass

Table 13.2   Freudian defense mechanisms.

Denial
    Denying the existence of an external threat or traumatic event; for example, a person with a terminal illness may deny the imminence of death.

Displacement
    Shifting id impulses from a threatening or unavailable object to an object that is available; for example, replacing hostility toward one's boss with hostility towards one's child.

Projection
    Attributing a disturbing impulse to someone else; for example, saying you don't really hate your professor—he hates you.

Rationalization
    Reinterpreting behavior to make it more acceptable and less threatening; for example, saying the job from which you were fired wasn't really a good job anyway.

Reaction formation
    Expressing an id impulse that is the opposite of the one that is driving the person; for example, someone disturbed by sexual longings may become a crusader against pornography.

Regression
    Retreating to an earlier, less frustrating period of life and displaying the childish and dependent behaviors characteristic of that more secure time.

Repression
    Denying the existence of something that causes anxiety; that is, involuntarily removing from consciousness some memory or perception that brings discomfort.

Sublimation
    Altering or displacing id impulses by diverting instinctual energy into socially acceptable behaviors; for example, diverting sexual energy into artistically creative behaviors.

---

swallowing, is the primary source of sensual satisfaction. Inadequate satisfaction at this stage—either too much or too little—may produce an oral type of personality, a person preoccupied with mouth habits such as smoking, kissing, and eating. Freud believed that a wide range of adult behaviors, from excessive optimism to sarcasm and cynicism, could be attributed to events that occurred during the oral stage of development.

In the *anal stage,* gratification shifts from the mouth to the anus, and children derive pleasure from the anal zone. This stage coincides with toilet training. Children may expel or withhold feces; both cases show defiance of their parents. Conflicts during this period can produce an anal-expulsive adult, who is dirty, wasteful, and extravagant, or an anal-retentive adult, who is excessively neat, clean, and compulsive.

During the *phallic stage,* which occurs around the fourth year, erotic satisfaction involves fondling and exhibiting of the genitals as well as sexual fantasizing. Freud described the development during this stage as the **Oedipus complex,** named for the Greek legend in which Oedipus unknowingly kills his father and marries his mother. Freud suggested that children become sexually attracted to the parent of the opposite sex and fearful of the parent of the same sex, who is perceived as a rival. He derived this notion from his own childhood experiences. "I have found love of the mother and jealousy of the father in my own case too," he wrote (Freud, 1954, p. 223).

OEDIPUS COMPLEX: At ages 4 to 5, the unconscious desire of a boy for his mother, accompanied by a desire to replace or destroy his father

Ordinarily, children overcome the Oedipus complex by identifying with the parent of the same sex and substituting affection for the sexual longing for the parent of the opposite sex. However, the attitudes toward the opposite sex that develop during this stage will persist and influence adult relationships with members of the opposite sex. One of the results of identifying with the parent of the same sex is the development of the superego. In adopting the mannerisms and attitudes of that parent, children also assume the parent's superego standards.

Children who outlast the struggles of these early stages enter a period of latency from about ages 5 to 12. Then, in Freud's view, the onset of puberty signals the beginning of the *genital stage.* Heterosexual behavior becomes important, and the person begins to prepare for marriage and parenthood.

MECHANISM AND DETERMINISM IN FREUD'S SYSTEM

The structuralists, and later the behaviorists, considered humans to be like machines. First the human mind and then human behavior were reduced to their most elemental components. It may come as a surprise to learn that Freud, who approached human nature from a different perspective, was also influenced by the mechanistic tradition. No less vigorously than the experimental psychologists, Freud believed that all mental events—even dreams—were predetermined. No thought or bit of behavior occurred by chance or by free will. To Freud, there was a cause—a conscious or unconscious motive—for every action. Further, Freud accepted the doctrine that all phenomena could be reduced to the principles of physics.

Freud in his Vienna study in 1937, surrounded by his collection of Greek, Roman, and Egyptian antiquities.

© Mary Evans, Sigmund Freud Copyrights

In 1895 Freud undertook the task of developing his view of a scientific psychology. He attempted to show that psychology must have a basis in physical principles and that mental phenomena exhibit many of the same characteristics as the neurophysiological processes on which they are based. Psychology, in Freud's view, must be a natural science whose aim is to "represent [mental] processes as quantitatively determined states of specifiable material particles" (Freud, 1895, p. 359).

His project was never completed, but we can see in his later writings the ideas with which he worked and the terminology he adopted from physics, especially mechanics, electricity, and hydraulics. His theorizing along these lines provides another example of data lost to history. His writings on this topic were not found for more than 50 years. Until then, no one knew Freud had ever considered such an approach to psychology. He did not publish this work, and one scholar suggests that "he seems to have been ashamed of it, never referring to it again publicly and apparently hoping that any surviving copies would be destroyed" (Gardner, 1993, p. 68).

Although Freud modified his original intention to model his psychology after physics (when he found that his subject matter was not amenable to physical and chemical techniques), he remained true to the positivist philosophy, especially determinism, that nurtured experimental psychology. And although Freud was obviously influenced by this view, he was not constrained by it. Where he saw that it would not fit, he altered or discarded it. In the end he demonstrated how restrictive the mechanistic conception of human beings was.

RELATIONS BETWEEN PSYCHOANALYSIS AND PSYCHOLOGY

Psychoanalysis developed outside the mainstream of academic psychology, where it remained for many years. "Academic psychology largely closed its doors to psychoanalytic doctrine. An unsigned editorial in a 1924 issue of the *Journal of Abnormal Psychology* bemoaned the endless stream of writings on the unconscious by European psychologists" (Fuller, 1986, p. 123). The editorial dismissed those writings as essentially worthless. Following that strong statement, few articles on psychoanalysis were accepted for professional publication, a prohibition that continued for at least 20 years.

Many academic psychologists offered forceful criticisms of psychoanalysis. In 1916, Christine Ladd-Franklin wrote that psychoanalysis was a product of the "undeveloped . . . German mind," making this judgment at a time when virtually everything associated with Germany was suspect because of German aggression in World War I. Robert Woodworth, at Columbia University, called psychoanalysis an "uncanny religion" that led "even apparently sane individuals" to draw absurd conclusions. John B. Watson called some of Freud's ideas "voodooism" (quoted in Hornstein, 1992, pp. 255, 256).

Despite these and other scathing attacks on psychoanalysis by psychology's leaders, and the quieter dismissals of it as another crackpot theory, some of Freud's ideas made their way into American psychology textbooks of the early 1920s. Defense mechanisms were discussed seriously, along with the unconscious, and the manifest and latent contents of dreams (Popplestone & McPherson, 1994). Still, behaviorism remained the dominant school of thought in psychology, and psychoanalysis as a whole was generally ignored.

By the 1930s and 1940s, however, psychoanalysis had become popular with the general public. The combination of sex, violence, and hidden motives, and the promise to cure a variety of emotional problems proved attractive, almost irresistible. The psychology establishment was furious because people were confusing psychoanalysis with psychology, assuming that the two fields were the same. Psychologists did not like the suggestion that sex and dreams and neurotic behavior were all psychology was about. "It had become clear to psychologists by the 1930s that psychoanalysis was not a passing craze but a serious competitor which threatened the foundations of scientific psychology, at least in the minds of the public" (Morawski & Hornstein, 1991, p. 114).

To deal with this threat, psychologists decided to apply the experimental method to test psychoanalysis to determine its scientific legitimacy. They conducted "hundreds of studies whose creativity was matched only by the uselessness of their findings" (Hornstein, 1992,

p. 258). This flurry of research, however ill-conceived much of it may have been, confirmed that psychoanalysis was inferior to a psychology based on experimentation—at least in the eyes of the experimental psychologists. They had restored their position as "arbiters of psychological truth" (Morawski & Hornstein, 1991, p. 114). In addition, the research showed that academic psychology could be just as relevant to the interests of the general public because it was studying the same things the psychoanalysts studied.

The 1950s and 1960s found behaviorists translating psychoanalytic terminology into the language of behavior. Watson began the trend earlier when he defined emotion as nothing more than sets of habits, and described neuroses as the results of faulty conditioning. Skinner recast the Freudian defense mechanisms in the language of operant conditioning.

Psychology eventually incorporated many of Freud's concepts and made them part of the mainstream. The role of the unconscious, the importance of childhood experiences, and the operation of the defense mechanisms are a few examples of psychoanalytic ideas that are widely accepted, no longer in danger of being ignored.

CRITICISMS OF PSYCHOANALYSIS

Freud's methods of collecting data have been the target of much criticism. He drew his insights and conclusions from the responses of his patients while they were undergoing analysis. Consider the deficiencies of this approach, compared with the experimental method of systematically collecting objective data under controlled conditions of observation.

First, the conditions under which Freud collected his data are unsystematic and uncontrolled. He did not make a verbatim transcript of each patient's words but worked from notes he made several hours after seeing the patient. Some of the original data (the patient's words) would surely have been lost in the time that had elapsed because of the vagaries of memory and the well-documented possibility of distortion and omission. Thus, the data consisted only of what Freud remembered.

Second, it is possible that while recalling his patients' words, Freud reinterpreted them. He may have been guided by his desire to find material that supported his ideas. In other words, he may have remembered and recorded only what he wanted to hear. Of course, we must also consider the possibility that Freud's notes were accurate, but it is impossible to know this because the original data have not survived.

A third criticism relates to discrepancies between Freud's notes on his therapy sessions and the case histories he eventually published, which supposedly were based on those notes. One researcher compared Freud's notes and the published case history and found several differences. Among these were a longer period of analysis, an incorrect sequence of events disclosed by the patient during analysis, and an unsubstantiated claim that the patient was cured (Eagle, 1988; Mahony, 1986). There is no way to determine whether Freud made these distortions deliberately to provide support for his position or whether they resulted from his own unconscious. Historians cannot trace any possible similar errors in Freud's other case studies, because he destroyed most of his patient files.

Also, Freud published only six case histories after his break with Breuer, and none of them provides compelling supporting evidence for his system of psychoanalysis. "Some of the cases present such dubious evidence in favor of psychoanalytic theory that one may seriously wonder why Freud even bothered to publish them. . . . Two of the cases were incomplete and the therapy ineffective. . . . A third case was not actually treated by Freud" (Sulloway, 1992, p. 160).

There is a fourth criticism to make of Freud's data. Even if a complete, word-for-word record had been kept, it would not always have been possible to determine the accuracy of what his patients reported. Freud made few attempts to verify his patients' accounts of their childhood experiences. Critics argue he should have tried to check these accounts by questioning relatives and friends about the events described. Thus, the first step in scientific theory building— data collection—must be characterized, in Freud's case, as incomplete, imperfect, and inaccurate.

As for the next step—drawing inferences and generalizations from the data—we do not know exactly how this was done because Freud never explained his reasoning. And because his data could not be quantified or analyzed statistically, historians cannot determine their reliability or statistical significance.

Freud's assumptions about human nature also have come under attack. Even Freudians agree that he often contradicted himself, and that his definitions of key concepts—such as id, ego, and superego— are unclear. Freud recognized this and noted in his later writings the difficulties of defining precisely some of his ideas.

Many scholars have challenged Freud's views on women. He suggested that women have poorly developed superegos and that they feel inferior about their bodies because they do not have penises. The analyst Karen Horney left Freud's psychoanalytic circle because of this issue and developed her own system, suggesting that instead of women having penis envy, men have womb envy. Most analysts today agree that Freud's ideas about female psychosexual development are unproven and incorrect.

In chapters 14 and 15 we examine the work of other theorists who disagreed with Freud and attempted to modify his position. They argued that he placed too much emphasis on biological forces, particularly sex, as the determinants of personality. They suggested that personality was influenced more by social forces.

Other neo-Freudians challenged Freud's denial of free will and his focus on past behavior to the exclusion of one's hopes and goals for the future. Some criticized Freud for developing a personality theory based only on observations of neurotics, thus ignoring the traits of emotionally healthy persons. All of these points were used to build competing views of the human personality. The rise of these alternative theories led to divisiveness within the psychoanalytic camp and to the formalization of several derivative schools of Freudian analysis.

The Scientific Validation of Psychoanalytic Concepts

Many of Freud's concepts were submitted to experimental testing in the 1930s and 1940s, with questionable results. In recent years, research having greater validity has been performed. An analysis of some 2,000 studies drawn from psychiatry, psychology, anthropology, and other disciplines examined the scientific credibility of Freud's formulations (Fisher & Greenberg, 1977).

Although some concepts resisted attempts at scientific validation —including id, ego, superego, death wish, libido, and anxiety—others were found to be amenable to scientific testing. The analysis showed that published studies have provided support for the following:

1.   some characteristics of the oral and anal personality types;

2.   some causative factors of homosexuality;

3.   the notion that dreams provide an outlet for tension;

4.   aspects of the Oedipus complex in boys (rivalry with the father, sexual fantasies about the mother, and castration anxiety).

Freudian concepts that were tested but were *not* supported by the experimental results include the following:

1.   dreams satisfy symbolically repressed wishes and desires;

2.   in resolving the Oedipus complex boys identify with the father and accept his superego standards out of fear;

3.   women have an inferior conception of their bodies, have less severe superego standards than men, and find it more difficult to achieve an identity.

Later research has shown support for the influence of unconscious processes on thoughts and behavior, suggesting that unconscious influences may be more pervasive than Freud claimed

(Bornstein & Pittman, 1992; Brody, 1987; Jacoby & Kelley, 1987; Silverman, 1976). Experiments on the so-called Freudian slip have shown that at least some of these verbal misstatements appear to be just what Freud said they were—unconscious conflicts and anxieties revealing themselves in embarrassing ways (Motley, 1985).

As we noted, not all of the research conducted on Freudian concepts supports his theory of psychoanalysis. Studies on personality development do not confirm the suggestion that personality is largely formed by age 5 and changes little after that. Personality continues to develop over time and can change dramatically after the age of 5 (Kagan, Kearsley, & Zelazo, 1978; Olweus, 1979). Further, research on instincts as the driving forces of personality shows that Freud's formulation is no longer a useful model for human motivation (Barron, Eagle, & Wolitzky, 1992).

The most important point about these scientific attempts to analyze Freudian ideas is that at least some psychoanalytic concepts can be reduced to propositions that are testable by the methods of science.

CONTRIBUTIONS OF PSYCHOANALYSIS

Why has psychoanalysis survived despite the criticisms against it? To some extent, all theories of behavior can be criticized for lacking scientific acceptability. Psychologists in search of a theory must sometimes choose it on the basis of criteria other than formal scientific precision. And those who choose psychoanalysis are not making their selection in the total absence of supporting evidence.

Psychoanalysis does offer evidence, although it is not the kind usually accepted by science. But if psychoanalytic evidence is not scientific in the traditional sense, that does not mean the theory is incorrect or misleading. Belief in psychoanalysis may be based instead on the grounds the system gives an intuitive appearance of plausibility.

In general, Freudian psychoanalysis has had a strong impact on American academic psychology, and interest in Freud's ideas remains high. However, the popularity of psychoanalysis as a method of therapy has declined when measured by the number of clients choosing that technique and the number of people training to become analysts. Expensive, long-term Freudian therapy is being superseded by briefer and less expensive psychotherapies (some of which derive from psychoanalysis) and by behavioral and cognitive therapies.

Drug treatments have reduced the need for psychoanalysis and similar therapies for certain types of mental disorders. The availability of medications such as Lithium and Prozac has led some psychiatrists and clinical psychologists to revise their thinking about the causes of mental illness, away from the psychic school of thought and back to the somatic.

The somatic or biochemical approach holds that mental disorders result from chemical imbalances in the brain. Why prescribe expensive and time-consuming psychotherapies, then, when the patient can take a pill and feel better right away? Drug therapy, however, does not work for all conditions or all patients. It should also be noted that Freud predicted this development in the treatment of mental disorders long before it took place.

Freud's impact on popular culture in the United States has been enormous and was evident immediately after his visit to Clark University in 1909. Newspapers featured many stories about Freud, and by 1920 more than 200 books had been published on Freudian psychoanalysis. Magazines such as *Ladies' Home Journal, The Nation,* and *The New Republic* carried articles about psychoanalysis. A major movie studio, MGM, offered Freud $100,000 to collaborate on a film about love; he refused. This public enthusiasm for Freud's ideas occurred much earlier than his acceptance by academic psychology.

The 20th century has seen a loosening of sexual restraint in behavior, the arts, literature, and entertainment. It is widely believed that inhibiting or repressing sexual impulses can be harmful. But it is ironic that Freud's message about sex has been so greatly misinterpreted. He never argued for a weakening of sexual codes of conduct or for increased sexual freedom. Rather, his view was that the inhibition of the sex drive was necessary for the survival of civilization. Despite his intention, the sexual liberation of modern times is partly a result of Freud's work, because his emphasis on sex helped to popularize his ideas. Even in scientific journals, articles about sex have a sensational appeal.

Despite the criticisms of a lack of scientific rigor as well as methodological weakness, Freudian psychoanalysis remains an important force in modern psychology. In 1929, E. G. Boring wrote in his textbook, *A History of Experimental Psychology,* that psychology had no truly great proponent of the stature of Darwin or Helmholtz. Twenty-one years later, in the second edition of his text, Boring revised his opinion. Reflecting the development of psychology during the intervening decades, he wrote of Freud with admiration:

> *Now he is seen as the greatest originator of all, the agent of the Zeitgeist who accomplished the invasion of psychology by the principle of the unconscious process. . . . It is not likely that the history of psychology can be written in the next three centuries without mention of Freud's name and still claim to be a general history of psychology. And there you have the best criterion of greatness: posthumous fame.* (BORING, 1950, PP. 743, 707)

DISCUSSION QUESTIONS

1. Describe the relationship between psychoanalysis and the other schools of thought we have discussed. What was the third great shock Freud delivered to humanity?
2. Discuss the two major sources of influence on the psychoanalytic movement. What school of thought within psychiatry did Freud revolt against?
3. How were Freud's theories influenced by Darwin's work, by the idea of mechanism, by the 19th-century attitude toward sex, and by his childhood experiences?
4. Describe the current controversy about Freud's view of childhood seduction experiences. Describe the psychosexual stages of development.
5. Discuss the role of the patient Anna O. in the development of Freudian theory. How did Freud define the following concepts: repression, instinct, id, ego, and superego? What are the life instincts and the death instinct?
6. Describe the relationship between psychoanalysis and mainstream academic psychology. Describe Freud's attempt to explain mental processes in mechanistic, deterministic terms.
7. On what points has psychoanalysis been criticized? What were the results of attempts to test Freudian concepts experimentally?

SUGGESTED READINGS

Decker, H. S. (1991). *Freud, Dora, and Vienna 1900.* New York: Free Press. Describes Freud's treatment of 18-year-old Dora, who expressed her emotional distress through a nervous cough and loss of voice.

Drinka, G. F. (1984). *The birth of neurosis: Myth, malady, and the Victorians.* New York: Simon and Schuster. Examines social and cultural influences on theories of neurosis before Freud's time.

Evans, R. B., & Koelsch, W. A. (1985). Psychoanalysis arrives in America: The 1909 psychology conference at Clark University. *American Psychologist, 40,* 942–948. Describes the meeting that introduced psychoanalysis to an American academic audience.

Freeman, L., & Strean, H. S. (1987). *Freud and women.* New York: Continuum. Explores Freud's relationships with his mother, sisters, wife, daughters, and female colleagues and patients.

Hornstein, G. A. (1992). The return of the repressed: Psychology's problematic relations with psychoanalysis, 1909–1960. *American Psychologist, 47,* 254–263. Describes how the popularity of psychoanalysis in the 1920s posed a threat to experimental psychology, and how psychologists responded by testing and adopting psychoanalytic concepts.

Roazen, P. (1975). *Freud and his followers.* New York: Knopf. Recounts Freud's life and his relationships with the men and women who became his disciples, some of whom later broke away to form their own movements.

CHAPTER 14

PSYCHOANALYSIS:
DISSENTERS AND
DESCENDANTS

PSYCHOANALYSIS AFTER THE FOUNDING

As was the case with Wundt and his experimental psychology, Freud did not long enjoy a monopoly on his new system of psycho-analysis. Barely 20 years after he founded the movement, it splintered into competing factions led by analysts who disagreed with him on basic points.

Freud did not react well to these dissenters. Those analysts who espoused the new positions met with "the sort of invective that was once heaped upon the heads of heretics" (Brown, 1963, p. 37). No matter how close they may have been to Freud, personally and pro-fessionally, once they abandoned his teachings, he cast them out and never spoke to them again.

We discuss three prominent dissenters: Carl Jung, Alfred Adler, and Karen Horney. All were orthodox Freudians before they left Freud's circle to promote their own views. We also deal with three descendants of the Freudian school—Gordon Allport, Henry Murray, and Erik Erikson—who developed their approaches after Freud's death. They were not dissenters, having never been orthodox Freudians; rather, they derived their ideas from the work of Freud, either elaborating on or opposing his theories.

THE NEO-FREUDIANS AND EGO PSYCHOLOGY

First, let us note that not all who followed Freud in the psychoanalytic tradition felt the need to alter, abandon, or overthrow his system. There remains a large group of neo-Freudian analysts who adhere to the central premises of psychoanalysis but who, nevertheless, have modified certain aspects of the system.

The major change these Freudian loyalists introduced into psychoanalysis is an expansion of the concept of the ego (Hartmann, 1964). Rather than being the servant of the id, the ego's role has been extended. The ego is now believed to be more independent of the id. The ego possesses its own energy, which is not derived from the id, and has its own functions separate from the id. Further, these neo-Freudian analysts suggest that the ego is free of the conflict produced when id impulses press for satisfaction.

In Freud's view, the ego was forever responsive to the id, never free of its demands. In the revised view, the ego can function independently of the id, a significant departure from orthodox Freudian thought.

Another change introduced by the neo-Freudians is the deemphasis of biological forces as influences on personality, and the favoring instead of social and psychological forces. The neo-Freudians have also minimized the importance of infantile sexuality and the Oedipus complex. They suggest that personality development is determined primarily by psychosocial rather than psychosexual forces. Social interactions in childhood assume greater importance than sexual interactions, either real or imagined.

ANNA FREUD (1895–1982)

One of the leaders of neo-Freudian ego psychology was Freud's daughter Anna.

Anna Freud's Life

The youngest of the Freuds' six children, Anna Freud wrote that she would never have been born if a safe form of contraception had been available to her parents. Her father announced her birth, with more resignation than enthusiasm, in a letter to a friend, commenting that he would have sent the news by telegram if the infant had been a son (Young-Bruehl, 1988). Yet the year of Anna's birth, 1895, was symbolic—or perhaps prophetic—because it coincided with the birth of psychoanalysis and because Anna would be the only Freud child to follow her father's path and become an analyst.

Anna had an unhappy childhood as the least favored girl in the family. She remembered "the experience of being left out by the big ones, of being only a bore to them, and of feeling bored and left alone" (Appignanesi & Forrester, 1992, p. 273). She was jealous of her sister Sophie, who was clearly her mother's favorite. Anna became her father's favorite; soon he was "as addicted to his youngest daughter as he was to his cigars" (Appignanesi & Forrester, 1992, p. 277).

Anna became interested in her father's work. From the age of 14, she would sit unobtrusively in a corner at the meetings of the Vienna Psychoanalytic Society, absorbing everything that was said. At 22, driven by her emotional attachment to her father and her worries about what he called "her sexuality," Anna entered into analysis with him. She reported violent dreams that involved shooting, killing, dying, and defending him from enemies.

Freud was later criticized for attempting to analyze his own daughter. It was called "an impossible and incestuous treatment. . . . a momentous and bizarre event" and "an Oedipal acting-in at both ends of the couch" (Mahony, 1992, p. 307). The analysis lasted 4 years, with sessions 6 nights a week beginning at 10:00.

In 1924, Anna read her first scholarly paper to the Vienna Psychoanalytic Society. Entitled "Beating fantasies and daydreams," it was allegedly based on the case history of an anonymous patient, but it was actually about her own fantasies. She described dreams of an incestuous father-daughter love relationship, a beating, and sexual gratification through masturbation. The paper was well received by Freud and his colleagues and earned her admission into the society.

ANNA FREUD

Anna Freud never married. She devoted her life to the application of psychoanalysis to emotionally disturbed children and to the care of her father during his long illness. "Anna's care and nursing had become indispensable to him. Over the final decade, she emerges as incomparably the most important person in his life—all her many arrivals and departures, her illnesses and her work, are recorded in [his] diary" (annotation in Freud, 1992, p. 255).

Despite these burdens, she developed a psychoanalytic practice and pioneered the analysis of the child. She wrote many articles and books and made substantial contributions to the field, refining and extending her father's ideas.

Contributions to Psychoanalysis

In 1927, Anna Freud published her first book, *Introduction to the Technique of Child Analysis,* which foretold the direction of her interests. She developed an approach to psychoanalytic therapy with children that took into account their relative immaturity and the low level of their verbal skills. (Sigmund Freud had never treated children in his private practice.)

Her innovations include the use of play materials and the observation of the child in the home. Most of her work was carried out in London, where the Freud family settled after escaping from the Nazis in 1938. She opened a clinic next door to the house in which her father died, and there she treated patients and established a psychoanalytic training center at which clinical psychologists from all over the world came to study. Her work was reported in annual volumes of *The Psychoanalytic Study of the Child*, which began publication in 1945. Her collected works were cumulated in eight volumes published between 1965 and 1981.

Anna Freud substantially revised orthodox psychoanalytic theory, expanding the role of the ego as it functions independently of the id. In *The Ego and the Mechanisms of Defense* (1936), she elaborated on and clarified the use of the defense mechanisms in protecting the ego from anxiety. "This book was immediately hailed as a major contribution and translated into a number of languages. It is still one of the core works on psychoanalytic ego psychology" (Fine, 1990, p. 99). The standard list of Freudian defense mechanisms, such as those we mentioned in chapter 13, was really the work of Anna Freud. She described them more clearly and contributed examples from her analyses of children.

Comment

Ego psychology, as developed by Anna Freud and others, became the primary American form of psychoanalysis from the 1940s to the early 1970s. These neo-Freudians set out to make psychoanalysis "part of scientific psychology. They did so by translating, simplifying, and operationally defining Freudian notions, by encouraging the experimental investigation of psychoanalytic hypotheses, and by modifying psychoanalytic psychotherapy" (Steele, 1985b, p. 222). In the process, they fostered a more conciliatory relationship between psychoanalysis and academic experimental psychology.

Another modification of psychoanalysis is object relations theory, which was brought from England to the United States in the 1960s. This approach, developed by Melanie Klein (1882–1960), focuses on the intense emotional relationship that forms between an infant and its mother. (Klein, incidentally, was permanently estranged from her own daughter, also an analyst, who accused Klein of excessive interference. The daughter maintained that her brother, who died while mountain climbing, had committed suicide because of his poor relationship with their mother.)

Klein described the infant-mother bond in social-cognitive rather than sexual terms. She studied the relationship through direct observation of the infants. In traditional psychoanalysis, adult patients would be asked to recall and reconstruct their early childhood experiences.

The neo-Freudians identify themselves, in general, as Freudians. That label, however, cannot be applied to the dissenters and the descendants.

CARL JUNG (1875–1961)

Jung was once regarded by Freud as a surrogate son and heir to the psychoanalytic movement. Freud called him "my successor and crown prince" (quoted in McGuire, 1974, p. 218). After his friendship with Freud disintegrated in 1914, Jung began what he called analytical psychology, which was totally at odds with Freud's theory.

Jung's Life

Carl Jung, an expert yodeler, was reared in a small village in northern Switzerland, near the famous Rhine Falls. By his own account, his childhood was lonely, isolated, and unhappy (Jung, 1961). His father was a clergyman who had apparently lost his faith and was moody and irritable. His mother suffered from emotional disorders. Her behavior was erratic, and she could change in an instant from a happy housewife to a bewitched demon who mumbled incoherently. The marriage was an unhappy one. Jung learned at an early age not to trust or confide in either parent and, by extension, not to trust the external world as a whole. He turned inward, to the world of his dreams, visions, and fantasies, the world of his unconscious. Dreams and the unconscious—not the conscious world of reason—became his guides in childhood and remained so through his adult life.

At critical times in his life, Jung resolved problems and made decisions on the basis of what his unconscious told him through his dreams. When he was ready to start college, the issue of what he should study was revealed to him in a dream. He saw himself unearthing the bones of prehistoric animals, and he interpreted this to mean he should study nature and science. That dream about digging beneath the earth's surface, plus a dream he recalled from age 3 in which he was in an underground cavern, foretold his future study of personality: He would deal with the unconscious forces that lie beneath the surface of the mind.

Jung attended the University of Basel, Switzerland, and graduated with a medical degree in 1900. He was interested in psychiatry, and his first professional appointment was at a mental hospital in Zurich. The director was Eugen Bleuler, a psychiatrist noted for his work on schizophrenia. In 1905 Jung was appointed lecturer in psychiatry at the University of Zurich, but after several years he resigned this position to devote his time to writing, research, and private practice.

In his work with patients, he did not follow Freud's habit of asking patients to lie on a couch, remarking that he had no wish to put them to bed! Jung and his patient sat in comfortable chairs facing each other. Occasionally he held therapy sessions aboard his sailboat, happily racing across the lake in a high wind. Sometimes he would

Archives of the History of American Psychology/University of Akron

CARL JUNG

sing to his patients, and at other times he was deliberately rude. "Oh no," he told one patient who appeared at the appointed time. "I can't stand the sight of another one. Just go home and cure yourself today" (quoted in Brome, 1981, p. 185).

Jung became interested in Freud's work in 1900 after reading *The Interpretation of Dreams,* which he described as a masterpiece. By 1906 the two men had begun to correspond, and a year later Jung went to Vienna to meet Freud. At their initial meeting, they talked with great animation for 13 hours, an exciting beginning for their intimate, father-son relationship. In 1909, Jung accompanied Freud to the United States for the Clark University ceremonies, at which they both delivered lectures.

Unlike most of Freud's disciples, Jung had already established a professional reputation before he became associated with Freud; he was the best known of all the early converts to psychoanalysis. As a result, he was perhaps less impressionable, less suggestible, than the younger analysts who joined Freud's psychoanalytic family, many of whom were still in medical school or graduate school, unsure of their professional identities.

Jung did, for a time, become a disciple of Freud's, but he was never an uncritical one. Early in their relationship, however, he tried to suppress his doubts and objections. While writing *The Psychology of the Unconscious* (1912), he reported that he was troubled, realizing that when his book was published, stating his own position, it would damage his standing with Freud because it differed in major ways from Freud's approach. For months Jung was unable to proceed with the project, so disturbed was he about Freud's possible reaction. Of course he did eventually publish, and the inevitable occurred.

In 1911, at Freud's insistence—and in the face of opposition from the Viennese members—Jung became the first president of the International Psychoanalytic Association. Freud believed that anti-Semitism would impede the growth of the psychoanalytic movement if the president of the group was Jewish. The Viennese analysts, almost all of whom were Jewish, resented and distrusted the Swiss-born Jung, who was clearly Freud's favorite. They not only had seniority in the movement, but they also believed that Jung himself was anti-Semitic.

Shortly thereafter, his friendship with Freud began to show signs of strain, and by 1912 the two men terminated their personal correspondence. In 1914 Jung resigned his position and withdrew from the association.

When Jung was 38 years old, he was stricken with intense emotional problems that lasted for 3 years; Freud had experienced a similar period of turmoil at the same stage of life. Believing he was going insane, Jung felt unable to do any intellectual work or even read a scientific book, but, interestingly, he did not stop treating his patients.

He resolved his crisis in essentially the same way Freud did, by confronting his unconscious mind. Although he did not analyze his dreams systematically, as Freud had done, Jung followed the impulses of his unconscious as they were revealed to him in dreams and fantasies. As with Freud, this became a time of immense creativity for Jung and led to the formulation of his personality theory.

In line with his interest in mythology, Jung made field expeditions to Africa in the 1920s, to study the mental processes of preliterate peoples. In 1932 he was appointed professor at the Federal Polytechnical University in Zurich, a position he held until poor health forced him to resign in 1942. A chair of medical psychology was founded for him at the University of Basel, Switzerland, but illness prevented him from keeping that position for more than a year. He remained active in research and writing for most of his 86 years, publishing an astonishing array of books.

Analytical Psychology

A major point of difference between Jung's **analytical psychology** and Freud's psychoanalysis concerns the nature of libido. Whereas Freud defined libido in predominantly sexual terms, Jung regarded it as a generalized life energy, of which sex was only one part. For Jung, this basic libidinal life energy expressed itself in growth and reproduction, and in other activities as well, depending on what was most important for a person at any given time.

ANALYTICAL PSYCHOLOGY: Jung's theory of personality

Jung rejected the Freudian Oedipus complex. He explained a child's attachment to its mother in terms of a dependency need associated with the mother's ability to provide food. As the child matures and develops sexual functioning, this nourishing function becomes overlaid with sexual feelings. Jung suggested that libidinal energy took a heterosexual form only after puberty. He did not deny the existence of sexual forces in childhood, but he reduced the role of sex to one of several drives.

Jung's life experiences undoubtedly influenced his theory. We have already noted how his acceptance of the forces of his unconscious mind predicted his later professional interests. With regard to sex, autobiographical evidence is also strong. Jung had no use for an Oedipus complex in his theory because it was not relevant to his own childhood. He described his mother as fat and unattractive, and he could never understand Freud's insistence that every little boy has a sexual longing for his mother.

Jung developed no adult insecurities, inhibitions, or anxieties about sex, as Freud did, and he made no attempt to limit his sexual activities, as Freud had. Jung had sexual relationships with women patients and disciples, some lasting for years. "To Jung, who freely and frequently satisfied his sexual needs, sex played a minimal role in human motivation. To Freud, beset by frustrations and anxious about his thwarted desires, sex played the central role" (Schultz, 1990, p. 148).

Another basic difference between the work of Jung and Freud is in the direction of the forces that influence the human personality. Freud viewed people as victims of childhood events; Jung believed we are shaped not only by our past, but also by our goals, hopes, and aspirations for the future. Jung proposed that behavior is not fully determined by our experiences during the first 5 years of life but that it can be changed throughout our lifetime.

A third difference between Jung and Freud is that Jung attempted to probe more deeply into the unconscious mind. He added a new dimension: the inherited experiences of humans as a species and those of their animal ancestors (the collective unconscious).

The Collective Unconscious

PERSONAL UNCONSCIOUS: The reservoir of material that was once conscious but has been forgotten or suppressed

Jung described two levels of the unconscious. Just beneath the level of consciousness is the **personal unconscious,** which consists of all the memories, impulses, wishes, faint perceptions, and other experiences in a person's life that have been suppressed or forgotten. This level of unconsciousness is not very deep. Incidents from the personal unconscious can easily be recalled to conscious awareness.

The experiences in the personal unconscious are grouped into complexes, which are patterns of emotions, memories, wishes, and the like with common themes. Complexes are manifested in the individual by a preoccupation with some idea, such as power or inferiority, that will influence behavior. Thus, a complex is essentially a smaller personality that forms within the total personality.

COLLECTIVE UNCONSCIOUS: The deepest level of the psyche containing the inherited experiences of human and prehuman species

Below the personal unconscious is a deeper level, the **collective unconscious,** which is unknown to the individual and which contains the cumulative experiences of previous generations, including our animal ancestors. The collective unconscious consists of universal evolutionary experiences, and it forms the basis of the personality. It is important to note that the experiences within the collective unconscious are, indeed, unconscious; we are not aware of them, nor do we remember them or have images of them, as we do of the experiences in the personal unconscious.

Archetypes

Inherited tendencies within the collective unconscious, called *archetypes,* are innate determinants of mental life that dispose a person to behave in a manner not unlike that of ancestors who confronted similar situations. We experience archetypes in the form of emotions and other mental events. Archetypes are typically associated with such significant life experiences as birth and death, with stages of life such as adolescence, and with reactions to extreme danger.

Jung investigated the mythical and artistic creations of earlier civilizations and uncovered archetypal symbols that were common to all, even in cultures so widely separated in time and place that there was no possibility of direct influence. He also found what he considered to be traces of these symbols in the dreams reported by his patients. All of this material supported his conception of the collective unconscious.

Four of the archetypes seemed to occur more frequently than others: the persona, the anima and animus, the shadow, and the self.

The *persona* is the mask each of us wears when we come in contact with other people; it presents us as we want to appear to society. The persona may not correspond to an individual's true personality. The notion of the persona is similar to the sociological concept of role playing, in which we may act as we think other people expect us to act in different situations.

The archetypes *anima* and *animus* reflect the idea that each person exhibits some of the characteristics of the other sex. The anima refers to feminine characteristics in man; the animus denotes masculine characteristics in woman. As with the other archetypes, these arise from the primitive past of the human species in which men and women each took on some of the behavioral and emotional tendencies of the other sex.

The *shadow* archetype, our darker self, is the most animalistic part of the personality. Jung considered it to be our heritage from lower forms of life. The shadow contains all immoral, passionate, and unacceptable desires and activities. Jung wrote that the shadow urges us to do those things that ordinarily we would not allow ourselves to do. Once having done such a thing, we are apt to insist that something came over us. That "something" is the shadow, the primitive part of our nature. The shadow also has a positive side; it is the source of spontaneity, creativity, insight, and deep emotion, all of which are necessary for full human development.

Jung considered the *self* to be the most important archetype. Balancing all aspects of the unconscious, the self provides unity and stability to the personality. Thus, the self attempts to integrate the different personality systems. Jung likened it to a drive or force toward self-actualization, by which he meant a harmony and completeness of the personality, the full development of the self.

He believed that self-actualization could not be attained until middle age, and he viewed these years (between 35 and 40) as crucial to personality development, a natural time of transition when the personality undergoes necessary and beneficial changes. This belief reveals another autobiographical element in Jung's theory: Middle age was the time in his own life when he achieved the integration of his self, following the resolution of his neurotic crisis. Thus, to Jung, the most important stage in personality development was not childhood, as in Freud's life and system, but middle age, the time of his own personal crisis and resolution.

Introversion and Extraversion

Jung's concepts of introversion and extraversion are well known. The extravert directs libido (life energy) outside the self to external events and people. A person of this type is strongly influenced by forces in the environment and is sociable and self-confident in a range of situations. The libido of the introvert is directed inward. Such a person is contemplative, introspective, and resistant to external influences, less confident in relations with other people and with the external world, and less sociable than the extravert. These opposing attitudes exist in everyone, to some degree, but one attitude is usually stronger than the other; no one is a complete extravert or introvert. The dominant attitude at any given moment can be influenced by the situation. For example, normally introverted people may become sociable and outgoing in situations that hold their interest.

Psychological Types

According to Jung's theory, personality differences are also expressed through four functions—thinking, feeling, sensing, and intuiting—that are ways in which we orient ourselves to both the external objective world and our internal subjective world. Thinking is a conceptual process that provides meaning and understanding. Feeling is a subjective process of weighing and valuing. Sensing is the conscious perception of physical objects. Intuiting involves perceiving in an unconscious way.

Jung considered thinking and feeling to be rational modes of responding, because they involve reason and judgment. Sensing and intuiting are considered nonrational because they do not involve the use of reason. Within each pair of functions, only one is dominant at a given time. The dominant functions combine with the attitude of extraversion or introversion to produce eight **psychological types** (for example, the extraverted thinking type or the introverted intuiting type).

PSYCHOLOGICAL TYPES:
Personality types based on interactions of the attitudes and functions

The Word-Association Test

Jung developed the word-association test after a colleague told him about Wilhelm Wundt's association experiments. In Jung's word-association procedure, the analyst reads a list of words to a patient, one word at a time; the patient responds to each word with the first word that comes to mind. Jung measured the time the patient took to respond to each word, as well as changes in breathing rate and in the electrical conductivity of the skin, all thought to be evidence of emotional reactions. If a particular word produced a long response time, breathing irregularities, and a change in skin conductivity, Jung deduced the existence of an unconscious emotional problem connected with the stimulus word or with the reply.

Jung used the word-association test as a lie detector device, and on two occasions he identified people who were guilty of theft. For many years, scholars believed that Jung was the first to apply the technique to the determination of guilt, but new data of history reveal that the Gestalt psychologist Max Wertheimer published similar findings a few weeks before Jung did (Wertheimer, King, Peckler, Raney, & Schaef, 1992).

Comment

Jung's ideas influenced such diverse fields as religion, history, art, and literature. Many historians, theologians, and writers acknowledge him as a source of inspiration. In general, however, scientific psychology has ignored his analytical psychology. Many of his books were not translated into the English language until the 1960s, and his difficult writing style has impeded a complete understanding of his work. "Jung never wrote the kind of introduction or survey that Freud wrote. There is no one work by him that integrates his many publications into a single whole. Although he wrote copiously, his bent was really strikingly unsystematic" (Kaufmann, 1992, pp. 291–292).

His disdain for traditional scientific methods repels many experimental psychologists, for whom Jung's theories, with their mystical and religious basis, hold even less appeal than Freud's. Further, the criticisms we noted about the supporting evidence for Freud's system of psychoanalysis also apply to Jung's work. Jung, too, relied on clinical observation and interpretation rather than on controlled laboratory investigation.

Jung's eight proposed psychological types have stimulated considerable research. Of particular importance is the *Myers-Briggs Type Indicator,* a personality test designed to measure psychological types. The test was constructed in the 1920s by Katharine Briggs and Isabel Briggs Myers. It has become the most frequently administered personality test and is used for research and applied purposes, especially for employee selection and counseling (Saunders, 1991; Wink, 1993).

The introversion/extraversion formulations inspired the English psychologist Hans Eysenck to develop the *Maudsley Personality Inventory,* a personality test to measure those two attitudes. Research using these tests has provided empirical support for Jung's ideas and demonstrates that at least some of his notions are amenable to experimental testing. As with Freud's work, however, the larger aspects of Jung's theory (such as complexes, the archetypes, and the collective unconscious) resist attempts at scientific validation.

The word-association test has become a standard projective technique and spurred the development of the *Rorschach Inkblot Test*. The concept of self-actualization anticipated the work of Abraham Maslow and the humanistic psychologists. Jung's suggestion that middle age is a crucial time of personality change was embraced by Maslow and Erik Erikson and has been accepted by contemporary personality theorists.

Despite these contributions, the bulk of Jung's work has not been popular within psychology. His ideas enjoyed a burst of public attention in the 1970s and 1980s, largely because of their mystical content.

SOCIAL PSYCHOLOGICAL THEORIES: THE ZEITGEIST STRIKES AGAIN

Sigmund Freud was influenced by the mechanistic and positivistic outlook that pervaded 19th-century science. Toward the end of the 19th century, however, new disciplines were suggesting other ways of viewing human nature, ways that went beyond the approaches of biology and physics. For example, research in anthropology, sociology, and social psychology supported the proposition that humans are products of social forces and institutions, suggesting that human nature should be studied in social rather than strictly biological terms.

As anthropologists publicized their studies of different cultures, it became clear that some of the neurotic symptoms and taboos Freud described were not universal, as he had believed. (For example, not all cultures had prohibitions against incest.) Further, sociologists and social psychologists had found that much human behavior stemmed from social conditioning rather than attempts to satisfy biological needs.

The intellectual spirit of the times, the Zeitgeist, was calling for a revised conception of human nature, but Freud, to the dismay of some of his followers, clung to his emphasis on biological determinants of personality. Younger analysts, less constrained by tradition, drifted away from orthodox psychoanalysis and began to reshape Freudian theory along the lines of the social sciences. Their idea—that personality is more a product of environment than of biology—was compatible with American culture and thought, and it offered a more optimistic picture of human nature than Freud's deterministic position.

We discuss two dissenters who developed social psychological theories: Alfred Adler and Karen Horney. They and others suggest that human behavior is determined not by biological forces but by the interpersonal relationships to which the person is exposed, particularly in childhood.

ALFRED ADLER (1870–1937)

Adler is usually considered the first proponent of the social psychological form of psychoanalysis because he broke with Freud in 1911. He developed a theory in which social interest plays a major role, and he is the only psychologist to have a string quartet named after him.

Adler's Life

Alfred Adler was born to wealthy parents in a suburb of Vienna, Austria. His childhood was marked by illness, jealousy of an older brother, and rejection by his mother. He thought of himself as puny and unattractive. Adler felt closer to his father than to his mother, and perhaps, like Jung, later rejected the Freudian concept of the Oedipus complex because it did not reflect his own childhood experiences. As a child, Adler worked intently to become popular with his peers, and as he grew older, he achieved a sense of self-esteem and acceptance from others that he had not found within his family.

Initially Adler was a poor student, so inept that a teacher told his father the only job the boy was fit for was shoemaker's apprentice. Through persistence and dedication, Adler rose from the bottom to the top of his class. He strove both academically and socially to overcome his handicaps and inferiorities; thus, he became a textbook example of his adult theory of the necessity of compensating for one's weaknesses. Inferiority feelings, which form the core of his system, are a direct reflection of his childhood, a debt Adler freely acknowledged.

At the age of 4, while recovering from a near-fatal bout with pneumonia, Adler decided to become a physician. He received his medical degree from the University of Vienna in 1895. After specializing in ophthalmology and practicing general medicine, he went into psychiatry. In 1902 he joined Sigmund Freud's weekly discussion group on psychoanalysis, as one of four charter members. Although he worked closely with Freud, their relationship was not a personal one. Freud once said that Adler bored him.

Over the next several years Adler developed a theory of personality that was different from Freud's in several ways, and he openly criticized Freud's emphasis on sexual factors. In 1910 Freud named Adler president of the Vienna Psychoanalytic Society, to reconcile their growing differences, but by 1911 their inevitable split was complete. The parting was bitter. Adler described Freud as a swindler and called psychoanalysis "filth" (Roazen, 1975, p. 210). Freud referred to Adler as "abnormal" and "driven mad by ambition" (Gay, 1988, p. 223).

Adler served as a physician in the Austrian army during World War I and later organized child guidance clinics in the Vienna school system. During the 1920s his social psychological system, which he called **individual psychology,** attracted many followers. In 1926 Adler made the first of several visits to the United States, and 8 years later was appointed professor of medical psychology at the Long

Archives of the History of American Psychology/University of Akron

ALFRED ADLER

INDIVIDUAL PSYCHOLOGY:

Adler's theory of personality

Island College of Medicine in New York. He died in Aberdeen, Scotland, while on a strenuous lecture tour.

Freud, replying to a letter from a friend who expressed sadness at Adler's death, wrote, "I don't understand your sympathy for Adler. For a Jewish boy out of a Viennese suburb a death in Aberdeen is an unheard-of career in itself and a proof of how far he had got on. The world really rewarded him richly for his service in having contradicted psychoanalysis" (quoted in Scarf, 1971, p. 47).

Individual Psychology

Social Interest: The innate human potential to cooperate with other people to achieve personal and societal goals

Adler believed that human behavior is determined not by biological forces but by social forces. He proposed that **social interest,** defined as an innate potential to cooperate with others to achieve personal and societal goals, develops, through learning experiences, in infancy. In contrast to Freud, Adler minimized the role of sex in shaping personality and focused on conscious rather than unconscious determinants of behavior. Whereas Freud stressed that human behavior was determined by past experiences, Adler believed we are more strongly affected by what we think the future holds. Striving for goals or anticipating future events can influence our present behavior. For example, a person who lives in fear of eternal damnation after death will behave differently from a person who does not have that expectation.

Freud divided the personality into separate parts (id, ego, and superego), but Adler emphasized the unity and consistency of the personality. He posited a single dynamic driving force that channels the resources of the personality toward one overriding goal. This goal, for which we all strive, is superiority, or perfection, and it encompasses the complete development, fulfillment, and realization of the self. Adler believed that this striving for superiority, for the betterment of the self, is innate and is evident in every aspect of the personality.

Inferiority Feelings

Adler did not agree with Freud's contention that the primary basis of motivation is sex. Instead, he proposed that a generalized feeling of inferiority is the determining force in behavior, as it was in his own life. Initially Adler related this feeling of inferiority to defective parts of the body. The child with a hereditary organic weakness will attempt to compensate for the defect, overemphasizing the deficient function. A child who stutters may, through speech therapy, become a great orator; a child with weak limbs may, through intensive exercise, excel as an athlete or a dancer.

Adler later broadened this concept to include any physical, mental, or social handicap, real or imagined. He also believed that an infant's smallness, helplessness, and dependence on its environment produced a sense of inferiority, a feeling experienced by everyone. Consciously aware of this inferiority and the need to overcome it, the child is also driven by the innate striving for superiority or perfection. This pushing and pulling process continues throughout life, propelling an individual toward ever greater accomplishments.

Inferiority feelings also operate to the advantage of both the individual and society, because they lead to continuous improvement. But if in childhood these feelings are met with excessive pampering or with rejection, the result can be abnormal compensatory behaviors. Failure to compensate adequately for inferiority feelings can lead to the development of an **inferiority complex,** which renders the person incapable of coping with life's problems.

INFERIORITY COMPLEX: A condition that develops when a person is unable to compensate for normal inferiority feelings

Style of Life

According to Adler, the human striving for superiority is universal, but there are various behaviors by which each of us may reach for that goal. We demonstrate our striving in different ways and develop a unique or characteristic mode of responding, what Adler called a style of life. This style of life involves the behaviors by which we compensate for real or imagined inferiority. In the example of the child with the weakened body, the style of life includes those activities, such as exercise or practice at sports, that will result in increased physical strength and stamina.

Formed at the age of 4 or 5, the style of life becomes fixed and difficult to change thereafter, and it provides the framework within which all later experiences are handled. Again we see that Adler recognized the importance of the early years of life, but he differed from Freud in his belief that we consciously create our own style—our own self.

The Creative Power of the Self

Adler's concept of the creative power of the self is the pinnacle of his theory. He suggested we have the capacity to determine our own personality in accordance with our unique style of life. This creative power represents an active principle of human existence that may be likened to the notion of soul. Certain abilities and experiences come to us through our heredity and our environment, but it is the way we actively use and interpret these experiences that provides the basis for our attitude toward life. This means we are consciously involved in shaping our personality and destiny. Adler wrote that we can determine our fate, rather than having it determined for us by past experience.

Birth Order

In examining the childhoods of his patients, Adler became interested in the relationship between personality and order of birth. He found that the oldest, middle, and youngest child, because of their positions in the family, have different social experiences that result in different personalities. The oldest child receives a great deal of attention until dethroned by the birth of the second child. The first-born may then become insecure and hostile, authoritarian and conservative, with a strong interest in maintaining order. Adler suggested that criminals, neurotics, and perverts are often first-born children. (Sigmund Freud was a first-born.)

Adler found the second child to be ambitious, rebellious, and jealous, constantly striving to surpass the first-born. (Adler was a second-born and had a lifelong competitive relationship with his older brother, whose name was Sigmund.) Adler considered the second-born to be better adjusted than the first-born or the youngest child. He believed the youngest child in the family to be spoiled and the one most likely to have behavior problems in childhood and adulthood.

Comment

Adler's theories were warmly received by those who were dissatisfied with Freud's image of human beings as dominated by sexual forces and governed by childhood experiences. It is certainly more pleasant to think we can consciously direct our own development, regardless of genetic limitations or childhood events. Adler presented a satisfying and optimistic view of human nature.

His individual psychology does not lack critics. Many psychologists claim that his theories are superficial and rely on commonsense observations from everyday life, although others consider his ideas to be shrewd and insightful. Freud said that Adler's system was too simple. It could take 2 years to learn psychoanalysis because of its complexity, but Adler's ideas could be "learned in two weeks because with Adler there is so little to know" (quoted in Sterba, 1982, p. 156). Adler said that was precisely his point; it had taken him 40 years to make his psychology simple!

The criticisms directed by experimental psychology toward Freud and Jung also apply to Adler. His observations of his patients cannot be repeated or verified, nor were they obtained in controlled and systematic fashion. He did not attempt to confirm the accuracy of his patients' reports, and, like Freud and Jung, he did not explain the procedures by which he analyzed his data and reached his conclusions.

Although many of his concepts resist attempts at scientific validation, the notion of birth order has been the subject of considerable research. For example, studies show that first-borns are high in intelligence and in the need for achievement and tend to experience anxiety when dethroned by the arrival of a second child. Further research suggests that our early memories of childhood give some indication of our adult style of life (Davidow & Bruhn, 1990).

Adler's influence on post-Freudian psychoanalysis has been substantial. The work of the ego psychologists, which focuses more on conscious and rational processes than on the unconscious, follows Adler's lead. His emphasis on social forces in personality is seen in the work of Karen Horney, and his focus on the unity of personality is reflected in the theory of Gordon Allport.

The creative power of the self to shape one's style of life influenced the thinking of Abraham Maslow. And Adler's stress on social variables influenced the work of the neo-neobehavioral social learning theorist Julian Rotter. Indeed, Adler may have been far ahead of his time with his emphases on social and cognitive variables, ideas that are more compatible with contemporary psychology than they were with the psychology of his own day.

KAREN HORNEY (1885-1952)

Horney, an early feminist, was trained as a Freudian psychoanalyst in Berlin. She described her work as an extension of Freud's system rather than an effort to supplant it.

Horney's Life

Karen Horney was born in Hamburg, Germany. Her father was a devout, morose ship's captain many years older than her mother, a liberal and vivacious woman. Her mother made it clear to Karen that she wished her husband was dead; she had married him only out of fear of remaining a spinster (Sayers, 1991). Horney's childhood was not ideal. Her mother rejected her in favor of an older brother (whom Karen envied for being a boy), and her father frequently belittled her appearance and intelligence, making her feel inferior, worthless, and hostile. This lack of parental love fostered what she later called basic anxiety, and it provides another instance of the impact of personal experience on a theorist's views of personality development.

Beginning at the age of 14, Horney experienced a series of adolescent crushes as part of her increasingly frantic search for the love and acceptance she could not find at home. She started a newspaper she called "a virginal organ for supervirgins" and took to walking the streets frequented by prostitutes. "In my imagination," she confided to her diary, "there is no spot on me that has not been kissed by a burning mouth. In my imagination there is no depravity I have not tasted, to the dregs" (Horney, 1980, p. 64).

National Library of Medicine

KAREN HORNEY

In spite of opposition from her father, Horney entered medical school at the University of Berlin and received her MD in 1913. She married, gave birth to three daughters, and endured a long period of emotional distress. She felt overwhelmingly unhappy and oppressed, suffered stomach pains, had sexual difficulties with her husband, and engaged in several affairs. She divorced her husband in 1927 and continued her restless quest for acceptance for the rest of her life.

Her longest and most ardent affair was with the psychoanalyst Erich Fromm (1900–1980), and she was devastated when the relationship ended. She underwent psychoanalysis to deal with her depression and sexual problems and was told by her Freudian analyst that her search for love and attraction to forceful men reflected childhood Oedipal longings for her powerful father (Sayers, 1991).

From 1914 to 1918 Horney took orthodox psychoanalytic training at the Berlin Psychoanalytic Institute. Later she became a faculty member at the institute and began a private practice. She wrote a number of journal articles about problems of the female personality, in which she outlined her disagreement with certain Freudian concepts. In 1932 she came to the United States as associate director of the Chicago Institute for Psychoanalysis. She continued to see patients and taught at the New York Psychoanalytic Institute, but a growing disaffection with orthodox Freudian theory led her to break with this group. She founded the American Institute of Psychoanalysis and remained its head until her death.

Disagreements With Freud

Horney did not agree with Freud that personality depends on unchangeable biological forces. She denied the preeminent position of sexual factors, challenged the validity of the Oedipal theory, and discarded the concepts of libido and the Freudian structure of personality. Opposed to Freud's belief that women are motivated by penis envy, Horney argued that men are motivated by womb envy, that they envy women for their ability to give birth. She believed that this womb envy and its accompanying resentment are manifested unconsciously in men through behaviors designed to harass and belittle women, to maintain their allegedly inferior status. By denying women equal rights, limiting their opportunities, and downgrading their efforts to achieve, men attempt to retain an alleged natural superiority. To Horney, the fundamental reason for such masculine behavior is a sense of inferiority resulting from womb envy.

Horney and Freud also differed in their views of human nature. Horney wrote: "Freud's pessimism as regards neuroses and their treatment arose from the depths of his disbelief in human goodness and human growth. Man, he postulated, is doomed to suffer or to destroy. . . . My own belief is that man has the capacity as well as the desire to develop his potentialities and become a decent human being. . . . I believe that man can change and go on changing as long as he lives" (Horney, 1945, p. 19).

Although Horney rejected much of Freud's system, she did accept unconscious motivation and the existence of emotional, nonrational motives.

Basic Anxiety

The fundamental concept in Horney's theory is **basic anxiety,** defined as "the feeling a child has of being isolated and helpless in a potentially hostile world" (Horney, 1945, p. 41). This definition characterizes her own feelings as a child. Basic anxiety results from various parental actions toward the child, including dominance, lack of protection, lack of love, and erratic behavior. Anything that disturbs the secure relationship between the child and the parents can produce basic anxiety. Thus, basic anxiety is not innate but results from social forces in the child's environment.

BASIC ANXIETY: Pervasive feelings of loneliness and helplessness; in Horney's system, these feelings are the foundation of neuroses

In place of Freud's instincts as major motivating forces, Horney believed that the helpless infant was seeking security in a threatening world. She proposed that the basic human motivation is the need for safety and freedom from fear.

Horney shared with Freud a belief that personality develops in early childhood, but she maintained that personality could change throughout life. Where Freud detailed psychosexual stages of development, Horney focused on the way the growing child is treated by the parents or caregivers. She denied universal developmental phases, such as oral or anal stages, and suggested that if a child developed any such tendencies, they were a result of parental behaviors. Nothing in a child's development was universal; everything depended on cultural, social, and environmental factors.

Neurotic Needs

Basic anxiety arises from the parent-child relationship. When this socially or environmentally produced anxiety appears, the child develops behavioral strategies to deal with the resulting feelings of helplessness and insecurity, as a response to the parents' behaviors. If any of the child's behavioral strategies becomes a fixed part of the personality, it is called a *neurotic need,* a mode of defense against anxiety. Horney listed 10 neurotic needs, including the needs for affection, personal achievement, and self-sufficiency.

In later writings she grouped the neurotic needs into three trends:

1. the compliant personality, who needs to move toward other people, expressing the needs for approval and affection and for a dominant partner;

2. the detached personality, who needs to move away from people, expressing the needs for independence and perfection and a withdrawn view of life;

3. the aggressive personality, who needs to move against people, expressing the needs for power, exploitation, prestige, admiration, and achievement.

Movement toward people implies an acceptance of helplessness and an attempt to win the affection of others; this is the only way the person can feel secure with other people. Movement away from people involves withdrawing, to appear self-sufficient and to avoid dependency. Movement against people involves hostility, rebellion, and aggression.

None of these responses is a realistic way to deal with anxiety. The needs can give rise to conflicts because of their incompatibility. Once we establish a behavioral strategy for coping with basic anxiety, it ceases to be flexible enough to permit alternative behaviors. When a fixed behavior proves to be inappropriate for a particular situation, we are unable to change in response to the situation's demands. These entrenched behaviors intensify our difficulties because they affect the total personality—our relations with other people, with ourselves, and with life as a whole (Horney, 1945).

The Idealized Self-Image

The idealized self-image provides a false picture of the personality. It is an imperfect and misleading mask that prevents neurotic persons from understanding and accepting their true selves. In donning the mask, neurotics deny the existence of their inner conflicts. Neurotics see the idealized self-images as genuine, and those images enable them to believe they are superior to the people they truly are.

Horney did not think neurotic conflicts were innate or inevitable, however. She suggested that they arose from undesirable situations in childhood. Neuroses could be prevented if the child's home life was full of warmth, understanding, security, and love.

Comment

Horney's optimism about the possibility of avoiding neurotic conflicts was welcomed by psychologists and psychiatrists as a relief from the pessimism of Freud's theory. In addition, her work is noteworthy because she described the development of personality in terms of social forces, attributing little if anything to innate factors.

The evidence to support Horney's theory, like that of Freud, Jung, and Adler, is taken from clinical observations of patients and thus is subject to the questions of scientific credibility noted previously. Little research has been conducted on the concepts in her system. Although

Freud did not comment directly on Horney's work, he once said of her, "she is able but malicious" (quoted in Blanton, 1971, p. 65).

Although Horney did not have a loyal band of disciples or a journal in which to disseminate her ideas, her work has had considerable impact. The Karen Horney Clinic and the Karen Horney Psychoanalytic Institute (a training center for analysts) are both active in New York City. With the feminist movement that began in the 1960s, her books have enjoyed renewed popularity. It is her writings on feminine psychology that today are considered her major contribution.

Horney was an early and ardent feminist, and many of her positions, stated more than 60 years ago, have a strong contemporary ring. She began work on her feminine psychology early in 1922 and was the first woman to present a paper on the topic at an international psychoanalytic congress. That meeting, held in Berlin, was chaired by Sigmund Freud (O'Connell, 1990).

In the 1930s Horney drew a distinction between the traditional woman, who seeks her identity through marriage and motherhood, and the modern woman, who seeks her identity through a career. This conflict between love and work, as she saw it, characterized her own life. Horney focused on work, which brought enormous satisfaction, but continued to search for love. Her dilemma is as relevant in the 1990s as it was to her in the 1930s, and she fought vigorously for women to have the right to choose, to make their own decisions in the face of restrictions imposed by a male-dominated society.

THE DESCENDANTS

Freudian psychoanalytic theory did not long remain the sole approach to explaining the human personality. The changes introduced by the neo-Freudian loyalists, by Jung, and by the social psychological theorists represent some of the alternatives developed during Freud's lifetime. The area of personality theory and research has since grown immensely and has splintered into more conflicting viewpoints. Contemporary textbooks typically discuss 15 to 20 theories. Although these approaches differ in both specifics and generalities, they have a common heritage. All owe their origin and form, in varying degrees, to the founding efforts of Sigmund Freud.

Freud served the same purpose on the psychoanalytic side of the history of psychology that Wilhelm Wundt served on the experimental side, as a source of inspiration as well as a force to oppose. Every structure, actual and theoretical, depends on the soundness of its foundation, and Freud, like Wundt, provided a solid and challenging base on which to build.

As examples of the evolution in personality theory since the time of Freud, we note the works of three descendants: Allport, Murray, and Erikson.

GORDON ALLPORT (1897–1967)

Over the course of a long and productive career at Harvard University, Gordon Allport, more than anyone else, made the study of personality academically respectable. Personality was not formally considered to be part of psychology until he published *Personality: A Psychological Interpretation* in 1937. Never psychoanalyzed or in private practice himself, Allport took the study of personality out of the clinical setting and brought it into the university.

GORDON ALLPORT

Allport's Life

As a child, Allport felt isolated and rejected by other children, but his home life was happy and marked by affection and trust. Unlike Freud and the early post-Freudians, Allport does not seem to have had any noteworthy or traumatic childhood experiences that bear directly on his adult view of personality. Perhaps that is why he chose to approach the field from an intellectual and academic standpoint, rather than from a more personal one.

Between his undergraduate and graduate school years at Harvard, Allport took time off to travel. In Vienna he visited Freud, an event that did have an impact on his approach to personality. Ushered into the great man's office, young Allport could think of nothing to say. Freud sat still, looking at him, waiting for him to start the conversation. Finally Allport blurted out an account of an incident he had witnessed involving a boy with an obvious and extreme fear of dirt. When Allport finished the story, Freud stared in silence for a moment and then asked, "Was that little boy you?"

Freud was expressing his belief that Allport was revealing his own inner conflicts by telling this story (Allport, 1968). Freud's question may have been insightful. "Allport was indeed a person who was neat, meticulous, orderly and punctual—possessing many of the characteristics associated by Freud with the compulsive personality" (Pervin, 1984, p. 267).

Allport was shaken by Freud's question. Years later he wrote, "My single encounter with Freud was traumatic" (Allport, 1967, p. 22). He suspected that psychoanalysis focused too greatly on unconscious forces and motives, to the neglect of conscious motives, and he went on to fashion a view of personality that differed from Freud's.

Allport minimized the role of the unconscious in mentally healthy adults, arguing that they function in more rational and conscious terms. Only neurotic persons, Allport said, are significantly influenced by their unconscious minds. He also disagreed with Freud about the impact of childhood experiences on conflicts in adult life, insisting that we are influenced much more by present experiences and by plans for the future than we are by the past.

Another major difference is Allport's conviction that the only way to investigate personality is to study normal adults, not neurotic adults. He did not believe there was a continuum between normal and neurotic behavior. Allport argued there were no similarities between normal and neurotic persons, and thus there was no basis for comparison. He emphasized the uniqueness of each individual personality and did not propose universal laws that could be applied to everyone.

Personality and Motivation

To Allport, the core of personality theory is its treatment of motivation. To explain motivation in the normal adult he proposed the concept of **functional autonomy,** the idea that a motive is not functionally related to any childhood experience. Human motives are independent of the original circumstances in which they appeared. An analogy can be made with a tree, which, in a sense, becomes self-determining; that is, the tree becomes independent of its origin, no longer functionally related to the seed from which it grew. Similarly, the adult human being becomes self-determining, independent of childhood experiences.

FUNCTIONAL AUTONOMY:
Allport's idea that adult motives are independent of childhood experiences

For example, when we begin our careers, we work hard, motivated perhaps to attain the goals of money and job security. Years later, when we have become successful and financially secure, we may continue to work hard, but for other reasons, because our original goals have been reached. Adult motivation, in Allport's view, cannot be traced to childhood but can be understood only in terms of our present behavior and intentions.

Allport's term for the self is the *proprium,* which is used in the sense of being appropriate. The self is what belongs to or is appropriate for each of us. It includes everything that is unique about us, and it is an important and conscious aspect of the personality. The proprium develops through seven stages from infancy to adolescence. These developmental stages are not psychosexual, nor do they involve Freudian conflicts centered on erogenous zones of the body. Instead, social relationships, particularly those with the mother, are crucial in the development of the proprium.

Allport's study of the traits of personality, the first undertaken in the United States, began with his doctoral dissertation. He distinguished between traits, which can be shared by any number of people, and personal dispositions, which are the traits unique to each person. Both can be inferred by observing behavior over a period of time, looking for consistencies and regularities.

Allport discussed three kinds of traits:

1. cardinal traits, which are ruling passions that dominate every aspect of life;

2.   central traits, which are behavioral themes, such as aggressiveness or sentimentality;

3.   secondary traits, which are behaviors displayed less frequently and consistently than the other traits.

Comment

Although Allport's theory has been influential in psychology, it has not inspired a great deal of research, because of the difficulty in translating his concepts into specific propositions that can be tested under laboratory conditions. Allport's own most notable research dealt with expressive behavior, the facial expressions, vocal inflections, gestures, and mannerisms that tend to reveal, to a trained observer, various facets of personality.

Allport's emphasis on the uniqueness of personality and on the importance of a person's goals and expectations influenced Abraham Maslow, Carl Rogers, and the humanistic school of thought. Allport's work on personality traits has become increasingly recognized as part of a renewal of interest in this topic. His ideas "look remarkably sound . . . and yield a large number of implications for conceptualizations and research in modern personality psychology" (Funder, 1991, p. 32).

Allport's books are written in a clear, readable style and his concepts are easy to understand. He developed a psychological test, the *Study of Values,* to measure the values and beliefs an individual holds. The test is considered to be a successful assessment device for research, counseling, and employee selection. Allport received the Gold Medal Award from the American Psychological Foundation and the Distinguished Scientific Contribution Award from the American Psychological Association; he was also elected president of the APA.

HENRY MURRAY (1893–1988)

PERSONOLOGY: Murray's theory of personality

Allport's personality theory was a complete rejection of Freudian psychoanalysis, but Murray's system, which he called **personology,** built on Freud's work. Like Allport, Murray chose to study personality in a university setting rather than in a clinic. Although he underwent psychoanalysis himself (and said that his analyst became bored), he did not maintain a private practice. He preferred to investigate the human personality through the intensive study of normal subjects at Harvard University. He believed that psychoanalysis was the only approach to psychology that dealt with the complexity of human behavior, and he urged that it be taught in the standard psychology curriculum (Triplet, 1992).

Murray's Life

Murray's childhood was distinguished by several events: His mother rejected him, which he believed led to lifelong bouts of depression; he developed an unusual sensitivity to the sufferings of others; and he applied Adlerian compensation to his physical defects (stuttering and ineptness at sports).

After graduating from Columbia University medical school, he completed an internship in surgery, and then earned a PhD in biochemistry from Cambridge University in England—certainly a circuitous route to becoming a psychologist. He had ample leisure time to pursue his diverse interests, thanks to a large inheritance and his marriage to an heiress to the DuPont fortune.

Murray had taken only one psychology course in college and reported that by the second lecture he was looking for the nearest exit. (The professor was Hugo Münsterberg.) The next psychology course he attended was the one he taught years later. He came to psychology because of a personal crisis: He fell in love with a young married woman, Christiana Morgan, but did not want to leave his wife. At Morgan's insistence, Murray went to Zurich to consult with Carl Jung.

At the time, Jung was also having an affair with a younger woman, which he maintained openly while living with his wife and family. He advised Murray to do the same, and Murray did so for 40 years. Not only did Jung resolve Murray's personal dilemma, he also steered Murray toward a career in psychology. Jung showed him that psychology—particularly the study of the unconscious—could provide answers to life's problems.

In 1927 Murray joined the new Harvard Psychological Clinic, which was formed specifically to study personality. He remained at Harvard for the rest of his career, except for the years 1941–1945, during World War II, when he established an assessment program for the Office of Strategic Services (a forerunner of the CIA). That program, in which candidates were observed in stressful real-life situations, evolved into the assessment-center approach to executive selection now widely used in business and government.

HENRY MURRAY

Personology

Given Murray's training in medicine and biochemistry, it is not surprising that he chose to emphasize physiological functioning in his theory of the human personality. He stressed the concept of tension reduction, which he considered to be the primary law of human behavior, much as Freud did. Also in the Freudian tradition, Murray noted the importance of the unconscious and the impact of childhood experiences on adult behavior. His system incorporated the id, ego, and superego, although with some modification of the orthodox Freudian position (Murray, 1938).

The id contains innate, impulsive tendencies and provides energy for the operation of the personality, a view virtually identical to Freud's. However, in addition to primitive and lustful impulses, the id in Murray's system contains socially desirable tendencies, such as empathy, identification, and love. Although parts of the id must be suppressed for normal development to occur, other parts must be allowed full expression. We see here the influence of Jung's concept of the shadow archetype, which also contained desirable and undesirable qualities.

In Murray's system, as in the work of the neo-Freudian ego psychologists, the ego assumes an active role in determining behavior. Murray believed that the ego is not merely the servant of the id but is also a conscious organizer of behavior. The ego acts to suppress undesirable id impulses and to facilitate the expression of desirable id impulses.

Murray agreed with Freud that the superego represents the internalization of cultural values and that individuals judge their behavior in terms of those values. He disagreed with Freud about the forces that shape the superego. Murray argued that the superego is influenced not only by the teachings of one's parents but also by one's peer group and by society's literature and mythology. The superego is not fixed by the age of 5 but continues to develop throughout life.

Motivation is central to Murray's personality theory. His classification of needs to explain motivation is his most significant contribution to psychology. Needs involve a chemical force in the brain that organizes intellectual and perceptual functioning. Needs arouse tension levels within the body, which can be reduced only by satisfying the needs. Thus, needs activate behavior, directing it in whatever ways are necessary to bring about satisfaction and tension reduction. Murray's research identified 20 needs, such as achievement, affiliation, aggression, autonomy, and dominance.

Like Freud, Murray believed that personality develops through a series of childhood stages. Each stage is marked by some condition that brings pleasure, and each leaves its imprint on the personality in the form of a complex, which is a normal behavior pattern that unconsciously affects the person's later development. The pleasurable conditions of childhood and their complexes are similar to some of Freud's psychosexual stages of development:

1. the claustral complex—the secure existence within the womb;

2. the oral complex—the sensuous enjoyment of sucking nourishment while being held;

3.   the anal complex—the pleasure resulting from defecation;

4.   the urethral complex—the pleasure accompanying urination;

5.   the genital complex—genital pleasures.

According to Murray, everyone passes through these same developmental stages. There was nothing abnormal about the complexes, except when manifested in the extreme.

The Thematic Apperception Test

Murray's classification of needs was the basis of his *Thematic Apperception Test* (TAT), which he developed with Christiana Morgan. For many years it was assumed the TAT was primarily Murray's work and that Morgan was the junior author. In 1985, Murray wrote that she had the "main role" in developing the test and noted that the original idea for the test had come from a woman student in one of his classes (Bronstein, 1988, p. 64).

The concept of the projective technique derives from Freud's defense mechanism of projection, in which a person attributes a disturbing impulse to someone else. In the TAT, the person creates a story about the people shown in an ambiguous picture and projects those impulses onto the figures depicted. The TAT is widely used in personality research and assessment and has been applied to clinical diagnosis and employee selection.

Comment

Murray's theory has generated considerable research on needs and on his techniques of personality assessment. Much of that research supports his ideas, especially the needs for affiliation and achievement. There is little scientific support for other aspects of his theory. In recognition of his contributions to the study of personality, Murray received the Gold Medal Award of the American Psychological Foundation and the Distinguished Scientific Contribution Award of the American Psychological Association.

ERIK ERIKSON (1902–1994)

Erikson was trained in orthodox psychoanalysis by Anna Freud. He developed a popular approach to personality that retained much of the psychoanalytic system while extending it in several ways. Erikson elaborated on the stages of development, argued that personality continued to grow throughout life, and recognized the impact of cultural, historical, and social forces.

Erik Erikson

Archives of the History of American Psychology/University of Akron

Identity Crisis: In Erikson's system, the failure in adolescence to achieve an ego identity (the integration of our ideas of what we are and what we want to be)

Psychosocial Stages: Eight developmental stages encompassing the life span; at each stage, the person copes with a crisis in an adaptive or a maladaptive way

Erikson's Life

Erik Erikson is well known for his concept of the **identity crisis,** an idea that arose from personal crises in his early years. "My best friends will insist," he wrote, "that I needed to name this crisis and see it in everybody else in order to really come to terms with it in myself" (Erikson, 1975, pp. 25–26). The first crisis involved his name. For many years he believed his last name was Homburger, the name of the stepfather whom Erikson believed was his natural father. He changed his name from Homburger to Erikson at age 39, when he became a United States citizen.

The second crisis of identity occurred during his school years in Germany. Erikson considered himself to be German, but his classmates rejected him because he was Jewish. At the same time, his Jewish classmates shunned him because of his blond Aryan appearance.

The third crisis occurred after his high school graduation. He dropped out of society and for several years wandered about Europe seeking his identity. When he was 25, he got a job teaching at a small school in Vienna that had been established for the children of Sigmund Freud's patients and friends. He trained in psychoanalysis and announced that he had found both a personal and a professional identity. Although he had no formal academic education beyond high school, Erikson eventually taught at Harvard and became one of the most influential psychoanalysts of modern times.

Psychosocial Stages of Development

Erikson's theory takes a developmental or life-span approach; that is, he focuses on personality growth over the individual's entire life, from birth to old age. His central theme in the development of personality is the search for an ego identity.

Erikson divided the life span into eight **psychosocial stages** of development, each of which involves a conflict or crisis that must be resolved. These conflicts arise in each developmental stage because the social and physical environments make new demands. The person is faced with a choice between two ways of coping, an adaptive way or a maladaptive way. Only when the crisis at each stage has been resolved, and the personality has changed, is the person prepared to deal with the next stage of development.

The first four stages Erikson proposed are similar to Freud's oral, anal, and phallic stages and the latency period, although Erikson emphasized social rather than biological and sexual factors. The last four developmental stages are unique to Erikson's system. They carry the individual from adolescence through old age, a period largely ignored by Freud.

Each of these stages of growth, although stressful enough to be labeled a crisis, can have a positive outcome if it is resolved in an adaptive way. If we fail at any one stage and are left with a maladaptive way of responding, that situation can be corrected by successful adaptation at a later stage of development. Thus, at all stages of personality growth, we can be hopeful about future outcomes.

Erikson proposed that we consciously direct our own growth at each stage of psychosocial development. This idea opposes Freud's view that we are products of childhood experiences and are unable to change our personalities later in life. Although Erikson recognized that childhood influences are important and can even be harmful, he argued that events at later stages can counteract or overcome negative childhood events and contribute to our ultimate goal: establishing a positive ego identity.

The Identity Crisis

The question of ego identity must be resolved during the stage of adolescence (approximately ages 12 to 18). This is a time of consolidation, when a person must shape an appropriate self-image that provides a continuity with the past and an orientation for the future. To Erikson, forming and accepting an identity is a difficult, anxiety-producing process. The adolescent must experiment with different roles and ideologies to determine the best fit.

People who achieve a strong sense of identity are equipped to deal with the problems of adulthood. Those who fail to achieve an identity are said to be experiencing an identity crisis. They may withdraw from the normal life sequence (education, job, marriage), as Erikson himself did for a time, and perhaps seek a negative identity in socially unacceptable behaviors such as drug addiction or crime.

Male-Female Personality Differences

A controversial aspect of Erikson's work is his argument that personality differences between the sexes are biologically based and arise from the presence or absence of a penis. He drew this conclusion not only from his agreement with Freud's work about male-female personality differences, but also from his research with children, notably a study in which boys and girls ages 10 to 12 constructed scenes out of toy figures and wooden blocks (Erikson, 1968).

The girls' constructions were low, static structures into which animals and male figures tried to force their way. The boys' constructions were action oriented and featured tall, towering structures (see Figure 14.1). Erikson interpreted these play constructions to mean that girls and boys were symbolically expressing their genitals. He conceded, however, that the differences could be the result of sex-role training in which boys are taught to be more aggressive than girls.

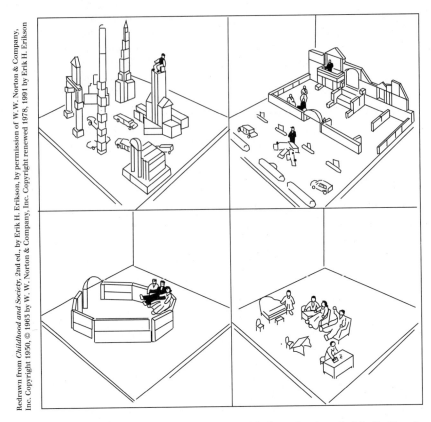

FIGURE 14.1   Play constructions created by boys (top) and girls (bottom).

Comment

Considerable research has been conducted on Erikson's concept of ego identity. In general, studies show that adolescents who developed a strong, positive identity had coped in an adaptive way with the crises of the earlier developmental stages. Adolescents who developed a weak ego identity had resolved the crises in a maladaptive way. These and similar findings support Erikson's predictions. Some research suggests that the identity crisis may occur later than Erikson proposed. One researcher found that the identity crisis begins late in adolescence and that up to 30% of the subjects were still searching for an identity at age 24 (Archer, 1982). Other findings indicate that adolescents who take full-time jobs after high school graduation are apt to achieve ego identity sooner than those who attend college; the college years may delay the formation of ego identity.

There is also a great deal of research support for the childhood stages of psychosocial development. Less attention has been paid to maturity, the final developmental stage, and critics charged that

Erikson had little to say about it himself. He responded to this criticism in 1986, at age 84, in his book, *Vital Involvement in Old Age* (Erikson, Erikson, & Kivnick, 1986), which shows his own vitality during his later years in continuing to develop and apply his theory.

Erikson's work has been influential in psychoanalysis, education, social work, vocational counseling, and marriage counseling. The growth in the field of life-span developmental psychology and the current interest in developmental problems of middle age and old age are direct outgrowths of his ideas. His books remain popular and his photograph appeared on the covers of *Newsweek* and the *New York Times Magazine,* unusual recognition for a psychologist.

THE PSYCHOANALYTIC TRADITION TODAY

We have described the divisions and the diversity within the psychoanalytic school during and after Freud's lifetime. Some contemporary positions bear little resemblance to Freud's views and may be labeled psychoanalytic only by default, to distinguish them from the behavioral/experimental tradition within psychology.

Psychoanalysis was left more fragmented by its revisionist developmental stages than was behaviorism. Despite the changes introduced by neobehaviorists and neo-neobehaviorists, all shared John B. Watson's belief that behavior, in some form, should remain a focus of study. In contrast, not all, or even most, of Freud's followers agreed that the focus of their study should be unconscious or biological forces, or that the motivators of human behavior are sex and aggression.

There are today many more subschools of psychoanalysis than of behaviorism. This multitude of viewpoints may be considered a sign of strength and vitality or of weakness and failing. At present these developments are too recent to judge. They are still history in the making. However, their number and diversity testify to the current importance of the approach begun by Sigmund Freud a century ago.

DISCUSSION QUESTIONS

1. Describe the changes the neo-Freudians made in Freud's system of psychoanalysis. Describe Anna Freud's approach to psychoanalysis. How did the changing Zeitgeist in the social sciences influence the development of psychoanalysis?
2. In what ways did Jung's life experiences influence his analytical psychology? Describe the Jungian concepts of the collective unconscious and the archetypes.

3. Discuss the issues on which Adler and Freud disagreed. Describe Adler's views on inferiority feelings, style of life, and birth order. What criticisms have been made of Adler's individual psychology?

4. Describe Horney's work on feminine psychology. Contrast her views on this topic with those of Freud. Explain the roles of basic anxiety and the idealized self-image.

5. How did Allport's view of personality differ from Freud's view? Define the following concepts: functional autonomy, proprium, and cardinal traits. How did Allport's work affect the academic acceptance of personality as a topic of study?

6. Describe the differences between Murray's conceptions and Freud's conceptions of the id, ego, and superego. What role does physiology play in Murray's system? What is the claustral complex? What is the urethral complex?

7. Compare Erikson's views with Freud's views on the issue of whether personality is fully determined in childhood.

SUGGESTED READINGS

Ellenberger, H. F. (1970). *The discovery of the unconscious: The history and evolution of dynamic psychiatry.* New York: Basic Books. Traces the study of the unconscious from primitive times to Freudian psychoanalysis and its derivatives; see especially chapter 8 on Adler and chapter 9 on Jung.

Maddi, S. R., & Costa, P. T. (1972). *Humanism in personology: Allport, Maslow, and Murray.* New York: Aldine-Atherton. Describes the background and work of these psychologists and explains similarities and differences among their theories.

Quinn, S. (1987). *A mind of her own: The life of Karen Horney.* New York: Summit Books. Describes Horney's life, her work on feminine psychology, and her conflicts with the orthodox Freudian establishment.

Sayers, J. (1991). *Mothers of psychoanalysis: Helene Deutsch, Karen Horney, Anna Freud, Melanie Klein.* New York: Norton. Describes the modification of psychoanalysis from patriarchal to matriarchal since the death of Sigmund Freud.

Young-Bruehl, E. (1988). *Anna Freud: A biography.* New York: Summit Books. Describes the life and work of Sigmund Freud's daughter, who developed a system of child analysis and served as her father's confidante.

CHAPTER 15

HUMANISTIC PSYCHOLOGY AND COGNITIVE PSYCHOLOGY

SCHOOLS OF THOUGHT IN PERSPECTIVE

WE HAVE described how the earlier schools of thought in psychology developed, prospered for a time, and then (with the exception of psychoanalysis) became part of or contributed to the mainstream of contemporary psychological thought. We have also seen that each movement grew strong through its opposition to an earlier school. When there was no longer a need to protest, when the new school had ousted its opposition, that school ceased to be a movement and became the established order, at least for a while.

Each school of thought was successful in its own way. Each made substantial contributions to the evolution of psychology. This is true even for structuralism, although it left little direct imprint on the modern psychological scene. There are no longer structuralist followers of Titchener in psychology, nor have there been for decades. Yet structuralism was an enormous success in that it promoted the enterprise begun by Wilhelm Wundt: the establishment of an independent science of psychology that was finally free of philosophy. That structuralism failed to dominate psychology for more than a short time does not detract from its revolutionary achievement as the first school of thought in a new science, and as a source of opposition for the schools that followed.

Consider the success of functionalism, which also has not endured as a separate school of thought. As an attitude or viewpoint, which is all its advocates hoped it would be, functionalism permeates contemporary American psychological thought. To the extent that American psychology today is as much a profession as science and is actively applying its findings to virtually every aspect of life, the functional, utilitarian attitude has indeed changed the nature of psychology. "The principles of functionalism, which encouraged intellectual exploration and diversification, continue to guide the activities of many psychologists" (Wagner & Owens, 1992, p. 10).

What of Gestalt psychology? It, too, on a more modest scale, accomplished its mission. Its opposition to elementism, its support of a "wholes" approach, and its continuing interest in consciousness have influenced psychologists in the areas of clinical psychology, learning, perception, social psychology, and thinking. Although the Gestalt school did not transform psychology the way its founders expected, it still had considerable impact and must therefore be described as a success.

As noteworthy as the accomplishments of structuralism, functionalism, and Gestalt psychology are, however, they take second place to the phenomenal impact of behaviorism and psychoanalysis. The effects of these movements have been profound, and they have maintained their identities as separate and unique schools of thought.

We discussed how both behaviorism and psychoanalysis splintered into various positions after the days of their founders, John B. Watson and Sigmund Freud. There is today no single form of behaviorism or of psychoanalysis that has won allegiance from all members of either school. The emergence of subschools divided both systems into competing factions, each with its own map of the true path.

Despite the internal diversity of the schools, behaviorists and psychoanalysts stand firmly opposed to each other in their definitions of and approaches to problems in psychology. Skinnerian behaviorists, for example, have more in common with sociobehaviorist followers of Bandura and Rotter than they do with followers of Jungian or Eriksonian psychoanalysis.

The vitality of these two major schools of thought is evident in their continuing evolution. We have seen that B. F. Skinner's psychology is not the last stage in the development of behaviorism any more than Alfred Adler's psychology is the final stage of psychoanalysis.

Let us examine two movements that arose in American psychology in the last half of the 20th century: humanistic psychology and cognitive psychology. Both have helped to reshape psychology by refocusing attention on consciousness.

HUMANISTIC PSYCHOLOGY: THE THIRD FORCE

In the early 1960s, a movement was developing in American psychology known as **humanistic psychology** or the "third force." It was not intended to be a revision or adaptation of any current school of thought, as was the case with some neo-Freudian and neobehaviorist positions. Instead, as the term *third force* implies, humanistic psychologists wanted to supplant behaviorism and psychoanalysis, the two major forces in psychology.

HUMANISTIC PSYCHOLOGY:
A system of psychology emphasizing the study of conscious experience and the wholeness of human nature and conduct

The basic themes of humanistic psychology are as follows:

1. an emphasis on conscious experience,

2. a belief in the wholeness of human nature,

3. a focus on free will, spontaneity, and the creative power of the individual,

4. the study of all factors relevant to the human condition.

Antecedent Influences on Humanistic Psychology

As with all movements, anticipations of the ideas of the humanistic psychologists can be found in the works of earlier psychologists. Consider Franz Brentano, an opponent of Wundt's and an anticipator of Gestalt psychology. Brentano criticized the mechanistic, reductionistic, natural-science approach to psychology and favored the study of consciousness as a molar quality rather than a molecular content.

Oswald Külpe demonstrated that not all conscious experience could be reduced to elementary form or be explained in terms of responses to stimuli. And William James argued against the mechanistic approach and urged a focus on consciousness and the whole individual.

The Gestalt psychologists believed that psychology should take a wholes approach to consciousness. In defiance of behaviorism's dominance, they continued to insist that conscious experience was a legitimate and fruitful area of study for psychology.

Roots of the humanistic position can also be found in psychoanalysis. Adler, Horney, Erikson, and Allport disagreed with Freud's notion that people are ruled by unconscious forces. These dissenters from orthodox psychoanalysis believed that we are primarily conscious beings who possess spontaneity and free will and are influenced by the present and the future as well as by the past. These theorists credit the personality with the creative power to shape itself.

With all movements in modern psychology, the Zeitgeist is influential in turning precedents and trends into a cohesive viewpoint.

Humanistic psychology reflected the disaffection and unrest voiced in the 1960s against mechanistic and materialistic aspects of Western culture. This so-called counterculture of the 1960s was composed primarily of college students and college dropouts, known as hippies, some of whom relied on hallucinogenic drugs to guide them to higher levels of consciousness. As a group they shared certain values that were consistent with the humanistic approach to psychology: a focus on personal fulfillment, a belief in human perfectibility, an emphasis on the present and on hedonism (satisfying one's pleasure-seeking instincts), and the tendency to self-disclose (to speak one's mind freely) (Smith, 1990).

The Nature of Humanistic Psychology

The humanistic psychologists saw behaviorism as a narrow, artificial, and sterile approach to the study of human nature. They believed that the emphasis on overt behavior was dehumanizing and reduced human beings to the status of animals or machines. They disputed the contention that people function in a deterministic manner, responding to environmental stimulus events. Further, the humanistic psychologists argued that we are more than laboratory rats or robots, and that we cannot be objectified, quantified, and reduced to stimulus-response units.

Behaviorism was not the only target of the humanistic psychologists. They opposed the deterministic tendencies in Freudian psychoanalysis as well, and the way it minimized the role of consciousness. They also criticized the Freudians for studying only neurotic and psychotic individuals.

If psychologists focused only on mental illness, the humanistic psychologists asked, how could they learn anything about mental health, about positive human qualities? By disregarding attributes such as joyfulness, contentment, ecstasy, kindness, and generosity— and concentrating on the darker side of the human personality—psychology was ignoring many distinctly human strengths and virtues. Thus, it was in response to the perceived limitations of both behaviorism and psychoanalysis that the humanistic psychologists advanced their third force in psychology. Humanistic psychology was intended as a serious study of heretofore neglected aspects of human nature. It is expressed in the works of Abraham Maslow and Carl Rogers.

ABRAHAM MASLOW (1908–1970)

Maslow has been called the spiritual father of humanistic psychology and probably did more than anyone else to spark the movement and

confer on it some degree of academic respectability. He wanted to understand the highest achievements humans are capable of reaching, and so he studied a small sample of psychologically outstanding people, to determine how they differed from those of average or normal mental health.

Maslow's Life

Born in Brooklyn, New York, Abraham Maslow had an unhappy childhood. His father was a distant figure, a womanizer and alcoholic who disappeared for long periods of time. His mother was intensely superstitious, and she punished the young Maslow for the slightest misbehavior, openly rejecting him in favor of her two younger children. He remembered watching her kill two cats he had brought home, bashing their heads against the wall. He never forgave her for the way she treated him. When she died, he refused to attend the funeral. These experiences had a lifelong effect on Maslow. He wrote: "The whole thrust of my life-philosophy and all my research and theorizing also has its roots in a hatred for and revulsion against everything she stood for" (quoted in Hoffman, 1988, p. 9).

Maslow felt a sense of inferiority in childhood, because of his scrawny physique and large nose, and he described his adolescence as consisting of a giant inferiority complex, for which he tried to compensate by developing athletic skills. Thus, the man who later became interested in Alfred Adler's work on inferiority and compensation was himself an example of Adler's theory. Maslow failed to gain acceptance and esteem on the athletic field, however, and turned to books instead.

He enrolled at Cornell University, where he reported that his first psychology course was "awful and bloodless and had nothing to do with people, so I shuddered and turned away from it" (Hoffman, 1988, p. 26). Maslow's professor for that course was E. B. Titchener. Maslow transferred to the University of Wisconsin and received his PhD in 1934.

Initially Maslow was an enthusiastic behaviorist, convinced that the mechanistic natural-science approach provided answers to all the world's problems. Then a series of personal experiences—the birth of his first child, the onset of World War II, and exposure to other ideas of human nature in philosophy, Gestalt psychology, and psychoanalysis—persuaded him that behaviorism was too limited to be relevant to enduring human issues.

Maslow was also influenced by his contact with some of the European psychologists who had fled Nazi Germany and settled in the United States—Adler, Horney, Koffka, Wertheimer. His feelings of awe toward Max Wertheimer and toward the American anthropologist Ruth Benedict led to his initial study of psychologically healthy self-actualizing persons. Wertheimer and Benedict were Maslow's models of the best of human nature.

Maslow's early attempts to humanize psychology, undertaken while teaching at Brooklyn College, had negative personal consequences. He was ostracized by the behaviorist psychological community. Although students found his work of interest, faculty colleagues avoided him because of his unorthodox views. He was considered far out of step with the dominant psychological position, and the major psychology journals would not publish his work (DeCarvallo, 1990).

It was at Brandeis University in Waltham, Massachusetts, from 1951 to 1969, that Maslow developed and refined his theory and presented it in a series of books. He supported the sensitivity group movement and became something of a celebrity in the 1960s. He was elected president of the APA in 1967.

Self-Actualization

SELF-ACTUALIZATION: The full development of one's abilities and the realization of one's potential

In Maslow's view, each person possesses an innate tendency toward **self-actualization** (Maslow, 1970). This state, the highest human need, involves the active use of all our qualities and abilities, the development and fulfillment of our potential. To become self-actualizing, we must first satisfy the needs that stand lower in the innate hierarchy of needs. Each need must be satisfied in turn before the next need in the hierarchy can motivate us.

The needs are, in the order in which they must be satisfied:

1.   the physiological needs for food, water, air, sleep, and sex,

2.   the safety needs for security, stability, order, protection, and freedom from fear and anxiety,

3.   the belonging and love needs,

4.   the needs for esteem from others and from oneself,

5.   the need for self-actualization.

Most of Maslow's research focused on the characteristics of persons who have satisfied the need for self-actualization and are thus considered to be psychologically healthy. He found that such persons share the following characteristics:

✦ an objective perception of reality

✦ a full acceptance of their own natures

✦ a commitment and dedication to some kind of work

✦ simplicity and naturalness in their behavior

✦ a need for autonomy, privacy, and independence

✦ intense mystical or peak experiences

✦ empathy with and affection for all humanity

✦ a resistance to conformity

✦ a democratic character structure

✦ an attitude of creativeness

✦ a high degree of social interest (an idea borrowed from Adler)

Self-actualizing persons are free of neuroses and are almost always middle-aged or older. Maslow said that they make up fewer than 1% of the population.

Comment

Maslow's research method and data have been criticized on the grounds that his sample was too small to allow for generalizations. Also, his subjects were selected according to his own subjective criteria of psychological health, and his terms are defined ambiguously and inconsistently. Maslow agreed that his investigations did not meet the requirements of scientific research, but he argued that there was no other way to study self-actualization. He referred to his research as preliminary and remained convinced his conclusions would one day be confirmed.

The self-actualization theory has limited empirical laboratory support; most research has failed to support the theory. It has been applied in business and industry, however, where many executives believe that the self-actualization need is a useful motivating force and a potential source of job satisfaction. Maslow's theory has also been applied in education, medicine, and psychotherapy.

CARL ROGERS (1902–1987)

Carl Rogers is known for a popular approach to psychotherapy called **person-centered therapy.** Based on data derived from his therapy, Rogers developed a personality theory that focuses on a single motivating factor that is similar to Maslow's concept of self-actualization. Unlike Maslow, however, Rogers's ideas did not come from the study of emotionally healthy people but from the application of person-centered therapy to the individuals who came to his university counseling centers for treatment.

The name of his therapy indicates his view of the human personality. By placing the responsibility for change on the person or client rather than on the therapist (as is the case in orthodox psychoanalysis), Rogers assumed that people can consciously and rationally alter their thoughts and behaviors from undesirable to desirable ones. He did not believe we are forever in the grasp of unconscious forces or childhood experiences. Personality is shaped by the present and by how we consciously perceive it.

Courtesy, Center for the Study of the Person, LaJolla

CARL ROGERS

PERSON-CENTERED THERAPY:
Rogers's approach to psychotherapy that places the responsibility for change on the client rather than on the therapist

Rogers's Life

Carl Rogers was born in Oak Park, Illinois, a suburb of Chicago. His parents espoused strict fundamentalist religious views, which, as Rogers put it, gripped him like a vise throughout his childhood and adolescence. Their beliefs—including the suppression of any display of emotion—forced him to live by their code and not his own. He said that these restrictions gave him something to revolt against, although the revolt would be long in coming.

He was a solitary child, reading incessantly. His isolation and loneliness led him to rely on his own experiences, but he could not yet break free of his parents' beliefs. When Rogers was 12, the family moved to a farm, and he developed a strong interest in nature. He read a great deal about agricultural experiments and learned about the scientific approach to knowledge.

Although his intellectual life was focused, his emotional life was in a turmoil. "My fantasies during this period were definitely bizarre," he wrote, "and probably would be classified as schizoid by a diagnostician, but fortunately I never came in contact with a psychologist" (Rogers, 1980, p. 30).

When he was 22 and attending a Christian student conference in China, he finally freed himself from his parents' fundamentalist beliefs and developed a more liberal philosophy of life (Rogers, 1967). He became convinced that people must guide their lives by their own interpretation of events, rather than relying on the beliefs of others. He was also persuaded that people can consciously and actively strive to improve themselves. These concepts became cornerstones of his personality theory.

Rogers received his PhD in clinical and educational psychology in 1931 from Teachers College of Columbia University. He spent the next nine years at the Society for the Prevention of Cruelty to Children, working with delinquent and disadvantaged youngsters. In 1940, he began his academic career, teaching at The Ohio State University, the University of Chicago, and the University of Wisconsin. It was during those years that he developed his theory and his unique approach to psychotherapy.

Self-Actualization

Rogers proposed that the major motivating force in personality is the drive to actualize the self (Rogers, 1961). Although this urge toward self-actualization is innate, it can be helped or hindered by childhood experiences and by learning.

He emphasized the importance of the mother-child relationship as it affects the child's growing sense of self. If the mother satisfies the infant's need for love, which Rogers called **positive regard,** then the infant will tend to become a healthy personality. If the mother makes her love for her child conditional on proper behavior (called *conditional positive regard*), then the child will internalize the mother's attitude and develop conditions of worth. In that situation, the child feels worthy only under certain conditions and will try to avoid those behaviors that bring the mother's disapproval. As a result, the child's self is not allowed to develop fully; the child cannot express all aspects of the self because some of them bring rejection.

POSITIVE REGARD: The unconditional love of a mother for her infant

Thus, the primary requisite for the development of psychological health is the receipt of unconditional positive regard in infancy. During that period the mother must demonstrate her love and acceptance of the child, regardless of the child's behavior. The child who receives such unconditional positive regard will not develop conditions of worth and will not have to repress any portion of the emerging self. Only in this way can a person achieve self-actualization.

Self-actualization is the highest level of psychological health. Rogers's conception is similar in principle to Maslow's proposed state of self-actualization. The two theories differ somewhat on the characteristics of the psychologically healthy person. To Rogers, psychologically healthy or fully functioning persons are characterized by the following:

✦ an openness to all experience

✦ a tendency to live fully in every moment

✦ an ability to be guided by one's own instincts rather than by reason or the opinions of others

✦ a sense of freedom in thought and action

✦ a high degree of creativity

Rogers described the fully functioning person as actualizing rather than actualized, to indicate that the development of the self is always a work in progress. This emphasis on our ability to be spontaneous and flexible and to continue to grow is neatly captured in the title of Rogers's most popular book, *On Becoming a Person* (Rogers, 1961).

Comment

Rogers's person-centered approach to psychotherapy has had a major impact on psychology. His theory of personality has also been well received, particularly its emphasis on the importance of the self. Criticism has been directed at Rogers's lack of specificity about our innate potential for self-actualization, and at his emphasis on subjective conscious experiences to the exclusion of unconscious influences. Both the theory and the therapy have generated considerable supportive research and are widely used in clinical settings.

Rogers was influential in the human potential movement, and his work was part of the overall trend toward humanizing psychology. He was elected president of the APA in 1946 and received their Distinguished Scientific Contribution Award and Distinguished Professional Contribution Award.

HUMANISTIC PSYCHOTHERAPIES

Because humanistic psychology, unlike psychoanalysis, focused on psychologically healthy rather than emotionally disturbed persons, its approach to therapy was different. Humanistic or growth therapies proliferated in the 1960s and 1970s when millions of people enrolled in encounter groups, sensitivity sessions, and human potential courses in schools, businesses, churches, clinics, and even prisons. The popularity of these programs has since declined dramatically.

Derived in part from the work of the Gestalt psychologist Kurt Lewin, humanistic psychotherapies were applied with persons of normal or average mental health to raise their levels of consciousness, help them relate better to themselves and to others, and release hidden potentials for creativity and self- development. In other words, the programs were designed to enhance psychological health and self-actualization rather than to cure neuroses, anxiety, or depression.

Unfortunately, the human potential movement attracted more than its share of well-intentioned but untrained and unqualified practitioners, along with self-styled gurus and teachers, who did more harm than good. Studies of the aftereffects of participation in encounter groups revealed psychological casualty rates of up to 50% in some cases (Hartley, Robach, & Abramowitz, 1976).

THE FATE OF HUMANISTIC PSYCHOLOGY

The humanistic psychology movement became formalized with the founding of the *Journal of Humanistic Psychology* in 1961, the American Association for Humanistic Psychology in 1962, and the Division of Humanistic Psychology of the American Psychological Association in 1971. Thus the distinguishing traits of a cohesive school of thought were evident.

Humanistic psychologists offered their own definition of psychology, distinct from the other two forces in the field, and promoted their subject matter, methods, and terminology. They possessed what every other school of thought boasted in its early days: a passionate conviction that theirs was the best path for psychology to follow.

Despite these attributes of a school of thought, humanistic psychology did not actually become a school. That was the judgment of humanistic psychologists themselves at a 1985 meeting, nearly 3 decades after the movement began. "Humanistic psychology was a great experiment, but it is basically a failed experiment in that there is no humanistic school of thought in psychology, no theory that would be recognized as a philosophy of science" (Cunningham, 1985, p. 18).

Carl Rogers agreed. "Humanistic psychology has not had a significant impact on mainstream psychology. We are perceived as having relatively little importance" (quoted in Cunningham, 1985, p. 16). Rogers told his supporters that if they wanted evidence for his statement they had only to examine any introductory psychology textbook. There they would find the same topics that characterized psychology 25 years before, with little mention of the study of the whole person.

A later review of textbooks agreed with Rogers's contention. Fewer than 1% of the subject matter of the books surveyed dealt with humanistic psychology, typically a brief mention of Maslow's hierarchy of needs and Rogers's person-centered therapy (Churchill, 1988).

Why didn't humanistic psychology become part of the mainstream of psychological thought? One reason is that most humanistic psychologists were in private clinical practice, rather than at universities. Unlike academic psychologists, humanistic psychologists did not, to the same extent, conduct research or publish papers or train new generations of graduate students to carry on their tradition. "The most striking and potentially serious trend has been the small amount of research in humanistic psychology in recent years" (Rice & Greenberg, 1992, p. 215).

Another reason has to do with the timing of the humanistic psychologists' protest. At its peak, the 1960s and early 1970s, humanistic psychology was attacking positions that were no longer so influential within psychology. Both Freudian psychoanalysis and Skinnerian behaviorism had already been weakened by divisiveness within their ranks, and both were already beginning to change in the direction urged by the humanistic psychologists. As a result, the humanistic protest was fighting against movements that were no longer dominant in their original form.

Although humanistic psychology has not transformed the field as a whole, it did strengthen the idea within contemporary psychoanalysis that people can consciously and freely shape their own lives. It may also have indirectly helped in the restoration of the study of consciousness in academic experimental psychology, because humanistic psychology arose at the same time as the cognitive psychology movement. Ulric Neisser, a founder of cognitive psychology, noted that he was "much moved by the spirit of humanistic psychologists [and] saw the cognitive approach as a more humanistic view of the human organism" (Baars, 1986, p. 273). Overall, humanistic psychology helped to ratify changes already taking place within the field, and from that standpoint, the movement may be called successful.

THE COGNITIVE MOVEMENT IN PSYCHOLOGY

"Psychology," wrote John B. Watson in his behaviorist manifesto of 1913, "must discard all reference to consciousness." The psychologists who followed Watson's dictates eliminated all mention of the mind and conscious processes, and banished all mentalistic terminology. For decades, introductory psychology textbooks described the functioning of the brain but refused to discuss any conception of the "mind." It was said that psychology had "lost consciousness" or "lost its mind" forever.

Suddenly, or so it seemed, although it had been building for some time, psychology began to regain consciousness. Once politically incorrect words were being uttered aloud in meetings and conferences and appearing in print in professional journals.

In 1979 the *American Psychologist* published an article entitled "Behaviorism and the Mind: A (Limited) Call for a Return to

Introspection" (Lieberman, 1979), invoking not only mind but also the suspect technique of introspection. A few months earlier the same journal had published an article with the simple title "Consciousness." "After decades of deliberate neglect," its author wrote, "consciousness is again coming under scientific scrutiny, with discussions of the topic appearing at entirely respectable locations in psychology's literature" (Natsoulas, 1978, p. 906).

The president of the American Psychological Association, delivering his annual address, told the assembled audience that the conception of psychology was changing and the change involved a return to consciousness. Psychology's image of human nature was becoming "human rather than mechanical" (McKeachie, 1976, p. 831).

When an officer of the APA and a prestigious journal discuss consciousness so optimistically, it seems obvious that a new movement, another revolution, is under way. Revisions in introductory textbooks followed, now defining psychology as the science of "behavior and mental processes" instead of just behavior, and as the science that "systematically studies and attempts to explain observable behavior and its relationship to the unseen mental processes that go on inside the organism" (Hilgard, Atkinson, & Atkinson, 1975, p. 12; Kagan & Havemann, 1972, p. 9).

College courses that dealt with the psychology of consciousness became popular for both undergraduate and graduate students (Spanos, 1993). A 1987 survey asked psychologists what aspects of modern psychology surprised them most, in light of the expectations they had held for the field 25 years before. They responded that they were most surprised by the rapid rise of the cognitive movement in psychology (Boneau, 1992).

Thus it came clear that psychology had progressed far beyond the desires and designs of Watson and Skinner. A new school of thought was taking hold.

Antecedent Influences on Cognitive Psychology

Like all revolutionary movements in psychology, **cognitive psychology** did not spring up overnight. Many of its features had been anticipated by the work of others. It has been suggested that "cognitive psychology is both the newest and the oldest strand in the history of the subject" (Hearnshaw, 1987, p. 272). What this means is that interest in consciousness was evident in the earliest days of psychology, even before it became a formal science. The writings of the Greek philosophers Plato and Aristotle deal with cognitive processes, as do the theories of the British empiricists and associationists.

When psychology became a separate scientific discipline, the focus remained on consciousness. Wilhelm Wundt is a forerunner of

COGNITIVE PSYCHOLOGY:
A system of psychology that focuses on the process of knowing, on how the mind actively organizes experiences

cognitive psychology because of his emphasis on the creative activity of the mind. Structuralism and functionalism dealt with consciousness, studying its elements in one case and its functions in the other. Behaviorism brought about a fundamental change, dismissing consciousness from the field for nearly 50 years.

The return to consciousness—the formal beginning of the cognitive psychology movement—can be traced to the 1950s, although signs were noticed in the 1930s. The behaviorist E. R. Guthrie, toward the end of his career, came to deplore the mechanistic model and argued that stimuli cannot always be reduced to physical terms. Psychologists must describe stimuli in perceptual or cognitive terms, he suggested, so that they will be meaningful for the responding organism (Guthrie, 1959). Psychologists cannot deal with the concept of meaning solely in behaviorist terms, because it is a mentalistic or cognitive process.

The purposive behaviorism of E. C. Tolman was another precursor of the cognitive movement. His form of behaviorism recognized the importance of cognitive variables and contributed to the decline of the stimulus-response approach. Tolman proposed the idea of cognitive maps, attributed purpose to animals, and emphasized intervening variables as a way of operationally defining internal, unobservable states.

Rudolf Carnap, a positivist philosopher, called for a return to introspection. In 1956 Carnap wrote that "a person's awareness of his own state of imagining, feeling, et cetera, must be recognized as a kind of observation, in principle not different from external observation, and therefore as a legitimate source of knowledge" (quoted in Koch, 1964, p. 22). Even Percy Bridgman, the physicist who gave behaviorism the notion of operational definitions, later renounced behaviorism and insisted that introspective reports be used to give meaning to operational analyses.

Gestalt psychology was an influence on the cognitive movement because of its focus on "organization, structure, relationships, the active role of the subject, and the important part played by perception in learning and memory" (Hearst, 1979, p. 32). The Gestalt school of thought helped keep alive at least a token interest in consciousness during the years when behaviorism dominated American psychology.

Another anticipator of the cognitive movement is the Swiss psychologist Jean Piaget (1896–1980), who produced important work on the development of the child—not in terms of psychosexual or psychosocial stages (as proposed by Freud and Erikson)—but in terms of cognitive stages. Piaget's initial formulations, published in the 1920s and 1930s, were highly influential in Europe. They were not so widely accepted in the United States, because they were incompatible with the behaviorist position. However, Piaget's emphasis on cognitive factors was welcomed by early proponents of the cognitive movement.

AP/Wide World Photos

JEAN PIAGET

As the ideas of the cognitive psychologists took hold in American psychology, the relevance of Piaget's ideas became clear. In 1969 Piaget became the first European psychologist to receive the APA's Distinguished Scientific Contribution Award. Because his work focused on the development of the child, it helped broaden the range of behavior to which cognitive psychology could be applied.

The Changing Zeitgeist in Physics

When we find such a major shift in the evolution of a science, we know it is reflecting changes that are already part of its intellectual Zeitgeist. We have seen that a science, like a living species, adapts to the changing demands and conditions of its environment. What was the intellectual climate that fostered the cognitive movement, that dictated a moderating of behaviorism by the readmission of consciousness? Once again we may look to the Zeitgeist in physics, long the role model for psychology, which has influenced the field since its beginnings as a science.

Early in the 20th century a new viewpoint was developing within physics as a result of the work of Albert Einstein, Neils Bohr, Werner Heisenberg, and others. They rejected the mechanistic Galilean-Newtonian model of the universe, the prototype from which psychology drew the mechanistic, reductionistic view of human nature expounded by psychologists from Wundt to Skinner. The new look in physics discarded the classical world of total objectivity and the complete separation of the external world from the observer.

Physicists recognized that we cannot observe the natural world without disturbing it. Thus, they attempted to bridge the artificial gap between the observer and the observed, the inner world and the outer world, the world of conscious experience and the world of matter. The focus of scientific investigation shifted from an independent and objectively knowable universe to our own observation of that universe. Modern scientists would no longer be so detached from the focus of their observation; they would become participant-observers.

The ideal of a totally objective reality was believed to be unattainable. Today physics is characterized by the belief that objective knowledge is actually subjective; that is, it is dependent on the observer. This position that all knowledge is personal sounds suspiciously like what George Berkeley proposed close to 300 years ago—that all knowledge is subjective because it depends on the nature of the person perceiving it. One writer described that situation as follows: Our picture of the world, "far from being a genuine photographic reproduction of an independent reality 'out there,' [is] rather more on the order of a painting: a subjective creation of the mind which can convey a likeness but can never produce a replica" (Matson, 1964, p. 137).

The physicists' rejection of an objective, machinelike subject matter and their recognition of subjectivity restored the vital role of conscious experience in obtaining information about our world. This revolution in physics was an effective argument for the acceptance of consciousness as a legitimate part of the subject matter of psychology. Although scientific psychology resisted the new physics for a half century, clinging to an outdated model by defining itself as an objective science of behavior, it eventually responded to the Zeitgeist and modified its form sufficiently to readmit cognitive processes.

The Founding of Cognitive Psychology

A retrospective look at the cognitive movement gives the impression of an orderly and rapid transition that shook the foundations of the psychological world in only a few short years. At the time, of course, this transition was not at all apparent. This dramatic change in psychology emerged slowly and quietly, with no beating drums and no fanfare. "No one announced its existence until long after the fact" (Baars, 1986, p. 141).

The progression of history is often clear only after the event. The founding of cognitive psychology did not happen overnight, nor could it be attributed to the persuasiveness of a single individual who, like John B. Watson, changed the field almost singlehandedly. Like functional psychology, the cognitive movement claims no solitary founder, perhaps because none of the psychologists working in the area had the personal ambition to lead a new movement. Their interest was simply in getting on with the work of redefining psychology.

History has identified two scholars who, although not founders in the formal sense of the term, did contribute groundbreaking work in the form of a research center and a book, now considered to be milestones in the development of cognitive psychology. They are George Miller and Ulric Neisser, and their stories highlight some of the personal factors involved in shaping new schools of thought.

GEORGE MILLER (1920–)

George Miller began his career by majoring in English and speech at the University of Alabama; he received his master's degree in speech in 1941. While a student at Alabama, he expressed an interest in psychology. He was given an instructorship to teach 16 sections of introductory psychology, having never taken a course in the field. He said that after teaching the same material 16 times a week, he began to believe it himself.

Miller went on to Harvard University, where he worked in the psychoacoustic laboratory on problems in vocal communication, and in 1946 he received his PhD. He embarked on the study of psycholinguistics, publishing *Language and Communication* in 1951. Miller accepted behaviorism as the primary school of thought in psychology, noting that he had little choice because behaviorists held all the leadership positions in the major universities and professional organizations.

> *The power, the honors, the authority, the textbooks, the money, everything in psychology was owned by the behavioristic school. . . . those of us who wanted to be scientific psychologists couldn't really oppose it. You just wouldn't get a job.* (MILLER, QUOTED IN BAARS, 1986, P. 203)

By the mid-1950s, after delving into statistical learning theory, information theory, and computer-based models of the mind, Miller reached the conclusion that behaviorism was not, as he put it, "going to work out." The similarities between the operation of computers and the human mind impressed him, and his interests shifted to a more cognitively oriented psychology. At the same time, he developed an allergy to animal hair and dander, which meant that he could not conduct research with laboratory rats. He could work only with human subjects, a disadvantage in a world ruled by behaviorists.

Miller's move toward a cognitive psychology was aided by his rebellious spirit, which typified many of his generation of psychologists. They were ready to revolt against the kind of psychology then being taught and practiced and to offer a new approach, one that would focus on cognitive rather than behavioral factors.

GEORGE MILLER

The Center for Cognitive Studies

Together with a colleague, Jerome Bruner (1915–), Miller established a research center at Harvard to investigate the human mind. They asked the university president for space, and in 1960 they were given a house in which William James had once lived, an appropriate site because James had dealt so exquisitely in his *Principles* book with the nature of mental life.

The choice of a name for the new enterprise was not a trivial question. Being associated with Harvard, it would have the potential for exerting an enormous influence on psychology; indeed, for defining a new movement. Miller and Bruner chose the word *cognition* to denote their subject matter, and they called the new facility the Center for Cognitive Studies.

> *In using the word "cognition" we were setting ourselves off from behaviorism. We wanted something that was* mental–*but "mental psychology" seemed terribly redundant. "Common-sense psychology" would have suggested some sort of anthropological*

investigation, and "folk psychology" would have suggested Wundt's social psychology. What word do you use to label this set of views? We chose "cognition." (Miller, quoted in Baars, 1986, p. 210)

Two students at the center recalled that no one there could tell them what the word *cognition* really meant or what they were supposed to be in favor of. The center "was not set up to be for anything in particular; it was set up to be against things. What was important was what it was not" (Norman & Levelt, 1988, p. 101).

It was not behaviorism. It was not the ruling authority, the establishment, the psychology of the present. In defining the center, its founders were demonstrating how strongly they differed from behaviorism. As we have seen with every new movement, proclaiming how their position or attitude differs from the ongoing school of thought is a necessary preliminary stage to later defining what they are about and how they propose to change the field.

Despite the revolutionary qualities of cognitive psychology, Miller did not believe it was a true revolution. He called it an accretion—a change by slow growth or accumulation. He saw the movement as more evolutionary than revolutionary and believed it was a return to a commonsense psychology, one that recognized and affirmed that psychology dealt with mental life as well as behavior.

A wide range of topics were investigated at the Center for Cognitive Studies: language, memory, perception, concept formation, thinking, and developmental psychology, most of which had been eliminated from the vocabulary of the behaviorists. Miller later established a program for cognitive sciences at Princeton University.

In recognition of his efforts, Miller became president of the American Psychological Association in 1969 and received their Distinguished Scientific Contribution Award and the Gold Medal Award for Life Achievement in the Application of Psychology. Perhaps the greater acknowledgment of his work can be found in the number of laboratories of cognitive psychology that followed his and in the rapid development of the approach to psychology that he did so much to define.

Ulric Neisser (1928–)

Born in Kiel, Germany, Ulric Neisser was brought to the United States by his parents at the age of 3. He began his college studies at Harvard, majoring in physics. Impressed with a young professor by the name of George Miller, he decided that physics did not "sing" to him and switched to psychology. He took an honors course with Miller dealing with the psychology of communications and was introduced to information theory. He reports also being influenced by Koffka's book, *Principles of Gestalt Psychology.*

After receiving his bachelor's degree from Harvard in 1950, Neisser took his master's degree at Swarthmore College, studying under the Gestalt psychologist Wolfgang Köhler. Neisser returned to Harvard for his PhD, which he received in 1956.

Despite the growing attraction of the cognitive approach to psychology, Neisser saw no escape from behaviorism for an academic career. "It was what you had to learn," he said. "That was the age when it was supposed that no psychological phenomenon was real unless you could demonstrate it in a rat. . . . A very peculiar enterprise, it seemed to me" (quoted in Baars, 1986, p. 275).

Neisser found behaviorism not only peculiar but a little "crazy" as well, and it was fortunate his first academic job was at Brandeis University, where the head of the psychology department was Abraham Maslow. At the time, Maslow was moving away from his own behaviorist training to develop a humanistic approach to the field. Maslow was not successful in turning Neisser into a humanistic psychologist, or in turning humanistic psychology into psychology's third force, but he provided an opportunity for Neisser to pursue his interests in cognitive issues. (Neisser later claimed that cognitive psychology, not humanistic psychology, was the "third force.")

© Emory University

ULRIC NEISSER

In 1967 Neisser published *Cognitive Psychology,* a book that "established and christened the field" (Goleman, 1983, p. 54). He reported that the book was a personal one, really an attempt to define himself—the kind of psychologist he was and wanted to be. The book also defined a new psychology. It became extremely popular, and Neisser was embarrassed to find himself designated the "father" of cognitive psychology. He had no desire to found a school of thought, but his book nevertheless helped to push psychology away from behaviorism and toward cognition.

Neisser defined cognition in terms of those processes "by which the sensory input is transformed, reduced, elaborated, stored, recovered, and used. . . . cognition is involved in everything a human being might possibly do" (Neisser, 1967, p. 4). Thus, cognitive psychology is concerned with sensation, perception, imaging, memory, problem solving, thinking, and all other mental activities.

Nine years after writing the book that launched the field, Neisser published *Cognition and Reality* (1976), in which he expressed his dissatisfaction with the narrowing of the cognitive position and its reliance on artificial laboratory situations for its data instead of on real-world settings. He became disillusioned, concluding that the cognitive psychology movement as then constituted had little to contribute to psychology's understanding of how people deal with reality.

And so Neisser, one of the most important figures in the founding of cognitive psychology, became a vocal critic, challenging the movement as he had earlier challenged behaviorism. He is currently affiliated with Emory University in Atlanta, Georgia, after spending 17 years at Cornell, where his office was not far from the pickled brain of E. B. Titchener.

THE COMPUTER METAPHOR

Clocks and automata were the 17th-century metaphors for the mechanical view of the universe and, by extension, for the human mind. Those machines were readily available and easily understood models of the way in which the mind was said to work. Today, the mechanical model of the universe and the behavioral psychology that derived from it have been superseded by other viewpoints; namely, the new look in physics and the cognitive movement in psychology.

The clock is no longer a useful example for the 20th-century view of the mind. A new metaphor is needed, and a 20th-century machine, the computer, has emerged to serve as our model. Psychologists are increasingly invoking the operation of the computer as a way of explaining cognitive phenomena. Computers are said to display artificial intelligence, and their functioning is often described in human terms. For example, the storage capacity of computers is its *memory,* programming codes are *languages,* and newer generations of computers are said to be *evolving* (Campbell, 1988; Roszak, 1986).

Computer programs, which are essentially sets of instructions for dealing with symbols, may be said to function similarly to the human mind. Both the computer and the mind receive and digest large amounts of information (stimuli or data) from the environment. They process this information, manipulating, storing, and retrieving it, and acting on it in various ways. Thus, computer programming is the pattern for the cognitive view of human information processing, reasoning, and problem solving. It is the program, not the computer itself (the software, not the hardware), that serves as the explanation for mental operations.

Cognitive psychologists are interested not in any physiological correlates of mental processes but in the sequence of symbol manipulation that underlies how we think. Their goal is to discover that "library of programs the human has stored away in memory—programs that enabled the person to understand and produce sentences, to commit certain experiences and rules to memory, and to solve novel problems" (Howard, 1983, p. 11).

This information-processing view of the human mind forms the basis of cognitive psychology. In the more than 100 years of its history, psychology has progressed from clocks to computers as models for its subject matter, but it is significant that both are machines. This demonstrates the historical continuity in psychology's evolution between older and newer schools of thought.

"For psychologists, always looking for reassurances that their theories refer to some physically possible reality, the lure of machine metaphors is well-nigh irresistible" (Baars, 1986, p. 154). We are left to wonder whether the old expression—the more things change, the more they stay the same—contains a lesson about history for those who try to learn from it.

THE NATURE OF COGNITIVE PSYCHOLOGY

We described how reference to cognitive factors in the social learning theories of Bandura and Rotter changed American behaviorism. But it is not only in behavioral psychology that the cognitive movement has had an impact. Cognitive factors are being considered in virtually every area: attribution theory in social psychology, cognitive dissonance theory, motivation and emotion, personality, learning, memory, perception, and the information-processing approach to decision making and problem solving. In applied areas such as clinical, community, school, and industrial/organizational psychology, there is also an emphasis on cognitive factors.

Cognitive psychology differs from behaviorism on several points. First, cognitive psychologists focus on the process of knowing, rather than simply responding to stimuli. The important factors are mental processes and events, not stimulus-response connections; the emphasis is on the mind, not on behavior. This does not mean that cognitive psychologists ignore behavior, only that behavioral responses are not the sole goals of their research. Behavioral responses are seen as sources for making inferences and drawing conclusions about the mental processes that accompany them.

Second, cognitive psychologists are interested in how the mind structures or organizes experience. The Gestalt psychologists, as well as Jean Piaget, argued that the tendency to organize conscious experience (sensations and perceptions) into meaningful wholes and patterns is innate. The mind gives form and coherence to mental experience, and it is this process that is the subject matter of cognitive psychology. The British empiricists and associationists and their 20th-century derivatives, the Skinnerian behaviorists, insisted that the mind did not possess any such inherent organizational abilities.

Third, in the cognitive view the individual is actively and creatively arranging the stimuli received from the environment. We are capable of participating in the acquisition and application of knowledge, deliberately attending to some events and choosing to commit them to memory. We are not, as the behaviorists claimed, passive responders to external forces or blank slates on which sensory experience will write.

The Role of Introspection

The emergence of cognitive psychology with its renewed focus on conscious experiences brought about the return of scientific psychology's first research method introduced by Wilhelm Wundt more than a century ago; namely, introspection. Some psychologists prefer the more scientific-sounding euphemism: *phenomenological assessment.* In a statement that could have been made by Wundt or Titchener, a contemporary psychologist noted the obvious fact that "if we are to study consciousness we must use introspection and introspective reports" (Farthing, 1992, p. 61). Introspective reports are used today to study a variety of research problems.

Attempts have been made to quantify introspective reports to render them more objective and amenable to statistical analyses. One approach, called retrospective phenomenological assessment, involves asking subjects to rate the intensity of the subjective experiences they underwent while they were responding to a stimulus situation presented earlier (Pekala, 1991). In other words, subjects retrospectively evaluate their subjective experiences from a specific time period during which they were responding to a specific stimulus.

Despite the resurgence of introspection and its application to a variety of research topics, some psychologists question whether individuals really do have access to their higher-order mental processes, especially those processes involved in making judgments and decisions. In a classic article, "Telling More Than We Can Know," psychologists Richard Nisbett and Timothy Wilson concluded we do not have free access to our thought processes and that introspection or self-report is therefore worthless (Nisbett & Wilson, 1977).

They described several studies designed to determine if human subjects could report the causes of their own behavior and concluded the subjects could not: They were unable to specify which stimuli affected their responses, or how the effects might have occurred. The psychologists also found that responses, or reported effects of stimuli, were not based on introspection but on prior beliefs about the causal links between stimuli and responses.

For example, if you have been taught that Event A always causes Event B, then you will tend to explain your response (Event B) to a stimulus (Event A) in terms of that long-standing belief, rather than performing any sort of genuine introspection of your thought processes. "We infer that a particular stimulus caused our behavior, not through introspection of our actual mental processes, but by judging whether the stimulus is representative of the category of stimuli that usually cause such behavior" (Farthing, 1992, p. 156).

Nisbett and Wilson's experimental demonstration that we may not have introspective access to the causes of our behavior has persuaded some psychologists that introspection is not a valid technique.

(If this conclusion sounds familiar, recall the behaviorists' protests against introspection many decades earlier.) Other researchers, however, are more optimistic about the value of introspection and argue it can be a valid technique (Farthing, 1992; Pekala, 1991). The resolution of this question is crucial for the future of cognitive psychology, because so much of its research has relied on the use of introspective reports.

Unconscious Cognition

The study of conscious mental processes has sparked a renewed interest in unconscious cognitive activities (Jacoby, Lindsay, & Toth, 1992). "After 100 years of neglect, suspicion, and frustration, unconscious processes have now taken a firm hold on the collective mind of psychologists" (Kihlstrom, Barnhardt, & Tataryn, 1992, p. 788).

This is not the unconscious mind of which Sigmund Freud spoke, overflowing with repressed desires and memories that can be brought into conscious awareness only through a lengthy period of psychoanalysis. The new unconscious is viewed as being more rational than emotional. It is involved in the first stage of human cognition in the act of responding to a stimulus. The unconscious is an integral part of learning and information processing, and it can be studied through several forms of controlled experiment.

To distinguish the cognitive unconscious from the psychoanalytic version of the unconscious (and from the physical state of being unaware, asleep, or comatose), some cognitive psychologists prefer the term *nonconscious*. So important has this concept of the nonconscious mind become in cognitive psychology that, in general, researchers agree that most of our mental processing takes place at the nonconscious level. This has been demonstrated experimentally in behavioral evidence of information processing when the subjects showed no conscious awareness of that information.

A popular research approach involves subliminal perception or subliminal activation, in which stimuli are presented to subjects below the subjects' levels of conscious awareness. Despite their inability to perceive the stimuli, the subjects' conscious processes and behavior are activated by those stimuli. The researchers concluded that we can be influenced by stimuli we can neither see nor hear (Greenwald, 1992).

These and similar findings have persuaded cognitive psychologists that the process of acquiring knowledge, whether in or out of the experimental laboratory, takes place at both conscious and nonconscious levels, but that most of the mental work involved in learning occurs at the nonconscious level (Loftus & Klinger, 1992). Research also indicates that nonconscious information processing is faster, more efficient, and more sophisticated than that which occurs at the conscious level.

If the bulk of our information processing is nonconscious, then it follows that no amount of introspecting will reveal how it works. There is little point in asking subjects to report on something of which they are not aware. "No matter how cooperative and well trained our subjects are, they cannot tell us how they go about processing information. . . . This is because subjects not only do not know how they do all those things, but have never known it" (Lewicki, Hill, & Czyzewska, 1992, p. 796). This conclusion certainly limits the applications of introspection as a research method for cognitive psychology.

Animal Cognition

The cognitive revolution restored consciousness not only to humans but to animals as well (Hulse, 1993). The work of the animal or comparative psychologists has come full circle—from observations of animal mental life reported by Romanes and Morgan in the 1880s and 1890s, through the mechanical stimulus-response conditioning research of the Skinnerian behaviorists in the 1950s and 1960s, to the restoration of consciousness by the cognitive psychologists.

Beginning in the 1970s, animal psychologists have attempted to demonstrate "how animals encode, transform, compute, and manipulate symbolic representations of the real world's spatial, temporal, and causal textures for the purposes of adaptively organizing their behavior" (Cook, 1993, p. 174). In other words, the computer-like system of information processing believed to occur in humans is now being studied in animals.

Early research on cognition in animals used simple stimuli such as colored lights, tones, and clicks. These stimuli may have been too simple to permit an understanding of the cognitive processes of animals, because they did not allow the animals to display the scope of their information-processing abilities. Later research used more complex and realistic stimuli, such as color photographs of familiar objects. These complex pictorial stimuli have revealed conceptual abilities not previously attributed to animals.

Current research has shown that animal memory is complex and flexible, and that at least some cognitive processes may operate in the same way in animals as in humans. Laboratory animals have been shown to be capable of learning diverse and sophisticated concepts. Mental processes such as coding and organizing symbols have been demonstrated, as well as the ability to form basic abstractions about space, time, and number (Gallistel, 1989; Roitblat, Bever, & Terrace, 1984; Wasserman, 1993).

Animal cognition has become popular enough to be discussed in the mass media; *Time* and *Newsweek* published long articles on the topic in 1993. However, some animal psychologists maintain that the research does not sufficiently support the supposition that animal cognition operates similarly to human cognition. The gap between human and animal functioning proposed by Descartes in the 17th century retains a strong appeal.

Behavioral psychologists continue to reject the notion of consciousness—in animals as well as humans. One behaviorist wrote this about the cognitive animal psychologists: "They are the George Romaneses of today. Speculating about memory, reasoning, and consciousness in animals is no less ridiculous today than it was a hundred years ago" (Baum, 1994, p. 138).

COMMENT

With the cognitive movement in experimental psychology and the emphasis on consciousness in humanistic psychology and post-Freudian psychoanalysis, we can see that consciousness has reclaimed the central position it held when the field began. An analysis of 95 presidential addresses to the American Psychological Association showed that the subject matter of psychology "has shifted dramatically from a dominant acceptance of subjective phenomena to a dominant acceptance of objective phenomena and then back to subjective phenomena" (Gibson, 1993, p. 43). Consciousness has made a substantial and vigorous comeback.

Cognitive psychology must be judged a success. By the early 1970s, the movement had attracted so many followers that it needed its own journals. Within a decade six journals were established: *Cognitive Psychology* (1970), *Cognition* (1971), *Memory and Cognition* (1983), *Journal of Mental Imagery* (1977), *Cognitive Therapy and Research* (1977), and *Cognitive Science* (1977).

Jerome Bruner described cognitive psychology as "a revolution whose limits we still cannot fathom" (Bruner, 1983, p. 274). Its impact has extended to most areas of psychology and has influenced psychological thought in Europe and Russia. It has also moved beyond psychology itself, attempting to consolidate the work of many major disciplines in a unified study of how the mind acquires knowledge.

This new perspective, dubbed *cognitive science*, is an amalgamation of cognitive psychology, linguistics, anthropology, philosophy, computer sciences, artificial intelligence, and the neurosciences. Although George Miller has questioned how united such disparate fields of study can become—suggesting they be spoken of in the plural as cognitive sciences—there is no denying the growth of this multidisciplinary approach. Cognitive science laboratories and institutes have been established at universities throughout the United States, and some psychology departments have been renamed cognitive science departments. This suggests that by whatever name, the cognitive approach to the study of mental phenomena and processes may dominate not only psychology but also other disciplines, well into the next century.

No revolution, however successful, is without its critics. Most Skinnerian behaviorists opposed the cognitive movement (Skinner, 1987b, 1989). Even those who supported it pointed out weaknesses and limitations. They note there are few concepts on which the majority of cognitive psychologists agree or even consider important, and that there is considerable confusion about terminology and definitions. "Now, some twenty years since the cognitive revolution marked a major turning point in the history of science, we still lack any satisfying consensus as to its exact nature and source, its driving rationale, or its precise meaning for the future" (Sperry, 1993, p. 880).

Another criticism relates to what some see as an overemphasis on cognition at the expense of other influences on thought and behavior, such as motivation and emotion. The professional literature dealing with motivation and emotion has declined over the past few decades, whereas the publications on cognition have increased. The result, Ulric Neisser suggested, is a narrowing and a sterility of the field. Neisser commented that "human thinking is passionate and emotional, people operate from complex motives. A computer program, by contrast . . . has no emotion and is monomaniacal in its singlemindedness" (quoted in Goleman, 1983, p. 57). There is, then, the danger that cognitive psychology is becoming fixated on thought processes to the same extent that behaviorism focused only on overt behavior.

Other critics charge that the progress of cognitive psychology is more illusory than real, because many psychologists have simply adopted the words *cognitive* or *cognition* without making any fundamental changes in the way they approach their research problems. The behaviorist B. F. Skinner said that it had become "fashionable to insert the word 'cognitive' wherever possible" (Skinner, 1983b, p. 194). George Miller agreed:

> *What seems to have happened is that many experimental psychologists who were studying human learning, perception, or thinking began to call themselves cognitive psychologists without changing in any obvious way what they had always been thinking and doing—as if they suddenly discovered they had been speaking cognitive psychology all their lives. So our victory may have been more modest than the written record would have led you to believe.* (QUOTED IN BRUNER, 1983, P. 126)

Support for the suggestion that cognitive psychology's victory may be more modest than previously thought was provided by a citation analysis of the leading journals in cognitive psychology, behaviorism, and psychoanalysis for the years 1979 to 1988. If cognitive psychology had displaced the other two approaches, we would expect to find declining citation rates in their journals; that was not the case (Friman, Allen, Kerwin, & Larzelere, 1993).

The citation numbers were highest for the cognitive psychology journals and exhibited the only significant positive trend, but there was no significant downward trend for journal citations for behaviorism. Citation rates for psychoanalytic journals were not as high as those for behaviorism, but the rate of decline was marginal. These findings indicate that cognitive psychology may be the dominant force in psychology today, but the other two positions remain strong. "Repeated declarations of a [cognitive] revolution may be more a reflection of the enthusiasms many cognitive psychologists have for their sub-discipline than of actual events. . . . reports on the death of behavioral psychology and psychoanalysis appear greatly exaggerated" (Friman, Allen, Kerwin, & Larzelere, 1993, pp. 662, 664).

Cognitive psychology is not complete. The movement is still developing, still history in the making, and it is too soon to judge its ultimate impact and contribution. It does already have the trappings and characteristics that define each of the earlier schools of thought: Cognitive psychology has its own journals, laboratories, meetings, jargon, and convictions, as well as the zeal of the righteous believers. We may now speak of cognitivism, as we do of functionalism and behaviorism. Cognitive psychology has become what other schools of thought became in their time—part of psychology's mainstream. And that, as we have seen, is the natural progression of revolutions when they become successful.

A FINAL NOTE

If the history of psychology as depicted in these chapters tells us anything, it is that when a movement becomes formalized into a school, it gains a momentum that can be stopped only by its success in overthrowing the established position. When that happens, the unobstructed arteries of the once vigorous and youthful movement begin to harden. Flexibility turns to rigidity, revolutionary passion turns to protection of position, and eyes and minds begin to close to new ideas. And in this way a new establishment is born. So it is in the progress of any science, an evolutionary building to ever higher levels of development. There is no completion, no finish, but instead a never-ending process of growth, as newer species evolve from older ones and attempt to adapt to a continually changing environment.

Discussion Questions

1. Discuss the accomplishments of the major schools of thought in psychology. Describe the status of humanistic psychology and the reasons for its fate.
2. What were the antecedent influences on humanistic psychology? Compare the views of Maslow and Rogers on self-actualization and on the characteristics of the psychologically healthy person.
3. Describe the antecedent influences on cognitive psychology. How did the changing Zeitgeist in physics influence cognitive psychology?
4. Describe the early signs of a cognitive revolution in psychology. What personal factors motivated Miller and Neisser to help shape the cognitive movement?
5. Discuss the notion of the computer as a metaphor for mental processes. Note three ways in which cognitive psychology differs from behavioral psychology.
6. What is the role of introspection in cognitive psychology? Describe the current ideas in psychology about unconscious cognitive activities.
7. What is the present status of animal cognition within psychology? What criticisms have been made of cognitive psychology? In your opinion, has the cognitive movement been successful? Why or why not?

Suggested Readings

Baars, B. J. (1986). *The cognitive revolution in psychology.* New York: Guilford. Describes the transition from post-Watsonian behaviorism to cognitive psychology. Includes interviews with Miller, Neisser, and other cognitive psychologists.

DeCarvalho, R. J. (1990). A history of the "third force" in psychology. *Journal of Humanistic Psychology, 30*(4), 22–44. Examines the history of the humanistic movement and its formalization as a school of psychological thought.

Evans, R. I. (1975). *Carl Rogers: The man and his ideas.* New York: Dutton. Interviews with Rogers on the evolution of the self, person-centered therapy, and applications of humanistic psychology to education.

Hoffman, E. (1988). *The right to be human: A biography of Abraham Maslow.* Los Angeles: Tarcher. Describes Maslow's life and career from early work with primates to the human potential movement.

Skinner, B. F. (1987). Whatever happened to psychology as the science of behavior? *American Psychologist, 42,* 780–786. Presents

Skinner's view that humanistic psychology and cognitive psychology are "obstacles" in the way of psychology's acceptance of his program for the experimental analysis of behavior.

CHAPTER 16

GENDER AND RACE IN THE HISTORY OF PSYCHOLOGY

ISSUES IN CONTEMPORARY PSYCHOLOGY

WE HAVE seen that psychology in every age has been faced with problems and challenges, with changing social and intellectual environments to which it has tried to adapt; the psychology of the final years of the 20th century is no exception. Psychology today, both as science and profession, is struggling with issues that will help define the future course of the field. One such problem relates to cognitive psychology, whether it will emerge as a defining paradigm to unite and give coherence to the discipline in a way no previous school of thought was able to do.

Other continuing problems include the dichotomies and divergences of the experimental versus the clinical, and the pure versus the applied approaches to the field. In addition, the impact of historiographical discoveries, such as new biographies and other unforeseen data of history, may change our perception and assessment of the development of psychology. The growing competition facing providers of clinical psychology services in the health care marketplace is also of major concern.

Although these issues are crucial to the continuing growth and adaptation of the field, we choose to close our discussion of the history of psychology with the problem posed by the social and political context to which so many aspects of American society are now trying to adapt; that is, the recognition of the multicultural nature of our population. Different gender, racial, and ethnic groups are proclaiming separate identities and demanding that society respond to their unique needs.

This diversity in the culture is manifested in classroom, clinic, and workplace. It represents a new Zeitgeist that may turn out to be the greatest contextual challenge facing psychology.

THE POLITICS OF IDENTITY

We have seen a great deal of diversity in the definitions and theories of psychology over the past century, yet there has been a relative lack of diversity in the personal attributes of the psychologists. Despite differences in ideas and methods, most of the psychologists we have discussed share certain identifying characteristics: They were, typically, White males from European countries or from the United States.

Almost all of the subjects in their experiments—subjects on whom their research and theories were based—were White. And, as one Black psychologist reminded us, only partially joking, even the laboratory rats were white (Guthrie, 1976)! In addition, often the observers, subjects, or patients were male. Recall, for example, that Henry Murray's theory of personality is based on 51 male college students.

Yet the major figures in the history of psychology offered theories of human nature that, by implication, were assumed to be valid for all people, regardless of gender, race, or cultural heritage. Few theorists acknowledged that their ideas might apply *only* to men or to Whites, to college students at Harvard or to neurotic middle-aged Viennese women. Few psychologists explained that their approach might not be appropriate to account for the behavior or mental functioning of people with other characteristics or from other backgrounds. Although recognizing the importance of a diversity of social and environmental factors—such as the influence of parents, siblings, and peers—not many scientists admitted that gender or race might have exerted a greater influence.

Throughout this book we have seen examples of how discrimination and prejudice restricted educational and career opportunities for women and for minorities. We noted in chapter 1 that some psychologists are challenging the contemporary psychology establishment to remedy past gender and racial bias. This movement, called identity politics, represents an attempt by people excluded from the field, or whose progress in the field has been restricted, to define their identities in terms of their unique life experiences and to end the exclusionary practices of socially dominant groups (Sampson, 1993). The psychologists subscribing to this view (including women,

Blacks and other ethnic minorities, gays and lesbians, and people questioning the Eurocentric world view) believe that psychology does not represent them, that it marginalizes their legitimate concerns and fails to reflect their interests and problems.

We explore in this chapter the impact of gender and racial bias in the history of psychology and describe how these practices led to the exclusion of qualified individuals from full participation in the field. In discussing racial bias, our focus is on African Americans. We noted that Hispanic Americans, Asian Americans, and American Indians have also experienced discrimination. In recent years, as we will see, they have organized professional associations and meetings and are publishing journals dealing with their unique concerns. However, their numbers are small and the available material on their contributions to the history of psychology is limited.

We also examine the steps mainstream psychology is taking to acknowledge and correct past injustices. But first, it is important to emphasize a frequently overlooked point: It is undeniably true that in this or any other textbook on the history of psychology, you will find few women and minority scholars. However, it is also true you will find few White men singled out for attention, relative to their numbers in the field. That is not the result of deliberate discrimination. Rather, it is a function of the way in which history in any field is written.

> *The history of a discipline such as psychology involves describing major discoveries, illuminating questions of priority, and identifying "great individuals" in the context of a national or international Zeitgeist. Those who carry out the day-to-day work of a discipline are unlikely to find themselves in this spotlight. . . . Psychologists who bring considerable talent to bear behind the scenes—teaching courses, seeing clients, performing experiments, sharing data with colleagues . . . seldom are publicly recognized beyond a small group of peers.* (PATE & WERTHEIMER, 1993, P. XV)

Thus, history ignores the everyday work of the *majority* of psychologists, regardless of their race or gender.

With this point in mind, we return to the basic issues of this chapter:

1. some people have been denied the opportunity to become psychologists solely because of their gender or race; and

2. some psychologists have faced discriminatory practices within the field that have kept them from making the best use of their abilities.

The Variability Hypothesis and the Myth of Male Superiority

In most academic fields of study in Europe and the United States, women were traditionally excluded from colleges and universities. When Harvard University was founded in 1636, for example, women were not admitted. It was not until the 1830s that some American colleges relaxed their prohibitions and accepted women as undergraduates.

The primary reason for this restriction was a belief in the so-called natural intellectual superiority of men. Even if women were granted educational opportunities similar to those for men, so this argument ran, women's innate intellectual deficiencies prevented them from reaping the benefits. Prominent 19th-century scientists such as Charles Darwin, as well as most of the psychologists of the day (including Hall, Thorndike, Cattell, and Freud), subscribed to this view.

Much of the myth of male superiority derives from Darwinian theories of male variability. Darwin found that in many species, males showed a wider range of development of physical characteristics and abilities than did females; the characteristics and abilities of females were found to be more clustered around the average. This female tendency toward averageness was thought to make women less likely to benefit from education and less likely to achieve in mental or scholarly work. It was a small step from that proposition to the idea that female brains were less highly evolved than male brains. Because males were more variable, they could adapt to and benefit from more varied and stimulating environments (Rossiter, 1982; Shields, 1982).

A popular related theory was that women who were exposed to higher education suffered physical and emotional damage. Hall, among others, argued that educating women endangered their biological imperative to motherhood by disrupting the menstrual cycle and weakening the maternal urge. If women were to be educated at all, Hall wrote, "they should be educated to motherhood" (quoted in Diehl, 1986, p. 872).

In 1873, a former Harvard medical school professor, Edward Clarke, described the effects of higher education on women as follows: "monstrous brains and puny bodies; abnormally active cerebration and abnormally weak digestion; flowing thought and constipated bowels" (quoted in Scarborough & Furumoto, 1987, p. 4). He also warned that "Identical education of the sexes is a crime before God and humanity" (Clarke, 1873, p. 127). Clarke's book was so popular it appeared in 17 editions over 13 years.

Today, more than half the graduates who receive PhDs in psychology are women. Two thirds of psychology graduate students are women, as are three fourths of psychology undergraduate students

(Martin, 1995). However, as we have seen, the history of psychology has been dominated by men. In part this is because women were discriminated against even after they were admitted to degree programs to pursue careers in psychology. They faced restrictions and inequities in graduate schools and in job opportunities. Recall that Margaret Washburn was not allowed to enroll at Columbia University because she was a woman. It was not until 1892 that Yale, the University of Chicago, and a few other institutions agreed to accept women graduate students. For nearly 20 years after the formal founding of psychology as a scientific discipline, it was difficult for women even to become psychologists, much less to make significant contributions to the development of the field.

It was also difficult for women to obtain faculty positions except at traditionally women's colleges. Even when women were hired at universities they faced restrictions on promotion and tenure. They tended to be kept at the lower faculty ranks and received lower pay than men in comparable jobs.

Despite these practices, psychology's record is more enlightened than that of other scholarly disciplines and professions. By the beginning of the 20th century, some 20 women had earned doctoral degrees in psychology. In the 1906 edition of *American Men of Science,* 12% of the listed psychologists are women, a high figure considering the barriers to their graduate education. These first women psychologists were actively encouraged to join the American Psychological Association.

Cattell was a leader in urging the acceptance of women in psychology, reminding male colleagues they ought not to "draw a sex line" (unpublished letter quoted in Sokal, 1992, p. 115). At APA's second annual meeting, in 1893, Cattell nominated two women for membership. Because of his and similar efforts, APA could claim that "no other society had women members earlier in its development" (Sokal, 1992, p. 115). Between 1893 and 1921, APA elected 79 women to membership, some 15% of the total of new members during that period (Scarborough, 1992). Mary Whiton Calkins became APA's first woman president in 1905, and in 1994, Dorothy Cantor was the eighth woman psychologist to be elected to serve as president of APA.

Other professional societies denied women full participation for many years. Women doctors were not permitted to join the American Medical Association until 1915, and women lawyers were excluded from the American Bar Association until 1918 (Furumoto, 1987).

WOMEN IN APPLIED PSYCHOLOGY

Because women were effectively prohibited from seeking university positions for much of psychology's history, they found employment in the applied fields, particularly the helping professions such as clinical and counseling psychology, child guidance, and school psychology. Many women psychologists made significant contributions in those areas, notably in the development and application of psychological tests (Denmark & Fernandez, 1992).

Florence L. Goodenough, who received her PhD in 1924 from Stanford University, developed the *Draw-A-Man Test* (now the *Goodenough-Harris Drawing Test*), a widely used nonverbal intelligence test for children. A pioneer in test construction, Goodenough worked at the Institute of Child Development at the University of Minnesota for more than 20 years. She also published a detailed review of the psychological testing movement (Goodenough, 1949) and several works on child psychology.

Maude A. Merrill James, director of a psychological clinic for children in California, coauthored, with Lewis Terman, the 1937 revision of the *Stanford-Binet Intelligence Test,* which became widely known as the Terman-Merrill test. Thelma Gwinn Thurstone, who received her PhD in 1927 from the University of Chicago, married psychologist L. L. Thurstone. Like many women who work with their husbands, her contributions were overlooked and uncredited. She helped develop the *Primary Mental Abilities* battery, a group intelligence test. She was professor of education at the University of North Carolina and director of the psychometric laboratory (Denmark & Fernandez, 1992).

The long career of Anne Anastasi (1908–) at Fordham University established her as an authority on psychological testing (see Anastasi, 1988, 1993). In 1971 she served as president of APA and has received many professional honors, including the National Medal of Science. One survey named Anastasi as the most prominent woman psychologist in the English-speaking world (Gavin, 1987). Her first academic job, after earning her PhD at Columbia University in 1930, was as an instructor in psychology at Barnard College, at an annual salary of $2400. In 1947 Anastasi joined the faculty of Fordham, retiring as Professor Emeritus in 1979 (Sexton & Hogan, 1990).

Although women psychologists became successful in areas such as testing, their work in applied psychology was a professional disadvantage. Jobs in nonacademic institutions rarely provide the time, financial support, and graduate-student assistance required to conduct research and to write scholarly articles, the primary vehicles for professional visibility. In an applied setting, one's contributions are rarely recognized beyond the confines of the organization. The tremendous growth of applied psychology in the United States—the legacy of the functionalist school of psychology—offered women psychologists employment opportunities. But it also meant that women remained largely separate from mainstream academic psychology, where the theories, research programs, and schools of thought—the themes of the history of psychology—were being developed.

Many academic psychologists retained a negative view of applied work, considering it menial and inferior; applied areas such as counseling were belittled as "women's work." The published histories of psychology tended to undervalue applied psychology, and with it the contributions of the many women psychologists who worked in hospitals, clinics, research institutes, and military and government agencies and who pioneered and developed applied areas. It is also interesting to note that no woman was ever elected president of the American Association of Applied Psychology, despite the fact that by 1941, one third of its members were women (Rossiter, 1982).

Those women psychologists who were able to secure university teaching appointments, and who conducted research and published their findings, faced another obstacle that deprived them of recognition. For many years now, the accepted method of citation lists last names followed by initials (Jones, M. instead of Jones, Mary, for example), making it impossible for readers to determine whether the author is male or female. Thus, our awareness of the contributions of women psychologists is lower than if first names were included in reference lists and bibliographies.

In addition, women professors and graduate students did not always receive credit for their work. "We will probably never know how much work was done by women but credited to men: how many footnotes of appreciation should rightfully have been coauthorship, how many times junior authorship should have been senior authorship, or how many times it was the male coauthor who should have received the footnote" (Bernstein & Russo, 1974, p. 131).

THE PSYCHOLOGY OF WOMEN

A number of women psychologists have worked to develop and promote a psychology of women. Within the psychoanalytic tradition, Karen Horney was an early feminist, presenting her first paper on the psychology of women in 1922 (see chapter 14). In academic experimental psychology, Helen Bradford Thompson Woolley and Leta Stetter Hollingworth studied issues in feminine psychology.

HELEN BRADFORD THOMPSON WOOLLEY (1874–1947)

Helen Bradford Thompson was born in Chicago in 1874. Her parents supported the idea of education for women; all three of the Thompson daughters attended college. Helen Thompson received her undergraduate degree at the University of Chicago in 1897 and her

Archives of the History of American Psychology/University of Akron

HELEN BRADFORD THOMPSON WOOLLEY

PhD in 1900. Her major professors were Angell and Dewey; Dewey called Thompson one of his most brilliant students (James, 1994). After a postgraduate fellowship in Paris and Berlin, she became director of the psychological laboratory at Mount Holyoke College in Massachusetts.

She married a physician, Paul Woolley, and accompanied him to the Philippines where he was director of a laboratory. In 1908 the couple moved to Cincinnati, Ohio, where Helen accepted the directorship of the vocation bureau of the public school system, concerned with child welfare issues. Her research on the effects of child labor led to changes in the state's labor laws. (In many states at that time, children as young as 8 were working in factories 10 hours a day, 6 days a week. Few states had protective legislation regarding age, working hours, or minimum wages for children.) In 1921 she served as president of the National Vocational Guidance Association.

That year the Woolleys relocated to Detroit, Michigan, where Helen joined the staff of the Merrill-Palmer Institute and established a nursery school program to study child development and mental abilities. In 1924 she became director of the new Institute of Child Welfare Research at Columbia University (Scarborough & Furumoto, 1987), continuing her work on learning in early childhood, vocational education, and school guidance counseling.

Helen Woolley's doctoral dissertation at the University of Chicago was the first experimental test of the Darwinian notion that women were biologically inferior to men, an idea assumed at the time to be so obvious that it needed no scientific study (James, 1994). She administered a battery of tests to 25 male and 25 female subjects to measure motor abilities, sensory thresholds (taste, smell, hearing, pain, and vision), intellectual abilities, and personality traits.

The results showed no sex differences in emotional functioning and only small nonsignificant differences in intellectual abilities. The data also revealed that women were slightly superior to men in abilities such as memory and sensory perception. Woolley took the unprecedented step of attributing the differences to social and environmental factors—the differences in child-rearing practices and expectations for boys and for girls—rather than to biological determinants (Rossiter, 1982).

Woolley published her results in *The Mental Traits of Sex: An Experimental Investigation of the Normal Mind in Men and Women* (Thompson, 1903). Her conclusions were not well received by male academic psychologists. For example, G. Stanley Hall accused her of giving a feminist interpretation to the data (Hall, 1904). The fact it was a *woman* whose research showed that women were not biologically inferior to men somehow tainted or biased the results (James, 1994). She later wrote two reviews of the growing research literature on the psychology of sex differences for the prestigious journal *Psychological Bulletin* (Woolley, 1910, 1914).

For 30 years Woolley worked as teacher, researcher, and mentor for women psychologists in the areas of child development and education. When poor health and a traumatic divorce forced her to retire prematurely, the focus on the psychology of women passed to others.

LETA STETTER HOLLINGWORTH (1886–1939)

Archives of the History of American Psychology/University of Akron

LETA STETTER HOLLINGWORTH

Born in Nebraska, Leta Stetter attended the University of Nebraska, graduating in 1906 with Phi Beta Kappa honors. She taught high school for 2 years while her fiancé, Harry Hollingworth, completed his PhD in psychology with Cattell at Columbia University. Leta and Harry married in 1908. He taught at Barnard College in New York City, but she was not permitted to continue teaching, to her surprise and regret. It was believed that if a married woman was employed outside the home, her husband and children would suffer.

She turned to writing but was unable to publish her short stories. The couple lived frugally, and Harry accepted consulting jobs to save enough money for Leta to go to graduate school. In 1916 she earned her PhD from Teacher's College, Columbia University, studying with Thorndike, and worked as a psychologist for the civil service in New York City. Five years later she was cited in *American Men of Science* for her contributions to the psychology of women.

Leta Hollingworth conducted extensive empirical research on the variability hypothesis, the idea that for physical, psychological, and emotional functioning, women were a more homogeneous and average group than men and thus showed less variation. Because of this belief, as we noted, it was assumed men would benefit more than women from diverse educational and career opportunities. Women, who were believed to be more alike in their abilities, had less capacity for mental challenges and little need to be educated for anything more demanding than keeping house and caring for their children.

Hollingworth's research between 1913 and 1916 focused on physical and sensorimotor functioning and intellectual abilities in a variety of subjects: infants, men and women college students, and women during their menstrual period (when it was assumed their mental and emotional conditions were affected by their natural bodily processes). Her data refuted the variability hypothesis and other notions of female inferiority. For example, she found that the menstrual cycle was not related to performance deficits in perceptual and motor skills or in intellectual abilities, as had long been assumed (Hollingworth, 1914).

Further, she challenged the concept of an innate instinct for motherhood, questioning the idea that women could find satisfaction only through bearing children, and she dismissed the notion that a woman's desire to achieve in other fields was somehow abnormal or unhealthy. She suggested that social and cultural attitudes rather than biological factors were influential in keeping women from becoming fully contributing members of society (Benjamin & Shields, 1990; Shields, 1975). Hollingworth also cautioned vocational and guidance counselors against advising women that they should restrict their aspirations to the then socially acceptable fields of child-rearing and housekeeping, where prominence and visibility are denied. "No one knows who is the best housekeeper in America," she wrote. "Eminent housekeepers do not and cannot exist" (quoted in Benjamin & Shields, 1990, p. 177).

Leta Hollingworth also made significant contributions to clinical, educational, and school psychology, especially the educational and emotional needs of "gifted" children, a term she coined (Benjamin, 1975). Despite the breadth and quality of her research, she was never able to obtain research grant support (H. Hollingworth, 1943). She was active in the woman's suffrage movement, campaigning for a woman's right to vote (finally achieved in 1920) and took part in parades and demonstrations in New York.

WOMEN IN PSYCHOLOGY TODAY: THE CALL TO ENGENDER PSYCHOLOGY

Historians of psychology are paying more attention to issues of discrimination and are striving to provide recognition for women psychologists where appropriate. The professional literature on the role of women in psychology has grown rapidly since the 1970s (see, for example, Bohan, 1990; Furumoto, 1989; O'Connell & Russo, 1983, 1988, 1990; Scarborough & Furumoto, 1987). The American Psychological Association established a task force on the status of women and a committee on women in psychology. The committee's purpose was to ensure that "women achieve equality as members of the psychological community" (*Women in the American Psychological Association*, 1986, p. 1). The APA's Division of Psychology of Women (Division 35) was formed to promote the study of women and the appreciation of the contributions of women psychologists. Among their priorities are greater participation of ethnic minority women and the development of a multicultural approach to examining the psychosocial aspects of women's lives.

Although women are no longer invisible within professional psychology, inequities still exist in universities. The vast majority of tenured college faculty are men (81%). Half of all male faculty members achieve full professor rank, compared with one fourth of female faculty members. Only 13% of graduate psychology departments are headed by women (Denmark, 1994).

A survey of a random sample of two APA divisions found gender inequities at all career levels. In graduate school, men were more likely than women to find role models among the faculty. Men were more apt to develop personal relationships with faculty members and to receive assistance in finding jobs. Men produced more publications and earned higher salaries from full-time jobs in psychology than did women. Some 96% of the men who relocated to advance their careers reported that their wives or companions moved with them. Among women, 32% reported that their partners went with them when their jobs required them to relocate (Cohen & Gutek, 1991).

Professors who identified themselves as feminists reported that colleagues and administrators were generally unsupportive, unsympathetic, and even hostile toward their views. They also reported being targets of sexual harassment. They were often denied tenure and were cautioned that discussions of gender issues were inappropriate in the classroom (Denmark, 1994). Other problems affecting women (and minority) faculty include heavier workloads than White men faculty, feelings of isolation, undervaluation of research on gender and ethnic issues, and lack of mentoring (Gainen & Boice, 1993).

Gender bias has been demonstrated in behavioral science and in biomedical research as well, where the subjects in most long-term research programs typically have been male. This is particularly common with health-related issues such as aging, cholesterol levels, AIDS, cancer, and heart disease. Research on drug effects is almost exclusively based on male subjects (Denmark, 1994).

Florence Denmark (1931–) received her PhD in social psychology in 1958 from the University of Pennsylvania. As a professor at Hunter College, she directed the first doctoral-level seminar on the psychology of women (Paludi & Russo, 1990). A past president of APA, Denmark has worked extensively on gender bias issues and recently issued a challenge to the psychology establishment: Psychologists must work to "engender" psychology. (To engender something means to bring it forth, to cause it to grow and develop.) Denmark argues that psychologists must generate and stimulate a new psychology, one that will be more sensitive to issues of gender and diversity. Although the number of women psychologists has increased over the last 2 decades, simply having more women working in the field has not made mainstream psychology more aware of these issues.

> *Our psychology must make visible women's viewpoints and experiences. It should also promote women and other underrepresented groups (including people of color and lesbians and gay men) into key positions where they can influence the direction taken by psychology. . . . From the classroom to the laboratory to [clinical] practice, we must make psychology more feminist.*
> (DENMARK, 1994, PP. 329, 334)

Whether that goal can be achieved remains for future history books to tell.

AFRICAN AMERICANS IN THE
HISTORY OF PSYCHOLOGY

African Americans have faced decades of racial prejudice and discrimination within psychology. In 1940, only four Black colleges in the United States offered undergraduate degree programs in psychology. In those instances when Blacks were permitted to enroll at predominantly White universities, they confronted a variety of barriers to achievement. In the 1930s and 1940s, for example, many colleges did not allow Black students to live on campus.

The major university providing psychology instruction for Black students was the department at Howard University in Washington, D.C., under the leadership of Francis Sumner, the first African American to earn a doctoral degree in psychology from a university in the United States. He received his PhD from G. Stanley Hall at Clark University in 1920.

James A. Bayton (1912–1990), who earned his bachelor's and master's degrees at Howard University, received his PhD in 1943 from the University of Pennsylvania and taught at Howard University from 1947 until his death. He had begun his doctoral program at Columbia, studying with Robert Woodworth, but transferred to the University of Pennsylvania to be closer to his family when his father became ill. One of his major professors at Pennsylvania was Lightner Witmer.

Bayton was instrumental in improving undergraduate education in psychology for African American students. At historically Black colleges, instruction in psychology was often the province of the department of education, largely because the Black community had a great need for teachers. Bayton helped promote scientific psychology as an independent discipline at several Black colleges, including Morgan State in Baltimore and Virginia State in Petersburg. He received the American Psychological Foundation's Distinguished Teaching Award in 1981. His research interests included self-concepts of African Americans, racial tension in military settings, and issues in marketing research. He was often called on to serve as an expert witness in school desegregation and job discrimination cases (Ross & Hicks, 1991).

A few Blacks were among the American scholars who went to Germany for graduate study during the early years of psychology's development. For example, Gilbert Haven Jones earned his PhD in 1901 from the University of Jena and later studied at the University of Göttingen (Guthrie, 1976). Recall that at that time, psychology was not yet a separate discipline at most universities, so Jones's degree was in philosophy. He was the first African American with a doctoral degree to teach psychology courses in the United States. He later became dean and vice president of Wilberforce University in Ohio. Although American Blacks did not face the same sort of prejudice at European universities that they did at home, few had the financial resources that would permit them to study abroad.

The first African American woman to earn a doctoral degree in the field was Inez Beverly Prosser (1897–1934), who studied the development of Black children in segregated and integrated schools. She taught at Tillotson College in Texas and at Tougaloo College in Mississippi before completing her graduate studies at the University of Cincinnati in 1933. Tragically, she was killed in an automobile accident a year later.

Between 1930 and 1938, only 36 Black students were enrolled in graduate psychology programs in universities outside the American South; the vast majority of these students were at Howard University (Guthrie, 1976). Between 1920 and 1950, 32 Blacks earned doctoral degrees in psychology. From 1920 to 1966, the 10 most prestigious psychology departments in the United States awarded eight doctorates to Blacks, out of a total of more than 3,700 doctoral degrees granted (Guthrie, 1976; Russo & Denmark, 1987).

Earning a PhD was only the first hurdle; finding a suitable job was next. Few universities hired Blacks as faculty members, and most business organizations that employed applied psychologists—a major source of jobs for women psychologists—were effectively closed to African Americans. The historically Black colleges were the primary sources of employment, but the working conditions rarely afforded opportunities for the type of scholarly research that led to professional visibility and recognition. In 1936, a professor at a Black college described the situation as follows:

> *Lack of money, overwork, and other unpleasant factors make it practically impossible for him to do anything outstanding in the field of pure scholarship. He cannot buy books on a large scale himself, and he cannot get them at his school libraries, because there are no really adequate libraries in the Negro schools. Probably the worst handicap of all is the lack of a scholarly atmosphere about him. There is no incentive, and, of course, no money for research in most schools.* (A. P. DAVIS, QUOTED IN GUTHRIE, 1976, P. 123)

Although the outlook for African American and other ethnic minority psychologists has improved in terms of educational and career opportunities, these psychologists remain underrepresented within the profession. However, this situation may not be wholly explained in terms of deliberate discrimination.

Beginning in the 1970s, American colleges and universities made intensive efforts to recruit minority students and faculty and offered significant amounts of financial aid. The number of minority psychology students increased but the rise proved temporary. Minority undergraduate student enrollment declined in the 1980s and has since remained stagnant at around 12%. The low percentage of psychology students leads inevitably to an underrepresentation of minority faculty. Only 6% of psychology college professors are minorities: 3% African Americans, 1% Hispanic, 1% Asian American, 1% Native American. These psychologists are less likely than White psychologists to hold senior faculty positions or to be granted tenure (Guzman, Schiavo, & Puente, 1992).

AFRICAN AMERICAN PSYCHOLOGY

Some African American psychologists suggest that non-Black psychologists cannot adequately comprehend the American Black experience because they do not share that heritage. They have called for an African American psychology to embrace African philosophy and traditions as well as the experiences of Blacks forcibly transplanted to the United States generations ago. One Black psychologist wrote:

> *It is critical to acknowledge that human beings of African origin as a group have experienced and are still experiencing a common core of stimuli that differs qualitatively and quantitatively from those of other peoples of the world [and that] results in ethnically distinct behavior. [It is] most improbable that a researcher who is not imbued with Black culture would have the perceptions, psychological sets, and other predispositions that would allow for Africentric interpretation of data.* (HOUSTON, 1990, PP. 23, 24)

Although not all Black psychologists subscribe to this separatist view, African American psychology is a viable enterprise with its own organizations, publications, and guidelines for the study of the Black experience. In 1968, the Association of Black Psychologists was formed to develop a psychology that would enhance the psychological well-being of Blacks and promote research on the Black experience.

Although their membership numbers are small, compared to APA, the Hispanic Psychological Association, the American Indian Psychological Association, and the Asian American Psychological Association are working to generate and amplify approaches to psychology from their individual perspectives. We may see these organizations as part of the identity-politics movement, motivated by the belief that explanations of human behavior and mental functioning developed largely by White males within the European tradition may not be wholly applicable to other groups. It should be noted again, however, that not all minority psychologists agree with this point of view.

A major purpose of these organizations is to encourage research on minority issues, which has been underreported in the mainstream psychology journals. A survey of APA journals in the areas of clinical, developmental, educational, social, and personality psychology found that in the 1970s and 1980s, fewer than 4% of the published articles dealt with African American issues. The author of the survey wrote: "African Americans have been increasingly marginalized in mainstream psychological research, as methodologically sound empirical articles on Blacks have all but vanished from the pages of major APA journals" (Graham, 1992, p. 636).

Several African American psychologists have had a significant impact on the education and training of Black psychologists in the United States and on issues of concern not only to the Black community but to American society as a whole. We will note briefly some of the contributions of Francis Sumner, Kenneth Clark, and Mamie Phipps Clark.

FRANCIS CECIL SUMNER (1895–1954)

Born in Arkansas in 1895, Francis Sumner was educated at elementary schools in Virginia and New Jersey, but did not attend high school because at that time opportunities for formal education at that level were rare for Blacks. He taught himself through his own program of reading as well as wide-ranging discussions with his parents, who provided him with old textbooks and a variety of other reading materials. After passing a written examination, Sumner was accepted at Lincoln University in Pennsylvania. He graduated *magna cum laude* and class valedictorian in 1915 with a bachelor's degree in philosophy. His goal was to become a writer.

He spent a year at Clark College in Massachusetts, earning a second bachelor's degree by taking courses in English, foreign languages, and psychology. Although he could not live on campus, a professor arranged for him to stay with a "fine colored family in Worcester" (Guthrie, 1976, p. 177). In the college dining hall, a special table was arranged for him and the few Whites who had befriended him. After Sumner worked for a year as an instructor in psychology and German at Lincoln, G. Stanley Hall awarded him a fellowship to enter the PhD program at Clark University. Although his studies were interrupted by a year of service as a sergeant with an infantry regiment in France during World War I, Sumner became, in 1920, the first Black American to earn a doctoral degree in psychology. His dissertation was on the psychoanalysis of Freud and Adler. Hall called the work "a genuinely new contribution" (Guthrie, 1976, p. 182).

Sumner's academic career included 7 years at West Virginia State College, where he conducted research and published several important articles on racial prejudice, education for Blacks, and the nature-nurture controversy (see, for example, Sumner, 1928). In

1928 he became acting chair of the psychology department at Howard University, where he remained until his death in 1954. He established the psychology department as a separate entity, independent of the education department, and assumed the chairmanship in 1930. Within 2 decades, he had made Howard University the leading institution for the recruiting and training of Black psychologists (Guthrie, 1976).

Sumner and his graduate students pursued an active research program in several areas including psychology of religion, psychology and the law, and attitudes of Blacks and Whites toward the criminal justice system in the United States. With his interest in languages, Sumner translated for the leading APA journals more than 3,000 articles from German, French, and Spanish.

KENNETH B. CLARK (1914–) AND MAMIE PHIPPS CLARK (1917–1983)

Archives of the History of American Psychology/University of Akron

KENNETH B. CLARK

Kenneth Clark was born in the Panama Canal Zone, where his parents had emigrated from Jamaica to find work. When Clark was 7 years old, his mother brought him to New York City to pursue, as most immigrants do, a better way of life. She took a job in a garment factory. She taught her son that he must excel at whatever he did, and she refused to accept race, color, or prejudice as excuses for not succeeding. "To hell with it," she told him. "Whatever anyone else can do, you can do" (Clark, 1978, p.77).

Despite the discrimination he faced, Clark did succeed. In high school, he worked to achieve the highest grade in the class to win the school's economics prize at graduation. Then he learned that he would be denied the prize because the teacher "wasn't ready at that time to award it to a black student" (Clark, 1978, p. 80).

He enrolled at Howard University in Washington, D.C., where he studied with Francis Sumner, who guided Clark into a career in psychology. Clark received his undergraduate and master's degrees from Howard, and applied to Cornell and to Columbia for admission to their doctoral programs. Cornell rejected his application, saying that because PhD candidates "worked so closely together," they couldn't admit Blacks (Clark, 1978, p. 82). Clark earned his PhD from Columbia University in 1940.

Much of Clark's professional career has been as professor of psychology at City University of New York, where he conducted research on the effects of segregation and on racial awareness of children. He founded a metropolitan research institute to examine problems of the urban poor and was the first Black psychologist to serve as president of the American Psychological Association.

Mamie Phipps was born in Hot Springs, Arkansas, and attended Howard University, where she met Kenneth Clark and was encouraged to switch her major from mathematics to psychology. She graduated *magna cum laude* with a bachelor's degree in 1938 and a master's degree in 1939. She spent a summer working as a secretary in a Washington law office that was involved in civil rights cases challenging racial segregation practices. Her experience there made Phipps aware of the importance of scientific research on the psychological effects of racial segregation on Black children. Her master's thesis, on the development in Black children of a sense of identity, stimulated her new husband's interest in the topic. Together they investigated several related problems in Black psychology (Clark & Clark, 1939a, 1939b, 1940). Mamie Clark was awarded a research fellowship to attend Columbia University, where she earned her PhD in 1944.

Despite her degrees and her impressive research record, prejudice against women and Blacks prevented her from obtaining a university faculty position, and she managed to find only a minor position analyzing research data, a job she described as "humiliating" (Guthrie, 1990, p. 69). She later found employment as a psychologist at a children's home in New York. She also worked as a research psychologist for the American Public Health Association and for the U. S. Armed Forces Institute. In 1946, Mamie and Kenneth Clark established the Northside Center for Child Development in Harlem, where she worked until her retirement in 1979, directing a wide-ranging program providing educational, social, and psychological services to children.

Her research on the self-concept and social identification in Black children, using brown dolls and white dolls as experimental stimuli, found that boys and girls, ages 3–7, accepted their racial identity as part of their self-concept. Black children reported that they looked more like a brown doll than like a white doll. When asked which doll they would prefer to play with, more than half the Black children chose the white doll because it was seen as somehow better. Mamie Clark suggested that this indicated a desire to be White and that the Black children were experiencing emotional conflicts because of their skin color, which they perceived to be less desirable than white skin (M. P. Clark, 1944).

Kenneth Clark discussed the results of Mamie Clark's research in a legal brief he helped prepare on the effects of racial segregation. This work was cited in the U. S. Supreme Court's landmark 1954 decision ending racial segregation in public schools. Thus, the research of Mamie and Kenneth Clark had an impact on the laws of the United States and brought about a massive change in social and government policy. It also fostered the idea that psychological research could be a tool for social change and made psychologists aware of the importance of differences in cultural perceptions.

TOWARD A MULTICULTURAL PSYCHOLOGY

Psychology has recognized that it must not ignore the multicultural nature of the American population, and it is making efforts to be responsive to the politics of identity. The APA's Office of Ethnic Minority Affairs has programs to recruit minority undergraduate students and guide them into graduate schools, and to facilitate the hiring of minority psychologists in colleges and universities. It also sponsors efforts to broaden the college psychology curriculum by emphasizing cultural diversity.

We are seeing an increase in the amount of research performed on the effects of cultural identity on personality, and the results are being more widely disseminated as journals become more receptive to publishing work on these issues.

Coursework focusing on cultural diversity has increased. The APA accreditation program for graduate training in psychology requires reference to cultural as well as individual differences. Massachusetts has become the first state to require that all those applying for certification as psychologists receive multicultural training. As of July 1996, doctoral students must take at least four credit hours of training in multicultural issues and, beginning July 1999, at least one course in race and ethnicity (DeAngelis, 1994).

There is a moral imperative for psychologists to act on the demands of the identity-politics movement, but there is also a practical reason for doing so. By the year 2000, African Americans and other minorities are expected to account for one third of the population of the United States. Unless psychology meets their needs, the field will become increasingly irrelevant to a substantial portion of students in college classrooms, clients in clinics and mental health centers, and employees and managers in organizations. Thus, identity politics is a significant contextual factor that will influence the continuing evolution of American psychology.

The United States is a multicultural and an ethnically diverse society. The field of psychology for more than a century has attempted, through its various definitions and schools of thought, to be a useful science of behavior and mental life. It must once again evolve and adapt to changes in its environment to reflect that diversity, as it has successfully adapted to other challenges throughout its history. The future of psychology requires it.

DISCUSSION QUESTIONS

1. Explain the term "identity politics." Name several groups of psychologists who believe that contemporary psychology does not represent them or is not responsive to their concerns. Why does

the writing of the history of any field restrict the number of people singled out for attention?

2. Describe the variability hypothesis and the notion of male superiority. How did the research of Helen Woolley and Leta Hollingworth refute these ideas?

3. Discuss some of the obstacles encountered by women who wished to pursue careers in psychology. What steps have been taken to reduce the marginalization of women in psychology?

4. What are the advantages and the disadvantages for women of careers in applied fields of psychology?

5. Discuss the issue of an African American psychology that is distinct from mainstream psychology. In your opinion, is the development of a separate psychology for each racial and ethnic minority the best way to promote attention to the unique problems and interests of these groups?

6. Discuss the problems faced by African Americans in pursuing careers in psychology. Describe the contributions of James Bayton, Francis Sumner, and Kenneth and Mamie Clark.

7. Why is it important for the future of psychology that it respond to the identity-politics movement? In your opinion, is the call to engender psychology being heeded? Give examples.

SUGGESTED READINGS

Bohan, J. S. (Ed.). (1992). *Seldom seen, rarely heard: Women's place in psychology.* Boulder, CO: Westview Press. Articles on feminist psychology and psychology's marginalization of women and women's experiences.

Goodchilds, J. D. (1991). *Psychological perspectives on human diversity in America.* Washington, DC: American Psychological Association. Master lectures by five prominent psychologists on bias in the history of psychology based on race, ethnicity, gender, and sexual orientation.

Guthrie, R. V. (1976). *Even the rat was white: A historical view of psychology.* New York: Harper & Row. Describes the contributions of Black psychologists to American psychology.

Jones, R. L. (Ed.). (1991). *Black psychology* (3rd ed.). Berkeley, CA: Cobb & Henry. Papers on the understanding and interpretation of behavior from a variety of viewpoints as alternatives to the Eurocentric perspective.

O'Connell, A. N., & Russo, N. F. (Eds.). (1990). *Women in psychology: A bio-bibliographic sourcebook.* New York: Greenwood Press. Brief biographies of 36 prominent women in the history of psychology including Anastasi, Calkins, Clark, Denmark, Freud, Hollingworth, and Horney.

REFERENCES

Abel, T. M. (1989). Some famous psychologists I have known. *History of Psychology Newsletter, 21*(2), 53–55.

Adams, G. (1928, December). The decline of psychology in America. *American Mercury,* pp. 450–454.

Adams, G. R., & Fitch, S. A. (1982). Ego stage and identity status development: A cross–sequential analysis. *Journal of Personality and Social Psychology, 43,* 574–583.

Adler, A. (1930). Individual psychology. In C. Murchison (Ed.), *Psychologies of 1930* (pp. 395–405). Worcester, MA: Clark University Press.

Agassiz, G. R. (Ed.). (1922). *Meade's headquarters, 1863–1865: Letters of Colonel Theodore Lyman from the Wilderness to Appomattox.* Boston: Atlantic Monthly Press.

Allen, G. W. (1967). *William James.* New York: Viking Press.

Allport, G. W. (1937). *Personality: A psychological interpretation.* New York: Holt.

Allport, G. W. (1967). Autobiography. In E. G. Boring & G. Lindzey (Eds.), *A history of psychology in autobiography* (Vol. 5, pp. 1–25). New York: Appleton-Century-Crofts.

Allport, G. W. (1968). *The person in psychology.* Boston: Beacon Press.

Altman, I. (1987). Centripetal and centrifugal trends in psychology. *American Psychologist, 42,* 1058–1069.

Amsel, A., & Rashotte, M. E. (Eds.). (1984). *Mechanisms of adaptive behavior: Clark L. Hull's theoretical papers with commentary.* New York: Columbia University Press.

Anastasi, A. (1988). *Psychological testing* (6th ed.). New York: Macmillan.

Anastasi, A. (1993). A century of psychological testing: Origins, problems, and progress. In T. K. Fagan & G. R. VandenBos (Eds.), *Exploring applied psychology* (pp. 9–36). Washington, DC: American Psychological Association.

Anderson, R. J. (1980). Wundt's prominence and popularity in his later years. *Psychological Research, 42,* 87–101.

Angell, J. R. (1904). *Psychology.* New York: Holt.

Angell, J. R. (1907). The province of functional psychology. *Psychological Review, 14,* 61–91.

Appignanesi, L. & Forrester, J. (1992). *Freud's women.* New York: Basic Books.

Archer, S. L., (1982). The lower age boundaries of identity development. *Child Development, 53,* 1551–1556.

Ash, M. G. (1987). Psychology and politics in interwar Vienna: The Vienna Psychological Institute, 1922–1942. In M. G. Ash & W. R. Woodward (Eds.), *Psychology in twentieth-century thought and society* (pp. 143–164). Cambridge, England: Cambridge University Press.

Ash, M. G. (1992). Cultural contexts and scientific change in psychology: Kurt Lewin in Iowa. *American Psychologist, 47,* 198–207.

Averill, L. A. (1990). Recollections of Clark's G. Stanley Hall. *Journal of the History of the Behavioral Sciences, 26,* 125–130.

Baars, B. J. (1986). *The cognitive revolution in psychology.* New York: Guilford Press.

Balance, W. D. G., & Bringmann, W. G. (1987). Fechner's mysterious malady. *History of Psychology Newsletter, 19*(1/2), 36–47.

Baldwin, B. T. (Ed.). (1980). In memory of Wilhelm Wundt. In W. G. Bringmann & R. D. Tweney (Eds.), *Wundt studies: A centennial collection* (pp. 280–308). Toronto: C. J. Hogrefe. (Original work published 1921)

Bandura, A. (1982). Self-efficacy mechanism in human agency. *American Psychologist, 37,* 122–147.

Bandura, A. (1986). *Social foundations of thought and action: A social cognitive theory.* Englewood Cliffs, NJ: Prentice-Hall.

Barron, J. W., Eagle, M. N., & Wolitzky, D. L. (1992). *Interface of psychoanalysis and psychology.* Washington, DC: American Psychological Association.

Baum, W. M. (1994). John B. Watson and behavior analysis: Past, present, and future. In J. T. Todd & E. K. Morris (Eds.), *Modern perspectives on John B. Watson and classical behaviorism* (pp. 133–140). Westport, CT: Greenwood Press.

Becker, E. (1973). *The denial of death.* New York: Free Press.

Beers, C. (1908). *A mind that found itself.* London: Longmans, Green.

Bekhterev, V. M. (1932). *General principles of human reflexology.* New York: International Publishers.

Belmont, L., & Marolla, F. A. (1973). Birth order, family size and intelligence. *Science, 182,* 1096–1101.

Ben–David, J., & Collins, R. (1966). Social factors in the origin of a new science: The case of psychology. *American Sociological Review, 31,* 451–465.

Benjamin, L. T., Jr. (1975). The pioneering work of Leta Hollingworth in the psychology of women. *Nebraska History, 56,* 493–505.

Benjamin, L. T., Jr. (1986). Why don't they understand us? A history of psychology's public image. *American Psychologist, 41,* 941–946.

Benjamin, L. T., Jr. (1987). Knee jerks, Twitmyer, and the Eastern Psychological Association. *American Psychologist, 42,* 1118–1120.

Benjamin, L. T., Jr. (1988a). E. B. Titchener and structuralism. In L. T. Benjamin, Jr. (Ed.), *A history of psychology: Original sources and contemporary research* (pp. 208–211). New York: McGraw-Hill.

Benjamin, L. T., Jr. (1988b). A history of teaching machines. *American Psychologist, 43,* 703–712.

Benjamin, L. T., Jr. (1991). A history of the New York branch of the American Psychological Association: 1903–1935. *American Psychologist, 46,* 1003–1011.

Benjamin, L. T., Jr. (1992). Introduction to the special issue: The history of American psychology. *American Psychologist, 47,* 109.

Benjamin, L. T., Jr. (1993). *A history of psychology in letters.* Dubuque, IA: Brown & Benchmark.

Benjamin, L. T., Jr., Bryant, W. H. M., Campbell, C., Fisher, J., & Holtz, C. (1994). *Between psoriasis and ptarmigan: American encyclopedia portrayals of psychology, 1880–1940.* Manuscript submitted for publication.

Benjamin, L. T., Jr., Durkin, M., Link, M., Vestal, M., & Acord, J. (1992). Wundt's American doctoral students. *American Psychologist, 47,* 123–131.

Benjamin, L. T., Jr., Rogers, A. M., & Rosenbaum, A. (1991). Coca-Cola, caffeine, and mental deficiency: Harry Hollingworth and the Chattanooga trial of 1911. *Journal of the History of the Behavioral Sciences, 27,* 42–55.

Benjamin, L. T., Jr., & Shields, S. (1990). Leta Stetter Hollingworth (1886-1939). In A. N. O'Connell & N. F. Russo (Eds.), *Women in psychology: A bio-bibliographic sourcebook* (pp. 173–183). New York: Greenwood Press.

Berkeley, G. (1957a). An essay towards a new theory of vision. In M. W. Calkins (Ed.), *Berkeley: Essay, principles, dialogues* (pp. 1–98). New York: Scribners. (Original work published 1709)

Berkeley, G. (1957b). A treatise concerning the principles of human knowledge. In M. W. Calkins (Ed.), *Berkeley: Essay, principles, dialogues* (pp. 99–216). New York: Scribners. (Original work published 1710)

Berliner, D. C. (1993). The 100-year journey of educational psychology: From interest, to disdain, to respect for practice. In T. K. Fagan & G. R. VandenBos (Eds.), *Exploring applied psychology: Origins and critical analyses* (pp. 37–78). Washington, DC: American Psychological Association.

Berman, L. (1927). *The religion called Behaviorism.* New York: Boni & Liveright.

Bernstein, M. D., & Russo, N. F. (1974). The history of psychology revisited: Or, up with our foremothers. *American Psychologist, 29,* 130–134.

Bettelheim, B. (1982). *Freud and man's soul.* New York: Knopf.

Binet, A. (1971). *The psychic life of micro-organisms.* West Orange, NJ: Saifer. (Original work published 1889)

Bjork, D. W. (1983). *The compromised scientist: William James in the development of American psychology.* New York: Columbia University Press.

Bjork, D. W. (1993). *B. F. Skinner.* New York: Basic Books.

Blanton, S. (1971). *Diary of my analysis with Sigmund Freud.* New York: Hawthorn Books.

Blumenthal, A. L. (1975). A reappraisal of Wilhelm Wundt. *American Psychologist, 30,* 1081–1088.

Blumenthal, A. L. (1977). Wilhelm Wundt and early American psychology: A clash of two cultures. *Annals of the New York Academy of Sciences, 291,* 13–20.

Blumenthal, A. L. (1979). Wilhelm Wundt: The founding father we never knew. *Contemporary Psychology, 24,* 547–550.

Blumenthal, A. L. (1985). Wilhelm Wundt: Psychology as the propaedeutic science. In C. E. Buxton (Ed.), *Points of view in the modern history of psychology* (pp. 19–50). Orlando, FL: Academic Press.

Boakes, R. (1984). *From Darwin to behaviourism: Psychology and the minds of animals.* Cambridge, England: Cambridge University Press.

Boas, M. (1961). *The scientific renaissance: 1450–1630.* London: Collins.

Bohan, J. S. (1990). Contextual history: A framework for replacing women in the history of psychology. *Psychology of Women Quarterly, 14,* 213–227.

Boneau, C. A. (1992). Observations on psychology's past and future. *American Psychologist, 47,* 1586–1596.

Boorstin, D. J. (1983). *The discoverers.* New York: Random House.

Bootzin, R. R., Kihlstrom, J. F., & Schacter, D. L. (Eds.). (1990). *Sleep and cognition: Information processing outside of awareness.* Washington, DC: American Psychological Association.

Boring, E. G. (1929). *A history of experimental psychology.* New York: Appleton.

Boring, E. G. (1950). *A history of experimental psychology* (2nd ed.). New York: Appleton-Century-Crofts.

Boring, E. G. (1967). Titchener's experimentalists. *Journal of the History of the Behavioral Sciences, 3,* 315–325.

Bornstein, R. F., & Pittman, T. S. (1992). *Perception without awareness: Cognitive, clinical, and social perspectives.* New York: Guilford Press.

Bottome, P. (1939). *Alfred Adler.* New York: Putnam.

Breland, H. M. (1974). Birth order, family configuration and verbal achievement. *Child Development, 45,* 1011–1019.

Breland, K., & Breland, M. (1961). The misbehavior of organisms. *American Psychologist, 16,* 681–684.

Brems, C., Thevenin, D. M., & Routh, D. K. (1991). The history of clinical psychology. In C. E. Walker (Ed.), *Clinical psychology: Historical and research foundations* (pp. 3–35). New York: Plenum Press.

Brentano, F. (1874). *Psychology from an empirical standpoint.* Leipzig: Duncker & Humblot.

Breuer, J., & Freud, S. (1895). Studies on hysteria. In *Standard edition* (Vol. 2). London: Hogarth Press.

Brewer, C. L. (1991). Perspectives on John B. Watson. In G. A. Kimble, M. Wertheimer, & C. White (Eds.), *Portraits of pioneers in psychology* (pp. 171–186). Hillsdale, NJ: Erlbaum.

Bridgman, P. W. (1927). *The logic of modern physics.* New York: Macmillan.

Bridgman, P. W. (1954). Remarks on the present state of operationism. *Scientific Monthly, 79,* 224–226.

Bringmann, W. G., & Balk, M. M. (1992). Another look at Wilhelm Wundt's publication record. *History of Psychology Newsletter, 24*(3/4), 50–66.

Bringmann, W. G., Bringmann, M. W., & Early, C. E. (1992). G. Stanley Hall and the history of psychology. *American Psychologist, 47,* 281–289.

Broad, W., & Wade, N. (1982). *Betrayers of the truth: Fraud and deceit in the halls of science.* New York: Simon & Schuster.

Brody, N. (1987). Introduction: Some thoughts on the unconscious. *Personality and Social Psychology Bulletin, 13,* 293–298.

Brome, V. (1981). *Jung: Man and myth.* New York: Atheneum.

Bronstein, P. (1988). Personality from a sociocultural perspective. In P. Bronstein & K. Quina (Eds.), *Teaching a psychology of people: Resources for gender and sociocultural awareness* (pp. 60–68). Washington, DC: American Psychological Association.

Brown, J. A. C. (1963). *Freud and the post-Freudians.* London: Cassell.

Brown, J. (1992). *The definition of a profession: The authority of metaphor in the history of intelligence testing, 1890–1930.* Princeton, NJ: Princeton University Press.

Brožek, J. (1980). The echoes of Wundt's work in the United States, 1887–1977: A quantitative citation analysis. *Psychological Research, 42,* 103–107.

Bruner, J. S. (1982, May). Psychology has been responding to the so-called postindustrial revolution. *Psychology Today,* pp. 42–43.

Bruner, J. S. (1983). *In search of mind: Essays in autobiography.* New York: Harper & Row.

Buckley, K. W. (1982). The selling of a psychologist: John Broadus Watson and the application of behavioral techniques to advertising. *Journal of the History of the Behavioral Sciences, 18,* 207–221.

Buckley, K. W. (1989). *Mechanical man: John Broadus Watson and the beginnings of behaviorism.* New York: Guilford Press.

Buckley, K. W. (1994). Misbehaviorism: The case of John B. Watson's dismissal from Johns Hopkins University. In J. T. Todd & E. K. Morris (Eds.), *Modern perspectives on John B. Watson and classical behaviorism* (pp. 19–36). Westport, CT: Greenwood Press.

Burnham, J. (1968). On the origins of behaviorism. *Journal of the History of the Behavioral Sciences, 4,* 143–151.

Burnham, J. (1994). John B. Watson: Interviewee, professional figure, symbol. In J. T. Todd & E. K. Morris (Eds.), *Modern perspectives on John B. Watson and classical behaviorism* (pp. 65–73). Westport, CT: Greenwood Press.

Burt, C. (1962). The concept of consciousness. *British Journal of Psychology, 53,* 229–242.

Cadwallader, T. C. (1984). Neglected aspects of the evolution of American comparative and animal psychology. In G. Greenberg & E. Tobach (Eds.), *Behavioral evolution and integrative levels* (pp. 15–48). Hillsdale, NJ: Erlbaum.

Cadwallader, T. C. (1987). Early zoological input to comparative and animal psychology at the University of Chicago. In E. Tobach (Ed.), *Historical perspectives and the international status of comparative psychology* (pp. 37–59). Hillsdale, NJ: Erlbaum.

Cadwallader, T. C. (1992). The historical roots of the American Psychological Association. In R. B. Evans, V. S. Sexton, & T. C. Cadwallader (Eds.), *The American Psychological Association: A historical perspective* (pp. 3–41). Washington, DC: American Psychological Association.

Camfield, T. M. (1992). The American Psychological Association and World War I: 1914 to 1919. In R. B. Evans, V. S. Sexton, & T. C. Cadwallader (Eds.), *The American Psychological Association: A historical perspective* (pp. 91–118). Washington, DC: American Psychological Association.

Campbell, J. (1988). *The improbable machine: What the upheavals in artificial intelligence research reveal about how the mind really works.* New York: Simon & Schuster.

Carr, H. A. (1925). *Psychology.* New York: Longmans, Green.

Carr, H. A. (1930). Functionalism. In C. Murchison (Ed.), *Psychologies of 1930* (pp. 59–78). Worcester, MA: Clark University Press.

Catania, A. C. (1992). B. F. Skinner, organism. *American Psychologist, 47,* 1521–1530.

Cattell, J. M. (1890). Mental tests and measurements. *Mind, 15,* 373–381.

Cattell, J. M. (1896). Address of the president before the American Psychological Association, 1895. *Psychological Review, 3,* 134–148.

Cattell, J. M. (1904). The conceptions amd methods of psychology. *Popular Science Monthly, 66,* 176–186.

Cattell, J. M. (1928). Early psychological laboratories. *Science, 67,* 543–548.

Chiesa, M. (1992). Radical behaviorism and scientific frameworks: From mechanistic to relational accounts. *American Psychologist, 47,* 1287–1299.

Chomsky, N. (1959). [Review of *Verbal Behavior* by B. F. Skinner.] *Language, 35,* 26–58.

Chomsky, N. (1972). *Language and mind.* New York: Harcourt Brace Jovanovich.

Churchill, S. D. (1988, August). *Humanistic psychology and introductory psychology textbooks: Wizards and straw men.* Paper presented at the meeting of the American Psychological Association, Atlanta, GA.

Clark, K. B. (1978). Kenneth B. Clark: Social psychologist. In T. C. Hunter (Ed.), *Beginnings* (pp. 76–84). New York: Crowell.

Clark, K. B., & Clark, M. P. (1939a). The development of consciousness of self and the emergence of racial identification in Negro preschool children. *Journal of Social Psychology, 10,* 591–599.

Clark, K. B., & Clark, M. P. (1939b). Segregation as a factor in the racial identification of Negro preschool children. *Journal of Experimental Education, 8,* 1961–1965.

Clark, K. B., & Clark, M. P. (1940). Skin color as a factor in racial identification of Negro preschool children. *Journal of Social Psychology, 11,* 159–169.

Clark, M. P. (1944). Changes in primary mental abilities with age. *Archives of Psychology, 291.* New York: Columbia University.

Clarke, E. H. (1873). *Sex and education.* Boston: Osgood.

Cohen, A. G., & Gutek, B. A. (1991). Sex differences in the career experiences of members of two APA divisions. *American Psychologist, 46,* 1292–1298.

Comte, A. (1896). *The positive philosophy of Comte.* London: Bell. (Original work published 1830)

Cook, R. C. (1993). The experimental analysis of cognition in animals. *Psychological Science, 4,* 174–178.

Coon, D. J. (1982). Eponymy, obscurity, Twitmyer, and Pavlov. *Journal of the History of the Behavioral Sciences, 18,* 255–262.

Coon, D. J. (1994). "Not a creature of reason": The alleged impact of Watsonian behaviorism on advertising in the 1920s. In J. T. Todd & E. K. Morris (Eds.), *Modern perspectives on John B. Watson and classical behaviorism* (pp. 37–63). Westport, CT: Greenwood Press.

Costall, A. (1993). How Lloyd Morgan's Canon backfired. *Journal of the History of the Behavioral Sciences, 29,* 113–122.

Cranston, A. (1986). Psychology in the Veterans Administration. *American Psychologist, 41,* 990–995.

Crewsdon, J. (1988). *By silence betrayed: Sexual abuse of children in America.* Boston: Little, Brown.

Cunningham, S. (1985, May). Humanists celebrate gains, goals. *APA Monitor,* pp. 16, 18.

Cuny, H. (1965). *Ivan Pavlov: The man and his theories.* New York: Eriksson.

Dallenbach, K. (1967). Autobiography. In E. G. Boring & G. Lindzey (Eds.), *A history of psychology in autobiography* (Vol. 5, pp. 57–93). New York: Appleton-Century-Crofts.

Danziger, K. (1987). Social context and investigative practice in early twentieth–century psychology. In M. G. Ash & W. R. Woodward (Eds.), *Psychology in twentieth-century thought and society* (pp. 13–33). Cambridge, England: Cambridge University Press.

Danziger, K. (1988). A question of identity: Who participated in psychological experiments? In J. G. Morawski (Ed.), *The rise of experimentation in American psychology* (pp. 35–52). New Haven, CT: Yale University Press.

Darwin, C. (1859). *On the origin of species by means of natural selection.* London: Murray.

Darwin, C. (1871). *The descent of man.* London: Murray.

Darwin, C. (1872). *The expression of the emotions in man and animals.* London: Murray.

Darwin, C. (1877). A biographical sketch of an infant. *Mind, 2*, 285–294.

Davidow, S., & Bruhn, A. R. (1990). Earliest memories and the dynamics of delinquency: A replication study. *Journal of Personality Assessment, 54*, 601–616.

DeAngelis, T. (1994, March). Massachusetts now requires multicultural training. *APA Monitor*, p. 41.

DeCarvallo, R. (1990). A history of the "third force" in psychology. *Journal of Humanistic Psychology, 30*, 22–44.

Decker, H. S. (1991). *Freud, Dora, and Vienna 1900.* New York: Free Press.

Demarest, J. (1987). Two comparative psychologies. In E. Tobach (Ed.), *Historical perspectives and the international status of comparative psychology* (pp. 127–155). Hillsdale, NJ: Erlbaum.

Denmark, F. L. (1994). Engendering psychology. *American Psychologist, 49*, 329–334.

Denmark, F. L., & Fernandez, L. C. (1992). Women: Their influence and their impact on the teaching of psychology. In A. E. Puente, J. R. Matthews, & C. L. Brewer (Eds.), *Teaching psychology in America: A history* (pp. 171–188). Washington, DC: American Psychological Association.

Dennis, P. M. (1984). The Edison questionnaire. *Journal of the History of the Behavioral Sciences, 20*, 23–37.

Dennis, P. M. (1991). Psychology's first publicist: H. Addington Bruce and the popularization of the subconscious and the power of suggestion before World War I. *Psychological Reports, 68*, 755–765.

Descartes, R. (1912). *A discourse on method.* London: Dent. (Original work published 1637)

Desmond, A., & Moore, J. (1991). *Darwin.* New York: Warner Books.

Dewey, J. (1886). *Psychology.* New York: Harper.

Dewey, J. (1896). The reflex arc concept in psychology. *Psychological Review, 3*, 357–370.

Dewey, J. (1900). Psychology and social practice. *Psychological Review, 7*, 105–124.

Dewsbury, D. A., & Pickren, W. E. (1992). Psychologists as teachers: Sketches toward a history of teaching during 100 years of American psychology. In A. E. Puente, J. R. Matthews, & C. L. Brewer (Eds.), *Teaching psychology in America: A history* (pp. 127–151). Washington, DC: American Psychological Association.

Diamond, S. (1980). A plea for historical accuracy [Letter to the editor]. *Contemporary Psychology, 25*, 84–85.

Diehl, L. A. (1986). The paradox of G. Stanley Hall: Foe of coeducation and educator of women. *American Psychologist, 41*, 868–878.

Distinguished Scientific Contribution Award. (1981). *American Psychologist, 36*, 27–42. [A. Bandura]

Domjan, M. (1987). Animal learning comes of age. *American Psychologist, 42*, 556–564.

Donnelly, M. E. (Ed.). (1992). *Reinterpreting the legacy of William James.* Washington, DC: American Psychological Association.

Duke, C., Fried, S., Pliley, W., & Walker, D. (1989). Rosalie Rayner Watson: The mother of a behaviorist's sons. *Psychological Reports, 65*, 163–169.

Eagle, M. N. (1988). How accurate were Freud's case histories? [Book review of *Freud and the Rat Man*]. *Contemporary Psychology, 33*, 205–206.

Ebbinghaus, H. (1885). *On memory.* Leipzig: Duncker & Humblot.

Ebbinghaus, H. (1902). *The principles of psychology.* Leipzig: Veit.

Ebbinghaus, H. (1908). *A summary of psychology.* Leipzig: Veit.

Eissler, K. R. (1971). *Talent and genius: The fictitious case of Tausk contra Freud.* New York: Quadrangle.

Ellenberger, H. F. (1970). *The discovery of the unconscious: The history and evolution of dynamic psychiatry.* New York: Basic Books.

Ellenberger, H. F. (1972). The story of "Anna O": A critical review with new data. *Journal of the History of the Behavioral Sciences, 8*, 267–279.

Erikson, E. H. (1968). *Identity: Youth and crisis.* New York: Norton.

Erikson, E. H. (1975). *Life history and the historical moment.* New York: Norton.

Erikson, E. H., Erikson, J. M., & Kivnick, H. Q. (1986). *Vital involvement in old age.* New York: Norton.

Evans, R. B. (1972). E. B. Titchener and his lost system. *Journal of the History of the Behavioral Sciences, 8*, 168–180.

Evans, R. B. (1991). E. B. Titchener on scientific psychology and technology. In G. A. Kimble, M. Wertheimer, & C. White (Eds.), *Portraits of pioneers in psychology* (pp. 89–103). Hillsdale, NJ: Erlbaum.

Evans, R. B. (1992). Growing pains: The American Psychological Association from 1903 to 1920. In R. B. Evans, V. S. Sexton, & T. C. Cadwallader (Eds.), *The American Psychological Association: A historical perspective* (pp. 73–90). Washington, DC: American Psychological Association.

Evans, R. B., & Scott, F. J. D. (1978). The 1913 International Congress of Psychology: The American congress that wasn't. *American Psychologist, 33*, 711–723.

Evans, R. B., Sexton, V. S., & Cadwallader, T. C. (1992). Preface: The American Psychological Association at 100. In R. B. Evans, V. S. Sexton, & T. C. Cadwallader (Eds.), *The American Psychological Association: A historical perspective* (pp. xv–xvi). Washington, DC: American Psychological Association.

Evans, R. I. (1968). *B. F. Skinner: The man and his ideas.* New York: Dutton.

Evans, R. I. (1989). *Albert Bandura: The man and his ideas.* New York: Praeger.

Fallon, D. (1992). An existential look at B. F. Skinner. *American Psychologist, 47,* 1433–1440.

Farthing, G. W. (1992). *The psychology of consciousness.* Englewood Cliffs, NJ: Prentice-Hall.

Fechner, G. (1966). *Elements of psychophysics.* New York: Holt, Rinehart and Winston. (Original work published 1860)

Fernald, D. (1984). *The Hans legacy: A story of science.* Hillsdale, NJ: Erlbaum.

Ferster, C. B., & Skinner, B. F. (1957). *Schedules of reinforcement.* New York: Appleton-Century-Crofts.

Fine, R. (1990). Anna Freud: 1895–1982. In A. N. O'Connell & N. F. Russo (Eds.), *Women in psychology: A bio-bibliographic sourcebook* (pp. 96–103). New York: Greenwood Press.

Fisher, S., & Greenberg, R. P. (1977). *The scientific credibility of Freud's theories and therapy.* New York: Basic Books.

Fishman, D. B., & Franks, C. M. (1992). Evolution and differentiation within behavior therapy: A theoretical and epistemological review. In D. K. Freedheim (Ed.), *History of psychotherapy: A century of change* (pp. 159–196). Washington, DC: American Psychological Association.

Fowler, R. D. (1990). In memorium: Burrhus Frederic Skinner, 1904–1990. *American Psychologist, 45,* 1203.

Freeman, L. (1972). *The story of Anna O.* New York: Walker.

Freud, A. (1936). *The ego and the mechanisms of defense.* London: Hogarth Press.

Freud, A. (1966). Introduction to the technique of child analysis. In *The writings of Anna Freud* (Vol. I, pp. 3–69). New York: International Universities Press. (Original work published as "Four lectures on child analysis," 1927)

Freud, S. (1895). On the origins of psychoanalysis. In J. Strachey (Ed. & Trans.), *The standard edition of the complete psychological works of Sigmund Freud* (Vol. 1). London: Hogarth Press.

Freud, S. (1896). Heredity and the etiology of the neuroses. In *Standard edition* (Vol. 3, pp. 142–156). London: Hogarth Press.

Freud, S. (1900). The interpretation of dreams. In *Standard edition* (Vols. 4, 5). London: Hogarth Press.

Freud, S. (1901). The psychopathology of everyday life. In *Standard edition* (Vol. 6). London: Hogarth Press.

Freud, S. (1905a). Fragment of an analysis of a case of hysteria. In *Standard edition* (Vol. 7, pp. 3–122). London: Hogarth Press. (Original work published 1901)

Freud, S. (1905b). Three essays on the theory of sexuality. In *Standard edition* (Vol. 7, pp. 125–243). London: Hogarth Press.

Freud, S. (1910). Five lectures on psychoanalysis. In *Standard edition* (Vol. 11, pp. 3–55). London: Hogarth Press. (Original work published 1909)

Freud, S. (1914). On the history of the psychoanalytic movement. In *Standard edition* (Vol. 14, pp. 3–66). London: Hogarth Press.

Freud, S. (1917). A difficulty in the path of psychoanalysis. In *Standard edition* (Vol. 17, pp. 136–144). London: Hogarth Press.

Freud, S. (1920). Beyond the pleasure principle. In *Standard edition* (Vol. 18, pp. 3–64). London: Hogarth Press.

Freud, S. (1933). New introductory lectures on psychoanalysis. In *Standard edition* (Vol. 22, pp. 3–182). London: Hogarth Press.

Freud, S. (1940). An outline of psychoanalysis. In *Standard edition* (Vol. 23, pp. 141–207). London: Hogarth Press.

Freud, S. (1941). Findings, ideas, problems. In *Standard edition* (Vol. 23, pp. 299–300). London: Hogarth Press. (Original work published 1938)

Freud, S. (1954). *The origins of psychoanalysis: Letters to Wilhelm Fliess, drafts and notes: 1887–1902.* New York: Basic Books.

Freud, S. (1964). *The letters of Sigmund Freud.* New York: McGraw-Hill. (Original letter published 1883)

Freud, S. (1992). *The diary of Sigmund Freud, 1929–1939: A record of the final decade.* New York: Charles Scribner's Sons. (Original work published 1939)

Friman, P. C., Allen, K. D., Kerwin, M. L. E., & Larzelere, R. (1993). Changes in modern psychology: A citation analysis of the Kuhnian displacement thesis. *American Psychologist, 48,* 658–664.

Fuller, R. C. (1986). *Americans and the unconscious.* New York: Oxford University Press.

Funder, D. C. (1991). Global traits: A neo-Allportian approach to personality. *Psychological Science, 2,* 31–39.

Furumoto, L. (1987). On the margins: Women and the professionalization of psychology in the United States, 1890–1940. In M. G. Ash & W. R. Woodward (Eds.), *Psychology in twentieth-century thought and society* (pp. 93–113). Cambridge, England: Cambridge University Press.

Furumoto, L. (1988). Shared knowledge: The Experimentalists, 1904–1929. In J. G. Morawski (Ed.), *The rise of experimentation in American psychology* (pp. 94–113). New Haven, CT: Yale University Press.

Furumoto, L. (1989). The new history of psychology. In I. S. Cohen (Ed.), *The G. Stanley Hall Lecture Series* (Vol. 9, pp. 5–34). Washington, DC: American Psychological Association.

Furumoto, L. (1990). Mary Whiton Calkins (1863–1930). In A. N. O'Connell & N. F. Russo (Eds.), *Women in psychology: A bio-bibliographic sourcebook* (pp. 57–65). New York: Greenwood Press.

Gainen, J., & Boice, R. (Eds.). (1993). *Building a diverse faculty.* San Francisco: Jossey-Bass.

Gallistel, C. R. (1989). Animal cognition: The representation of space, time, and number. *Annual Review of Psychology, 40,* 155–189.

Galton, F. (1869). *Hereditary genius.* London: Macmillan.

Galton, F. (1874). *English men of science: Their nature and nurture.* London: Macmillan.

Galton, F. (1889). *Natural inheritance.* London: Macmillan.

Gantt, W. H. (1941). Introduction. In I. P. Pavlov, *Lectures on conditioned reflexes.* New York: International Publishers.

Gantt, W. H. (1979, February). Interview with Professor Emeritus W. Horsley Gantt. *Johns Hopkins Magazine,* pp. 26–32.

Gardner, H. (1993). *Creating minds.* New York: Basic Books.

Gavin, E. (1987). Prominent women in psychology, determined by ratings of distinguished peers. *Psychotherapy in Private Practice, 5,* 53–68.

Gay, P. (1983). *Education of the senses.* New York: Oxford University Press.

Gay, P. (1988). *Freud: A life for our time.* New York: Norton.

Gazzaniga, M. S. (1988). Life with George: The birth of the Cognitive Neuroscience Institute. In W. Hirst (Ed.), *The making of cognitive science: Essays in honor of George A. Miller* (pp. 230–241). Cambridge, England: Cambridge University Press.

Gelfand, T. (1992). Sigmund-sur-Seine: Fathers and brothers in Charcot's Paris. In T. Gelfand & J. Kerr (Eds.), *Freud and the history of psychoanalysis* (pp. 29–57). Hillsdale, NJ: Analytic Press.

Gelman, D. (1988, June 27). Where are the patients? *Newsweek.*

Gengerelli, J. A. (1976). Graduate school reminiscences: Hull and Koffka. *American Psychologist, 31,* 685–688.

Gerow, J. R. (1986). *Psychology through Time: The first ten years.* Paper presented at the meeting of the Southeastern Psychological Association.

Geuter, U. (1987). German psychology during the Nazi period. In M. G. Ash & W. R. Woodward (Eds.), *Psychology in twentieth-century thought and society* (pp. 165–187). Cambridge, England: Cambridge University Press.

Geuter, U. (1992). *The professionalization of psychology in Nazi Germany.* Cambridge, England: Cambridge University Press.

Gibson, K. R. (1993). The presidential addresses of the American Psychological Association, 1892–1992: A qualitative analysis. *History of Psychology Newsletter, 25*(4), 43–53.

Gilgen, A. R. (1982). *American psychology since World War II: A profile of the discipline.* Westport, CT: Greenwood Press.

Goleman, D. (1983, May). A conversation with Ulric Neisser. *Psychology Today,* pp. 54–62.

Goleman, D. (1987, August 30). B. F. Skinner: On his best behavior. *New York Times.*

Goodenough, F. L. (1949). *Mental testing: Its history, principles, and applications.* New York: Rinehart.

Goodstein, L. D. (1988). The growth of the American Psychological Association. *American Psychologist, 43,* 491–498.

Gould, S. J. (1976). Darwin and the captain. *Natural History, 85*(1), 32–34.

Gould, S. J. (1981). *The mismeasure of man.* New York: Norton.

Gould, S. J. (1986). Knight takes bishop? *Natural History, 95*(5), 18–33.

Graham, S. (1992). "Most of the subjects were White and middle class": Trends in published research on African Americans in selected APA journals, 1970–1989. *American Psychologist, 47,* 629–639.

Greenwald, A. G. (1992). New look 3: Unconscious cognition reclaimed. *American Psychologist, 47,* 766–779.

Grieser, C., Greenberg, R., & Harrison, R. H. (1972). The adaptive function of sleep: The differential effects of sleep and dreaming on recall. *Journal of Abnormal Psychology, 80,* 280–286.

Gruber, C. (1972). Academic freedom at Columbia University, 1917–1918: The case of James McKeen Cattell. *American Association of University Professors Bulletin, 58*(3), 297–305.

Gundlach, H. U. K. (1986). Ebbinghaus, nonsense syllables, and three-letter words [Book review]. *Contemporary Psychology, 31,* 469–470.

Guthrie, E. R. (1935). *The psychology of learning.* New York: Harper.

Guthrie, E. R. (1959). Association by contiguity. In S. Koch (Ed.), *Psychology: A study of a science* (Vol. 2, pp. 158–195). New York: McGraw-Hill.

Guthrie, R. V. (1976). *Even the rat was white: A historical view of psychology.* New York: Harper & Row.

Guthrie, R. V. (1990). Mamie Phipps Clark (1917–1983). In A. N. O'Connell & N. F. Russo (Eds.), *Women in psychology: A bio-bibliographic sourcebook* (pp. 66–74). New York: Greenwood Press.

Guzman, L. P., Schiavo, R. A., & Puente, A. E. (1992). Ethnic minorities in the teaching of psychology. In A. E. Puente, J. R. Matthews, & C. L. Brewer (Eds.), *Teaching psychology in America: A history* (pp. 189–217). Washington, DC: American Psychological Association.

Hale, M., Jr. (1980). *Human science and social order: Hugo Münsterberg and the origins of applied psychology.* Philadelphia: Temple University Press.

Hall, G. S. (1904). *Adolescence.* New York: Appleton.

Hall, G. S. (1912). *Founders of modern psychology.* New York: Appleton.

Hall, G. S. (1917). *Jesus, the Christ, in the light of psychology.* Garden City, NY: Doubleday.

Hall, G. S. (1919). Some possible effects of the war on American psychology. *Psychological Bulletin, 16,* 48–49.

Hall, G. S. (1920). *Recreations of a psychologist.* New York: Appleton.

Hall, G. S. (1922). *Senescence.* New York: Appleton.

Hall, G. S. (1923). *The life and confessions of a psychologist.* New York: Appleton.

Hannush, M. J. (1987). John B. Watson remembered: An interview with James B. Watson. *Journal of the History of the Behavioral Sciences, 23,* 137–152.

Harris, B. (1979). Whatever happened to little Albert? *American Psychologist, 34,* 151–160.

Harrison, R. (1963). Functionalism and its historical significance. *Genetic Psychology Monographs, 68,* 387–423.

Hartley, D. (1749). *Observations on man, his frame, his duty, and his expectations.* London: Leake & Frederick.

Hartley, D., Robach, H. B., & Abramowitz, S. I. (1976). Deterioration effects in encounter groups. *American Psychologist, 31,* 247–255.

Hartmann, E. (1884). *Philosophy of the unconscious.* London: Trübner. (Original work published 1869)

Hartmann, H. (1964). *Essays on ego psychology.* New York: International Universities Press.

Hearnshaw, L. S. (1987). *The shaping of modern psychology.* London: Routledge & Kegan Paul.

Hearst, E. (Ed.). (1979). *The first century of experimental psychology.* Hillsdale, NJ: Erlbaum.

Heidbreder, E. (1933). *Seven psychologies.* New York: Appleton.

Helmholtz, H. (1856–1866). *Handbook of physiological optics.* Leipzig: Voss.

Helmholtz, H. (1954). *On the sensations of tone.* New York: Dover. (Original work published 1863)

Helson, H. (1925, 1926). The psychology of Gestalt. *American Journal of Psychology, 36,* 342–370, 494–526; *American Journal of Psychology, 37,* 25–62, 189–223.

Henle, M. (1974). E. B. Titchener and the case of the missing element. *Journal of the History of the Behavioral Sciences, 10,* 227–237.

Henle, M. (1978). One man against the Nazis—Wolfgang Köhler. *American Psychologist, 33,* 939–944.

Hilgard, E. R. (1956). *Theories of learning* (2nd ed.). New York: Appleton-Century-Crofts.

Hilgard, E. R. (1987). *Psychology in America: A historical survey.* San Diego: Harcourt Brace Jovanovich.

Hilgard, E. R. (1994). Foreword. In J. T. Todd & E. K. Morris (Eds.), *Modern perspectives on John B. Watson and classical behaviorism* (pp. xv–xvii). Westport, CT: Greenwood Press.

Hilgard, E. R., Atkinson, R., & Atkinson, R. (1975). *Introduction to psychology* (6th ed.). New York: Harcourt Brace Jovanovich.

Hilgard, E. R., Leary, D. E., & McGuire, G. R. (1991). The history of psychology: A survey and critical assessment. *Annual Review of Psychology, 42,* 79–107.

Hirschmüller, A. (1989). *The life and work of Josef Breuer: Physiology and psychoanalysis.* New York: New York University Press.

Hoffman, E. (1988). *The right to be human: A biography of Abraham Maslow.* Los Angeles: Tarcher.

Hoffman, R. R., Cochran, E. L., & Nead, J. M. (1990). Cognitive metaphors in experimental psychology. In D. E. Leary (Ed.), *Metaphors in the history of psychology* (pp. 173–229). Cambridge, England: Cambridge University Press.

Holder, A. (1988). Reservations about the *Standard edition.* In E. Timms & N. Segal (Eds.), *Freud in exile: Psychoanalysis and its vicissitudes* (pp. 210–214). New Haven, CT: Yale University Press.

Hollingworth, H. L. (1943). *Leta Stetter Hollingworth.* Lincoln: University of Nebraska Press.

Holt, R. R. (1989). *Freud reappraised: A fresh look at psychoanalytic theory.* New York: Guilford Press.

Horney, K. (1945). *Our inner conflicts.* New York: Norton.

Horney, K. (1980). *The adolescent diaries of Karen Horney, 1899–1911.* New York: Basic Books.

Hornstein, G. A. (1992). The return of the repressed: Psychology's problematic relations with psychoanalysis, 1909–1960. *American Psychologist, 47,* 254–263.

Houston, L. N. (1990). *Psychological principles and the Black experience.* Lanham, MD: University Press of America.

Howard, D. V. (1983). *Cognitive psychology: Memory, language and thought.* New York: Macmillan.

Hull, C. L. (1928). *Aptitude testing.* Yonkers, NY: World.

Hull, C. L. (1933). *Hypnosis and suggestibility.* New York: Appleton.

Hull, C. L. (1943). *Principles of behavior.* New York: Appleton.

Hull, C. L. (1951). *Essentials of behavior.* New Haven, CT: Yale University Press.

Hull, C. L. (1952). *A behavior system.* New Haven, CT: Yale University Press.

Hull, C. L., Hovland, C. L., Ross, R. T., Hall, M., Perkins, D. T., & Fitch, F. G. (1940). *Mathematico-deductive theory of rote learning: A study in scientific methodology.* New Haven, CT: Yale University Press.

Hulse, S. H. (1993). The present status of animal cognition: An introduction. *Psychological Science, 4,* 154–155.

Hume, D. (1739). *A treatise of human nature.* London: Noon.

Innis, N. K. (1992). Tolman and Tryon: Early research on the inheritance of the ability to learn. *American Psychologist, 47,* 190–197.

Isbister, J. N. (1985). *Freud: An introduction to his life and work.* Cambridge, England: Polity Press.

Jackson, M., & Sechrest, L. (1962). Early recollections in four neurotic diagnostic categories. *Journal of Individual Psychology, 18,* 52–56.

Jacobson, J. Z. (1951). *Scott of Northwestern: The life story of a pioneer in psychology and education.* Chicago: Mariano.

Jacoby, L. L., & Kelley, C. M. (1987). Unconscious influences of memory for a prior event. *Personality and Social Psychology Bulletin, 13,* 314–336.

Jacoby, L. L., Lindsay, D. S., & Toth, J. P. (1992). Unconscious influences revealed: Attention, awareness, and control. *American Psychologist, 47,* 802–809.

James, E. M. (1994). *Sowing the seeds of the psychology of women: Helen Bradford Thompson Woolley and The Mental Traits of Sex.* Manuscript submitted for publication.

James, W. (1890). *The principles of psychology.* New York: Holt.

James, W. (1899). *Talks to teachers.* New York: Holt.

James, W. (1902). *The varieties of religious experience.* New York: Longmans, Green.

James, W. (1907). *Pragmatism.* New York: Longmans, Green.

Jaynes, J. (1970). The problem of animate motion in the seventeenth century. *Journal of the History of Ideas, 31,* 219–234.

Johnson, M. G., & Henley, T. B. (Eds.). (1990). *Reflections on the principles of psychology: William James after a century.* Hillsdale, NJ: Erlbaum.

Johnson, R. C., McClearn, G. E., Yuen, S., Nagoshi, C. T., Ahern, F. M., & Cole, R. E. (1985). Galton's data a century later. *American Psychologist, 40,* 875–892.

Jončich, G. (1968). *The sane positivist: A biography of Edward L. Thorndike.* Middletown, CT: Wesleyan University Press.

Jones, E. (1953, 1955, 1957). *The life and work of Sigmund Freud* (3 vols.). New York: Basic Books.

Jones, M. C. (1924). A laboratory study of fear: The case of Peter. *Pedagogical Seminary, 31,* 308–315.

Jones, M. C. (1974). Albert, Peter, and John B. Watson. *American Psychologist, 29,* 581–583.

Jones, R. A. (1987). Psychology, history, and the press: The case of William McDougall and the *New York Times. American Psychologist, 42,* 931–940.

Jung, C. G. (1912). *The psychology of the unconscious.* Leipzig: Franz Deuticke.

Jung, C. G. (1961). *Memories, dreams, reflections.* New York: Random House.

Kagan, J., & Havemann, E. (1972). *Psychology: An introduction* (2nd ed.). New York: Harcourt Brace Jovanovich.

Kagan, J., Kearsley, R., & Zelazo, P. (1978). *Infancy.* Cambridge, MA: Harvard University Press.

Kaufmann, W. (1992). *Freud, Adler, and Jung: Discovering the mind* (Vol. 3). New Brunswick, NJ: Transaction Publishers.

Keiger, D. (1993, March). A profession built through metaphor. *Johns Hopkins Magazine,* pp. 48–49.

Keller, F. (1991). Burrhus Frederic Skinner, 1904–1990. *Journal of the History of the Behavioral Sciences, 27,* 3–6.

Kerr, J. (1993). *A most dangerous method: The story of Jung, Freud, and Sabina Spielrein.* New York: Knopf.

Kihlstrom, J. F. (1987). The cognitive unconscious. *Science, 237,* 1445–1452.

Kihlstrom, J. F., Barnhardt, M., & Tataryn, D. J. (1992). The psychological unconscious: Found, lost, and regained. *American Psychologist, 47,* 788–791.

Koch, S. (1964). Psychology and emerging conceptions of knowledge as unitary. In T. Wann (Ed.), *Behaviorism and phenomenology* (pp. 1–41). Chicago: University of Chicago Press.

Koch, S. (1993). "Psychology" or "the psychological studies"? *American Psychologist, 48,* 902–904.

Koelsch, W. A. (1970). Freud discovers America. *Virginia Quarterly Review, 46,* 115–132.

Koelsch, W. A. (1987). *Clark University: 1887–1987.* Worcester, MA: Clark University Press.

Koenigsberger, L. (1965). *Hermann von Helmholtz.* New York: Dover.

Koffka, K. (1921). *The growth of the mind.* New York: Harcourt.

Koffka, K. (1922). Perception: An introduction to Gestalt-theorie. *Psychological Bulletin, 19,* 531–585.

Koffka, K. (1935). *Principles of Gestalt psychology.* New York: Harcourt.

Köhler, W. (1917, 1924, 1927). *The mentality of apes.* Berlin: Royal Academy of Sciences; New York: Harcourt Brace.

Köhler, W. (1920). *Static and stationary physical Gestalts.* Braunschweig: Vieweg.

Köhler, W. (1929). *Gestalt psychology.* New York: Liveright.

Köhler, W. (1947). *Gestalt psychology: An introduction to new concepts in modern psychology.* New York: Liveright.

Köhler, W. (1959). Gestalt psychology today. *American Psychologist, 14,* 727–734.

Köhler, W. (1969). Gestalt psychology. In D. Krantz (Ed.), *Schools of psychology* (pp. 69–85). New York: Appleton-Century-Crofts.

Kohout, J., & Wicherski, M. (1990). *Doctorate employment survey: 1989.* Washington, DC: American Psychological Association.

Konorski, J. (1974). Autobiography. In G. Lindzey (Ed.), *A history of psychology in autobiography* (Vol. 6, pp. 183–217). Englewood Cliffs, NJ: Prentice-Hall.

Koppes, L. L., Landy, F. J., & Perkins, K. N. (1993). First American female applied psychologists. *The Industrial-Organizational Psychologist, 31*(1), 31–33.

Korn, J. H., Davis, R., & Davis, S. F. (1991). Historians' and chairpersons' judgments of eminence among psychologists. *American Psychologist, 46,* 789–792.

Kreshel, P. J. (1990). John B. Watson at J. Walter Thompson: The legitimation of "science" in advertising. *Journal of Advertising, 19*(2), 49–59.

Krüll, M. (1986). *Freud and his father.* New York: Norton.

Kuhn, T. S. (1970). *The structure of scientific revolutions* (2nd ed.). Chicago: University of Chicago Press.

Külpe, O. (1893). *Outline of psychology.* Leipzig: Engelmann.

Kuna, D. P. (1976). The concept of suggestion in the early history of advertising psychology. *Journal of the History of the Behavioral Sciences, 12,* 347–353.

Landy, F. J. (1992). Hugo Münsterberg: Victim or visionary? *American Psychologist, 47,* 787–802.

Landy, F. J. (1993). Early influences on the development of industrial/organizational psychology. In T. K. Fagan & G. R. VandenBos (Eds.), *Exploring applied psychology: Origins and critical analyses* (pp. 83–118). Washington, DC: American Psychological Association.

Larson, C. (1979, May). Highlights of Dr. John B. Watson's career in advertising. *The Industrial-Organizational Psychologist,* pp. 3–5.

Larson, C., & Sullivan, J. J. (1965). Watson's relation to Titchener. *Journal of the History of the Behavioral Sciences, 1,* 338–354.

Lashley, K. (1929). *Brain mechanisms and intelligence.* Chicago: University of Chicago Press.

Lattal, K. A. (1992). B. F. Skinner and psychology: Introduction to the special issue. *American Psychologist, 47,* 1269–1272.

Leahey, T. H. (1981). The mistaken mirror: On Wundt's and Titchener's psychologies. *Journal of the History of the Behavioral Sciences, 17,* 273–282.

Leahey, T. H. (1992). The mythical revolutions of American psychology. *American Psychologist, 47,* 308–318.

Leary, D. E. (1987). Telling likely stories: The rhetoric of the new psychology, 1880–1920. *Journal of the History of the Behavioral Sciences, 23,* 315–331.

Leonard, G. (1983, December). Abraham Maslow and the new self. *Esquire,* pp. 326–336.

Lerner, G. (1979). *The majority finds its past: Placing women in history.* New York: Oxford University Press.

Levinson, D. J. (1978). *The seasons of a man's life.* New York: Knopf.

Lewicki, P., Hill, T., & Czyzewska, M. (1992). Nonconscious acquisition of information. *American Psychologist, 47,* 796–801.

Lewin, K. (1936). *Principles of topological psychology.* New York: McGraw-Hill.

Lewin, K. (1939). Field theory and experiment in social psychology: Concept and methods. *American Journal of Sociology, 44,* 868–896.

Lewin, K., Lippitt, R., & White, R. (1939). Patterns of aggressive behavior in experimentally created social climates. *Journal of Social Psychology, 10,* 271–299.

Lewis, R. W. B. (1991). *The Jameses: A family narrative.* New York: Farrar, Straus and Giroux.

Ley, R. (1990). *A whisper of espionage: Wolfgang Köhler and the apes of Tenerife.* Garden City Park, NY: Avery Publishing Group.

Lieberman, D. A. (1979). Behaviorism and the mind: A (limited) call for a return to introspection. *American Psychologist, 34,* 319–333.

Ljunggren, B. (1990). *Great men with sick brains and other essays.* Park Ridge, IL: American Association of Neurological Surgeons.

Lloyd, M. A., & Brewer, C. L. (1992). National conferences on undergraduate psychology. In A. E. Puente, J. R. Matthews, & C. L. Brewer (Eds.), *Teaching psychology in America: A history* (pp. 263–284). Washington, DC: American Psychological Association.

Locke, J. (1959). *An essay concerning human understanding.* New York: Dover. (Original work published 1690)

Loeb, J. (1918). *Forced movements, tropisms, and animal conduct.* Philadelphia: Lippincott.

Loevinger, J. (1987). *Paradigms of personality.* New York: Freeman.

Loftus, E. (1979). *Eyewitness testimony.* Cambridge, MA: Harvard University Press.

Loftus, E., & Klinger, M. R. (1992). Is the unconscious smart or dumb? *American Psychologist, 47,* 761–765.

Loftus, E., & Monahan, J. (1980). Trial by data: Psychological research as legal evidence. *American Psychologist, 35,* 270–283.

Logue, A. W. (1978). Behaviorist John B. Watson and the continuity of the species. *Behaviorism, 6*(1), 71–79.

Logue, A. W. (1985a). The growth of behaviorism: Controversy and diversity. In C. E. Buxton (Ed.), *Points of view in the modern history of psychology* (pp. 169–196). Orlando, FL: Academic Press.

Logue, A. W. (1985b). The origins of behaviorism: Antecedents and proclamation. In C. E. Buxton (Ed.), *Points of view in the modern history of psychology* (pp. 141–167). Orlando, FL: Academic Press.

Lowry, R. (1982). *The evolution of psychological theory: A critical history of concepts and presuppositions* (2nd ed.). Hawthorne, NY: Aldine.

Lubek, I., & Apfelbaum, E. (1987). Neobehaviorism and the Garcia effect: A social psychology of science approach to the history of a paradigm clash. In M. G. Ash & W. R. Woodward (Eds.), *Psychology in twentieth-century thought and society* (pp. 59–91). Cambridge, England: Cambridge University Press.

Mach, E. (1914). *The analysis of sensations.* Chicago: Open Court. (Original work published 1885)

Mackenzie, B. (1977). *Behaviourism and the limits of scientific method.* Atlantic Highlands, NJ: Humanities Press.

MacLeod, R. B. (1959). Review of *Cumulative record* by B. F. Skinner. *Science, 130,* 34–35.

MacLeod, R. B. (Ed.). (1969). *William James: Unfinished business.* Washington, DC: American Psychological Association.

Madigan, S., & O'Hara, R. (1992). Short-term memory at the turn of the century: Mary Whiton Calkins's memory research. *American Psychologist, 47,* 170–174.

Mahony, P. (1986). *Freud and the Rat Man.* New Haven, CT: Yale University Press.

Mahony, P. (1992). Freud as family therapist: Reflections. In T. Gelfand & J. Kerr (Eds.), *Freud and the history of psychoanalysis* (pp. 307–317). Hillsdale, NJ: Analytic Press.

Malcolm, J. (1984). *In the Freud archives.* New York: Knopf.

Malthus, T. (1914). *Essay on the principle of population.* New York: Dutton. (Original work published 1789)

Martin, S. (1995, January). Field's status unaltered by the influx of women. *APA Monitor,* p. 9.

Marx, M. H., & Cronan-Hillix, W. A. (1987). *Systems and theories in psychology* (4th ed.). New York: McGraw-Hill.

Marx, M. H., & Hillix, W. A. (1979). *Systems and theories in psychology* (3rd ed.). New York: McGraw-Hill.

Maslow, A. H. (1970). *Motivation and personality* (2nd ed.). New York: Harper & Row.

Masson, J. M. (1984). *The assault on truth: Freud's suppression of the seduction theory.* New York: Farrar, Straus and Giroux.

Masson, J. M. (Ed.). (1985). *The complete letters of Sigmund Freud to Wilhelm Fliess, 1887–1904.* Cambridge, MA: Harvard University Press.

Matarazzo, J. D. (1987). There is only one psychology: No specialties, but many applications. *American Psychologist, 42,* 893–903.

Matarazzo, J. D. (1990). There is only one psychology, no specialties, but many applications. In L. Bickman & H. Ellis (Eds.), *Preparing psychologists for the 21st century* (pp. 87–108). Hillsdale, NJ: Erlbaum.

Matson, F. W. (1964). *The broken image.* New York: Braziller.

Maurice, K., & Mayr, O. (Eds.). (1980). *The clockwork universe: German clocks and automata, 1550–1650.* New York: Neale Watson.

May, W. W. (1978). A psychologist of many hats: A tribute to Mark Arthur May. *American Psychologist, 33,* 653–663.

Mazlish, B. (1993). *The fourth discontinuity: The co-evolution of humans and machines.* New Haven, CT: Yale University Press.

McAdams, D. P., Ruetzel, K., & Foley, J. M. (1986). Complexity and generativity at midlife: Relations among social motives, ego development, and adults' plans for the future. *Journal of Personality and Social Psychology, 50,* 800–807.

McDougall, W. (1908). *Introduction to social psychology.* London: Methuen.

McDougall, W. (1912). *Psychology: The study of behavior.* London: Oxford University Press.

McDougall, W. (1930). Autobiography. In C. Murchison (Ed.), *A history of psychology in autobiography* (Vol. 1, pp. 191–223). Worcester, MA: Clark University Press.

McGovern, T. V. (1990, July). Goals for major in psychology outlined. *APA Monitor,* p. 50.

McGovern, T. V. (1992). Evolution of undergraduate curricula in psychology, 1892–1992. In A. E. Puente, J. R. Matthews, & C. L. Brewer (Eds.), *Teaching psychology in America: A history* (pp. 13–38). Washington, DC: American Psychological Association.

McGraw, M. B. (1990). Memories, deliberate recall, and speculations. *American Psychologist, 45,* 934–937.

McGuire, W. (Ed.). (1974). *The Freud/Jung letters.* Princeton, NJ: Princeton University Press.

McKeachie, W. J. (1976). Psychology in America's bicentennial year. *American Psychologist, 31,* 819–833.

McKinney, F. (1978). Functionalism at Chicago: Memories of a graduate student, 1929–1931. *Journal of the History of the Behavioral Sciences, 14,* 142–148.

McReynolds, P. (1987). Lightner Witmer: Little-known founder of clinical psychology. *American Psychologist, 42,* 849–858.

Merton, R. (1957). Priorities in scientific discovery. *American Sociological Review, 22,* 635–659.

Meyer, M. (1911). *The fundamental laws of human behavior.* Boston: Badger.

Mill, J. S. (1961). Autobiography. In M. Lerner (Ed.), *Essential works of John Stuart Mill* (pp. 1–182). New York: Bantam Books. (Original work published 1873)

Mill, J. (1829). *Analysis of the phenomena of the human mind.* London: Baldwin & Cradock.

Miller, G. A. (1951). *Language and communication.* New York: McGraw-Hill.

Miller, G. A. (1962). *Psychology: The science of mental life.* New York: Harper & Row.

Miller, G. A. (1985). The constitutive problem of psychology. In S. Koch & D. Leary (Eds.), *A century of psychology as science* (pp. 40–45). New York: McGraw-Hill.

Miller, G. A., & Buckhout, R. (1973). *Psychology: The science of mental life* (2nd ed.). New York: Harper & Row.

Misceo, G., & Samelson, F. (1983). On textbook lessons from history, or how the conditioned reflex discovered Twitmyer. *Psychological Reports, 52,* 447–454.

Moore, D. L. (1992). The Veterans Administration and the training program in psychology. In D. K. Freedheim (Ed.), *History of psychotherapy: A century of change* (pp. 776–800). Washington, DC: American Psychological Association.

Morawski, J. G., & Hornstein, G. A. (1991). Quandary of the quacks: The struggle for expert knowledge in American psychology, 1890–1940. In J. Brown & D. K. van Keuren (Eds.), *The estate of social knowledge* (pp. 106–133). Baltimore: Johns Hopkins University Press.

Morgan, C. D., & Murray, H. A. (1935). A method for investigating fantasies. *Archives of Neurology and Psychiatry, 34,* 289–306.

Moses, S. (1991, March). APA calls for recast psychology major. *APA Monitor,* p. 37.

Motley, M. T. (1985). Slips of the tongue. *Scientific American, 253,* 116–127.

Mueller, C. G., & Schoenfeld, W. N. (1954). Edwin R. Guthrie. In W. Estes et al. (Eds.), *Modern learning theory* (pp. 345–379). New York: Appleton-Century-Crofts.

Müller, J. (1883–1840). *Handbook of the physiology of mankind* (3 vols.). Coblenz: Hölscher.

Münsterberg, H. (1909). *Psychotherapy.* New York: Moffat Yard.

Münsterberg, H. (1913). *Psychology and industrial efficiency.* Boston: Houghton Mifflin.

Münsterberg, M. (1922). *Hugo Münsterberg: His life and work.* New York: Appleton.

Murphy, G. (1963). Robert Sessions Woodworth, 1869–1962. *American Psychologist, 18,* 131–133.

Murray, H. A. (1938). *Explorations in personality.* New York: Oxford University Press.

Murray, H. A. (1940). What should psychologists do about psychoanalysis? *Journal of Abnormal and Social Psychology, 35,* 150–175.

Myers, G. E. (1986). *William James: His life and thought.* New Haven, CT: Yale University Press.

Myers, R. A. (1990). Issues of cultural diversity in graduate education in psychology. In L. Bickman & H. Ellis (Eds.), *Preparing psychologists for the twenty-first century: Proceedings of the National Conference on Graduate Education in Psychology* (pp. 189–190). Hillsdale, NJ: Erlbaum.

Natsoulas, T. (1978). Consciousness. *American Psychologist, 33,* 904–916.

Neisser, U. (1967). *Cognitive psychology.* New York: Appleton-Century-Crofts.

Neisser, U. (1976). *Cognition and reality.* San Francisco: W. H. Freeman.

Nisbett, R. E., & Wilson, T. D. (1977). Telling more than we can know: Verbal reports on mental processes. *Psychological Review, 84,* 231–259.

Norman, D. A., & Levelt, W. J. M. (1988). Life at the Center. In W. Hirst (Ed.), *The making of cognitive science: Essays in honor of George A. Miller* (pp. 100–109). Cambridge, England: Cambridge University Press.

O'Connell, A. N. (1990). Karen Horney: 1885–1952. In A. N. O'Connell & N. F. Russo (Eds.), *Women in psychology: A bio-bibliographic sourcebook* (pp. 184–196). New York: Greenwood Press.

O'Connell, A. N., & Russo, N. F. (1983). *Models of achievement: Reflections of eminent women in psychology.* New York: Columbia University Press.

O'Connell, A. N., & Russo, N. F. (1988). *Models of achievement: Reflections of eminent women in psychology* (Vol. 2). Hillsdale, NJ: Erlbaum.

O'Connell, A. N., & Russo, N. F. (1990). *Women in psychology: A bio-bibliographic sourcebook.* New York: Greenwood Press.

O'Donnell, J. M. (1979). The crisis of experimentalism in the 1920s: E. G. Boring and his uses of history. *American Psychologist, 34,* 289–295.

O'Donnell, J. M. (1985). *The origins of behaviorism: American psychology, 1870–1920.* New York: New York University Press.

Olweus, D. (1979). The stability of aggressive reaction patterns in human males: A review. *Psychological Bulletin, 86,* 852–875.

Paludi, M. A., & Russo, N. F. (1990). Florence L. Denmark (1931–   ). In A. N. O'Connell & N. F. Russo

(Eds.), *Women in psychology: A bio-bibliographic sourcebook* (pp. 75–87). New York: Greenwood Press.

Paskauskas, R. A. (1988). The Jones-Freud era, 1908–1939. In E. Timms & N. Segal (Eds.), *Freud in exile: Psychoanalysis and its vicissitudes* (pp. 109–125). New Haven, CT: Yale University Press.

Pate, J. L. (1993). The Southern Society for Philosophy and Psychology. In J. L. Pate & M. Wertheimer (Eds.), *No small part: A history of regional organizations in American psychology* (pp. 1–19). Washington, DC: American Psychological Association.

Pate, J. L., & Wertheimer, M. (1993). Preface. In J. L. Pate & M. Wertheimer (Eds.), *No small part: A history of regional organizations in American psychology* (pp. xv–xvii). Washington, DC: American Psychological Association.

Pauly, P. J. (1979, December). Psychology at Hopkins: Its rise and fall and rise and fall and. . . . *Johns Hopkins Magazine*, pp. 36–41.

Pauly, P. J. (1986). G. Stanley Hall and his successors: A history of the first half–century of psychology at Johns Hopkins. In S. H. Hulse & B. F. Green, Jr. (Eds.), *One hundred years of psychological research in America: G. Stanley Hall and the Johns Hopkins tradition* (pp. 21–51). Baltimore: Johns Hopkins University Press.

Pauly, P. J. (1990). *Controlling life: Jacques Loeb and the engineering ideal in biology.* Berkeley: University of California Press.

Pavlov, I. P. (1927). *Conditioned reflexes.* Oxford, England: Oxford University Press.

Pavlov, I. P. (1955). *Selected works.* Moscow: Foreign Languages Publishing House.

Pearce, J. M. (1987). *An introduction to animal cognition.* Hillsdale, NJ: Erlbaum.

Peel, J. D. Y. (1971). *Herbert Spencer: The evolution of a sociologist.* London: Heinemann.

Pekala, R. J. (1991). *Quantifying consciousness: An empirical approach.* New York: Plenum.

Pervin, L. (1984). *Personality: Theory and research* (4th ed.). New York: Wiley.

Pervin, L. (1985). Personality: Current controversies, issues and directions. *Annual Review of Psychology, 36*, 83–114.

Pickering, G. (1974). *Creative malady.* New York: Oxford University Press.

Pillsbury, W. (1911). *Essentials of psychology.* New York: Macmillan.

Planck, M. (1949). *Scientific autobiography.* New York: Philosophical Library.

Popplestone, J. A., & McPherson, M. W. (1994). *An illustrated history of American psychology.* Dubuque, IA: Brown & Benchmark.

Quinn, S. (1987). *A mind of her own: The life of Karen Horney.* New York: Summit Books.

Rapp, D. (1988). The reception of Freud by the British press: General interest and literary magazines, 1920–1925. *Journal of the History of the Behavioral Sciences, 24,* 191–201.

Reed, J. (1987a). Robert M. Yerkes and the comparative method. In E. Tobach (Ed.), *Historical perspectives and the international status of comparative psychology* (pp. 91–101). Hillsdale, NJ: Erlbaum.

Reed, J. (1987b). Robert M. Yerkes and the mental testing movement. In M. M. Sokal (Ed.), *Psychological testing and American society, 1890–1930* (pp. 75–94). New Brunswick, NJ: Rutgers University Press.

Reizenzein, R., & Schönpflug, W. (1992). Stumpf's cognitive-evaluative theory of emotion. *American Psychologist, 47,* 34–45.

Rice, B. (1968, March 17). Skinner agrees he is the most important influence in psychology. *New York Times Magazine,* pp. 27ff.

Rice, L. N., & Greenberg, L. S. (1992). Humanistic approaches to psychotherapy. In D. K. Freedheim (Ed.), *History of psychotherapy: A century of change* (pp. 197–224). Washington, DC: American Psychological Association.

Richards, R. J. (1980). Wundt's early theories of unconscious inference and cognitive evolution in their relation to Darwinian biopsychology. In W. G. Bringmann & R. D. Tweney (Eds.), *Wundt studies: A centennial collection* (pp. 42–70). Toronto: Hogrefe.

Richards, R. J. (1987). *Darwin and the emergence of evolutionary theories of mind and behavior.* Chicago: University of Chicago Press.

Roazen, P. (1975). *Freud and his followers.* New York: Knopf.

Roback, A. A. (1952). *History of American psychology.* New York: Library Publishers.

Robinson, D. N. (1981). *An intellectual history of psychology* (Rev. ed.). New York: Macmillan.

Roethlisberger, F. J., & Dickson, W. J. (1939). *Management and the worker: An account of a research program conducted by the Western Electric Company, Chicago.* Cambridge, MA: Harvard University Press.

Rogers, C. R. (1961). *On becoming a person.* Boston: Houghton Mifflin.

Rogers, C. R. (1967). Autobiography. In E. G. Boring & G. Lindzey (Eds.), *A history of psychology in autobiography* (Vol. 5, pp. 341–384). New York: Appleton-Century-Crofts.

Rogers, C. R. (1980). *A way of being.* Boston: Houghton Mifflin.

Roitblat, H. L., Bever, T. G., & Terrace, H. S. (Eds.). (1984). *Animal cognition.* Hillsdale, NJ: Erlbaum.

Romanes, G. J. (1883). *Animal intelligence.* London: Routledge & Kegan Paul.

Rose, P. (1983). *Parallel lives: Five Victorian marriages.* New York: Knopf.

Rosenzweig, S. (1985). Freud and experimental psychology: The emergence of idiodynamics. In S. Koch & D. Leary (Eds.), *A century of psychology as science* (pp. 135–207). New York: McGraw-Hill.

Rosenzweig, S. (1992). *Freud, Jung, and Hall the kingmaker: The historic expedition to America (1909).* Seattle: Hogrefe & Huber.

Ross, D. (1972). *Granville Stanley Hall: The psychologist as prophet.* Chicago: University of Chicago Press.

Ross, S., & Hicks, L.H. (1991). James A. Bayton (1912–1990) [obituary]. *American Psychologist, 46,* 1345.

Rossiter, M. W. (1982). *Women scientists in America: Struggles and strategies to 1940.* Baltimore: Johns Hopkins University Press.

Roszak, T. (1986). *The cult of information: The folklore of computers and the true art of thinking.* New York: Pantheon.

Rotter, J. B. (1966). Generalized expectancies for internal versus external control of reinforcement. *Psychological Monographs, 80* (Whole No. 609).

Rotter, J. B. (1982). *The development and applications of social learning theory: Selected papers.* New York: Praeger.

Rotter, J. B. (1990). Internal versus external control of reinforcement: A case history of a variable. *American Psychologist, 45,* 489–493.

Ruckmick, C. A. (1913). The use of the term "function" in English textbooks of psychology. *American Journal of Psychology, 24,* 99–123.

Russo, N. F., & Denmark, F. L. (1987). Contributions of women to psychology. *Annual Review of Psychology, 38,* 279–298.

Samelson, F. (1980). J. B. Watson's little Albert, Cyril Burt's twins, and the need for a critical science. *American Psychologist, 35,* 619–625.

Samelson, F. (1981). Struggle for scientific authority: The reception of Watson's behaviorism, 1913–1920. *Journal of the History of the Behavioral Sciences, 17,* 399–425.

Sampson, E. E. (1993). Identity politics: Challenges to psychology's understanding. *American Psychologist, 48,* 1219–1230.

Sand, R. (1992). Pre-Freudian discovery of dream meaning. In T. Gelfand & J. Kerr (Ed.), *Freud and the history of psychoanalysis* (pp. 215–229). Hillsdale, NJ: Analytic Press.

Sanua, V. D. (1993). Wundt's American students reminisce: "We like thee not Professor Wundt!" *History of Psychology Newsletter, 25*(4), 54–61.

Sarton, G. (1936). *The study of the history of science.* New York: Dover.

Saunders, F. (1991). *Mother's light, daughter's journey: Katherine and Isabel.* Palo Alto, CA: Consulting Psychologists Press.

Sayers, J. (1991). *Mothers of psychoanalysis.* New York: Norton.

Scarborough, E. (1990). Margaret Floy Washburn, 1871–1939. In A. N. O'Connell & N. F. Russo (Eds.), *Women in psychology: A bio-bibliographic sourcebook* (pp. 342–349). New York: Greenwood Press.

Scarborough, E. (1992). Women in the American Psychological Association. In R. B. Evans, V. S. Sexton, & T. C. Cadwallader (Eds.), *The American Psychological Association: A historical perspective* (pp. 303–325). Washington, DC: American Psychological Association.

Scarborough, E., & Furumoto, L. (1987). *Untold lives: The first generation of American women psychologists.* New York: Columbia University Press.

Scarf, M. (1971, February 28). The man who gave us "inferiority complex," "compensation," "aggressive drive" and "style of life." *New York Times Magazine,* pp. 10ff.

Scarr, S. (1987, May). Twenty years of growing up. *Psychology Today,* pp. 24–28.

Schachter, S. (1963). Birth order, eminence, and higher education. *American Sociological Review, 28,* 757–767.

Scheere, E. (1988). Fifty volumes of *Psychological Research/Psychologische Forschung:* The history and present status of the journal. *Psychological Research, 50,* 71–82.

Scheibe, K. E. (1988). Metamorphoses in the psychologist's advantage. In J. G. Morawski (Ed.), *The rise of experimentation in American psychology* (pp. 53–71). New Haven, CT: Yale University Press.

Schneider, W. H. (1992). After Binet: French intelligence testing, 1900–1950. *Journal of the History of the Behavioral Sciences, 28,* 111–132.

Schultz, D. (1990). *Intimate friends, dangerous rivals: The turbulent relationship between Freud and Jung.* Los Angeles: Tarcher.

Schultz, D. P. (1969). The human subject in psychological research. *Psychological Bulletin, 72,* 214–228.

Schur, M. (1972). *Freud: Living and dying.* New York: International Universities Press.

Schwartz, A. E. (1988). Freud and the feminine fallacy [Book review of *A mote in Freud's eye: From psychoanalysis to the psychology of women*]. *Contemporary Psychology, 33,* 501–502.

Scott, W. D. (1903). *The theory and practice of advertising: A simple exposition of the principles of psychology in their relation to successful advertising.* Boston: Small, Maynard.

Seaman, J. D. (1984). On phi-phenomena. *Journal of the History of the Behavioral Sciences, 20,* 3–8.

Segal, E. M., & Lachman, R. (1972). Complex behavior or higher mental process: Is there a paradigm shift? *American Psychologist, 27,* 46–55.

Sexton, V. S., & Hogan, J. D. (1990). Anne Anastasi. In A. N. O'Connell & N. F. Russo (Eds.), *Women in psychology: A bio-bibliographic sourcebook* (pp. 13–22). New York: Greenwood Press.

Shapiro, A. E., & Wiggins, J. C. (1994). A PsyD degree for every practitioner: Truth in labeling. *American Psychologist, 49,* 207–210.

Shea, W. R. (1991). *The magic of numbers and motion: The scientific career of René Descartes.* Canton, MA: Science History Publications.

Shepherd, N. (1993). *A price below rubies: Jewish women as rebels and radicals.* Cambridge, MA: Harvard University Press.

Sherrill, R., Jr. (1991). Natural wholes: Wolfgang Köhler and Gestalt theory. In G. A. Kimble, M. Wertheimer, & C. White (Eds.), *Portraits of pioneers in psychology* (pp. 257–273). Hillsdale, NJ: Erlbaum.

Shevrin, H., & Dickman, S. (1980). The psychological unconscious: A necessary assumption for all psychological theory? *American Psychologist, 35,* 421–434.

Shields, S. (1975). Ms. Pilgrim's progress: The contributions of Leta Stetter Hollingworth to the psychology of women. *American Psychologist, 30,* 852–857.

Shields, S. (1982). The variability hypothesis: The history of a biological model of sex differences in intelligence. *Signs: Journal of Women in Culture and Society, 7,* 769–797.

Siegel, A. W., & White, S. H. (1982). The child study movement. In H. W. Reese (Ed.), *Advances in child development and behavior* (Vol. 17, pp. 233–285). New York: Academic Press.

Silverman, L. H. (1976). Psychoanalytic theory: "The reports of my death are greatly exaggerated." *American Psychologist, 31,* 621–637.

Skinner, B. F. (1938). *The behavior of organisms.* New York: Appleton.

Skinner, B. F. (1945a, October). Baby in a box. *Ladies Home Journal,* pp. 30ff.

Skinner, B. F. (1945b). The operational analysis of psychological terms: Rejoinders and second thoughts. *Psychological Review, 52,* 291–294.

Skinner, B. F. (1948). *Walden Two.* New York: Macmillan.

Skinner, B. F. (1953). *Science and human behavior.* New York: Macmillan.

Skinner, B. F. (1956). A case history of scientific method. *American Psychologist, 11,* 221–233.

Skinner, B. F. (1957). *Verbal behavior.* New York: Appleton.

Skinner, B. F. (1963). Behaviorism at fifty. *Science, 140,* 951–958.

Skinner, B. F. (1967). Autobiography. In E. G. Boring & G. Lindzey (Eds.), *A history of psychology in autobiography* (Vol. 5, pp. 387–413). New York: Appleton-Century-Crofts.

Skinner, B. F. (1968). *The technology of teaching.* New York: Appleton-Century-Crofts.

Skinner, B. F. (1969). *Contingencies of reinforcement.* New York: Appleton-Century-Crofts.

Skinner, B. F. (1971). *Beyond freedom and dignity.* New York: Knopf.

Skinner, B. F. (1976). *Particulars of my life.* New York: Knopf.

Skinner, B. F. (1979). *The shaping of a behaviorist.* New York: Knopf.

Skinner, B. F. (1983a). Intellectual self-management in old age. *American Psychologist, 38,* 239–244.

Skinner, B. F. (1983b). *A matter of consequences.* New York: Knopf.

Skinner, B. F. (1986). What is wrong with daily life in the Western world? *American Psychologist, 41,* 568–574.

Skinner, B. F. (1987a). *Upon further reflection.* Englewood Cliffs, NJ: Prentice-Hall.

Skinner, B. F. (1987b). Whatever happened to psychology as the science of behavior? *American Psychologist, 42,* 780–786.

Skinner, B. F. (1989). The origin of cognitive thought. *American Psychologist, 44,* 13–18.

Skinner, B. F. (1990). Can psychology be a science of mind? *American Psychologist, 45,* 1206–1210.

Smith, C. (1987). David Hartley's Newtonian neuropsychology. *Journal of the History of the Behavioral Sciences, 23,* 123–136.

Smith, D. (1986, March 31). What would Freud think? The uproar in the shrine of psychoanalysis. *New York,* pp. 38–45.

Smith, M. B. (1989). Comment on "The case of William McDougall." *American Psychologist, 44,* 446.

Smith, M. B. (1990). Humanistic psychology. *Journal of Humanistic Psychology, 30,* 6–21.

Sokal, M. M. (1971). The unpublished autobiography of James McKeen Cattell. *American Psychologist, 26,* 626–635.

Sokal, M. M. (1981a). *An education in psychology: James McKeen Cattell's journal and letters from Germany and England, 1880–1888.* Cambridge, MA: MIT Press.

Sokal, M. M. (1981b). The origins of the Psychological Corporation. *Journal of the History of the Behavioral Sciences, 17,* 54–67.

Sokal, M. M. (1984). The Gestalt psychologists in behaviorist America. *American Historical Review, 89,* 1240–1263.

Sokal, M. M. (1987). James McKeen Cattell and mental anthropometry: Nineteenth-century science and reform and the origins of psychological testing. In M. M. Sokal (Ed.), *Psychological testing and American society, 1890–1930* (pp. 21–45). New Brunswick, NJ: Rutgers University Press.

Sokal, M. M. (1990). G. Stanley Hall and the institutional character of psychology at Clark, 1889–1920. *Journal of the History of the Behavioral Sciences, 26,* 114–124.

Sokal, M. M. (1992). Origins and early years of the American Psychological Association, 1890–1906. *American Psychologist, 47,* 111–122.

Spanos, N. P. (1993). Coming to grips with consciousness [Book review of *The psychology of consciousness*]. *Contemporary Psychology, 38,* 682.

Spence, K. W. (1952). Clark Leonard Hull: 1884–1952. *American Journal of Psychology, 65,* 639–646.

Spencer, H. (1855). *The principles of psychology.* London: Smith & Elder.

Sperry, R. W. (1993). The impact and promise of the cognitive revolution. *American Psychologist, 48,* 878–885.

Spillmann, J., & Spillmann, L. (1993). The rise and fall of Hugo Münsterberg. *Journal of the History of the Behavioral Sciences, 29,* 322–338.

Staats, A. W. (1991). Unified positivism and unification psychology: Fad or new field? *American Psychologist, 46,* 899–912.

Steele, R. S. (1985a). Paradigm found: A deconstruction of the history of the psychoanalytic movement. In C. E. Buxton (Ed.), *Points of view in the modern history of psychology* (pp. 197–219). Orlando, FL: Academic Press.

Steele, R. S. (1985b). Paradigm lost: Psychoanalysis after Freud. In C. E. Buxton (Ed.), *Points of view in the modern history of psychology* (pp. 221–257). Orlando, FL: Academic Press.

Stepansky, P. E. (Ed.) (1986). *Freud: Appraisals and reappraisals.* New York: Analytic Press.

Sterba, R. F. (1982). *Reminiscences of a Viennese psychoanalyst.* Detroit: Wayne State University Press.

Stumpf, C. (1883, 1890). *Psychology of tone.* Leipzig: Hirzel.

Sulloway, F. J. (1979). *Freud: Biologist of the mind.* New York: Basic Books.

Sulloway, F. J. (1992). Reassessing Freud's case histories: The social construction of psychoanalysis. In T. Gelfand & J. Kerr (Eds.), *Freud and the history of psychoanalysis* (pp. 153–192). Hillsdale, NJ: Analytic Press.

Sumner, F. C. (1928). Environic factors which prohibit creative scholarship among Negroes. *School and Society, 22,* 558.

Thompson, H. (1903). *The mental traits of sex: An experimental investigation of the normal mind in men and women.* Chicago: University of Chicago Press.

Thompson, T. (1988). Benedictus behavior analysis: B. F. Skinner's magnum opus at fifty [Book review of *The behavior of organisms: An experimental analysis*]. *Contemporary Psychology, 33,* 397–402.

Thorndike, E. L. (1898). Animal intelligence: An experimental study of the associative processes in animals (monograph supplement no. 8). *Psychological Review, 5,* 68–72.

Thorndike, E. L. (1905). *The elements of psychology.* New York: Seiler.

Thorndike, E. L. (1931). *Human learning.* New York: Appleton.

Titchener, E. B. (1896). *An outline of psychology.* New York: Macmillan.

Titchener, E. B. (1898a). The postulates of a structural psychology. *Philosophical Review, 7,* 449–465.

Titchener, E. B. (1898b). *Primer of psychology.* New York: Macmillan.

Titchener, E. B. (1901–1905). *Experimental psychology.* New York: Macmillan.

Titchener, E. B. (1909). *A textbook of psychology.* New York: Macmillan.

Titchener, E. B. (1912a). Prolegomena to a study of introspection. *American Journal of Psychology, 23,* 427–448.

Titchener, E. B. (1912b). The schema of introspection. *American Journal of Psychology, 23,* 485–508.

Titchener, E. B. (1921). Wilhelm Wundt. *American Journal of Psychology, 32,* 161–178.

Todd, J. T. (1994). What psychology has to say about John B. Watson: Classical behaviorism in psychology textbooks, 1920–1989. In J. T. Todd & E. K. Morris (Eds.), *Modern perspectives on John B. Watson and classical behaviorism* (pp. 75–107). Westport, CT: Greenwood Press.

Tolman, C. W. (1993). Is there a functionalist psychology? [Review of *Progress in modern psychology: The legacy of American functionalism*]. *Contemporary Psychology, 38,* 1318–1319.

Tolman, E. C. (1932). *Purposive behavior in animals and men.* New York: Appleton.

Tolman, E. C. (1945). A stimulus-expectancy need-cathexis psychology. *Science, 101,* 160–166.

Tolman, E. C. (1952). Autobiography. In E. G. Boring, H. S. Langfeld, H. Werner, & R. Yerkes (Eds.), *A history of psychology in autobiography* (Vol. 4, pp. 323–339). Worcester, MA: Clark University Press.

Triplet, R. G. (1992). Henry A. Murray: The making of a psychologist? *American Psychologist, 47,* 299–307.

Turner, C. H. (1906). A preliminary note on ant behavior. *Biological Bulletin, 12,* 31–36.

Turner, F. J. (1947). *The significance of the frontier in American history.* New York: Holt.

Turner, M. (1967). *Philosophy and the science of behavior.* New York: Appleton-Century-Crofts.

Turner, R. S. (1982). Helmholtz, sensory physiology, and the disciplinary development of German psychology. In W. R. Woodward & M. G. Ash (Eds.), *The problematic science: Psychology in nineteenth-century thought* (pp. 147–166). New York: Praeger.

Tuzin, D. (1994). The forgotten passion: Sexuality and anthropology in the ages of Victoria and Bronislaw. *Journal of the History of the Behavioral Sciences, 30,* 114–137.

Tweney, R. D. (1987). Programmatic research in experimental psychology: E. B. Titchener's laboratory investigations, 1891–1927. In M. G. Ash & W. R. Woodward (Eds.), *Psychology in twentieth-century thought and society* (pp. 35–57). Cambridge, England: Cambridge University Press.

Twitmyer, E. B. (1905). Knee-jerks without stimulation of the patellar tendon. *Psychological Bulletin, 2,* 43–44.

Urban, W. J. (1989). The black scholar and intelligence testing: The case of Horace Mann Bond. *Journal of the History of the Behavioral Sciences, 25,* 323–334.

Vande Kemp, H. (1992). G. Stanley Hall and the Clark school of religious psychology. *American Psychologist, 47,* 290–298.

VandenBos, G. R., Cummings, N. A., & Deleon, P. H. (1992). A century of psychotherapy: Economic and environmental influences. In D. K. Freedheim (Ed.), *History of psychotherapy: A century of change* (pp. 65–102). Washington, DC: American Psychological Association.

Von Mayrhauser, R. T. (1989). Making intelligence functional: Walter Dill Scott and applied psychological testing in World War I. *Journal of the History of the Behavioral Sciences, 25,* 60–72.

Wagner, M., & Owens, D. A. (1992). Introduction: Modern psychology and early functionalism. In D. A. Owens & M. Wagner (Eds.), *Progress in modern psychology: The legacy of American functionalism* (pp. 3–16). Westport, CT: Praeger.

Washburn, M. F. (1908). *The animal mind: A textbook of comparative psychology.* New York: Macmillan.

Washburn, M. F. (1932). Autobiography. In C. Murchison (Ed.), *A history of psychology in autobiography* (Vol. 2, pp. 333–358). Worcester, MA: Clark University Press.

Wasserman, E. A. (1993). Comparative cognition: Beginning the second century of the study of animal intelligence. *Psychological Bulletin, 113,* 211–228.

Waterman, C. K., Buebel, M. E., & Waterman, A. S. (1970). Relationship between resolution of the identity crisis and outcomes of previous psychosocial crises. *Proceedings of the Annual Convention of the American Psychological Association, 5,* 467–468.

Watson, J. B. (1903). *Animal education.* Chicago: University of Chicago.

Watson, J. B. (1907). [Review of C. H. Turner, "A preliminary note on ant behavior"]. *Psychological Bulletin, 4,* 296–297.

Watson, J. B. (1908). [Review of Pfungst's *Das Pferd des Herrn Von Osten*]. *Journal of Comparative Neurology and Psychology, 18,* 329–331.

Watson, J. B. (1913). Psychology as the behaviorist views it. *Psychological Review, 20,* 158–177.

Watson, J. B. (1914). *Behavior: An introduction to comparative psychology.* New York: Holt.

Watson, J. B. (1916). The place of the conditioned reflex in psychology. *Psychological Review, 23,* 89–116.

Watson, J. B. (1919). *Psychology from the standpoint of a behaviorist.* Philadelphia: Lippincott.

Watson, J. B. (1925). *Behaviorism.* New York: Norton.

Watson, J. B. (1928). *Psychological care of the infant and child.* New York: Norton.

Watson, J. B. (1929). Behaviorism. *Encyclopaedia Britannica* (Vol. 3, pp. 327–329).

Watson, J. B. (1930). *Behaviorism* (Rev. ed.). New York: Norton.

Watson, J. B. (1936). Autobiography. In C. Murchison (Ed.), *A history of psychology in autobiography* (Vol. 3, pp. 271–281). Worcester, MA: Clark University Press.

Watson, J. B., & McDougall, W. (1929). *The battle of behaviorism.* New York: Norton.

Watson, J. B., & Morgan, J. J. B. (1917). Emotional reactions and psychological experimentation. *American Journal of Psychology, 28,* 163–174.

Watson, J. B., & Rayner, R. (1920). Conditioned emotional reactions. *Journal of Experimental Psychology, 3,* 1–14.

Watson, R. (1978). *The great psychologists* (4th ed.). Philadelphia: Lippincott.

Wehr, G. (1987). *Jung: A biography.* Boston: Shambhala.

Wertheimer, Max (1912). Experimental studies of the perception of movement. *Zeitschrift für Psychologie, 61,* 161–265.

Wertheimer, Max (1938). Gestalt theory. In W. D. Ellis (Ed.), *A source book of Gestalt psychology* (pp. 1–11). London: Routledge & Kegan Paul.

Wertheimer, Max (1945). *Productive thinking.* New York: Harper.

Wertheimer, Michael (1978). Humanistic psychology and the humane but tough-minded psychologist. *American Psychologist, 33,* 739–745.

Wertheimer, Michael (1979). *A brief history of psychology* (2nd ed.). New York: Holt, Rinehart and Winston.

Wertheimer, Michael, & King, D. B. (1994). Max Wertheimer's American sojourn, 1933–1943. *History of Psychology Newsletter, 26*(1), 3–15.

Wertheimer, Michael, King, D. B., Peckler, M. A., Raney, S., & Schaef, R. W. (1992). Carl Jung and Max Wertheimer on a priority issue. *Journal of the History of the Behavioral Sciences, 28,* 45–56.

White, A. D. (1965). *A history of the warfare of science with theology in Christendom.* New York: Free Press. (Original work published 1896)

White, S. H. (1990). Child study at Clark University, 1894–1904. *Journal of the History of the Behaviorol Sciences, 26,* 131–150.

Wiggins, J. G., Jr. (1994). Would you want your child to be a psychologist? *American Psychologist, 49,* 485–492.

Wilcox, S. B. (1992). Functionalism then and now. In D. A. Owens & M. Wagner (Eds.), *Progress in modern psychology: The legacy of American functionalism* (pp. 31–51). Westport, CT: Praeger.

Wilson, F. (1991). Mill and Comte on the method of introspection. *Journal of the History of the Behavioral Sciences, 27,* 107–129.

Windholz, G. (1986). A comparative analysis of the conditional reflex discoveries of Pavlov and Twitmyer, and the birth of a paradigm. *Pavlovian Journal of Biological Science, 21,* 141–147.

Windholz, G. (1990). Pavlov and the Pavlovians in the laboratory. *Journal of the History of the Behavioral Sciences, 25,* 64–74.

Windholz, G., & Lamal, P. A. (1985). Köhler's insight revisited. *Teaching of Psychology, 12,* 165–167.

Wink, P. (1993). Does Jung need rescuing? [Book review of *In search of Jung: Historical and philosophical enquiries*]. *Contemporary Psychology, 38,* 1231–1232.

Witmer, L. (1896). Practical work in psychology. *Pediatrics, 2,* 462–471.

Wittels, F. (1924). *Sigmund Freud.* New York: Dodd, Mead.

Women in the American Psychological Association. (1986). Washington, DC: Committee on Women in Psychology, American Psychological Association.

Woodworth, R. S. (1918). *Dynamic psychology.* New York: Columbia University Press.

Woodworth, R. S. (1921). *Psychology.* New York: Holt.

Woodworth, R. S. (1930). Dynamic psychology. In C. Murchison (Ed.), *Psychologies of 1930* (pp. 327–336). Worcester, MA: Clark University Press.

Woodworth, R. S. (1938, 1954). *Experimental psychology.* New York: Holt.

Woodworth, R. S. (1943). The adolescence of American psychology. *Psychological Review, 50,* 10–32.

Woodworth, R. S. (1948). *Contemporary schools of psychology* (2nd ed.). New York: Ronald Press.

Woodworth, R. S. (1958). *Dynamics of behavior.* New York: Holt.

Woolley, H. T. (1910). Psychological literature: A review of the recent literature on the psychology of sex. *Psychological Bulletin, 7,* 335–342.

Woolley, H. T. (1914). The psychology of sex. *Psychological Bulletin, 11,* 353–379.

Wrightsman, L. S. (1981). Personal documents as data in conceptualizing adult personality development. *Personality and Social Psychology Bulletin, 7,* 367–385.

Wundt, W. (1858–1862). *Contributions to the theory of sensory perception.* Leipzig: Winter.

Wundt, W. (1863). *Lectures on the minds of men and animals.* Leipzig: Voss.

Wundt, W. (1873–1874). *Principles of physiological psychology.* Leipzig: Engelmann.

Wundt, W. (1888). Zur Erinnerung an Gustav Theodor Fechner. *Philosophische Studien, 4,* 471–478.

Wundt, W. (1896). *Outline of psychology.* Leipzig: Engelmann.

Wundt, W. (1900–1920). *Cultural psychology.* Leipzig: Engelmann.

Yerkes, R. M., & Morgulis, S. (1909). The method of Pavlov in animal psychology. *Psychological Bulletin, 6,* 257–273.

Young-Bruehl, E. (1988). *Anna Freud: A biography.* New York: Summit Books.

Zeigarnik, B. (1938). On finished and unfinished tasks. In W. D. Ellis (Ed.), *A source book of Gestalt psychology* (pp. 300–314). London: Routledge & Kegan Paul. (Original work published 1927)

Name Index

SUBJECT INDEX